CATALOGUE OF EXHIBITS

WHY MONEY?

The introduction of coinage in the ancient Greek world is a product of human ingenuity intended to meet everyday needs, under a convention aimed at preserving equity in a society of reciprocity, in which the value of all goods of a certain weight or a certain affinity could be estimated comparatively, fairly and logically, using one medium. This was achieved by the adoption of money in the form of the coin, i.e. a metal piece weighed and tested, imprinted with the stamp of the issuing authority, as a sign of sovereignty and a guarantee of credit. In consequence, coinage, initially with an intrinsic value (deriving from precious metals, particularly silver) and later with a nominal value (bronze coins), became the vehicle of various monetized exchanges and transactions, as well as a means for savings. Thus, it acquired a dynamic role in people's lives and with its *continuum mobile* contributed decisively to the expansion of the economy.

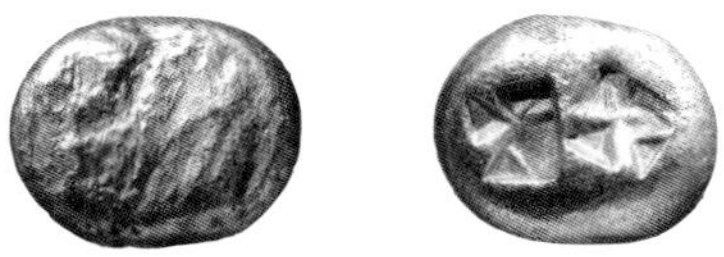

CAT. 1
Electrum *hekte*, uncertain Ionian mint, *ca*. 630–600 BC.
Roughened surface / Two incuse squares.
2.16 g; 9 mm
KIKPE Collection, Athens
See *Essays II* and *VI*

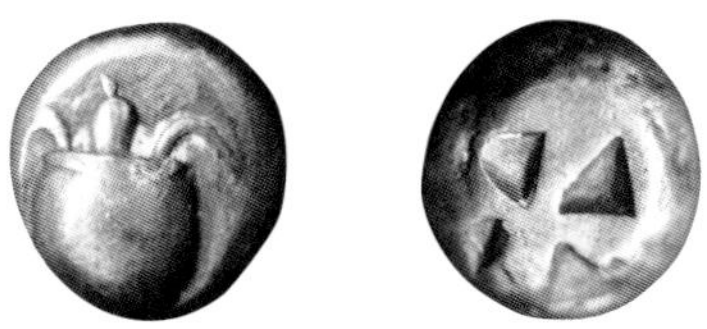

CAT. 2
Silver stater, Aegina, *ca*. 550–500 BC.
Turtle / Incuse (windmill pattern).
12.04 g; 17 mm
Fondation Martin Bodmer, Cologny
See *Essay IV*

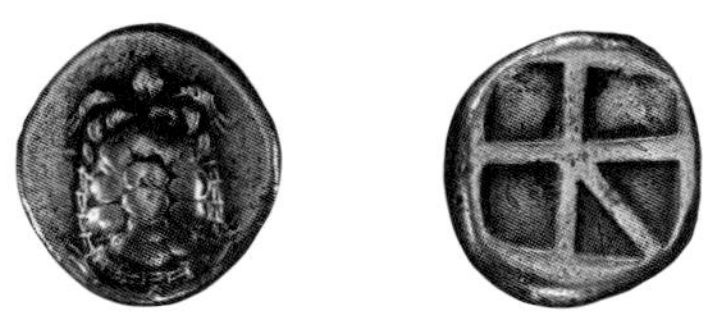

CAT. 3
Silver stater, Aegina, *ca*. 456–431 BC.
Tortoise / Incuse with five skewed compartments.
11.34 g; 20 mm
Fondation Martin Bodmer, Cologny
See *Essay IV*

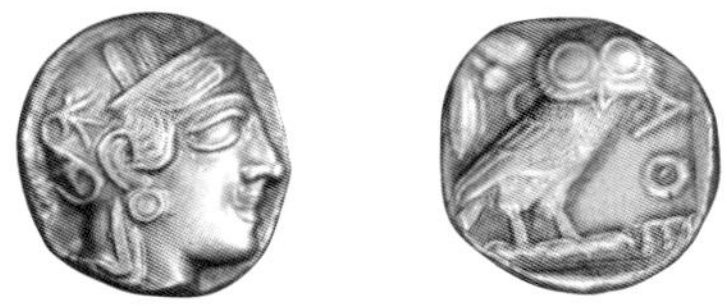

CAT. 4
Silver tetradrachm, Athens, *ca*. 454–404 BC.
Head of Athena / Owl.
17.14 g; 23 mm
Fondation Martin Bodmer, Cologny
See *Essays IV* and *VI*

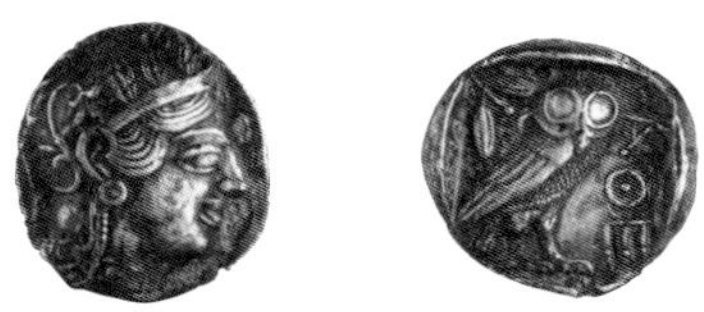

CAT. 5
Subaerate tetradrachm, Athens, 406/5 BC.
Head of Athena / Owl.
13.91 g; 26 mm
KIKPE Collection, Athens
See *Essays II* and *VI*

* *All the images of the coins in the catalogue and the essays are illustrated at random scale.*

The introduction of the bronze coinage

Coins of base metal are now part and parcel of everyday life. In Antiquity, however, the establishment of copper or bronze coinage met with considerable reservation, even though bronze, as a solid mass or even in the form of vessels, had played a decisive role in the transition from the pre-coinage period to that of coinage. With sole exception the peculiar cast coins from the area of the Euxine Pontus (mod. Black Sea). which first appeared in the mid-sixth century BC, the first issues of bronze coins in the Hellenic world date from the second half of the fifth century BC. The Greek colonies in South Italy – Thurium, Rhegium, Poseidonia, Hyele, Metapontum, Croton, Caulonia – led the way in establishing bronze coinage in the ancient world. Nevertheless, the words of Plato (427–347 BC) on the need for a coin suitable for everyday transactions, in his Laws – his last work –, herald the Athenian bronze coinage.

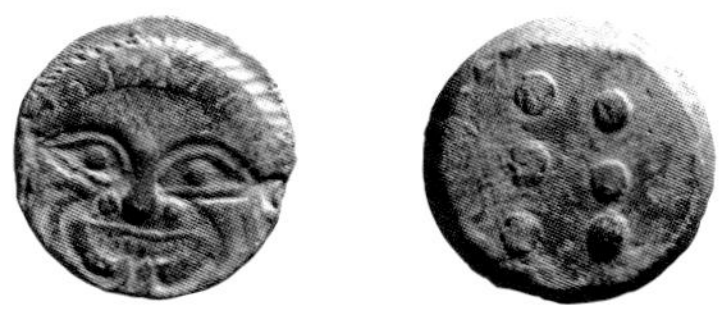

CAT. 6
Bronze *hemilitron*, Himera, after *ca*. 430 BC.
Gorgoneion / Six pellets.
14.45 g; 23 mm
KIKPE Collection, Athens: *SNG KIKPE* 184

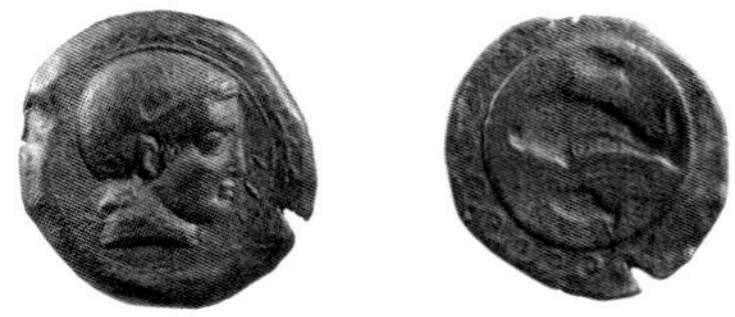

CAT. 9
Bronze coin, uncertain mint in central Etruria, 3rd century BC.
Head of Minerva / Incuse dolphin and incuse fish.
11.93 g; 28 mm
KIKPE Collection, Athens: *SNG KIKPE* 46

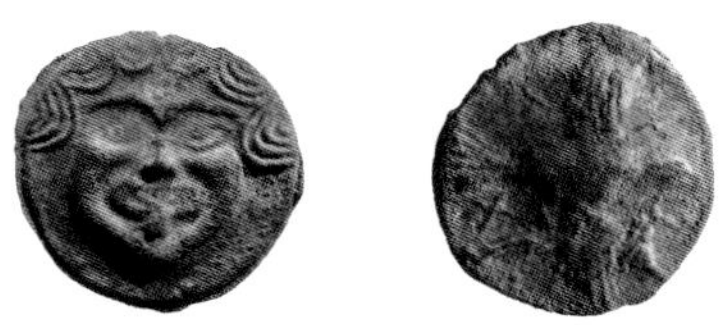

CAT. 7
Bronze cast coin, Olbia, 5th–4th century BC.
Gorgoneion / Eagle holding dolphin.
109.52 g; 70 mm
KIKPE Collection, Athens: *SNG KIKPE* 286

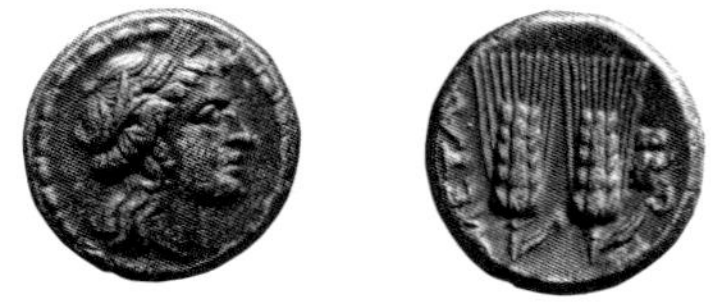

CAT. 10
Bronze coin, Metapontum, late 3rd century BC (?).
Head of Demeter / Two ears of barley.
5.21 g; 17 mm
KIKPE Collection, Athens: *SNG KIKPE* 103

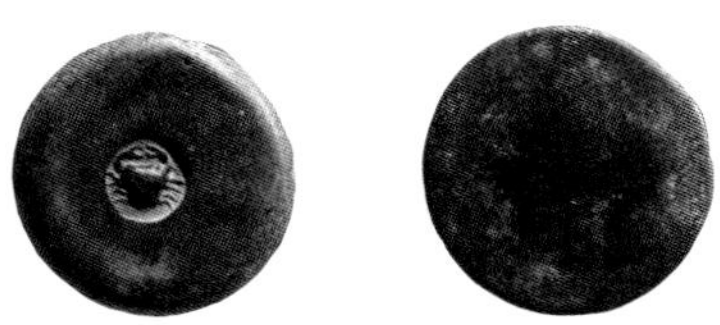

CAT. 8
Bronze *hemilitron*, Akragas, *ca*. 412–406 BC and later
(date of countermarking).
Smoothened surface; countermark (crab) / Smoothened surface.
19.81 g; 30 mm
KIKPE Collection, Athens: *SNG KIKPE* 151

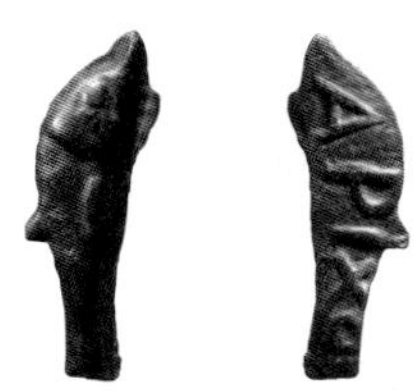

CAT. 11
Bronze dolphin-shaped coin, Olbia, 5th century BC.
4.50 g; H: 39 mm, W: 8 mm
KIKPE Collection, Athens: *SNG KIKPE* 285

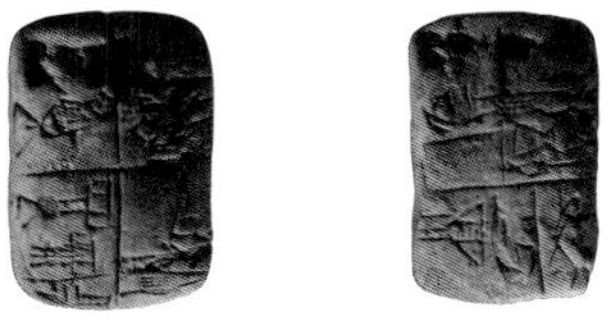

CAT. 12

Texts in pictographic script on red clay tablets, Mesopotamia, Uruk, reign of Gemdet-Nasr, *ca.* 3100–2850 BC, Uruk III period.

These tablets record commercial transactions of cereals, particularly barley. One tablet was stamped on the reverse with a cylinder seal (possibly a merchant's seal).

Fondation Martin Bodmer, Cologny, Inv. 26/3 and 26/5

See *Essay VI*

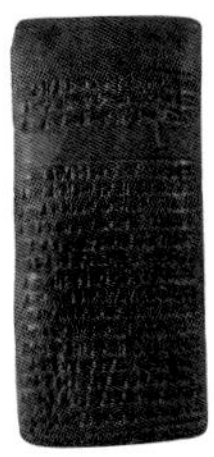

CAT. 13

Cuneiform tablet, Mesopotamia, Ur, reigns of Shulgi and his son Amar-Sîn, between 2093 and 2037 BC, Third Dynasty of Ur.

This tablet is inscribed (in a single column) with a list of various natural products: wood (cedar, cypress), plants (reeds) and oil. It gives the products' weight in *mana* (or *mina* = approx. 500 g) and *shekel* (approx. 8.5 g). The small quantities mentioned in the list suggest that these were ingredients used in the preparation of a medicine or cosmetic (probably perfume).

Fondation Martin Bodmer, Cologny, Inv. 39

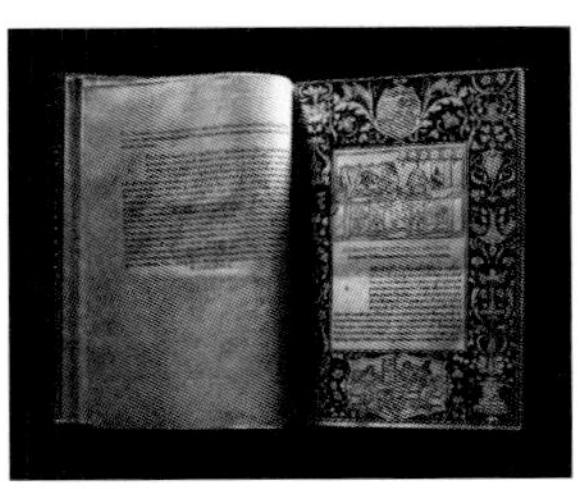

CAT. 14

Herodotus, *Historiae*…, Venice, Johannes et Gregorius de Gregoriis, 8 March 1494.

Latin edition, translated by the Italian humanist Lorenzo della Valle (1407–1457), produced by Antonio Mancinelli (1451–1505), first published in 1474. This volume is particularly noteworthy for its *incipit*, which is decorated with sumptuous vignettes engraved on wood and a large framing band with black background.

Fondation Martin Bodmer, Cologny, Inc. Bod. 123

See *Essays II* and *VI*

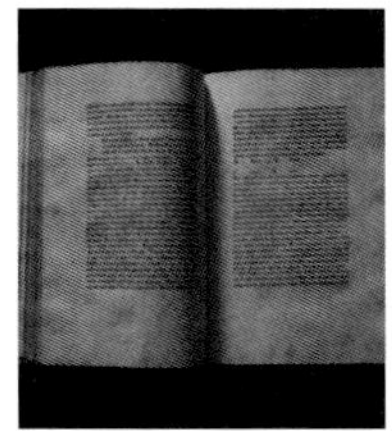

CAT. 15

Aristotle, *Ethica ad Nicomachum – Politica – Œconomica*…, Strasburg, Johann Mentelin, [before 3 July 1469].

First Latin edition of Aristotle, translated by the famous humanist Leonardo Bruni (also known as Leonardo Aretino, 1370–1444), apostolic secretary, then chancellor of Florence.

Fondation Martin Bodmer, Cologny, Inc. Bod. 24

See *Essay II*

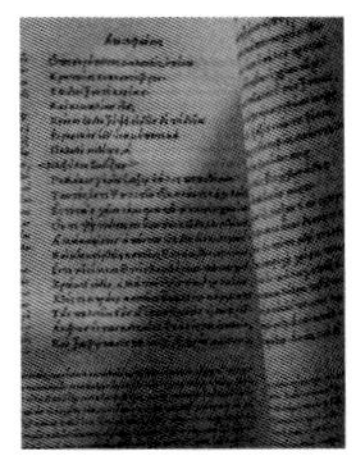

CAT. 16

Aristophanes, *Comediae Novem*…, Venice, Aldo Manuzio, 15 July 1498.

Greek *editio princeps*, edited and commented by the Cretan humanist Marco Musuro (1470–1517), long time professor of Greek at the universities of Padua and Venice.

Fondation Martin Bodmer, Inc. Bod. 20

See *Essays II* and *VI*

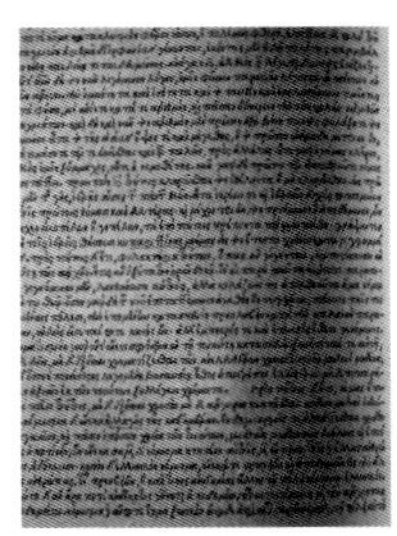

CAT. 17

Plato, [*Opera Omnia*…] (Gr.), Venice, Aldo [Manuzio] et Andrea [d'Asola], September 1513.

Greek *editio princeps*, edited by the Cretan humanist Marco Musuro (1470–1517), who also composed a Greek poem in praise of Plato at the beginning of the volume.

Fondation Martin Bodmer, Cologny

FROM HAND TO HAND
TO KEEP MEMORY ALIVE

Coinage, aside from its traditional role as standard of value, medium of transaction and means of storing wealth, has been, since the beginning of its history and through its iconography, an ideal medium for projecting political prestige. On the small circular flan of the coins, city-states, rulers and kings, alliances and empires, imprinted a variety of devices: gods and patron deities, temples, sacred symbols, holy animals and birds, mythical heroes and monsters, kings, emperors and potentates, eminent persons of the past, products that were a source of a city's wealth and prosperity were represented. Through its use and circulation, coinage functioned as a transmitter relaying messages to a wide audience inside and outside the geographical boundaries of each issuing authority.
Moreover, through the ages, old coins found in the soil attracted the interest of collectors and scholars, and their narrative and pictorial language became an eyewitness of humanity's past, a visual didactic discourse and an instrument of cultural transmission (*translatio*). The engravings stamped on coins help people to approach actual events and beliefs of the past. It is noteworthy that with the invention of printing, coin designs were used as models to transmit the glory that was Greece and the grandeur that was Rome.

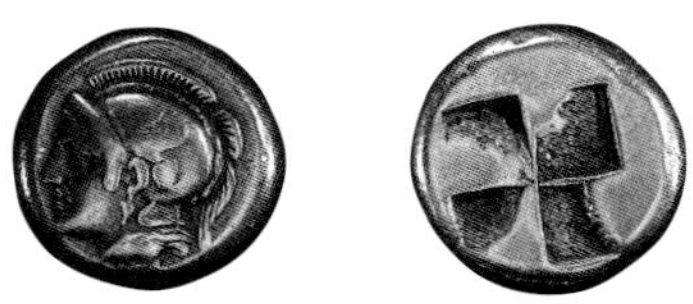

CAT. 18
Electrum *hekte*, Phocaea, early 4th century BC.
Head of Athena / Incuse square.
2.53 g; 10 mm
Fondation Martin Bodmer, Cologny

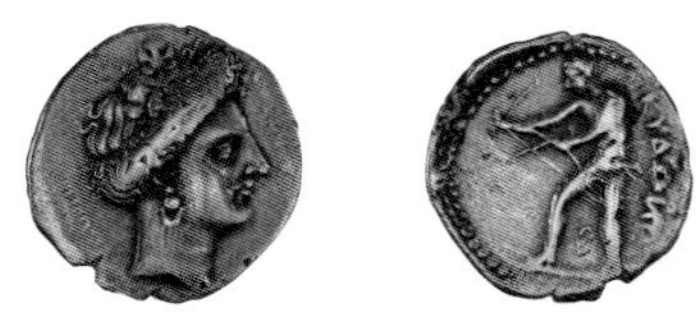

CAT. 20
Silver stater, Kydonia, *ca*. 320–280 BC.
Head of nymph / The hero Kydon stringing bow.
11.13 g; 30 mm
Fondation Martin Bodmer, Cologny
See *Essay V*

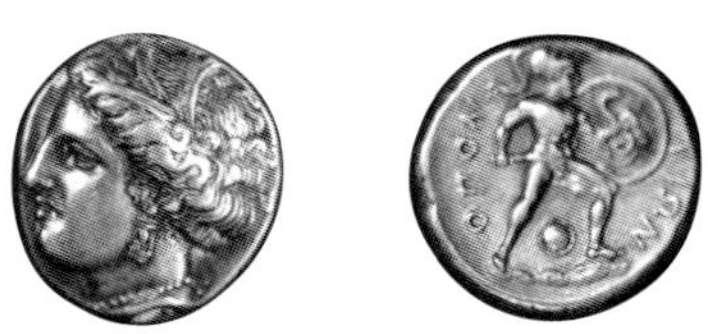

CAT. 19
Silver stater, Lokri Opuntii, *ca*. 360 BC.
Head of Demeter / Ajax, son of Oileus.
12.22 g; 25 mm
Fondation Martin Bodmer, Cologny
See *Essay III*

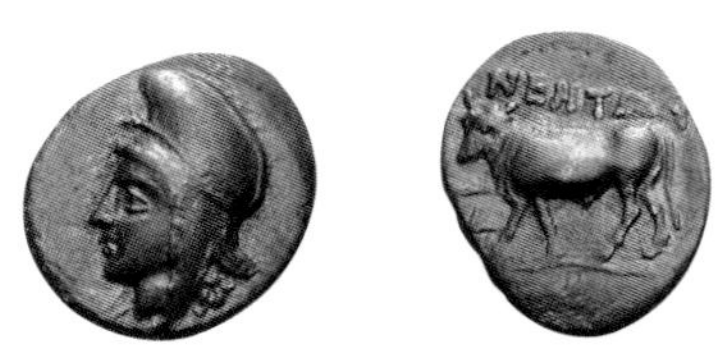

CAT. 21
Bronze coin, Aineia, *ca*. 400–357/349 BC.
Head of Aeneas / Bull.
3.95 g; 17 mm
KIKPE Collection, Athens: *SNG KIKPE* 388
See *Essays* V and *VI*

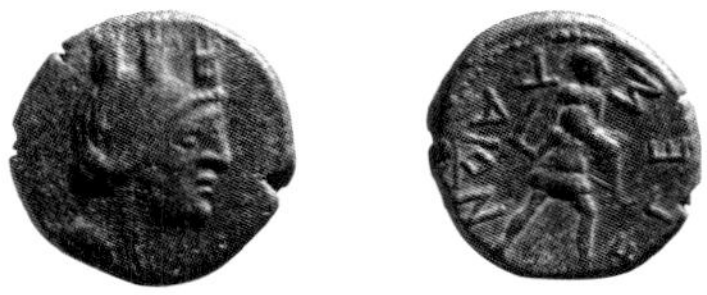

CAT. 22

Bronze coin, Segesta, *ca.* 190–180? BC.
Turreted bust of Segesta / Aeneas carrying Anchises on his shoulders.
7.28 g; 21 mm
KIKPE Collection, Athens: *SNG KIKPE* 224
See *Essay V*

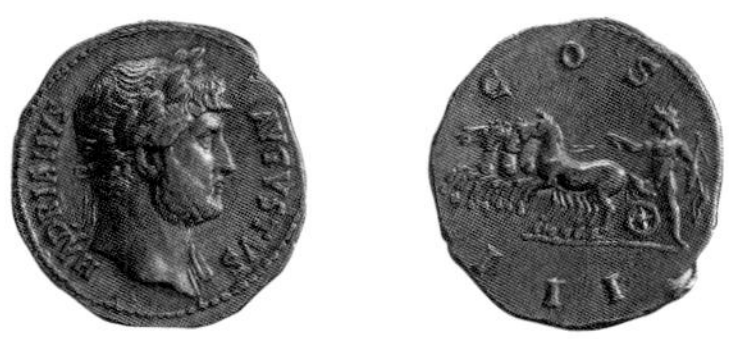

CAT. 23

Gold *aureus*, Hadrian (117–138 AD), Rome, *ca.* 125–128 AD.
Head of Hadrian / Quadriga.
7.28 g; 20 mm
Fondation Martin Bodmer, Cologny
See *Prooemium* and *Essay VIII*

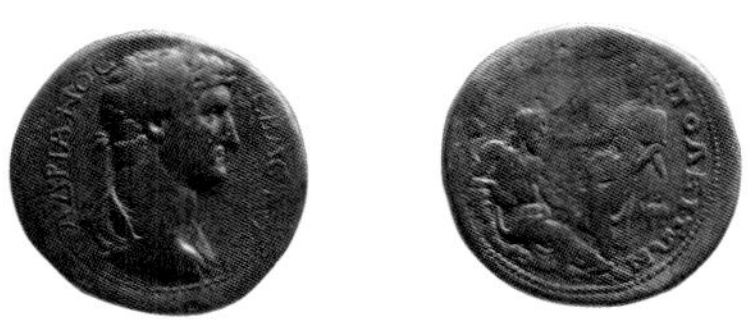

CAT. 24

Bronze coin, Philippopolis under Hadrian (117–138 AD).
Bust of Hadrian / Hebros and Tyche of Philippopolis.
27.48 g; 34 mm
KIKPE Collection, Athens
See *Prooemium* and *Essay V*

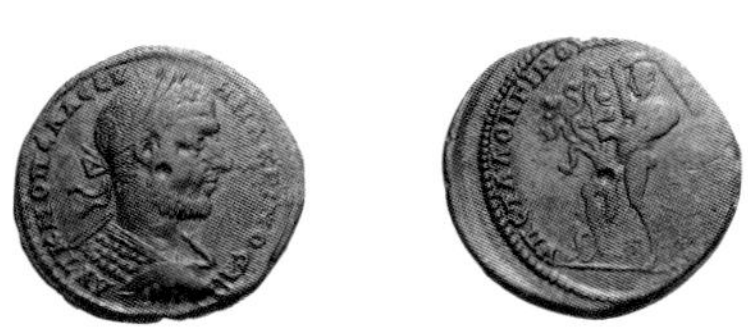

CAT. 25

Bronze coin, Nicopolis ad Istrum under Macrinus (217–218 AD).
Bust of Macrinus / Heracles and the Lernaea Hydra.
10.55 g; 26 mm
KIKPE Collection, Athens
See *Prooemium* and *Essay I*

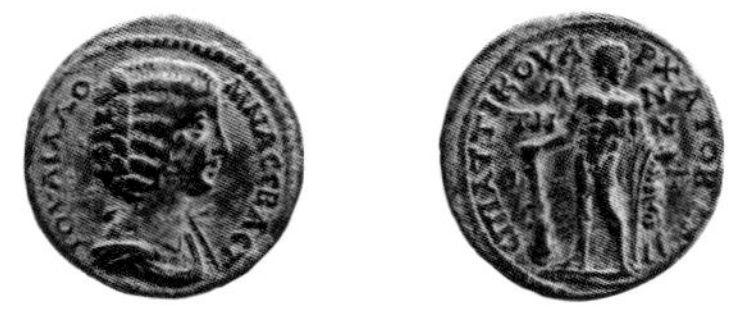

CAT. 26

Bronze coin, Saittae in the name of Iulia Domna (193–217 AD).
Bust of Iulia Domna / Heracles.
14.91 g; 29 mm
KIKPE Collection, Athens

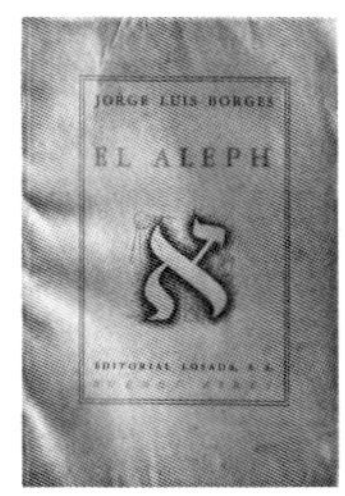

CAT. 27

Borges, Jorge Luis, *El Aleph*, Buenos Aires, Editorial Losada, 1949.

First edition. In this first edition, the collection numbered only thirteen short stories already published in various periodicals between 1944 and 1949. Four new texts were added for the second edition in 1952. Apart from the esoteric new eponym (a reference to a specific point in the universe, which allows a global and integral understanding of it), this volume proposes several texts that are relevant to Greco-Roman antiquity, such as *The House of Asterion*, which presents with the famous Minotaur myth from the beast's point of view.

Fondation Martin Bodmer, Cologny
See *Essay I*

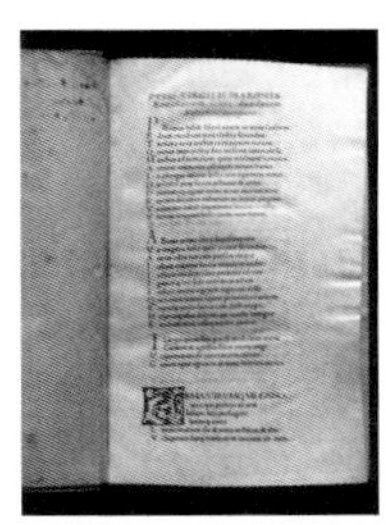

CAT. 28

Virgil, *Opera*..., Venice, Wendelin von Speyer, 1470.

Copy printed on *vellum*, with illuminated initials. Only one on two years later than the first edition, which was printed in Rome, and almost as rare, this Venetian edition is noteworthy for the more correct text version and for the presence of the printing date below the colophon, which makes it the first dated edition of Virgil.

Fondation Martin Bodmer, Cologny, Inc. Bod. 248
See *Essay IV*

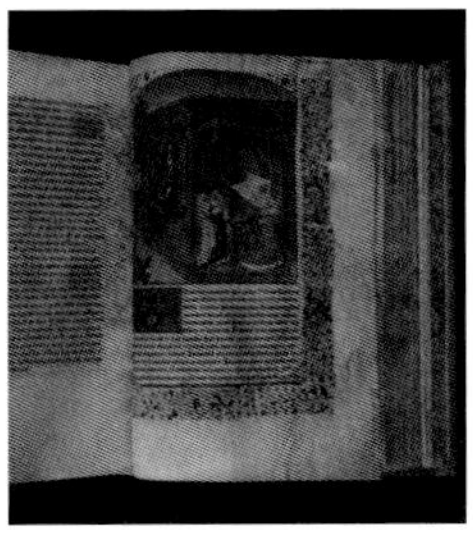

CAT. 29

[Imolensis, Beneventus], *Romuleon*, Latin manuscript on *vellum*, France, *ca.* 1461–1465 (?).

According to an ancient tradition, this famous compilation of Roman history is attributed to the erudite grammarian Benvenuto (dei) Rambaldi (*ca.* 1338–1390), better known by the name Benvenuto da Imola (or Beneventus Imolensis). This volume was probably copied and decorated for Charles of France (1446–1472), Duke of Berry, during the reign of his father King Charles VII.

Fondation Martin Bodmer, Cologny (Cod. Bodmer 143)
See *Procemium*

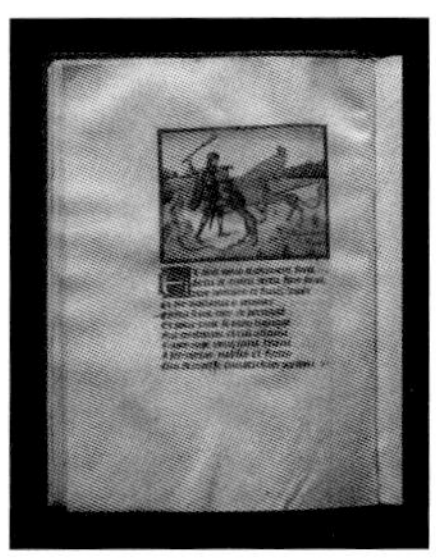

CAT. 30

Pisan, Christine de, *Epître d'Othéa*, French manuscript on *vellum*, Bruges, *ca.* 1480.

French literature's first veritable authoress, Christine de Pisan delivered with this *Epître*, or *Letter*, written in 1400–1401, a 'mirror of the princes' both with a moralizing intention and as an epitome of Greco-Roman mythology. Through her *Cent Histoires de Troie* (*Hundred Stories of Troy*: short texts in verse always followed by an explanatory *Glose*, or linguistic commentary, and by an interpretative *Allegory* in the form of moralizing tale), a mysterious goddess Othea (the personification of Prudence) addresses Hector of Troy, then a young knight of fifteen years of age, in order to inculcate the duties of his office. This work, which combined famous episodes of pagan mythology (used as *exempla*) with a Christian moral education, was also provided with a very specific iconographic programme by its author. Although this manuscript belongs to a family of copies from which the dedication (and therefore the author's name) is missing, it preserves the entire cycle of miniatures. Apart from the notably different large opening vignette, all of the other miniatures were executed in *grisaille*, with only a few highlights in colour, probably by an illuminator in Bruges. This copy was made for Antoine, the Great Bastard of Bourgogne (1421–1504), illegitimate son of Duke Philip the Good and, like his father, a refined bibliophile. Apart from the handwritten *ex-libris* '*Nul ne s'i frote*' (May no one chafe it), the manuscript also features its owner's coat of arms painted inside the acanthus leafs border of one of the margins. The presence of the collar of the Order of Saint Michael around the shield allows a probable dating of the manuscript to the early 1480s, when the Burgundian prince entered the order.

Fondation Martin Bodmer, Cologny, Cod. Bodmer 49
See *Procemium*

THE LEGEND OF ALEXANDER THE GREAT

Alexander the Great (356–323 BC) was, from the beginning of his reign (336 BC), envelopped in a legend that presented him as a deified hero, Heracles and heir to Zeus. His military campaigns in the East took him to many lands – Syria, Egypt, Persia, Bactria, India – and everywhere he founded new cities, each named Alexandria. He left behind a legacy of Greek culture and his fame lived on long after the demise of Antiquity. His achievements had a significant impact from his era to the present day and have been spotlighted in high art and popular culture, in several traditions from Persia and Islam, and from the Age of Chivalry to modern Greece. Alexander's life and history are represented in sculptures, paintings, tapestries, works in the decorative arts, illuminated books, etc., visually bridging the 'reality' of the man and his 'journey' to immortality, focusing on Alexander's colourful legend and his divine origins.

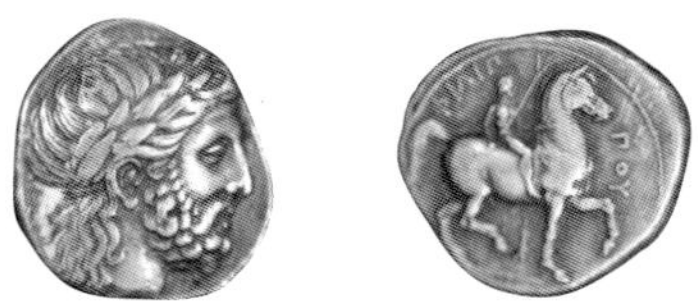

CAT. 31
Silver tetradrachm, Philip II of Macedon (360/359–336 BC), Pella, 342/1–337/6 BC.
Head of Zeus / Young rider with palm-branch.
14.34 g; 24 mm
Fondation Martin Bodmer, Cologny
See *Essays III* and *VII*

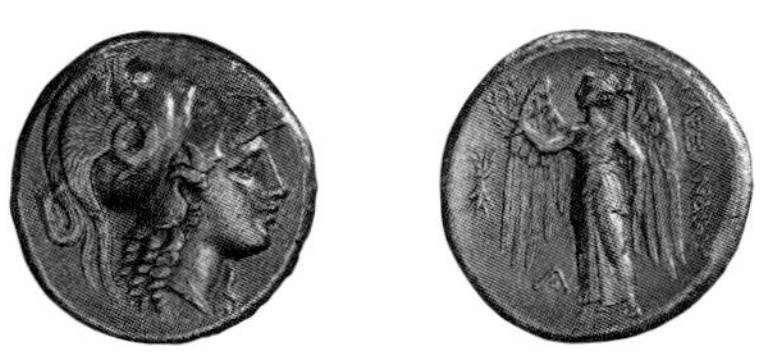

CAT. 32
Gold double stater, Alexander the Great (336–323 BC), Aigeai(?).
Head of Athena / Nike.
17.23 g; 20 mm
Fondation Martin Bodmer, Cologny
See *Essays III* and VII

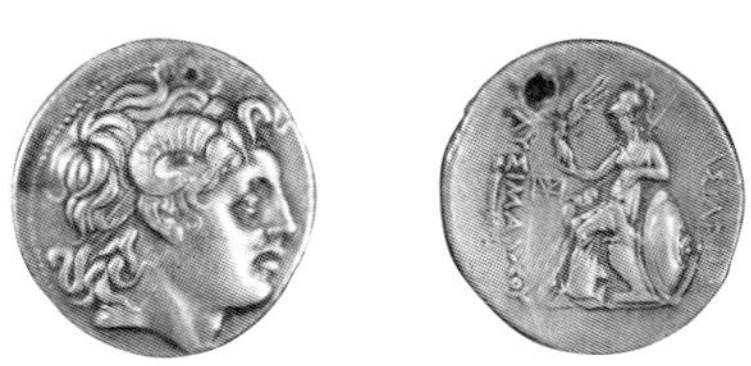

CAT. 33
Silver tetradrachm, Lysimachus (306–281 BC), Lampsacus, 297/6–282/1 BC.
Head of Alexander the Great as Zeus Ammon / Athena seated.
16.58 g; 30 mm
Fondation Martin Bodmer, Cologny
See *Essays III* and *VII*

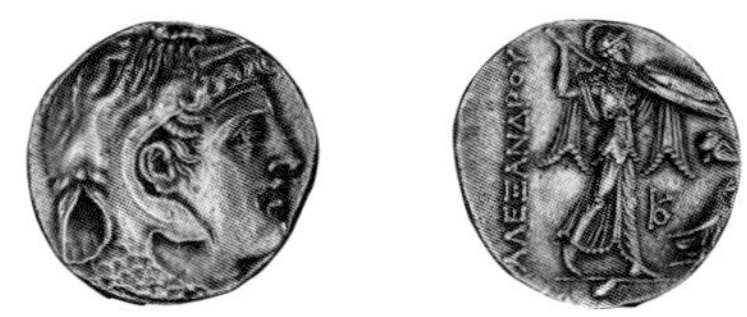

CAT. 34
Silver tetradrachm, Ptolemy I Soter (311–281 BC), Alexandria, *ca*. 310–305 BC.
Head of Alexander the Great with elephant-scalp / Athena Promachos.
15.62 g; 25 mm
Fondation Martin Bodmer, Cologny
See *Essays III* and *VII*

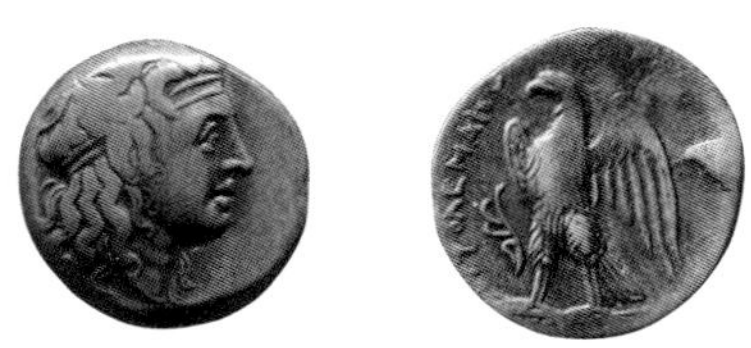

CAT. 35
Bronze coin, Ptolemy I Soter (311–281 BC), Cyrene, *ca*. 300–285 BC.
Head of Alexander the Great / Eagle on thunderbolt.
5.08 g; 20 mm
KIKPE Collection, Athens: *SNG KIKPE* 1173
See *Essay III*

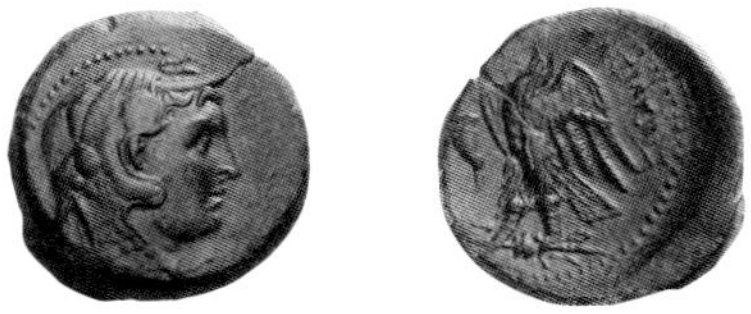

CAT. 36
Bronze coin, Ptolemy II Philadelphus (285/281–246 BC), Sidon(?), *ca.* 271/261–246 BC.
Head of Alexander the Great with elephant-scalp / Eagle on thunderbolt.
11.33 g; 25 mm
KIKPE Collection, Athens: *SNG KIKPE* 1176
See *Essay III*

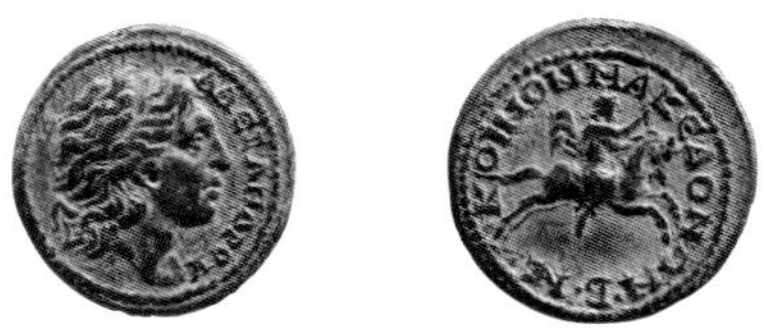

CAT. 37
Bronze coin, Macedonian *koinon* under Severus Alexander (222–235 AD), Beroia, *ca.* 231–235 AD.
Head of Alexander the Great / Alexander on horseback.
13.59 g; 26.5 mm
KIKPE Collection, Athens
See *Essay III*

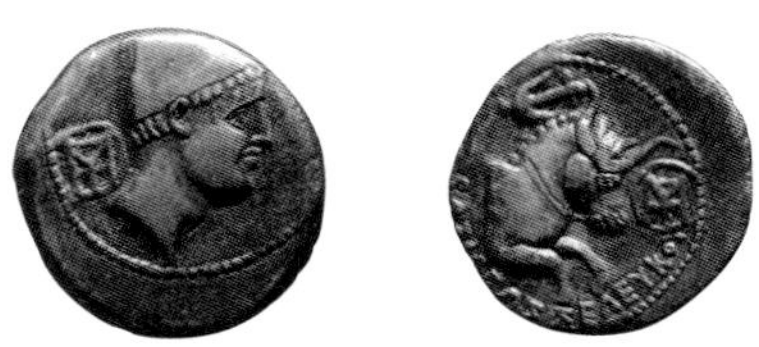

CAT. 38
Bronze coin, Seleucus I Nicator (312–281 BC), uncertain mint in Bactria, *ca.* 290/286–281 BC.
Head of Dioscurus / Forepart of horned horse (Bucephalus?).
6.77 g; 20 mm
KIKPE Collection, Athens: *SNG KIKPE* 1038
See *Procemium*

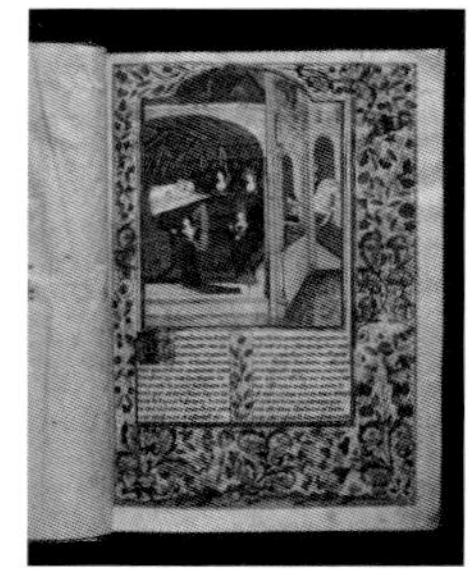

CAT. 39
Quintus Curtius, *Faits et gestes du grand Alexandre*, French manuscript on *vellum*, France, late 15th century.

This translation of the nine books of the *Histories of Alexander the Great* is followed here by Plutarch's *Alexander* in Vasco de Lucena's version of the Latin translation by Guarino Veronese.

Fondation Martin Bodmer, Cologny, Cod. Bodmer 53
See *Procemium*

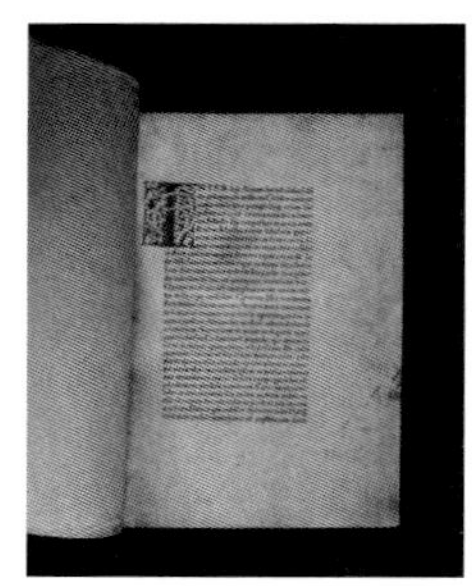

CAT. 40
Quintus Curtius, *Historiae Alexandri Magni*, [Venice], Wendelin von Speyer, [*ca.* 1471].

First edition. Inspired by the great conqueror's biography written by his contemporary Cleitarchus of Alexandria, the Latin historian composed this work in approximately the mid-first century AD. Although filled with imprecisions and with an all-Roman moralizing condemnation of the Orient's corruptions, this text circulated widely, as suggested by the more than one hundred surviving manuscripts. Even so, the narrative's first three books are missing and the other eight are incompletely preserved.

Fondation Martin Bodmer, Cologny, Inc. Bodmer 80

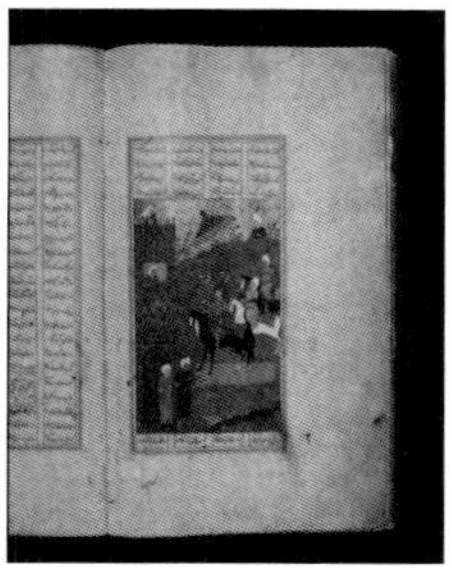

CAT. 41

Nizami Ganjavi, Abou Mohammad Elyas, *Khamsah* [*Quintet*], Persian manuscript on paper, Persia, Shiraz, 1516–1521.

Established at Ganja (in modern Azerbaijan), where he spent most of his life, Nizami Ganjavi (*ca.* 1141–1209) was the greatest Persian epic poet of his time. His main poetry collection, the *Khamsah* (also known as the *Panj Ganj*, or 'Five Treasures'), consists of fine narrative poems in different metres. Composed in the last years of the twelfth century and entitled *Eskandar-nameh*, or *Alexander's Book*, the fourth poem consists of two books inspired by the myths developed around the great conqueror in the Muslim world and by the *Romance of Alexander* by pseudo-Callisthenes and its many derivatives. Decorated with thirty miniatures, this book was copied by the calligrapher Mihammed Katib in Nastaliq script.

Fondation Martin Bodmer, Cologny, Cod. Bodmer 524

DESCRIBING THE WORLD

From early on, humans followed an essential need to understand the world in which they live and to pinpoint their position in relation to the surrounding space. Gradually, the initial mythological approaches gave way to more pragmatic interpretations and in the process the first conventions for mapmaking were established. Greek writers laid the foundations of geographical knowledge, which was systematized under the Roman Empire. The ancient view of the world was continued and reinterpreted in the Middle Ages, with additions and advances coming particularly from Islamic cartography. From another perspective, there are intriguing glimpses at the way in which elements and parts of the earth were visualized on a number of ancient and medieval coins. In general, the prevailing trend was to represent personifications of regions, cities, rivers, etc., while naturalistic depictions of areas, mountains, harbours, etc. are less common. Within this context, dialogues between texts and coins can be traced, in an attempt to highlight interesting connotations.

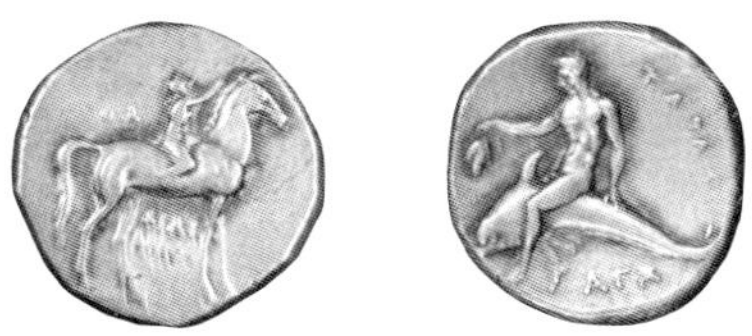

CAT. 42
Silver *nomos*, Taras, *ca.* 302–281 BC.
Young rider / The hero Taras on dolphin.
7.86 g; 21 mm
Fondation Martin Bodmer, Cologny
See *Essay V*

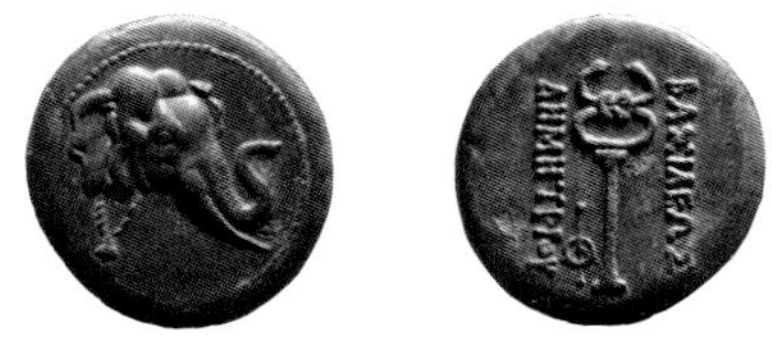

CAT. 45
Bronze coin, Demetrius I of Bactria and India (*ca.* 200–190 BC).
Elephant's head / Caduceus.
11.97 g; 29 mm
KIKPE Collection, Athens: *SNG KIKPE* 1131
See *Essay V*

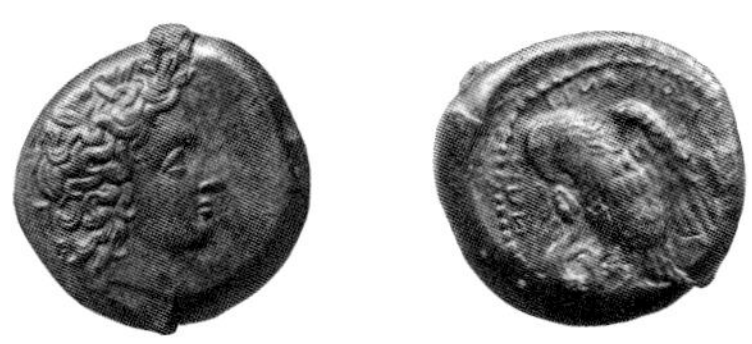

CAT. 43
Bronze coin, Morgantina, *ca.* 340 BC.
Head of Sicilia / Eagle holding serpent.
9.55 g; 20 mm
KIKPE Collection, Athens: *SNG KIKPE* 208
See *Essay V*

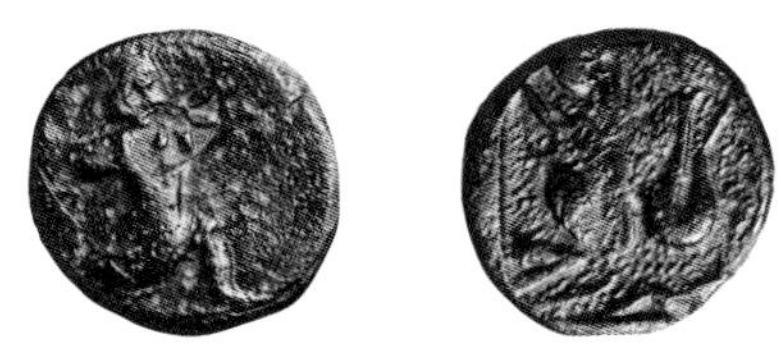

CAT. 46
Bronze coin, uncertain satrap, Ephesus(?), early 4th century BC (?).
Persian king; countermark (star) /
Incuse square (map of the hinterland of Ephesus?).
1.87 g; 13 mm
KIKPE Collection, Athens: *SNG KIKPE* 873
See *Essay V*

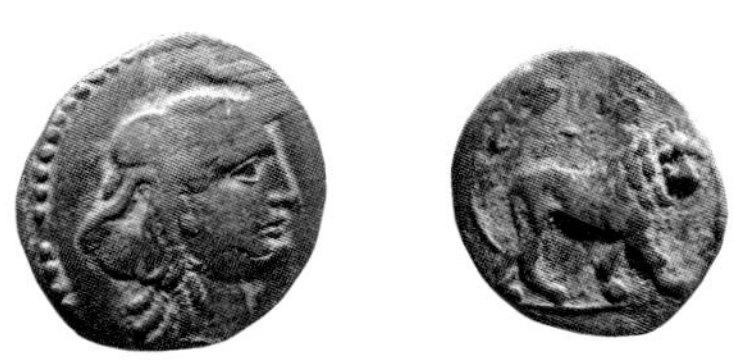

CAT. 44
Bronze coin, Juba I of Numidia (60–46 BC), Cirta.
Head of Africa or Numidia / Lion.
5.57 g; 20 mm
KIKPE Collection, Athens: *SNG KIKPE* 1224
See *Essay V*

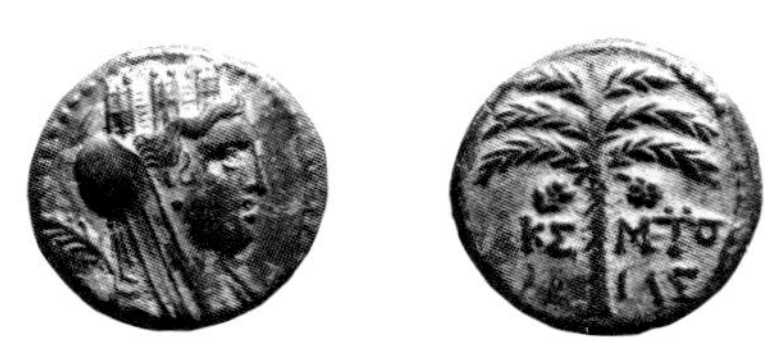

CAT. 47
Bronze coin, Tyrus, 94/5 AD.
Turreted head of Tyrus / Palm tree.
3.57 g; 17 mm
KIKPE Collection, Athens
See *Essay V*

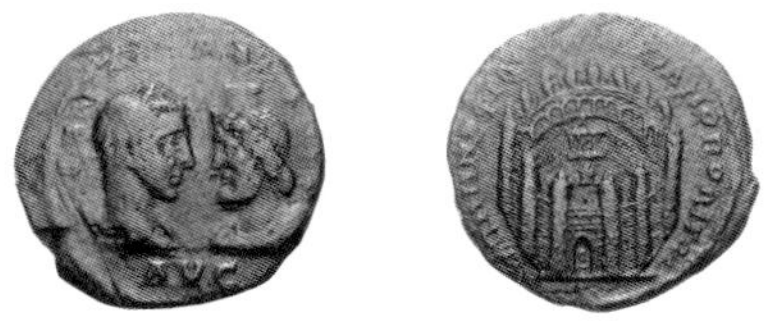

CAT. 48
Bronze coin, Marcianopolis under Gordian III (238–244 AD).
Busts of Gordian III and Sarapis / City-view from aerial perspective.
12.23 g; 28 mm
KIKPE Collection, Athens
See *Essays V* and *VIII*

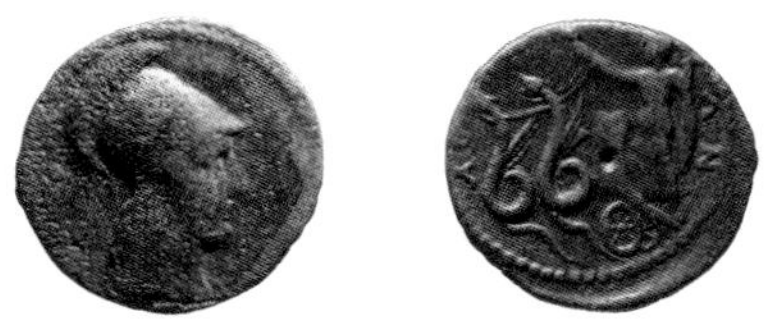

CAT. 49
Bronze coin, Athens, *ca*. 145/155–175 AD.
Head of Athena / Triptolemus on serpent-drawn chariot.
7.03 g; 24 mm
KIKPE Collection, Athens

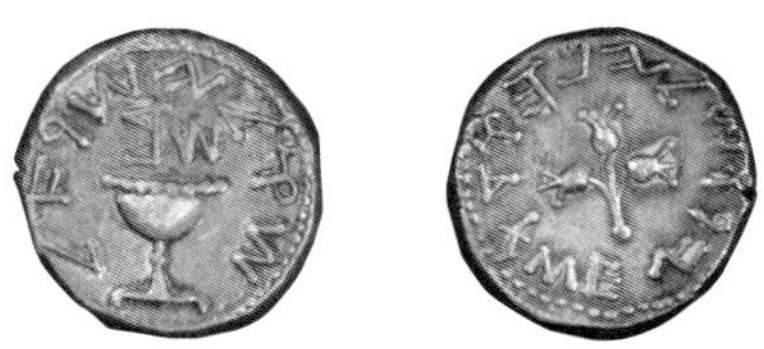

CAT. 50
Silver shekel, Judaea, Jerusalem, 68/9 AD.
Omer cup / Sprig of three pomegranates.
14.00 g; 20 mm
Fondation Martin Bodmer, Cologny
See *Essay V*

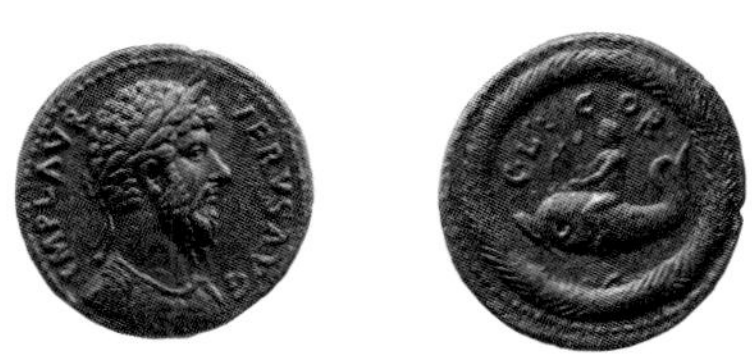

CAT. 51
Bronze coin, Corinth under Lucius Verus (161–169 AD).
Bust of Lucius Verus / Melicertes on dolphin.
10.97 g; 27 mm
KIKPE Collection, Athens

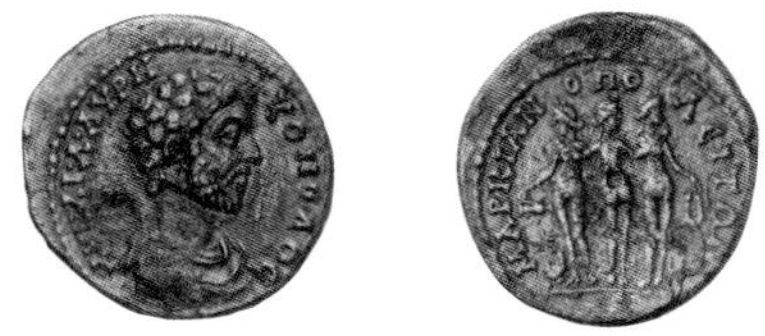

CAT. 52
Bronze coin, Marcianopolis under Commodus (177–192 AD).
Bust of Commodus / The Three Graces.
9.75 g; 25 mm
KIKPE Collection, Athens

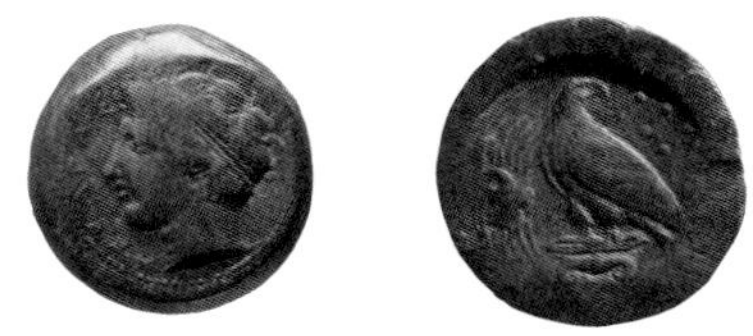

CAT. 53
Bronze coin, Akragas, late 5th century BC.
Head of river god Akragas / Eagle on Ionic capital.
17.48 g; 26 mm
KIKPE Collection, Athens: *SNG KIKPE* 149
See *Essay V*

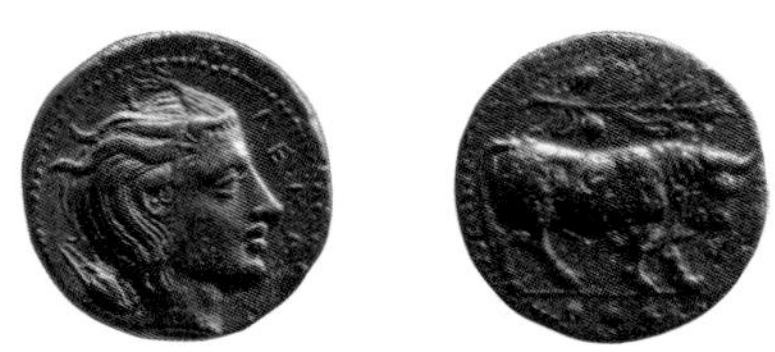

CAT. 54
Bronze coin, Gela, *ca*. 420–405 BC.
Head of river god Gelas / Bull.
3.94 g; 16 mm
KIKPE Collection, Athens: *SNG KIKPE* 175
See *Essay V*

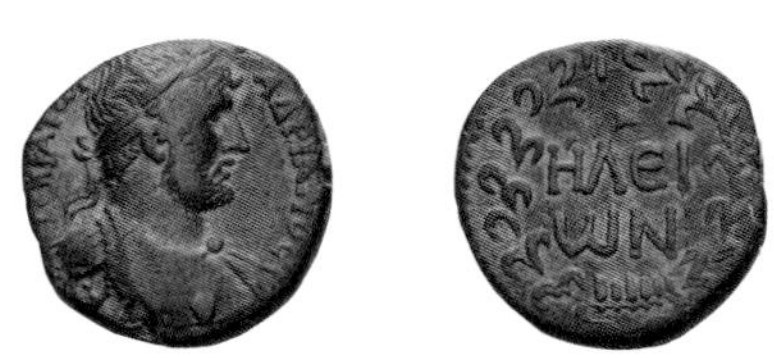

CAT. 55
Bronze coin, Elis/Olympia under Hadrian (117–138 AD), *ca*. 125 AD.
Bust of Hadrian / Legend within wreath.
14.95 g; 25 mm
KIKPE Collection, Athens

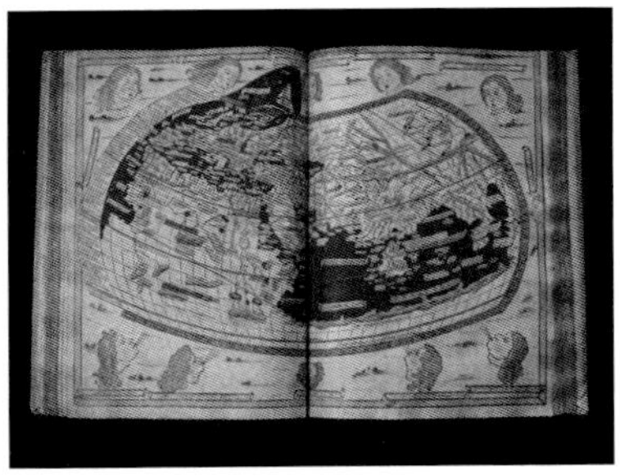

CAT. 56

Ptolemy, *Cosmographia*, Ulm, Leonhard Holl, 16 July 1482.

Latin edition, translation by the Florentine humanist Giacomo d'Angelo (or Jacobus Angelus), produced by the German cartographer Nicolaus Germanus (*ca.* 1420–1490). The wood engravings (above all the impressive double-paged *mappa mundi*) and the initials were enhanced with watercolour.

Fondation Martin Bodmer, Cologny, Inc. Bod. 207
See *Essay V*

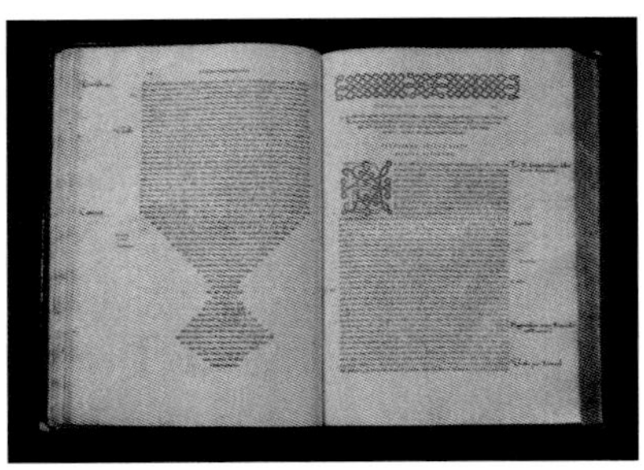

CAT. 57

Strabo, [*De situ orbis*] (Gr.), Venice, Aldo [Manuzio] and Andrea [d'Asola], November 1516.

Greek *editio princeps*. According to the preface, this edition was supervised by the humanist Benedictus Tyrrhenus. This copy features several marginal annotations in Greek and Latin by the Swiss humanist, poet and geographer Heinrich Loriti (1488–1563), also known as Glareanus, a friend of Erasmus.

Fondation Martin Bodmer, Cologny
See *Essay V*

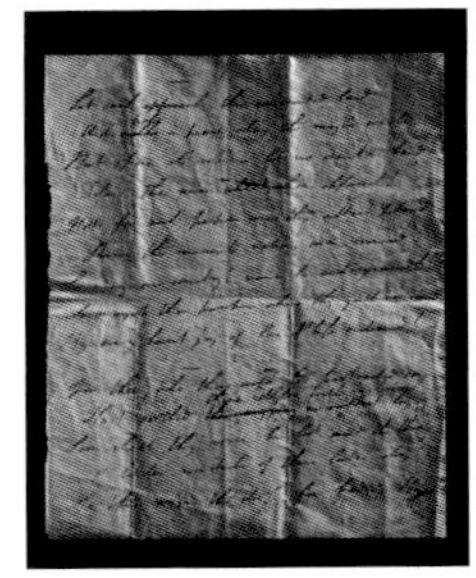

CAT. 58

Byron, George Gordon, '*Let such approach this consecrated land* …'. Autograph manuscript, with corrections, 1809/10.

This fragment of the second *Canto* of *Childe Harold's Pilgrimage* (first published in 1812 and largely inspired by the poet's first sojourn in Greece) comprises stanzas 93 ('*Let such approach this consecrated land…*') and 94 ('*For thee, who thus in too protracted song…*'). Whereas the poem contains many references to prestigious sites (such as Thebes, Delphi, Athens), Byron, to use the words of his friend John Galt, who was also his first biographer, 'laid down his pen' after his stay at Athens: '*Childe Harold* there disappears'. Once in Athens, however, on 13 January 1810, the poet and his travelling companions rode to Eleusis and the ruined temple of Demeter, seat of the 'mysteries' established by the city's mythical King Triptolemus. But, according to Galt, 'neither of [the battle of Salamine] nor of the mysteries for which the Temple of Ceres was for so many ages celebrated, has the poet given us description or suggestion; and yet few topics among all his wild and wonderful subjects were so likely to have furnished such «ample room, and verge enough» to his fancy'.

Fondation Martin Bodmer, Cologny, B-102.2

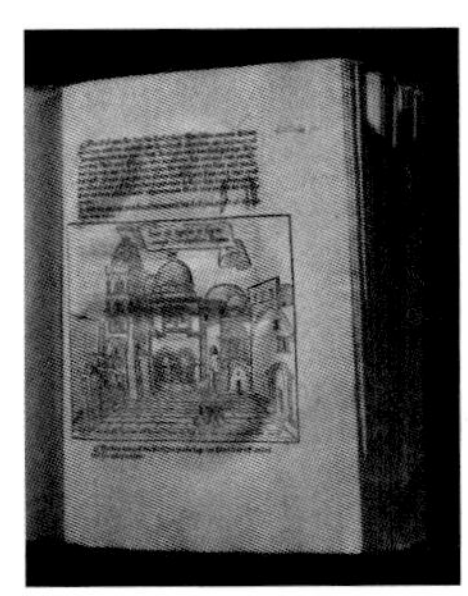

CAT. 59

Breidenbach, Bernhard von, *Peregrinatio in Terram Sanctam*, Mainz, Erhard Reuwich, 21 June 1486.

First German edition, with handwritten annotations in Latin and German. *Canon* Bernhard von Breidenbach (*ca.* 1440–1497), bailiff of the Mainz cathedral, went on a pilgrimage to the Holy Land in 1483–1484, during which he visited Jerusalem and Mount Sinai. Upon his return, he wrote the narrative of his journey. Illustrated with numerous wood engravings, this volume also contains the first printed Armenian and Arabic alphabets.

Fondation Martin Bodmer, Cologny, Inc. Bod. 56

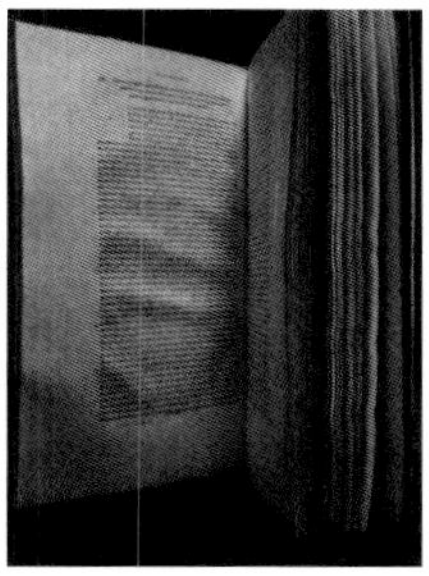

CAT. 60

Pausanias, [*Descriptio Graeciae*] (Gr.), Venice, Aldo [Manuzio] and Andrea [d'Asola], 1516.

Greek *editio princeps*, produced by the Cretan humanist Marco Musuro (1470–1517). A native of Lydia, Pausanias (*ca*. AD 115–180) composed towards the end of his life the *Periegesis*, a vast and well-documented geographic description of Greece in ten books, the second of which is dedicated to Corinthia. According to Pausanias, near the town of Crommyon, 'by the waterside, was a pine tree and an altar to Melicertes. The natives say that his body was carried there by a dolphin and that it was found by Sisyphus, who buried it in the Isthmus and founded the Isthmian Games in his honour'. The *Periegesis* manuscript used as a source for this edition was probably unreliable, hence the many erroneous readings. On the other hand and may be because of the publishers' negligence, entire passages were omitted or excised, making this first edition of Pausanias a faulty and incomplete one.

Fondation Martin Bodmer, Cologny
See *Essay V*

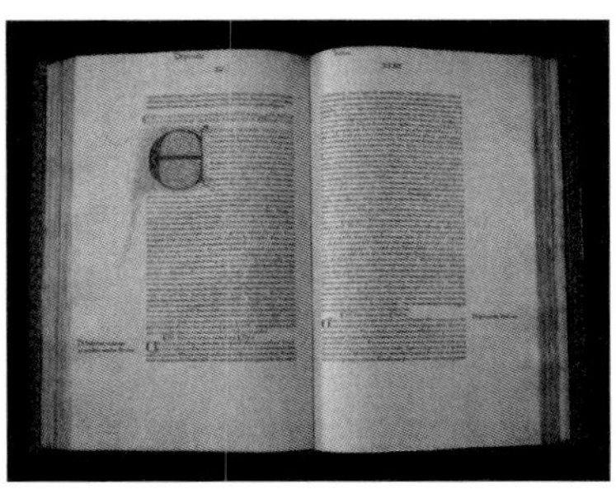

CAT. 61

Pliny the Elder, *Naturalis historia*, Venice, Nicolas Jenson, [before 18 September] 1472 (volume I only).

Published by Giovanni d'Andrea (or Johannes Andreae, *ca*. 1270–1348). Before receiving its new name in honour of Ulpia Marciana, emperor Trajan's sister, in 106, the city of Marcianopolis in Lower Moesia was called Parthenopolis. It is thus mentioned by Pliny the Elder in his list of the seven main cities of the Danubian province, formerly '*totum eum tractum Scythæ Aroteres cognominati tenuere*' (entirely occupied by the Scythes dubbed 'Aroteres' [labourers]) (*Naturalis historia*, Book IV, Ch. 11).

Fondation Martin Bodmer, Cologny (Inc. Bod. 199)
See *Essay V*

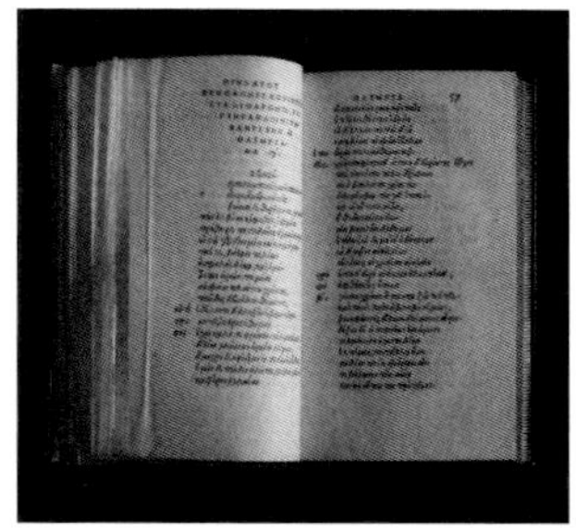

CAT. 62

Pindar, [*Olympia. Pythia. Nemea. Isthmia*] (Gr.), Venice, Aldo [Manuzio] and Andrea [d'Asola], 1513.

Greek *editio princeps*. It is to the grammarian Aristophanes of Byzantium, director of the Alexandria Library, that we owe the grouping of Pindar's odes into four books. These poems celebrated the victories of famous athletes in the four major ancient Panhellenic games: the Olympian, Pythian, Nemean, and Isthmian Games. This first edition of Pindar also includes both a first edition of Lycophron's *Alexandra*, and new editions of Callimachus's *Hymns* (already published in print in 1494) and of Dionysius of Alexandria's *De situ orbis* (first published in Ferrara in 1512). Also known as Dionysius the Periegetes, this last author probably composed his short geographical poem during the reign of emperor Hadrian. This highly didactic text, which divides the world into three regions (Libya, Europe, and Asia), became a teaching manual and remained so throughout the Byzantine period, after the addition of a commentary by Eustathius of Thessalonike in the twelfth century. Two Latin translations were made by a certain Avienus and a certain Priscianus, in the fourth and the sixth century AD respectively.

Fondation Martin Bodmer, Cologny

THE COSMOS

Coming to terms with the great unknown of the universe was a significant parameter for mankind. Traditional views of religious aspect or superstitious character were shaken by pioneering interpretations of the Hellenic genius; reason (*logos*) took centre stage and new theories were proposed concerning the basic elements of the Cosmos and its order. Cosmology and cosmography had a fair share in the quests of inquiring minds during Antiquity and the Middle Ages. Moreover, charting the sky was important to ancient and medieval societies beyond scientific reasons, as many people turned their eyes to the heavens in search of omens giving guidance or a deeper meaning to their lives. These attitudes were projected also through coinage, and a number of stars, constellations and zodiac signs are to be found on coins. It is not surprising that such subjects were often incorporated in the ideology expressed by the issuing authority, usually becoming part of propaganda images addressed to the public. In association with a selection from the extant texts, particular examples of ancient Greek or Turkoman coins featuring representations of celestial bodies provide some thought-provoking insights into concepts of the Cosmos.

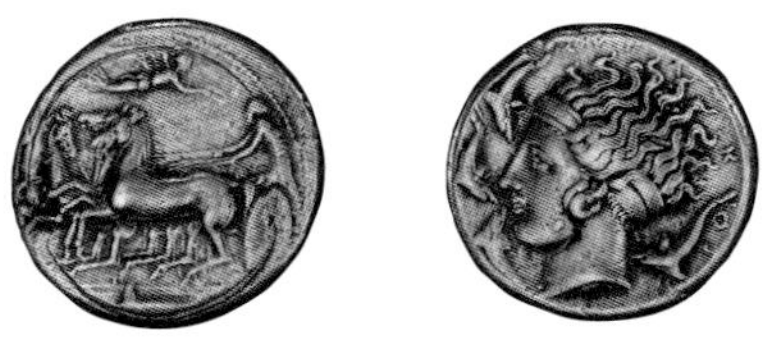

CAT. 63
Silver tetradrachm, Syracuse, *ca.* 405–367 BC.
Quadriga / Head of Arethusa.
17.08 g; 25 mm
Fondation Martin Bodmer, Cologny
See *Procemium* and *Essay V*

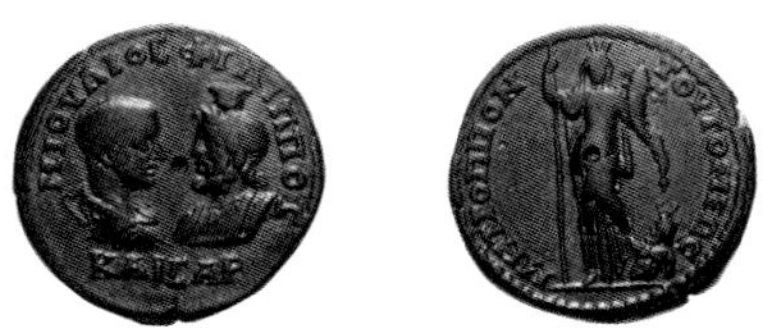

CAT. 64
Bronze coin, Tomis in the name of caesar Philip (II), 244–247 AD.
Busts of Philip II and Sarapis / Tyche of Tomis and Pontus.
14.20 g; 27 mm
KIKPE Collection, Athens
See *Essay V*

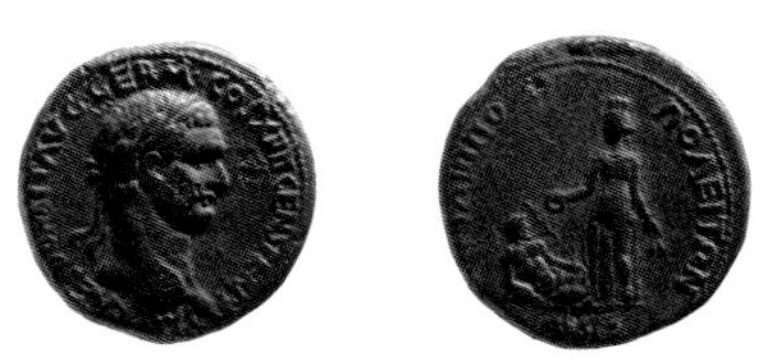

CAT. 65
Bronze coin, Philippopolis under Domitian (81–96 AD), 88–89 AD.
Head of Domitian / River god Hebros and the Tyche of Philippopolis.
25.18 g; 35 mm
KIKPE Collection, Athens
See *Essay V*

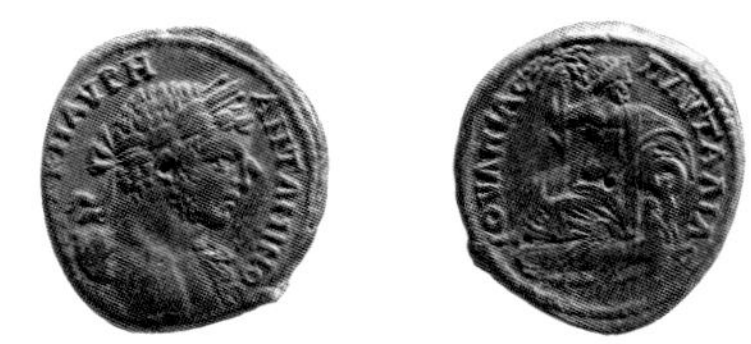

CAT. 66
Bronze coin, Pautalia under Caracalla (198–217 AD).
Bust of Caracalla / River god Strymon.
17.06 g; 29 mm
KIKPE Collection, Athens
See *Essay V*

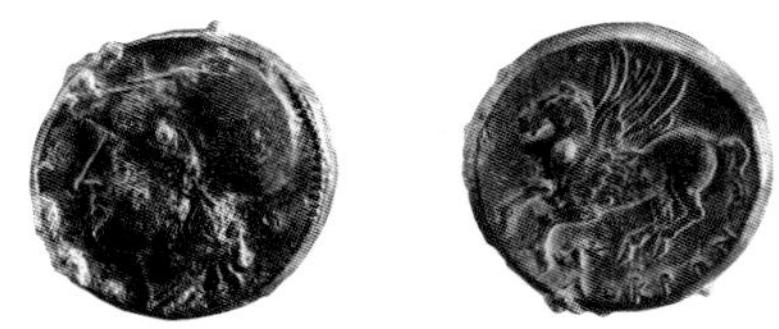

CAT. 67
Bronze coin, Lokroi Epizephyrioi, *ca.* 280–275 BC.
Head of Athena / Pegasus (the winged horse, symbolizes the element of air).
14.88 g; 24 mm
KIKPE Collection, Athens: *SNG KIKPE* 124

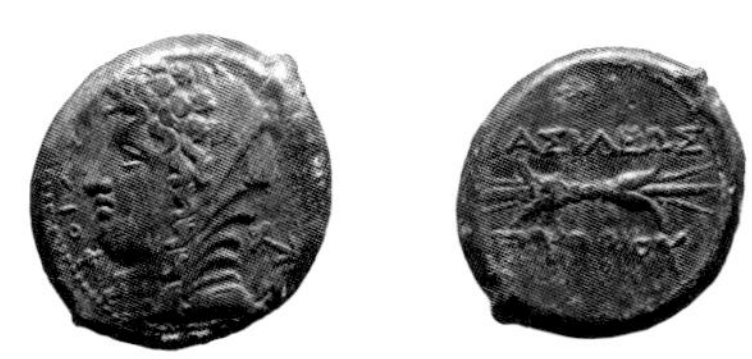

CAT. 68
Bronze coin, Pyrrhos of Epirus (319/8–272 BC), Syracuse, *ca.* 278–276 BC.
Head of Phthia / Thunderbolt (the element of fire in the element of air).
11.55 g; 26 mm
KIKPE Collection, Athens: *SNG KIKPE* 249

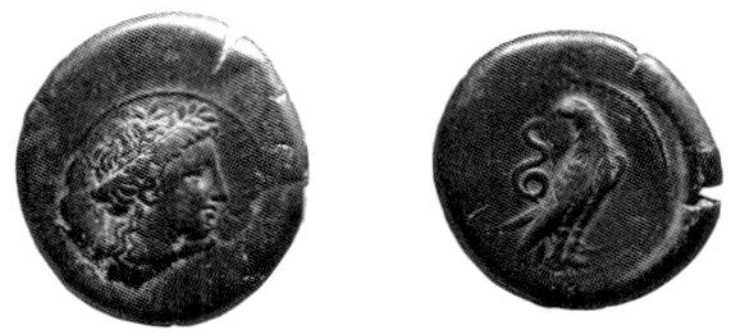

CAT. 69
Bronze coin, Herbessos, *ca.* 344–336 BC.
Head of Sicilia / Eagle holding serpent.
18.90 g; 28 mm
KIKPE Collection, Athens: *SNG KIKPE* 182
See *Essay V*

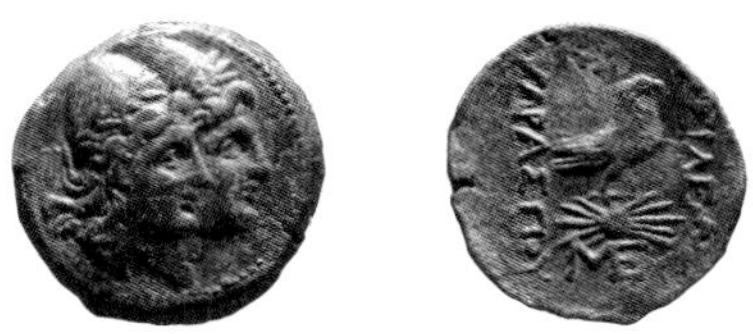

CAT. 70
Bronze coin, Charaspes (*ca.* 180–150 BC), Scythian ruler.
Heads of Dioscuri / Eagle on thunderbolt.
9.52 g; 23 mm
KIKPE Collection, Athens: *SNG KIKPE* 381
See *Essay V*

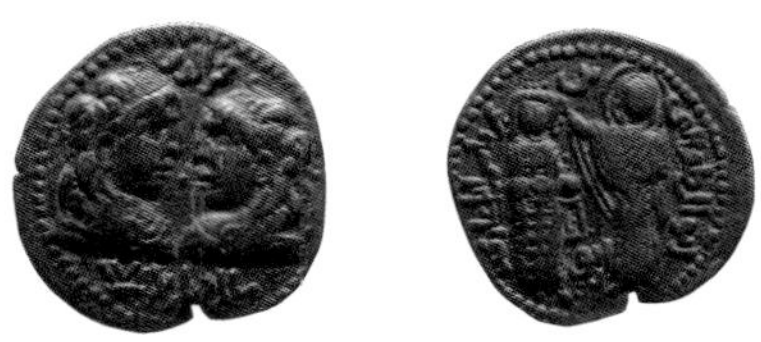

CAT. 71
Bronze coin, Najm al-Din Alpi (1152–1176 AD), Artuqid ruler of Mardin (Mardes), *ca.* 1154 AD.
Busts of Gemini / Emperor crowned by Virgin Mary.
15.43 g; 34 mm
KIKPE Collection, Athens
See *Essay V*

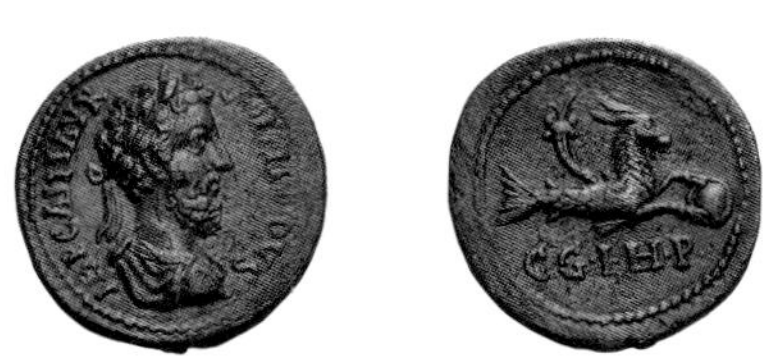

CAT. 72
Bronze coin, Parium under Commodus (180–192 AD).
Bust of Commodus / Capricorn.
8.17 g; 25 mm
KIKPE Collection, Athens
See *Essay V*

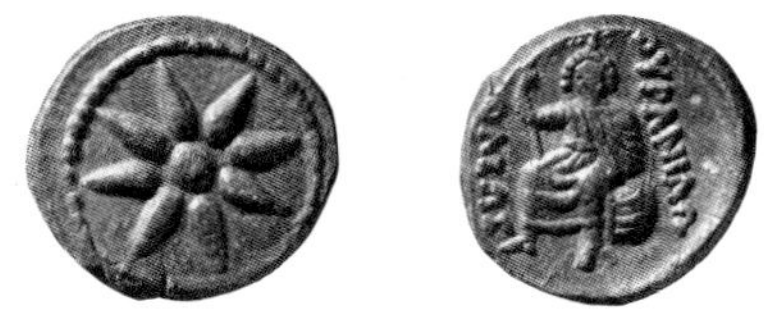

CAT. 73
Bronze coin, Ouranopolis, *ca.* 300 BC.
Eight-rayed star / Ouranos (Sky) on globe.
3.51 g; 16 mm
KIKPE Collection, Athens: *SNG KIKPE* 404
See *Essay V*

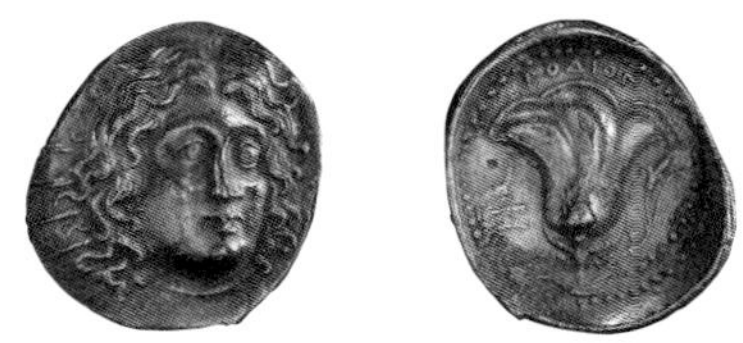

CAT. 74
Silver tetradrachm, Rhodos, *ca.* 250–190 BC.
Head of Helios / Rose.
12.71 g; 30 mm
Fondation Martin Bodmer, Cologny
See *Essay V*

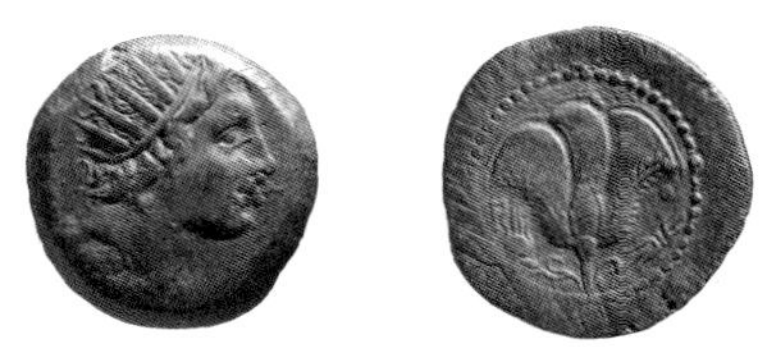

CAT. 75
Bronze coin, Rhodos, 88 BC and a little later.
Head of Helios / Rose.
17.35 g; 30 mm
KIKPE Collection, Athens: *SNG KIKPE* 913
See *Essay V*

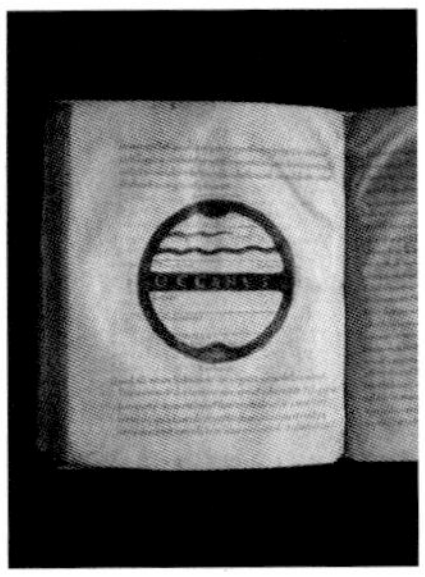

CAT. 76

Macrobius, *Commentarius in Ciceronis Somnium Scipionis*. Latin manuscript on *vellum*, South Germany or Austria, 10th century [*ca*. 970?].

This manuscript contains, from a ninth century archetype, an abridged version of the commentary by Macrobius (*ca*. AD 370 – post 430) of Cicero's *Dream of Scipio*. Concerned both with cosmogony and with the question of the immortality of the soul as explained in a dream to the young Scipio Emilianus by his forefathers, this text is only a passage from Cicero's *De re publica* (Book VI). Macrobius's interest in the passage accounts for its preservation when most of this Cicero's treatise is lost. This copy formerly belonged to the Benedictine Abbey of Saint Blaise at Admont (diocese of Salzburg) and was kept in its library from at least the twelfth century.

Fondation Martin Bodmer, Cologny, Cod. Bodmer 111
See *Essay V*

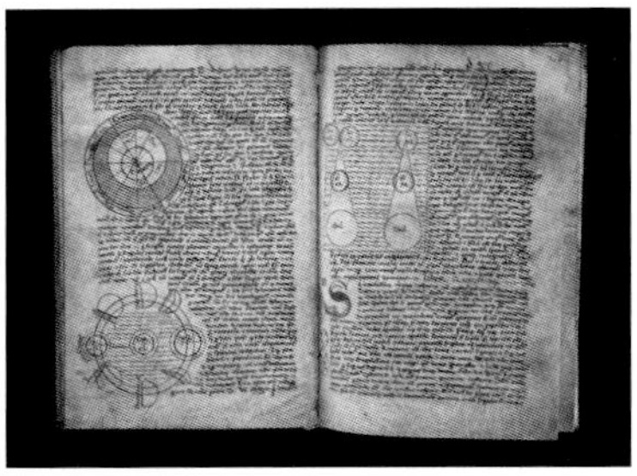

CAT. 77

Guillaume de Conches, *Dragmaticon*, Latin manuscript on *vellum*, West Germany, Rheinland, *ca*. 1230.

Magnum opus of Guillaume de Conches (*ca*. 1080–1160), one of the masters of the celebrated École de Chartres, the *Dragmaticon* was a particularly popular philosophical treatise. This copy, which was probably produced in a scholastic environment in the region of Cologne, is one of the earliest surviving copies. Its handy format, thirty-four diagrams and tables, and cursive Gothic script suggest that it was intended for university use. Typical of the *Zackenstil*, the impressive illuminated frontispiece depicts in two horizontal bands Plato conversing with Philosophy and the author (*Magister Wilhelmus*) questioned by the dedicatee Geoffrey the Handsome, Duke of Normandy.

Fondation Martin Bodmer, Cologny, Cod. Bodmer 188
See *Essay V*

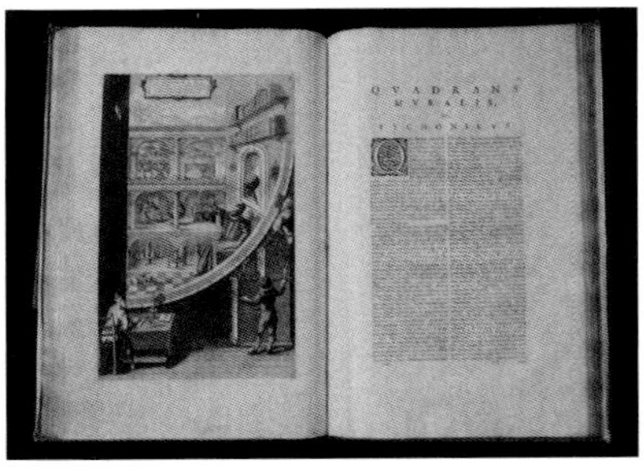

CAT. 78

Blaeu, Johannes, *Atlas Major*, Amsterdam, Blaeu, 1662.

With 597 maps distributed into eleven *in-folio* volumes, this atlas, probably the most sumptuous ever printed, exemplifies the Golden Age of Dutch cartography. Engraved with the intaglio technique, the plates of this copy are enhanced with handpainted colours.

Fondation Martin Bodmer, Cologny

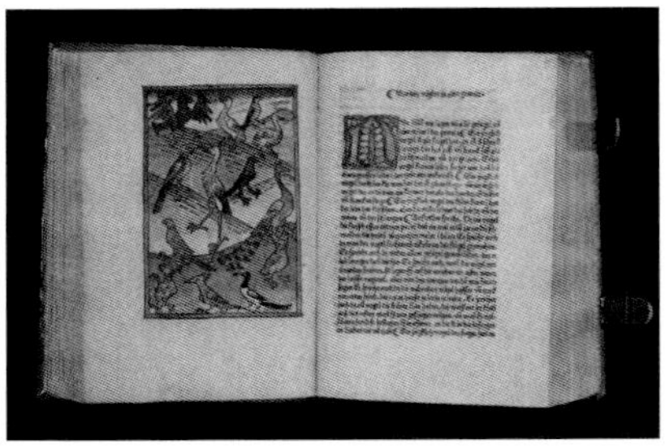

CAT. 79

Megenberg, Konrad von, *Buch der Natur*, Augsburg, Johann Bämler, 30 October 1475.

Editio princeps. Also known as *Buch von den natürlichen Dingen*, this encyclopedia was composed in the mid-fifteenth century by the German erudite Konrad von Megenberg (*ca*. 1309–1374), erstwhile professor of philosophy and theology at the Sorbonne. The first book of natural sciences produced in German, it was divided into eight chapters and addressed the various aspects of Creation: man, cosmogony, flora and fauna, precious stones and metals, and waterways.

Fondation Martin Bodmer, Cologny, Inc. Bod. 158

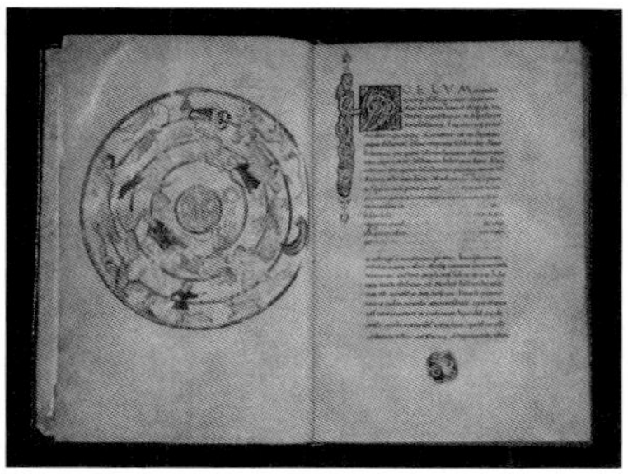

CAT. 80

Genus Arati. Latin manuscript on *vellum*, Italy, [probably Naples], 15th century.

A collection of astronomical treatises by Germanicus, Pliny the Elder, and Hyginus, this manuscript is decorated with several watercolours, including one of a planisphere with five gold concentric circles containing the constellations in the form of human figures and animals. These illustrations were probably created by the illuminator Antonio di Mario in the region of Naples, where two other contemporary manuscripts of identical content were produced.

Fondation Martin Bodmer, Cologny, Cod. Bodmer 7
See *Essay V*

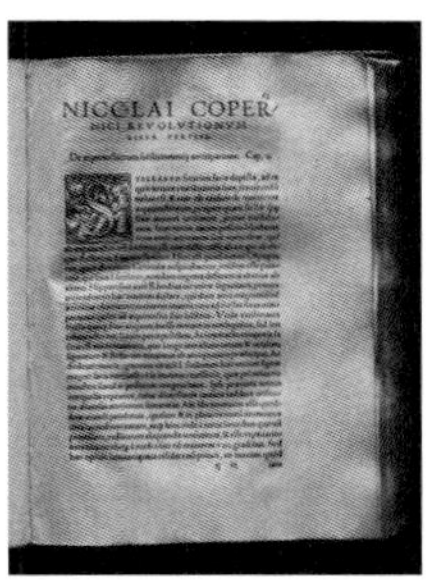

CAT. 81

Copernicus, Nicolaus, *De Revolutionibus Orbium Cœlestium*, Nuremberg, Johann Petreius, 1543.

First edition. Probably begun in the 1510's and completed in the 1530's, this revolutionary work, the first modern manifestation of the heliocentric theory, was printed only thirteen years later, shortly before its author's death, thanks to the perseverance of his disciple Joachim von Lauchen (also known as Rheticus).

Fondation Martin Bodmer, Cologny

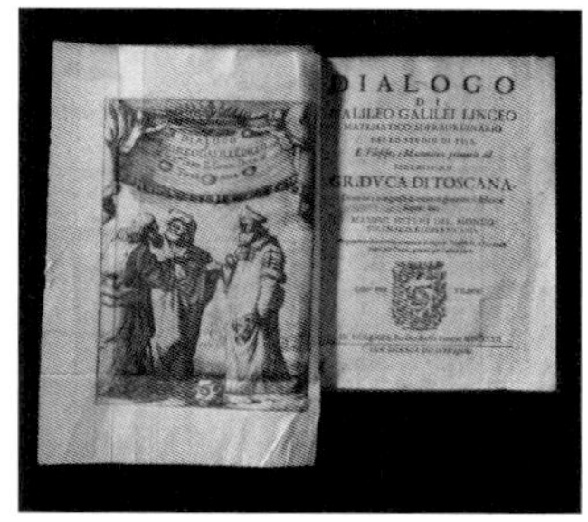

CAT. 82

Galilei, Galileo, *Dialogo di Galilei Galileo linceo matematico sapraordinario dello studio di Pisa… sopra i due massimi sistemi del mondo…*, Florence, Giovanni Batista Landini, 1632.

First edition, decorated with a frontispiece by Stefano della Bella. Originally commissioned by Pope Urban VIII, the *Dialogue Concerning the Two Chief World Systems* involved three characters: Filippo Salviati (named after Galileo's astronomer friend, who died in 1614) who spoke in favour of the Copernican system; a certain Simplicio, who supported the Aristotelian vision of the world; and the Venetian Giovan Francesco Sagredo, informed mediator, but without a clear position. Although supposed to present impartially both designs, the text was actually an advocacy for heliocentrism, which led to the rapid condemnation of the book and its author.

Fondation Martin Bodmer, Cologny

GODS AND MYTHS

Ancient Greek religion continues to be known to this day, through its celebrated myths and gods. It was revived for modern scholarship, art and literature from the Renaissance onwards, and particularly in the eighteenth and nineteenth centuries. A learned person of that period might well have read the *Iliad*, known the Muses, or at any rate been familiar with the principal myths from Antiquity. Where the surviving literature ends, the stories of ancient myth are taken up today by archaeological research, prominently including Numismatics. Indeed, Greek and Roman coins are among our sources on ancient Greek religion. The deity is a cosmic mind that creates nature, history, justice and morality, and its engraving on coins is an interpretation, a secret window through which man can glimpse at the inexhaustible forces of the universe and the powers controlling the world, as well as at the relation between man and the places where he lived and was animated by these powers.

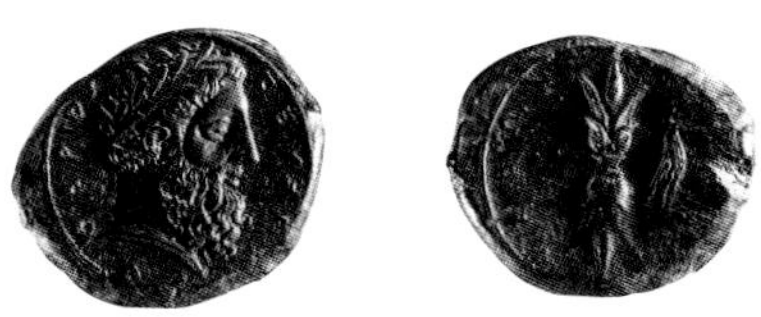

CAT. 83
Bronze coin, Syracuse, 357–354 BC.
Head of Zeus / Thunderbolt and eagle.
12.55 g; 23 mm
KIKPE Collection, Athens: *SNG KIKPE* 235

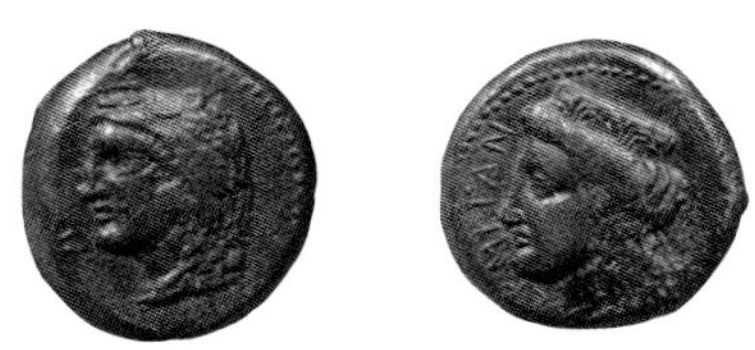

CAT. 84
Bronze coin, Thermae Himeraeae, 407–406 BC.
Head of Heracles / Head of Hera.
8.33 g; 19 mm
KIKPE Collection, Athens: *SNG KIKPE* 262

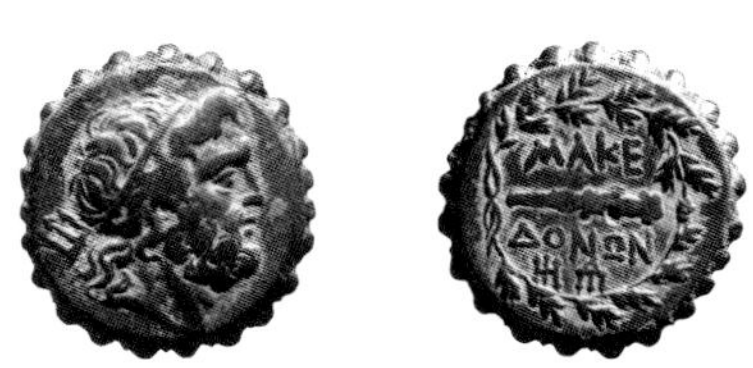

CAT. 85
Bronze coin, Macedonian kingdom, *ca*. 187–168 BC.
Head of Poseidon / Club.
13.00 g; 23 mm
KIKPE Collection, Athens: *SNG KIKPE* 457

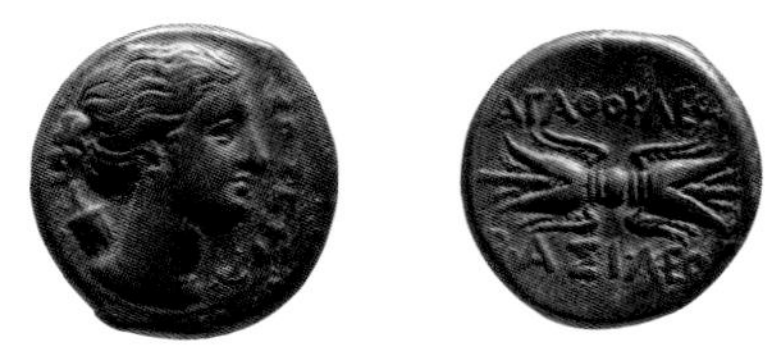

CAT. 86
Bronze coin, Agathocles (*ca*. 317–289 BC), Syracuse.
Head of Artemis / Winged thunderbolt.
10.10 g; 21 mm
KIKPE Collection, Athens: *SNG KIKPE* 237

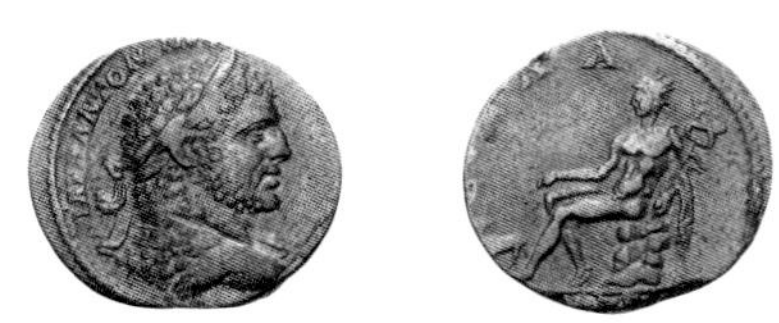

CAT. 87
Bronze coin, Patrae under Caracalla (198–217 AD), 213–217 AD.
Bust of Caracalla / Hermes on rock.
8.25 g; 23 mm
KIKPE Collection, Athens
See *Essay VIII*

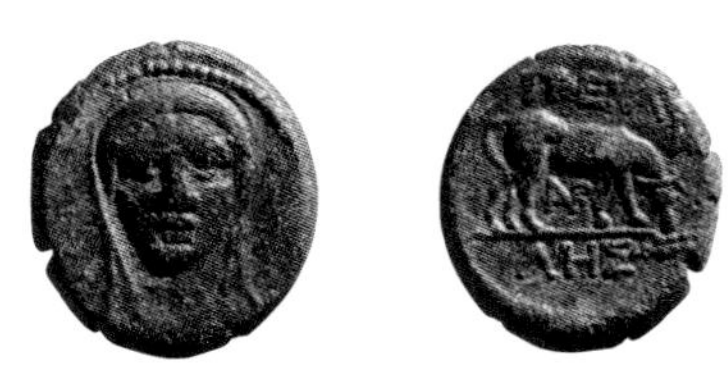

CAT. 88
Bronze coin, Pella, *ca*. 187–168 BC.
Head of Demeter / Cow grazing.
6.36 g; 17 mm
KIKPE Collection, Athens: *SNG KIKPE* 405

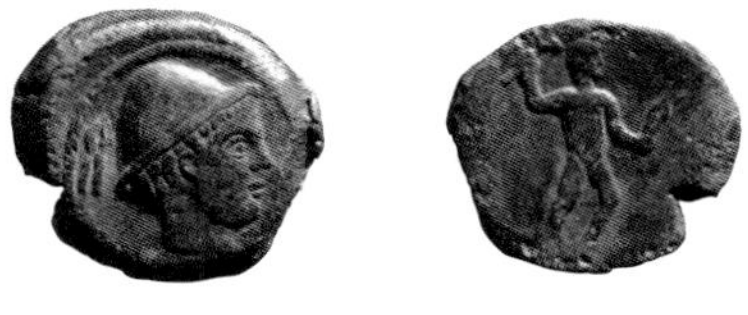

CAT. 89

Bronze coin, Lipara, after 210 BC.
Head of Hephaistus / Hephaistus holding tongs and hammer.
5.00 g; 19 mm
KIKPE Collection, Athens: *SNG KIKPE* 271

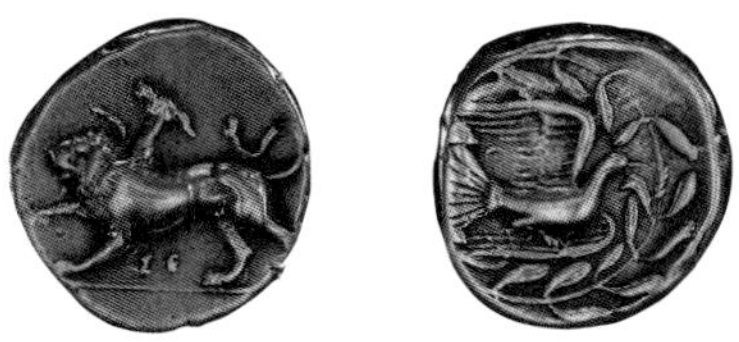

CAT. 90

Silver stater, Sicyon, early 4th century BC.
Chimaera / Dove within wreath.
12.08 g; 23 mm
Fondation Martin Bodmer, Cologny

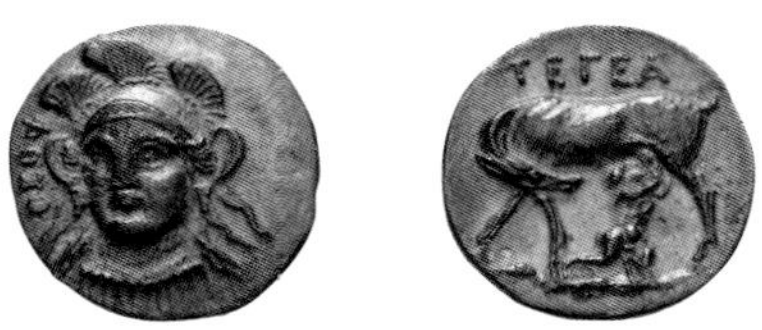

CAT. 91

Bronze coin, Tegea, *ca.* 250 BC.
Head of Athena / Doe suckling Telephos.
3.77 g; 17 mm
KIKPE Collection, Athens: *SNG KIKPE* 649
See *Procemium*

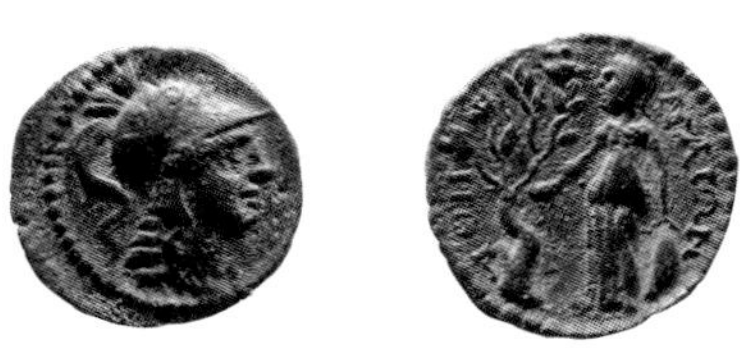

CAT. 92

Bronze coin, Athens, *ca.* 264–267 AD.
Head of Athena / Athena Parthenos and olive–tree.
5.26 g; 21 mm
KIKPE Collection, Athens
See *Essay I*

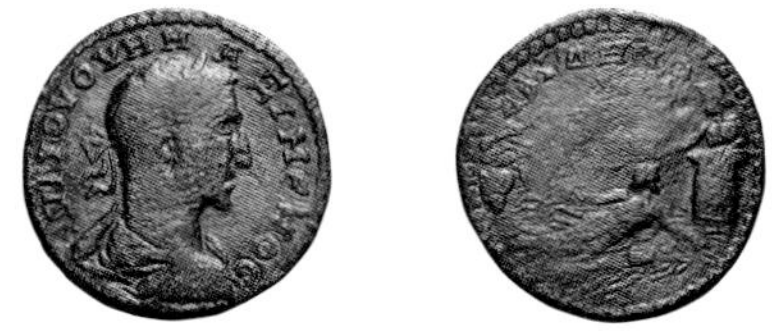

CAT. 93

Bronze coin, Abydos under Maximinus I Thrax (235–238 AD).
Bust of Maximinus / Leander and Hero.
20.42 g; 35 mm
KIKPE Collection, Athens
See *Essays I* and *V*

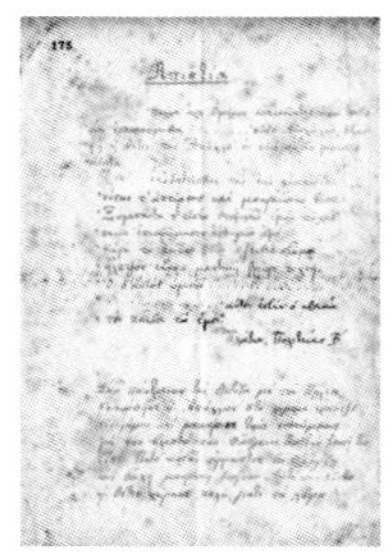

CAT. 94

Cavafy, Constantine P., autograph manuscript
(the poem *Unfaithfulness*):

"*... that he would not know sickness, would live long, / and that every blessing would be his; / and he sang such praises that he rejoiced my heart. / And I had hopes that the divine lips of Apollo, / fluent with the art of prophecy, would not prove false. / But he who proclaimed these things ... / he it is who killed my son ...*" (Plato, *Republic*, 383b)
At the marriage of Thetis and Peleus / Apollo stood up during the sumptuous wedding feast / and blessed the bridal pair / for the son who would come from their union ... (transl. E. Keeley)

Benaki Museum, Historical Archives, inv. no. 175/18

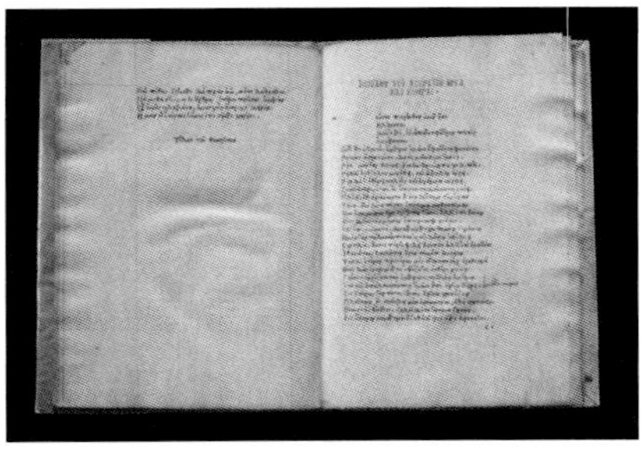

CAT. 95

Hesiod, [*Opera et Dies*] (Gr.), [Milan, Bonus Accursius, *ca.* 1479/1480].

Editio princeps. This *in-folio*, which appeared without publisher's name or date, brought together the works of Hesiod and Theocritus's *Idylls*, an association repeated in several subsequent editions, most notably that by Aldes in 1495.

Fondation Martin Bodmer, Cologny, Inc. Bod. 237
See *Essay VI*

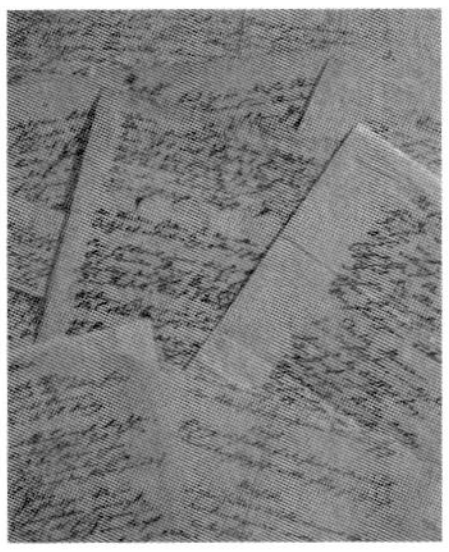

CAT. 96

Goethe, Johann Wolfgang von, [*Faust, eine Tragödie. Zweiter Teil*]. Autograph manuscript, [*ca.* 1825–1831].

A set of twenty-five autographed fragments of the play's five acts, amounting to a total of 420 verses. In Act I of his second *Faust* (written between 1825 and 1831), Goethe staged a large group of mythological figures. Various beings and imaginary monsters succeeded one another during a carnival masquerade scene located in a great hall of the imperial palace: the Graces, the Fates and the Furies, then the Fauns, a Satyr and the Nymphs, and, finally, a procession of Gnomes praising the great Pan. The last, who is none other than the emperor, almost burns himself when he tries to get hold of the treasure conspicuously left by Pluto (in other words Mephistopheles or Faust himself).

Fondation Martin Bodmer, Cologny, G-30.1 to G-30.19

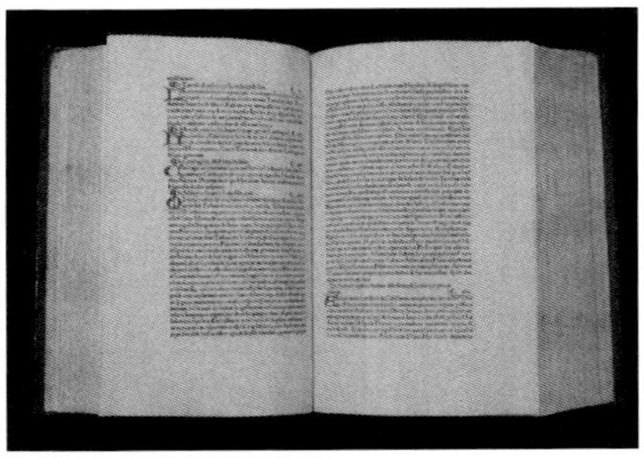

CAT. 97

Boccaccio, Giovanni, *Genealogiæ Deorum gentilium*, Venice, Wendelin von Speyer, 1472. *Editio princeps*, with additions by Dominicus Silvester and Raphael Zovenzonius.

Commissioned by Hugo IV of Lusignan, King of Cyprus and the book's dedicatee, this compilation of the principal Greek myths and their interpretations was completed in around 1360, although Boccaccio continued to rewrite, augment, and correct his work until 1374.
Each divinity is accompanied by a 'biographical note' according to the best ancient and medieval *auctoritates*. Thus, information on *Minerva secundi Jovis filia* is drawn from both Cicero's *The Nature of Gods* and Alberic of London, a twelfth-century mythographer.

Fondation Martin Bodmer, Cologny, Inc. Bod. 51

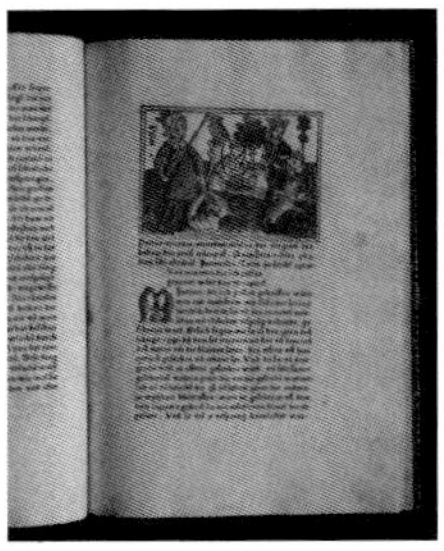

CAT. 98

Boccaccio, Giovanni, *De claris Mulieribus*, Ulm, Johann Zainer, [1473].

First German edition, translated by Heinrich Steinhöwel. Written in the early 1360's, this collection of women's biographies, the first of its kind, aimed at becoming the equivalent to Plutarch's *De viris illustribus*. Dedicated by Boccaccio to Andrea Acciaiuoli, Countess of Altavilla, the book treats female rulers of the past, contemporary ladies of the Florentine and Siennese bourgeoisie, and mythological figures. The sixth portrait is dedicated to the goddess '*Minerva die öch pallas gehaissen wurt*', or Athena Parthenos, the '*dea virginum*'. One of the 76 wood engravings with watercolour accents illustrating the volume depicts Athena fully armed, her *gorgoneion*-decorated shield at her feet. The artist also represented her principal attributes, the owl and the olive tree, at her sides.

Fondation Martin Bodmer, Cologny, Inc. Bod. 48
See *Essay I*

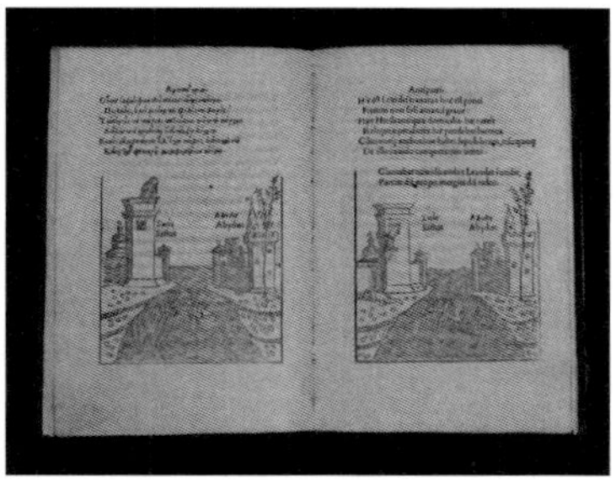

CAT. 99

Musaeus the Grammarian, *Opusculum de Herone et Leandro*, Venice, Aldo Manuzio, [before November 1495 for the Greek part, 1497 for the Latin part].

Editio princeps and first Latin edition (translated by the Cretan humanist Marco Musuro [1470–1517]).
An Egyptian poet writing in Greek, Musaeus is known only by this short epyllion relating the tragic love of Hero and Leander. Leander would swim every night across the Hellespont to be with his loved one. One night, he lost his way and was drowned, so Hero took her life to be with him. This volume includes a striking double engraving depicting the death of the two lovers. The undated juxtalinear Greco-Roman translation was long considered (wrongly) the first print to be produced in the famous workshop of Aldo Manuzio, which began its activity in 1494.

Fondation Martin Bodmer, Cologny, Inc. Bod. 181

See *Essay V*

THE WORLD OF HOMER

In the Western classical tradition, Homer is the author of the *Iliad* and the *Odyssey*, and the greatest ancient Greek epic poet. In actual fact, we know very little about him. His birthplace is doubtful, although Smyrna, Colophon, Chios, Amastris, Nicaea, Tios, Ios, and other cities have all contended for this honour, and his birth date is likewise controversial. However, almost everyone knows of the Trojan War and the legendary tales of the gods and heroes who battled around the impregnable walls of Troy: Zeus, Athena, Ares, Apollo, Menelaus, Agamemnon, Helen, Achilles, Hector, Ajax. Homer's world is a realm of splendid wars, of gleaming gold and bronze, of noble men and of the most beautiful of women, a world that has had an enormous influence on the history of literature. The high-walled city of Troy was more fable than reality to everyone except Heinrich Schliemann, who from his boyhood was determined to discover the celebrated city and the treasure reputed to lie within it.

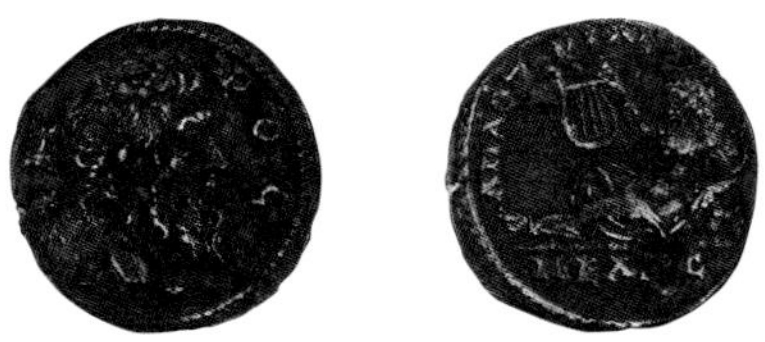

CAT. 100
Bronze coin, Amastris, 2nd century AD.
Bust of Homer / River god Meles.
9.56 g; 22 mm
Fondation Martin Bodmer, Cologny
See *Essay III*

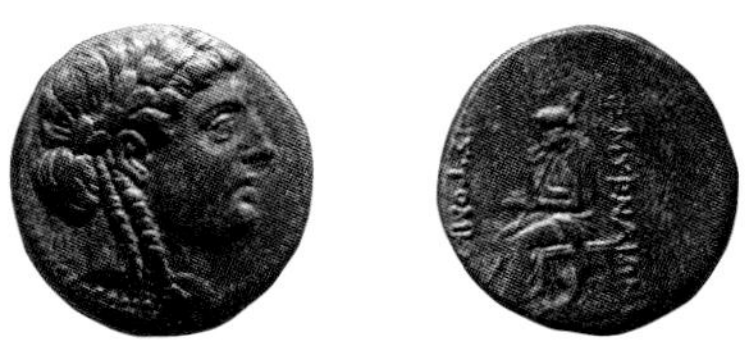

CAT. 101
Bronze coin, Smyrna, shortly after *ca.* 190 BC.
Head of Apollo / Homer seated.
8.63 g; 21 mm
KIKPE Collection, Athens: *SNG KIKPE* 868
See *Essay III*

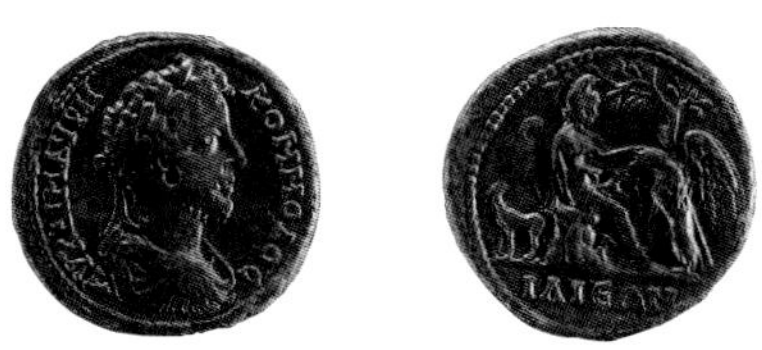

CAT. 102
Bronze coin, Ilium under Commodus (180–192 AD).
Bust of Commodus / Ganymedes and eagle (Zeus).
21.66 g; 35 mm
KIKPE Collection, Athens

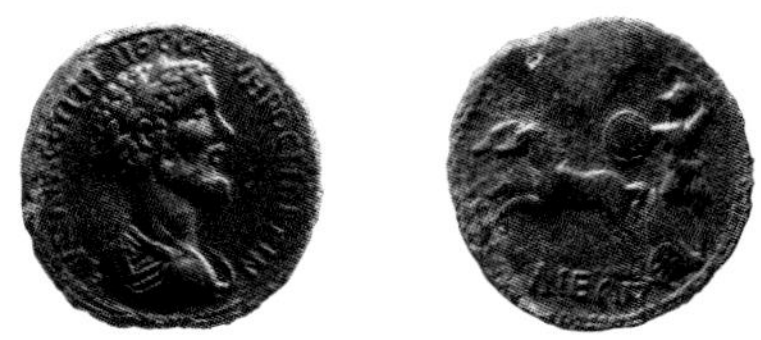

CAT. 103
Bronze coin, Ilium under Septimius Severus (193–211 AD).
Bust of Septimius Severus / Hector on chariot.
21.61 g; 37 mm
KIKPE Collection, Athens

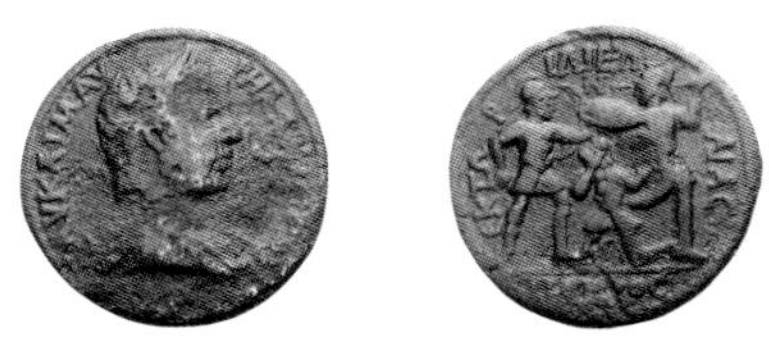

CAT. 104
Bronze coin, Ilium under Caracalla (198–217 AD).
Bust of Caracalla / Hector fighting Teucros and Ajax.
24.06 g; 33 mm
KIKPE Collection, Athens
See *Essay I*

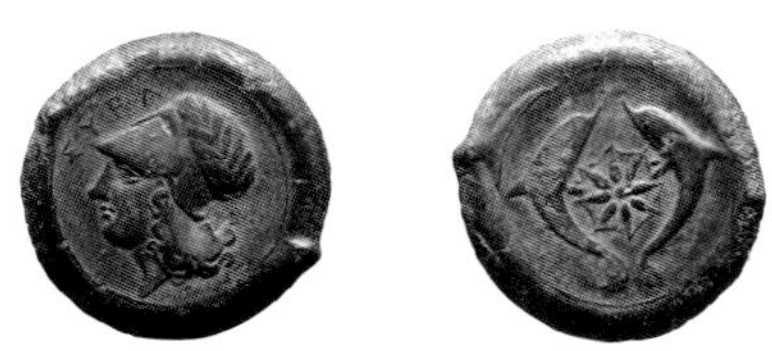

CAT. 105
Bronze coin, Syracuse, from *ca.* 395 BC onwards.
Head of Athena / Sea-star between two dolphins.
30.72 g; 30 mm
KIKPE Collection, Athens: *SNG KIKPE* 234

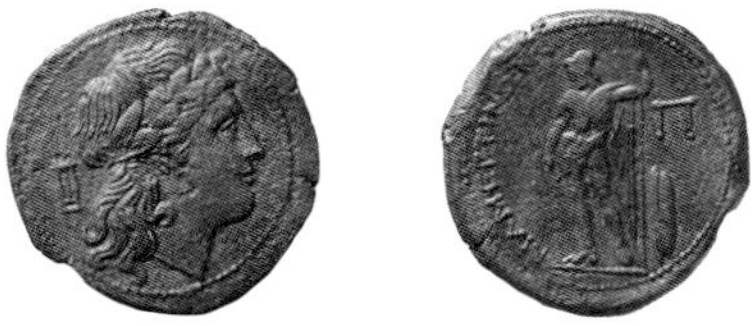

CAT. 106
Bronze coin, the Mamertini, Messana, *ca.* 211–208 BC.
Head of Apollo / Warrior.
11.79 g; 25 mm
KIKPE Collection, Athens: *SNG KIKPE* 206

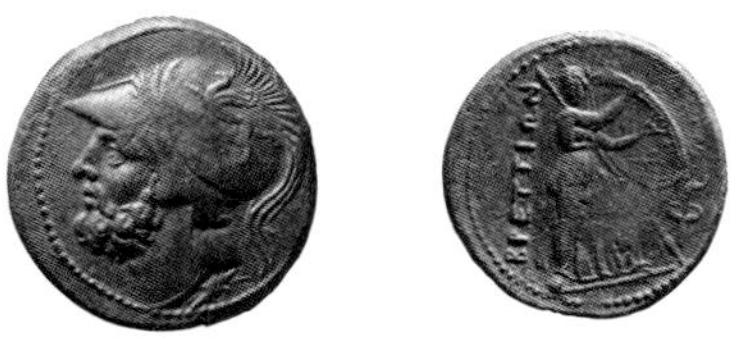

CAT. 107
Bronze coin, Brettii, *ca.* 211–208 BC.
Head of Ares / Athena.
15.76 g; 26 mm
KIKPE Collection, Athens: *SNG KIKPE* 116

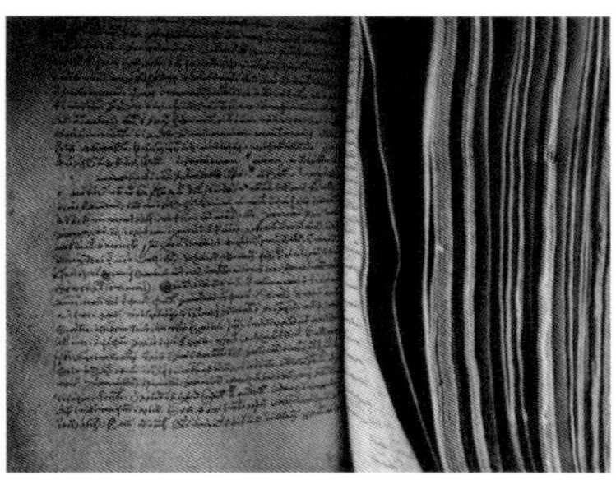

CAT. 108
Homer, *Iliad*. Greek manuscript on *vellum* and paper, Italy, region of Otranto, 3rd third of 13th century.

Created in the region of Otranto, centre of Greek culture in southern Italy, this copy of the Homeric text is completed with interlinear and marginal scholia, primarily excerpts from the commentary composed a century earlier by the Byzantine erudite Ioannis Tzetzes (*ca.* 1110–1180/1185).

Fondation Martin Bodmer, Cologny, Cod. Bodmer 7

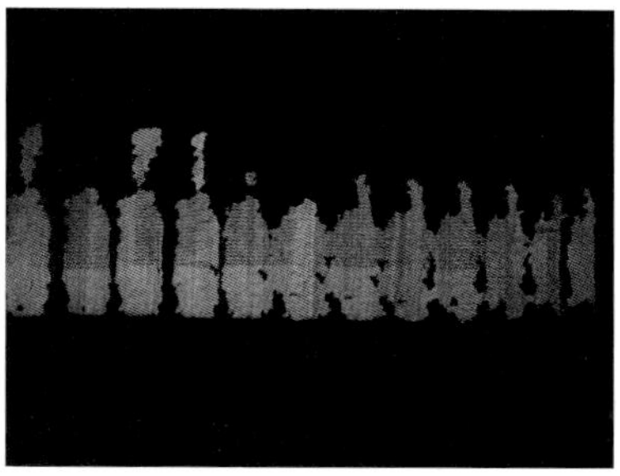

CAT. 109
Homer, *Iliad*, [Chapter V]. Greek manuscript on papyrus, Egypt, probably Panopolis [modern Akhmim], *ca.* AD 250–350.

Written on the reverse of an administrative register dating to the reign of emperor Septimius Severus (AD 208 or 209), this copy of Chapter V was obviously intended as an independent scroll. This manuscript is characteristic of the division of original works into chapters or books (Kleinrollensystem) allowing for smaller scrolls, which were easier for the reader to handle than the earlier bulky *volumina*.

Fondation Martin Bodmer, Cologny, Pap. Bodmer I

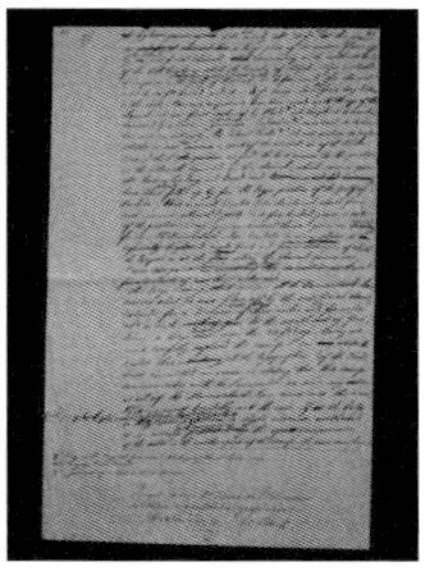

CAT. 110
Schliemann, Heinrich, [*On the canal of Bournbashi Sou*]. Autograph manuscript in English, [*ca.* 1880].

In his *Ilios, the city and country of the Trojans* (London, J. Murray, 1880), Heinrich Schliemann (1822–1890) provided a synthesis of the 'results of researches and discoveries on the site of Troy and throughout the Troad in the years 1871–72–73–78–79'. This excerpt (included on page 98 of the London edition) refers to the canal that regulates the course of Bournabashi Sou, one of the tributaries of the Homeric Scamander River. Unlike most of his predecessors, of which some thought of the canal as being Ottoman, Schliemann attributed this work to Antiquity on archaeological grounds: to him the thickness of the sediments accumulated at the canal's opening could only be explained by 'several thousands years' of alluvial deposits.

Fondation Martin Bodmer, Cologny, S-30.1

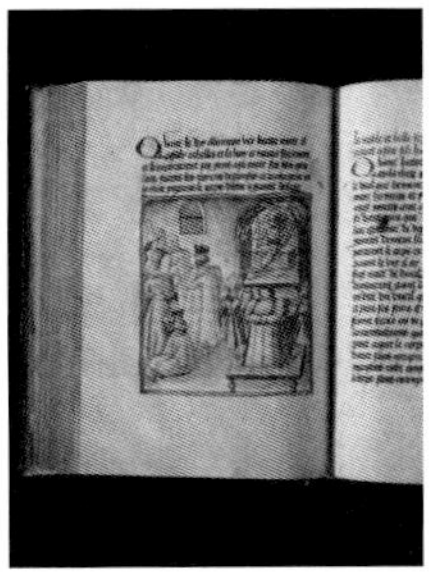

CAT. 111

Histoire de Thèbes, [followed by:] *Histoire de Troie*, French manuscript on paper, France, 1469.

This *Histoire de Troie* (History of Troy) is a free and abridged translation in prose of Guido delle Colonne's *Historia destructionis Troiae*. Written between 1270 and 1287, the latter work was also a translation in Latin prose of the *Romance of Troy*, a long poem composed a century earlier by Benoît de Sainte-Maure. Delle Colonne's book was a phenomenal success throughout Europe, with translations in French (first by Raoul Le Fèvre in 1464), but also in Neapolitan, English, and Catalan. Copied by a certain Jacotin de Lespluc, this manuscript is illustrated with 128 ink and watercolour drawings (possibly created in the workshop of Jean d'Ardenay).

Fondation Martin Bodmer, Cologny, Cod. Bodmer 160

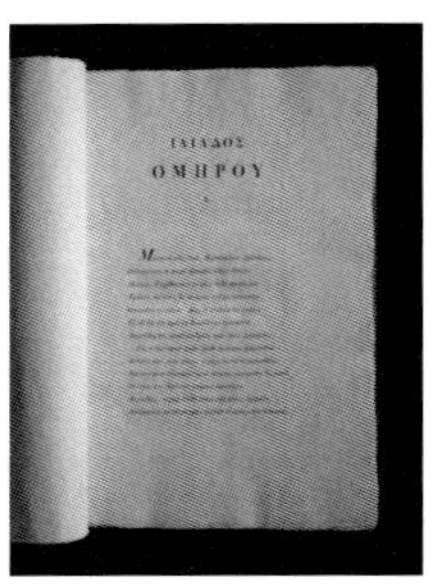

CAT. 112

Homer, [*Iliad*] (Gr.), Parma, Giambattista Bodoni, 1808.

A most ambitious typographic enterprise, this edition of the *Iliad* in three *in-folio* volumes required no less than five years of work, primarily in order to engrave and cast the simple, elegant letters desired by the publisher Bodoni (1740–1813). This monumental edition to the glory of Homer was limited to 168 copies.

Fondation Martin Bodmer, Cologny
See *Essay IV*

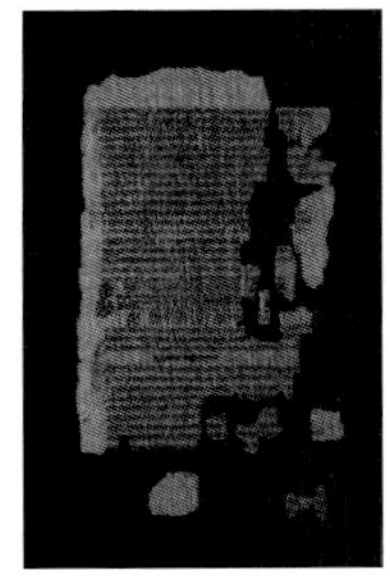

CAT. 113

Dorotheos, *The Vision*. Greek manuscript on papyrus, end of 4th or beginning of 5th century.

Studded with reminiscences of Homer, Hesiod, and Apollonius Rhodius, this poem of 360 verses retranscribed in the first person the mystical experience, close to a trance, of Dorotheos (possibly the son of the poet Quintus of Smyrna), a pagan erudite suddenly converted to Christianity. The protagonist might also be identified as Dorotheos, priest of the Church of Antioch in *ca.* AD 290, friend of Eusebius of Caesaria and martyred under Diocletian.

Fondation Martin Bodmer, Cologny, Pap. Bodmer XXIX

IN SEARCH OF IMMORTALITY

The anxiety over death, the inability to comprehend the transience of life, the discomfiture before the gateway to the Underworld and the hope of a life after death are enduring concepts that are identified with all the watersheds in the history of mankind, regardless of religious or cultural environment. The symbolisms of these mental yet conscious emotions are an alloy in which variations of myths, legends and traditions with a historical kernel, popular beliefs and poetic imagination are fused. Dramatic narratives are limited to the domain of divine protection and intervention, in an austere and summary manner, in a head-on dialogue between the representations on the two sides of the coins, where solitary figures predominate. Man's angst is intensified during the transitional period when the old religion gave way to Christianity.

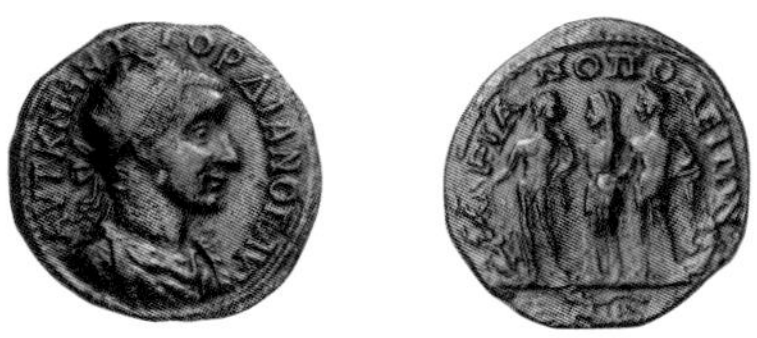

CAT. 114
Bronze coin, Hadrianopolis under Gordian III (238–244 AD).
Bust of Gordian III / Orpheus, Eurydice and Hermes.
13.91 g; 30 mm
KIKPE Collection, Athens
See *Procemium*

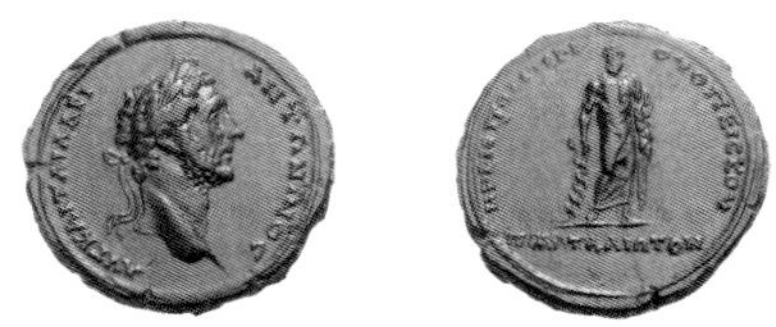

CAT. 117
Bronze coin, Pautalia under Antoninus Pius (138–161 AD).
Bust of Antoninus Pius / Asclepius.
20.41 g; 32 mm
KIKPE Collection, Athens
See *Essay III*

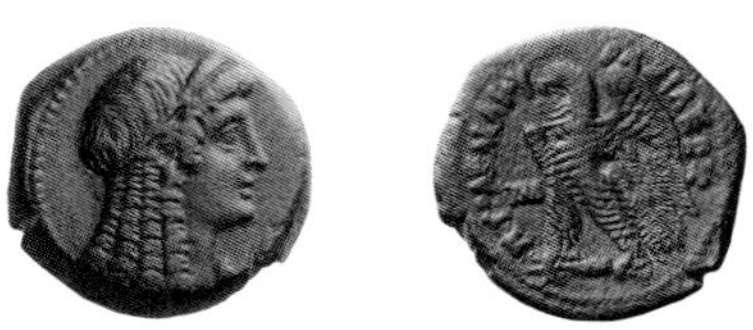

CAT. 115
Bronze coin, Ptolemy VI (180–145 BC), Alexandria, *ca.* 180–176 BC.
Head of Isis / Eagle on thunderbolt.
14.94 g; 27 mm
KIKPE Collection, Athens: *SNG KIKPE* 1185
See *Essay III*

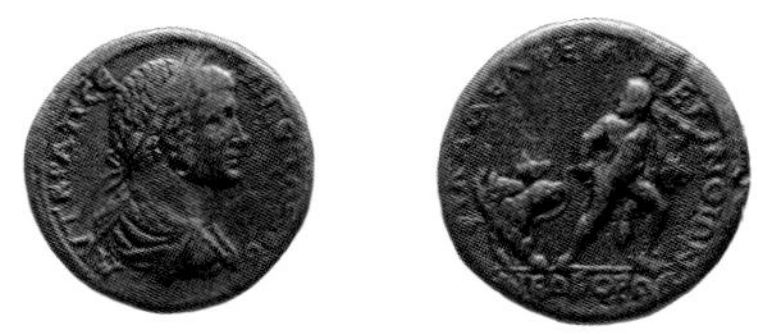

CAT. 118
Bronze 'medallion', Perinthus in the name of Geta (*ca.* 209–212 AD).
Bust of Geta / Heracles and the Cerberus.
36.04 g; 39 mm
KIKPE Collection, Athens
See *Procemium* and *Essay III*

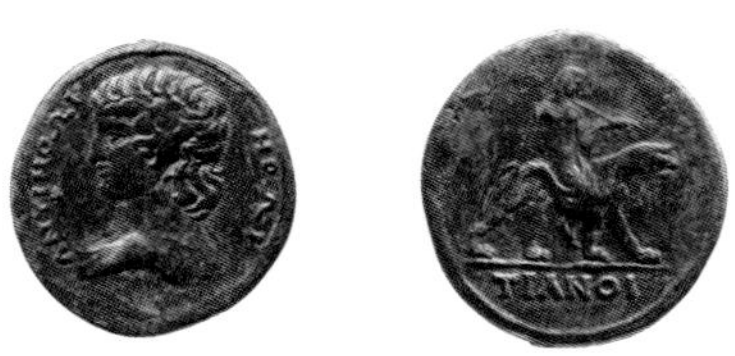

CAT. 116
Bronze 'medallion' in honour of Antinous, Tium under Hadrian (117–138 AD), after 130 AD.
Bust of Antinous / Antinous as Dionysus on panther.
41.13 g; 37 mm
KIKPE Collection, Athens
See *Procemium, Essays I* and *III*

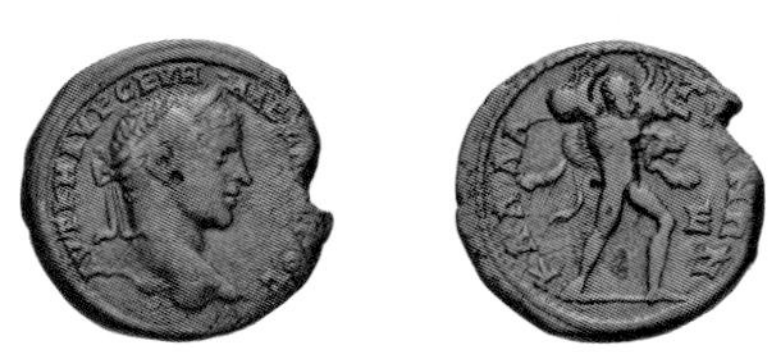

CAT. 119
Bronze coin, Callatis under Severus Alexander (222–235 AD).
Bust of Severus Alexander / Heracles and the Erymanthian Boar.
10.04 g; 25 mm.
KIKPE Collection, Athens
See *Essay III*

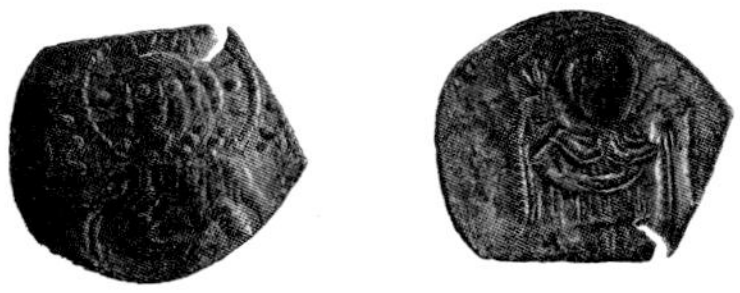

CAT. 120

Billon *trachy*, Demetrios Komnenos Doukas (1244–1246 AD.), Thessalonike.
Bust of Christ Emmanuel / Archangel Michael.
1.64 g; 24 mm
KIKPE Collection, Athens

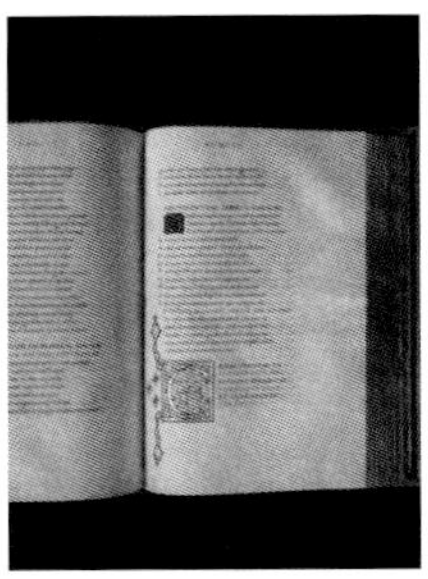

CAT. 121

Ovid, *Metamorphoseon* [and] *Fasti*. Latin manuscript on *vellum*, Italy, Naples, 15th century [*ca*. 1480?].

With its exquisite *bianchi girari* (white vine scrolls) decoration, this copy is typical of Italian productions of the early Renaissance and more particularly of the Neapolitan creations imitating the style of the royal illuminator Cola Rapicano. In fact, this manuscript was copied by the artist Ippolito Lunense (active between 1479 and 1492) for Antonello Petrucci (†1487), secretary of Ferdinand I of Aragon, King of Naples.

Fondation Martin Bodmer, Cologny, Cod. Bodmer 124
See *Procemium* and *Essay IV*

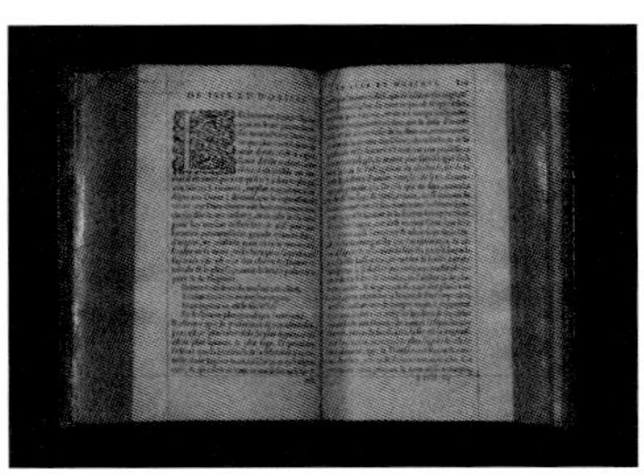

CAT. 122

Plutarch, *Les Œuvres morales et meslees*, Paris, Michel Vascosan, 1574.

Published in seven beautifully printed volumes, this edition is the second of the French translation by the humanist Jacques Amyot (1513–1593), Bishop of Auxerre and Grand Almoner of France. Praised by Montaigne, this very faithful version remained for a long time the reference edition, often combined with the *Vies des hommes illustres* (*Lives of Illustrious Men*), also translated by Amyot.

Fondation Martin Bodmer, Cologny

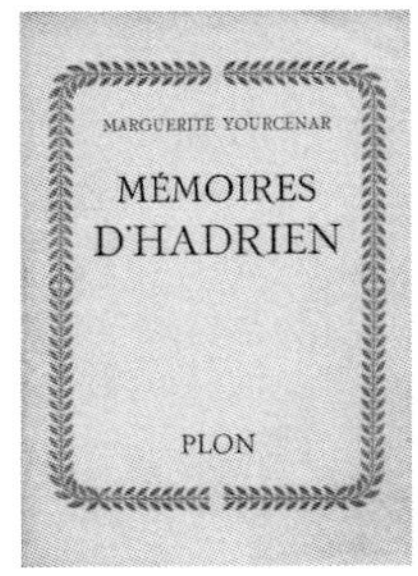

CAT. 123

Yourcenar, Marguerite, *Memoirs of Hadrian*. Plon, 1951.

Presented in the form of a long letter addressed by the elderly emperor to his adoptive grandson and future successor Marcus Aurelius, this novel retraces in first person the career of this enlightened ruler, symbol of the apogee of the Roman Empire, based on solid historical documentation.

See *Procemium* and *Essay V*

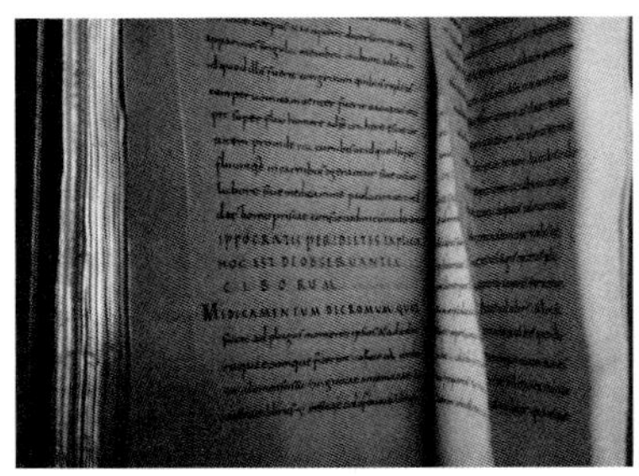

CAT. 124

Pseudo-Hippocrates, *De victus ratione liber II, seu De observantia ciborum*. Latin manuscript on *vellum*, Germany, Fulda, first half of 9th century.

Produced in the *scriptorium* of the famous Benedictine Abbey of Fulda, this manuscript is the only known example of the Latin version of the treatise *De victus ratione*, formerly (and wrongly) attributed to Hippocrates. This book, which laid the foundation of dietetics and influenced many physicians, is followed here by a collection of the *Recepta medica* and was originally bound together with Apicius's *De coquiniaria*.

Fondation Martin Bodmer, Cologny, Cod. Bodmer 124

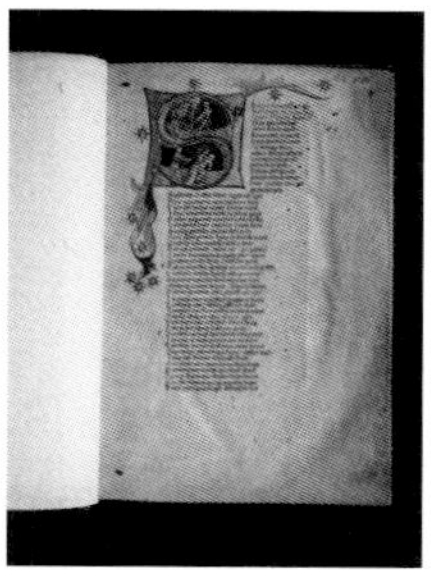

CAT. 125

Seneca, *Tragœdiae*, Latin manuscript on *vellum*, Italy, 15th century.

This copy, which belongs to the so-called 'Family A' of manuscripts of these tragedies, comprises ten plays, including one clearly apocryphal (*Octavia*). The attribution of *Hercules Oetaeus* (ff. 101-121) is still debated, as it differs significantly from the other plays most notably because of its length. Each play's *incipit* is illustrated here by a handsome historiated initial depicting one of the play's episodes.

Fondation Martin Bodmer, Cologny, Cod. Bodmer 152

See *Procemium*

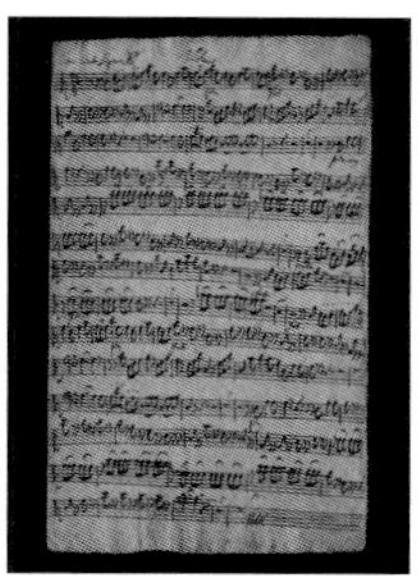

CAT. 126

Bach, Johann Sebastian, *Der alte Drache brennt vor Neid...* Autograph score, 1732–1735.

This viola piece from the bass aria *Der alte Drache brennt vor Neid...* (from the cantata *Herr Gott, dich loben alle wie...* [BWV 130]) was composed for the celebration of the archangel Michael in Leipzig in 1724 and intended to be reworked.

Fondation Martin Bodmer, Cologny, B-2.1

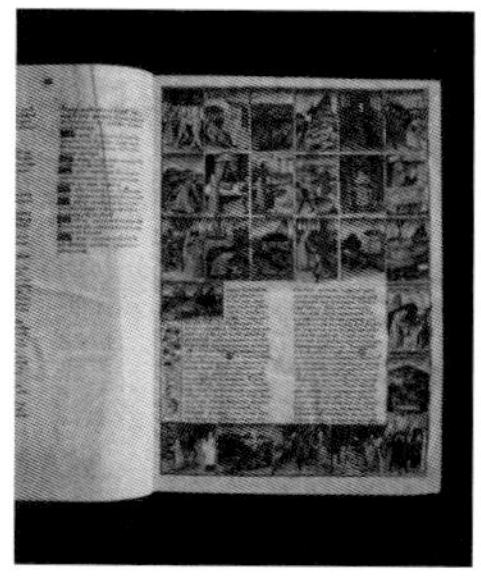

CAT. 127

Boccaccio, Giovanni, *Des cas des nobles hommes et femmes*. French manuscript on *vellum*, France, 15th century.

French translation by Laurent de Premierfait of the *De casibus virorum illustrium*. This manuscript is richly illustrated with 10 large and 150 small miniatures. The *incipit* of each of the nine books is framed by a veritable mosaic of historiated vignettes depicting the 'cases' referred to in the subsequent chapter.

Fondation Martin Bodmer, Cologny, Cod. Bodmer 174

CHRISTIAN IMAGES

Christian art is produced in an endeavour to illustrate, supplement and portray in tangible form the sacred. According to the Christian ideals and principles, the sacred was formulated in words and images, and when in liturgies it was accompanied by chant. Over the centuries the Christians developed an easy and very precise visual language for their religious art. One of this art's rules is that it gives the viewer hints at or guides how a picture is to be read. Images of Jesus Christ, the Virgin Mary, various saints, holy symbols and narrative scenes are the most common subjects. The tardiness in the appearance of religious themes in Byzantine coinage and their rather restricted presence on coins seem to confirm that from a secular viewpoint there were different worlds relating to the holy, which should not be confused. Holy figures were placed on coins in an attempt to define the relation of the emperor to the divine, as representative and servant of Christ on earth, or to solicit intervention through the presence of the Virgin or of certain saints.

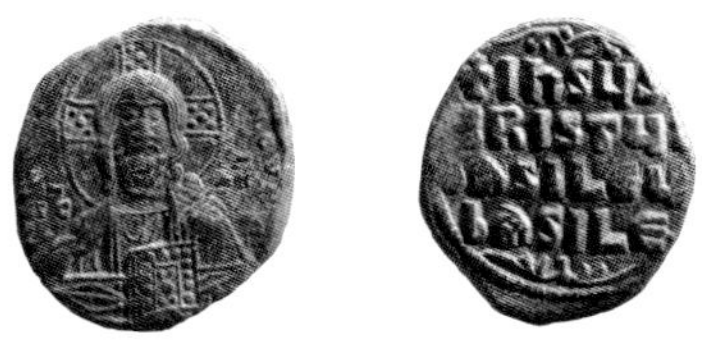

CAT. 128
Bronze anonymous *follis*, Class A2, Constantinople, 976–1030/1035 AD.
Bust of Christ Pantokrator / Legend in four lines.
9.77 g; 29 mm
KIKPE Collection, Athens
See *Essay X*

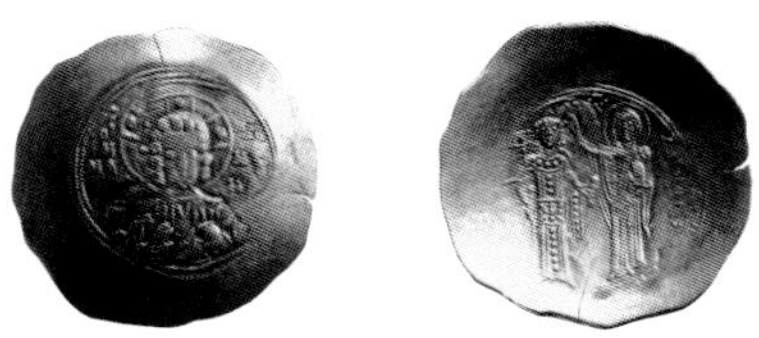

CAT. 129
Electrum aspron trachy, Manuel I Komnenos (1143–1180 AD), Constantinople, *ca*. 1143–11154 AD.
Bust of Christ Emmanuel / Virgin Mary crowning the emperor
4.40 g; 32 mm
KIKPE Collection, Athens
See *Essay X*

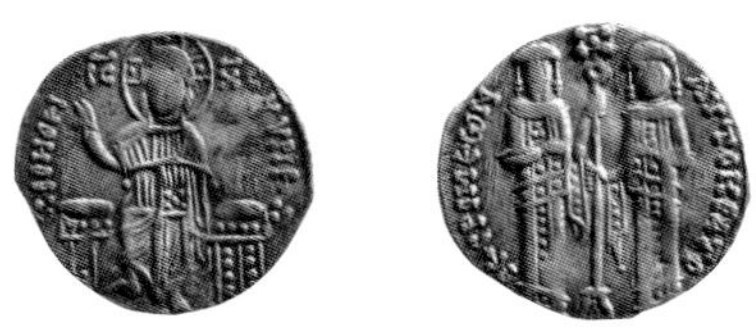

CAT. 130
Silver *basilikon*, Andronikos II Palaiologos (1261–1328 AD), Constantinople, *ca*. 1294–1320 AD.
Christ enthroned / Two emperors (Andronikos II and his son Michael IX) holding labarum.
1.81 g; 20 mm
KIKPE Collection, Athens

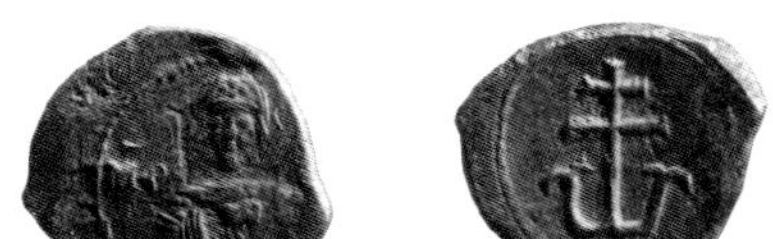

CAT. 131
Bronze half *tetarteron*, Latin Kingdom of Thessalonike, Thessalonike, 1204–1224 AD.
Bust of Virgin Mary / Patriarchal cross with tendrils.
2.12 g; 18 mm
KIKPE Collection, Athens

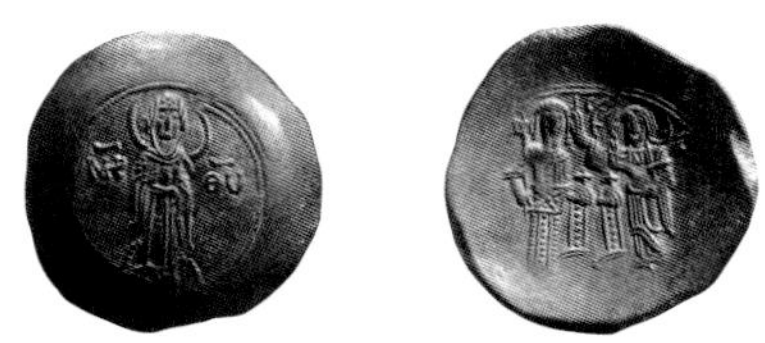

CAT. 132
Billon *trachy*, Andronikos I Komnenos (1183–1185 AD), Constantinople.
Virgin Mary / Christ crowning the emperor.
4.91 g; 27 mm
KIKPE Collection, Athens
See *Essay X*

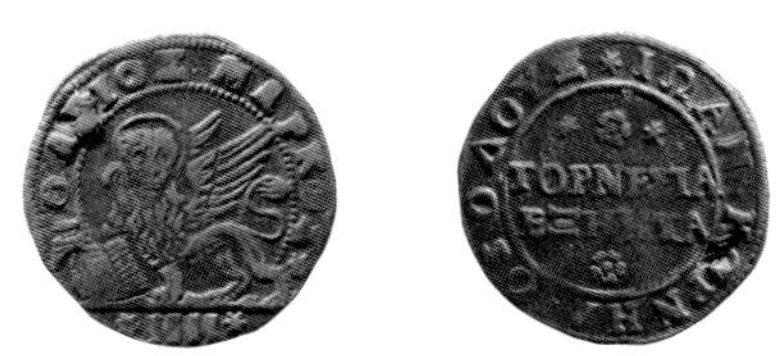

CAT. 133
Bronze coin, Giovanni I Corner, doge of Venice, Crete, (1625–1629 AD).
St. Mark's lion / Legend in two lines (60 *tornesia*); legend around bearing the name of doge.
6.11 g; 29 mm
KIKPE Collection, Athens

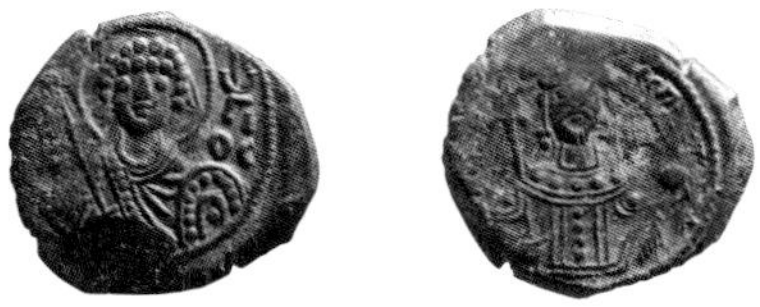

CAT. 134

Bronze *tetarteron*, Manuel I Komnenos (1143–1180 AD), Thessalonike, *ca.* 1152–1160 AD.
Bust of St. George / The imperial bust.
4.61 g; 21 mm
KIKPE Collection, Athens
See *Essay I*

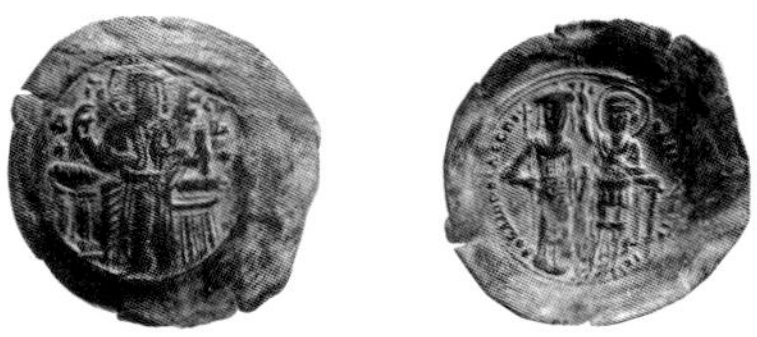

CAT. 135

Bronze *trachy*, Theodoros Komnenos Doukas (1216–1230 AD), Thessalonike, *ca.* 1227 (?) AD.
Christ enthroned / St. Demetrios crowning the emperor.
2.53 g; 29 mm
KIKPE Collection, Athens
See *Essay IX*

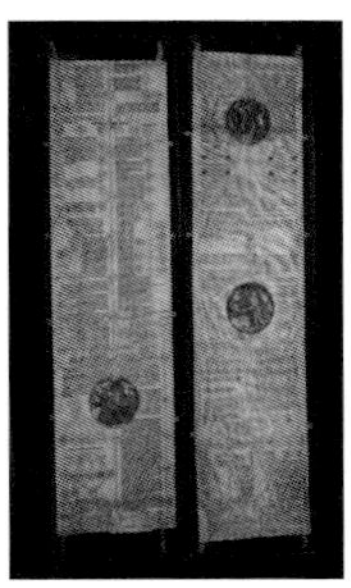

CAT. 136

Pierre de Poitiers (Petrus Pictaviensis), *Compendium historiae in genealogia Christi*. Latin scroll on *vellum*, divided into seven sheets, France or England, middle [?] of 13th century.

Developed by the successor of Pierre Comestor as chancellor of the Cathedral-School of Paris, this genealogical tree of Christ, which goes back to the Genesis, is interpolated with various quotes, particularly from Comestor's *Historia scholastica*. Six circular miniatures and several vignettes illustrate the main episodes of Christ's family life.

Fondation Martin Bodmer, Cologny, Cod. Bodmer 183

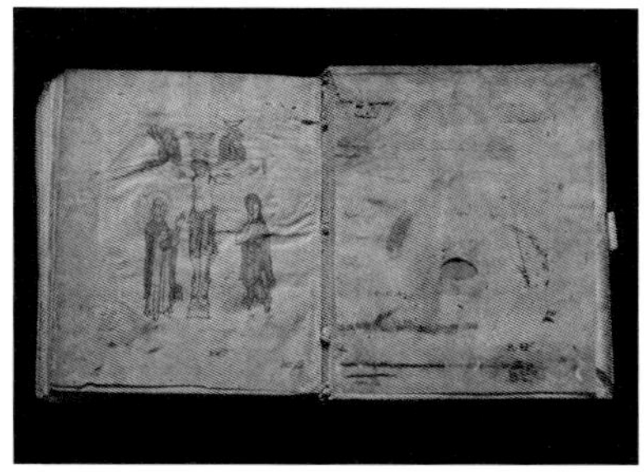

CAT. 137

Institutio canonicorum Aquisgranensis. Latin manuscript on *vellum*, Germany, first half of 9th century.

Long attributed to Amalaire of Metz, counsel to Charlemagne, this collection regarding the obligations of the monastic state was born out of the reformist decisions of the Council of Aix (816) and is probably a collective work, to which Benoit of Aniane, author of the *Concordia regularum*, contributed. This early manuscript, which post-dates the Council by only a few years, belonged to the Benedictine Abbey of Saint James in Mainz. A full-page drawing of the Crucifixion was added at the end of the volume (f. 154v) in the twelfth or thirteenth century.

Fondation Martin Bodmer, Cologny, Cod. Bodmer 68

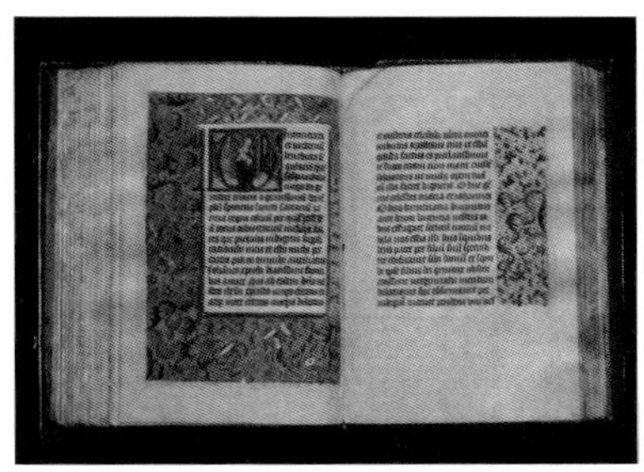

CAT. 138

Horae Beatae Mariae Virginis. Latin manuscript on *vellum*, Northern France [diocese of Cambrai?], 15th century.

Decorated with fourteen half-page vignettes (of which one represents the Virgin), borders with scrolls and acanthus leaves, and numerous historiated initials, this book of hours was probably created for the nuns of the Benedictine Abbey of Sainte Waudru at Mons.

Fondation Martin Bodmer, Cologny, Cod. Bodmer 180

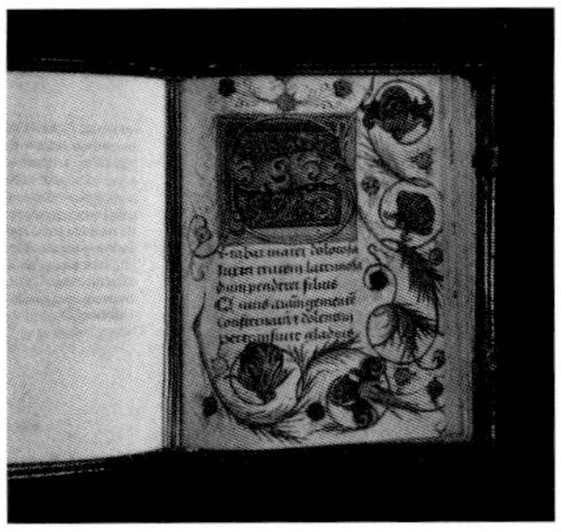

CAT. 139

Egbert de Schönau, *Stimulus dilectionis*. Latin manuscript on *vellum*, Germany, Maulbronn, 1480.

Copied at the Cistercian Abbey of Maulbronn (diocese of Spire, Wurtemberg), this manuscript combines Egbert de Schönau's treatise (here attributed to Saint Bernard of Clairvaux) and a collection of prayers to the Virgin.

Fondation Martin Bodmer, Cologny, Cod. Bodmer 19

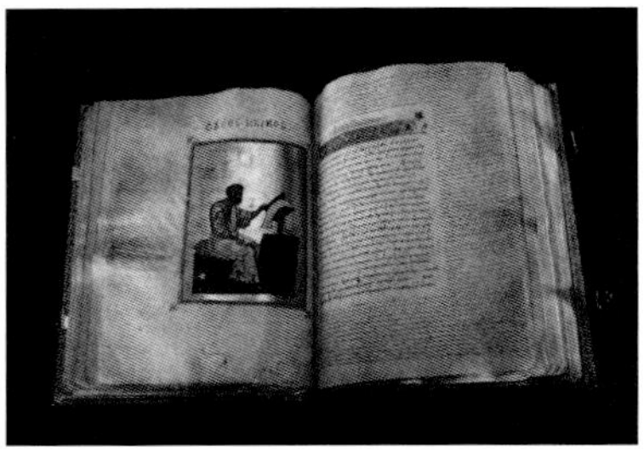

CAT. 140

Tetraevangelium. Greek manuscript on *vellum*, Constantinople or Smyrna, end of 10th century.

This manuscript of the four Gospels features a lengthy marginal linguistic commentary by Peter of Laodicae in cursive script. The volume is illustrated with two full-page miniatures depicting the evangelists Luke and Mark on a gold ground.

Fondation Martin Bodmer, Cologny, Cod. Bodmer 25

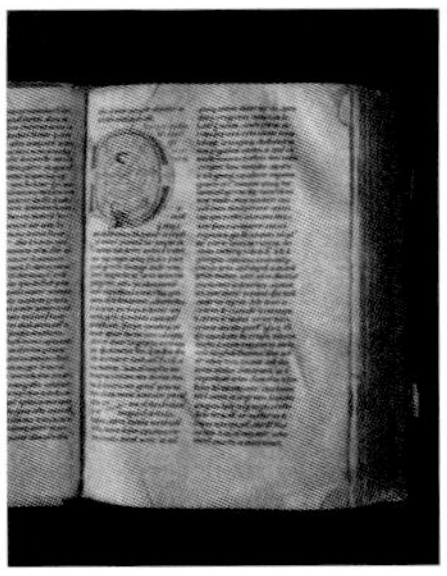

CAT. 141

Vitae sanctorum [*Passionale*], Latin manuscript on *vellum*, Germany, [Weissenau?], 12th century.

This passionary, or collection of saints' lives, from the Norbertine Abbey of Saint Peter at Weissenau (diocese of Constance), was probably copied and illuminated in this monastery's *scriptorium*. Particularly noteworthy among its many illustrations are a self-portrait of the monk and illustrator Rufillus (f. 44r) and a stunning representation of the martyrdom of Saint George (f. 48r).

Fondation Martin Bodmer, Cologny, Cod. Bodmer 127

THE GREEK WORLD BEFORE AND AFTER ALEXANDER

Without doubt, a turning point in the course of Hellenic history was the era of Alexander the Great. Although his reign was brief, Alexander transformed a large part of the then-known world by chasing his vision. Before him the power of Persia had been felt to the far reaches of the Greek world, extending its large arm even into Greece proper. After the death of the young campaigner the Persian Empire was no more, and in the wake of the new age that then dawned, the kingdoms and federations that arose enjoyed more or less glorious fortunes and rather brief lives. The powerful Hellenistic dynasties established by the late 4th century BC, as well as the federal states of mainland Greece, saw their might decline and they were eventually to yield to the prowess of the Roman war machine.

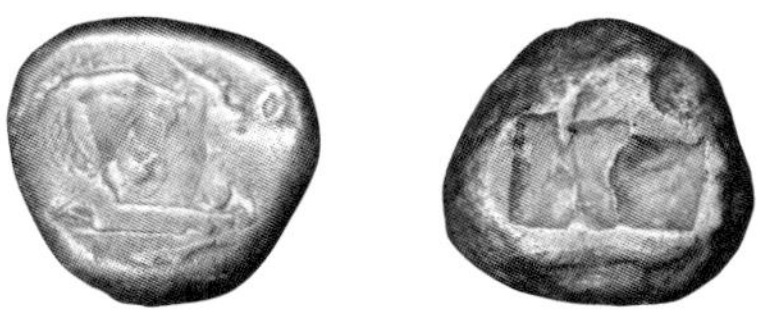

CAT. 142
Silver double *siglos*, Lydia, mid-6th century BC or later.
Foreparts of lion and bull / Incuse square.
9.75 g; 18 mm
Fondation Martin Bodmer, Cologny

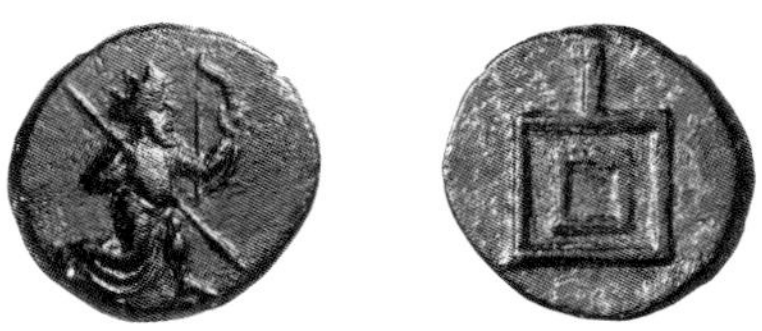

CAT. 143
Bronze coin, uncertain satrap, uncertain mint in Ionia, *ca*. 350–334 BC.
Persian king / Ground plan of fire altar?
1.73 g; 11 mm
KIKPE Collection, Athens: *SNG KIKPE* 873

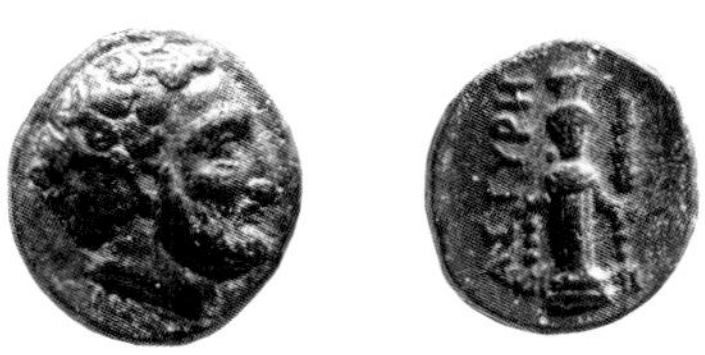

CAT. 144
Bronze coin, Tissaphernes, (*ca*. 400–395 BC.), Astyra.
Head of Tissaphernes / Cult statue of Artemis Astyrene.
1.65 g; 11 mm
KIKPE Collection, Athens: *SNG KIKPE* 929
See *Essay III*

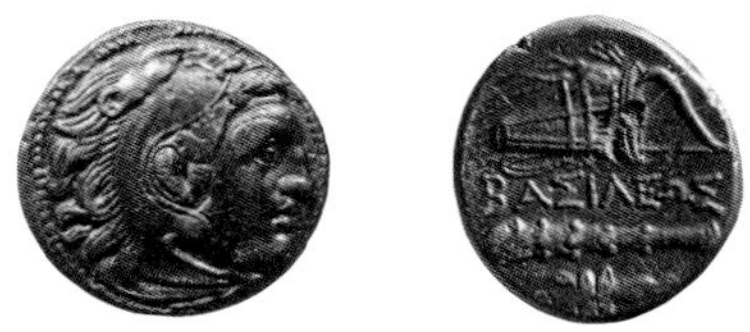

CAT. 145
Bronze coin, in the name of Alexander the Great of Macedonia (336–323 BC), uncertain mint in western Asia Minor, *ca*. 323–310 BC.
Head of Heracles / Weapons of Heracles.
5.59 g; 19 mm
KIKPE Collection, Athens: *SNG KIKPE* 438
See *Essay III*

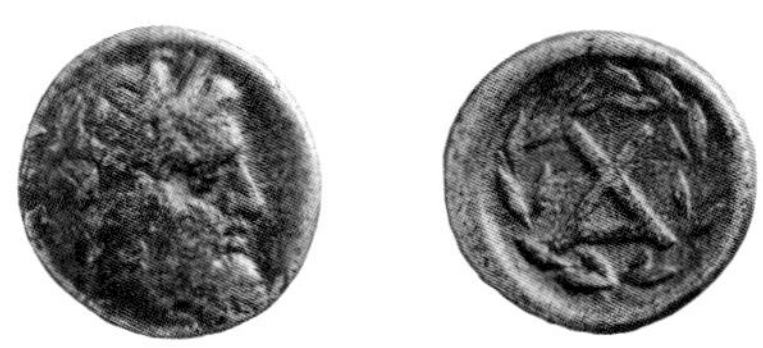

CAT. 146
Bronze *dichalkon*, Achaean League (280–146 BC), Achaea, *ca*. 250 BC.
Head of Zeus / Monogram.
2.97 g; 14 mm
KIKPE Collection, Athens: *SNG KIKPE* 601

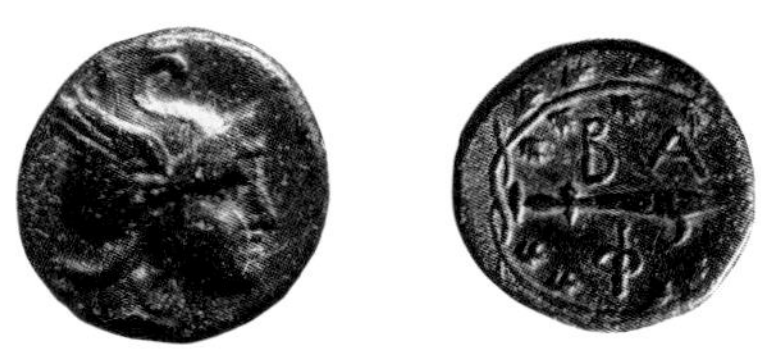

CAT. 147
Bronze coin, Philip V of Macedonia (222/1–179 BC), *ca*. 187–179 BC.
Head of Perseus / *Harpe*.
3.52 g; 16 mm
KIKPE Collection, Athens: *SNG KIKPE* 453

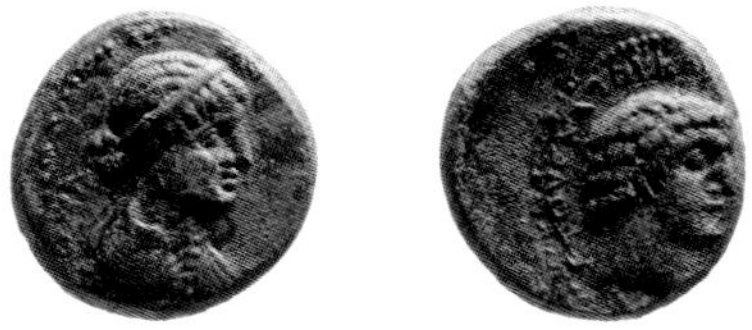

CAT. 148
Bronze coin, Cleopatra VII and Mark Antony (51–30 BC),
Chalcis sub Libano, 32/31 BC.
Bust of Cleopatra / Head of Antony.
8.00 g; 20 mm
KIKPE Collection, Athens: *SNG KIKPE* 1085
See *Essays I* and *VI*

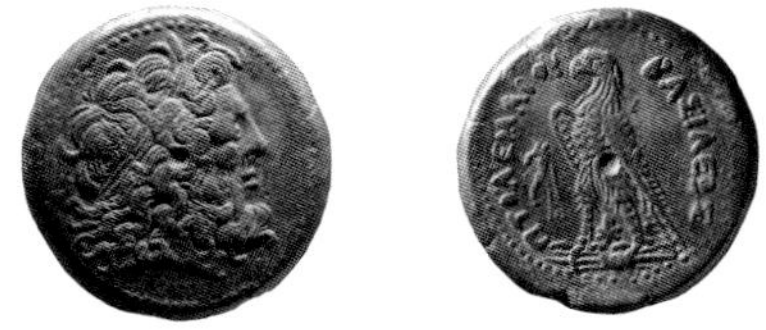

CAT. 152
Bronze coin, Ptolemy III Euergetes (247/6–221 BC),
Alexandria, *ca.* 245–222 BC.
Head of Zeus / Eagle on thunderbolt.
33.11 g; 34 mm
KIKPE Collection, Athens: *SNG KIKPE* 1178
See *Essay VI*

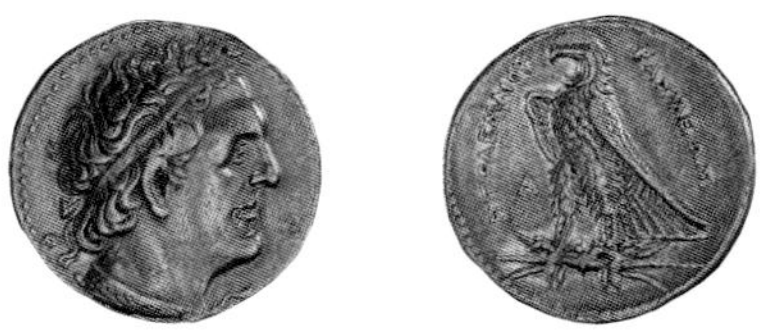

CAT. 149
Gold pentadrachm, Ptolemy I Soter (311–281 BC), Alexandria,
ca. 305–282 BC.
Head of Ptolemy / Eagle on thunderbolt.
17.74 g; 24 mm
Fondation Martin Bodmer, Cologny
See *Essay III*

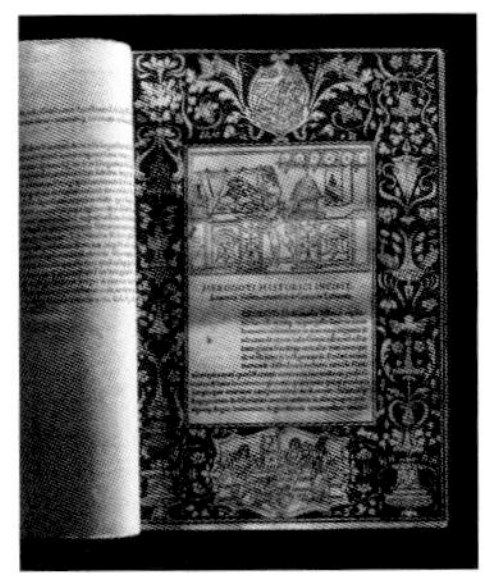

CAT. 153
Herodotus, *Historiae libri IX*, [Geneva], Henri II Estienne, 1566.

Although the original Greek version of Herodotus's 'investigations' was not published before 1502 by the Aldes, a Latin translation by the great Roman humanist Lorenzo Valla (*ca.* 1407–1457) had been printed in 1474. This new 1566 edition features additions to the text by Conrad Heresbach and an *Apologia pro Herodoto* by the printer himself. In this text, Henri Estienne intended to defend the Greek historian against accusations of gullibility or even of naivety. Very fond of Herodotus, Estienne published his *Apology* in French before producing the Greek edition of the *Historia* in 1570 and then a new Latin edition, revised and corrected in 1592. This copy is covered in red morocco binding decorated 'à la fanfare' with the coats of arms and monograms of Count Charles of Mansfeld (1543–1595). It was probably produced in the Parisian workshop dubbed 'à la première palmette', which also bound books for Catherine di Medici and Jacques-Auguste de Thou.

Fondation Martin Bodmer, Cologny

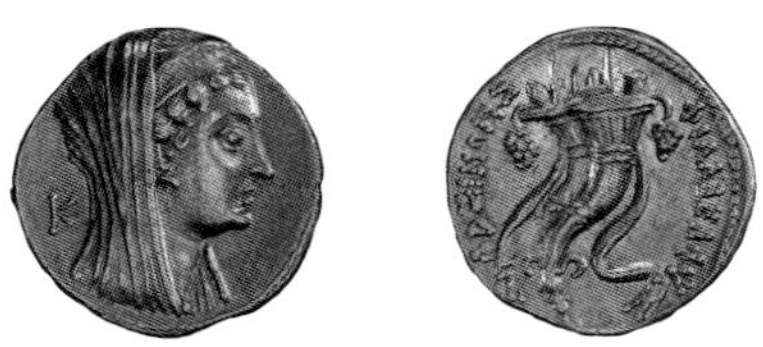

CAT. 150
Gold octadrachm, in the name of Arsinoe II (316–270/268 BC),
ca. 180–116 BC.
Head of Arsinoe / Double *cornucopia*.
27.87 g; 29mm
Fondation Martin Bodmer, Cologny

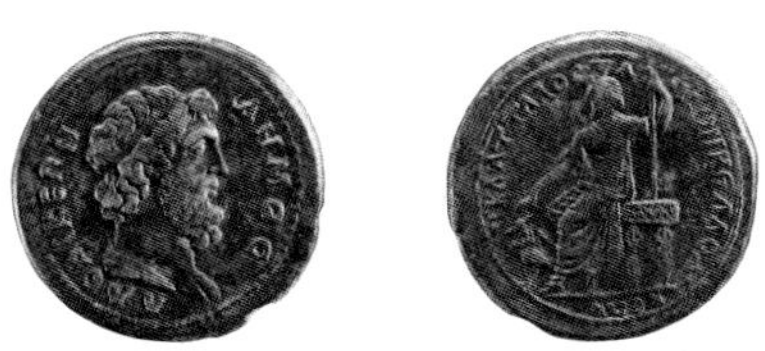

CAT. 151
Bronze 'medallion', Laodicea ad Lycum, 2nd century AD.
Bust of *Demos* of Laodicea / Sarapis seated; Cerberus.
6.97 g; 37 mm
KIKPE Collection, Athens

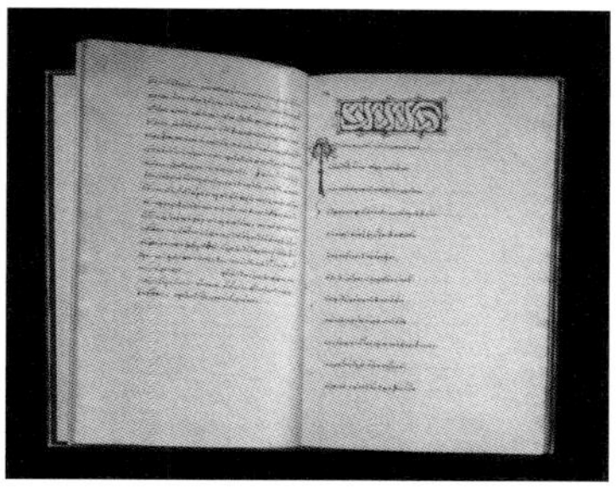

CAT. 154

Aeschylus, [*Persæ*] (Gr.). Greek manuscript on paper, end of 15th century.

Presented in 472 BC, only eight years after the Greek victories at Salamis and Plataiai, this tragedy, the earliest entirely preserved play, gives the point of view of the vanquished by staging the return of the defeated 'Great King' Xerxes to Susa. It was another Greek, Alexander the Great, who ended the Persian dynasty of the Achaemenids 150 years later.

Fondation Martin Bodmer, Cologny, Cod. Bodmer 3

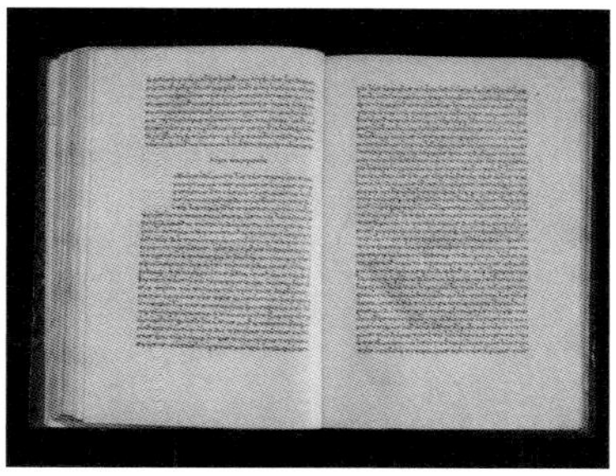

CAT. 155

Isocrates, [*Orationes*] (Gr.), Milan, Ulrich Scinzenzeller and Sebastianus de Ponte Tremolo, 24 January 1493.

Editio princeps. Apart from his talent as a logographer, Isocrates also sang the praises of Panhellenism, the concord and union between Greeks against Persia, the common enemy. Beginning with a *Life* of the orator by Plutarch, this first printed edition of Isocrates's speeches was supervised by the Athenian humanist Demetrios Chalkokondyles (1423–1511), who had already overseen the *editio princeps* of Homer (in 1488) and would subsequently publish the work of Suidas (*Souda*, 1499).

Fondation Martin Bodmer, Cologny, Inc. Bod. 138

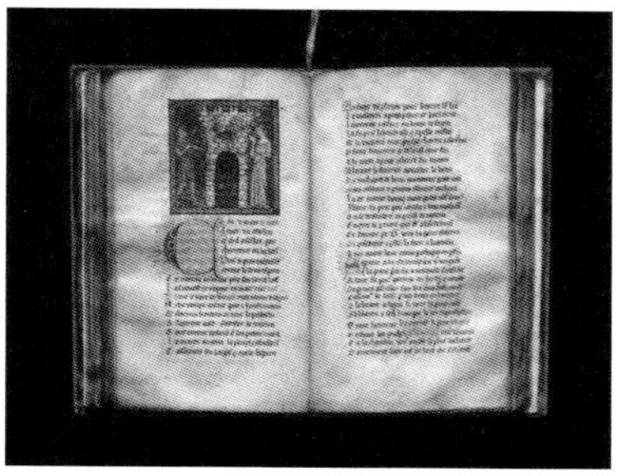

CAT. 156

Longuyon, Jacques de, *Les Vœux du Paon*. French manuscript on *vellum*, France, *ca*. 1310.

Composed at the request of Thibaut de Bar, Bishop of Liege (between 1303 and 1312), this poem in Alexandrine verse continues the then fashionable tradition of the *Romance of Alexander*. Towards the middle of the poem, Porrus, son of the king of India, is taken prisoner at the city of Epheson besieged by his father. While strolling in one of the palace courts, the captive prince shoots down a peacock with his bow and arrow. When presented at a banquet, the noble bird provides the occasion for an exchange of chivalresque vows between the ruler of Epheson and his hostage (hence the title). Of all thirty-five known copies, this one, which was probably created in Lorraine (possibly at Metz or Verdun), appears to be the earliest and might even be identified as the dedication copy. Thirteen miniatures (of which one depicts the hunting and the peacock's death) and several filigree initials adorn the volume.

Fondation Martin Bodmer, Cologny, Cod. Bodmer 189

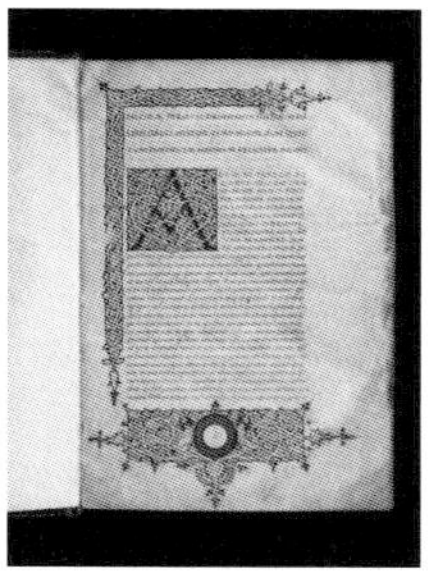

CAT. 157

Polybius, *Historiae*. Latin manuscript on *vellum*, Italy, Florence, 15th century [*ca*. 1460–1470?].

Of the forty books comprising the work of Polybius, Greek general turned historian (*ca*. 208–126 BC), only the first five are preserved complete. These refer to the years 264–216 BC (including an account of the first two Punic Wars). This manuscript contains the text of the Latin translation by Nicolo Perotti (1429–1480), which was dedicated to Pope Nicholas V. Still in its original binding of brown leather, cold-stamped and mounted on a wooden frame, this manuscript is characteristic of the humanist Florentine productions, with large initials decorated with *bianchi girari* (white vine scrolls) at the beginning of each book.

Fondation Martin Bodmer, Cologny, Cod. Bodmer 139

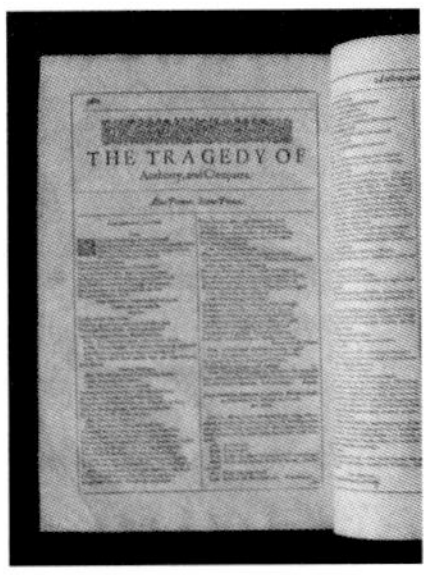

CAT. 158

Shakespeare, William, *Comedies, Histories, and Tragedies. Published according to the true Originall Copies*, London, by Thomas Cotes, for Robert Allot, 1632.

Second collected edition, published nine years after the *First Folio*, of which it is, despite the many minor corrections, a fairly accurate reprint. It includes the author's famous portrait on the title page and *The Tragedy of Anthony, and Cleopatra*, written and staged in 1606–1607, but first published in the *First Folio*. Among the first pages is a laudatory epitaph to Shakespeare, which constitutes John Milton's first published English poem.

Fondation Martin Bodmer, Cologny

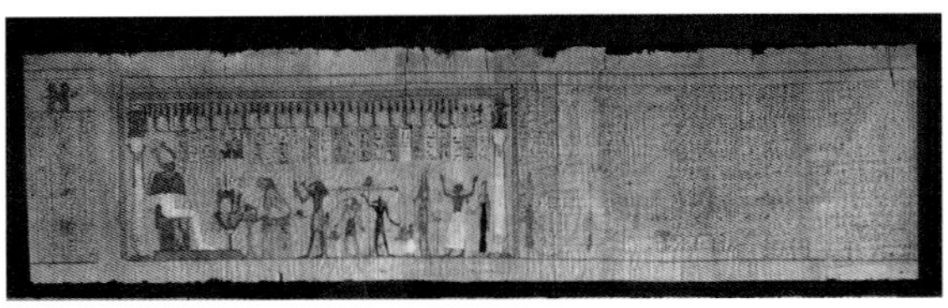

CAT. 159

Book of the Dead of Hor, priest of Amun. Polychrome hieroglyphic manuscript on papyrus, Egypt, Thebes, XXXth Dynasty or beginning of Ptolemaic period, 4th–3rd century BC.

Viaticum of the deceased on their way to *Amenti* (the Egyptian afterlife), the *Book of the Dead* contained 190 spells intended to inform the deads of the tests awaiting them on their journey and especially on how to overcome them. This journey ends in the court of Osiris, where the judgement of the deceased in the Weighing of the Heart ritual takes place, the heart being the centre of emotions and thought, according to the ancient Egyptians, and therefore the organ that best reflects the acts of a lifetime. Originally sixteen metres long, this papyrus has polychrome illustration typical of the ephemeral XXXth Dynasty or the beginning of the Lagid period. It was commissioned by a certain Hor from Thebes, priest of Amun-Ra at the temple of Karnak and of Osiris, Min, Horus, and Isis at Thebes and Koptos.

Fondation Martin Bodmer, Cologny, Pap. Bodmer 105

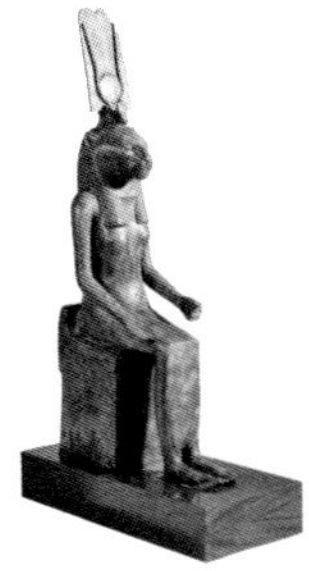

CAT. 160

Lion-headed goddess (Sekhmet?). Bronze statuette, hollow cast, Egypt, Late Period or early Ptolemaic period, 4th–3rd century BC

This polymorphous divinity can be identified either as the fearsome lion-goddesses Pakhet ('the Reaver') or Sekhmet (warrior and healing goddess), or as their appeased form, the cat Bastet. The gods and symbols engraved on the statuette's pedestal-throne (the god Ra-Horakhty, the god Heh, and the lotus flower) refer to the renewal of the year on the first day of the season of *akhet* (flooding of the Nile), a crucial period with either beneficial, or dramatic (when farmland was either insufficiently, or too heavily flooded) consequences: it was therefore important to ingratiate the lion-goddess.

Fondation Martin Bodmer, Cologny, Inv. 13

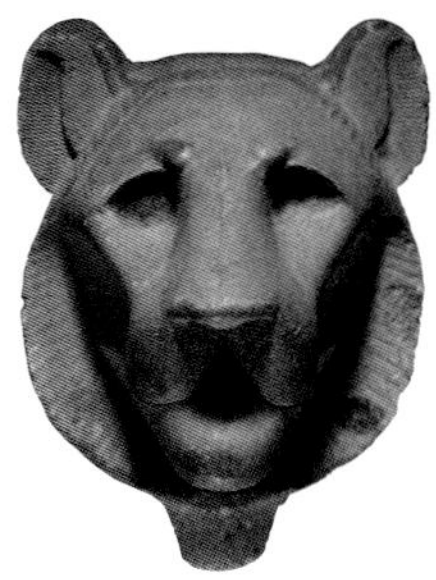

CAT. 161

Lion head (sculptor's model). Plaster, Egypt, end of Late Period – early Ptolemaic period, 4th–3rd century BC

Fondation Martin Bodmer, Cologny, Inv. 16

ROME

The history of Rome commences with the existence of a city that grew from a small village in the Italian peninsula into the centre of a mighty civilization that for centuries dominated a vast geographical area encircling the Mediterranean and stretching from northern England to the Euphrates, and from the Rhine to North Africa. Rome traced its founding back to the Trojan hero Aeneas, according to the epic of the poet Virgil. However, according to another tradition, the twin brothers Romulus and Remus, direct descendants of Aeneas, were the 'historical' founders of Rome, perhaps on 21 April 753 BC. From monarchy to Republic and then to Empire, Rome's prominent political and military evolution spans more than 1,000 years. The Roman Empire made remarkable achievements in creating a highly uniform culture and in inspiring loyalty. The Romans developed important ideas about law, government and political order; they honed to perfection the tactical use of power; they organized the best army in the world at that time; they had fine engineering and they built roads, cities and outstanding monuments; they remained largely faithful to their traditions and they worshipped their emperors, who in turn claimed absolute control over land and sea.

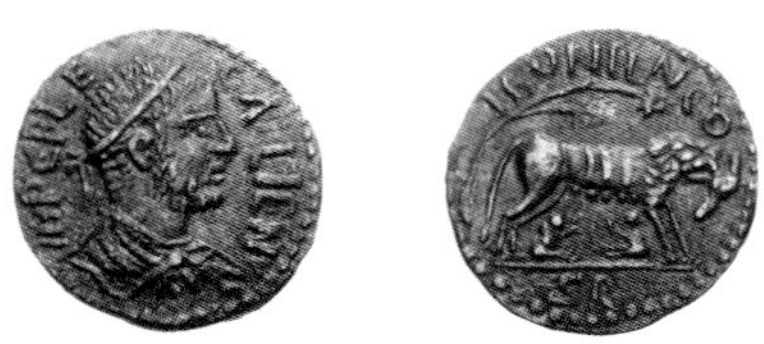

CAT. 162
Bronze coin, Iconium under Gallienus (253–268 AD).
Bust of Gallienus / She-wolf suckling Romulus and Remus.
13.96 g; 27 mm
KIKPE Collection, Athens

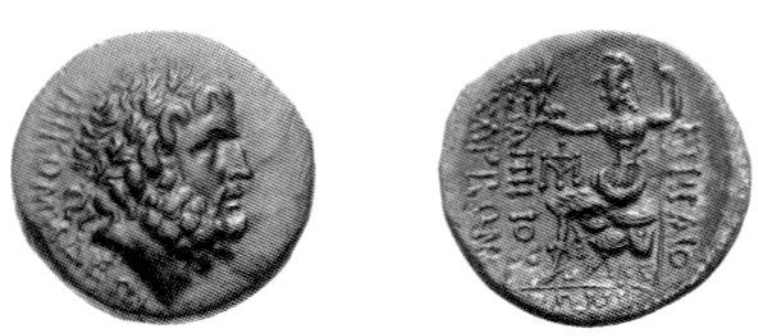

CAT. 163
Bronze coin, Nicomedia, C. Papirius Carbo, 59/8 BC.
Head of Zeus / Roma seated on shields.
8.61 g; 25 mm
KIKPE Collection, Athens: *SNG KIKPE* 742
See *Essays* V and *VIII*

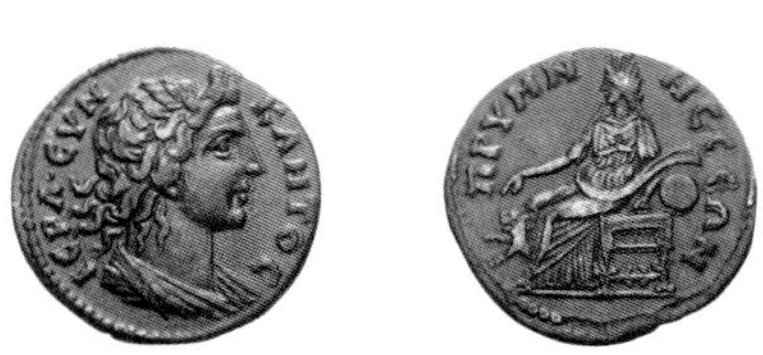

CAT. 164
Bronze coin, Prymnessos, *ca*. 193–217 AD.
Bust of the Senate / Kybele enthroned.
7.06 g; 24 mm
KIKPE Collection, Athens

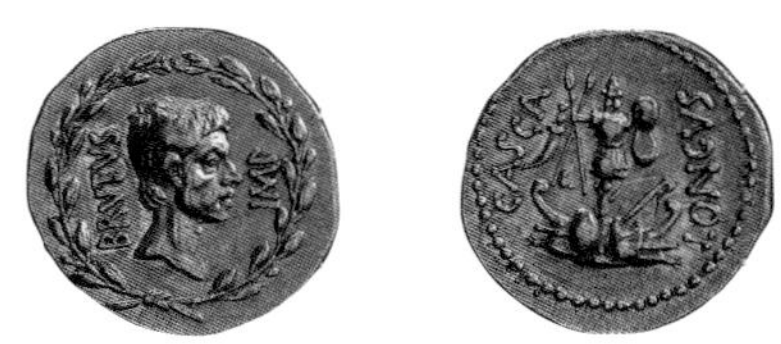

CAT. 165
Gold *aureus*, M. Iunius Brutus, mint in Macedonia, 42 BC.
Head of Brutus / Trophies.
8.02 g; 20 mm
Fondation Martin Bodmer, Cologny
See *Essay I*

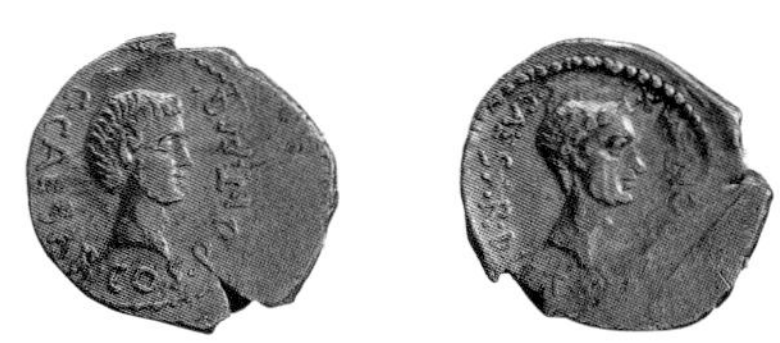

CAT. 166
Gold *aureus*, mint in Gaul, 43 BC.
Head of Octavian / Head of Julius Caesar.
8.05 g; 21 mm
Fondation Martin Bodmer, Cologny
See *Procemium* and *Essay I*

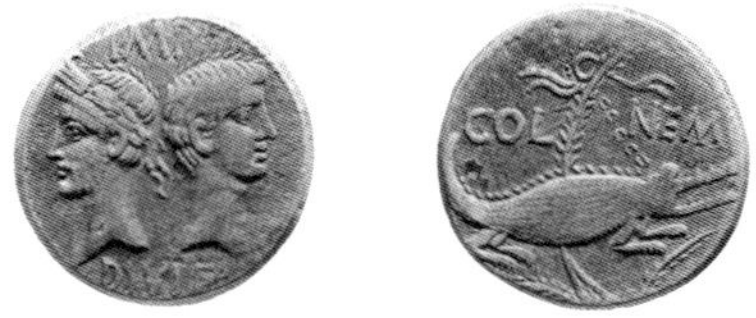

CAT. 167

Bronze coin, Nemausus under Augustus (27 BC–14 AD), *ca*. 16–10 BC.
Heads of Agrippa and Augustus / Crocodile chained to palm-branch.
12.56 g; 25 mm
KIKPE Collection, Athens
See *Essay V*

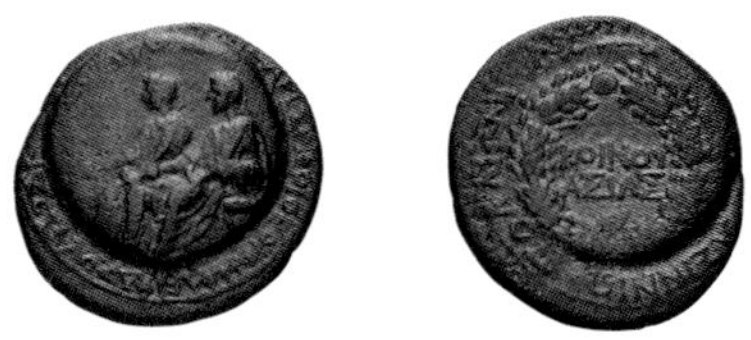

CAT. 168

Bronze coin, Sardis, in the name of caesars Drusus and Germanicus, *ca*. 28–29 AD.
Drusus and Germanicus seated / Legend in two lines within wreath.
10.10 g; 27 mm
KIKPE Collection, Athens

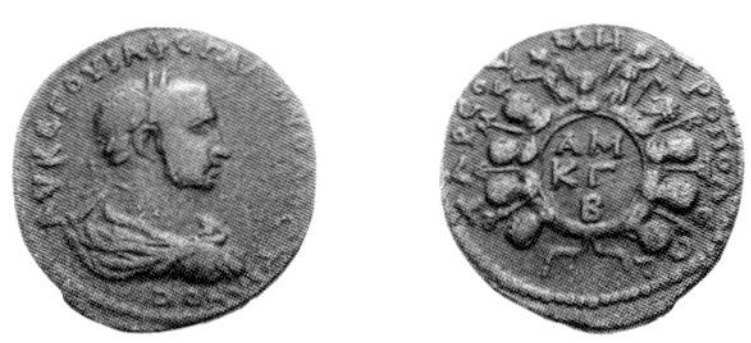

CAT. 169

Bronze coin, Tarsus under Volusian (251–253 AD).
Bust of Volusian / Cilicarch crown with eight imperial heads.
12.28 g; 28 mm
KIKPE Collection, Athens

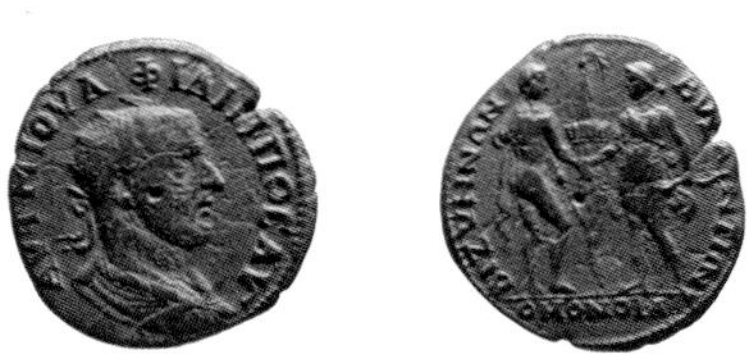

CAT. 170

Bronze coin, Bizye (in *Homonoia* with Byzantium) under Philip I, 244–249 AD.
Bust of Philip / Apollo and Artemis clasping hands.
17.83 g; 33 mm
KIKPE Collection, Athens

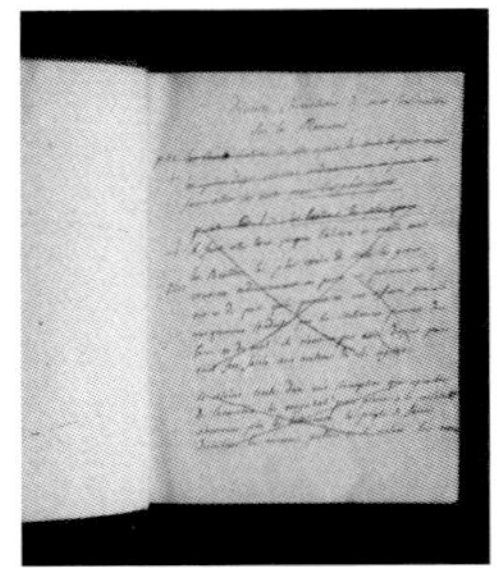

CAT. 171

Montesquieu, Charles-Louis de Secondat, baron of, *Diverses corrections de mes Considération sur les Romains*. Authograph manuscript on paper, between 1734 and 1748.

This thick manuscript contains the author's corrections for his *Considérations sur les causes de la grandeur des Romains et de leur décadence* (*Considerations on the Causes of the Greatness of the Romans and their Decline*) after the text's first edition in 1734. The passages used in the new edition of 1748 were crossed out by his hand and marked 'Mis'.

Fondation Martin Bodmer, Cologny, M-60.2

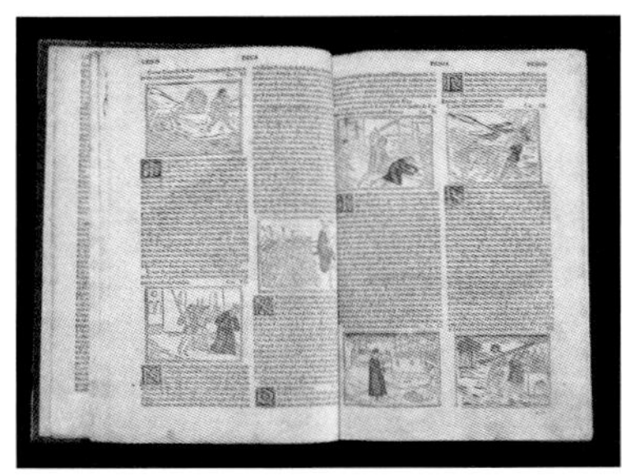

CAT. 172

Titus Livius, *Historiae Romanae decades*, Venice, Johann Rubeus (for Lucantonio Giunta), 11 February 1493.

Titus Livius's *Histories* are here published for the first time in Italian, Books III and IV using the translation by Boccaccio. This edition is also famous for its rich illustration: it includes no less that 420 wood engravings created for it and reused in seven subsequent editions of this work.

Fondation Martin Bodmer, Cologny, Inc. Bod. 166

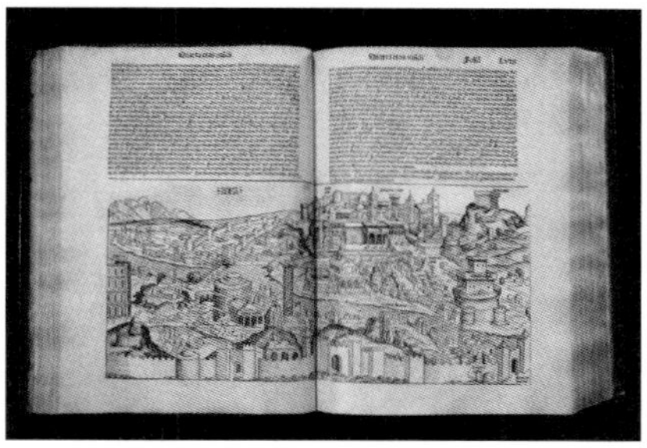

CAT. 173

Schedel, Hartmann, *Liber chronicarum*, Nuremberg, Anton Koberger, 12 July 1493.

First edition, illustrated with several wood engravings (some enhanced with watercolour). Doctor Hartmann Schedel's (1440–1514) chronicle or world history is one of the most sumptuously illustrated books of the fifteenth century with a total of 1,809 vignettes depicting cities (often rather fancifully) and famous people (rulers, saints and prelates, but also writers and thinkers). The product of a close collaboration between Schedel, his publisher, and two talented engravers, this work saw two editions, a Latin edition and a German edition, published in the same year, the second six months after the first.

Fondation Martin Bodmer, Cologny, Inc. Bod. 217

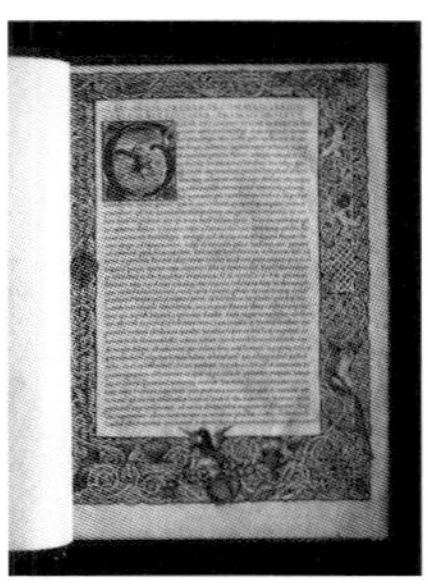

CAT. 174

Caesar, *Commentarii*, Latin manuscript on *vellum*, Italy, probably Naples, *ca*. 1480.

With its *bianchi girari* (white vine scrolls) decoration and historiated initials at the beginning of each book, this manuscript may have been produced in the workshop of the Neapolitan royal illuminator Cola Rapicano (†1488). The initial decorating the *incipit* depicts Caesar on horseback, fully armoured, holding a sword; this unusual representation of the Roman General was possibly the emblem of the Ordine della Banda founded by Alfonso the Magnanimus, King of Aragon and Naples.

Fondation Martin Bodmer, Cologny, Cod. Bodmer 44

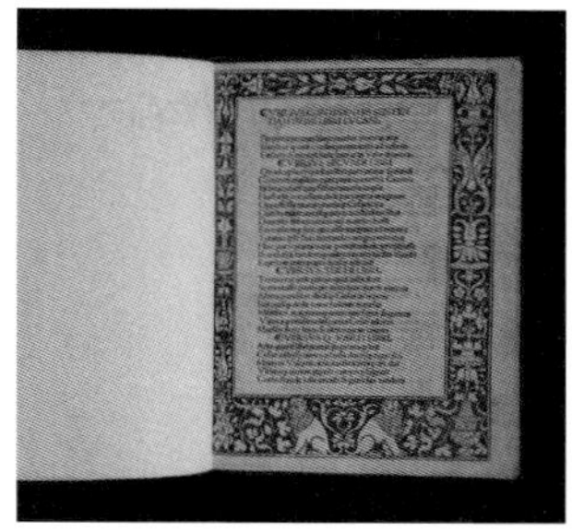

CAT. 175

Lucan, *Pharsalia*, Venice, Manfredus de Bonellis, 4 August 1495.

Third edition. This translation or, rather, Italian adaptation by Cardinal Luca Manzoli (*ca*. 1331–1411) in octosyllabic verse is illustrated with several elegant wood engravings. The first edition of this text was given by the printer Silber in Rome (1492).

Fondation Cologny Bodmer, Cologny, Inc. Bod. 167
See *Procemium*

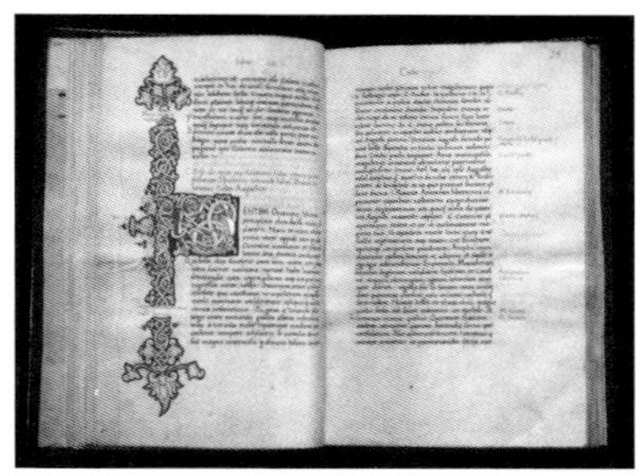

CAT. 176

Suetonius, *Vitae Caesarum*. Latin manuscript on *vellum*, Italy, [Lombardy?], 15th century.

This humanist manuscript containing the 'life' of the first twelve Caesars (several sheets of the life of Domitian are missing) is decorated with three large borders in the traditional style of *bianchi girari* (white vine scrolls).

Fondation Martin Bodmer, Cologny, Cod. Bodmer 156

THE NEW ROME

Byzantium, the old Greek colony founded by the homonymous hero Byzas at the mouth of the Bosphorus, was chosen by Constantine the Great (306–337) as his imperial seat in AD 324; renamed Constantinople, the city was transformed gradually into the New Rome. The curtains came down on the so-called Byzantine Empire when its capital city, Constantinople, fell to the Ottoman Turks on 29 May 1453. The conventional term Byzantium or Byzantine Empire was adopted by scholarship in the sixteenth century, in order to designate the State that survived for over a millennium. Byzantium was in fact the direct continuation of the Roman Empire in the eastern half of the Mediterranean, unlike the western part, which crumbled under the Germanic warlords. The empire's longevity attests that it commanded the loyalty of its inhabitants, who depended heavily on the imperial authority and were embedded in a highly centralized and sophisticated administrative system.

The empire as a whole evolved into a predominantly Christian and Greek-speaking milieu, although its population was multinational and its territory was constantly in flux, mainly due to the various invasions it suffered in the course of its long history; notably in the Arab-Byzantine Wars of the seventh and eighth centuries, in 1071, after the loss of the larger part of Asia Minor to the Seljuk Turks, and in 1204, when Constantinople was captured by the Franks during the Fourth Crusade.

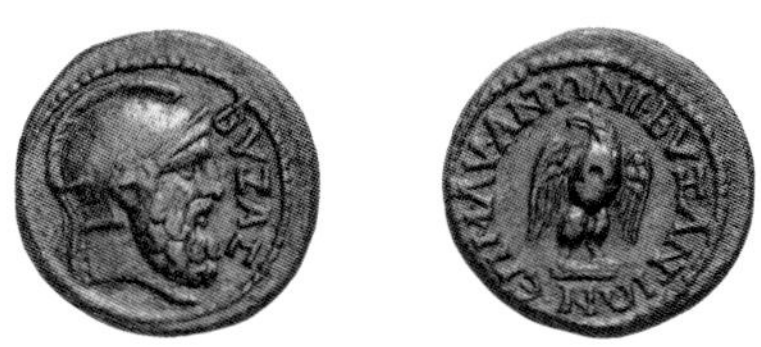

CAT. 177

Bronze coin, Byzantium, *ca*. 202–205 AD.
Head of Byzas / Eagle.
9.76 g; 25 mm
KIKPE Collection, Athens
See *Procemium, Essays III* and *V*

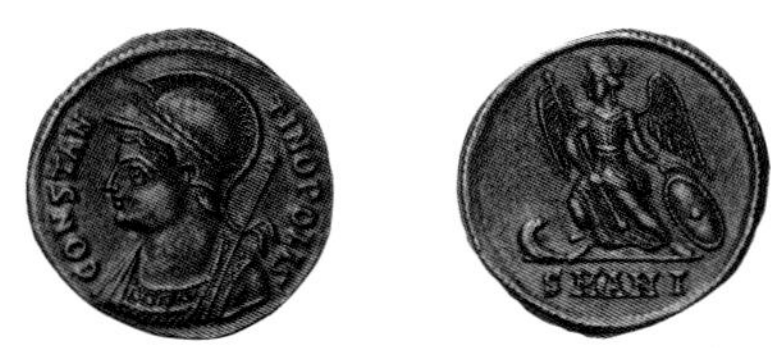

CAT. 179

Bronze coin, Antiochia, 335–337 AD.
Bust of Constantinopolis / Victory on prow.
2.34 g; 17 mm
KIKPE Collection, Athens
See *Essay X*

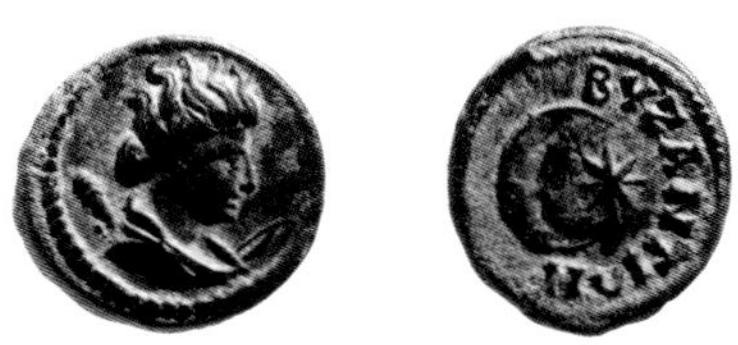

CAT. 178

Bronze coin, Byzantium, late 1st century BC – 1st century AD.
Bust of Artemis / Crescent and moon.
4.03 g; 18 mm
KIKPE Collection, Athens

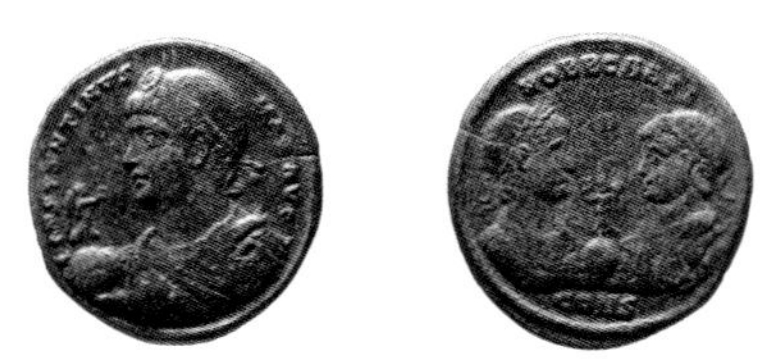

CAT. 180

Bronze 'medallion', Constantine I (306–337 AD), Constantinople, 328–330 AD.
Bust of Constantine / Busts of caesars.
5.50 g; 24 mm
KIKPE Collection, Athens
See *Procemium, Essays I* and *X*

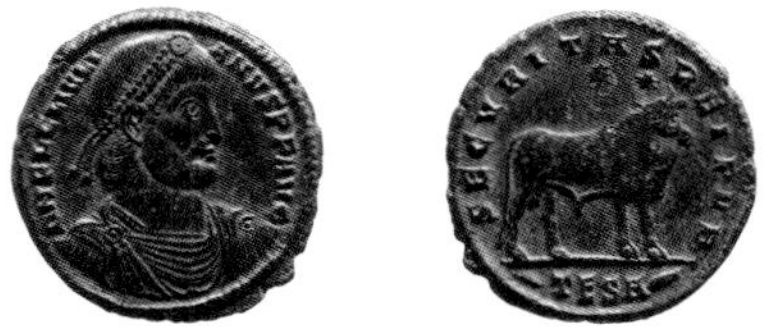

CAT. 181

Bronze coin, Julian (355–363 AD), Thessalonike, 361–363 AD.
Bust of Julian / Bull.
8.50 g; 28 mm
KIKPE Collection, Athens
See *Essays III*, *V* and *X*

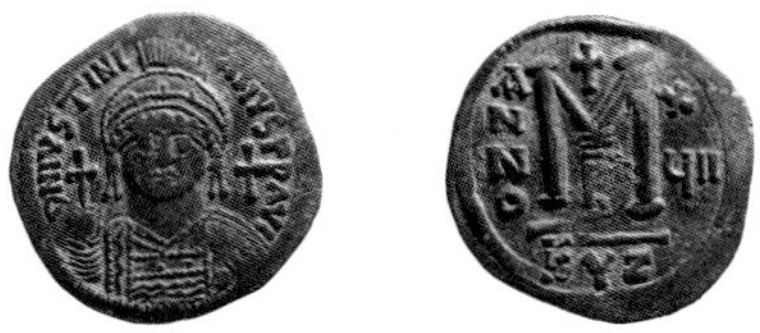

CAT. 182

Bronze *follis*, Justinian I (527–565 AD), Cyzicus, 543/4 AD.
Bust of Justinian / M (=40, mark of value).
19.49 g; 36 mm
KIKPE Collection, Athens
See *Proœmium* and *Essay X*

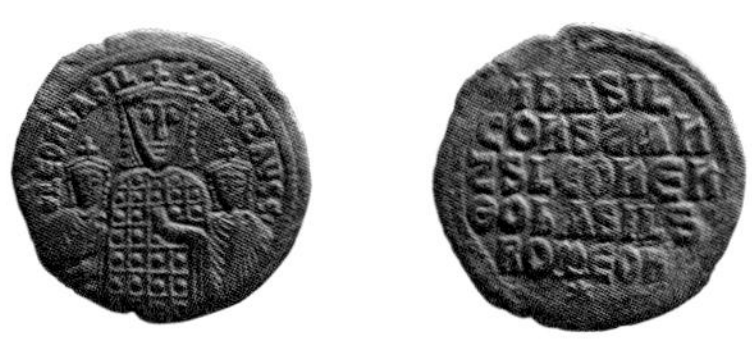

CAT. 183

Bronze *follis*, Basil I (867–886 AD), Constantinople, 870–879 AD.
Busts of Basil and his sons, Constantine and Leo /
Legend in five lines.
6.01 g; 27 mm
KIKPE Collection, Athens
See *Proœmium*

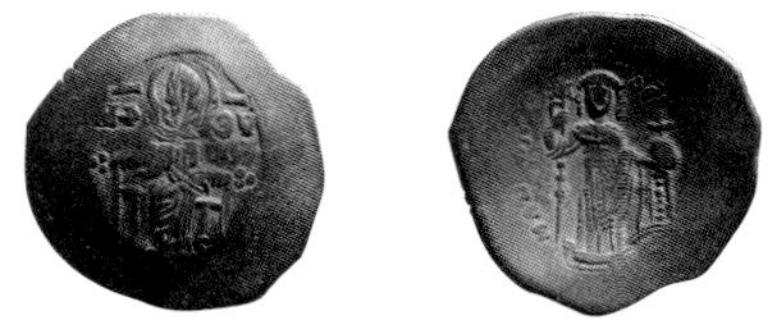

CAT. 184

Billon *trachy*, Manuel I Komnenos (1143–1180 AD), Constantinople, *ca.* 1160–1164 AD.
Virgin Mary enthroned / Manuel standing.
4.35 g; 30 mm
KIKPE Collection, Athens

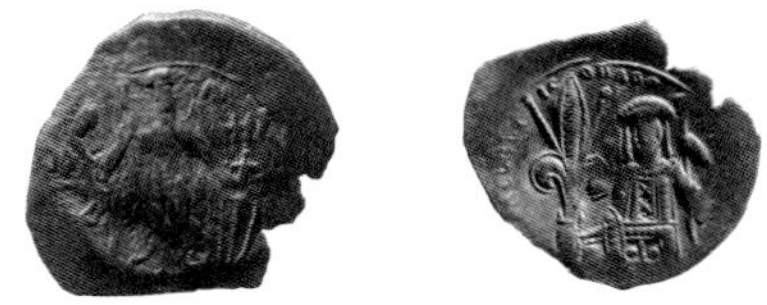

CAT. 185

Bronze *trachy*, Michael VIII Palaiologos (1259–1282 AD), Thessalonike, 1261–1282 AD.
St. Demetrius / Three-quarter-length imperial figure with large fleur-de-lis.
2.05 g; 27 mm
KIKPE Collection, Athens
See *Essay X*

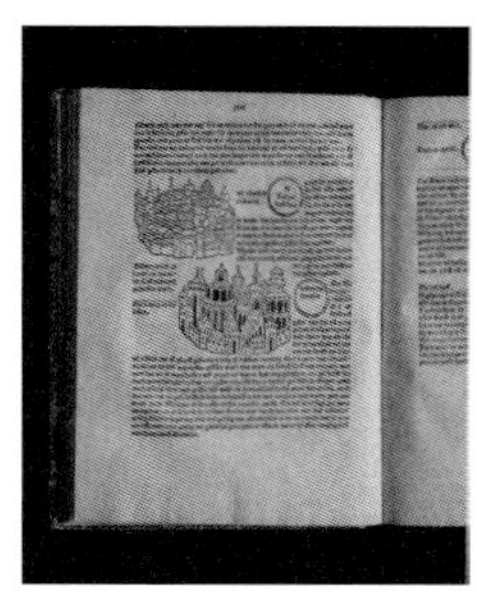

CAT. 186

Rolewinck, Werner, *Fasciculus temporum*, Basel, Bernhard Richel, 31 August 1481.

First German edition. A monk in the monastery of Saint Barbara in Cologne, Werner Rolewinck (1425–1502) was a prolific writer, mostly known for his universal history from the Creation until his time, which was intended as a continuation of Orosius's *Historia*. Published in 1474, the Latin version of this *Fasciculus* was followed by a German translation seven years later. All of these *incunabulae* are illustrated with remarkable wood engravings, including representations, both faithful and fanciful, of several large cities, including Byzantium.

Fondation Martin Bodmer, Cologny, Inc. Bod. 214
See *Essay X*

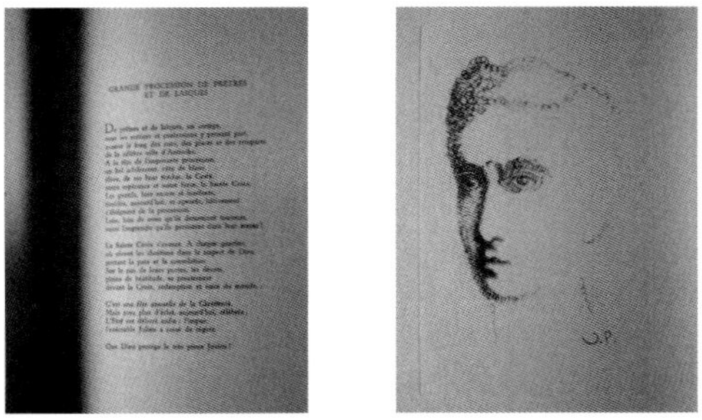

CAT. 187

Cavafy, Constantine P., *Poèmes*, Lausanne, Abbaye du Livre, 1947.

Translated from Greek into French by Theodore Griva, Cavafy's (1863–1933) poems are preceded by a portrait-frontispiece of the author and a study of his work by the academician Edmond Jaloux. The original Greek edition was published posthumously in Alexandria in 1935.

I. Fikioris Collection, Athens

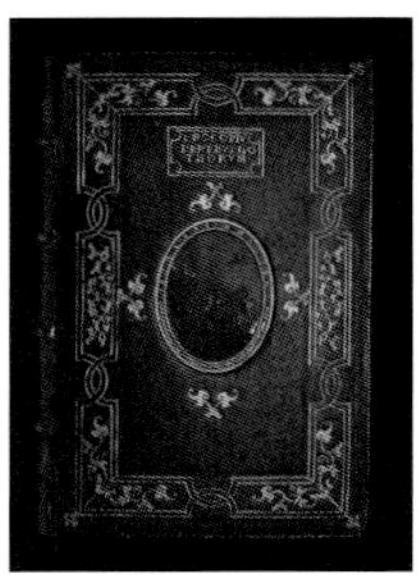

CAT. 188

Procopius of Caesaria, *De Rebus Gothorum, Persarum ac Vandalorum libri VII*, Basel, Johann Hervagius, 1531.

Editio princeps. Secretary of the famous General Belissarius, Procopius of Caesaria (*ca*. 500–560) left among other historical works (including his juicy *Anecdota*) a scrupulous chronicle of his master's campaigns against the Goth, Persian, and Vandal aggressors along the Empire's *limes*. After two partial editions (*De bello Gothorum* in 1506 and *De bello Persico* in 1509), this Latin translation by Cristoforo Persona (1416–1485) and Raffaele Maffei (1455–1522) is also the first complete edition. This volume was luxuriously bound for the Genoese banker Giovanni Battista Grimaldi during his studies in Rome. As in all 200 volumes of this 'libbraria finita', the first plate is decorated with a stamped allegorical medallion depicting Apollo guiding his chariot towards Mount Parnassus, on top of which stands Pegasus.

Fondation Martin Bodmer, Cologny

See *Prooemium*

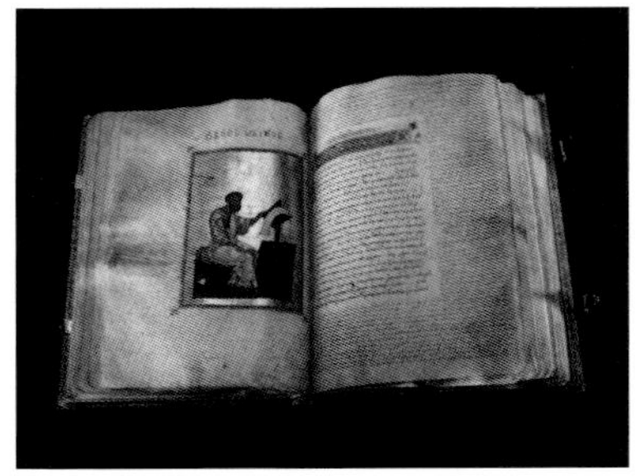

CAT. 189

Tetraevangelium: see no. 140.

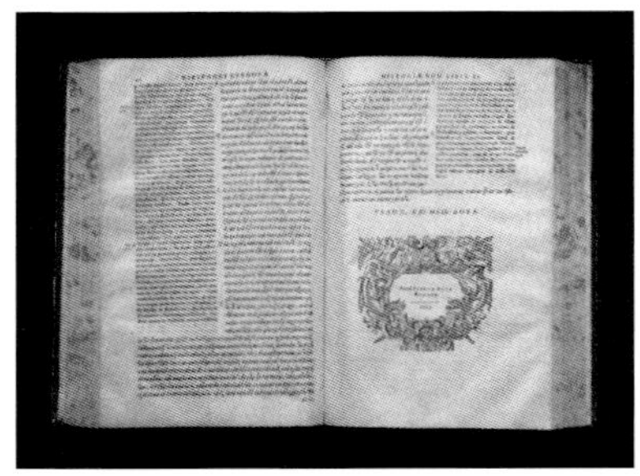

CAT. 190

Nicephoros Gregoras, Laonikos Chalkokondyles, and Georgios Akropolites, *Historiae Byzantinae scriptores tres graeco-latini*, Cologny [i.e. Geneva], Pierre de La Rovière, 1615.

Published under the false address 'Coloniae Allobrogum' (or Cologny, to avoid mentioning the name of Geneva, suspect beyond Protestant lands, in the title), this collection unites the work of three Byzantine historians: Nicephoros Gregoras (*ca*. 1295–1360) with his *Romanae, hoc est Byzantinae historiae Libri X*; Laonikos Chalkokondyles (*ca*. 1423–1490) and his *Historia origine ac rebus gestis Imperatorum Turcicorum*; and, finally, Georgios Akropolites and his *Chronicon Constantinopolitanum* (1217–1282). This edition, in which the work of Chalkokondyles is published for the first time, includes the Greek text and a juxtalineary Latin translation.

Fondation Martin Bodmer, Cologny

See *Essay X*

FACETS OF BYZANTIUM

Bridging the world of Late Antiquity with that of *Medium Aevum*, Byzantium stood as the heir of fallen Rome after AD 476. Taking pride in its Roman character, the empire lasted for almost another thousand years after the demise of its predecessor. The initial stage, aptly deemed as an Age of Spirituality, saw aspects of triumphant Christianity merging with parameters of the structure of the Graeco-Roman society, such as the methodical codification of *Ius Romanum* and the well-organized administrative hierarchy and bureaucratic mentality. The Byzantine Empire revelled in applying its rule both by military force and by diplomatic persuasion, often using its coinage reserves in order to avoid invasions or strategically employ foreign assistance against its foes. A multifaceted entity and a melting pot for peoples and ideas, Byzantium managed to sustain adversities and regenerate at times, both remaining loyal to its origins and to some point evolving through the centuries. In the end it shrunk to a remnant of its glorious past, but its legacy to posterity resonated for long after.

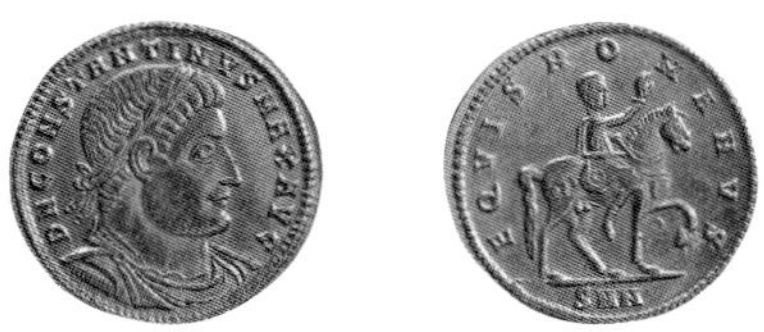

CAT. 191
Gold 'medallion', Constantine I (306–337 AD), Nicomedia, 324–325.
Head of Constantine / Constantine on horseback.
6.61 g; 23 mm
Fondation Martin Bodmer, Cologny
See *Essays I* and *III*

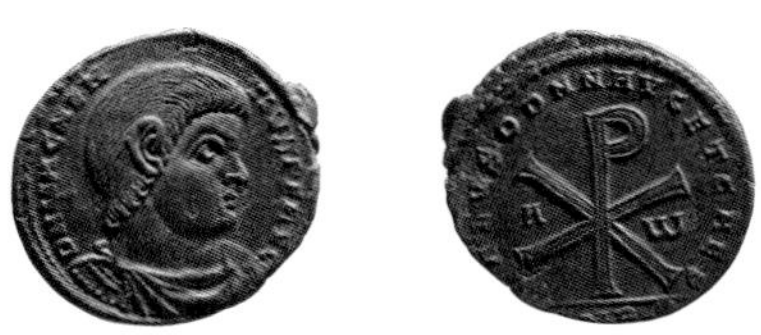

CAT. 192
Bronze coin, Magnentius (350–353 AD), Amiens, 351–353.
Bust of Magnentius / Christogram.
7.62 g; 29 mm
KIKPE Collection, Athens
See *Essays I* and *X*

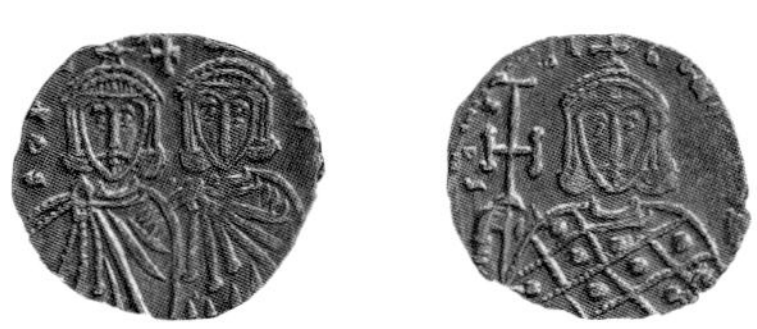

CAT. 193
Gold *solidus*, Constantine V (741–775 AD), Syracuse, *ca.* 751–775.
Busts of Constantine V and Leo IV / Bust of Leo III.
3.88 g; 20 mm
Fondation Martin Bodmer, Cologny
See *Procemium*

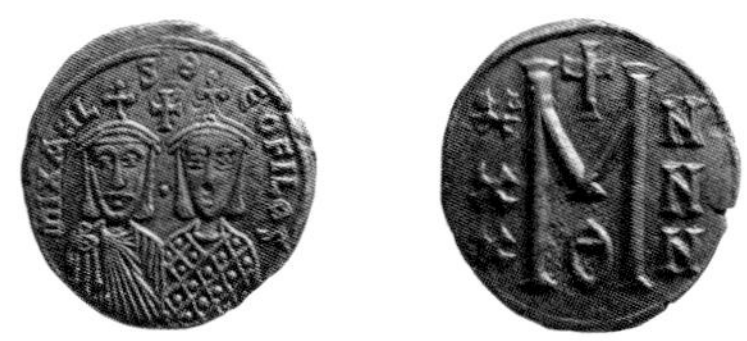

CAT. 194
Bronze *follis*, Michael II (820–829 AD), Constantinople.
Two imperial busts: Michael II and his son Theophilos /
M (=40, mark of value).
7.21 g; 29 mm
KIKPE Collection, Athens
See *Procemium* and *Essay X*

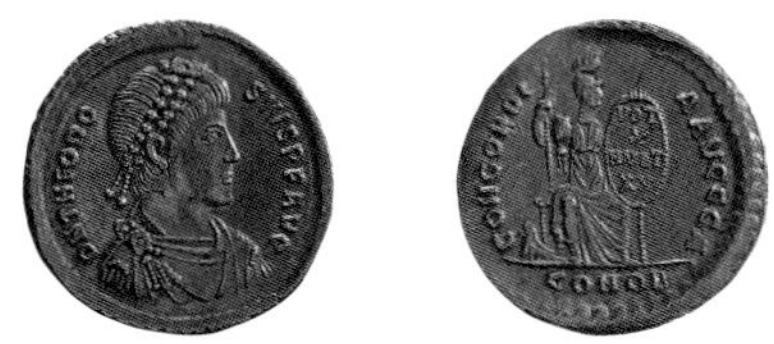

CAT. 195
Gold *solidus*, Theodosios I (379–395 AD), Constantinople, 383–388.
Imperial bust / Constantinopolis seated.
4.39 g; 21 mm
Fondation Martin Bodmer, Cologny
See *Procemium*

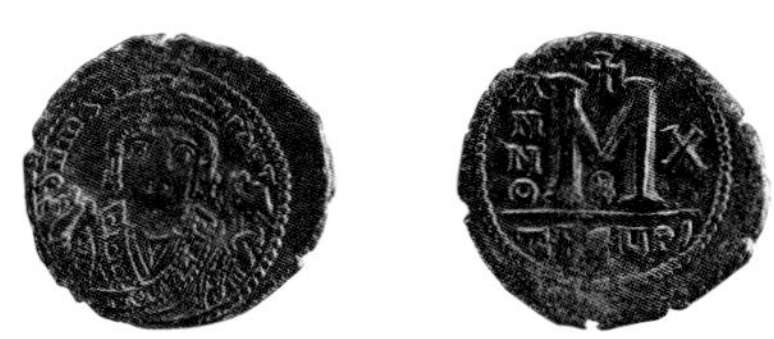

CAT. 196
Bronze *follis*, Maurice (582–602 AD), Antiochia, 591/2.
Bust of Maurice / M (=40, mark of value).
12.72 g; 30 mm
KIKPE Collection, Athens

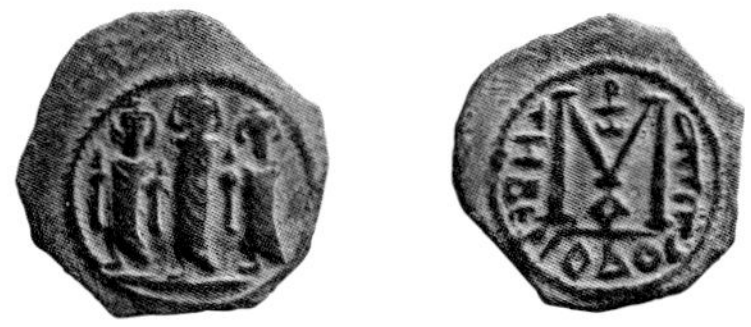

CAT. 197

Bronze *fals*, Tiberias, Arab-Byzantine issue under Umayyad rule, *ca*. 661–680 AD.
Three imperial figures / M (=40, mark of value).
3.32 g; 24 mm
KIKPE Collection, Athens
See *Essay X*

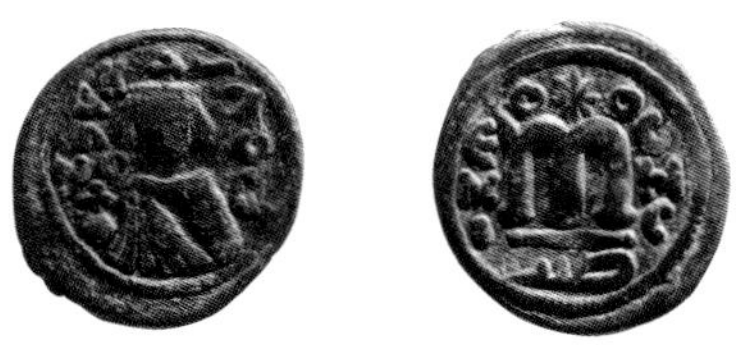

CAT. 198

Bronze *fals*, Emesa, Arab-Byzantine issue under Umayyad rule, *ca*. 680–696 AD.
Imperial bust / M (=40, mark of value).
4.6 g; 22 mm
KIKPE Collection, Athens
See *Essay X*

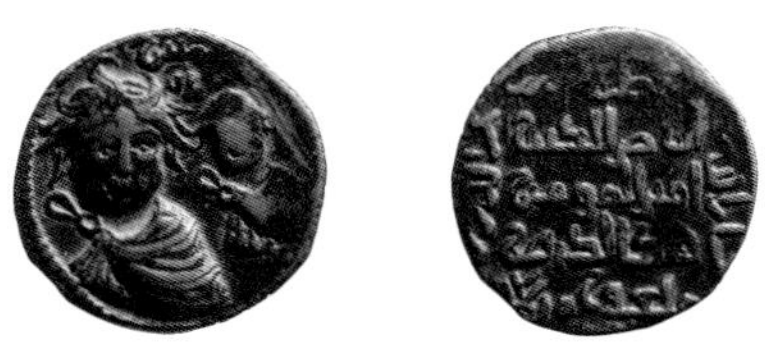

CAT. 199

Bronze coin, Qutb al-Din Il-Ghazi (1176–1184 AD), Artuqid ruler of Mardin (Mardes), 1181–1184.
Busts of emperor and his son / Legend in five lines.
14.10 g; 32 mm
KIKPE Collection, Athens

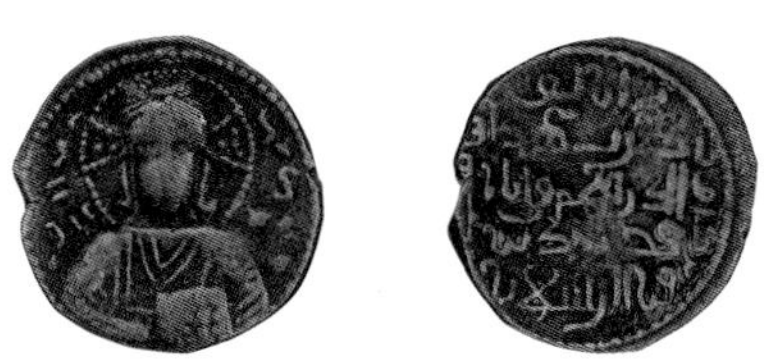

CAT. 200

Bronze coin, Fakhr al-Din Qara Arslan, Artuqid ruler of Hisn Kayfa (Kephas), 1144–1174 AD.
Crude bust of Christ / Legend in four lines.
5.97 g; 25 mm
KIKPE Collection, Athens
See *Essay X*

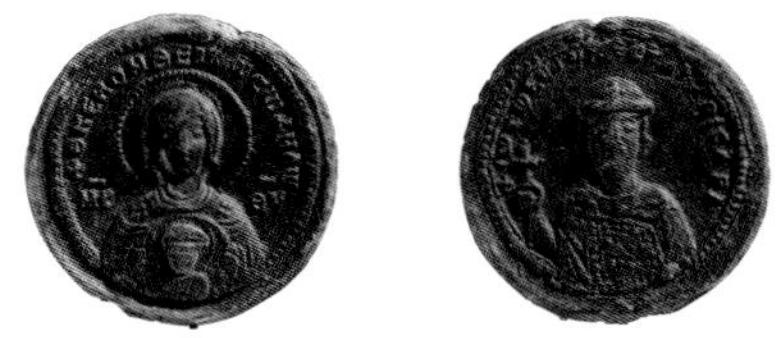

CAT. 201

Lead seal, John Doukas Caesar, *ca*. 1060–1071 AD.
Bust of Virgin Mary holding Christ in medallion / Bust of John Doukas.
25.14 g; 31 mm
KIKPE Collection, Athens
See *Essay I*

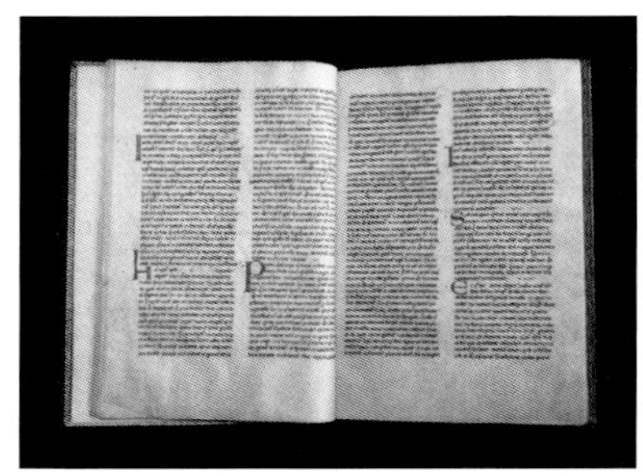

CAT. 202

Eusebius of Caesaria, *Historia ecclesiastica*. Latin manuscript on *vellum*, France [?], second half of 12th century.

With this extensive summary, Eusebius (*ca*. 265–339), Bishop of Caesaria, is recognized as the founding father of the history of Christianity. His work was continued and imitated by many over the centuries both in Greek (Socrates Scolasticus, Theodoret of Cyrus, Sozomen) and in Latin translation (Rufin of Aquileia).

Fondation Martin Bodmer, Cologny, Cod. Bodmer 65
See *Essay X*

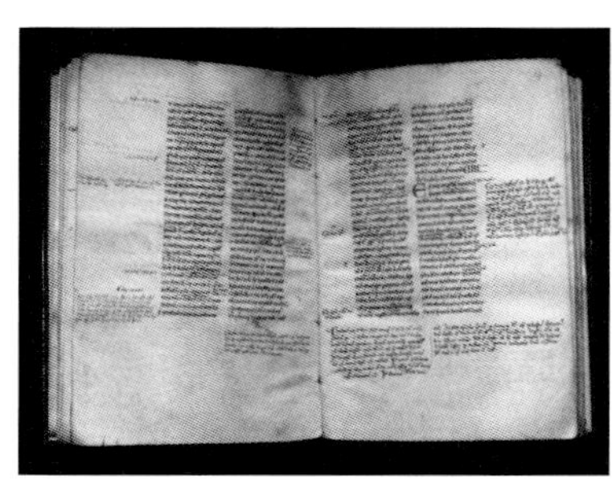

CAT. 203

John of Damascus, *De fide orthodoxa*, Latin manuscript on *vellum*, Italy, [Bologna?], 13th century.

This doctrinal summary, one of the main works of the Byzantine theologian, is here translated by Burgundi of Pisa during the reign of Pope Eugene III (1145–1153).

Fondation Martin Bodmer, Cologny, Cod. Bodmer 97
See *Procœmium*

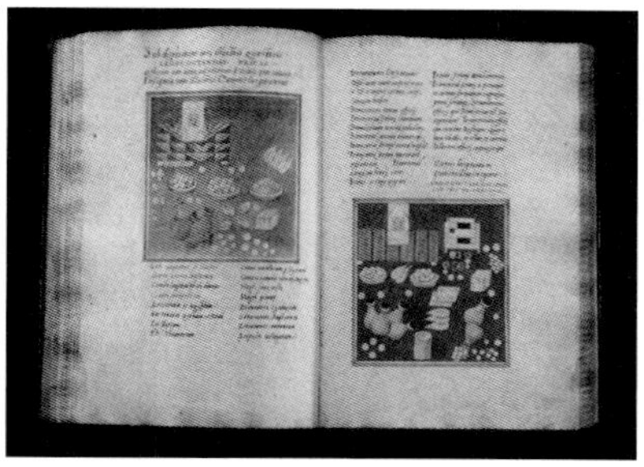

CAT. 204

De rebus bellicis [and] *Notitia dignitatum*, Latin manuscript on paper, Switzerland, [region of Basel?], *ca*. 1520–1530 [?].

Written in the fourth or early fifth century, these military treatises are among the most important evidence on the Roman army in Late Antiquity. The first describes the different war machines then in use; the second draws a picture of the empire's military and administrative organization, with lists of grades, functions, and offices. Decorated with several full and half-page watercolours, this manuscript probably copies a fifteenth century manuscript (BnF, Ms. Lat. 9661), which itself copies the *Codex Spirensis*, a unique archetype probably dating to the ninth or tenth century and now lost. This copy was probably used by S. Gelenius for his edition of the two works, published in Basel in 1552.

Fondation Martin Bodmer, Cologny, Cod. Bodmer 118
See *Procemium* and *Essay X*

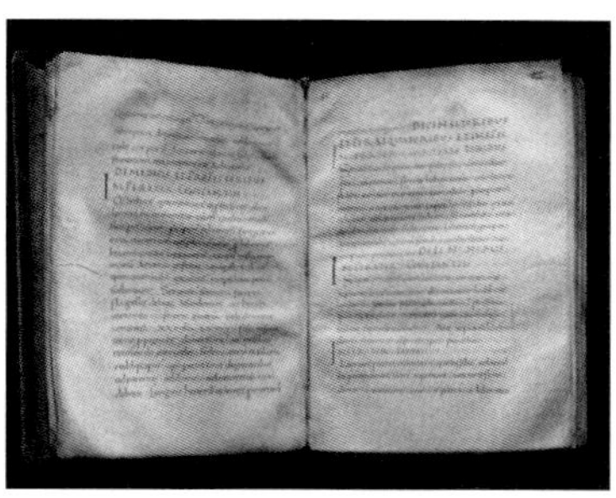

CAT. 205

Codex Theodosianus. Latin manuscript on *vellum*, Northwestern Germany, end of 9th century.

Formerly known as the Codex of Klitschdorf or Codex Solmsianus (from the name of its owner in the late eighteenth century), this collection consists of several legal treatises and texts, both complete and fragmentary, such as the Salic Law '*emendata*', the *leges Alamannorum et Baivuariorum*, and excerpts from Isidore of Seville and Charlemagne's laws. It also includes a compilation of passages from Books IX to XVI of the fundamental *Codex Theodosianus*, which, decreed in 438, became one of the pillars of Roman law.

Fondation Martin Bodmer, Cologny, Cod. Bodmer 107
See *Procemium*

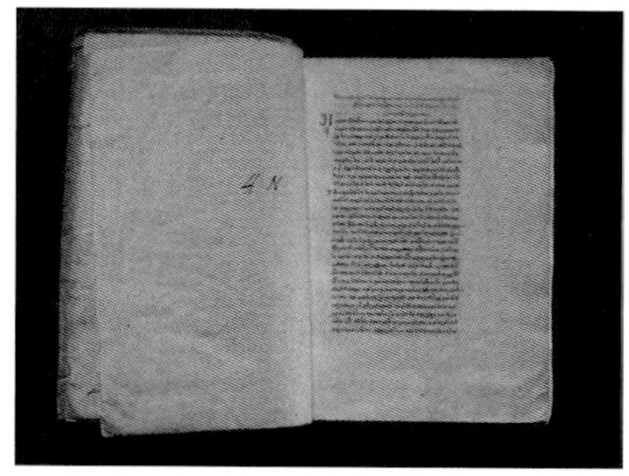

CAT. 206

Pseudo-Maurice, [*Strategikon*] (Gr.), Greek manuscript on paper, 1561.

Although tradition attributes the *Strategikon* to the Byzantine emperor Maurice (539–602), this classic 'art of war' in twelve books was probably the work of his brother, the *curopalates* Peter (*ca*. 545–602), or of a general of their entourage. This volume contains two other important military treatises: the *De velitatione bellica*, one of the first manuals of guerrilla warfare, attributed to emperor Nicephorus Phocas (*ca*. 912–969), and the *Apparatus bellicus*, attributed to Julius the African.

Fondation Martin Bodmer, Cologny, Cod. Bodmer 115
See *Essay X*

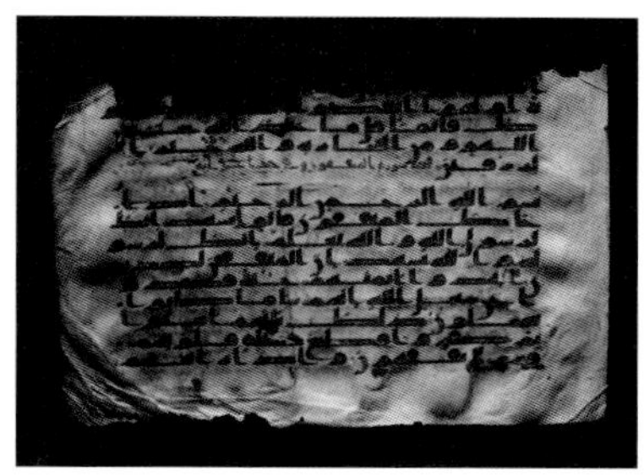

CAT. 207

Quran. Arab manuscript on *vellum*, 8th–9th centuries.

Written in Kufic calligraphy, this fragment contains the text of surat 62 (*Al-Juma*, Friday), verses 6-10, and surat 63 (*Al-Munafiqun*, The hypocrits), verses 4-8.

Fondation Martin Bodmer, Cologny, Cod. Bodmer 539

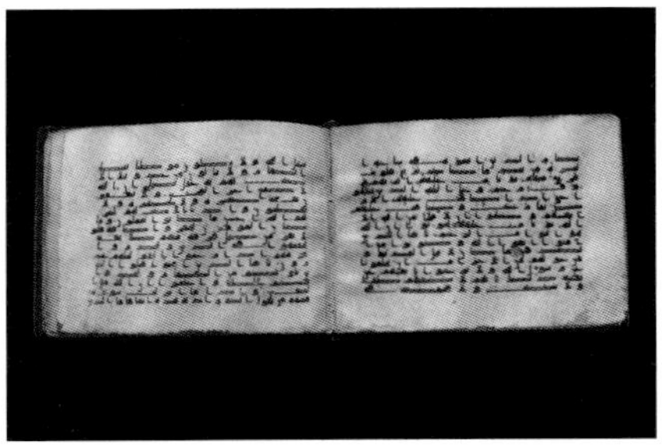

CAT. 208

Quran. Arab manuscript on *vellum*, 10th century, written in Kufic calligraphy.

Fondation Martin Bodmer, Cologny, Cod. Bodmer 540

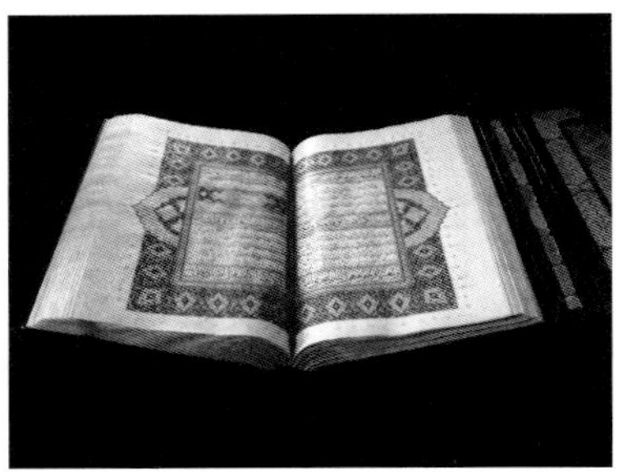

CAT. 209

Quran. Arab manuscript on paper, Persia, [Shiraz?], 16th century.

Unlike the two copies of the sacred text presented above, this large manuscript has been copied in Naskhi calligraphy. This more untied and cursive writing no longer uses angular Kufic characters and is easier to read. This manuscript is sumptuously illuminated: surats stand out against a gold foil ground, embellished with deep blue motifs and endless floral garlands. This copy may have been created in a workshop of Shiraz, one of the major cultural centres of the Persian Empire and, along with Tabriz and Herat, one of the three main cities producing illuminated manuscripts.

Fondation Martin Bodmer, Cologny, Cod. Bodmer 544

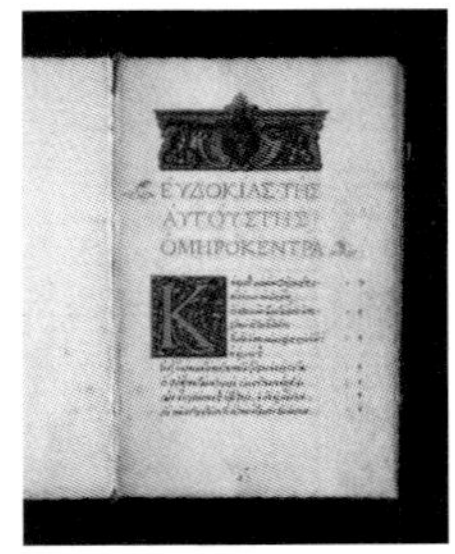

CAT. 210

[Eudocia] (attr. to), [*Homeric centos*] (Gr.).
Greek manuscript on paper, Paris, 1559.

A popular literary genre in Late Antiquity and kind of extreme paraphrase, these centos reuse Homeric verses to compose a poem with Christian flair and evocation of the salvation of humanity through the incarnation of Christ, in approximately 2000 verses. Their author's identity is still debated as various different names are mentioned in the earliest manuscripts. First composed by a bishop or priest named Patrikios (whom a later testimony by the Byzantine historian George Kedrenos wrongly identifies as the patrician Pelagios, who would have written these verses by order of his master the emperor Zeno), the poem was rewritten and completed (according to various ancient sources, including the Byzantine historian Ioannis Tzetzes) by the Empress Eudocia (*ca.* 400–460), wife of Theodosios II and a known poetess, author of biblical and hagiographical paraphrases, including a poem on Cyprian of Antioch. The otherwise unknown Optimus the Philosopher probably also participated in this collection, as did Cosmo of Jerusalem (whose identification with Cosmo of Maiouna is probable, but not certain). Penned by the Cretan scribe Angelos Vergikios (or Ange Vergèce, †1569) for Henry II, this copy has a luxurious red morocco binding, probably crafted in the Parisian workshop working for this ruler. Apart from the scattered triple gold dots, large mesh border, and ornate spandrels, the plates also feature beautiful central painted medallions depicting Athena and Hermes.

Fondation Martin Bodmer, Cologny, Cod. Bodmer 63

DE VIRIS ILLUSTRIBUS

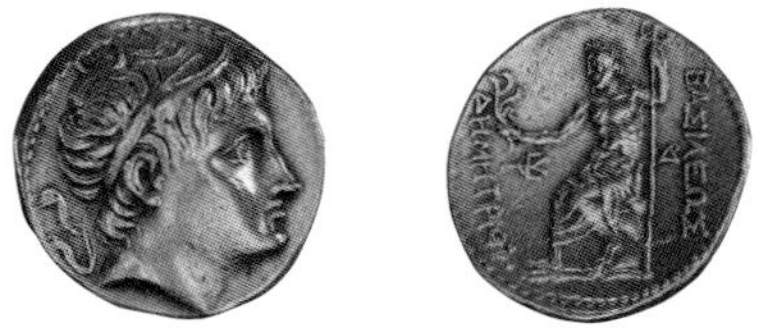

CAT. 211
Silver tetradrachm, Demetrius Poliorcetes (306/305–283 BC), Amphipolis, 291–290 BC.
Diademed head of Demetrius / Poseidon seated on rock.
16.96 g; 28 mm
Fondation Martin Bodmer, Cologny
See *Essay III*

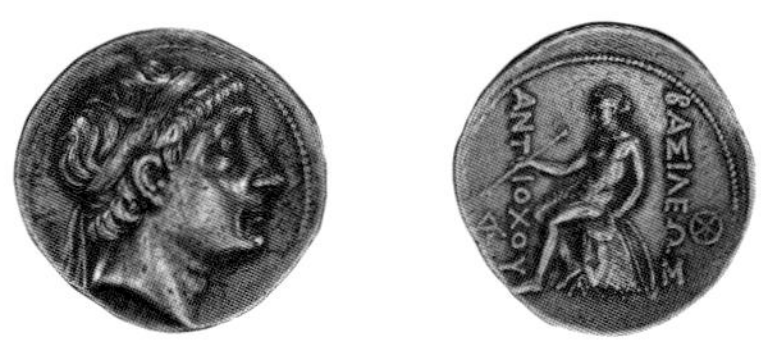

CAT. 212
Silver tetradrachm, Antiochus I Soter (280–261 BC), Seleucia on the Tigris.
Diademed head of Antiochus I / Apollo seated on omphalos.
29 mm
Fondation Martin Bodmer, Cologny
See *Essay III*

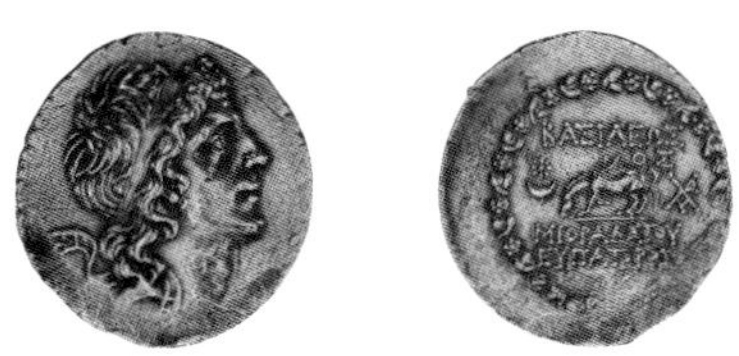

CAT. 213
Silver tetradrachm, Mithridates VI Eupator Dionysus (120–63 BC), Pontus.
Diademed head of Mithridates VI / Pegasus grazing.
16.49 g; 31 mm
Fondation Martin Bodmer, Cologny
See *Essay III*

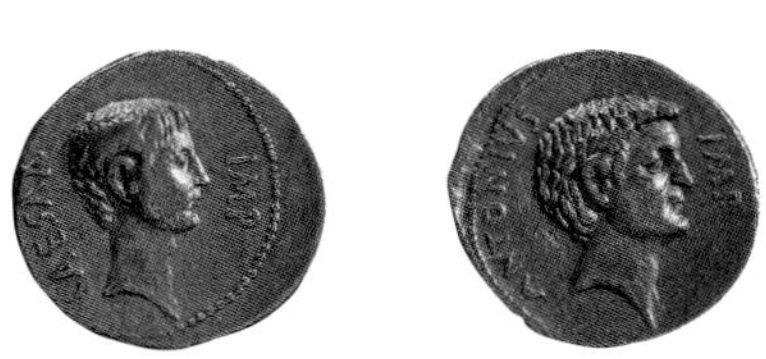

CAT. 214
Gold *aureus*, Octavian and Mark Antony, Second Triumvirate (43–33 BC), mint in South or Central Italy, *ca.* 40–39 BC.
Head of Octavian / Head of Mark Antony.
8.10 g; 20 mm
Fondation Martin Bodmer, Cologny

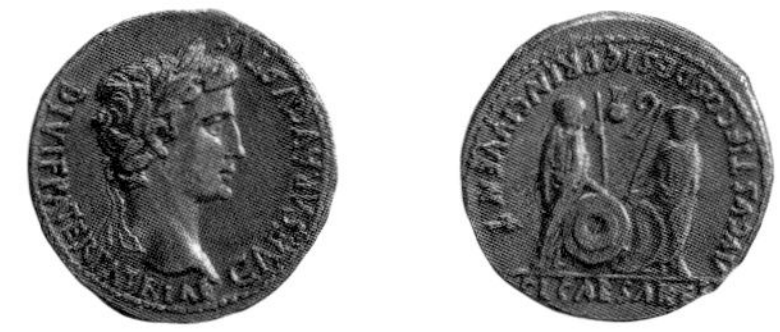

CAT. 215
Gold *aureus*, Augustus (27 BC–14 AD), Lugdunum, 7–6 BC.
Laureate head of Augustus /
Gaius and Lucius Caesares as *Principes Iuventutis*.
7.92 g; 18 mm
Fondation Martin Bodmer, Cologny
See *Essay VIII*

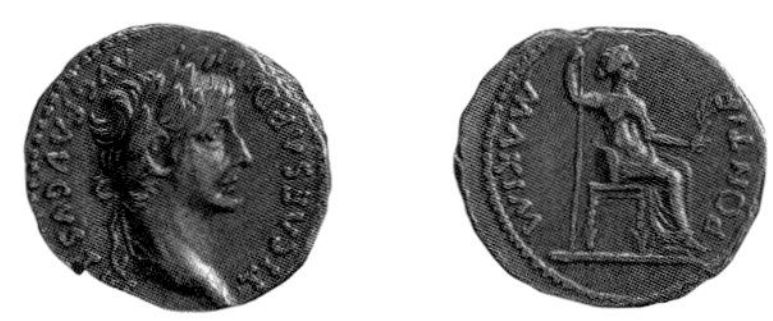

CAT. 216
Gold *aureus*, Tiberius (14–37 AD), Lugdunum.
Laureate head of Tiberius / Seated female figure.
7.77 g; 19 mm
Fondation Martin Bodmer, Cologny

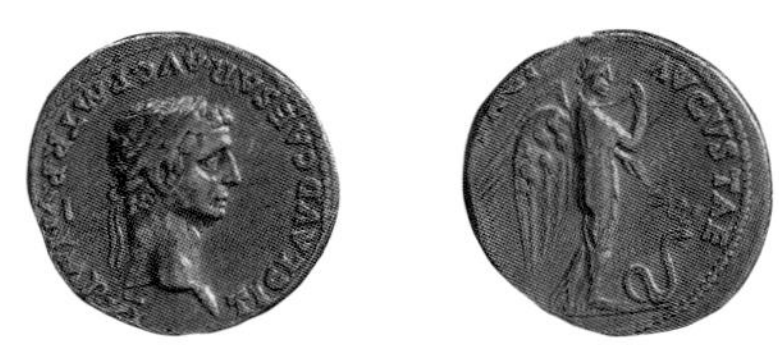

CAT. 217
Gold *aureus*, Claudius (41–54 AD), Rome, 46–47 AD.
Laureate head of Claudius / Winged Pax-Nemesis.
7.85 g; 18 mm
Fondation Martin Bodmer, Cologny

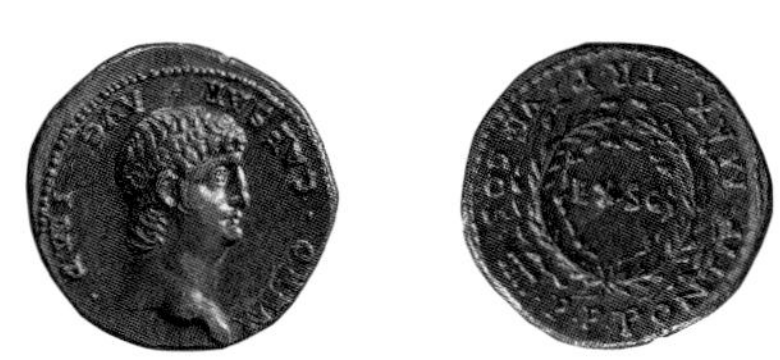

CAT. 218
Gold *aureus*, Nero (54–68 AD), Rome, 59–60 AD.
Head of Nero / EX SC within oak-wreath.
7.64 g; 17 mm
Fondation Martin Bodmer, Cologny

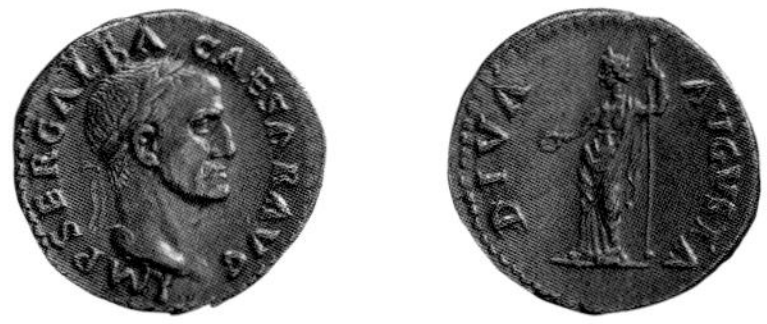

CAT. 219
Gold *aureus*, Galba (68–69 AD), Rome.
Laureate head of Galba / Livia standing.
7.29 g; 20 mm
Fondation Martin Bodmer, Cologny

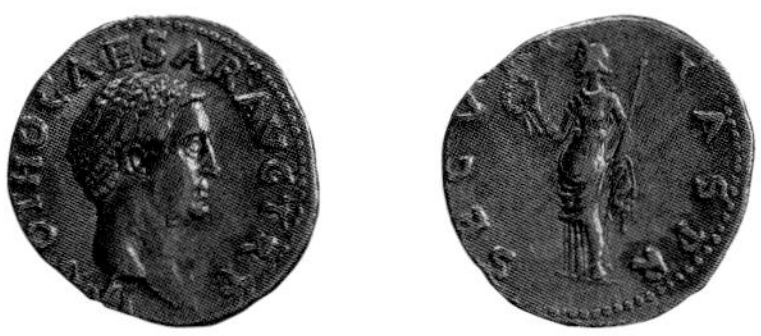

CAT. 220
Gold *aureus*, Otho (69 AD), Rome.
Head of Otho / Securitas standing.
7.26 g; 19 mm
Fondation Martin Bodmer, Cologny

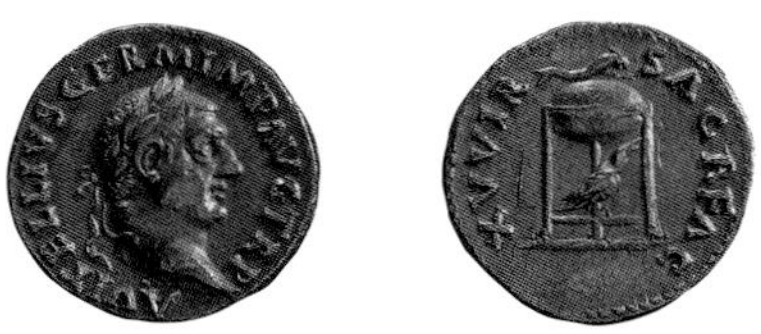

CAT. 221
Gold *aureus*, Vitellius (69 AD), Rome.
Laureate head of Vitellius / Tripod-lebes, dolphin and raven.
7.20 g; 19 mm
Fondation Martin Bodmer, Cologny
See *Essay VIII*

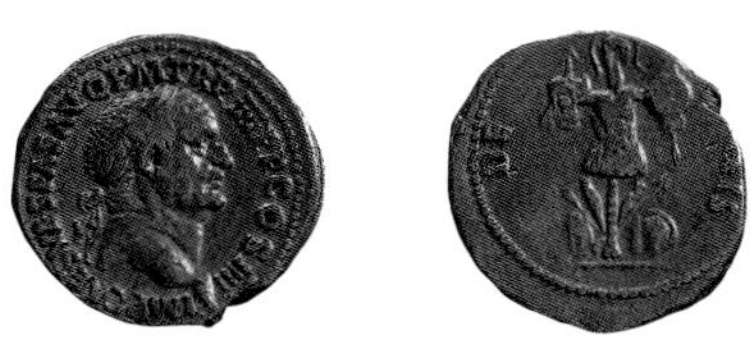

CAT. 222
Gold *aureus*, Vespasian (69–79 AD), Lugdunum, 72 AD
Laureate head of Vespasian / Trophy.
7.24 g; 20 mm
Fondation Martin Bodmer, Cologny

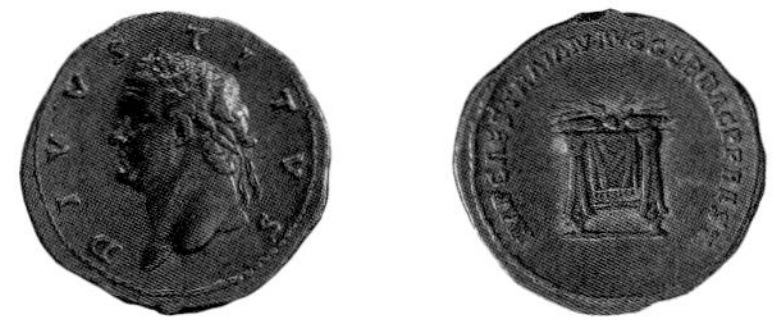

CAT. 223
Gold *aureus*, Trajan in the name of Titus (79–81 AD), Rome, *ca.* 107 AD.
Laureate head of Titus / Winged thunderbolt on throne.
7.18 g; 20 mm
Fondation Martin Bodmer, Cologny

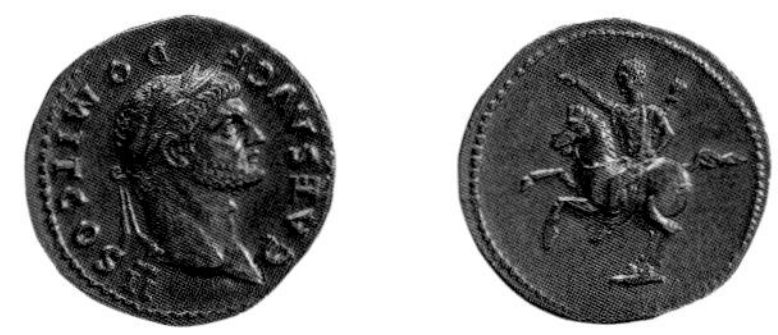

CAT. 224
Gold *aureus*, Domitian under Vespasian (73–75 AD), Rome, 73 AD.
Laureate head of Domitian / Domitian on horseback.
7.09 g; 20 mm
Fondation Martin Bodmer, Cologny

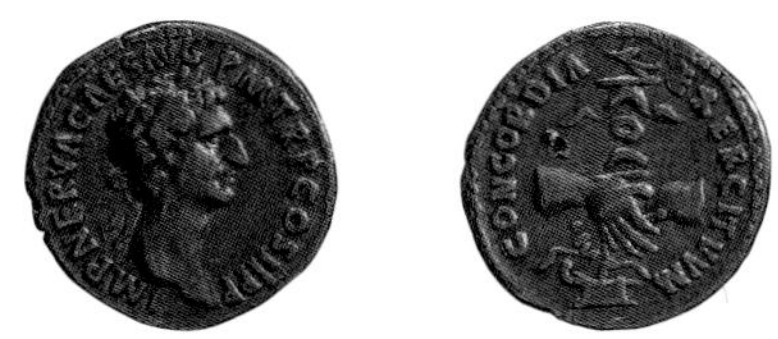

CAT. 225
Gold *aureus*, Nerva (96–98 AD), Rome, 96 AD.
Laureate head of Nerva / Clasped hands holding *aquila* set on prow.
7.56 g; 20 mm
Fondation Martin Bodmer, Cologny

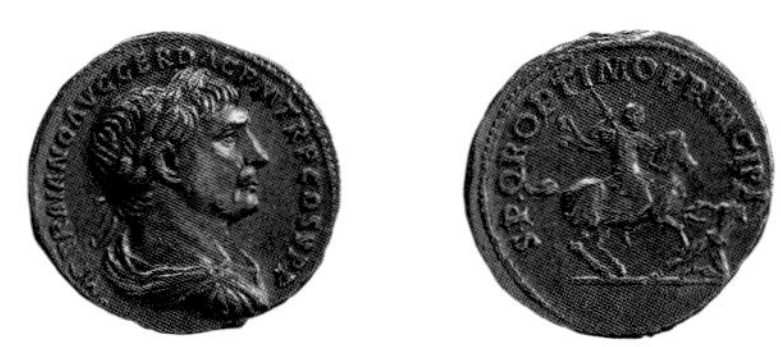

CAT. 226
Gold *aureus*, Trajan (98–117 AD), Rome, 103–111 AD.
Laureate head of Trajan / Trajan galloping and thrusting spear at fallen Dacian in front of horse.
7.28 g; 19 mm
Fondation Martin Bodmer, Cologny
See *Essay VIII*

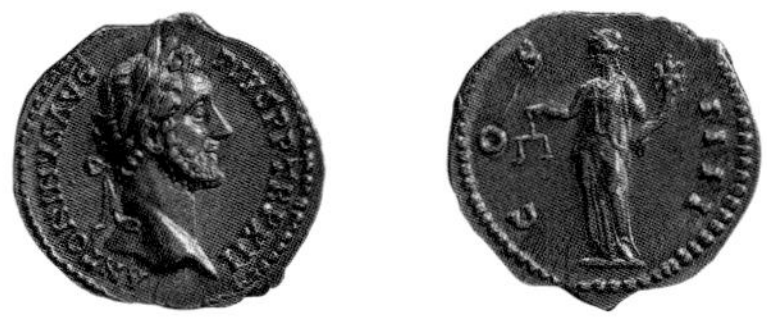

CAT. 227

Gold *aureus*, Antoninus Pius (138–161 AD), Rome, 148–149 AD.
Laureate head of Antoninus / Nemesis standing.
7.16 g; 20 mm
Fondation Martin Bodmer, Cologny
See *Essay VIII*

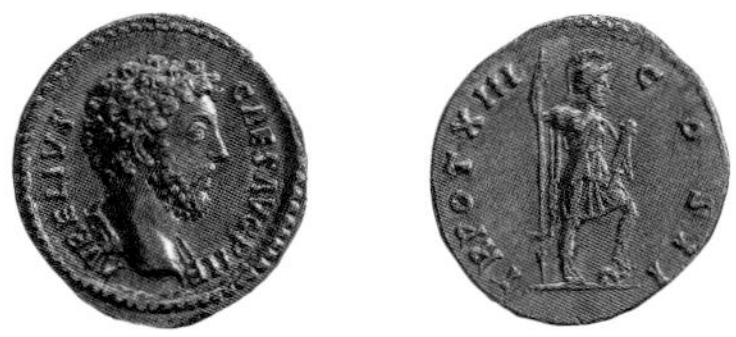

CAT. 228

Gold *aureus*, Marcus Aurelius under Antoninus Pius, Rome, 158–159 AD.
Head of Marcus Aurelius / Virtus standing.
7.24 g; 20 mm
Fondation Martin Bodmer, Cologny

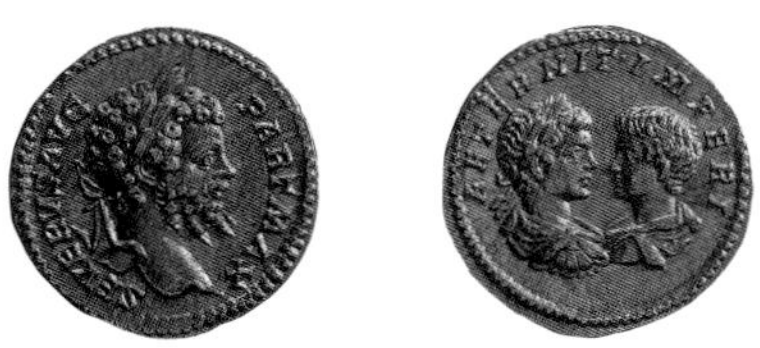

CAT. 229

Gold *aureus*, Septimius Severus (193–211 AD), Rome, 200–201 AD.
Laureate head of Septimius Severus / Busts of Caracalla and Geta.
7.07 g; 20 mm
Fondation Martin Bodmer, Cologny
See *Essay VIII*

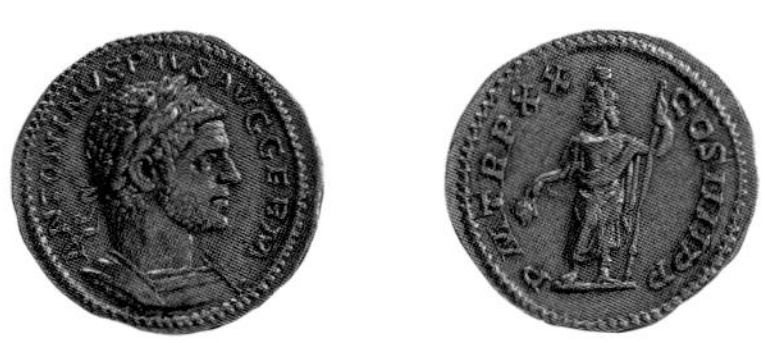

CAT. 230

Gold *aureus*, Caracalla (198–211 AD), Rome, 213 AD.
Laureate head of Caracalla / Serapis standing.
6.38 g; 20 mm
Fondation Martin Bodmer, Cologny
See *Essay VIII*

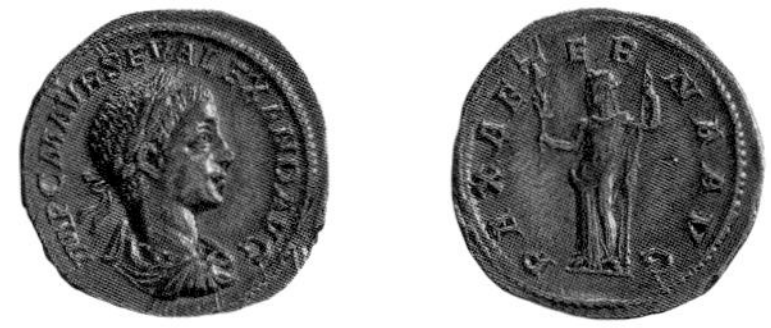

CAT. 231

Gold *aureus*, Alexander Severus (222–235 AD), Rome.
Laureate bust of Alexander Severus / Pax standing.
6.25 g; 21 mm
Fondation Martin Bodmer, Cologny

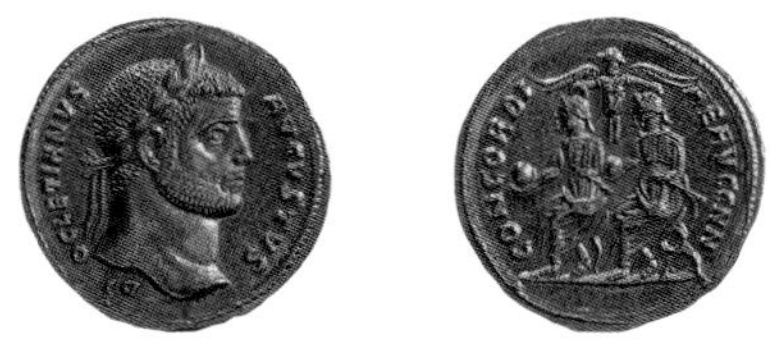

CAT. 232

Gold *aureus*, Diocletian (284–305 AD), Cyzicus, 293 AD.
Laureate head of Diocletian / Diocletian and Maximian holding globus and sword in their right and left hands respectively, crowned by Victory.
5.49 g; 20mm
Fondation Martin Bodmer, Cologny
See *Essay VIII*

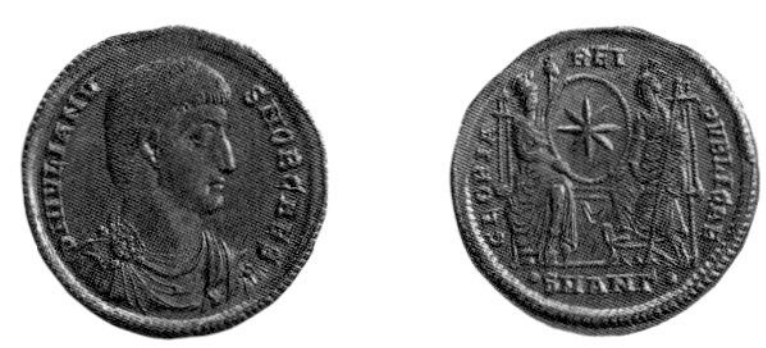

CAT. 233

Gold *solidus*, Julian II as a caesar (355–360 AD), Antioch.
Bust of Julian /
Rome and Constantinople holding between them shield with star.
4.45 g; 20 mm
Fondation Martin Bodmer, Cologny
See *Essay V*

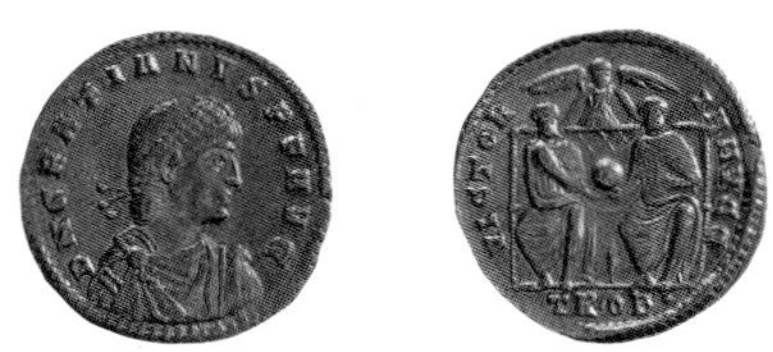

CAT. 234

Gold *solidus*, Gratian (375–383 AD), Trier, 367–375.
Diademed head of Gratian / Gratian and Teodosios I seated, crowned by Victory.
4.46 g; 21 mm
Fondation Martin Bodmer, Cologny

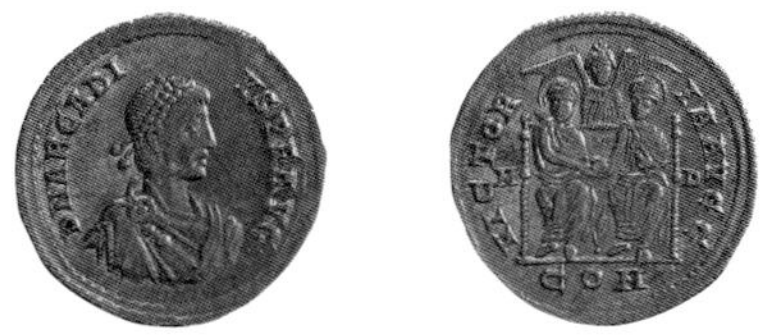

CAT. 235

Gold *solidus*, Arkadios (395–408 AD), Thessalonike, 383–388 AD. Diademed bust of Arkadios / Theodosios I and Arkadios seated, crowned by Victory.

4.43 g; 20 mm

Fondation Martin Bodmer, Cologny

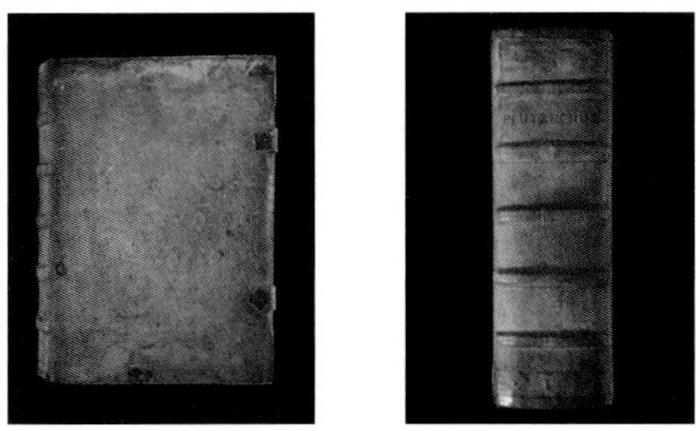

CAT. 236

Plutarch, *Vitae illustrium virorum, sive Parallelae*, [Strasbourg, Adolf Rusch, *ca*. 1470–1471].

Second edition of the Latin translation of Plutarch by the humanist and prelate Giovanni Antonio Campano (1429–1477), Bishop of Croton. Dedicated to Cardinal Francisco Piccolomini (future Pope Pius III), this version was first printed in Rome in 1470 (the Greek *editio princeps* was published forty-seven years later). Apart from some isolated biographies (probably later additions), the work of the Greek historian, written around AD 100–110, presented the *Lives* of forty-six great men, the entries organized in pairs juxtaposing a Roman to a Greek portrait (hence the title Βίοι Παράλληλοι, or *Parallel Lives*). Still in its original binding of cold-stamped pigskin, this copy features a gutter decorated with three ink motifs: a radiating medallion containing a Greek monogram (possibly the Christian *alpha-omega*), crowned by a *titulus* and framed by two interlace lozenges. In the middle of the sixteenth century, this volume belonged to Erasmus of Limburg (Bishop of Strasburg in 1541–1568), who, according to a handwritten *ex-dono*, donated it to the Franciscan monastery at Saverne.

Fondation Martin Bodmer, Cologny, Inc. Bod. 202

ARTEFACTS FROM THE BENAKI MUSEUM COLLECTIONS

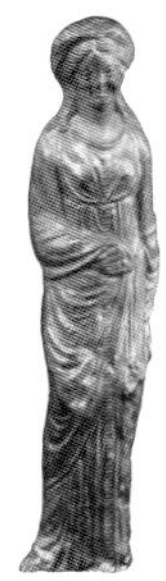

CAT. I

Gold statuette with clay core, representing Aphrodite holding a hare in her left hand, 1st century BC.

Benaki Museum, Athens, Inv. 27511

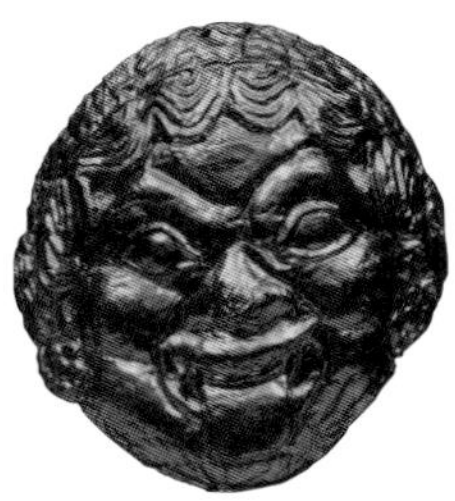

CAT. II

Gold repoussé Gorgon mask (*gorgoneion*), mid-6th century BC.

Benaki Museum, Athens, Inv. 27513

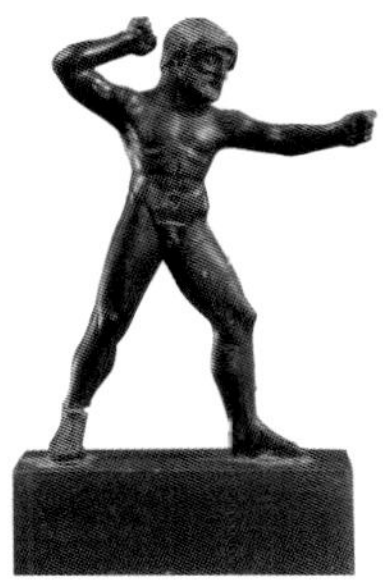

CAT. III

Bronze inscribed figurine of Heracles, from the Boeotian sanctuary of Apollo Ptoios, *ca*. 480–460 BC.

Benaki Museum, Athens, Inv. 8059

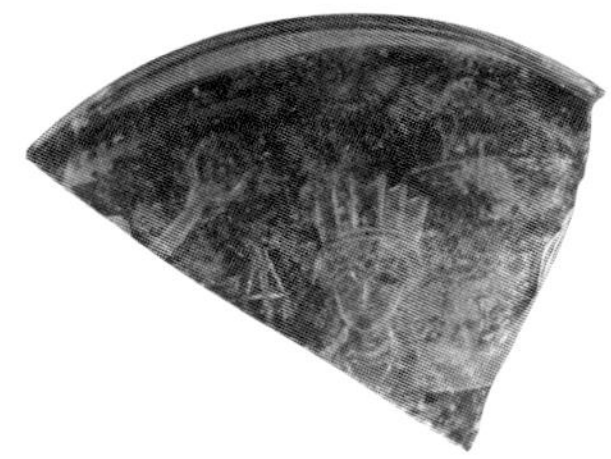

CAT. IV

Fragment of an inscribed glass cup with the personification of the city of Tyrus, from Tyrus, Phoenice, late 3rd – early 4th century AD.

Benaki Museum, Athens, Inv. 3240

See *Essay V*

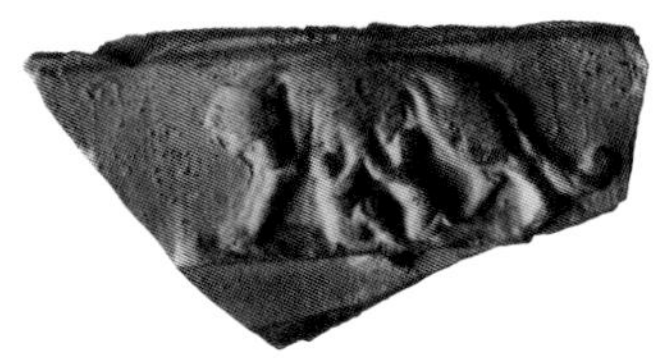

CAT. V

Terra sigillata vase fragment with the legendary she-wolf suckling Romulus and Remus, from Egypt, late 1st century – early 1st century AD.

Benaki Museum, Athens, Inv. 22243

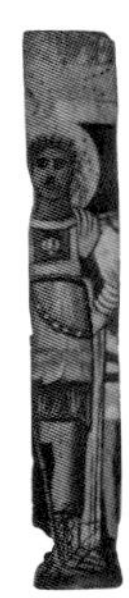

CAT. VI

Painted wood icon with a military figure (saint?), from Egypt, 7th century AD.

Athens, Benaki Museum, Inv. 21873

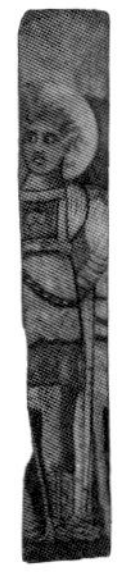

CAT. VII

Painted wood icon with a military figure (saint?), from Egypt, 7th century AD.

Benaki Museum, Athens, Inv. 21831

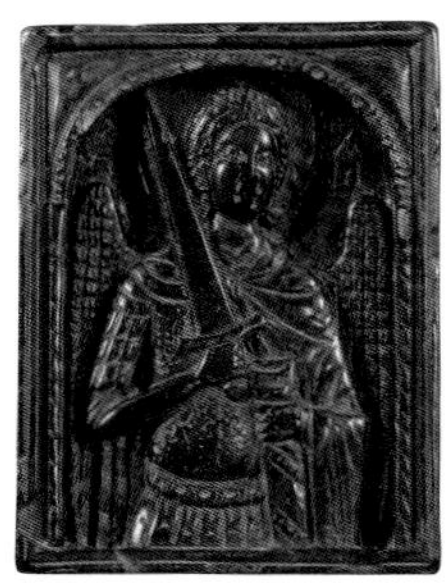

CAT. VIII

Small steatite icon of the Archangel Michael carved in relief, second half of the 13th century AD.

Benaki Museum, Athens, Inv. 13507

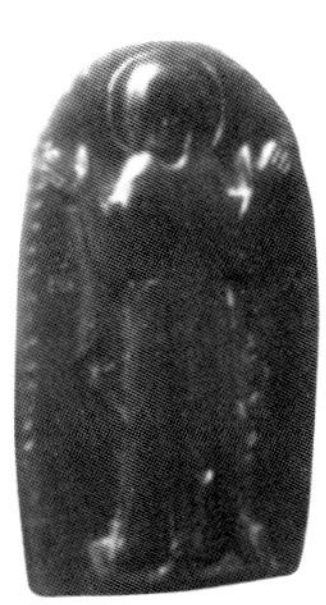

CAT. IX

Double-sided cameo of hematite (?) with the Virgin Orans on one side and Christ Pantokrator on the other, 11th century AD.

Benaki Museum, Athens, Inv. 13511

See *Essay IX*

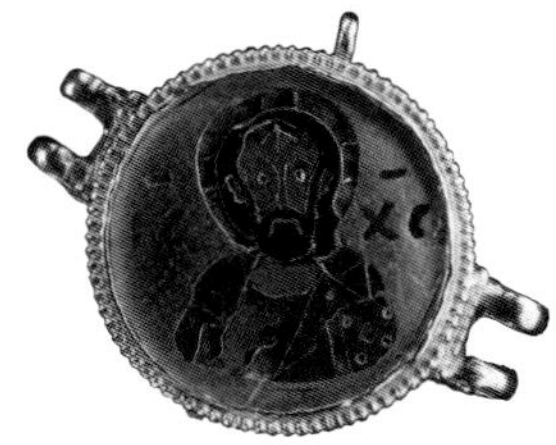

CAT. X

Double-sided circular jewellery attachment with Christ Pantokrator on one side and the Virgin Orans on the other, early 12th century AD.

Benaki Museum, Athens, Inv. 36343

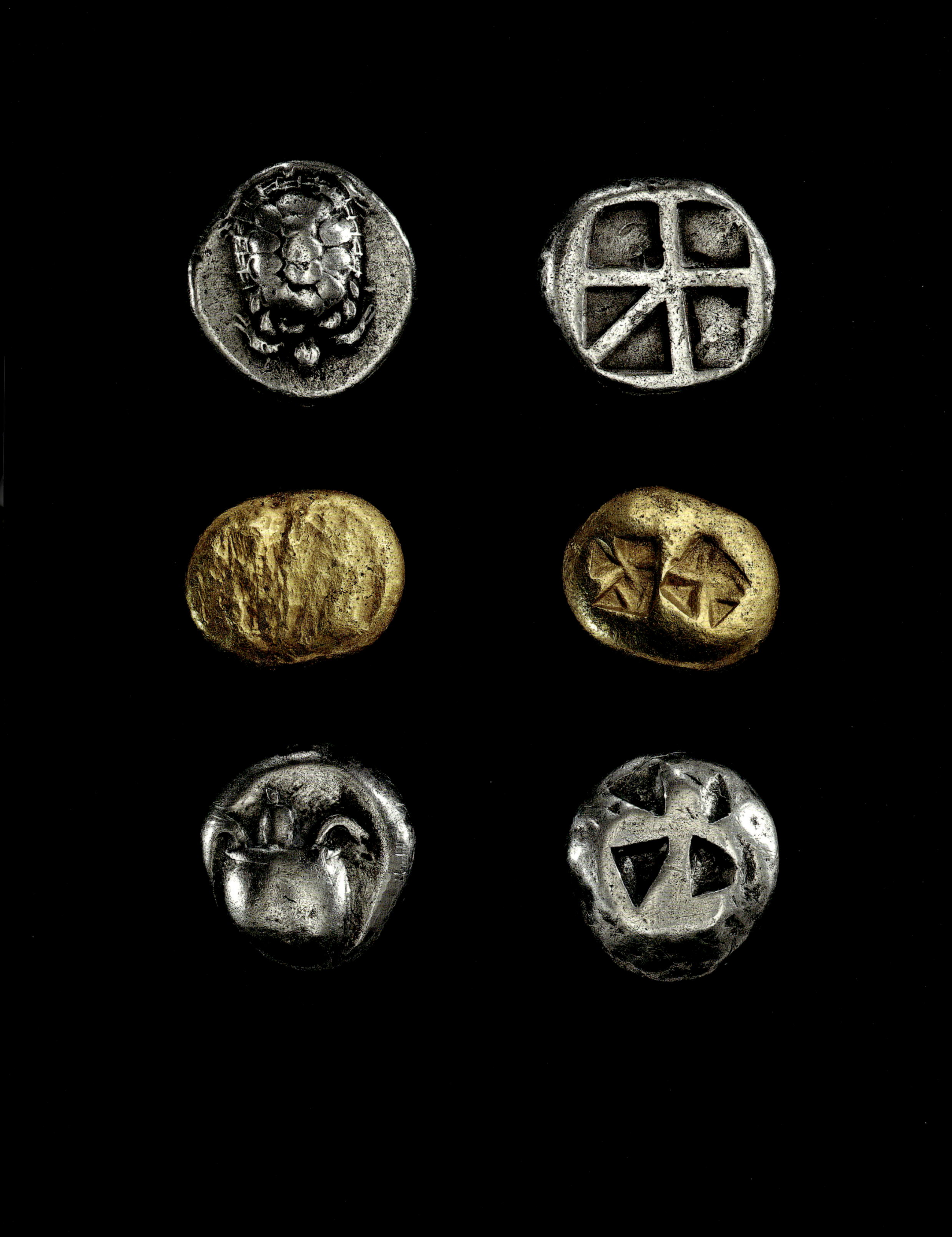

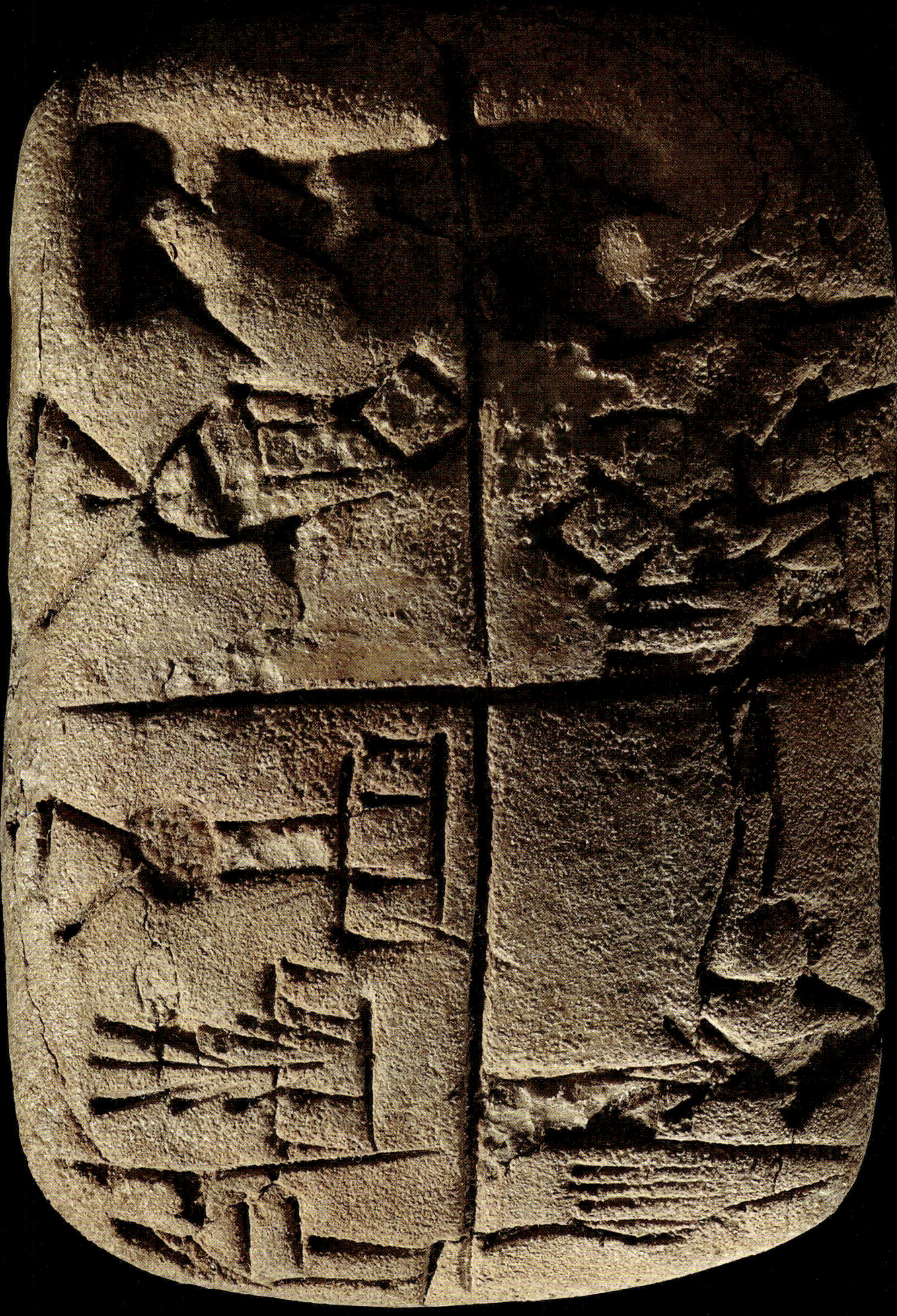

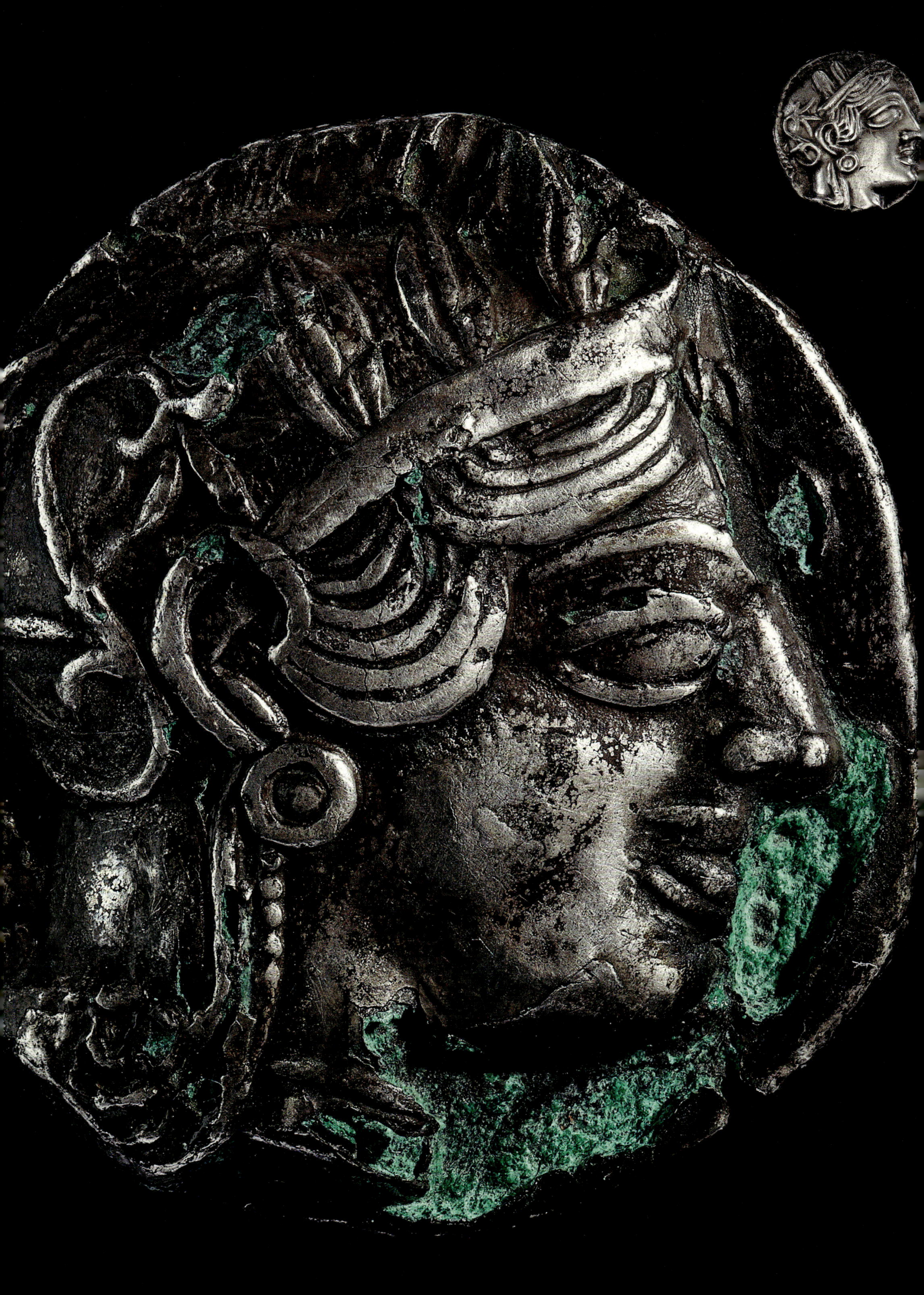

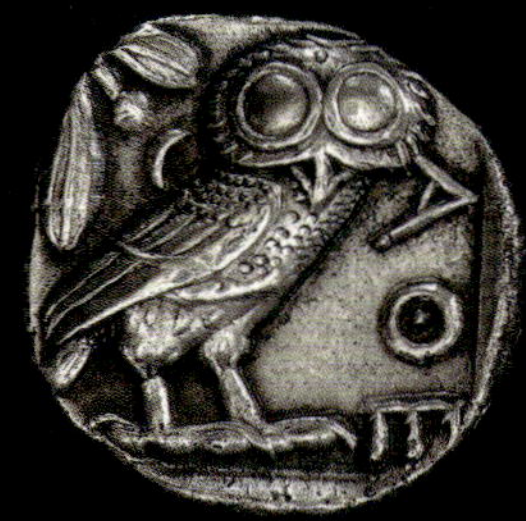

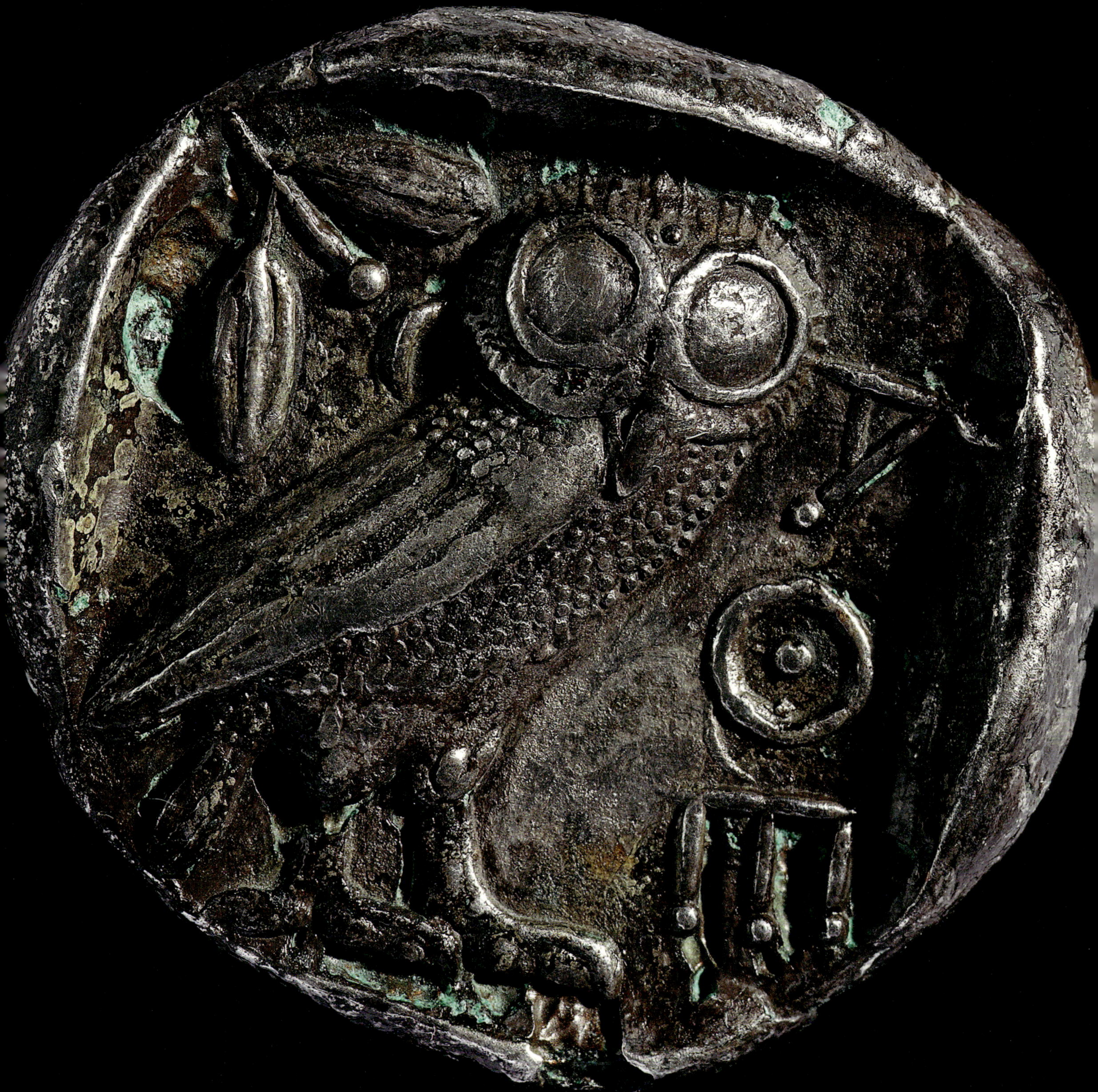

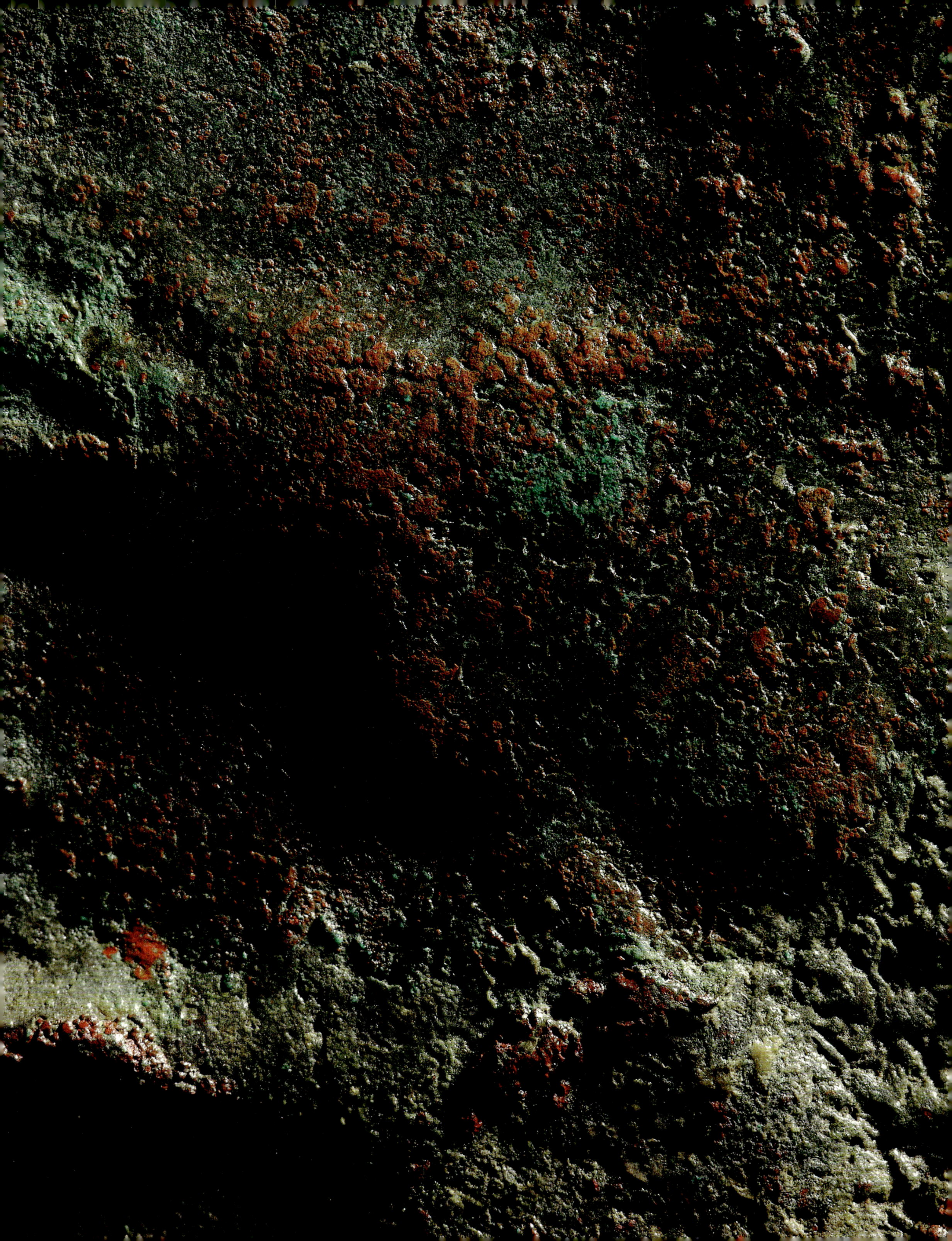

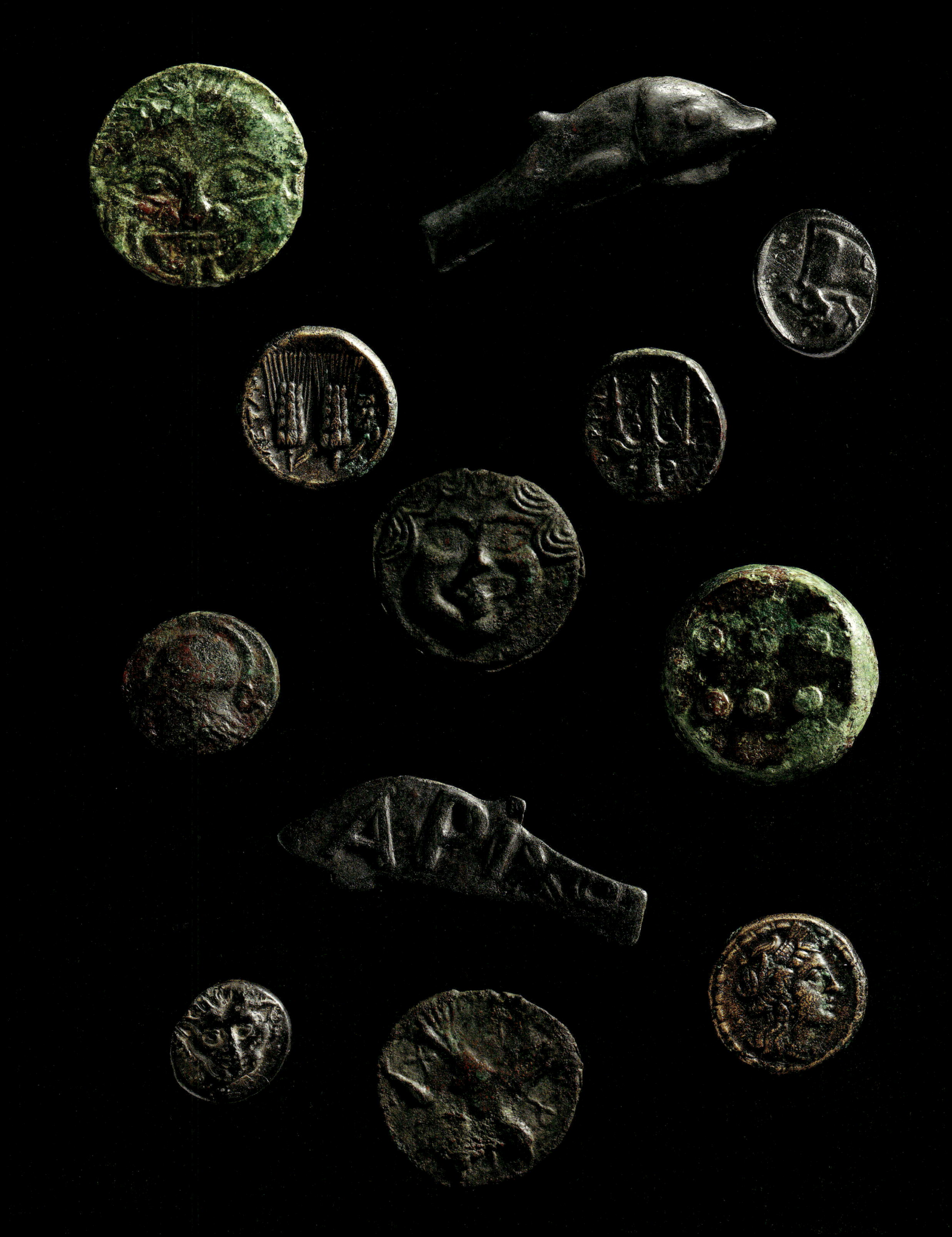

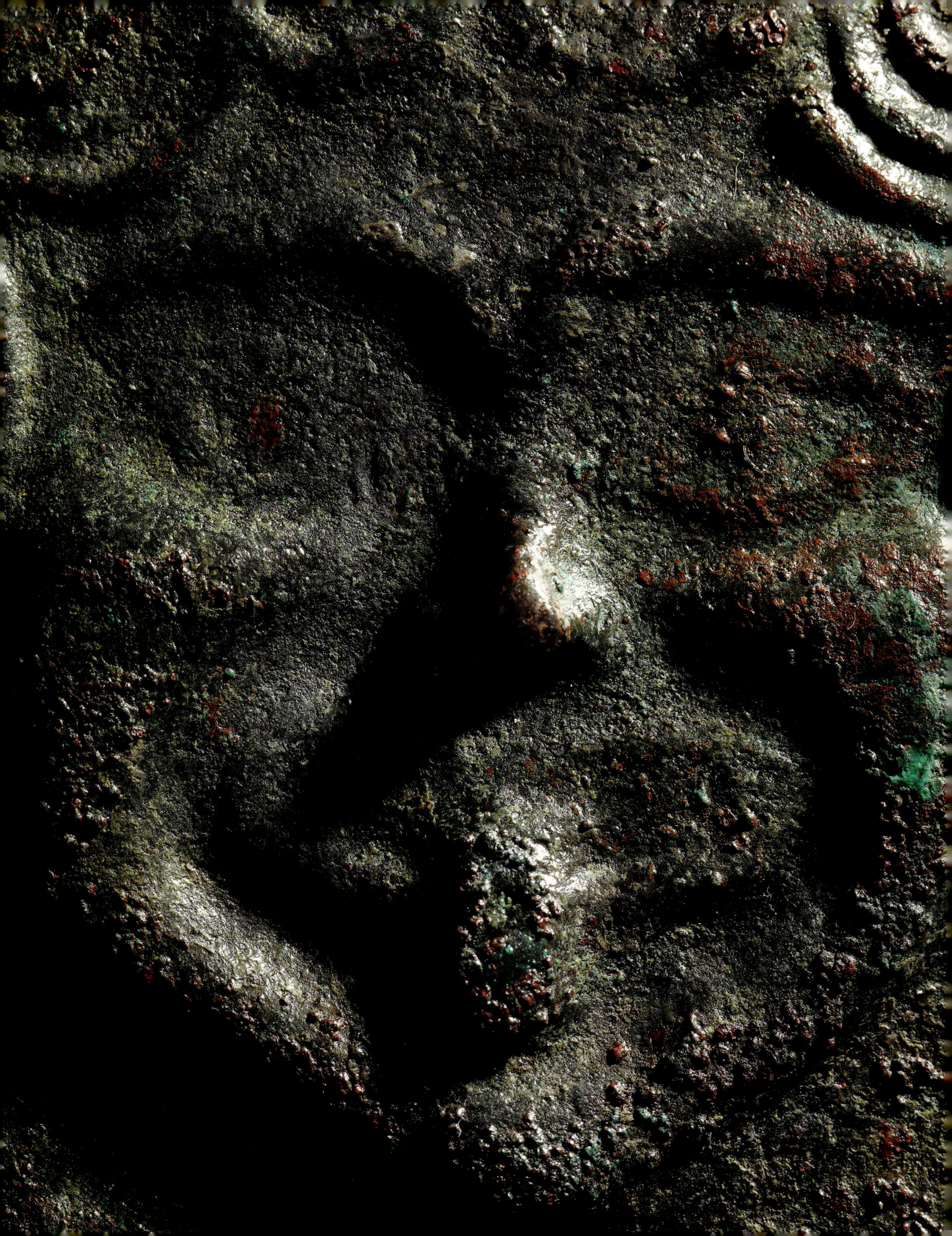

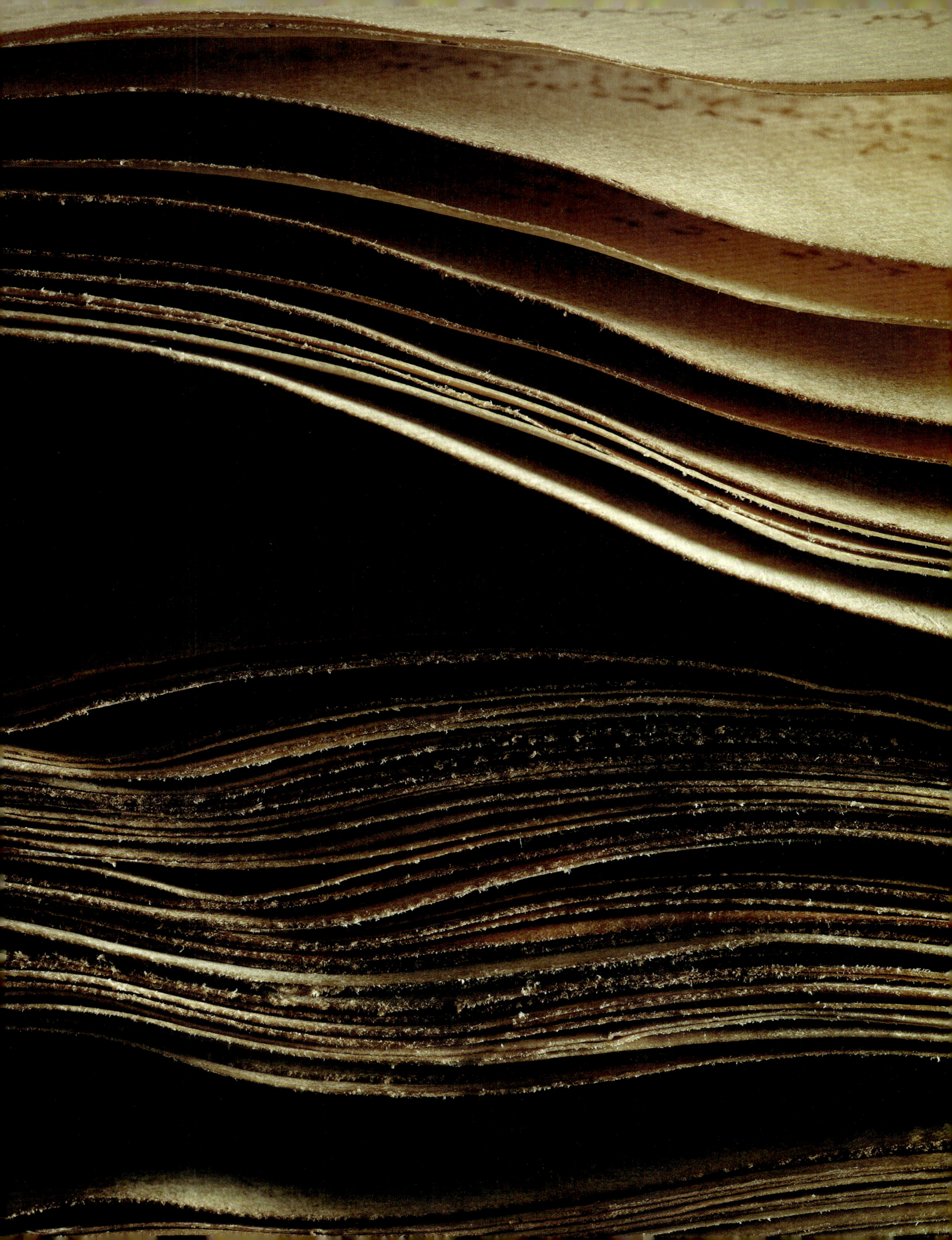

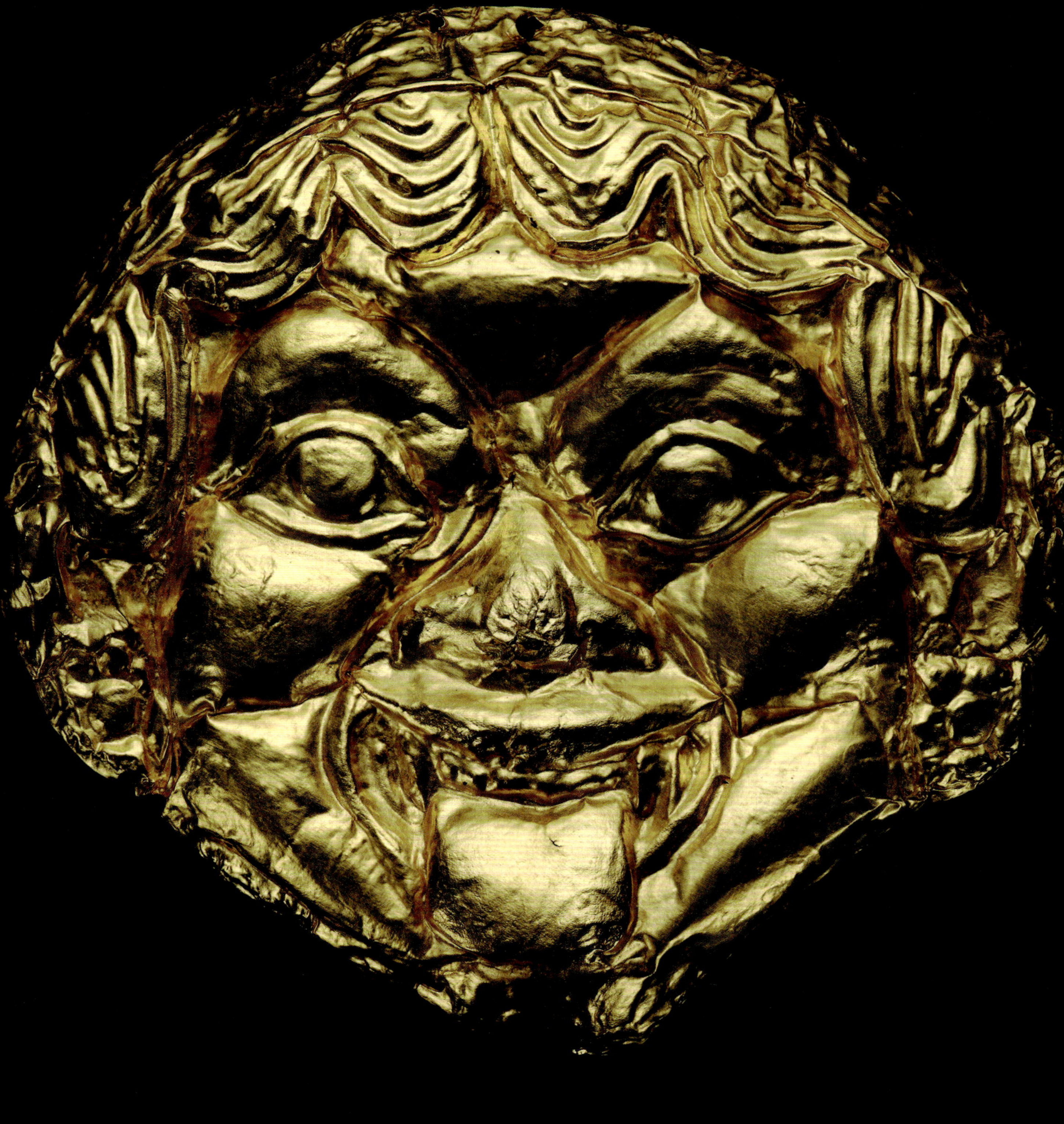

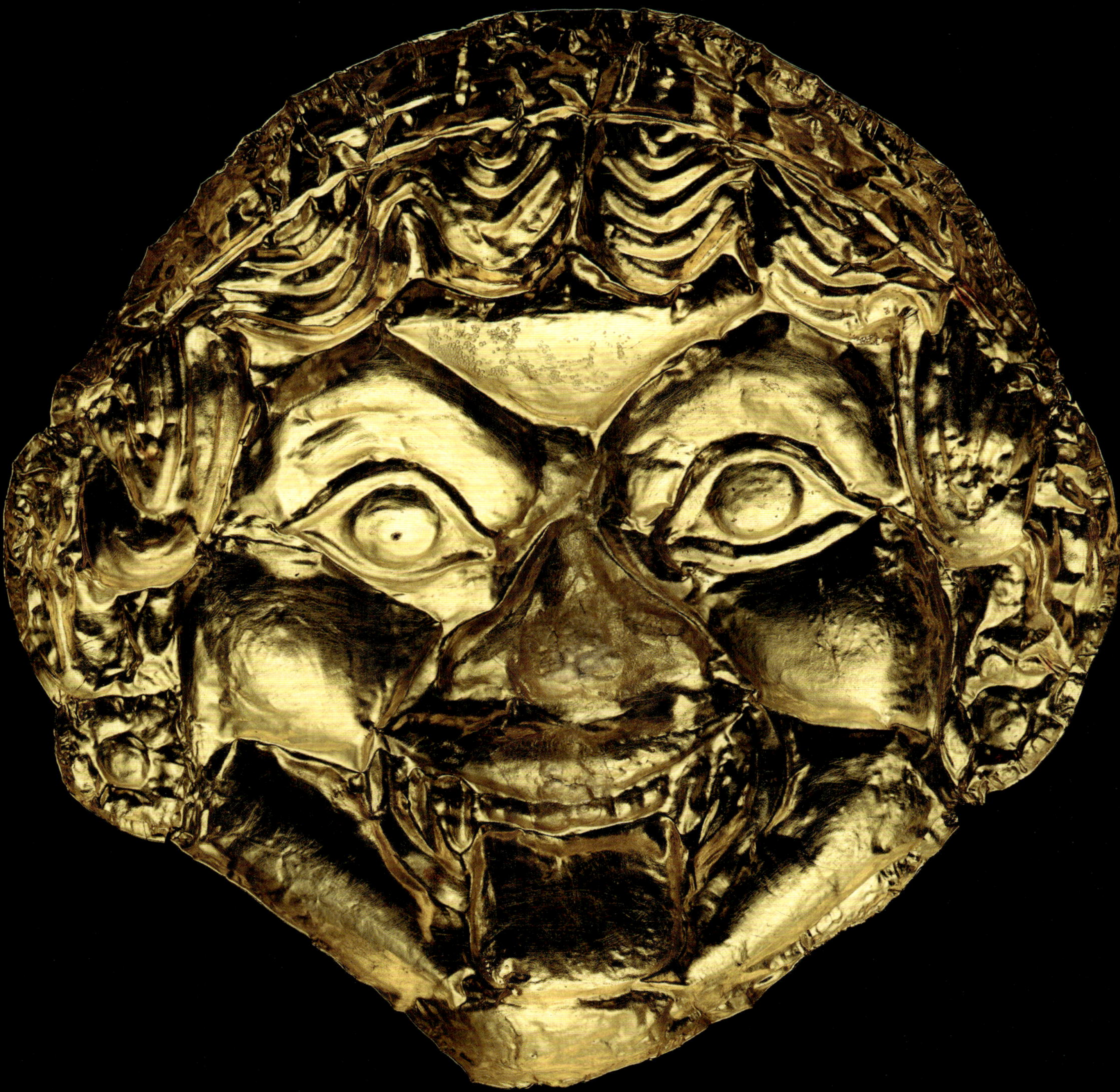

ὅτε κῦμα κατακλυσμοῦ φοροῦ … ὕδατος, ἢ πολέμων φθορά, ἐλάττους δὲ πολὺ τῶ
γμένου ἀριθμοῦ δι᾽ ὀρφανίας γένωνται, ἑκόντας μὲν οὐ δεῖ πολίτας παρεμβάλ
όθῃ παιδείᾳ πεπαιδευμένους. ἀνάγκῃ δέ, οὐδὲ θεὸς εἶναι λέγεται δυνατὸς βιάζεσθαι
οὕτω δὴ τὸν νῦν λεγόμενον λόγον, ἡμῖν φῶμεν παραινεῖν λέγοντα· ὦ πάντων ἀ
ἄριστοι. τὴν ὁμοιότητα καὶ ἰσότητα καὶ τὸ ταὐτὸν καὶ ὁμολογούμενον τιμῶντες
φύσιν, μὴ ἀνίετε κατά τε ἀριθμόν, καὶ πᾶσαν δύναμιν τὴν τῶν καλῶν κἀγαθῶ
μάτων· καὶ δὴ καὶ νῦν τὸν ἀριθμὸν μὲν πρῶτον διὰ βίου παντὸς φυλάξατε τὸ
μον· εἶτα τὸ τῆς οὐσίας ὕψος τε καὶ μέγεθος, ὃ τὸ πρῶτον ἐνείμασθε μέτριον ὂν
τιμάσητε τῷ τε ὠνεῖσθαι καὶ τῷ πωλεῖν, πρὸς ἀλλήλους· οὔτε γὰρ ὁ νείμας κλῆρον
ς ὑμῖν ξύμμαχος, οὔτε ὁ νομοθέτης. νῦν γὰρ δὴ πρῶτον τῷ ἀπειθοῦντι νόμο
τάττει. προειπὼν ἐπὶ τούτοις κληροῦσθαι τὸν ἐθέλοντα ἢ μὴ κληροῦσθαι. ὡς πρ
ὲν τῆς γῆς, ἱερᾶς οὔσης τῶν πάντων θεῶν. εἶτα ἱερέων τε καὶ ἱερειῶν εὐχὰς ποιησομένω
ς πρώτοις θύμασι καὶ δευτέροις· καὶ μέχρι τρίτων, τὸν πριάμενον ἢ ἀποδόμενον, ἢ
ὧν οἰκοπέδων ἢ γηπέδων, τὰ ἐπὶ τούτοις πρέποντα πάσχειν πάθη· γράψαντ
τοῖς ἱεροῖς θήσουσι κυπαριττίνας μνήμας εἰς τὸν ἔπειτα χρόνον καταγεγραμμ
πρὸς τούτοις δ᾽ ἔτι, φυλακτήρια τούτων, ὅπως ἂν γίγνηται, καταστήσουσιν
ῃ τῶν ἀρχῶν. ἥτις ἂν ὀξύτατον ὁρᾶν δοκῇ. ἵν᾽ αἱ παρὰ ταῦτα ἑκάστοτε παραγι
γνόμεναι μή, λανθάνωσιν αὐτούς, ἀλλὰ κολάζωσι τὸν ἀπειθοῦντα ἅμα νόμ
τῷ θεῷ. ὅσον γὰρ δὴ τὸ νῦν ἐπιταττόμενον ἀγαθὸν ὂν τυγχάνει, πάσαις ταῖς τ
ναις πόλεσι, τὴν ἑπομένην κατασκευὴν προσλαβὸν κατὰ τὴν παλαιὰν παρ
, οὐδεὶς εἴσεταί ποτε κακὸς ὤν· ἀλλ᾽ ἔμπειρός τε καὶ ἐπιεικὴς ἔθεσι γενόμενο
ατισμὸν γὰρ οὔτ᾽ ἔνεστι σφόδρα ἐν τῇ τοιαύτῃ κατασκευῇ. ξυνέπεταί τε αὐτ
λεῖν, μὴ δ᾽ ἐξεῖναι χρηματίζεσθαι τῶν ἀνελευθέρων χρηματισμῶν μηδενὶ μηδέ
σου ἐπονείδιστος λεγομένη βαναυσία ἦθος ἀποτρέπει ἐλεύθερον· μὴ δὲ τὸ παρ
ἀξιοῦν ἐκ τῶν τοιούτων ξυλλέγειν χρήματα.   Πρὸς τούτοις δ᾽ ἔτι, νόμος ἐ
πᾶσι τούτοις, μὴ δ᾽ ἐξεῖναι χρυσὸν μὴ δὲ ἄργυρον κεκτῆσθαι μηδένα μηδενὶ ἰδι
μισμα δ᾽ ἕνεκα ἀλλαγῆς τῆς καθ᾽ ἡμέραν. ἣν δημιουργοῖς τε ἀλλάττεσθαι σχε
καῖον, καὶ πᾶσιν ὁπόσων χρεία τῶν τοιούτων, μισθοὺς μισθωτοῖς δούλοις καὶ ἐπ
ποτίνειν; ὧν ἕνεκά φαμεν τὸ νόμισμα κτητέον· αὐτοῖς μὲν ἔντιμον· τοῖς δὲ ἄλλοις ἀν
ἀδόκιμον· κοινὸν δ᾽ ἑλληνικὸν νόμισμα, ἕνεκά τε στρατειῶν καὶ ἀποδημιῶν εἰς τοὺς
ἀνθρώπους, οἷον πρεσβειῶν ἢ καί τινος ἀναγκαίας ἄλλης τῇ πόλει νόμισμα ἑλληνικ

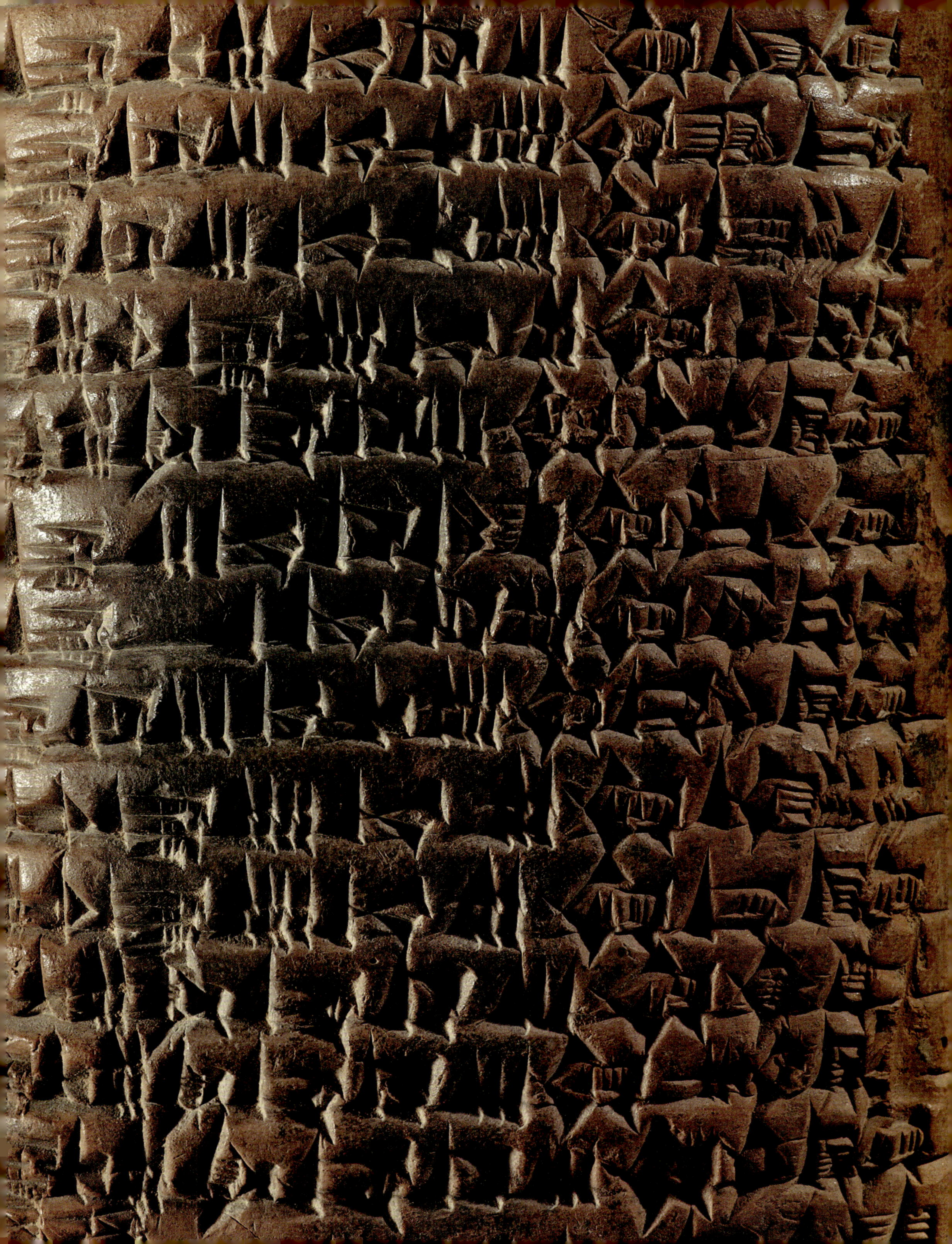

Ὁ πονηρότατος βαλανεύς, ὁπόσοι
Κρατοῦσι κυκησιτέφρου·
Ψευδονίτρου τε κονίας·
Καὶ κιμωλίας γῆς·
Χρόνον ἐνδιατρίψει· εἰδὼς δὲ τάδ᾽ οὐκ
Εἰρηνικὸς ἔσθ᾽· ἵνα μήποτε κἀ
Ποδυθῇ μεθύων, ἄ
<Νευξύλου βαδίζων.>

Πολλάκις γ᾽ ἡμῖν ἔδοξεν ἡ πόλις πεπονθέναι·
Ταυτόν, ἔς τε τῶν πολιτῶν τοὺς καλούς τε κἀγαθούς,
Ἔς τε τἀρχαῖον νόμισμα καὶ τὸ καινὸν χρυσίον·
Οὔτε γὰρ τούτοισιν οὖσιν οὐ κεκιβδηλευμένοις,
Ἀλλὰ καλλίστοις ἁπάντων ὡς δοκεῖ νομισμάτων·
Καὶ μόνοις ὀρθῶς κοπεῖσι, καὶ κεκωδωνισμένοις,
Ἔν τε τοῖς ἕλλησι καὶ τοῖς βαρβάροισι πανταχοῦ,
Χρώμεθ᾽ οὐδέν, ἀλλὰ τούτοις τοῖς πονηροῖς χαλκίοις,
Χθές τε καὶ πρώην κοπεῖσι τῷ κακίστῳ κόμματι·
Τῶν πολιτῶν θ᾽ οὓς μὲν ἴσμεν εὐγενεῖς καὶ σώφρονας·
Ἄνδρας ὄντας καὶ δικαίους· καὶ καλούς τε κἀγαθούς·
Καὶ τραφέντας ἐν παλαίστραις, καὶ χοροῖς, καὶ μουσικῇ,

τεπίρρημα ὅμοιον κατὰ πάντα τῷ ἐπιρρήματι, ἐν στίχοις κ΄ τροχαϊ-
ταληκτικῶν συγκείμενον· ὧν ὁ τελευταῖος ἤ τι καὶ πάσχη τε πάσχειν τοῖς
τέλει δὲ πλὴν ἐξωνενευκυῖα. τὸ δὲ ἑξῆς, τὸ αὐτὸ πέπονθεν ἡ πόλις εἰς τοὺς
ῶν εἰς τὸ ἀρχαῖον νόμισμα. ὥσπερ γὰρ τῷ παλαιῷ νομίσματι οὐ χρώ

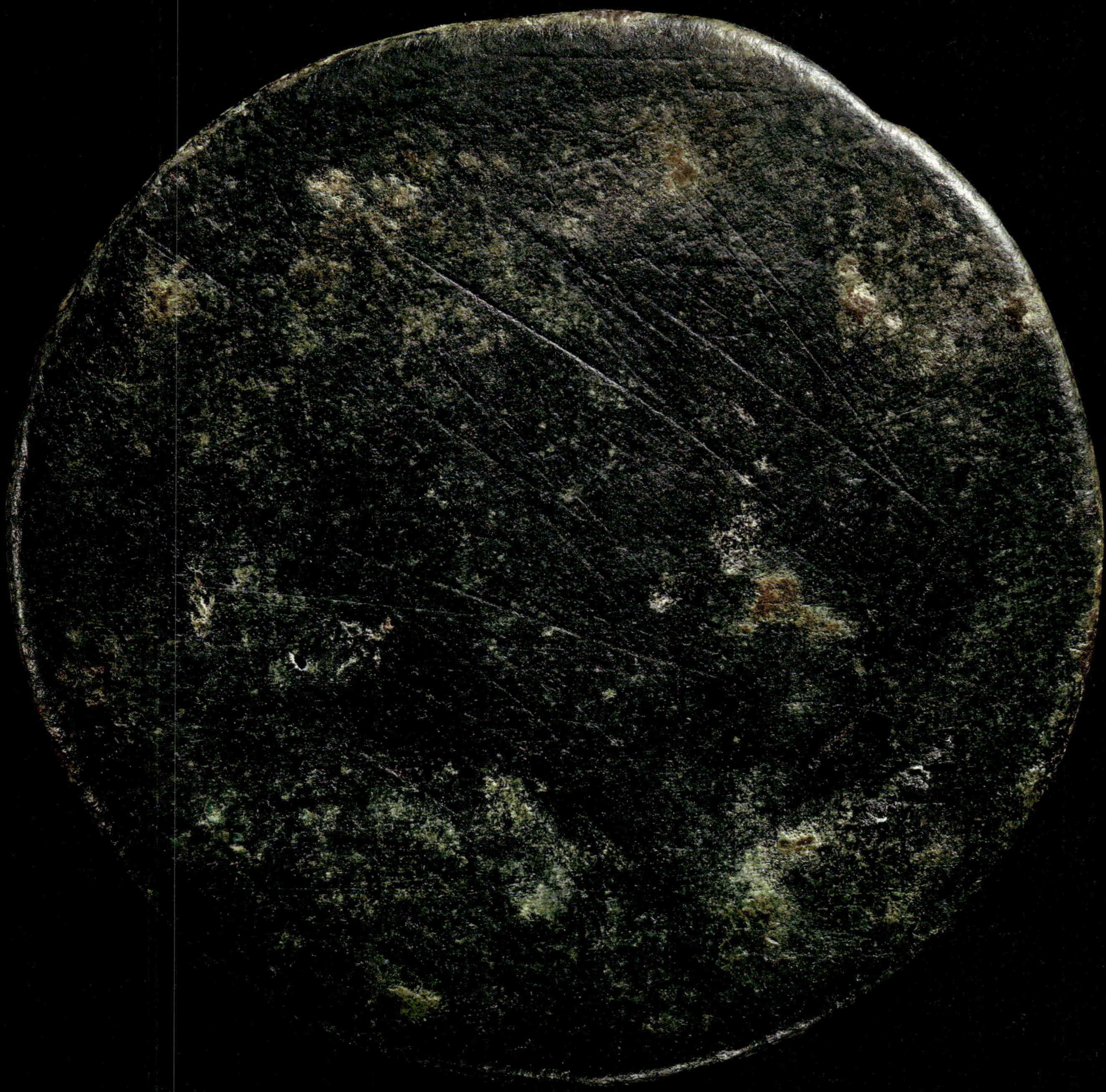

quā suū · lucrari dicit · minꝰ aūt quā ab inicio dāpnari · Et
in empcione et vendicōne ac in alijs quibuscūqꝫ licēciam le
pmiserit · Quādo aūt nec plus nec minꝰ sꝫ ipsa p ipsa ha
sua se habere dicunt · et nec lucrari nec dāpnum pati · Ja
lucri cuiusdā ac dāpni mediū ē iustū preter volūtariū eq
habēdo et prius ꝛ posterius ·

Et videt aliqbꝫ repassum quiddā simpliciť esse iu
vt pythagorici dixerūt · Diffiniebāt eni simplici
iustū esse id quod repassū sit alteri · Verꝫ hoc nō con
gruit neqꝫ ei iusto quod ē ꝯm leges neqꝫ ciuili · Voco autem
ciuile id quod est sociabile · Repassū nō cōgruit neqꝫ ei iusto
quod in distribuēdo cōsistit · neqꝫ ei quod ad corrigēdū perti
At qui volunt hec quidē dicē et rhadamātis iustū · Si pati
que fecit rectū ē iudiciū · Multifariā eni discordat · Ceu si
magistratu cōstitutꝰ pcusserit repcuti nō licet · At si magi
stratū quis pcusserit nō solū repcuciēdus ipe est · Verꝫ etiam
supplicio afficiēdus · Jnuolūtariū eciam et voluntariū mlt
differūt · sed in cōibus societatibꝫ cōmercioꝝ huiōi iustū con
tinet id quod repatit ꝯm pporcionē ꝛ non ꝯm eqlitatē · Nam
in repaciēdo ꝯm pporcionē cōsistit ciuitas · Aut eni quod ma
le ē querūt ꝛ seruitus videt esse nisi repēderit · aut quod b
et si nō retribucō tollit · At retribucōe cōsistunt · Jtaqꝫ gra
ciaꝝ sacꝝ in pmptu faciūt vt retribucō sit · hec eni gra
est ppria · Remunerādus ē eni qui munꝰ ꝯtulit · At rursu
ipe incipere debet qui suscepit · Facit autē retribucōnem ꝯm
pporcionē per dyametꝝ cōiunctio · Veluti faber in q̄ a · sutor
in quo · b · domꝰ in quo · c calceꝰ i quo · d · Oportet ergo reci
fabrū · a · sutore ex illius opere et ipsū sibi tradere de suo
ergo primū sit equū ꝯm pporcōnem · postea repassio fiat
quod dicit · alias vero nec equū ē neqꝫ cōsistit · Nichil eni
vetat melius ēē vnꝰ opus quā alterius · Oportet igit illa
equari · Est autem hoc et in alijs artibꝫ · Nam interiret vtiq

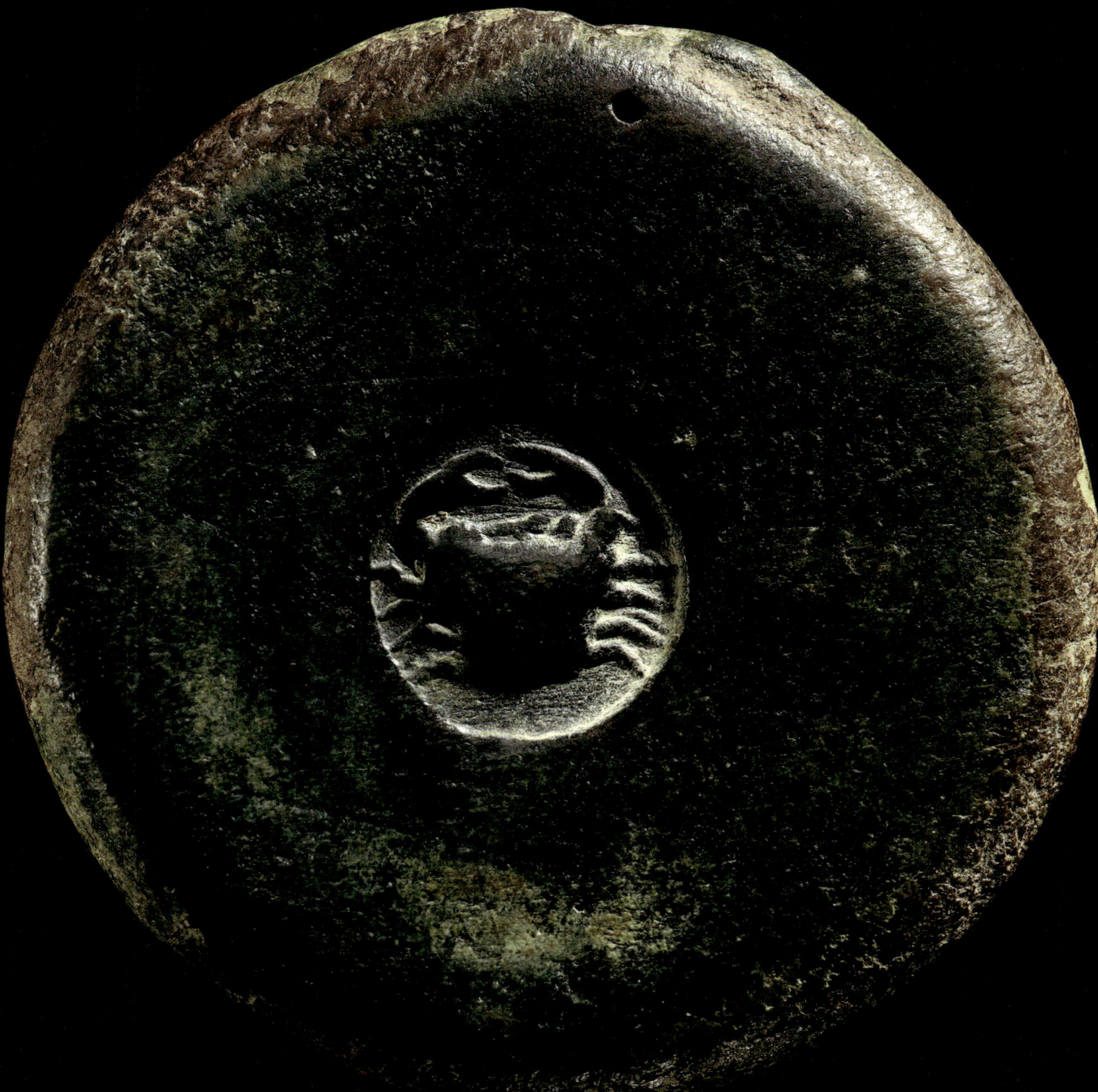

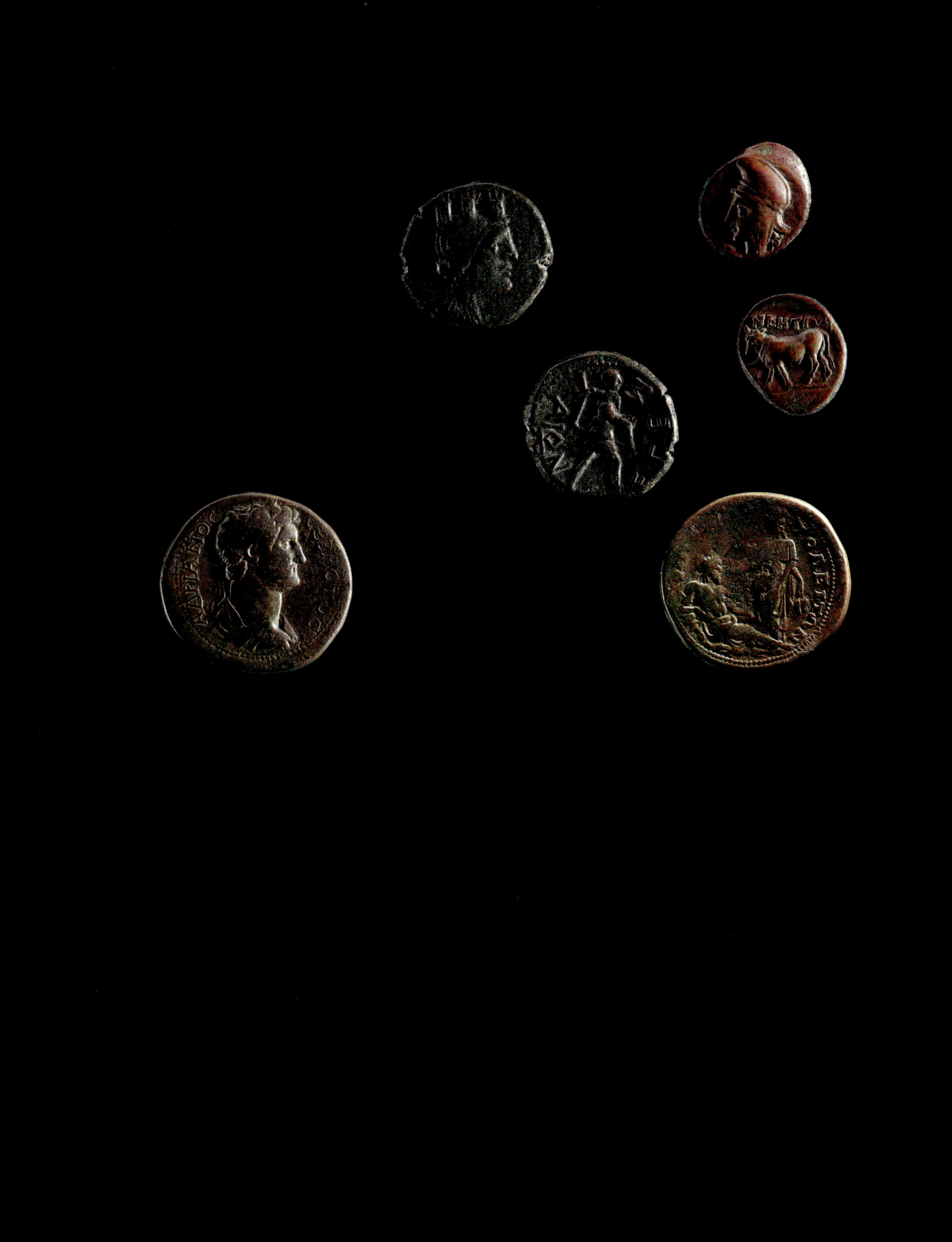

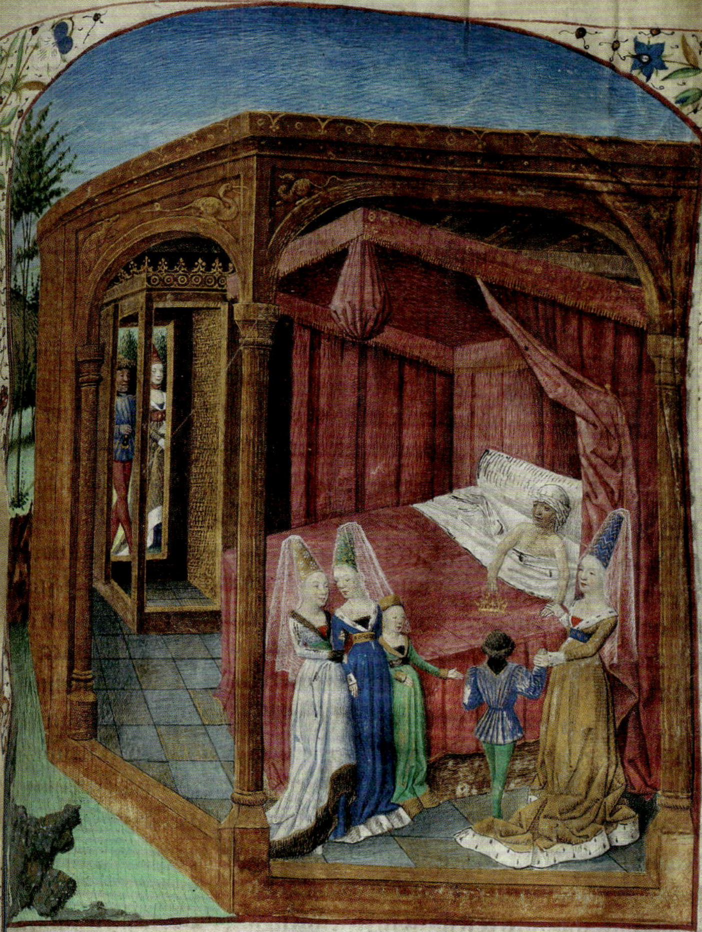

Drianus imperator sicut scribit Helius spartianus
narrat in libro quem de vita sua scripsit. maiores
fuisse de ytalia sub temporibus scipionum. Pat[er]
eius fuit helius adrianus consobrinus traiani
imperatoris. mater domitia paulina nata de g
dibus in hispania. Atavus eius nomine ma
rulinus primus in sua familia fuit senator populi romani. Adrianus
decimo anno etatis sue. orbatus patre. habuit tutorem traianum. qui
postea imperium tenuit. Adrianus autem ita dedit studiis grecis ani
mum: q[uod] a multis greculus diceretur. Adrianus anno quintodecimo
rediit in patriam. et continuo miliciam incepit. in venatione delectat[us]
usq[ue] ad reprehentionem. Quare traianus eum pro filio habuit. et sci

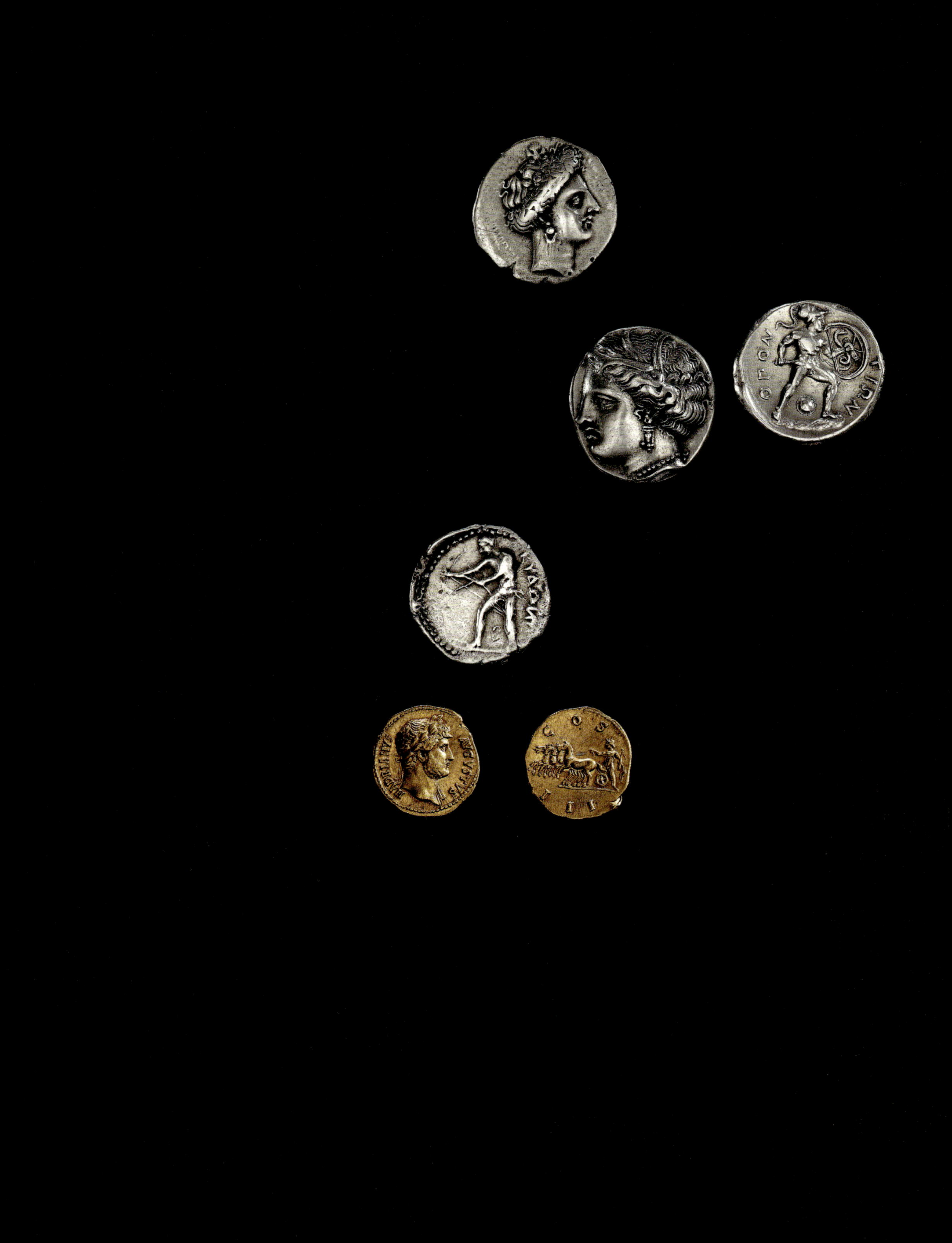

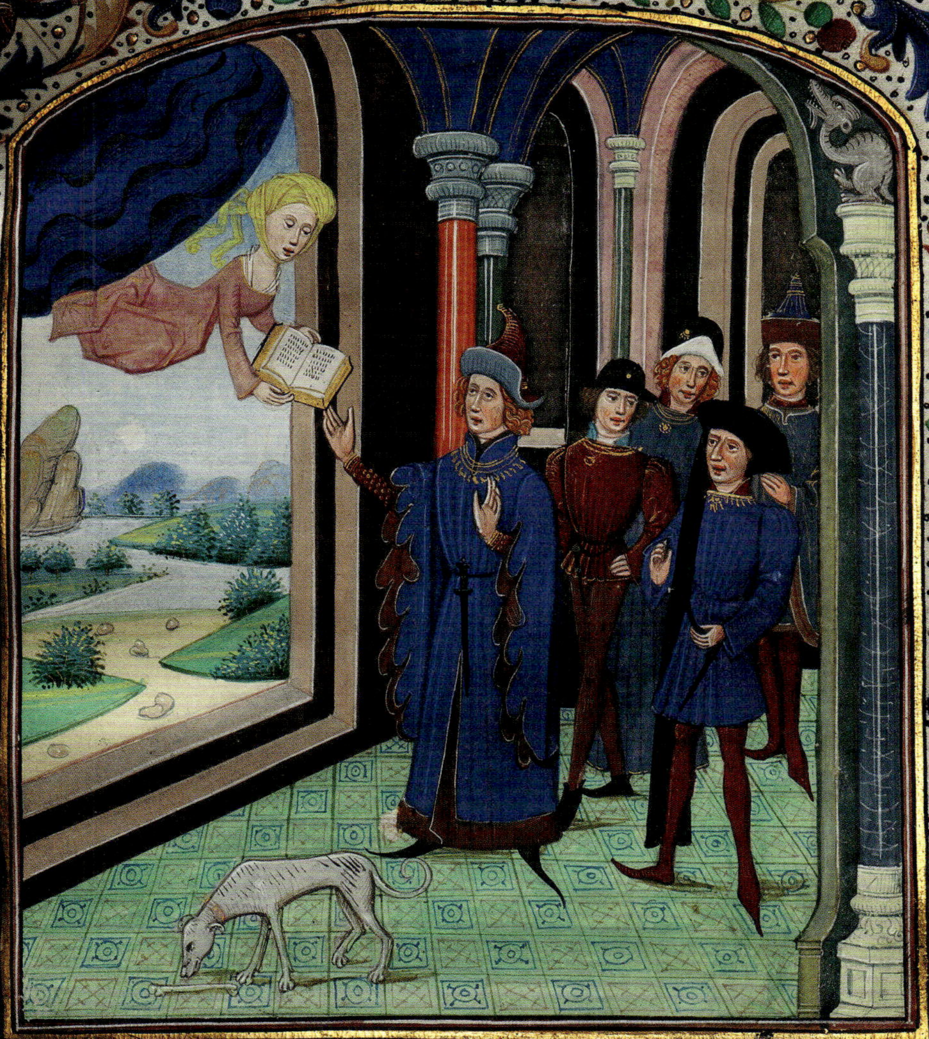

Othea deesse de prudence
Qui adresse les bons en vaillance
A toy hector noble prince puissant
Qui en armes es adez flourissant
Filz de mars le dieu de bataille
Qui les fais darmes livre et taille

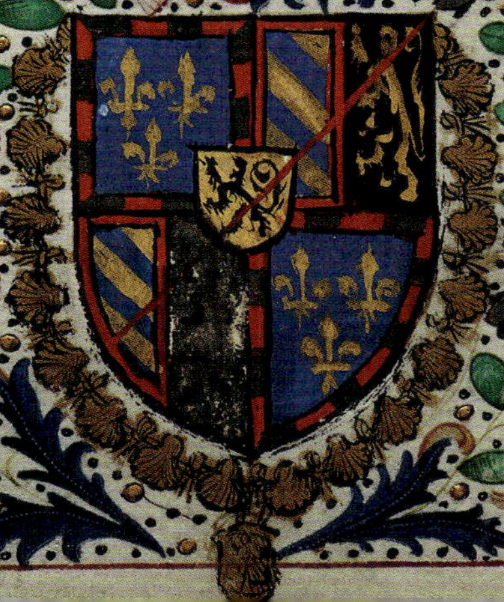

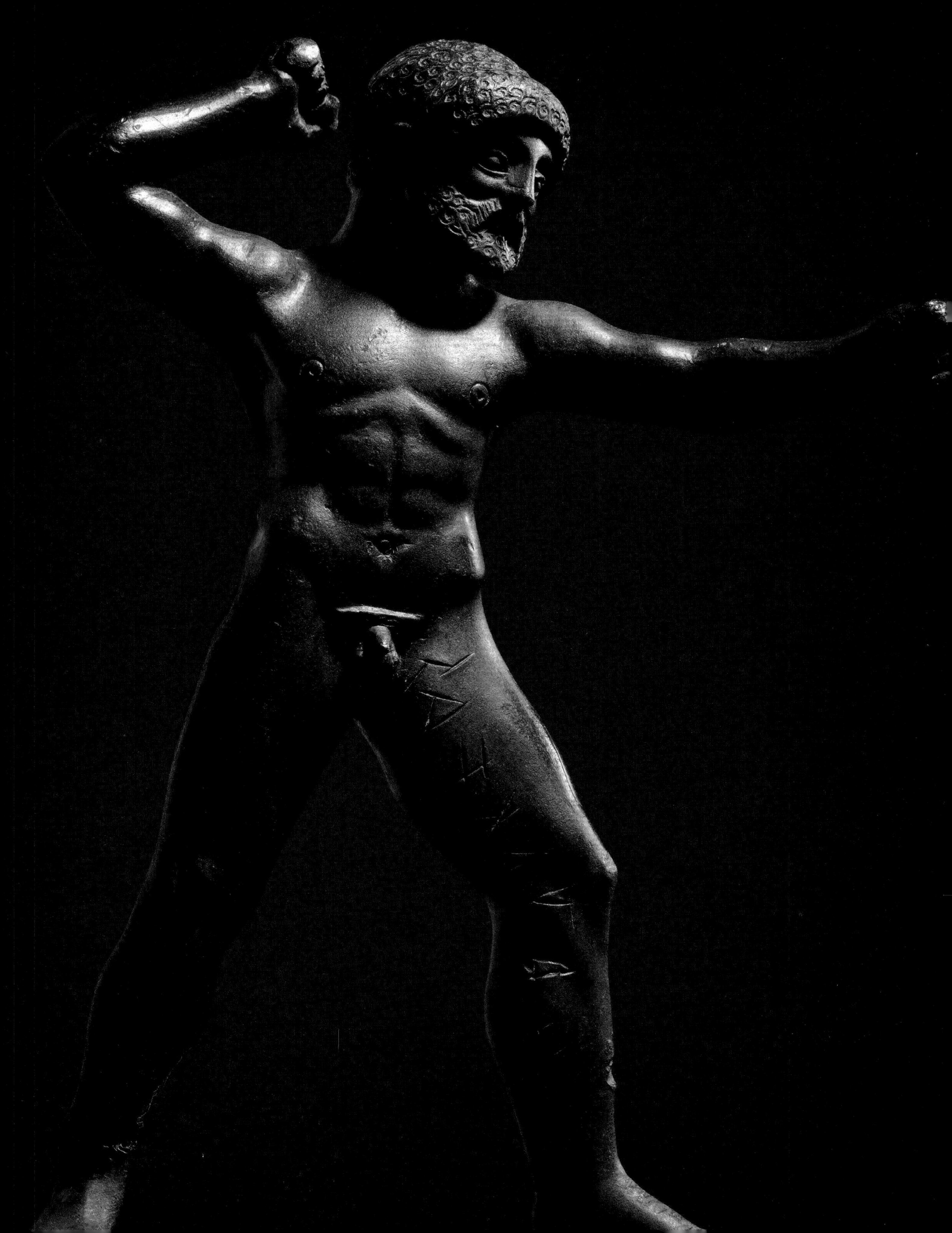

PVBLI VIRGILII MARONIS Æneidorum libri duodecim Feliciter incipiunt

PRimus hab& libycā ueniāt ut troes ī urbem.
Edoc& excidium troię cladēq; secundus.
Tertius a troia uectos canit ęquore teucros.
Quartus item miserę duo uulnera narrat elissę.
Manibus ad tumulum quīto celebrant̃ honores.
Aeneam memorat uisentem tartara sextus.
In phrygas italiam bello iam septimus armat.
Dat simul ęneę socios octauus: & arma.
Daunius expugnat nono noua moenia troię.
Exponit decimus tuscorum in littore pugnas.
Vndecimo rutuli superantur morte camillę.
Vltimus imponit bello turni nece finem.

Descriptio Primi libri.

AEneas primo libyę depellitur oris
Vir magnus bello nulli pietate secundus.
Aeneas odiis iunonis pressus iniquę
Italiam quęrens siculis errauit in undis:
Iactatus tandem libyę peruenit ad oras:
Ignarusq; loci fido comitatus achate
Indicio matris regnum cognouit elissę.
Quin etiam nebula septus peruenit ad urbem.
Ereptosq; undis socios cum classe recepit.
Hospitioq; usus didonis per cuncta benigne
Excidium troię iussus narrare parabat.

ILle qui quondam gracili modulatus auena
Carmen: & egressus siluis uicina coegi
Vt quanuis auido parerent arua colono
Gratum opus agricolis. at nunc horrētia martis

En. liber Primus Incipit.

ARMA: VIRVMQVE CANO:
troię qui primus ab oris
Italiam fato profugus:
lauinaq; uenit
Littora: multum ille & terris iactatus: & alto
Vi superum: sęuę memorem iunonis ob iram.

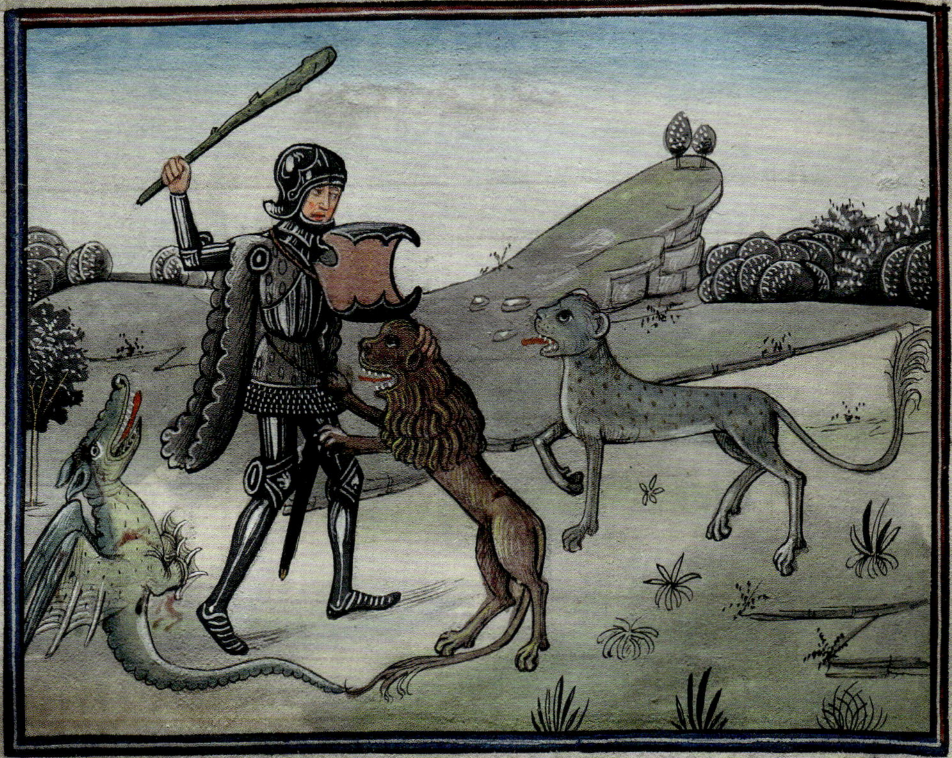

Et avec nous te couvient force
Se tu de grant vertu fais force
Deux hercules te fault suiver
Et ses vaillances ensuiver
En qui si eut trop de bernage
Et pour tant se a ton lignage
Fut contraire et eut attaine
N'aies mie pour tant hayne
A ses vertus nobles et fortes
Qui de prouesse euvrent les portes

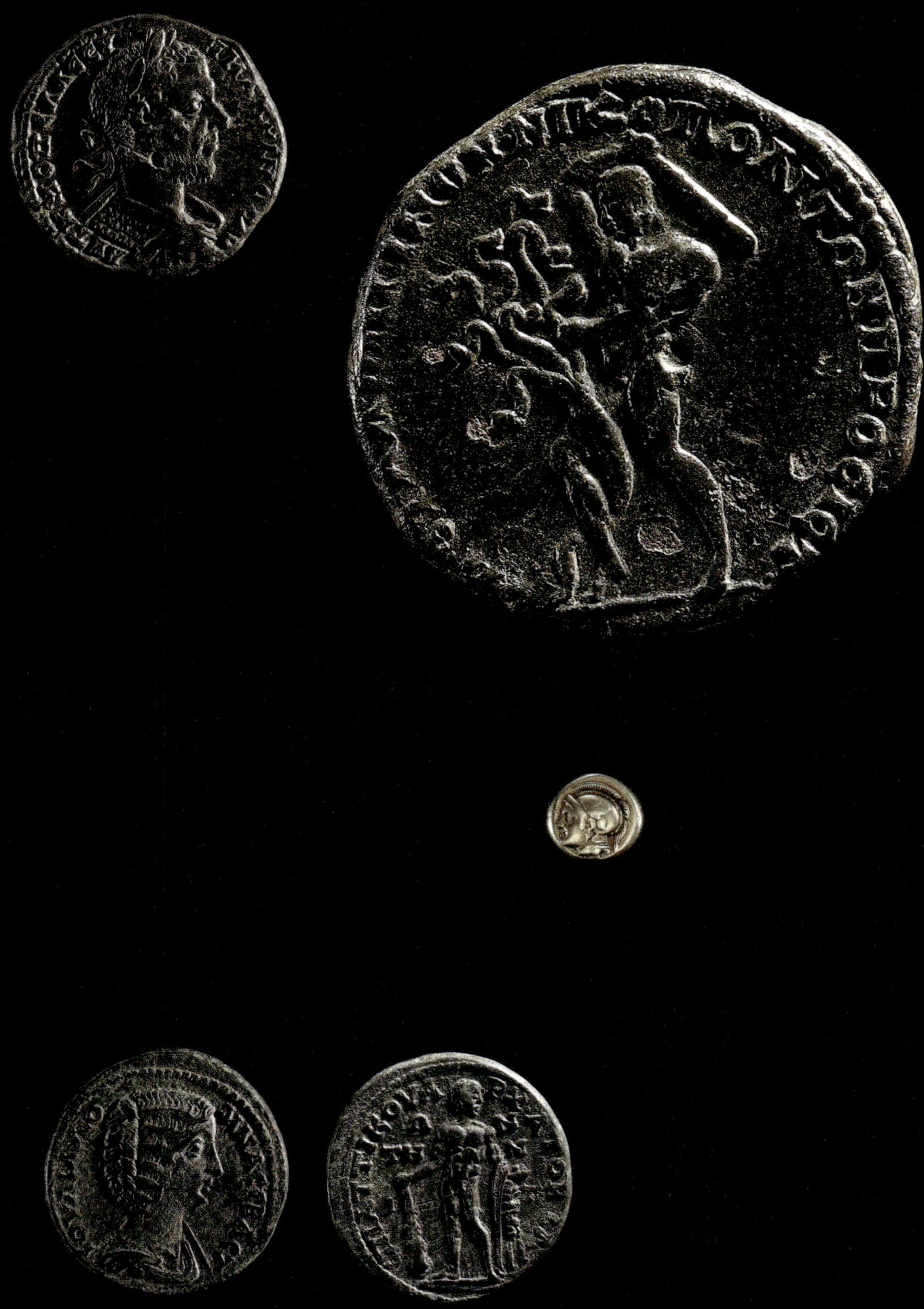

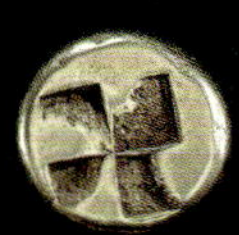

JORGE LUIS BORGES

EL ALEPH

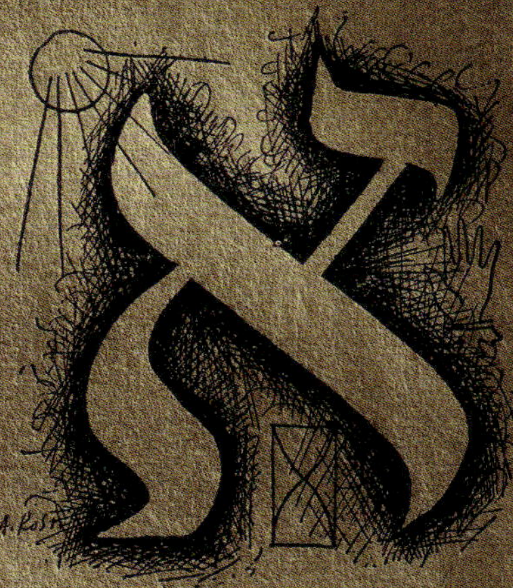

EDITORIAL LOSADA, S. A.

BUENOS AIRES

INTER hęc Alexander ad cōducēdū
ex peloponeſo militem Cleādro cum pe
cunia miſſo: lytie pamphilięq; rebus cō/
poſitis: ad urbē celenas exercitū admo/
uit. Media illa tempeſtate moenia inter
fluebat Marſus amnis fabuloſis gręco/
rum carminibus inclytus fons eius ex ſū
mo montis cacumine excurrens: in ſub/
iectam petram magno ſtrepitu aquarum cadit In
de diffuſus circumiectos rigat campos: liquidus et
ſuas duntaxat undas trahens. Itaq; color eius placi/
do mari ſimilis: locum poetarum mendacio fecit.
Quippe traditum eſt: nymphas amore amnis retē/
tas in illa rupe conſidere. Cęterum q̄diu ītra muros
fluit nomen ſuum retinet. At cum extra munimen
ta ſe euoluit: maiore ui ac molle agentem undas: ly
cum appellant. Alexander quidem urbem deſtitutā
a ſuis intrat. Arcem uero in quam confugerāt oppu
gnare adorſus Caduceatorē pręmiſit: qui denuntia
ret ni dederent: ipſos ultima eſſe paſſuros. Illi cadu
ceatorem ī turrim et ſitu et ope multum editā pdu
ctum: quanta eſſet altitudo intueri iubent: ac nunti/
are alexandro non eadem ipſum et incolas extimati
one munimenta metiri: ſe ſcire inexpugnabiles eē:
ad ultimum pro fide morituros. Cęterum ut circū/
ſideri arcem et omnia ſibi indies arctiora uiderunt
eſſe: ſexaginta dierum indutias pacti: ut niſi ītra eos
auxilium Darius ipſe miſiſſet: dederent urbē. Poſtq̄
nihil inde pręſidii mittebatur ad pręſtitutam diem

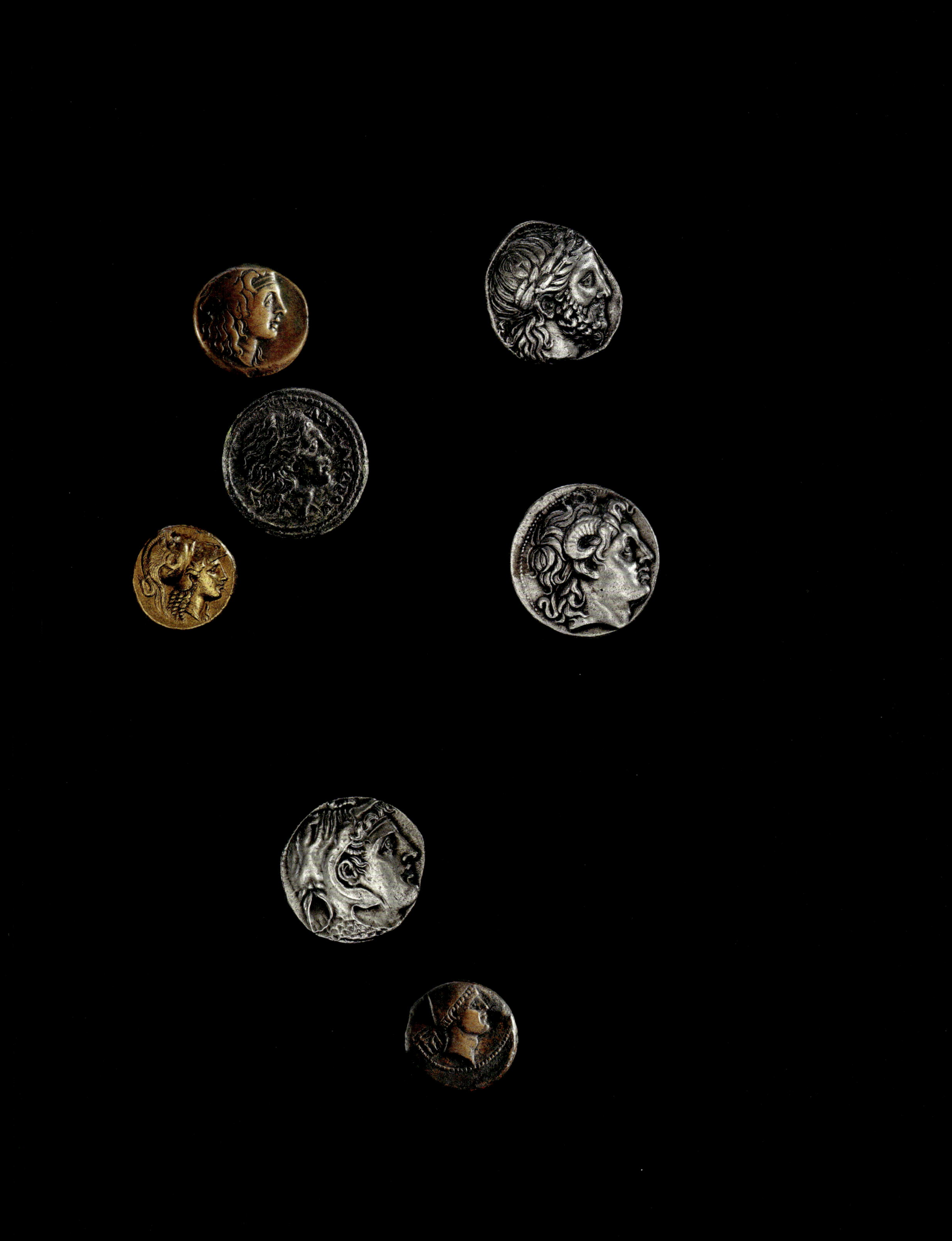

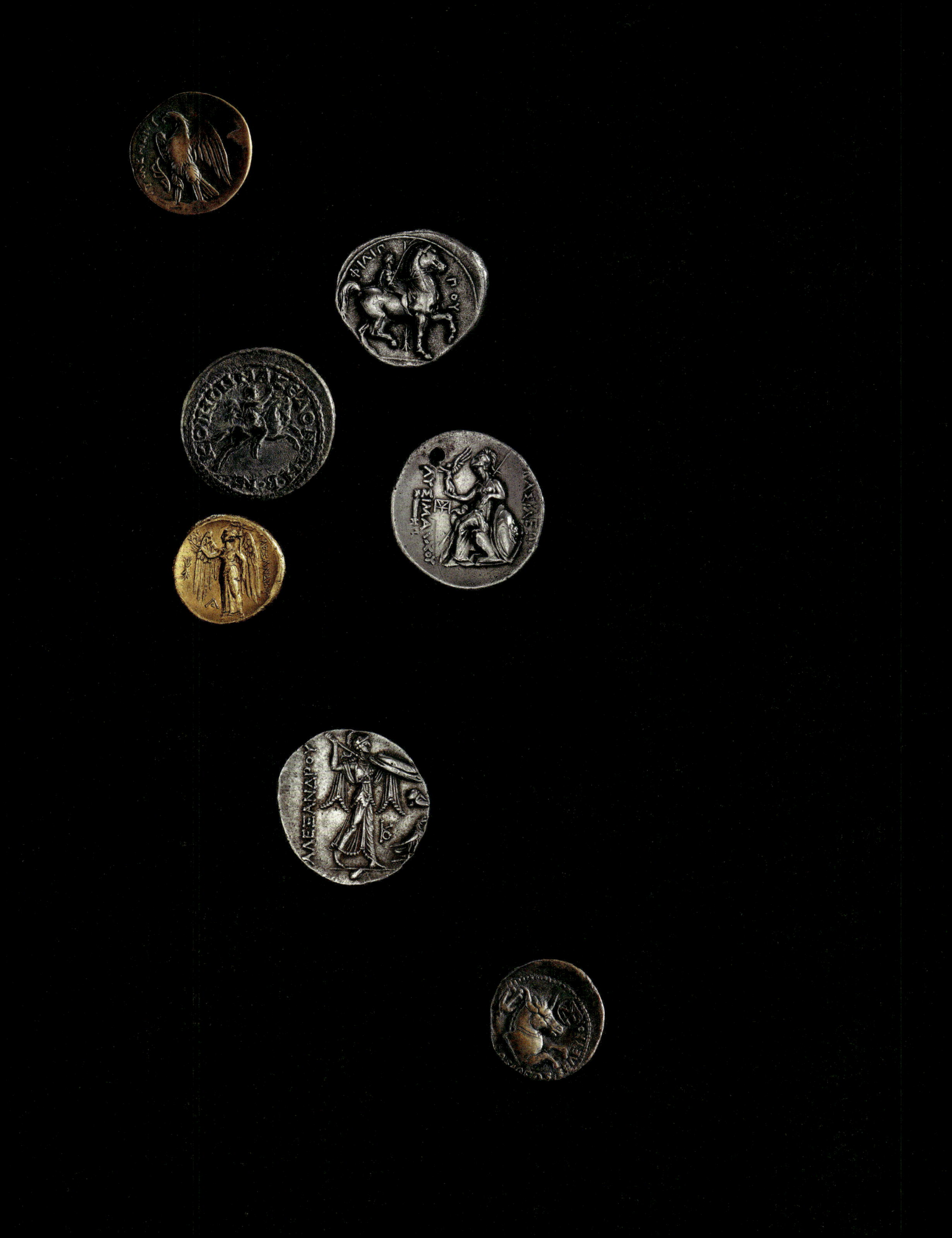

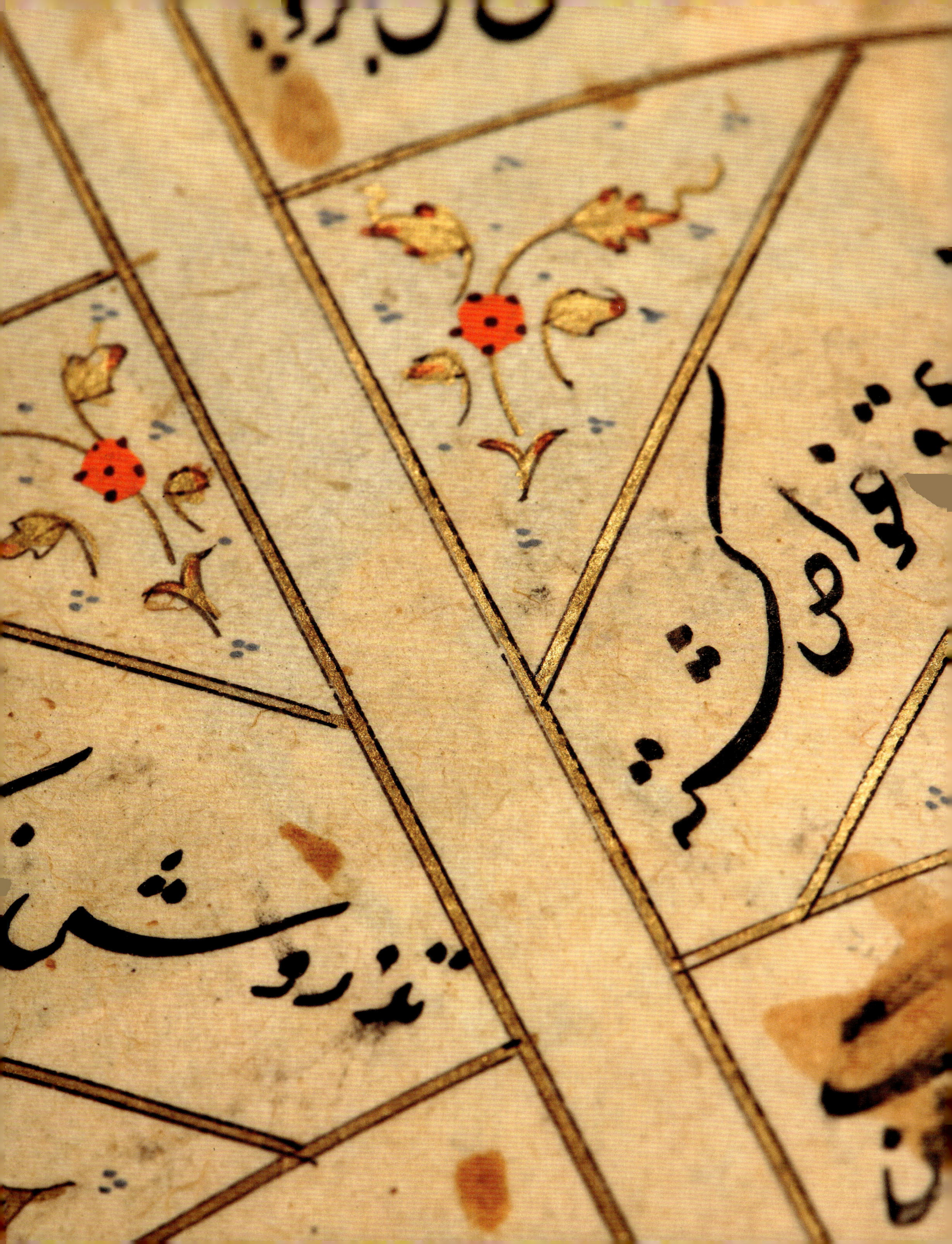

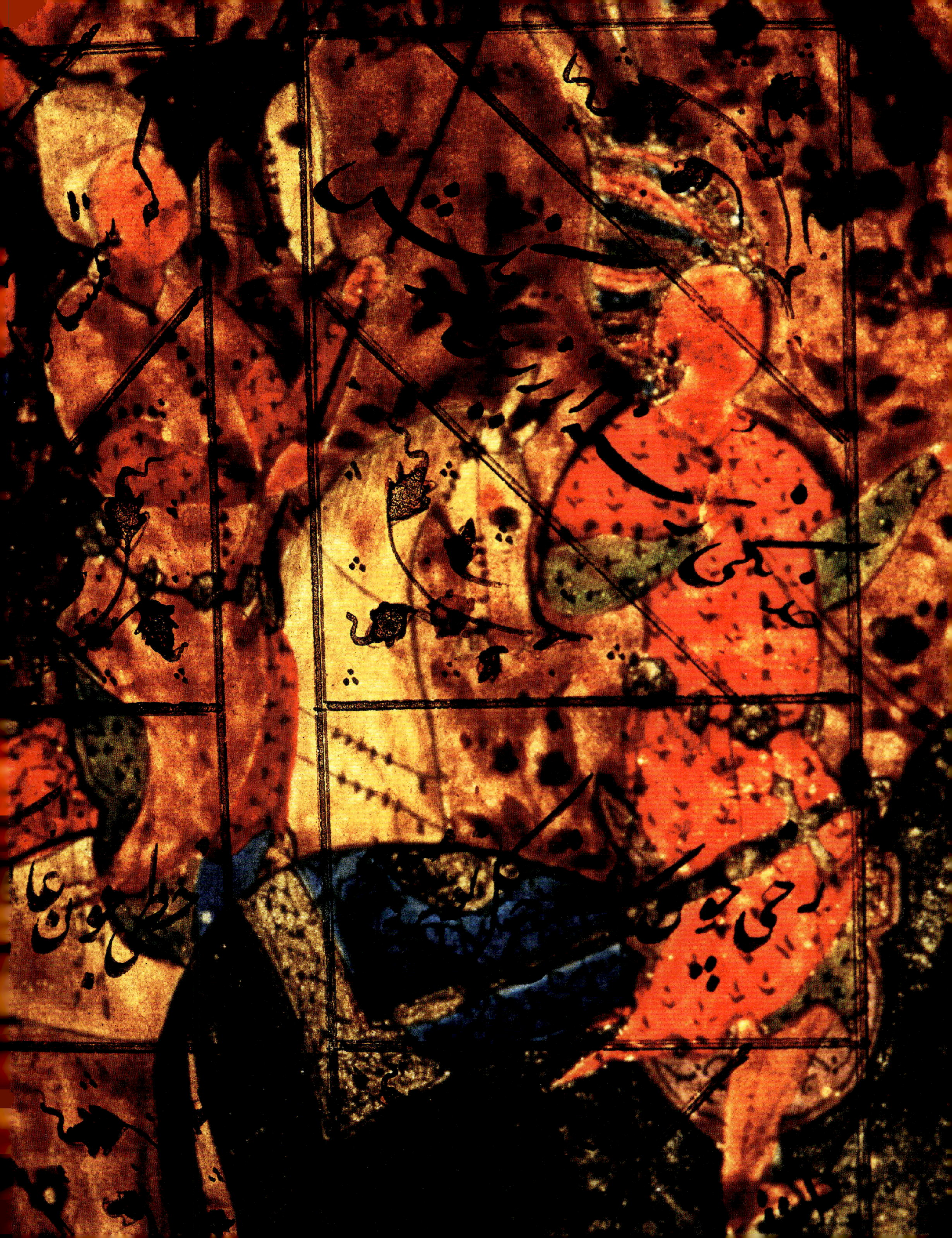

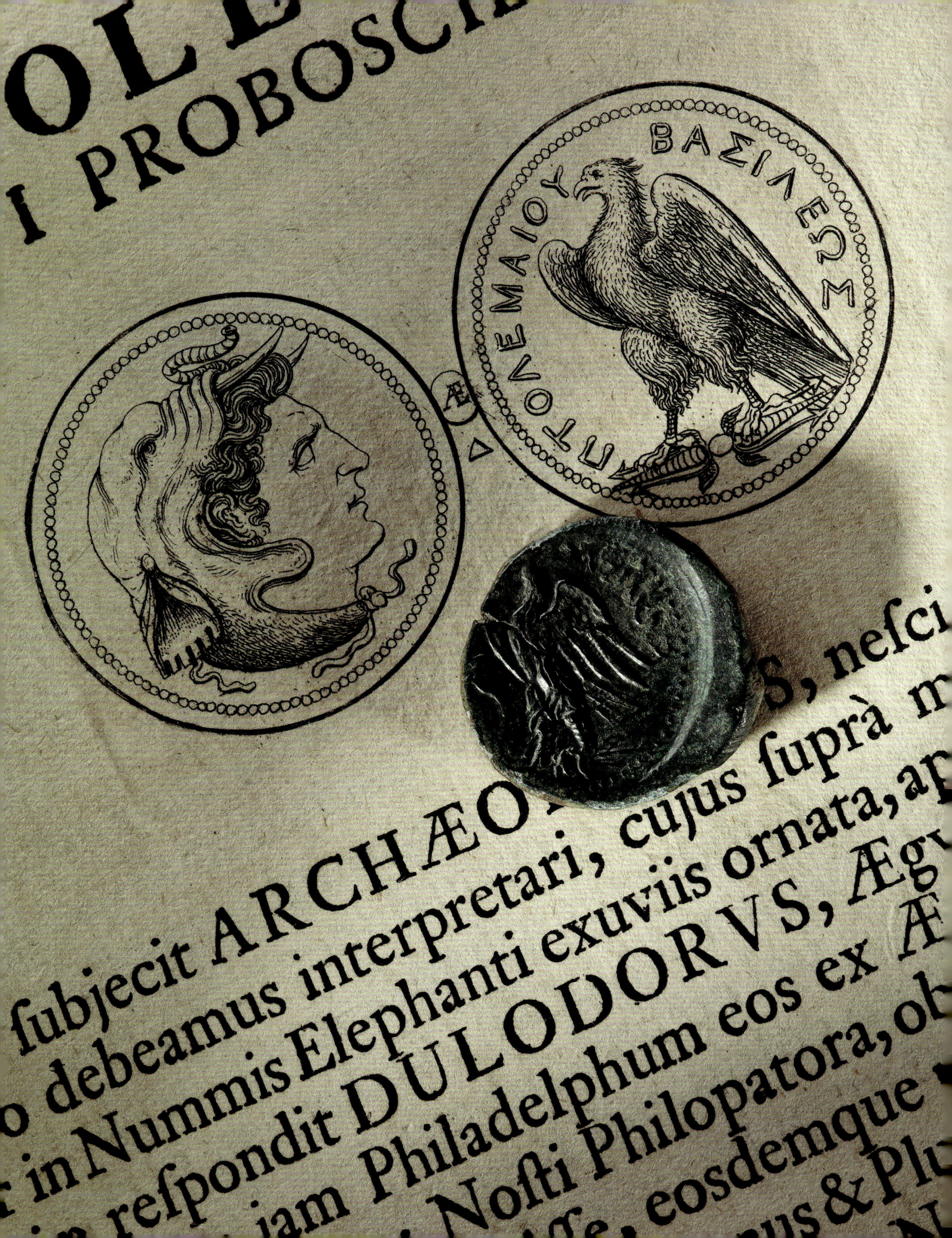
OLE
I PROBOSCI
ΒΑΣΙΛΕΩΣ
ΠΤΟΛΕΜΑΙΟΥ
Æ
ſubjecit ARCHÆO
S, neſci
o debeamus interpretari, cujus ſuprà
in Nummis Elephanti exuviis ornata, ap
in reſpondit DULODORVS, Æg
jam Philadelphum eos ex Æ
Noſti Philopatora, ob
eoſdemque
& Plu

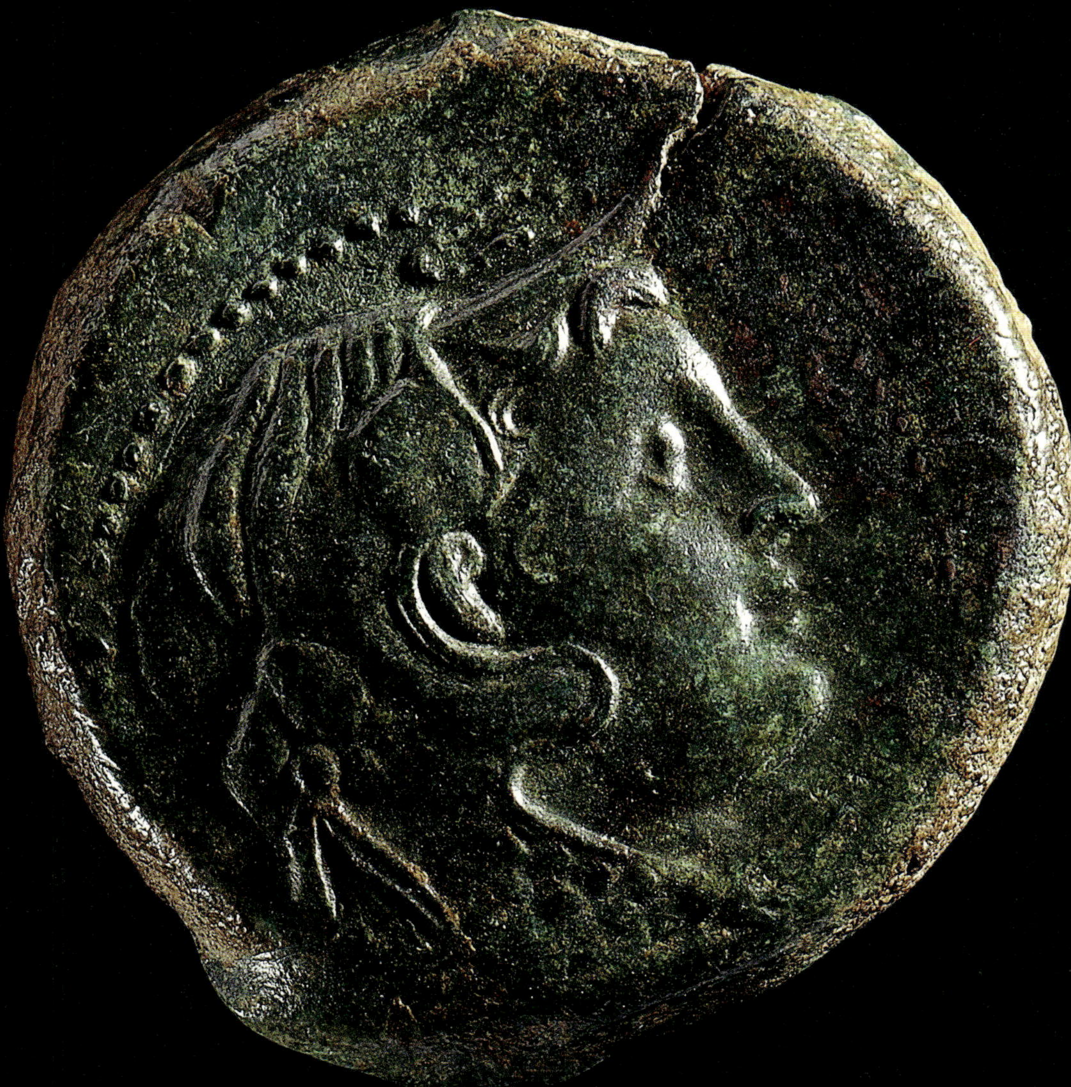

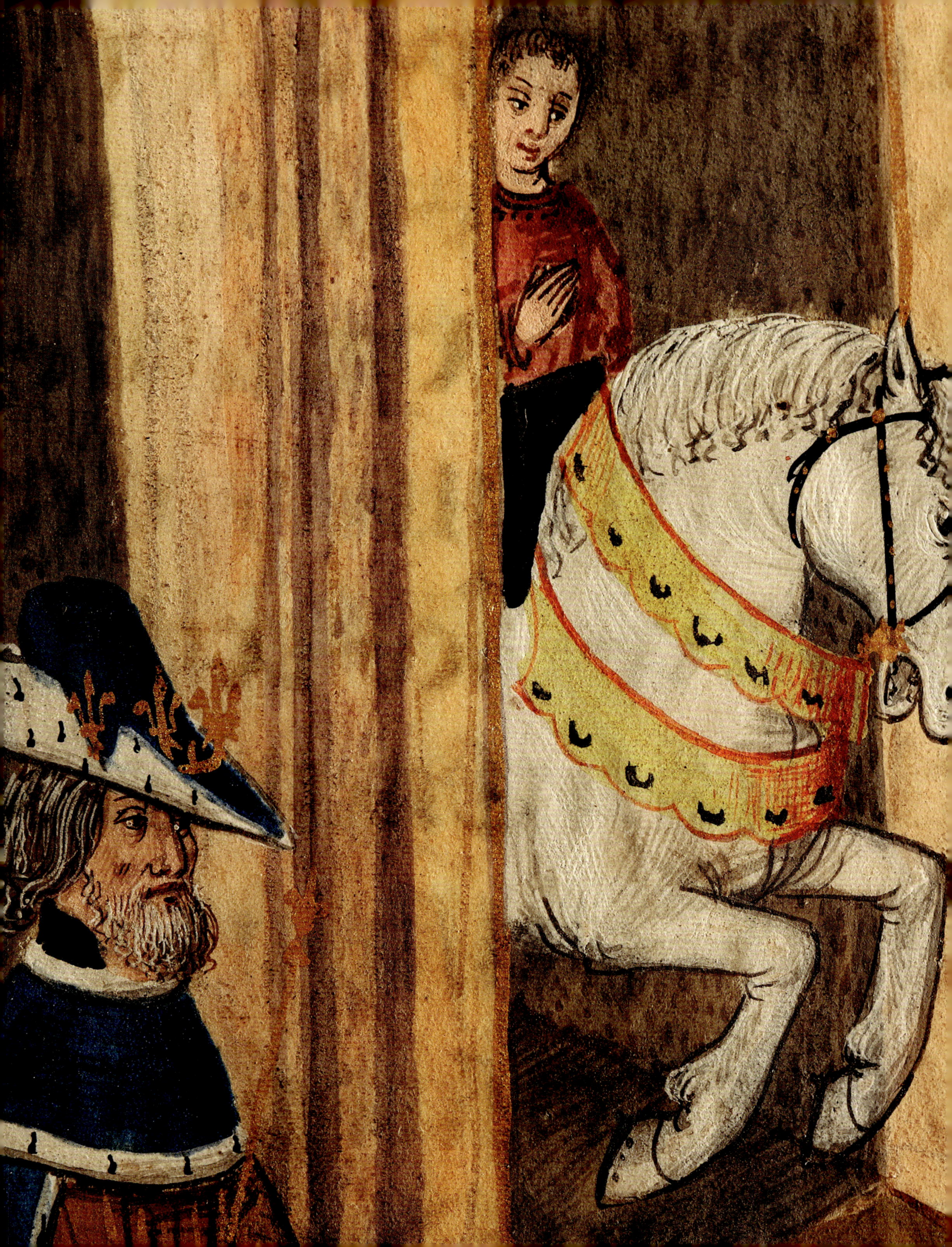

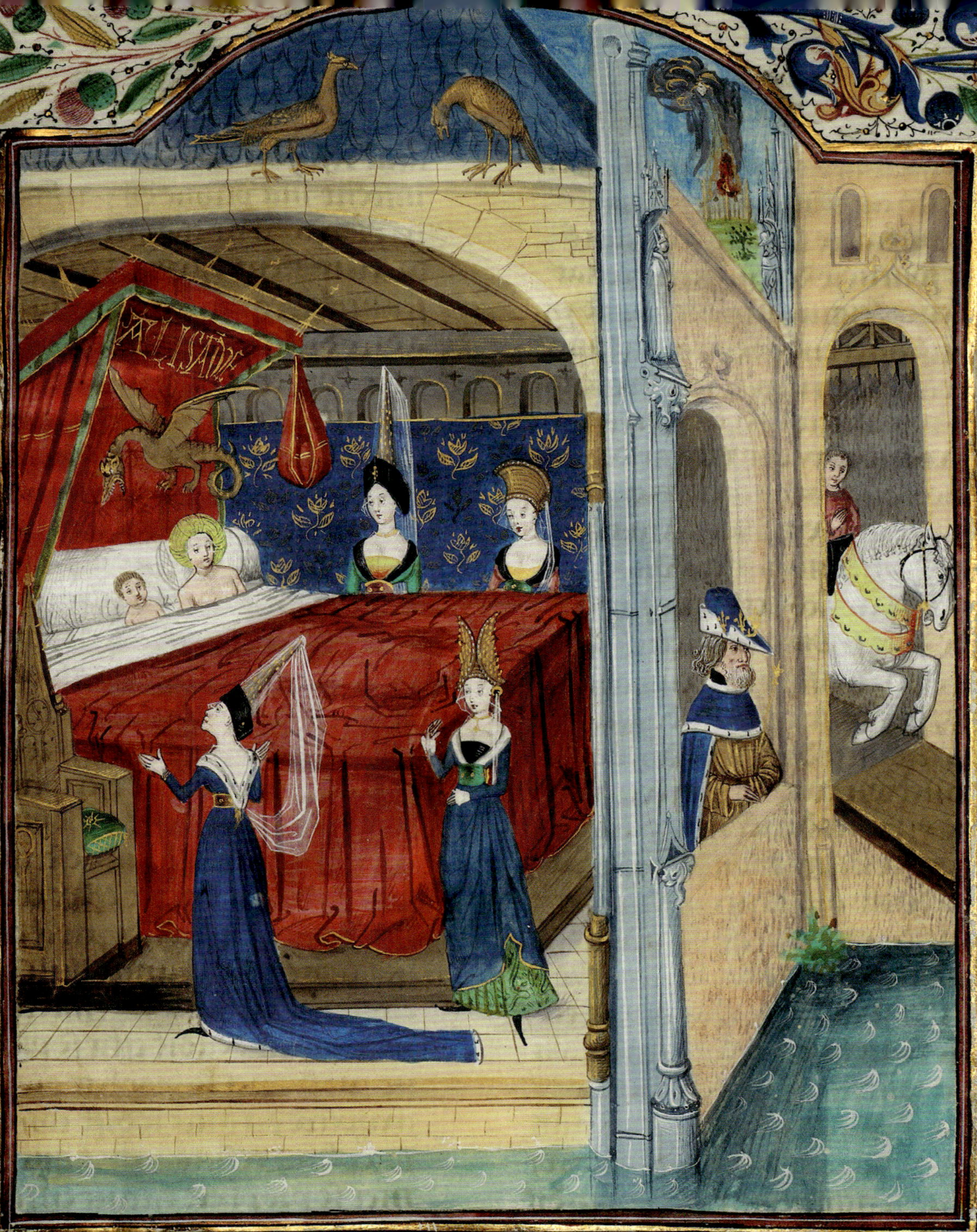

Regardant les discors
et infelicitez des sei
gnouries et royau
mes. et veullant mo
strer que en leurs maleurtez a tort
servissent les roys sur faulte de
bon peuple / le peuple sur faulte de
bons roys / et tous deux sur la vo
lenté de dieu et de fortune. Je treu
ve que la divine providence pour
voit tousiours et assortist telz
roys de telz peuples / telz peuples de
telz roys et que fortune ny fait rien.
Car en regardant les croissances
et les cheutes des choses publicque
principautez royaumes. ou empi
res. qui ont esté depuis Ninus roy
des assiriens iusques a ores. Il
est tout notoire que en tous temps
et en tous lieux ou les regnans
ont esté bons. vaillans. et vertu
eux. illec lestat de leurs seignouri

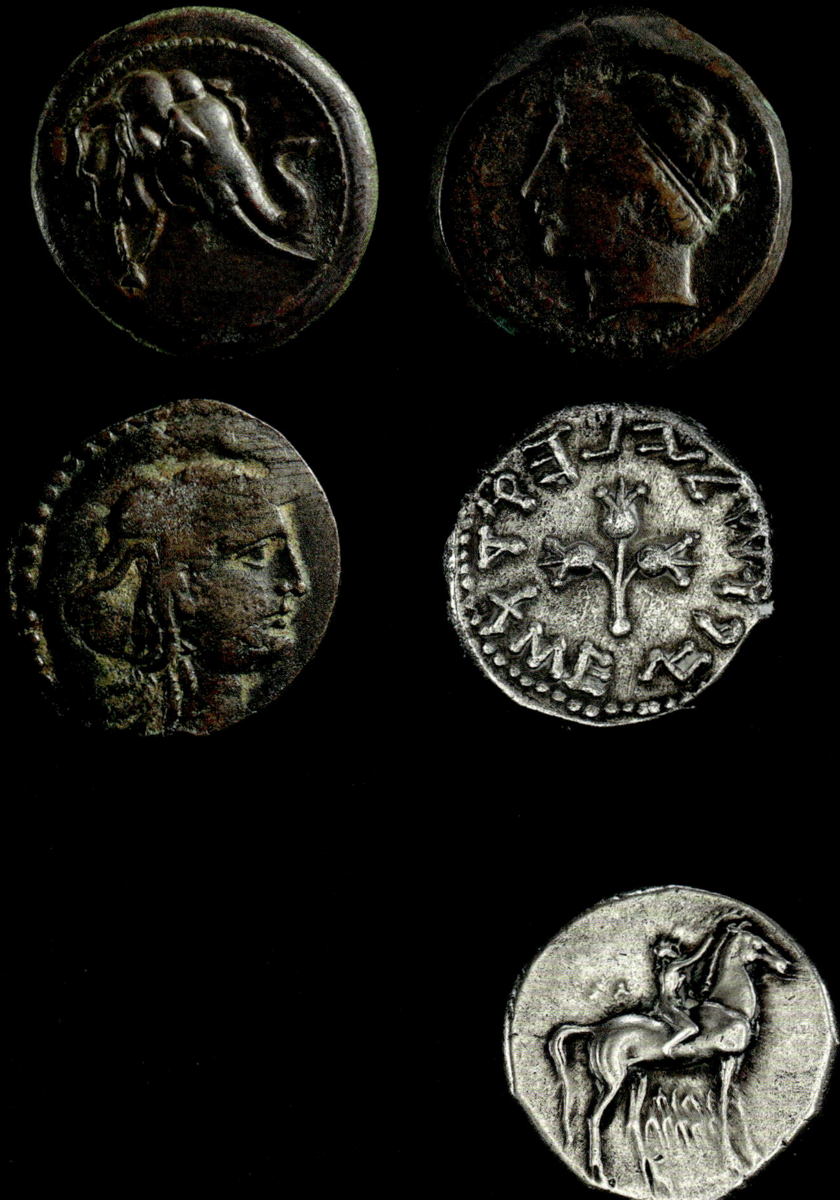

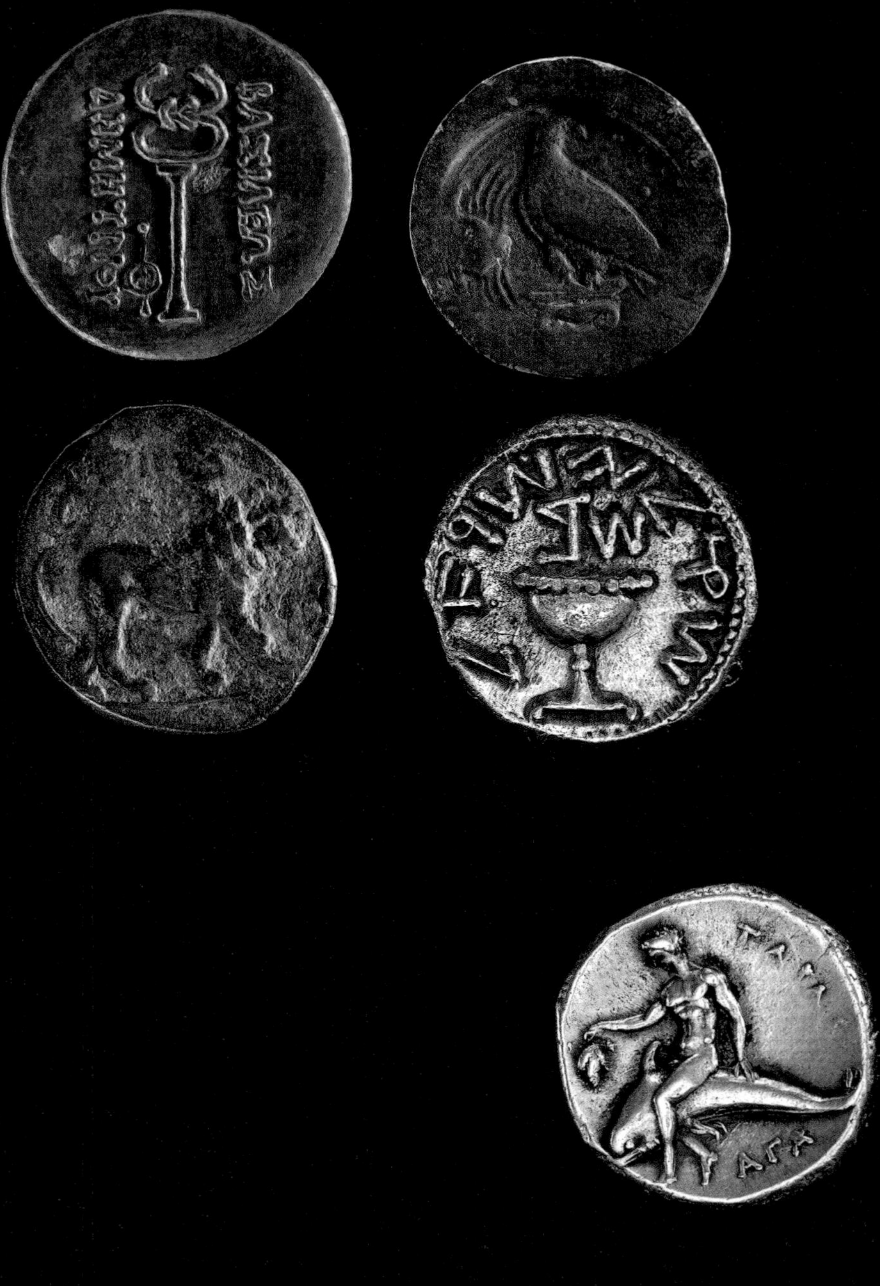

Eratosthenes

οἱ δὲ τοῖς ἰσθμοῖς· τῷ τε μεταξὺ τῆς κασπίας, καὶ τῆς ποντικῆς θαλάσσης, καὶ τῷ μεταξὺ τῆς ἐρυθρᾶς, καὶ τοῦ ἐκρήγματος· τοὺς δὲ χερρονήσους αὐτὰς λέγειν, εἶτ' οὐχ ὁρᾶν φησι πῶς ἂν εἰς πράγματα καταστρέφοι ἡ ζήτησις αὕτη. ἀλλὰ μόνον ἐρίζειν διαιτώντων μᾶλλον κατὰ δημόκριτον εἶναι. μὴ ὄντων γὰρ ἀκριβῶν ὅρων καθάπερ κολυττοῦ, καὶ μελίτης οἷον στηλῶν ἢ περιβόλων, τοῦτο μὲν ἔχειν φάναι ἡμᾶς· ὅτι τουτὶ μέν ἐστι κολυττός· τουτὶ δὲ μελίτη. τοὺς ὅρους δὲ μὴ ἔχειν εἰπεῖν· διὸ καὶ συμβαίνειν κρίσεις πολλάκις περὶ χωρίων τινῶν· καθάπερ ἀργείοις μὲν, καὶ λακεδαιμονίοις περὶ θυρέας· ἀθηναίοις δὲ, καὶ βοιωτοῖς, περὶ ὠρωποῦ. ἄλλως τε τοὺς ἕλληνας τὰς τρεῖς ἠπείρους ὀνομάσαι, οὐκ εἰς τὴν οἰκουμένην ἀποβλέψαντας· ἀλλ' εἰς τὴν σφετέραν, καὶ τὴν ἀπαντικρὺ τὴν καρικήν, ἐφ' ἣ νῦν ἴωνες, καὶ οἱ ἑξῆς· χρόνῳ δ' ἐπὶ πλέον προϊόντας ἀεὶ καὶ πλειόνων γνωριζομένων χωρῶν, εἰς τοῦτο καταστρέψαι τὴν διαίρεσιν. πότερον οὖν οἱ πρῶτοι διορίσαντες τὰς τρεῖς ἵνα ἀπὸ τῶν ἐσχάτων ἄρξωμαι διαιτῶντες τὴν ἔριν μὴ κατὰ δημόκριτον ἀλλὰ κατ' αὐτόν, οὗτοι ἦσαν οἱ πρῶτοι τὴν σφετέραν ἀπὸ τῆς ἀντικειμένης τῆς τῶν καρῶν διορίσαι ζητοῦντες, ἢ οὗτοι μὲν τὴν ἑλλάδα ἐπενόουν μόνην, καὶ τὴν καρίαν καὶ τὴν ὀλίγην τὴν συνεχῆ· οὔτε δ' εὐρώπην οὔτε ἀσίαν οὔτε λιβύην ὡσαύτως· οἱ δὲ λοιποὶ ἐπιόντες ὅσοι ἱκανοὶ ἐπιγράψαι τὴν τῆς οἰκουμένης ἐπίνοιαν, οὗτοι εἰσὶν οἱ εἰς τρία μέρη διαιροῦντες· πῶς οὖν οὐ τῆς οἰκουμένης ἐποιοῦντο διαίρεσιν· τίς δὲ τρία μέρη λέγων· καὶ καλῶν ἤπειρον ἕκαστον τῶν μερῶν οὐ προσεπινοεῖ τὸ ὅλον οὗ τὸν μερισμὸν ποιεῖται· εἰ δὲ μὴ ἐπινοεῖ μὲν τὴν οἰκουμένην, μέρους δέ τινος τὸν μερισμὸν αὐτῆς ποιεῖτο· τίνος ἄν τις μέρους εἶπε τὴν ἀσίαν ἢ τὴν εὐρώπην ἢ ὅλως ἤπειρον. ταῦτα γὰρ εἴρηται παχυμερῶς· ἔτι δὲ παχυμερέστερον τὸ φήσαντα μὴ ὁρᾶν εἰς τί πραγματικὸν καταστρέφει τὸ τοὺς ὅρους ζητεῖν, παραθεῖναι τὸ κολυττὸν καὶ τὴν μελίτην, εἶτ' εἰς τἀναντία περιτρέπεσθαι. εἰ γὰρ οἱ περὶ θυρέας καὶ ὠρωποῦ πόλεμοι διὰ τὰς τῶν ὅρων ἀγνοίας ἀπέβησαν, εἰς πραγματικόν τι καταστρέφον τὸ διακρίνειν τὰς χώρας, ἢ τοῦτο λέγει, ὡς ἐπὶ μὲν τῶν χωρίων καὶ νὴ δία τῶν καθ' ἕκαστα ἐθνῶν πραγματικὸν τὸ διορίζειν ἀκριβῶς, ἐπὶ δὲ τῶν ἠπείρων περιττόν· καίτοι οὐδὲ ἐνταῦθα ἧττον. γένοιτο γὰρ ἂν καὶ ἐπὶ τούτων, ἡγεμόσι μεγάλοις ἀμφισβήτησις, τῷ μὲν ἔχοντι τὴν ἀσίαν, τῷ δὲ τὴν λιβύην· ὁποτέρου δή ἐστιν ἡ αἴγυπτος, δηλονότι ἡ κάτω λεγομένη τῆς αἰγύπτου χώρα. Catanas κἂν ἐάσῃ δέ τις τοῦτο διὰ τὸ σπάνιον ἄλλως φατέον διαιρεῖσθαι τὰς ἠπείρους κατὰ μέγαν διορισμόν· καὶ πρὸς τὴν οἰκουμένην ὅλην ἀναφερόμενον· καθ' ὃν οὐδὲ τούτου φροντιστέον εἰ οἱ τοῖς ποταμοῖς διορίσαντες ἀπολείπουσί τινα χωρία ἀδιόριστα, cor. τῶν ποταμῶν μὴ μέχρι τοῦ ὠκεανοῦ διηκόντων· μηδὲ νήσους ὡς ἀληθῶς ἀπολιπόντων τὰς ἠπείρους.

Barbari Graeci Alexander

Ἐπὶ τέλει δέ φησι τοῦ ὑπομνήματος οὐκ ἐπαινέσας τοὺς δίχα διαιροῦντας ἅπαν τὸ τῶν ἀνθρώπων πλῆθος· εἴς τε ἕλληνας καὶ βαρβάρους καὶ τοὺς ἀλεξάνδρῳ παραινοῦντας τοῖς μὲν ἕλλησιν ὡς φίλοις χρῆσθαι, τοῖς δὲ βαρβάροις ὡς πολεμίοις, βέλτιον εἶναί φησιν ἀρετῇ καὶ κακίᾳ διαιρεῖν ταῦτα, πολλοὺς γὰρ καὶ τῶν ἑλλήνων εἶναι κακούς, καὶ τῶν βαρβάρων ἀστείους καθάπερ ἰνδοὺς καὶ ἀριανούς· ἔτι δὲ ῥωμαίους καὶ καρχηδονίους οὕτω θαυμαστῶς πολιτευομένους. διόπερ τὸν ἀλέξανδρον ἀμελήσαντα τῶν παραινούντων, ὅσους οἷόν τ' ἦν ἀποδέχεσθαι τῶν εὐδοκίμων ἀνδρῶν, καὶ εὐεργετεῖν. ὥσπερ δὲ δι' ἄλλο τι τοὺς μὲν οὕτω διελόντων τοὺς μὲν ἐν ψόγῳ τοὺς δ' ἐν ἐπαίνῳ τιθεμένων, ἢ διότι τοῖς μὲν ἐπικρατεῖ τὸ νόμιμον καὶ τὸ πολιτικὸν καὶ τὸ παιδείας καὶ λόγων οἰκεῖον· τοῖς δὲ τἀναντία. καὶ ὁ ἀλέξανδρος οὖν οὐκ ἀμελήσας τῶν παραινούντων ἀλλ' ἀποδεξάμενος τὴν γνώμην, τὰ ἀκόλουθα οὐ τὰ ἐναντία ἐποίει. πρὸς τὴν διάνοιαν σκοπῶν τὴν τῶν ἐπεσταλκότων.

ὙΠΟΘΕΣΙΣ ΤΟΥ ΔΕΥΤΕΡΟΥ ΒΙΒΛΙΟΥ

Ἐν τῷ δευτέρῳ κατὰ λέξιν προσβαλλόμενος τὰ ἐρατοσθένους, αἰτιᾶται καὶ διελέγχει ὅσα μὴ ὀρθῶς εἴρηται. ἢ διαγέγραπται. καὶ ἱππάρχου δὲ τῶν πολλῶν μιμνήσκεται ἐπιλαμβανόμενος. καὶ ἐπὶ τέλει ἔκθεσις σύντομος. καὶ τρόπον τινὰ σύνοψις τῆς ὅλης πραγματείας, τουτέστι τῆς γεωγραφικῆς ἱστορίας.

ΣΤΡΑΒΩΝΟΣ ΓΕΩΓΡΑΦΙΚΩΝ ΒΙΒΛΙΟΝ ΔΕΥΤΕΡΟΝ.

Ἐν δὲ τῷ τρίτῳ τῶν γεωγραφικῶν καθιστάμενος, τὸν τῆς οἰκουμένης πίνακα, γραμμῇ τινι διαιρεῖ. δίχα ἀπὸ δύσεως ἐπ᾽ ἀνατολὴν παραλλήλῳ τῇ ἰσημερινῇ γραμμῇ. πέρατα δ᾽ αὐτῆς τίθησι πρὸς δύσει μὲν τὰς ἡρακλείους στήλας. ἐπ᾽ ἀνατολῇ δὲ τὰ ἄκρα καὶ ἔσχατα ὄρη τῶν ἀφοριζόντων ὀρῶν, τὴν πρὸς ἄρκτον τῆς ἰνδικῆς πλευράν. γράφει δὲ τὴν γραμμὴν ἀπὸ στηλῶν διά τε τοῦ σικελικοῦ πορθμοῦ, καὶ τῶν μεσημβρινῶν ἄκρων τῆς τε πελοποννήσου καὶ τῆς ἀττικῆς. καὶ μέχρι τῆς ῥοδίας καὶ τοῦ ἰσσικοῦ κόλπου. μέχρι μὲν δὴ δεῦρο διὰ τῆς θαλάττης φησὶν εἶναι τὴν λεχθεῖσαν γραμμὴν καὶ τῶν παρακειμένων ἠπείρων. καὶ γὰρ αὐτὴν ὅλην τὴν καθ᾽ ἡμᾶς θάλατταν οὕτως ἐπὶ μῆκός τε τετάσθαι μέχρι τῆς κιλικίας. εἶτα ἐπ᾽ εὐθείας πως ἐκβάλλεσθαι παρ᾽ ὅλην τὴν ὀρεινὴν τοῦ ταύρου μέχρι τῆς ἰνδικῆς. τὸν γὰρ ταῦρον ἐπ᾽ εὐθείας τῇ ἀπὸ στηλῶν θαλάττῃ τεταμένον, δίχα τὴν ἀσίαν διαιρεῖν ὅλην ἐπὶ μῆκος. τὸ μὲν αὐτῆς μέρος βόρειον ποιοῦντα. τὸ δὲ νότιον. ὥστ᾽ ὁμοίως καὶ αὐτὸν ἐπὶ τοῦ διὰ ἀθηνῶν ἱδρῦσθαι παραλλήλου. καὶ τὴν ἀπὸ στηλῶν μέχρι δεῦρο θάλατταν. ταῦτα δ᾽ εἰπὼν οἴεται δεῖν διορθῶσαι τὸν ἀρχαῖον γεωγραφικὸν πίνακα. πολὺ γὰρ ἐπὶ τὰς ἄρκτους παραλλάττειν τὰ ἑωθινὰ μέρη τῶν ὀρῶν κατ᾽ αὐτόν. συνεπισπᾶσθαι δὲ καὶ τὴν ἰνδικὴν ἀρκτικωτέραν ἤδη γινομένην. πίστιν δὲ τούτου φέρει. μίαν μὲν τοιαύτην. ὅτι τὰ τῆς ἰνδικῆς ἄκρα, τὰ μεσημβρινώτατα, ὁμολογοῦσι πολλοὶ τοῖς κατὰ μερόην ἀνταίρειν τόποις. ἀπό τε τῶν ἀέρων, καὶ τῶν οὐρανίων τεκμαιρόμενοι. ἐντεῦθεν δ᾽ ἐπὶ τὰ βορειότατα τῆς ἰνδικῆς τὰ πρὸς τοῖς καυκασίοις ὄρεσι, πατροκλῆς ὁ μάλιστα πιστεύεσθαι δίκαιος. διά τε τὸ ἀξίωμα καὶ διὰ τὸ μὴ ἰδιώτης εἶναι τῶν γεωγραφικῶν, φησὶ σταδίους μυρίους καὶ πεντακισχιλίους. ἀλλὰ μὴν καὶ τὸν ἀπὸ μερόης ἐπὶ τὸν δι᾽ ἀθηνῶν παράλληλον τοσοῦτόν πως ἐστίν, ὥστε τῆς ἰνδικῆς τὰ προσάρκτια μέρη συνάπτοντα τοῖς καυκασίοις ὄρεσιν εἰς τοῦτον τελευτᾶν τὸν κύκλον. ἄλλην δὲ πίστιν φέρει τοιαύτην. ὅτι τὸ ἀπὸ τοῦ ἰσσικοῦ κόλπου διάστημα ἐπὶ τὴν θάλατταν τὴν ποντικήν, τρισχιλίων πως ἐστὶ σταδίων πρὸς ἄρκτον ἰόντι. καὶ τοὺς περὶ ἀμισὸν ἢ σινώπην τόπους. ὅσον, καὶ τὸ πλάτος τῶν ὀρῶν λέγεται. ἐκ δὲ ἀμισοῦ πρὸς τὴν ἰσημερινὴν ἀνατολὴν φερομένῳ, πρῶτον μὲν ἡ κολχίς ἐστιν. ἔπειτα ἡ ἐπὶ τὴν ὑρκανίαν θάλατταν ὑπέρθεσις. καὶ ἡ ἐφεξῆς ἡ ἐπὶ βάκτρα καὶ τοὺς ἐπέκεινα σκύθας ὁδὸς δεξιὰ ἔχοντι τὰ ὄρη. αὕτη δ᾽ ἡ γραμμὴ διὰ ἀμισοῦ πρὸς δύσιν ἐκβαλλομένη διὰ τῆς προποντίδος ἐστὶ καὶ τοῦ ἑλλησπόντου. ἀπὸ δὲ μερόης ἐπὶ τὸν ἑλλήσποντον, οὐ πλείους εἰσὶ τῶν μυρίων καὶ ὀκτακισχιλίων σταδίων. ὅσοι καὶ ἀπὸ τοῦ μεσημβρινοῦ πλευροῦ τῆς ἰνδικῆς, πρὸς τὰ περὶ τοὺς βακτρίους μέρη. προστεθέντων τρισχιλίων τοῖς μυρίοις καὶ πεντακισχιλίοις. ὧν οἱ μὲν, τοῦ πλάτους ἦσαν τῶν ὀρῶν, οἱ δὲ τῆς ἰνδικῆς. πρὸς δὲ τὴν ἀπόφασιν ταύτην ὁ ἵππαρχος ἀντιλέγει διαβάλλων τὰς πίστεις. οὔτε γὰρ πατροκλέα πιστὸν εἶναι δυεῖν, ἀντιμαρτυρούντων αὐτῷ δηιμάχου τε καὶ μεγασθένους. οἳ καθ᾽ οὓς μὲν τόπους δισμυρίων εἶναι σταδίων τὸ διάστημά φασι τὸ ἀπὸ τῆς κατὰ μεσημβρίαν θαλάττης. καθ᾽ οὓς, δὲ καὶ τρισμυρίων. τούτους γε δὴ τοιαῦτα λέγειν, καὶ τοὺς ἀρχαίους πίνακας τούτοις ὁμολογεῖν, ἀπίθανον δήπου νομίζει τὸ μόνῳ δεῖν πιστεύειν πατροκλεῖ, παρέντας τοσούτους τοὺς ἀντιμαρτυροῦντας αὐτῷ, καὶ διορθοῦσθαι παρ᾽ αὐτὸ τοῦτο τοὺς ἀρχαίους πίνακας. ἀλλὰ μὴ ἐᾶν οὕτως, ἕως ἄν τι πιστότερον περὶ αὐτῶν γνῶμεν. οἶμαι δὴ πολλὰς ἔχειν εὐθύνας τοῦτον τὸν λόγον. πρῶτον μὲν ὅτι πολλαῖς μαρτυρίαις ἐκεῖνος χρησάμενος, μιᾷ φησι, τῇ πατροκλέους αὐτὸν χρῆσθαι. τινὲς οὖν ἦσαν οἱ φάσκοντες τὰ μεσημβρινὰ ἄκρα

Ex III Eratosthenis libro terrae descriptio.

Taurus

I pistis

Patrocles

II pistis

Hipparchus contra Patroclis testimonium

Strabo pro Patrocle

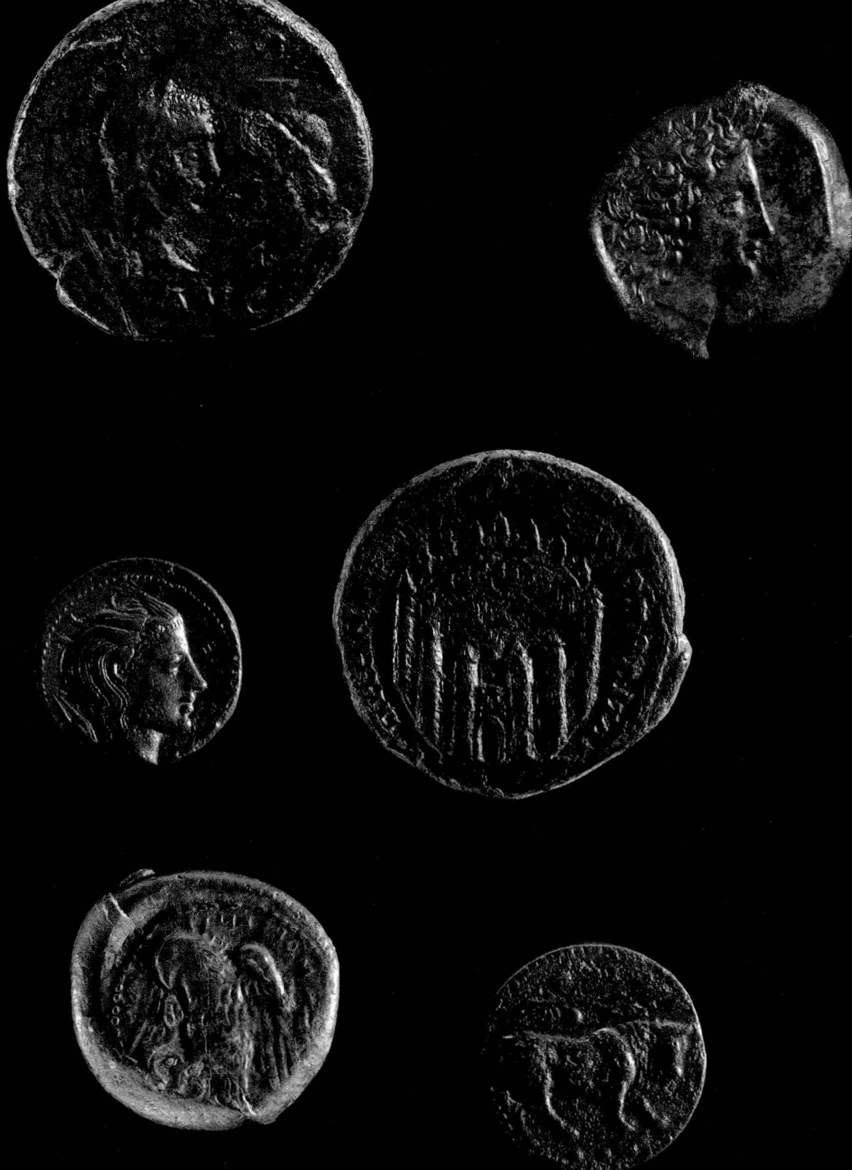

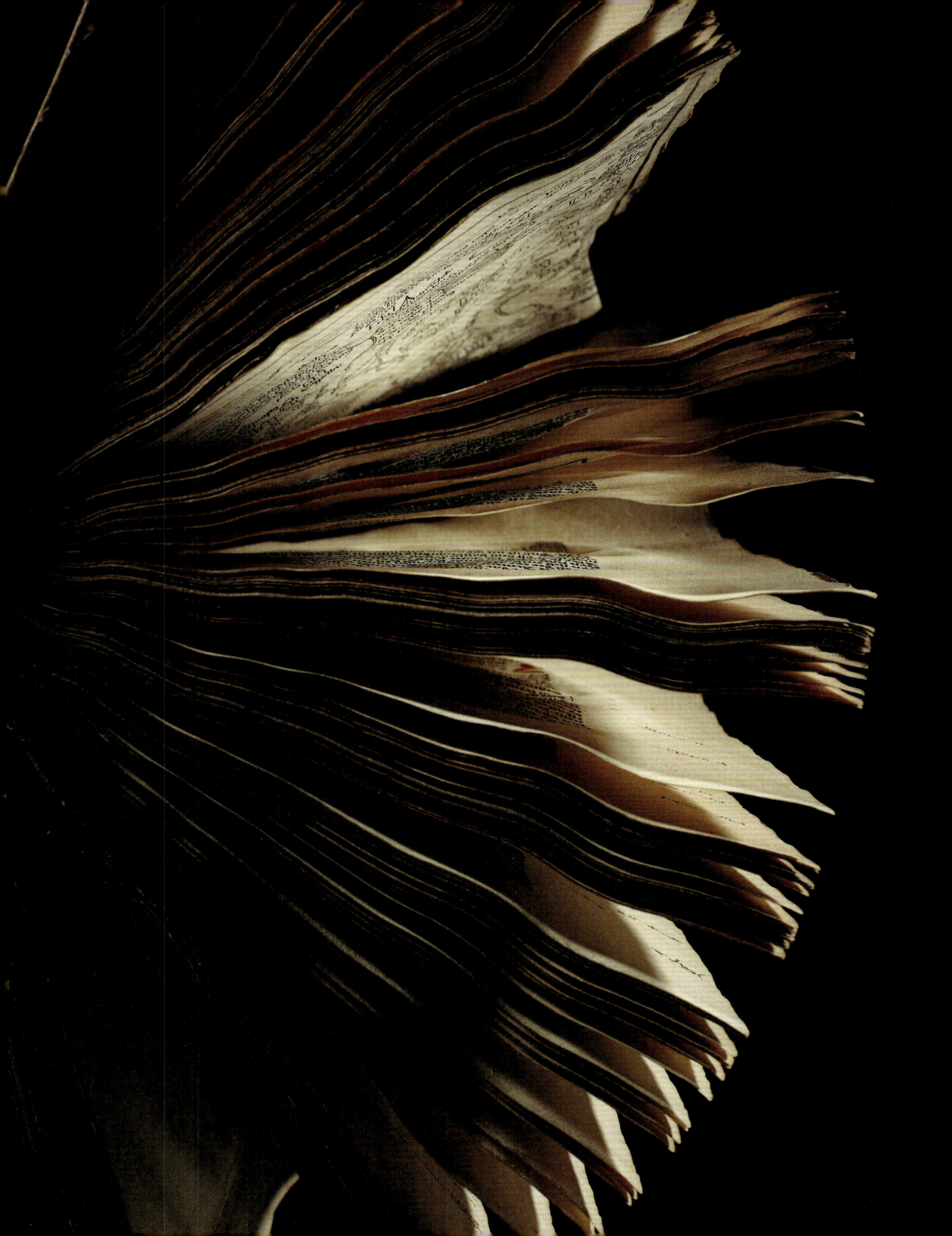

Εὔμηλος συγγραφεύς. μαραθῶνος υἱοί, σικυὼν καὶ κόρινθος. ἀνάστασις καὶ ἀνοικισμὸς κο-
ρίνθου. πιτυοκάμπτης σίνις. ἀδελφίτης κορωνίτης. ἰσθμοῦ διώρυχ. θεοὶ κο-
ρίνθου ἀμφισβητοῦντες. ἡρώδου πολυτελὲς ἀνάθημα.

δὲ κορινθία χώρα μοῖρα οὖσα τῆς ἀργείας, ἀπὸ κορίνθου τὸ ὄνομα ἔσχηκε. διὸς
δὲ εἶναι κόρινθον οὐδένα οἶδα εἰπόντα πω σπουδῇ. πλὴν κορινθίων τῶν πολ-
λῶν. εὔμηλος δὲ ὁ ἀμφιλύτου τῶν βακχιαδῶν καλουμένων ὃς καὶ τὰ ἔπη λέγε-
ται ποιῆσαι, φησὶν ἐν τῇ κορινθίᾳ συγγραφῇ. (εἰ δὴ εὐμήλου γε ἡ συγγραφή) ἐφύ-
ραν ὠκεανοῦ θυγατέρα οἰκῆσαι πρῶτον ἐν τῇ γῇ ταύτῃ. μαραθῶνα δὲ ὕστερον τὸν
ἐπωπέως τοῦ ἀλωέως τοῦ ἡλίου, φεύγοντα ἀνομίαν καὶ ὕβριν τοῦ πατρὸς ἐς τὰ 2
παραθαλάσσια μετοικῆσαι τῆς ἀττικῆς. ἀποθανόντος δὲ ἐπωπέως, ἀφικόμενον ἐς πελοπόννησον, καὶ
τὴν ἀρχὴν διανείμαντα τοῖς παισίν, αὐτὸν ἐς τὴν ἀττικὴν αὖθις ἀναχωρῆσαι. καὶ ἀπὸ μὲν σικυῶνος,
τὴν ἀσωπίαν. ἀπὸ δὲ κορίνθου τὴν ἐφυραίαν μετονομασθῆναι. Κόρινθον δὲ οἰκοῦσι κορινθίων
3 μὲν οὐδεὶς ἔτι τῶν ἀρχαίων. ἔποικοι δὲ ἀποσταλέντες ὑπὸ ῥωμαίων. αἴτιον δὲ τὸ συνέδριον τὸ ἀ-
χαιῶν. συντελοῦντες γὰρ ἐς αὐτὸ καὶ κορίνθιοι, μετέσχον τοῦ πολέμου τοῦ πρὸς ῥωμαίους. ὃν κρι-
τόλαος στρατηγεῖν ἀχαιῶν ἀποδειχθείς, παρεσκεύασε γενέσθαι. τούς τε ἀχαιοὺς ἀναπείσας ἀποστῆ-
ναι καὶ τῶν ἔξω πελοποννήσου τοὺς πολλούς. ῥωμαῖοι δὲ ὡς ἐκράτησαν τῷ πολέμῳ, παρείλοντο μὲν
καὶ τῶν ἄλλων ἑλλήνων τὰ ὅπλα. καὶ τείχη περιεῖλον ὅσαι τετειχισμέναι πόλεις ἦσαν. κόρινθον
δὲ ἀνάστατον μεμμίου ποιήσαντος, τοῦ τότε ἡγουμένου τῶν ἐνταῦθα στρατοπέδων ῥωμαίων, ὕστερον λέγου-
σιν ἀνοικίσαι καίσαρα. ὃς πολιτείαν ἐν ῥώμῃ πρῶτος τὴν ἐφ' ἡμῶν κατεστήσατο. ἀνοικίσαι δὲ καὶ καρ-
χηδόνα ἐπὶ τῆς ἀρχῆς τῆς αὐτοῦ. τῆς δὲ κορινθίας ἐστὶ γῆς καὶ ὁ καλούμενος κρομμύων, ἀπὸ τοῦ κρό-
4 μου τοῦ ποσειδῶνος. ἐνταῦθα τραφῆναι λέγουσι καὶ τὸν λεγόμενον θησέως πιτυοκάμπτην καὶ κατ'
αὐτὸν τὸν τόπον ἐστὶν ἔργον. προϊοῦσι γάρ, ἡ πίτυς ἄχρι γε ἐμοῦ ἐπεφύκει παρὰ τὸν αἰγιαλόν, καὶ με-
λικέρτου βωμὸς ἦν. ἐς τοῦτον τὸν τόπον, ἐκκομισθῆναι τὸν παῖδα ὑπὸ δελφῖνος λέγουσι. κειμένῳ
δὲ ἐπιτυχόντα σίσυφον, θάψαι τε ἐν τῷ ἰσθμῷ. καὶ τὸν ἀγῶνα ἐπ' αὐτῷ ποιῆσαι τῶν ἰσθμίων. ἔστι δὲ
5 ἐπὶ τοῦ ἰσθμοῦ τῆς ἀρχῆς ἔνθα ὁ λῃστὴς σίνις λαμβανόμενος πιτύων, ἦγεν ἐς τὸ κάτω σφᾶς. ὁπόσων
δὲ μάχῃ κρατήσειεν, ἀπ' αὐτῶν δήσας ἀφῆκεν ἂν τὰ δένδρα ἄνω φέρεσθαι. ἐνταῦθα ἑκατέρα τῶν πι-
τύων τὸν δεθέντα ἐπ' αὐτὴν εἷλκε καὶ τοῦ δεσμοῦ μηδ' ἑτέρωσε εἴκοντος, ἀλλ' ἀμφοτέρωθεν ἐπίσης βια-
ζομένου, διεσπᾶτο ὁ δεδεμένος. τοιούτῳ διεφθάρη τρόπῳ καὶ αὐτὸς ὑπὸ θησέως ὁ σίνις. ἐκάθηρε
γὰρ θησεὺς τῶν κακούργων τὴν ὁδὸν τὴν ἐς ἀθήνας ἐκ τροιζῆνος. οὕς τε πρότερον κατηρίθμησα ἀ-
6 νελών, καὶ ἐν ἐπιδαύρῳ τῇ ἱερᾷ περιφήτην ἡφαίστου νομιζόμενον, κορύνῃ χαλκῇ χρώμενον ἐς
τὰς μάχας. καθήκει δὲ ὁ τῶν κορινθίων ἰσθμός, τῇ μὲν ἐς τὴν ἐπὶ κεγχρέαις. τῇ δὲ ἐς τὴν ἐπὶ λεχαίῳ
θάλασσαν. τοῦτο γὰρ ἤπειρον ποιεῖ τὴν ἐντὸς χώραν. ὃς δὲ ἐπεχείρησε πελοπόννησον ἐργάσασθαι νῆσον,
7 προαπέλιπε διορύσσων ἰσθμόν. καὶ ὅθεν μὲν διορύσσειν ἤρξαντο, δῆλόν ἐστιν. ἐς δὲ τὸ πετρῶδες οὐ προε-
χώρησαν ἀρχήν. μένει δὲ ὡς ἐπεφύκει καὶ νῦν ἤπειρος ὤν. ἀλεξάνδρῳ τε τῷ φιλίππου, διασκάψαι
μίμαντα ἐθελήσαντι, μόνον τοῦτο οὐ προεχώρησε τῶν ἔργων. κνιδίους δὲ ἡ πυθία τὸν ἰσθμὸν ὀρύσσοντας
ἔπαυσεν. οὕτω χαλεπὸν ἀνθρώπῳ τὰ θεῖα βιάσασθαι. τὸ δὲ οὐ κορινθίοις μόνον περὶ τῆς χώρας ἐ-
στιν εἰρημένον. ἀλλὰ ἐμοὶ δοκεῖ ἀθηναῖοι πρῶτοι περὶ τῆς ἀττικῆς ἐσεμνολόγησαν. λέγουσι δὲ καὶ κο-
ρίνθιοι ποσειδῶνα ἐλθεῖν ἡλίῳ περὶ τῆς γῆς ἐς ἀμφισβήτησιν. βριάρεων δὲ διαλλακτὴν γενέσθαι
8 σφίσιν. ἰσθμὸν μὲν καὶ ὅσα ταύτῃ δικάσαντα εἶναι ποσειδῶνος. τὴν δὲ ἄκραν ἡλίῳ δόντος τὴν ὑ-
πὲρ τῆς πόλεως. ἀπὸ μὲν τούτου λέγουσιν εἶναι τὸν ἰσθμὸν ποσειδῶνος. θέας δὲ αὐτόθι ἄξια ἔστι μὲν
θέατρον. ἔστι δὲ στάδιον λίθου λευκοῦ. ἐλθόντι δὲ ἐς τοῦ θεοῦ τὸ ἱερόν, τοῦτο μὲν ἀθλητῶν νικησάντων
τὰ ἴσθμια ἑστήκασιν εἰκόνες. τοῦτο δὲ πιτύων δένδρα ἐστὶ πεφυτευμένα ἐπὶ στοίχου τὰ πολλὰ ἐς εὐ-
θὺ αὐτῶν ἀνήκοντα. τῷ ναῷ δὲ ὄντι μέγεθος οὐ μείζονι ἐφεστήκασι τρίτωνες χαλκοῖ. καὶ ἀγάλματα ἔ-
στιν ἐν τῷ προνάῳ. δύο μὲν ποσειδῶνος. τρίτον δὲ ἀμφιτρίτης. καὶ θάλασσα καὶ αὕτη χαλκῆ. τὰ δὲ
ἔνδον ἐφ' ἡμῶν ἀνέθηκεν ἡρώδης ἀθηναῖος. ἵππους τέσσαρας ἐπιχρύσους πλὴν τῶν ὁπλῶν. ὁπλαὶ
9 δέ σφισιν εἰσὶν ἐλέφαντος. καὶ τρίτωνες δύο παρὰ τοὺς ἵππους εἰσὶ χρυσοῖ. τὰ μετ' ἰξὺν καὶ οὗ-
τοι ἐλέφαντος. τῷ δὲ ἅρματι ἀμφιτρίτη καὶ ποσειδῶν ἐφεστήκασι. καὶ παῖς ὀρθός ἐστιν ἐπὶ δελ-
φῖνος ὁ παλαίμων. ἐλέφαντος δὲ καὶ χρυσοῦ καὶ οὗτοι πεποίηνται. τῷ βάθρῳ δὲ ἐφ' οὗ τὸ ἅρ-
μα, μέσῃ μὲν ἐπείργασται θάλασσα ἀνέχουσα ἀφροδίτην παῖδα. ἑκατέρωθεν δέ εἰσιν αἱ νηρηίδες καλού-
μεναι. ταύταις καὶ ἑτέρωθι τῆς ἑλλάδος βωμοὺς οἶδα ὄντας. τοῦ δὲ καὶ τεμένη σφίσιν ἀναθέντας ποιμέ-
νας, ἔνθα καὶ ἀχιλλεῖ τιμαί. δωτοῦς δὲ ἐν γαβάλοις ἱερόν ἐστιν ἅγιον. ἔνθα πέπλος ἔτι ἐλείπετο ὃν ἕλ-
ληνες ἐριφύλην λέγουσιν ἐπὶ τῷ παιδὶ λαβεῖν ἀλκμαίωνι. τοῦ ποσειδῶνος δέ εἰσιν ἐπειργασμένοι τῷ
βάθρῳ καὶ οἱ τυνδάρεω παῖδες. ὅτι δὴ σωτῆρες καὶ οὗτοι νεῶν καὶ ἀνθρώπων εἰσὶ ναυτιλλομένων.

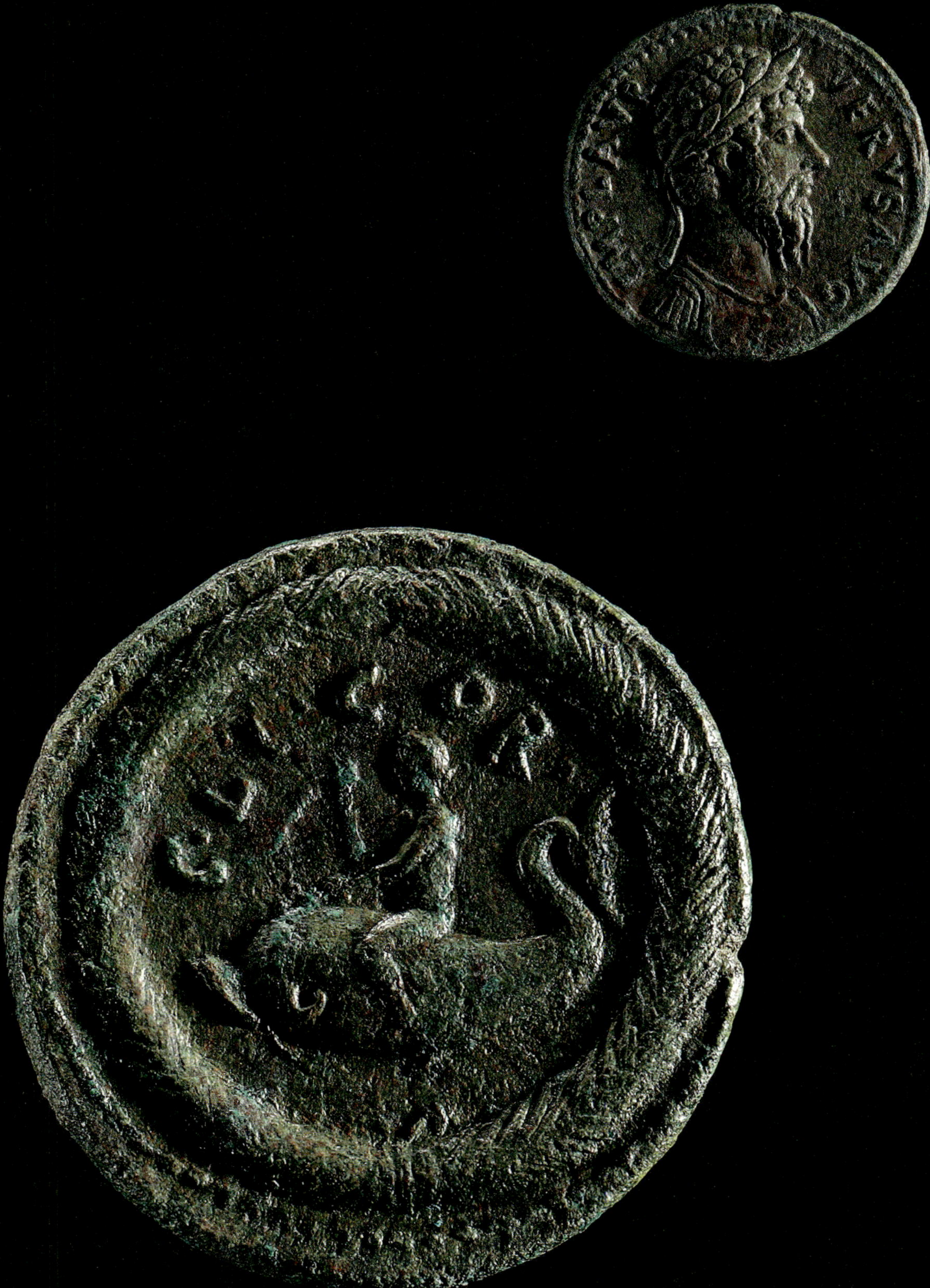

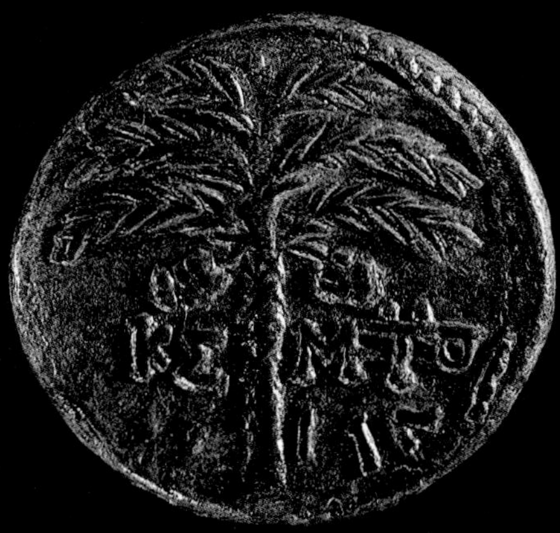

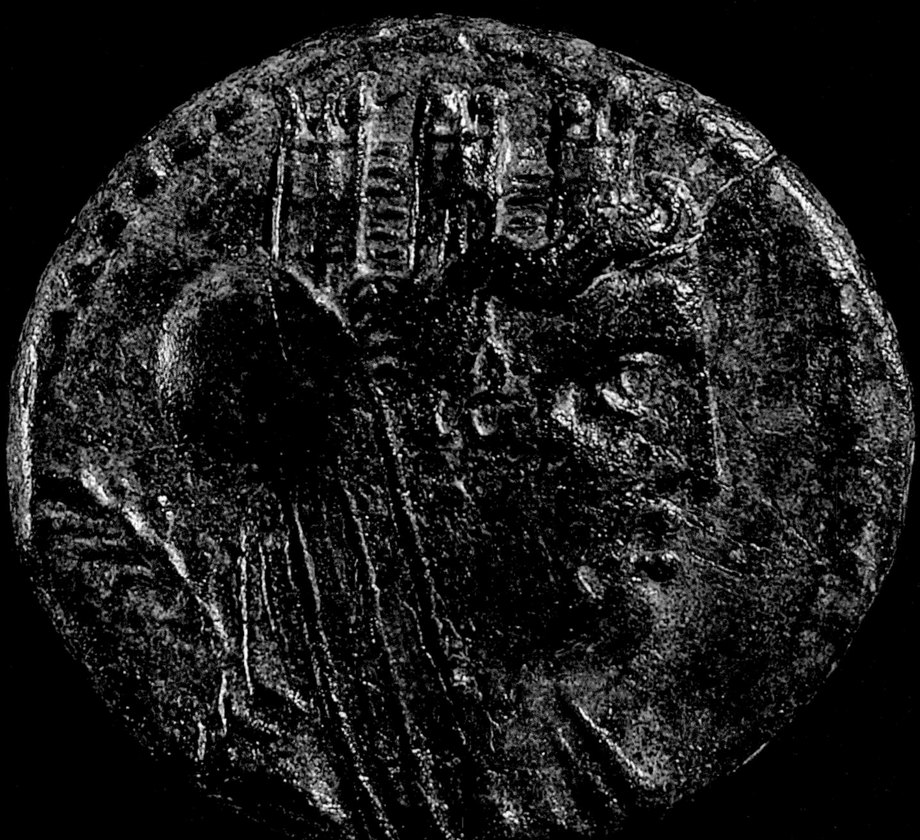

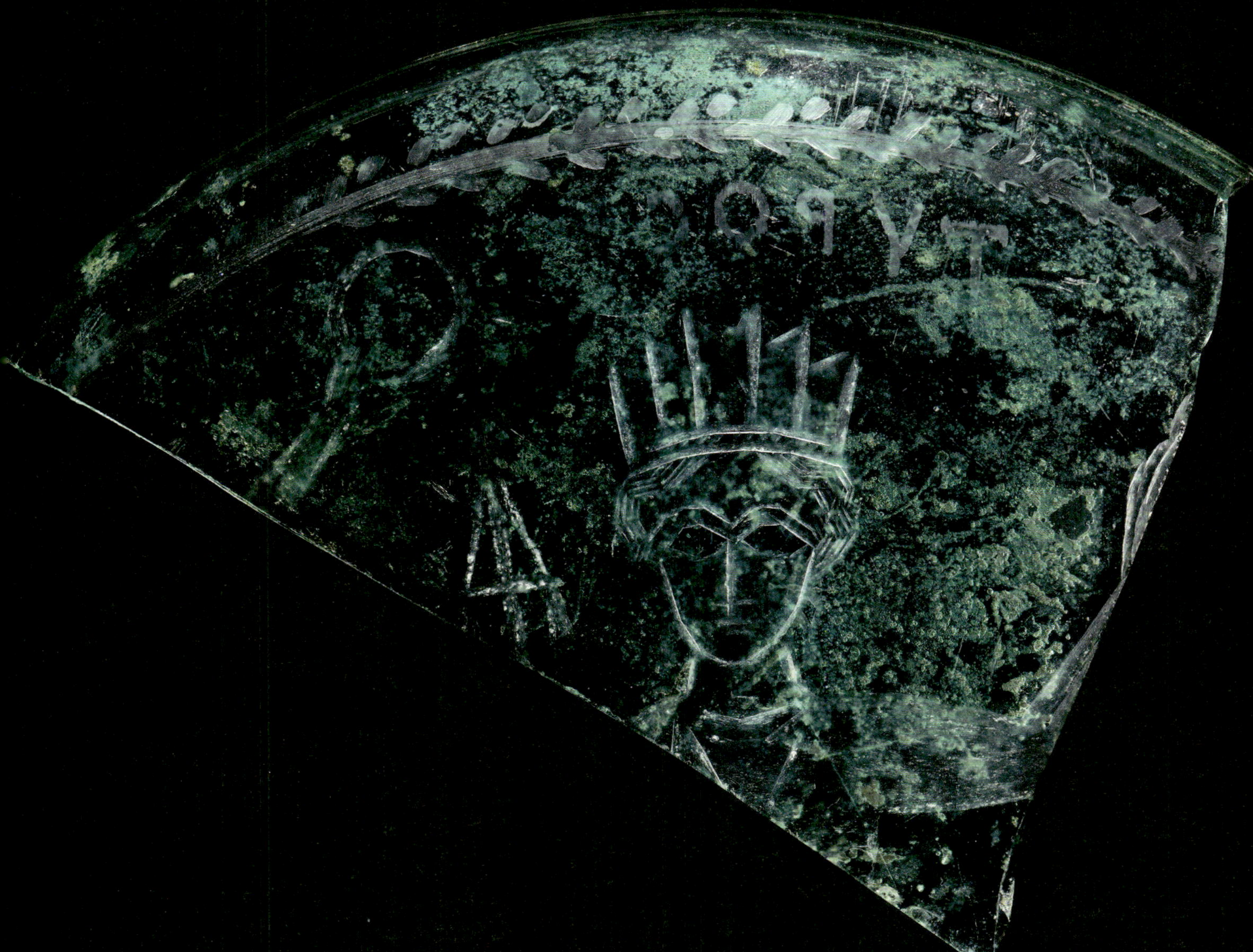

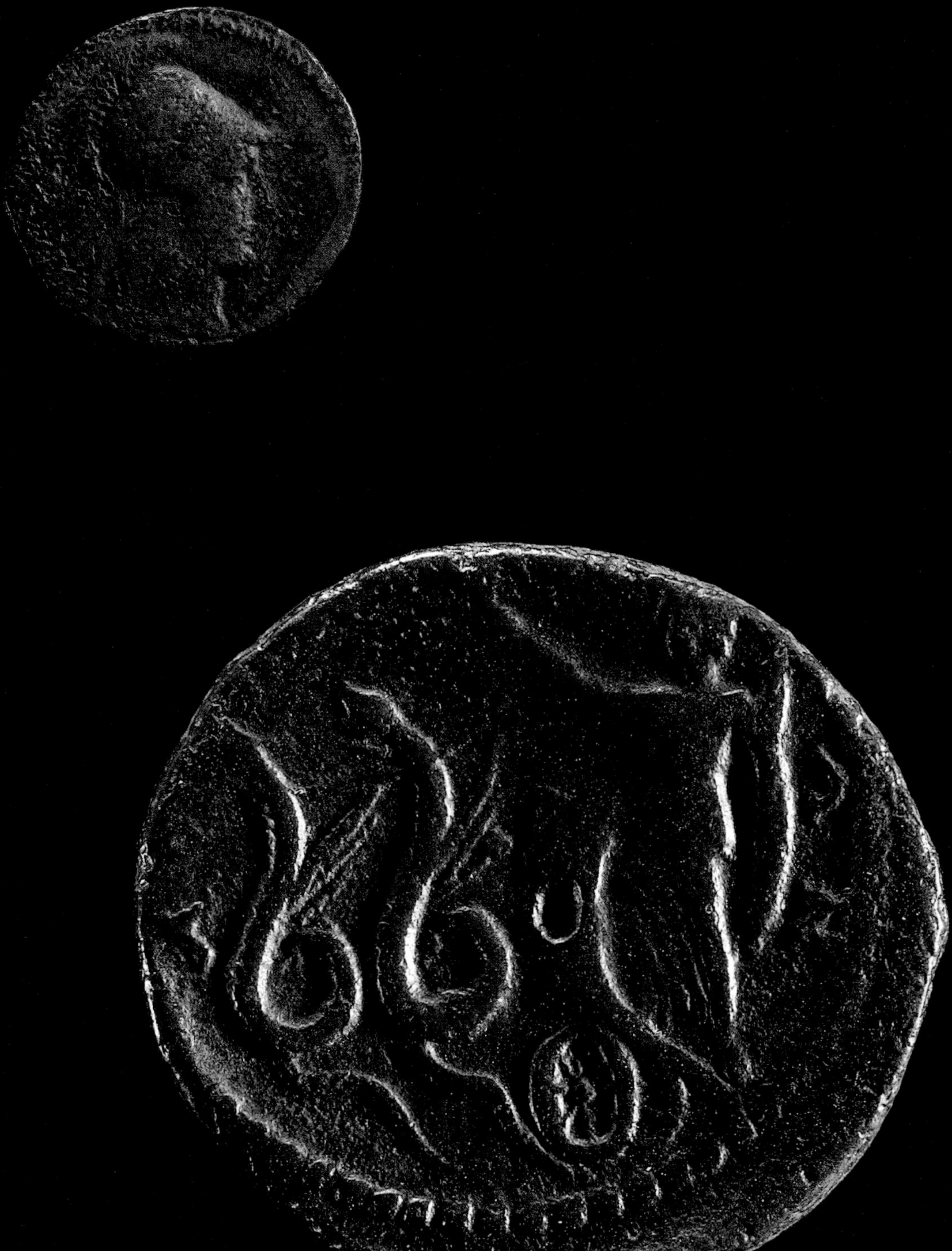

1

Let such approach this consecrated land
And ~~walk~~ pass in peace along the magic waste
But spare it's relics — let no wanton hand
Deface the scenes ~~already~~ how defaced!
Not for such purpose were these altars placed
Revere the remnants nations once revered
So may our country's name be undisgraced
So mayst thou prosper where thy youth was reared
By every honest joy of love & life endeared! —

2

For thee, who thus ~~with~~ in too protracted song
Hast soothed ~~[illegible]~~ thine idlesse with inglorious ~~wildest~~ lays,
Soon shall thy voice be lost amid the throng
Of louder minstrels of these later days,
To these resign the strife for fading Bays

ΠΙΝΔΑΡΟΥ
ΞΕΝΟΦΩΝΤΙ ΚΟΡ
ΣΤΑΔΙΟΔΡΟΜΩ
ΠΕΝΤΑΘΛΩ ΝΙ
ΣΑΝΤΙ ΤΗΝ
ΟΛΥΜΠΙΑ-
ΔΑ ιγ΄.

Στροφή.

Τ ρισολυμπιονίκαν ἐ
οἶκον, ἅμερον ἀστοῖς
ξένοισι δὲ θεράποντ
τὰν ὀλβίαν Κόρινθον, Ἰσθ
πρόθυρον Ποτειδᾶνος ἀγλ
ἐν τᾷ γὰρ εὐνομία ναίει, κα
ταί τε, βάθρον πολίων
ἀσφαλὴς δίκα, καὶ ὁμό-
τροφος εἰράνα, ταμίαι
ἀνδράσι πλούτου χρύσεαι,
παῖδες εὐβούλου θέμιτος,
ἀντί ἐθέλοντι δ᾽ ἀλέξειν ὕβριν κο
στρο ματέρα θρασύθυμον
φος. ἔχω καλά τε φράσαι. τόλμα
εὐθεῖα γλῶσσαν ὀρνύει λέγει
ἄμαχον δὲ κρύψαι τὸ συγγενὲ
ὔμμιν δὲ παῖδες ἀλάτα, πολλ
νικαφόρον ἀγλαΐαν

ὤπασαν ἄκραις ἀρεταῖς
ὑπερελθόντων ἱεροῖς
ἐν ἀέθλοισι. πολλὰ δ' ἐν
καρδίαις ἀνδρῶν ἔβαλον
ἐπῳ ὧραι πολυάνθεμοι ἀρ-
δός. χαῖα σοφίσμαθ'. ἅπαν δ' εὑρόντος ἔργον
ταὶ διονύσου πόθεν ἐξέφανε
σὺν βοηλάτᾳ χάριτες
διθυράμβῳ· τίς γὰρ ἱππεί-
οις ἐν ἔντεσι μέτρα,
ἢ θεῶν ναοῖσιν οἰω-
νῶν βασιλῆα δίδυμον
ἐπέθηκ'; ἐν δὲ μοῖσ' ἁδύπνοος
ἐν δ' ἄρης ἀνθεῖ, νέων
οὐλίαις αἰχμαῖσιν ἀνδρῶν
στρο ὕπατ' εὐρὺ ἀνάσσων ὀλυμπίας,
φὴ ἀφθόνατος ἔπεσι
β'. γένοις χρόνον ἅπαντα ζεῦ πάτερ·
καὶ τόνδε λαὸν ἀβλαβῆ νέμων,
ξενοφῶντος εὔθυνε δαίμονος οὖρον·
δέξαι δέ οἱ στεφάνων ἐγκώμιον
τεθμόν. τὸν ἄγει πεδίων
ἐκ πίσας, πεντάθλῳ ἅμα
σταδίου νικῶν δρόμον. ἀν-
τεβόλησεν τῶν· ἀνὴρ
θνατὸς οὔπω τις πρότερον.

mutato colore ĩ nigrũ durescere. Cũ cadat: frāgi. Item aliũ q̃ uocet̃ charitoblephar
efficacem ĩ amatoriis. Spatalia eo facere & monilia fœmĩas. Sẽtire eũ se capi: durar
cornus mõ: & hebetare aciẽ ferri. Quod si fefellerint ĩsidiæ: ĩ lapidẽ trãsfigurari.

CAII PLYNII SECVNDI NATVRALIS HISTORIAE LIBER. XIIII. I
QVO FRVCTIFERAE ARBORES TRADVNTVR. PROOEMIVI

EXTERNAE ARBORES INDOCILE
que nasci alibi q̃ ubi cœpere: & quæ in alienas
cõmeant terras: hactenus fere sũt. Licetq; iam
communibus loq: q̃ꝝ omnium peculiaris pare
uideri põt italia. Noscentes tantum meminer
naturas eaꝝ a nobis ĩterim dici: non culturas.
& colendi maxima ĩ natura portio est. Illud sa
mirari nõ queo: ĩterisse q̃rũdam memoriam: a
etiam nominum quæ auctores ꝓdidere: notic
Quis enim nõ communicato orbe terrarum m
iestate romãi impii ꝓfecisse uitam putet cõm
cio reꝝ? Ac societate festæ pacis? omniaque: e
quæ occulta ante fuerant: in ꝓmiscuo usu facta? At hercule non repiunt̃: qui non
multa ab antiquis prodita: tantum priscorum cura fertilior aut ĩdustria fœlicior fu
ante milia annorum: inter principia litterarum Hesiodo præcepta agricolis pand
orso: subsecutisq; non paucis hanc curã eius: unde nobis creuit labor. Quippe
requirenda sint non solum postea inuenta: uerum etiam ea quæ inuenerant pri
desidia rerum internitione memoriæ indicta. Cuius uitii causas quis alias q̃ public
mundi inuenerit? nimirum alii subiere ritus. Circaq; alia mentes hominum detin
& auariciæ tantum artes colunt̃: antea inclusis gentium imperiis intra ipsas. Ideo
& ingeniis q̃dam sterilitate fortunæ necesse erat animi bona exercere. Reges ĩnum
honore artium colebant̃: & in ostentatione has præferebant: opem & immortalit
sibi ꝑ illas prorogari arbitrantes. Quare abundabant & premia & opere uitæ. Post
ris laxitas mundi & rerum amplitudo damno fuit: postq̃ senator censu legi cœptu
iudex fieri censu: magistratum ducemq; nil magis exornare q̃ census: postq̃ cœpe
orbitas in auctoritate summa & potentia esse: captatio in quæstu fertilissimo: ac so
gaudia in possidendo: pessum iere uitæ precia: omnesq; a maximo bono liberales d
tæ artes in contrarium cecidere: ac seruitute sola profici cœptum. Alius hanc alio m
& ĩ aliis adorare: eodem tñ habendi quæstu ad spes hominum tendente uoto. Passi
uero etiam egregii aliena uitia q̃ bona sua colere malle. Ergo hercule uoluptas uiue
cœpit: uita ipsa desiit. Sed nos oblitterata quoq; scrutabimur. Nec deterreb
quarundam rerum humilitas: sicut nec ĩ aĩalibus fecit. Quãq̃ uidemus Virgiliu
præcellentissimum uatem eadem causa hortorum dotes fugisse: e tãtisq; quæ rettul
flores mõ rerum decerpsisse. Beatum fœlicemq; græciæ quindecim omnino generib
uuarum nominatis: tribus oleæ: totidem pirorum: malo uero tantum assyrio: cæte
õnibus neglectis. Vnde autem potius incipiemus q̃ a uitibus? q̃rum pricipatus ĩtã
peculiaris italiæ est: ut uel hoc uno omnia gentium uicisse: quanq̃ odorifera poss
uideri bona: q̃q̃ ubicũq; pubescentium odori nulla suauitas præfert̃.

DE Vitiũ natã: & q̃bus modis ferant. Cap. i.

De vitium natura: et quibus modis ferant

VItes iure apud priscos magnitudine quoq; inter arbores numerabant̃. Iouis
simulacꝝ ĩ urbe populonio ex una conspicimus uite tot æuis incorruptum. Ite
massiliæ pateram. Metaponti templum Iunonis uitigineis columnis stetit. Etiamn
scalis tectum ephesiæ Dianæ scãdit̃ uite una cypria (ut ferũt) quoniã ibi ad præcipu

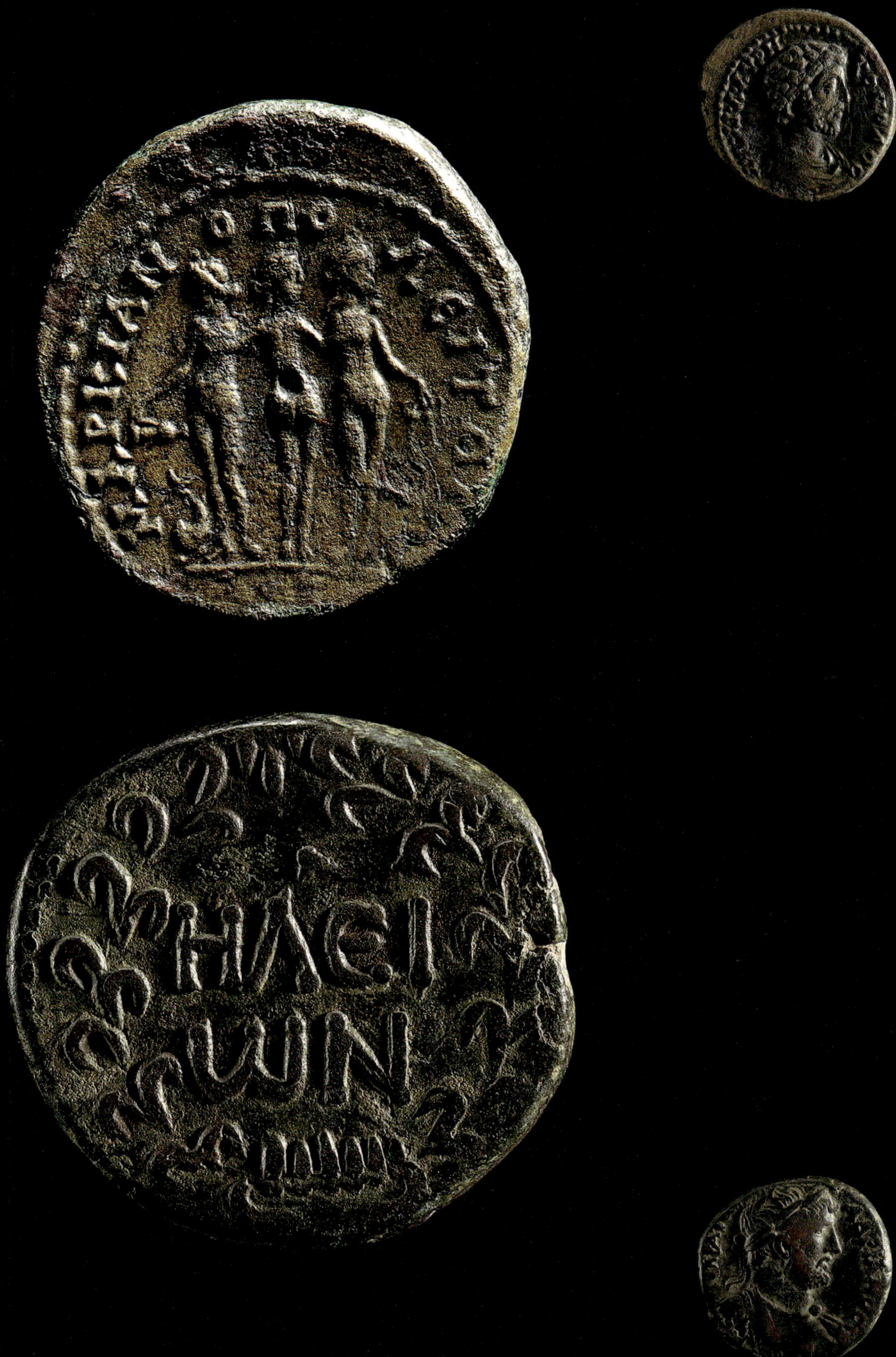
ΗΛΕΙ
ωΝ

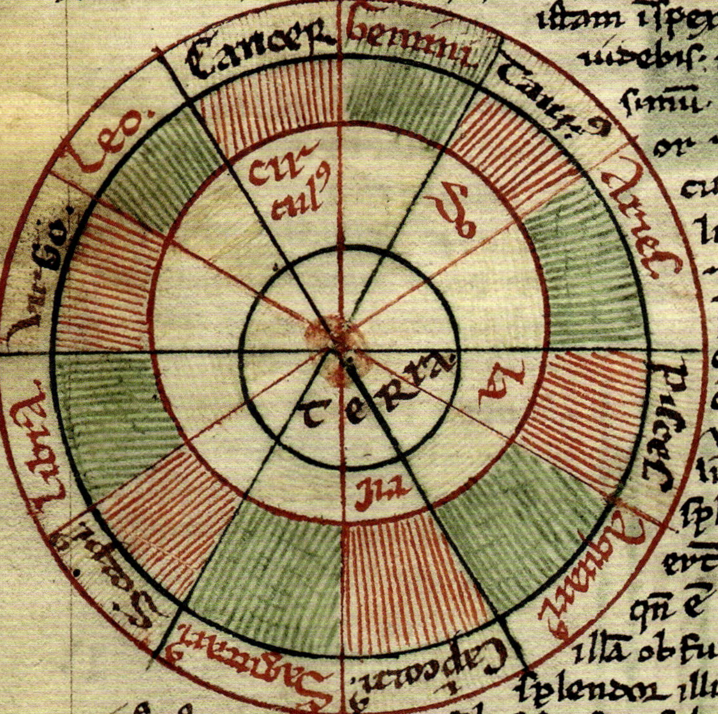

xii v linea ... figurare circulum vera. Si inspicis figu-
ram istam in speris. circulum solis in xii partes inequales divisum
videbis: ipsum quoque circulum sub geminis a terra remotis-
simum. sub sagittario proximum. Sol vero cum sit infe-
rior zodiaco. sub eo non in eo. per suum circulum dis-
currit et cum in illa parte sui circuli fuit que eis
lineis clauditur que gemini dicuntur esse in geminis
et cum illam transierit dicitur geminos transisse.
Illa vero xii pars sui circuli est latissima. ideo di-
ebus diebus super xxx. sol in ea immoratur pars vero
que est in sagittario est brevissima. ideo sol illam xx
viii diebus transcurrit iuxta predicta de a-
liis signis iudica. V. Placet mihi si dicas unde
splendor lune crescat vel minuatur. P. Fu-
erunt qui dixerunt lunam proprium habere splendorem. sed illius
quando est in eodem signo cum sole premio splendore
illa obfuscari. quando vero elongatur a sole in parte incipit
splendor illius apparere. et quanto plus ab ea removetur
minus. quod si verum esset plus de suo splendore appareret quanto illi est propior tanto
numquam a parte occidentis sed a parte orientis que est a sole re-
motior accenderetur. sed semper oritur opposita in parte soli. Sani quidem dixerunt quidam
qui dixerunt lunam ex propinquitate terre et aque spissius habere corpus quam cetere stel-
le habent. unde non ex se ipsa habet splendorem nec calorem. Si enim proprium haberet calorem cum vi-
cina sit terre et per singulos menses ascendat ad cancrum et descendat ad capri-
cornum per singulos menses fervore estatis et frigore hiemis terris ageret tamque
continuis inequalitatibus nichil vivere posset in eis. Caruit ergo proprio lumine et ca-
lore. a sole tamen supposito illustratur non semper equaliter apud nos. Cum enim
recto modo sub sole illustratur. sol superiorem illius partem illuminans umbram versus
terram iacit. unde a nobis non videtur. quando vero elongatur a sole incipit parum splen-
doris in modum gracilis cornu apparere. dicitur que monoi-
des. quanto plus elongatur a sole plus splendoris descen-
dit. itaque vii die dicothomos. id est divisa
per medium videtur. Et nota quod quantum splendor
descendit tantum umbra ascendit. vel econverso. Post
vii dies usque ad xiiii diem amphicir-
cos dicitur minor videtur plena. maior
dimidia. Quarto decimo die quia
per diametrum remota est a sole. quod ex
hoc probari potest quod sole occidente ipsa
oritur iam tota umbra ascendit. tota-
que splendor descendit. Et quod pan-
selenos. id est plenilunium. Hinc incipit so-
li appropinquare. unde umbra descendit
et splendor ascendit. et fit primum descen-
do amphicircos deinde dicothomos. ad ul-
timum monoydes. Hoc ita apta erit talis fi-
gura ante oculos posita. V. Unde contingit quod lune

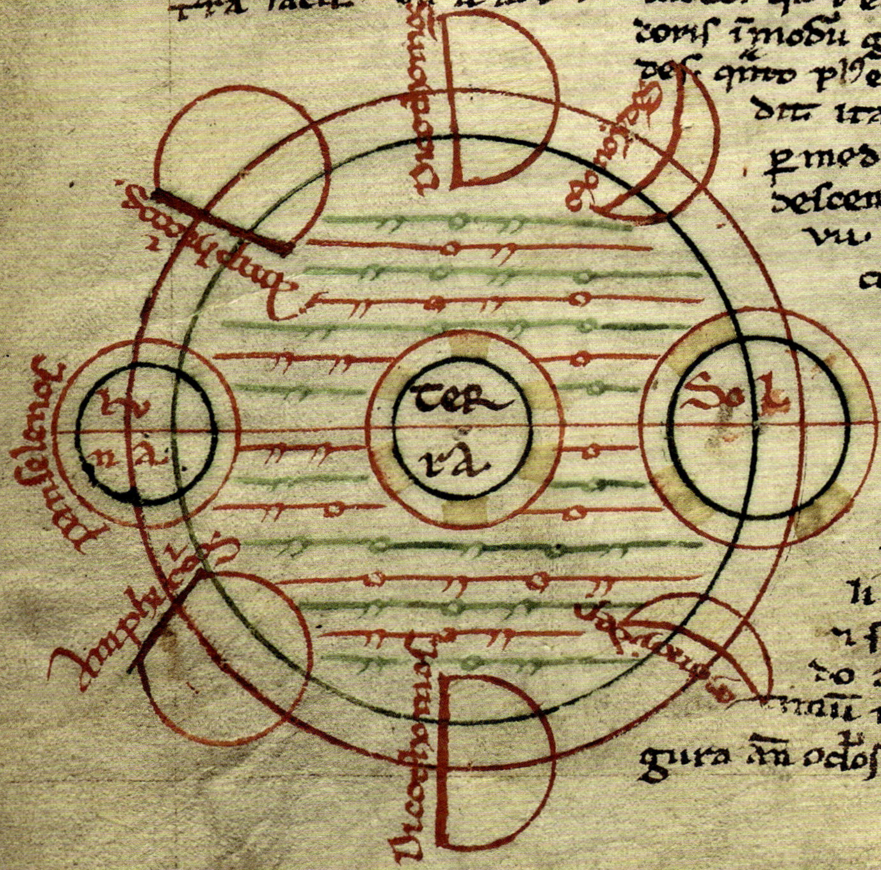

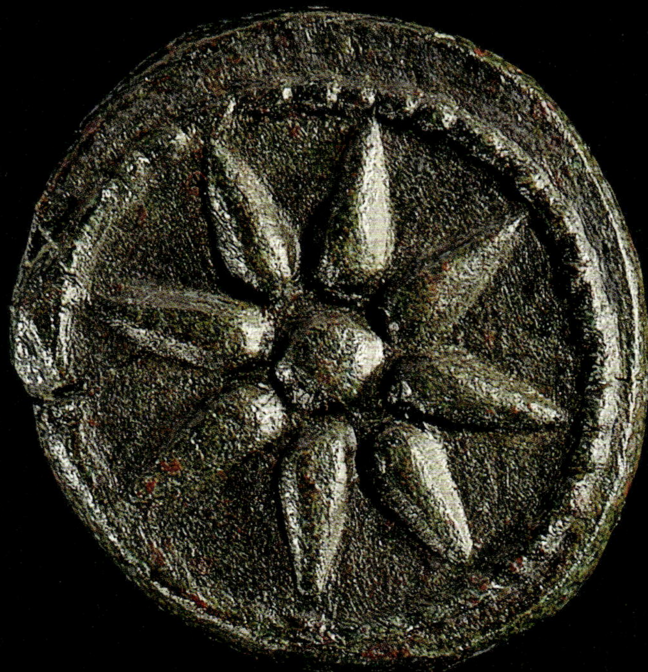

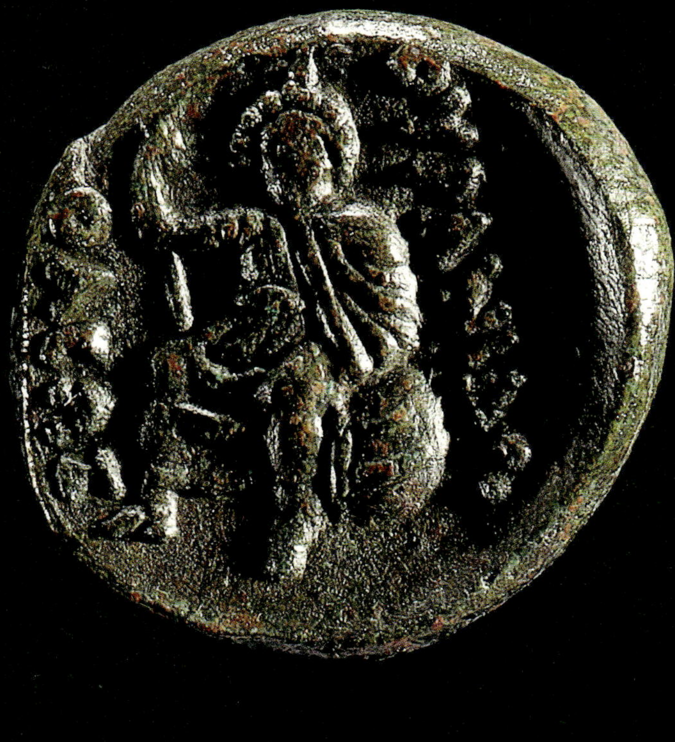

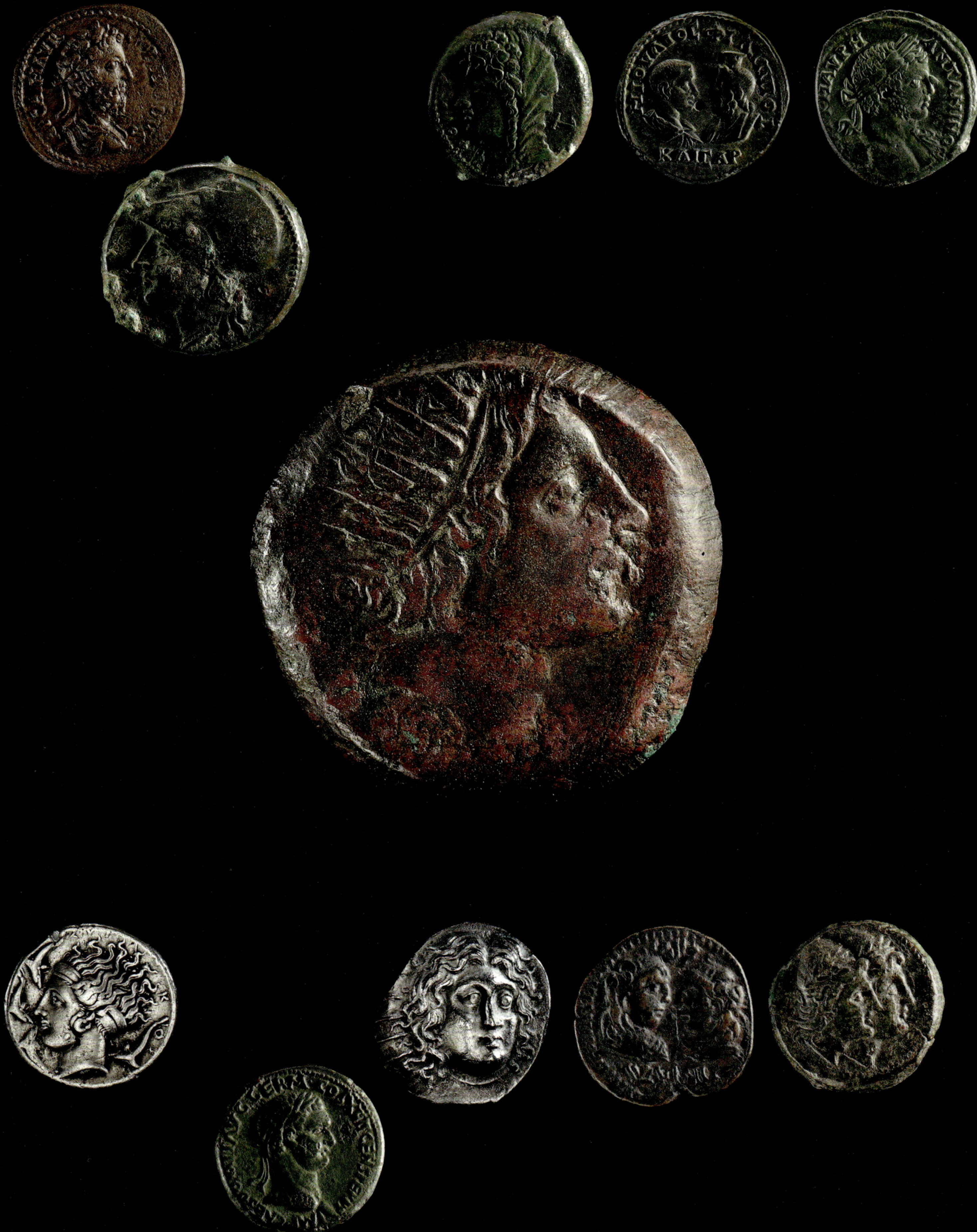

…US, MERCURIUS ΕΠΙΠΟΛΙ.
Et
SERPENTIFERA.

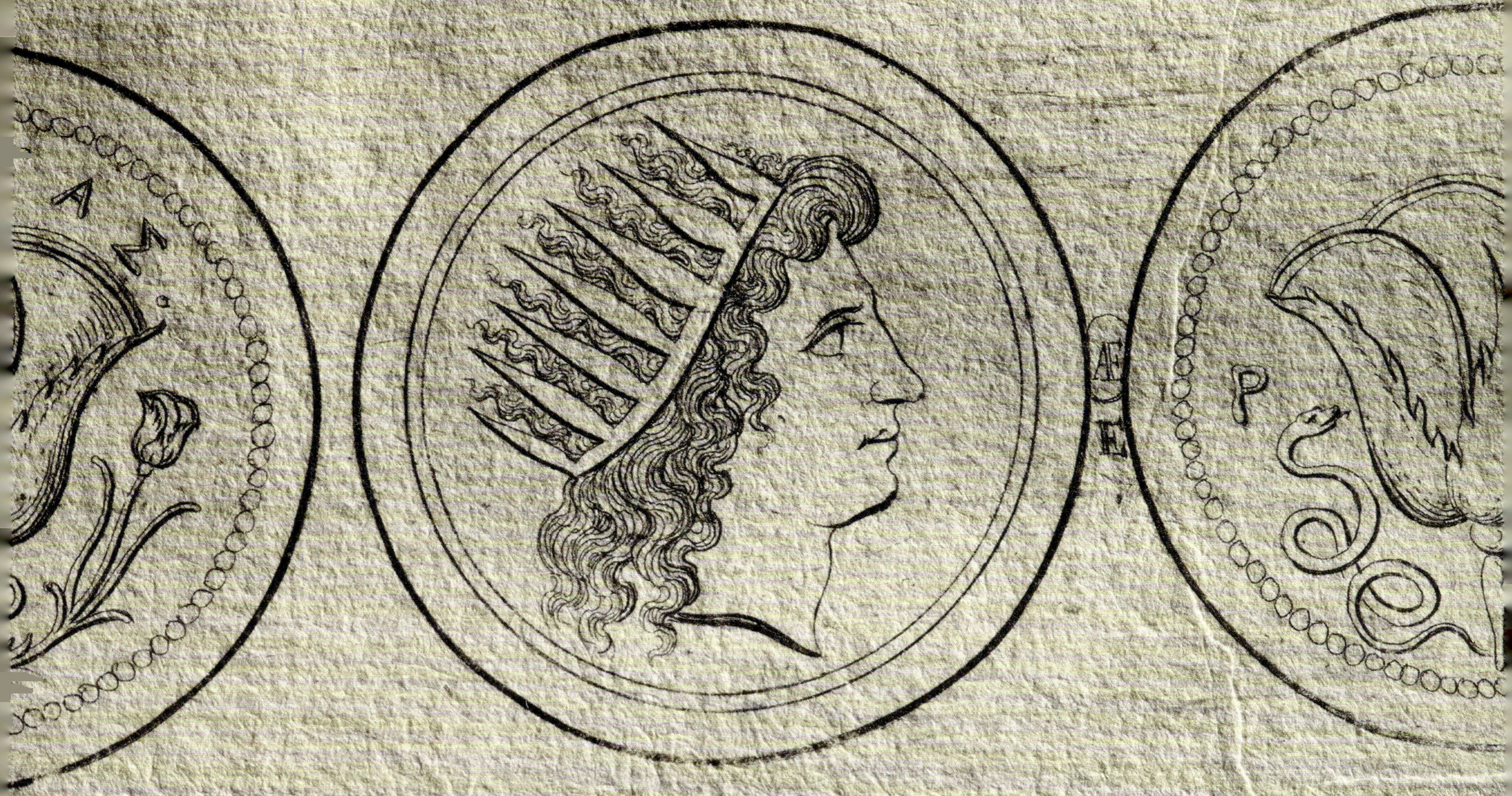

…aduceus est, cognomento Ἐπιπολιαῖο…
…niô constat. Ἐπιπολιαῖος, inquit, Ἑρμῆ…
…eus Rhodi, ut refert Gorgon. De Serp…
…ὠνείσης ὄφεις ὑπερμεγέθεις, συνέβη πολλοὺς…
…um terra Rhodiorum, inquit, *ingentes S…*

ēē nonnullos qui ei de oceano ingressum negent. Nec dubium in illā quoq; australis generis temperatā mare de oceano simil influere. sed describi hoc nr̄a adtestatione non debuit. cuius situs nob incognitus p̄seuerat.

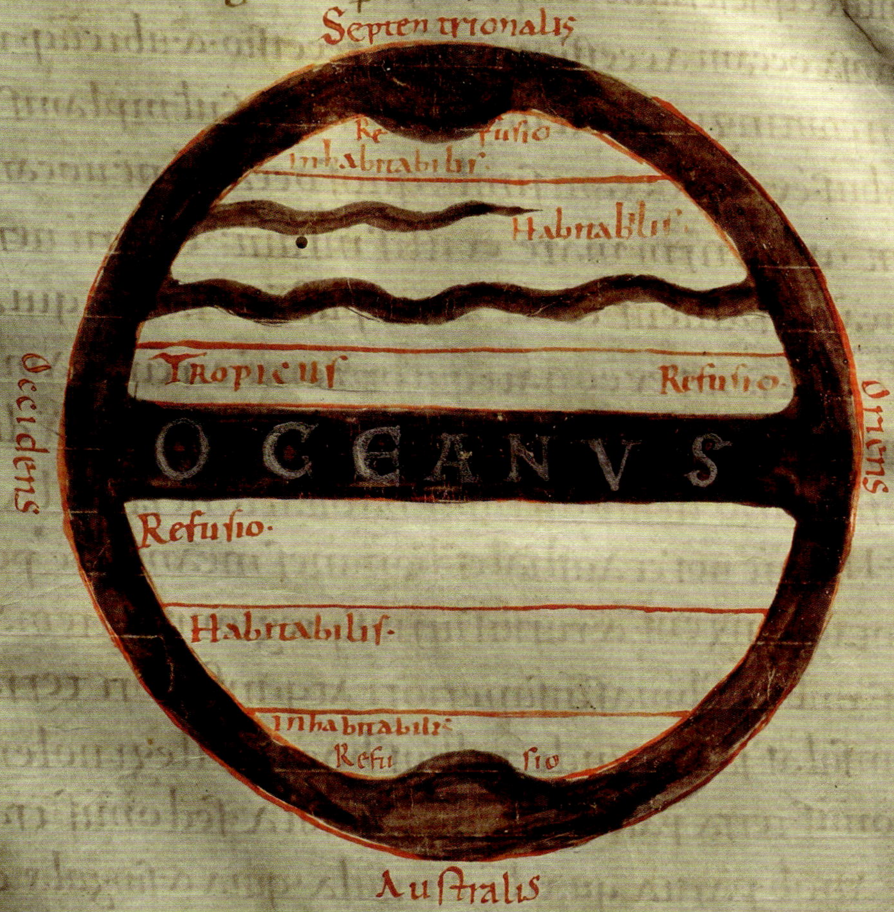

Quod aūt nr̄am habitabilē dix angustā uerticib; lateribus latiorē. in eadē descriptione poterimus aduertere. Nā quā longior ē tropicus circus septētrionali circo tanto con uerticib; quā laterib; angustior ē. quia summitas eius in arcū extremi circuli breuitate contrahit. Deductio a

Q

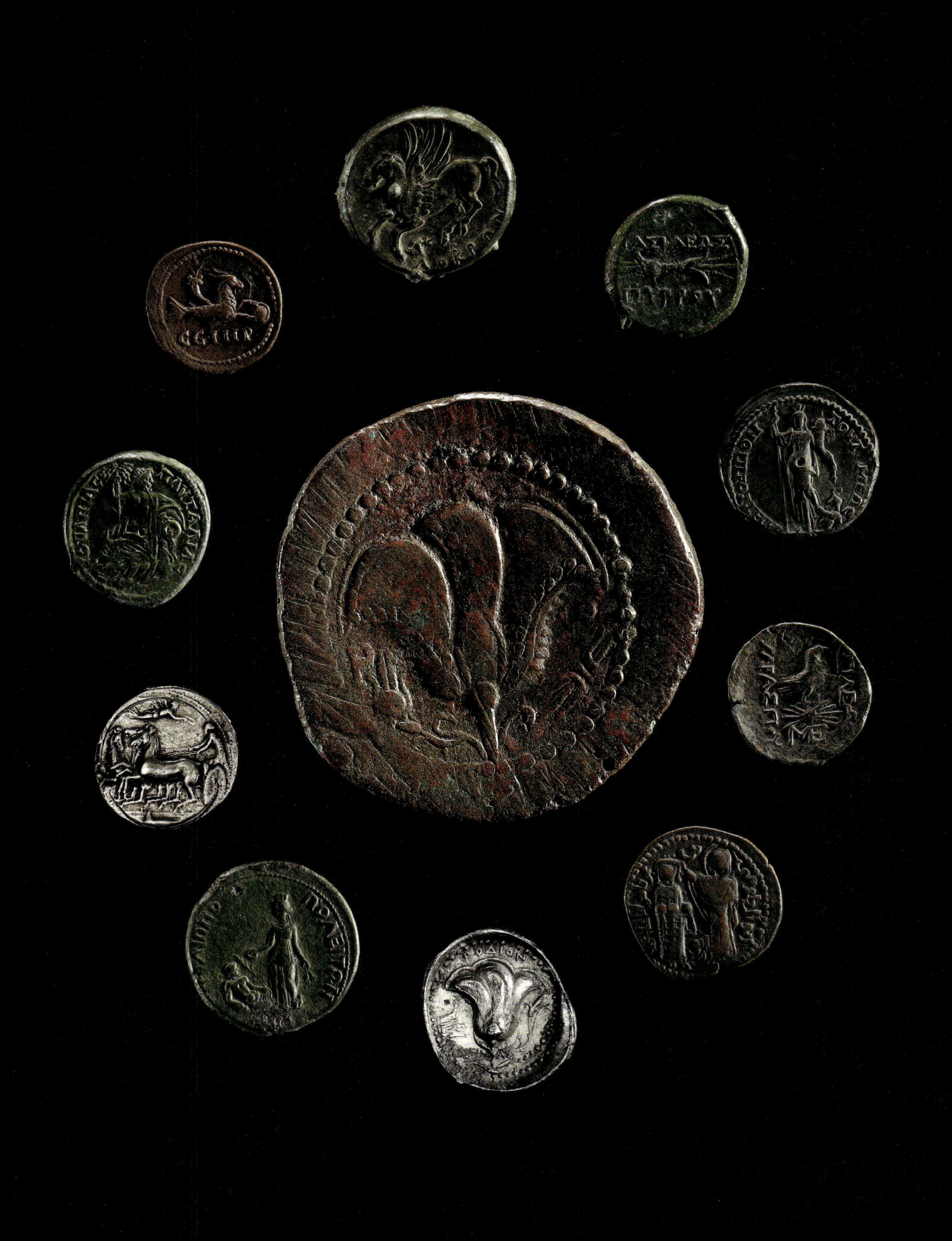

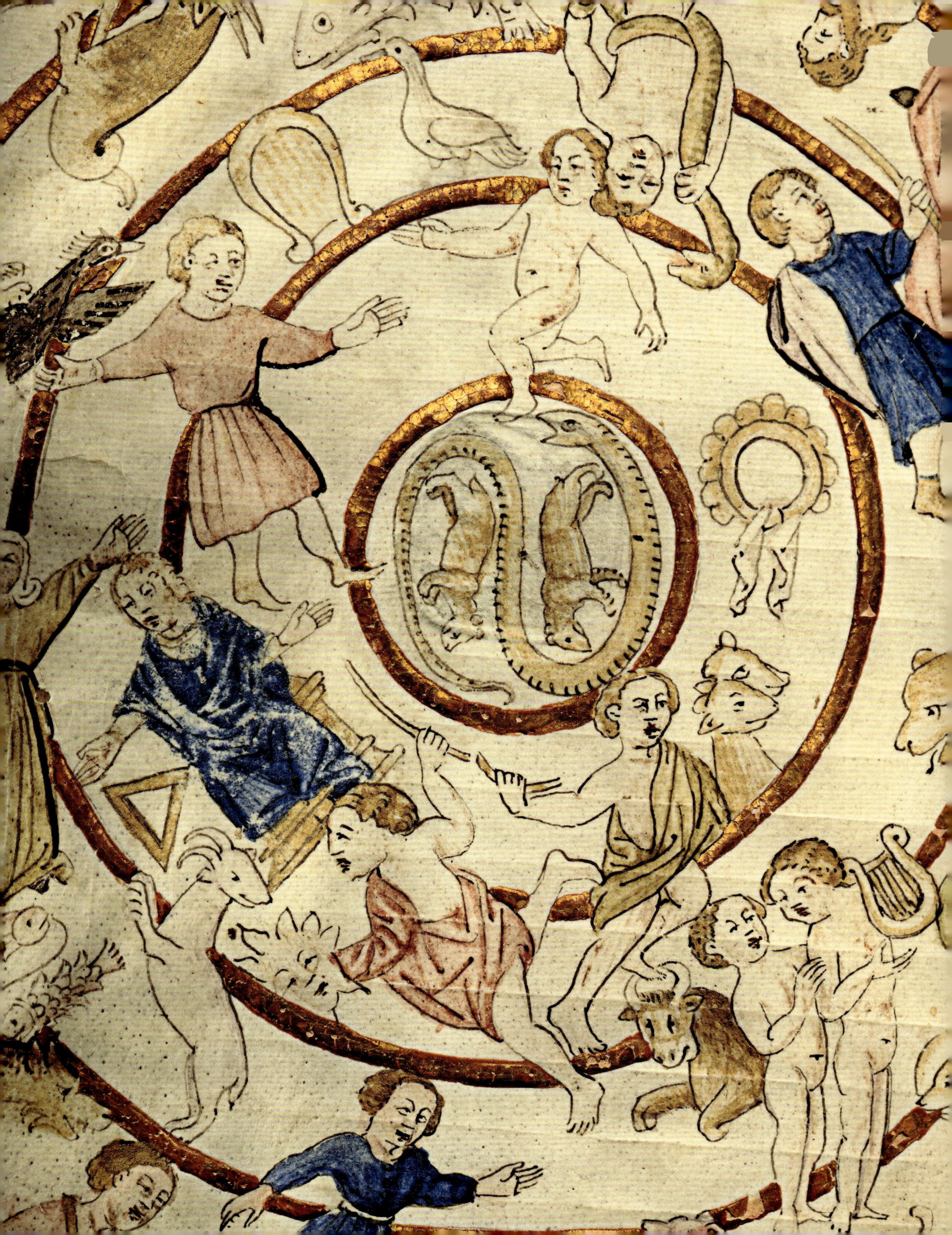

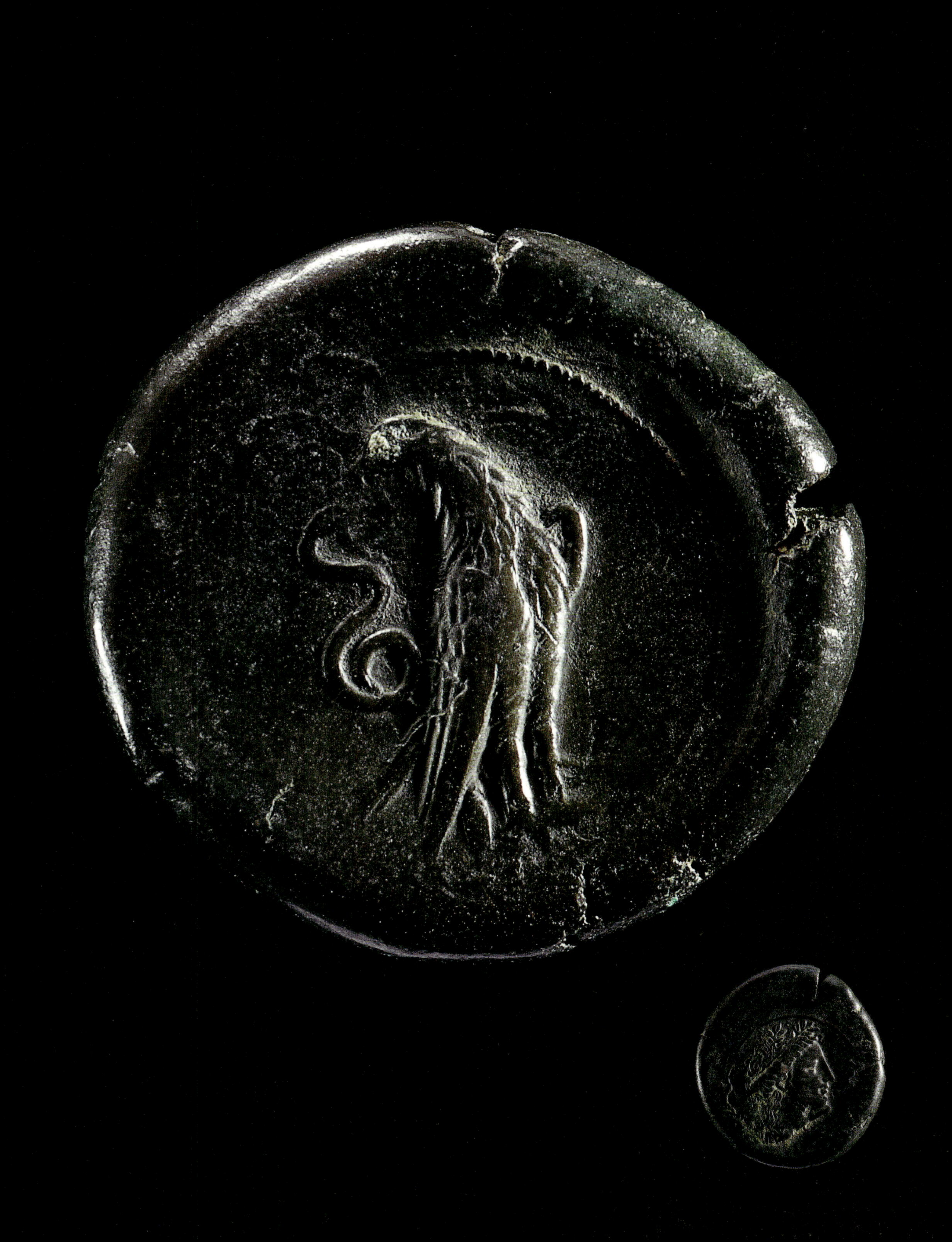

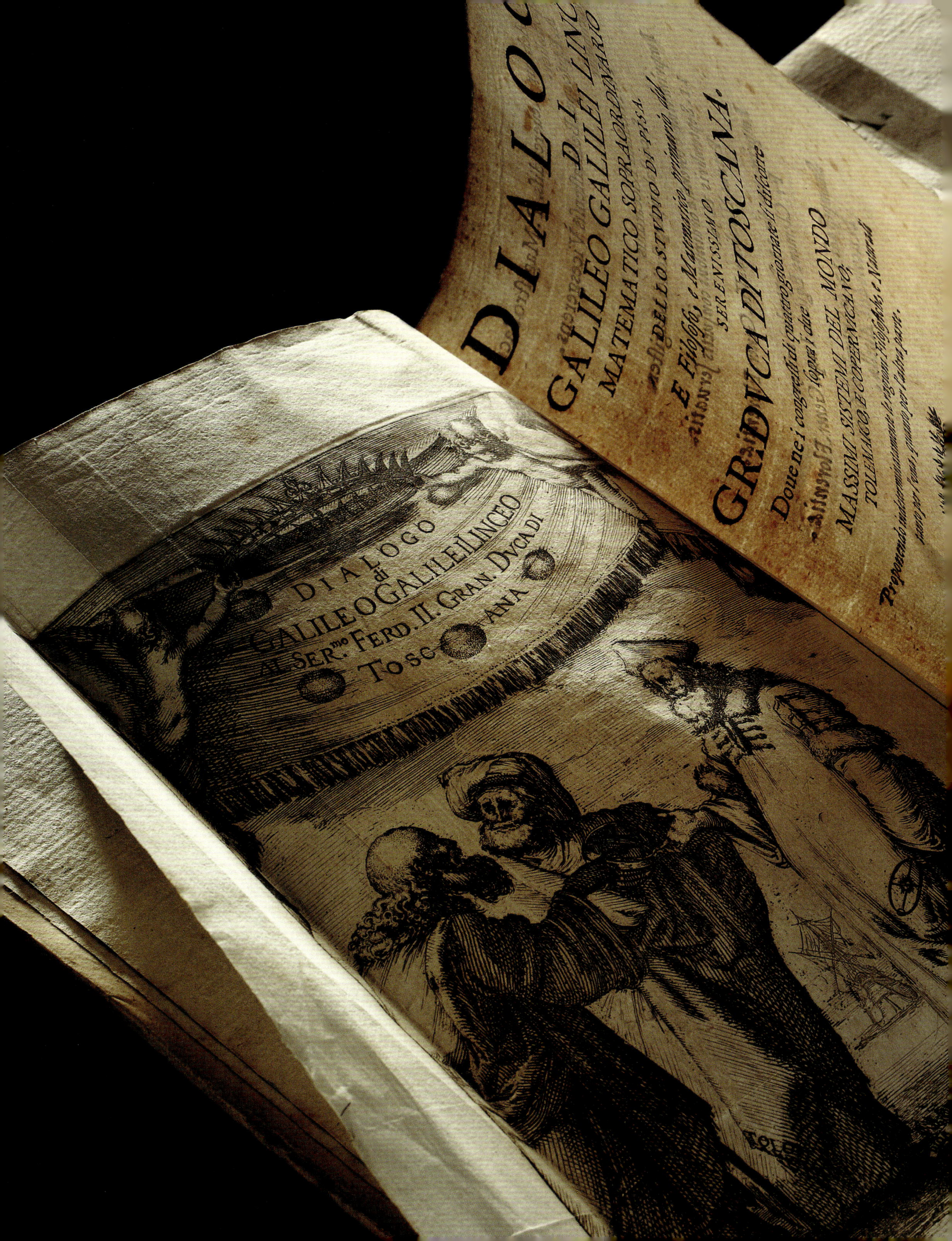
DIALO
DI
GALILEO GALILEI LINC
MATEMATICO SOPRAORDINARIO
DELLO STUDIO DI PISA.
E Filosofo, e Matematico primario del
SERENISSIMO
GR. DVCA DI TOSCANA.
Doue ne i congressi di quattro giornate si discorre
sopra i due
MASSIMI SISTEMI DEL MONDO
TOLEMAICO, E COPERNICANO;
DIALOGO
di
GALILEO GALILEI LINCEO
AL SER.mo FERD. II. GRAN DVCA DI
TOSCANA

NICOLAI COPERNICI REVOLVTIONVM

LIBER TERTIVS.

De æquinoctiorum solstitiorumq́ anticipatione. Cap. I.

STELLARVM fixarum facie depicta, ad ea quæ annuæ reuolutionis sunt, transeundũ nobis est, & eam ob causam de mutatione æquinoctiorum, propter quam stellæ quoq́ fixæ moueri creduntur, primo tractabimus. Inuenimus autem priscos Mathematicos annũ uertentem siue naturalem, qui ab æquinoctio uel solsticio est, non distinxisse ab eo, qui ab aliqua stellarum fixarum sumitur. Hinc est quod annos Olympiacos, quos ab exortu Caniculæ auspicabantur, eosdem esse putarent, qui sunt à solstitio, nondum cognita differentia alterius ab altero. Hipparchus autẽ Rhodius uir miræ sagacitatis, primus animaduertit hæc inuicem distare, qui dum anni magnitudinẽ attentius obseruaret: maiorem inuenit eum ad stellas fixas comparatum quàm ad æquinoctia siue solstitia. Vnde existimauit stellis quoq́ fixis aliquem inesse motum in consequẽtia, sed lentulum adeo nec statim perceptibilem. At iam tractu temporis factus est euidentissimus, quo longe iam alium ortum & occasum signorum & stellarum cernimus ab antiquorum præscripto. Ac dodecatemoria signorum circuli à stellarum hærentium signis magno satis interuallo à se inuicem recesserũt, quæ primitus nominibus simul ac positione congruebant. Ipse præterea motus inæqualis reperitur, cuius diuersitatis causam reddere uollentes, diuersas attulerunt sententias. Alij libramentum esse quoddam mundi pendentis, qualem & in planetis motũ inuenimus circa latitudines eorum, atq́ hinc inde à certis limitibus quantũ processerit, rediturum aliquando censuerunt, & esse expatiationem eius utrobiq́ à medio suo nõ maiorem VIII. gradibus. Sed hæc opinio iam antiquata residere nõ potuit, eo maxime quod

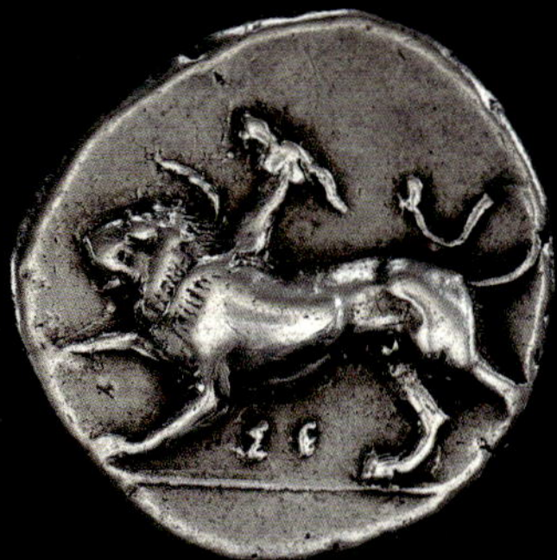

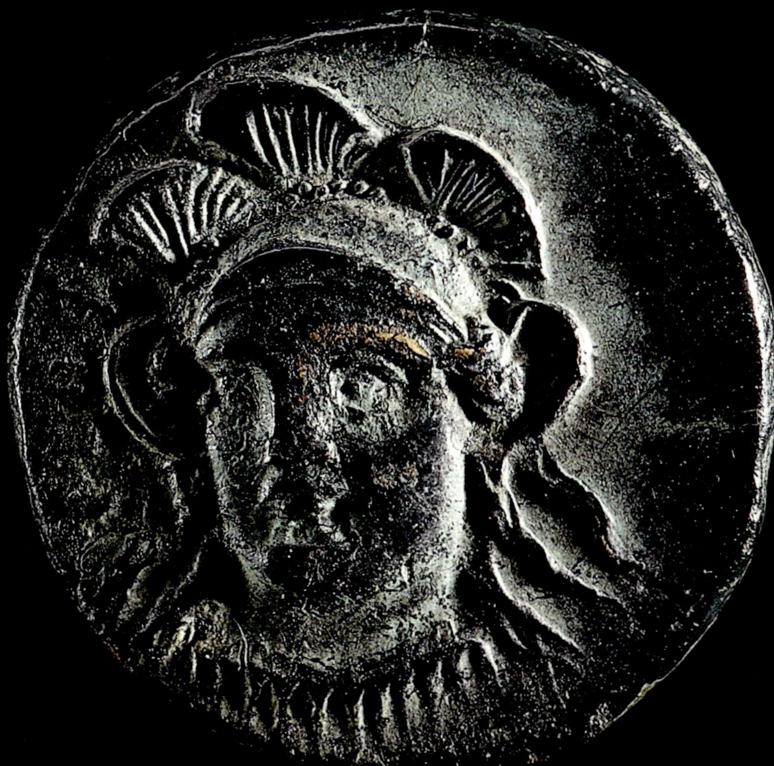

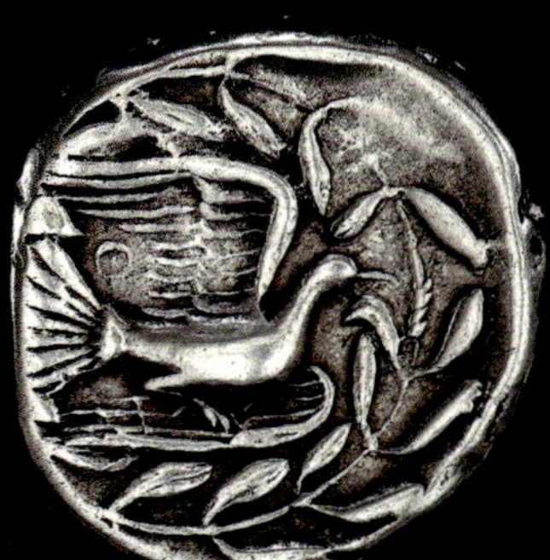

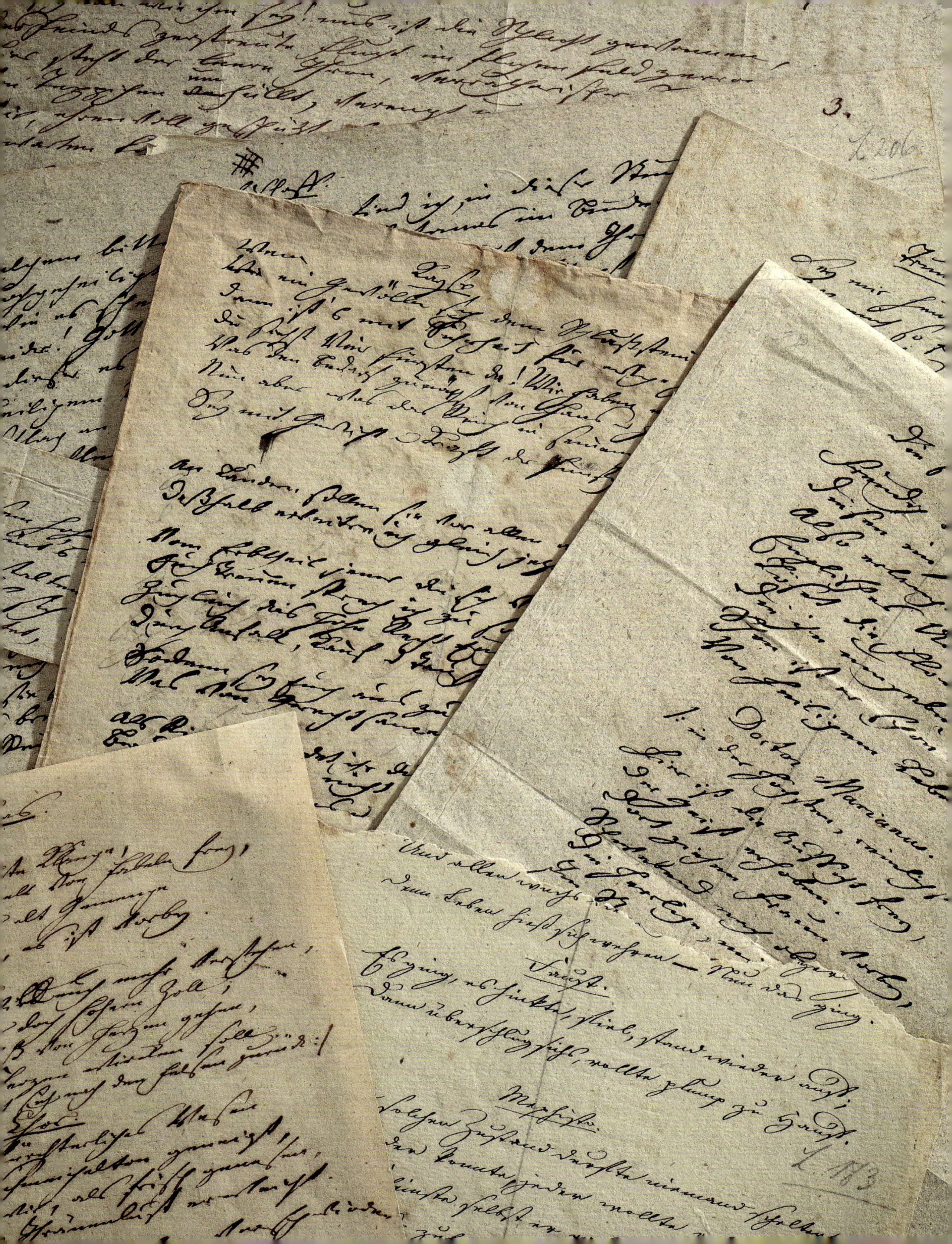
3.
1. Doctor Marianus.
Faust.
Mephisto.

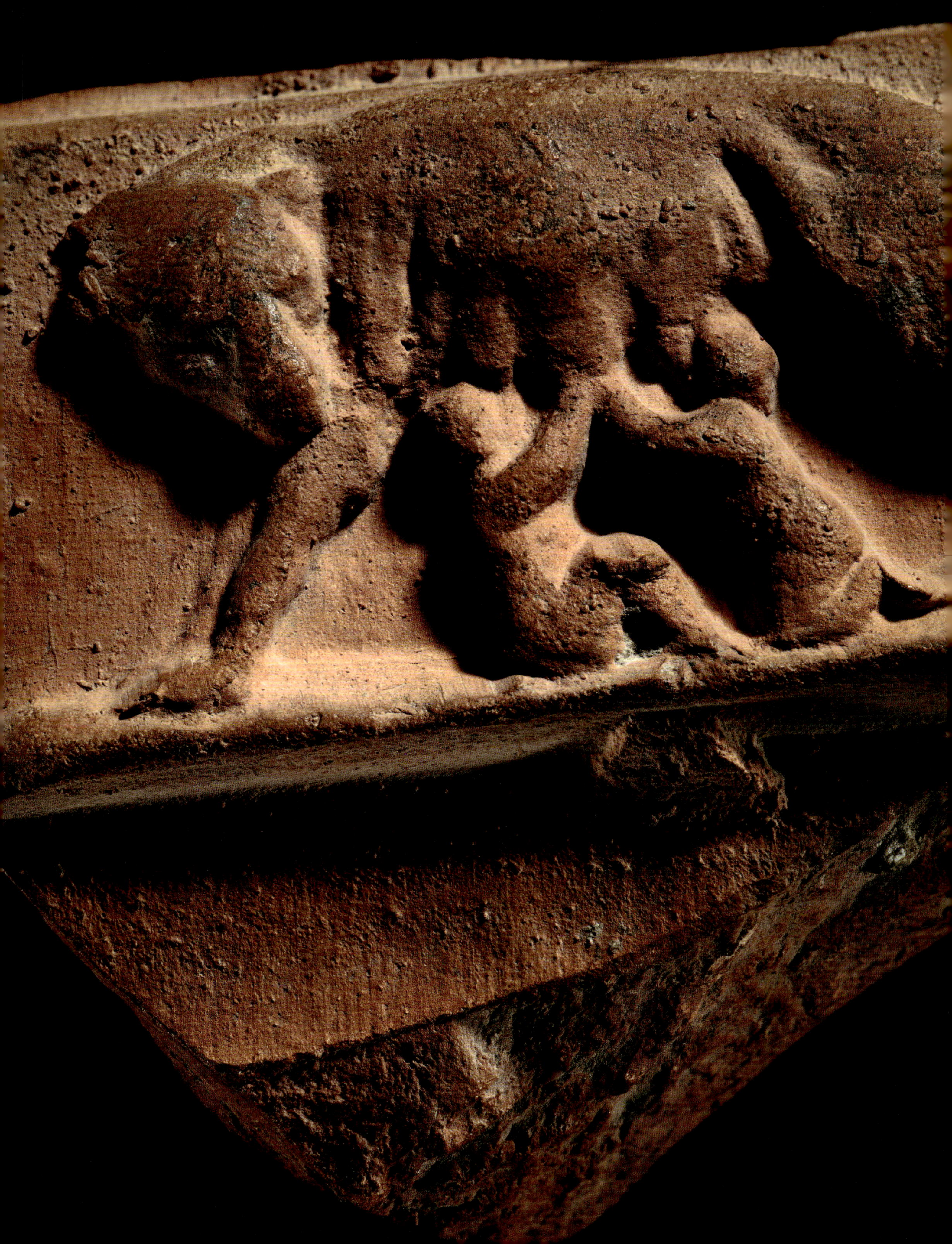

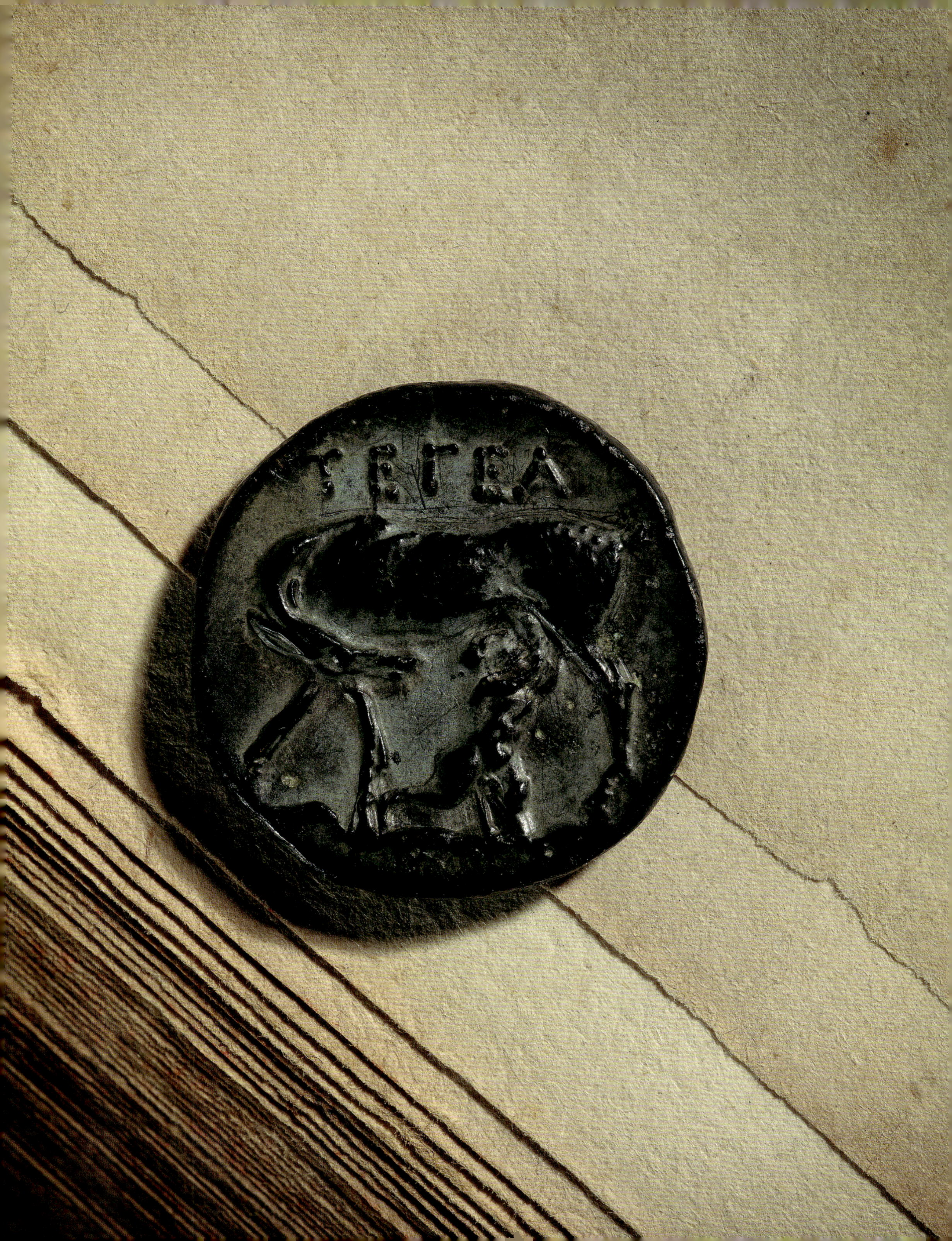
ΤΕΓΕΑ

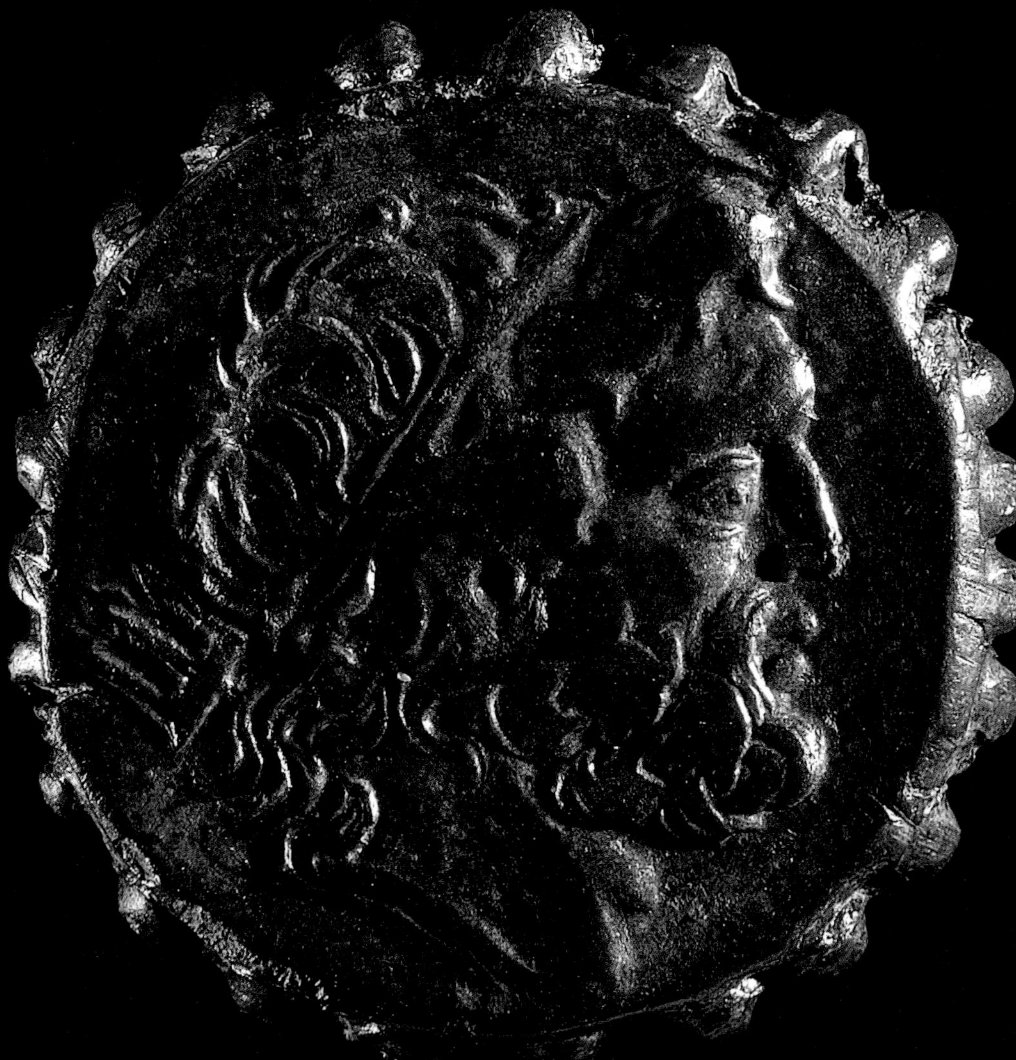

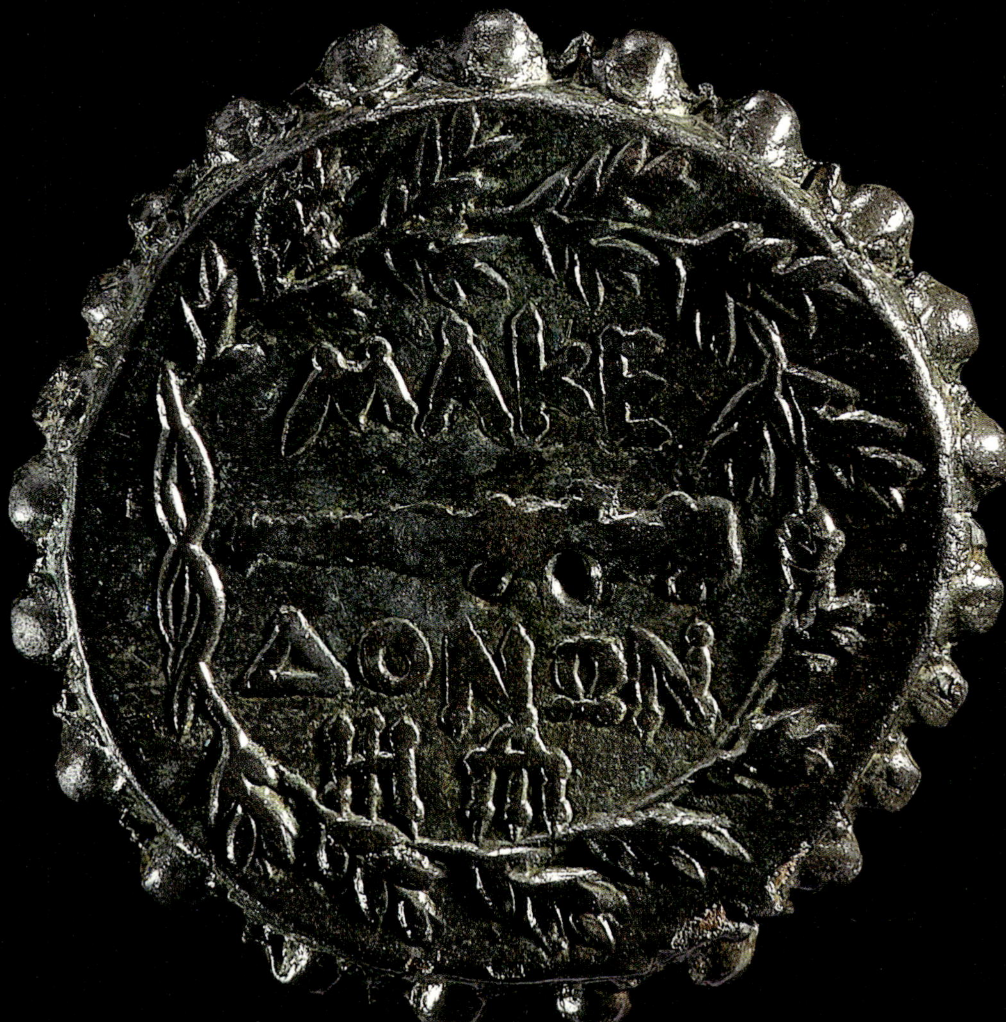
ΜΑΚΕ
ΔΟΝΩΝ

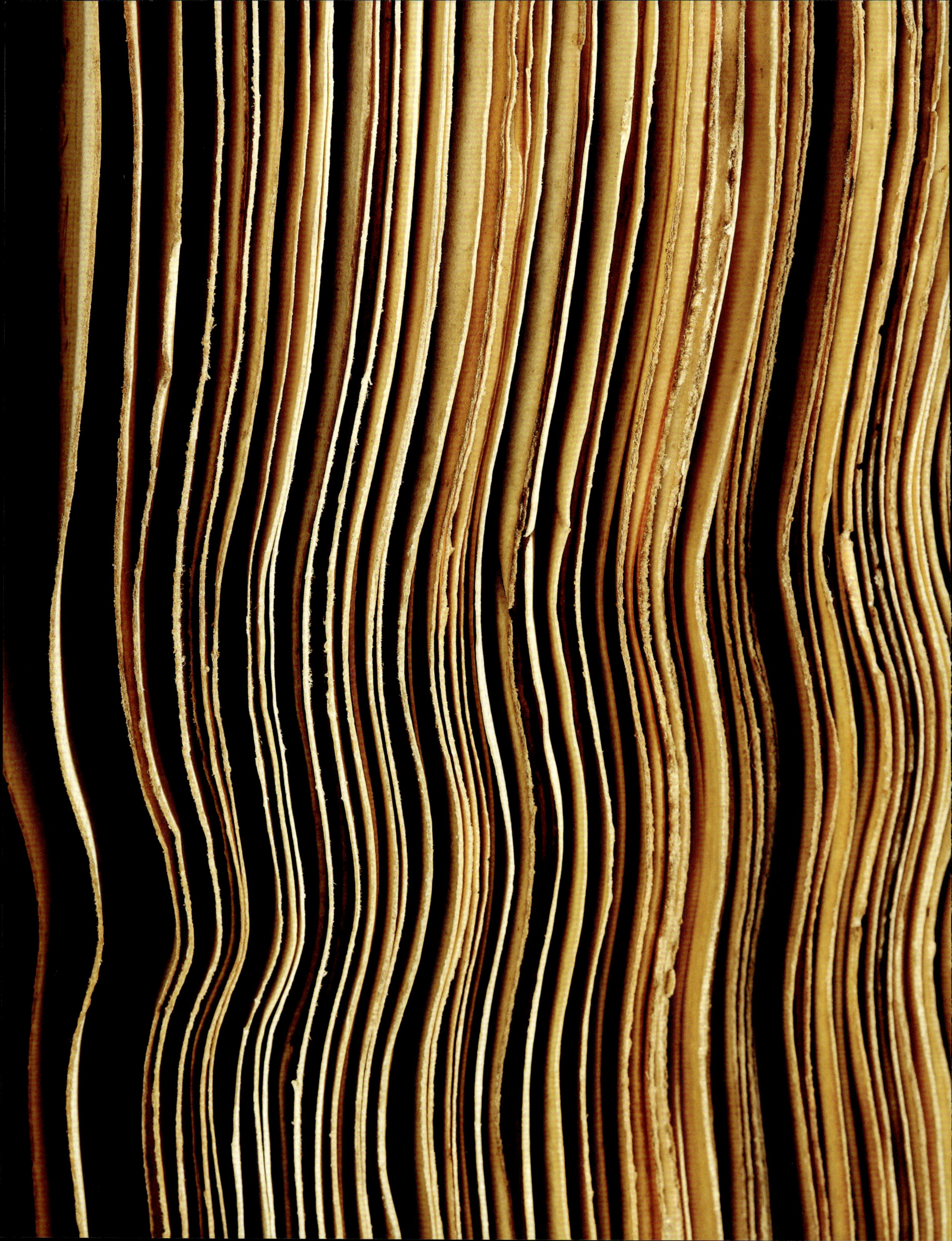

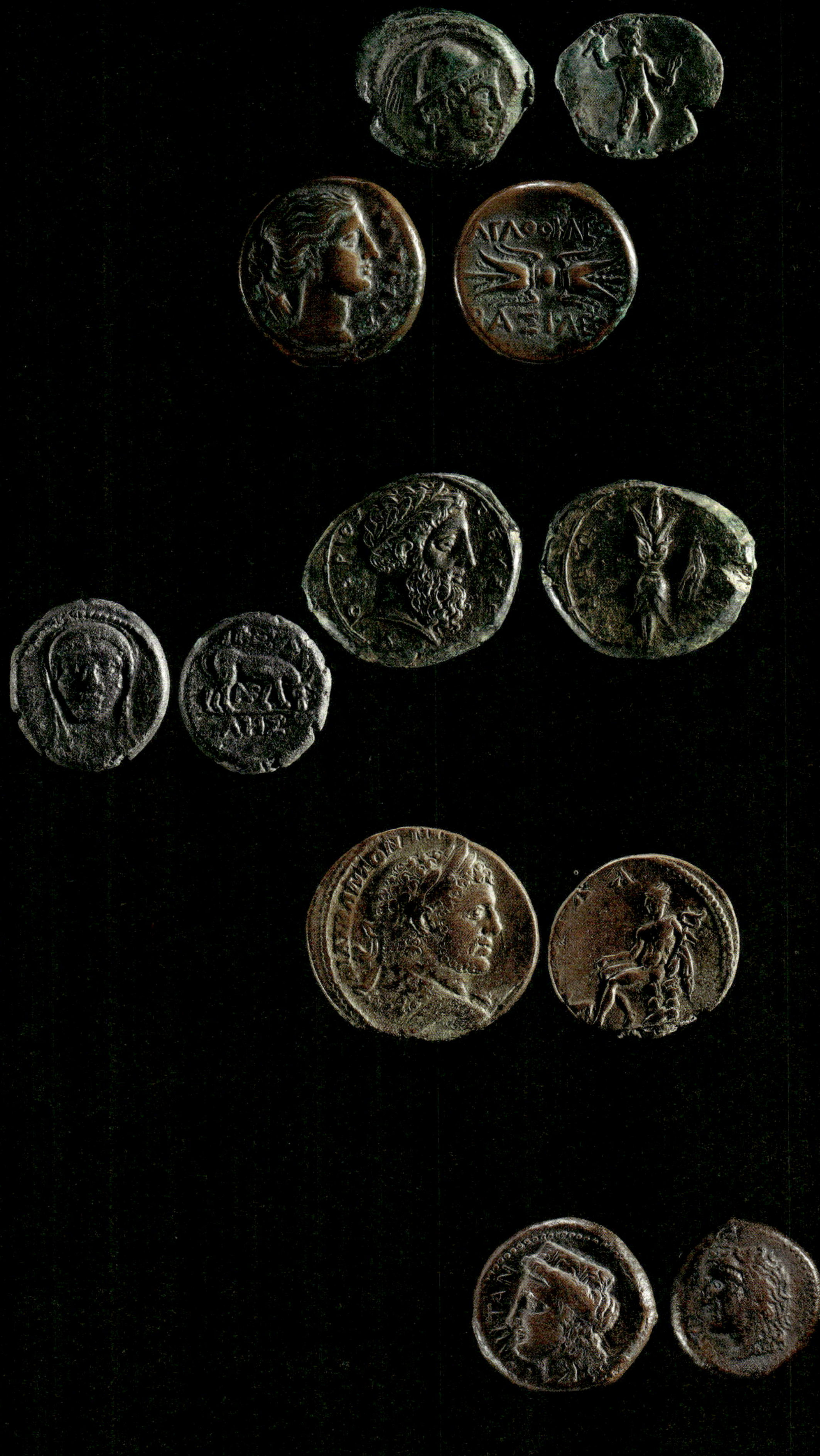

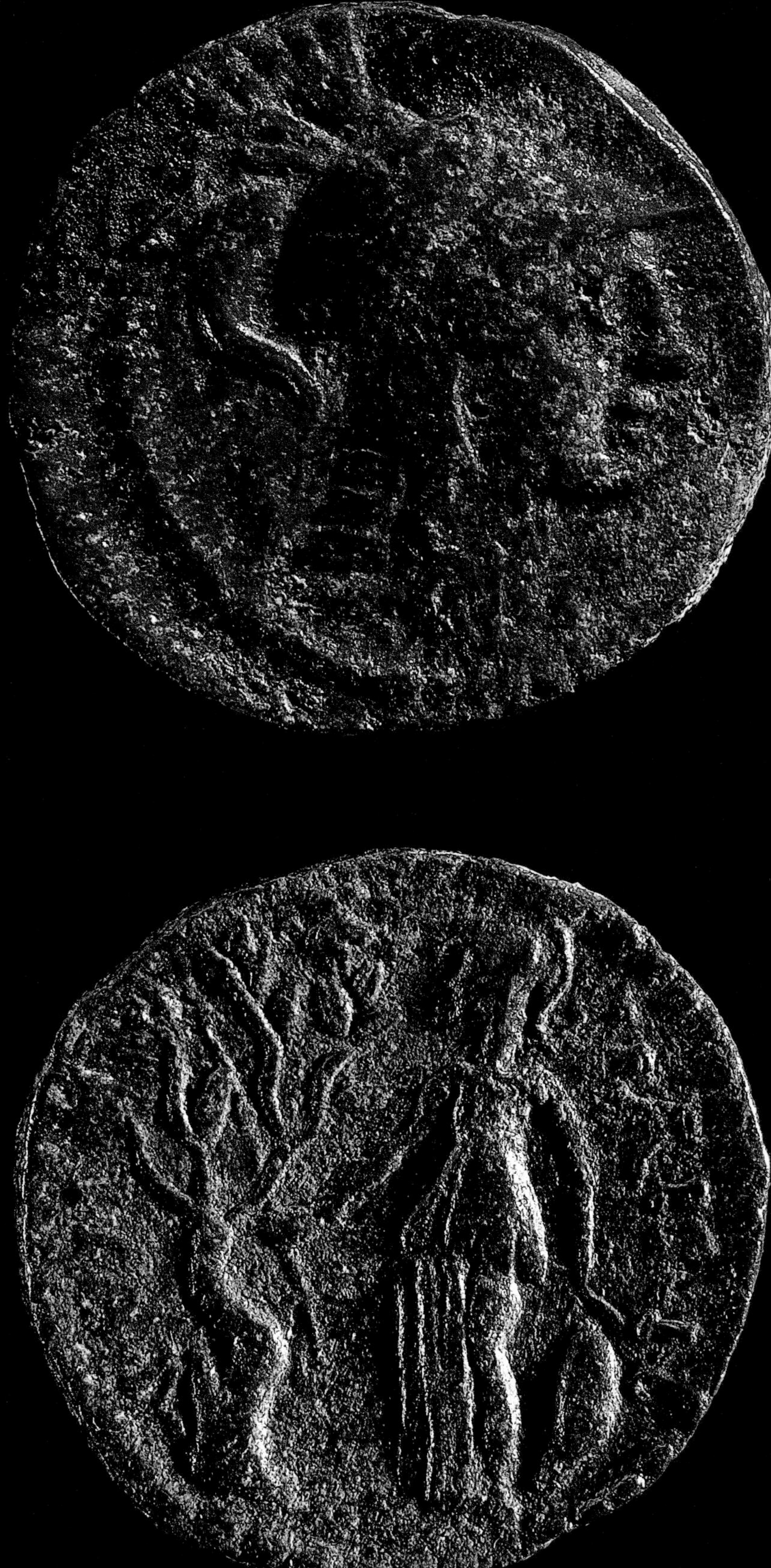

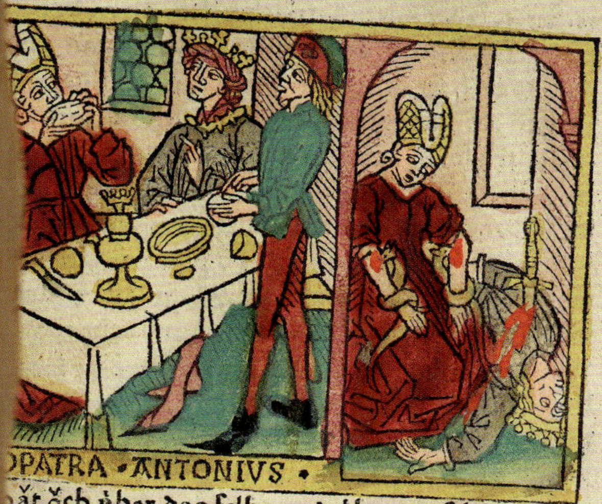

ät öch über das selb / vnd über die schöny ieres
kain wäre durchlüchtikait an ir gehabt / wan̄
erwiderum̄ / durch ir gytikait / vnküsche werk /
ortliche übel / ō ganczen welt schamloß gesenh
an̄ dionisi? oder mine? ir vatter / was der römer
ly deß kaisers / öbrister fründ / das erst jär syner
ing / vnd als er sterben solt / ließ er ain testamēt
m dz ō eltist sun / lisania gehaissen / syne schwest
rä ze wyb neme / die öch die eltist tochter was /
äch ierer gesaczt wol tün mochten / vnd die
ch synem tod regieren sölten. Wan̄ die schant-
ikait was in egipten gemain / dz kain lyplich
ee wenden solt / wan̄ allain der vätter vn̄ müt
gen ieren kinden / das ward volbrächt / aber
ie tag die ynbrünstige begirlikait / das küng-
in zeregierē wachsen ward / fiel sie in sollich
s übel / das sie den selben jüngling / erst funft-
alten / ieren brüder vn̄ man / mit vergifftem

Καὶ πόθον. ἔρχεσθε δὲ πρὸς ἀῶ, μή τι λάθησθαι.
Νεύμεθα κἄμμες ἐς ὄρθρον, ἐπεί κα πρᾶτος ἀοιδὸς
ἐξ εὐνᾶς κελαδήσῃ, ἀνασχὼν εὔτριχα δειρήν.
Ὑμὰν ὦ Ὑμέναιε γάμῳ ἐπὶ τῷδε χαρείης.

Τέλος τοῦ Θεοκρίτου

ἩΣΙΟΔΟΥ ΤΟΥ ἈΣΚΡΑΙΟΥ ἘΡΓΑ ΚΑΙ ἩΜΕΡΑΙ.

μ οῦσαι πιερίηθεν ἀοιδῆσι
κλείουσαι
δεῦτε δή, ἔννεπετε σφέτερον πατέρ'
ὑμνείουσαι.
ὅντε διὰ βροτοὶ ἄνδρες ὁμῶς ἄφατοί τε φατοί τε
ῥητοί τ' ἄρρητοί τε. διὸς μεγάλοιο ἕκητι.
ῥέα μὲν γὰρ βριάει. ῥέα δὲ βριάοντα χαλέπτει.
ῥεῖα δ' ἀρίζηλον μινύθει. καὶ ἄδηλον ἀέξει.
ῥεῖα δέ τ' ἰθύνει σκολιὸν καὶ ἀγήνορα κάρφει.
Ζεὺς ὑψιβρεμέτης. ὃς ὑπέρτατα δώματα ναίει.
Κλῦθι ἰδὼν ἀΐων τε δίκῃ δ' ἴθυνε θέμιστας
τύνη. ἐγὼ δέ κε πέρσῃ ἐτήτυμα μυθησαίμην
οὐκ ἄρα μοῦνον ἔην ἐρίδων γένος. ἀλλ' ἐπὶ γαῖαν
εἰσὶ δύω. τὴν μέν κεν ἐπαινήσειε νοήσας.
ἡ δ' ἐπιμωμητή. διὰ δ' ἄνδιχα θυμὸν ἔχουσιν
ἡ μὲν γὰρ πόλεμόν τε κακὸν καὶ δῆριν ὀφέλλει
σχετλίη. οὔτις τήνγε φιλεῖ βροτὸς ἀλλ' ὑπ' ἀνάγκης
ἀθανάτων βουλῆσιν ἔριν τιμῶσι βαρεῖαν
τὴν δ' ἑτέρην προτέρην μὲν ἐγείνατο νὺξ ἐρεβεννὴ
θῆκε δέ μιν κρονίδης ὑψίζυγος αἰθέρι ναίων
γαίης τ' ἐν ῥίζῃσι καὶ ἀνδράσι πολλὸν ἀμείνω
ἥτε καὶ ἀπάλαμόν περ ὁμῶς ἐπὶ ἔργον ἐγείρει. bella super
εἰς ἕτερον γάρ τίς τε ἰδὼν ἔργοιο χατίζων
πλούσιον, ὃς σπεύδει μὲν ἀρόμμεναι, ἠδὲ φυτεύειν.
οἶκόν τ' εὖ θέσθαι. ζηλοῖ δέ τε γείτονα γείτων.
εἰς ἄφενον σπεύδοντ'. ἀγαθὴ δ' ἔρις ἥδε βροτοῖσι.

εἰ

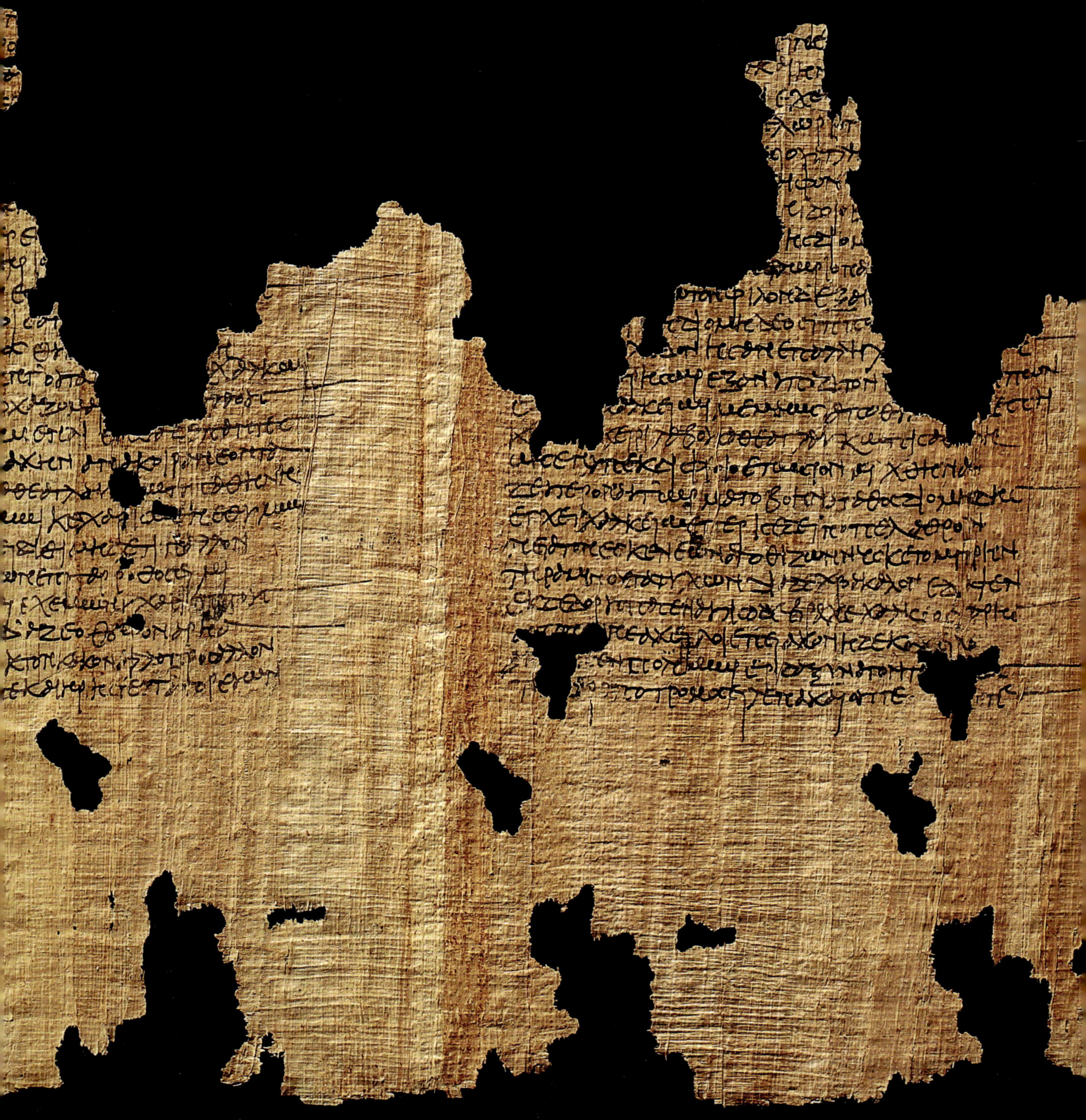

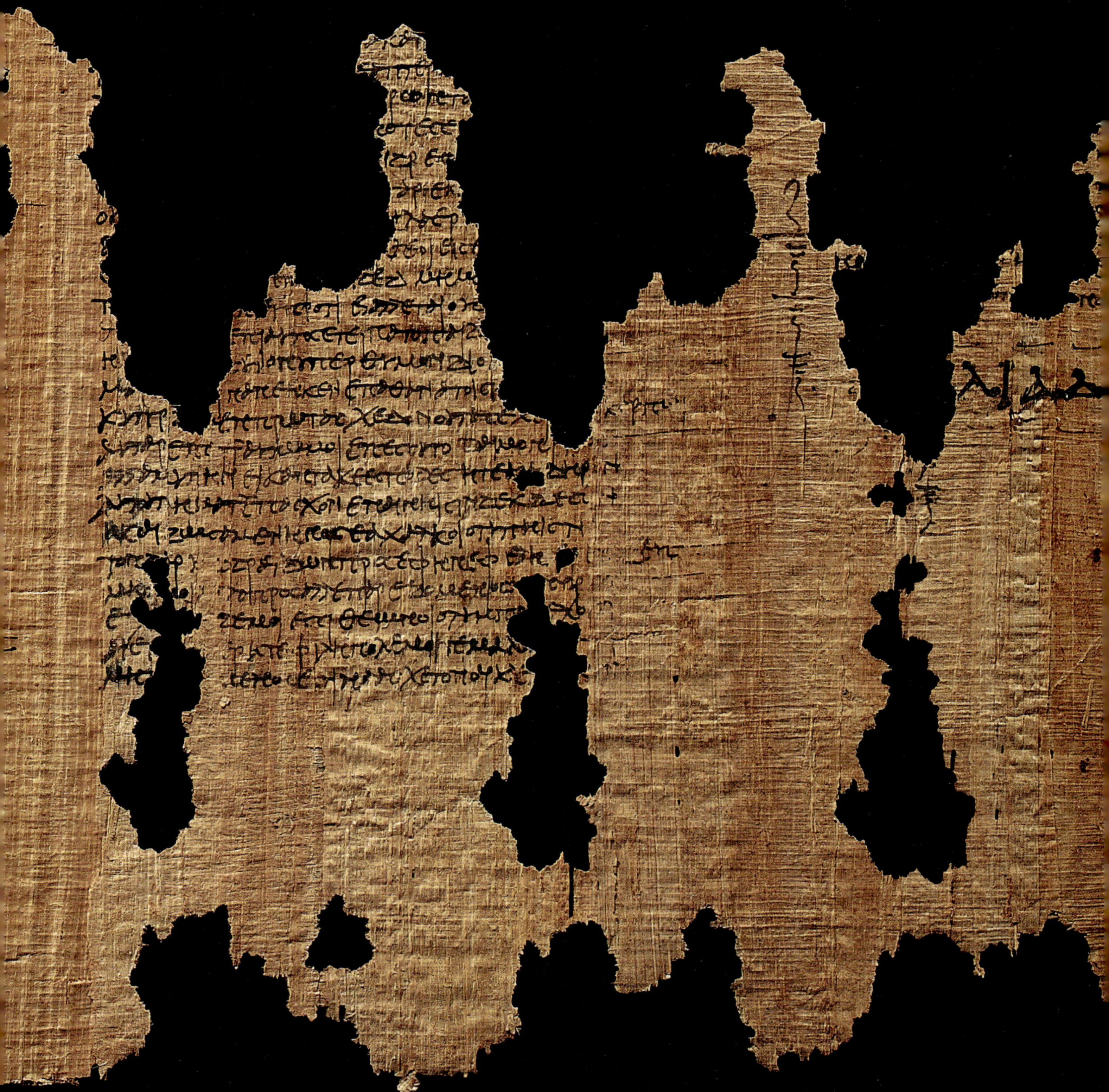

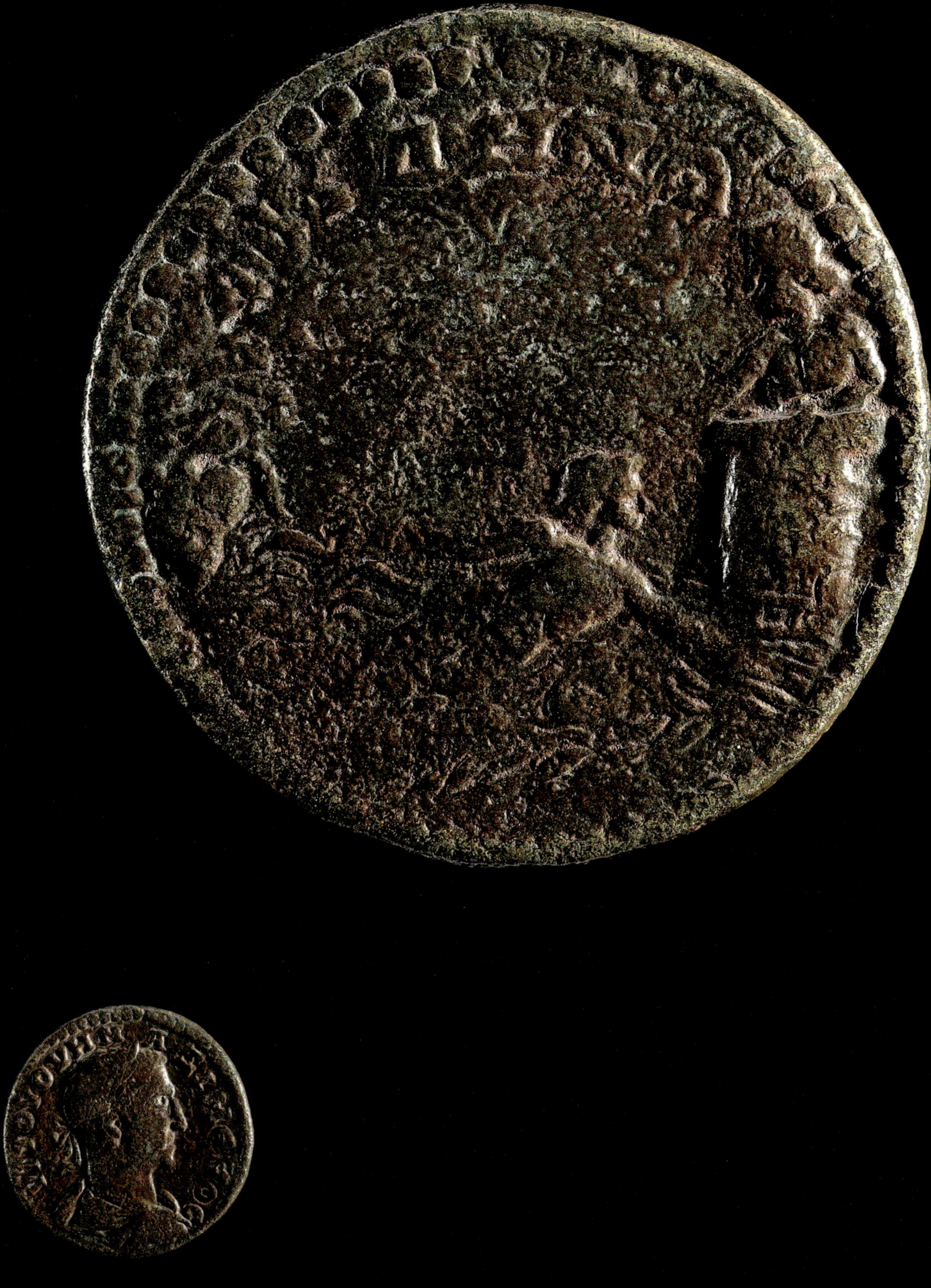

maliloquus.

De Tantalo duodecimo Iouis ſecundi filio. C. xlv.

Lacedęmonis expedita proſapia: ad reliquos Iouis ſecundi filios redeundum eſt: ex quibus duodecimum Tantalum dicit Theodontius Iouis fuiſſe filium. Fuit enim is antiquiſſimus Corinthiorum rex: & pius homo: atq; deorum menſis ſępe accubuit. Quod ideo fictũ puto: quia cęlſiſſima ſit arx Corinthiorum adeo: ut ſi quis eam aſcẽdat: in cęlum uideatur conſcendere: & eſſe cum ſuperis.

De Hercule.xiiii.ſecũdi Iouis filio: qui genuit Carthaginẽ. C. xlvi.

Hercules hic a Cicerone in libro de naturis deorum cognominatꝰ .iiii.& ab eodem dicitur Iouis filius ex Aſterie ſorore Latonę ſuſceptus. Hunc pręterea ſũme a Tyriis coli dicit: & ex eo Carthaginem filiam genitam.

De Carthagine. iiii. Herculis filia. C. xlvii.

Carthago (ut proximo ſupra mõſtratũ eſt) Herculis q̃rti fuit filia: quam nos Carthaginem nuncupamus: quę ideo Herculis filia dicta eſt: quia a Phoenicibus: qui Herculem ſumme colebant poſita eſt Herculis dei ſui auſpicio.

De Minerua ſecundi Iouis filia.xiiii. C. xlviii.

Minerua: non ea cui cognomen tritonia fuit: iouis ſecũdi fuit filia: ut ſcribit Tullius de naturis deoꝝ: quã ideȝ Tullius inuẽtricẽ aſſerit fuiſſe bellorum atq; principem: & ob id a nõnullis bellona appellata eſt: & ſoror Martis: & auriga: ut teſtari Statius uidetur dicens. Regit atra iugales Sanguinea bellona manu: longaq; fatigat Cuſpide. & cętera. Nec ea fuit hęc: quam ueteres uirginem & ſterilem aſſeruere: quinimmo (ut idem dicit Tullius) ex Vulcano Cęli filio antiquiſſimo Apollinem primum peperit. Pręterea (ut dicit Leõtius) hęc eſt: quam armis inſignem finxere: oculis toruam: haſtamq; gerentem longiſſimam cũ cryſtallino clypeo: & hoc magis ad oſtẽtationem inuenti a ſe belli: q̃ ob aliquod aliud ſignificatũ: quod ego non credo: quinimo inſignia illa ad aliquod myſterium oſtendendũ appoſita omnia puto. Nam cũ omnes aſſiduis infeſtemur bellis: armatam fingi puto: ut doceamur prouidos uiros ſemper in armis cõſiſtere. i. cõſiliis: quibus ad emergentia poſſint obſiſtere. Qꝫ oculos habeat toruos: oſtendit ſapientem de facili capi nõ poſſe: cum utplurimũ exterioribus actibus longe aliud ſe oſtendat agere: q̃ gerat animo: uti toruus alibi reſpicit: q̃ intuentes eius faciem arbitrentur. haſta autẽ illi dicatur longiſſima: ut noſcamus prudentem uirũ etiam longinqua cognoſcere: & ex longinquo ictus infigere: atq; a ſe inſidiantes repellere. Cryſtallinum autem ideo illi clypeum attributum ẽ: ut appareat ĩ tranſparenti cryſtallo atq; ſolido corpore ſapientem uirũ ęque ſimul & hoſtis uidere opa: & ſeipſũ remediis opportunis ꝑtegere

Huic inſuper dici
minis ciuitati At
ariopago agitatur
cuſſa laudabiliore
ob quam rem Ne
nerua autem haſt:
ſit equo: Minerua
uit Athenas: nam
figmenti eſt: ſic A
& huic Mineruae
fuiſſet aliq̃diu an
ualebat: an cõmod
naretur: quam ma
& mare uehat: ut e
oſus: & furore nim
oliuaꝝ abundans
cerneret circũſpe
trahi: & terreſtria
nominandã cenſui
Ego autem puto:
inter nautas & me
mum augeri naui
tem contra artibu
per oliuam demor
Quãobrem a diis.
ta eſt: & hic optim
nerua: quę artium
Iouem primum re
pe: & hic Cecropẽ
paucis abſoluit Le
a Cicrope: ſed ma
oliuam in arcem n

De Archade q
Ionium.

Archas Iouis
dius. Huius e
a Ioue: ut refert Pa
tam agens: cum ęt
dius) ab eodem ſu
oppreſſa eſt. Qu
ſotiis ad lauacrum

Ἀντιπάτρου.

Οὗτος ὁ λεάνδροιο διάπλοος· οὗτος ὁ πόντου
Πορθμὸς, ὁ μὴ μούνῳ τῷ φιλέοντι βαρύς.
Ταῦθ' ἥρους τὰ πάροιθε ἐπαύλια· τοῦτο τὸ πύργου
Λείψανον· ὁ προδότης ὧδ' ἐπέκειτο λύχνος.
Κοινὸς δ' ἀμφοτέρους ὅδ' ἔχει τάφος, εἰσέτι καὶ νῦν
Κείνῳ τῷ φθονερῷ μεμφομένους ἀνέμῳ.

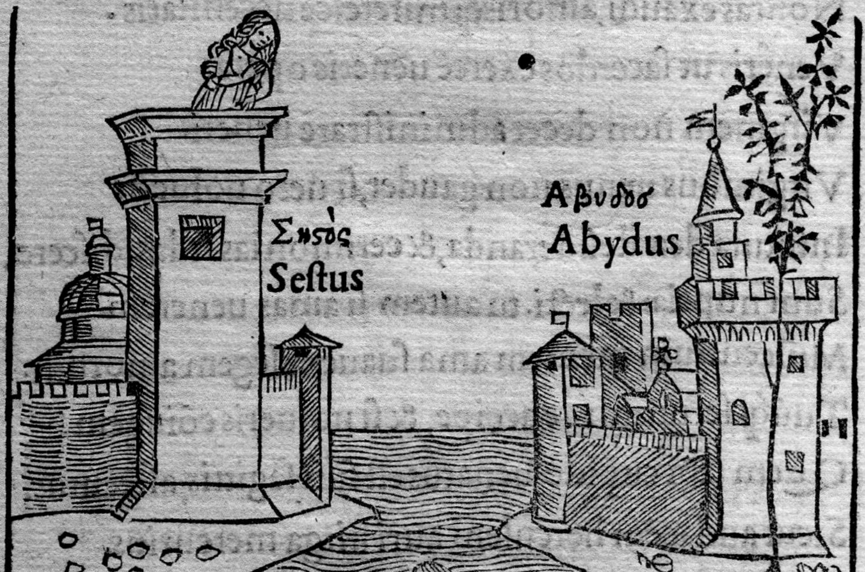

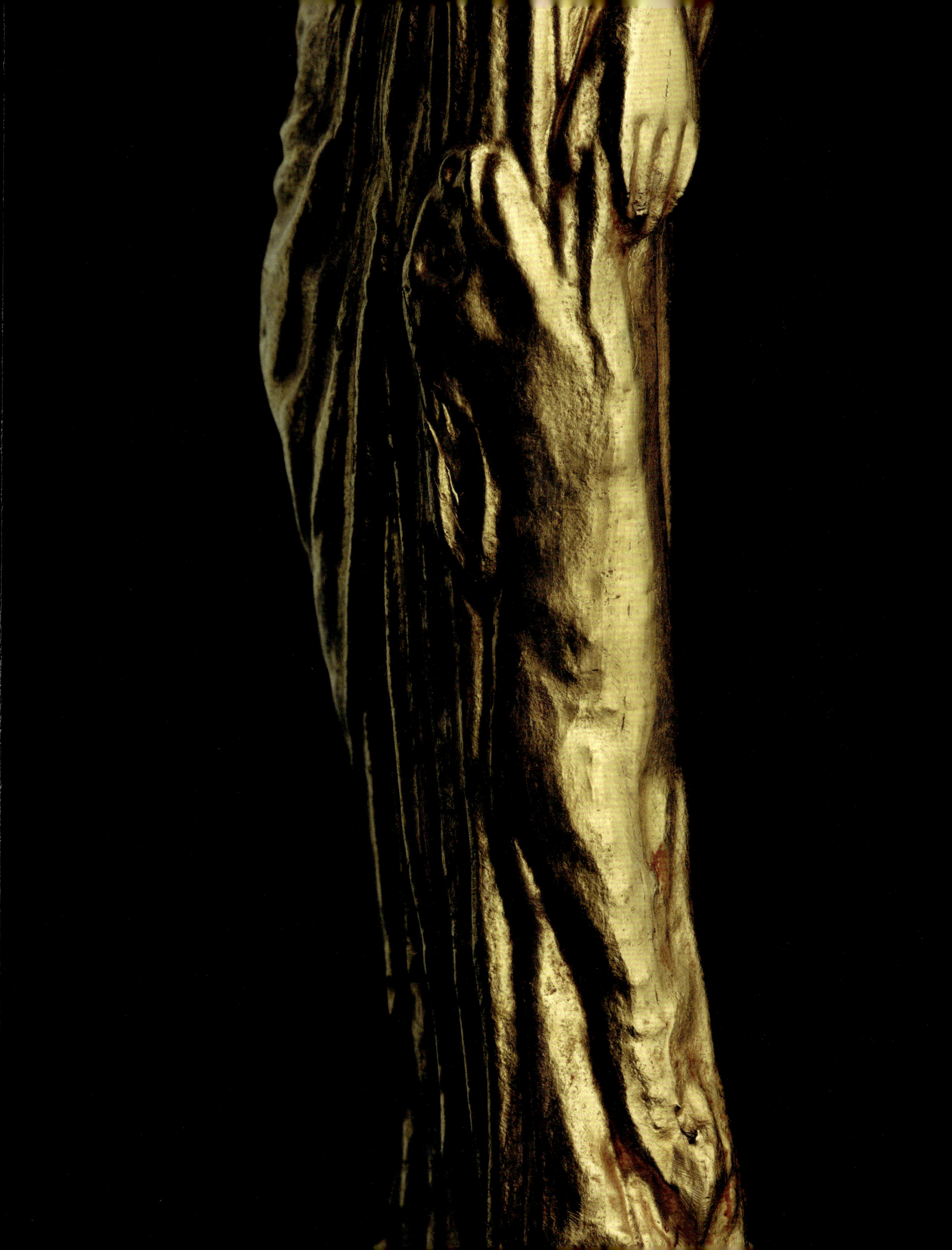

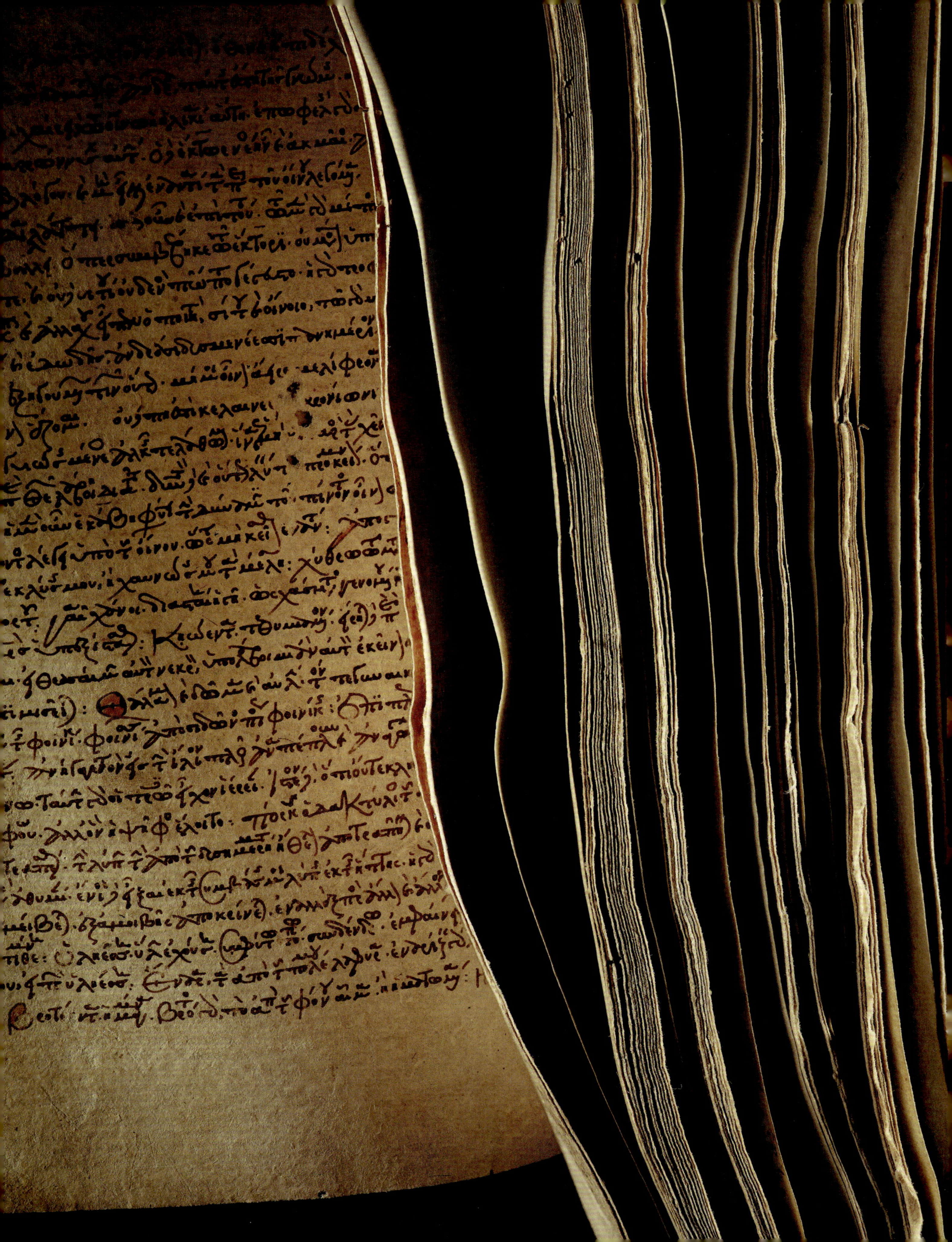

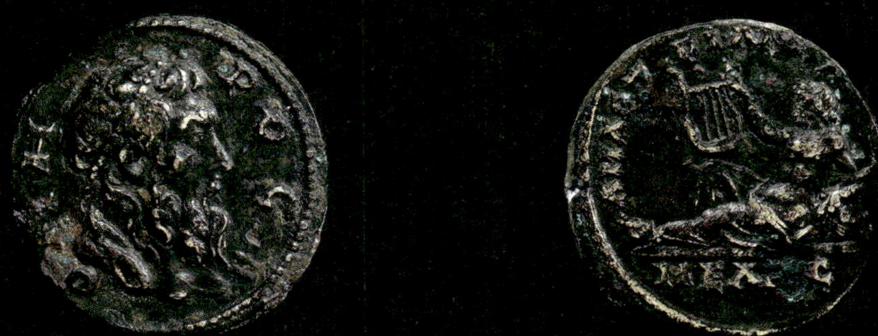

ΙΛΙΑΔ

ΟΜΗΡ

Α.

ΙΛΙΑΔΟΣ

ΟΜΗΡΟΥ

Α.

Μῆνιν ἄειδε, θεὰ, Πηληϊάδεω Ἀχιλῆος,
Οὐλομένην, ἣ μυρί' Ἀχαιοῖς ἄλγε' ἔθηκε,
Πολλὰς δ' ἰφθίμους ψυχὰς Ἄϊδι προΐαψεν
Ἡρώων, αὐτοὺς δὲ ἑλώρια τεῦχε κύνεσσιν
Οἰωνοῖσί τε πᾶσι· Διὸς δ' ἐτελείετο βουλή·
Ἐξ οὗ δὴ τὰ πρῶτα διαστήτην ἐρίσαντε
Ἀτρείδης τε, ἄναξ ἀνδρῶν, καὶ δῖος Ἀχιλλεύς.

Τίς τ' ἄρ σφωε θεῶν ἔριδι ξυνέηκε μάχεσθαι;
Λητοῦς καὶ Διὸς υἱός. ὁ γὰρ βασιλῆϊ χολωθεὶς,
Νοῦσον ἀνὰ στρατὸν ὦρσε κακὴν, ὀλέκοντο δὲ λαοὶ,
Οὕνεκα τὸν Χρύσην ἠτίμησ' ἀρητῆρα
Ἀτρείδης. ὁ γὰρ ἦλθε θοὰς ἐπὶ νῆας Ἀχαιῶν,
Λυσόμενός τε θύγατρα, φέρων τ' ἀπερείσι' ἄποινα,

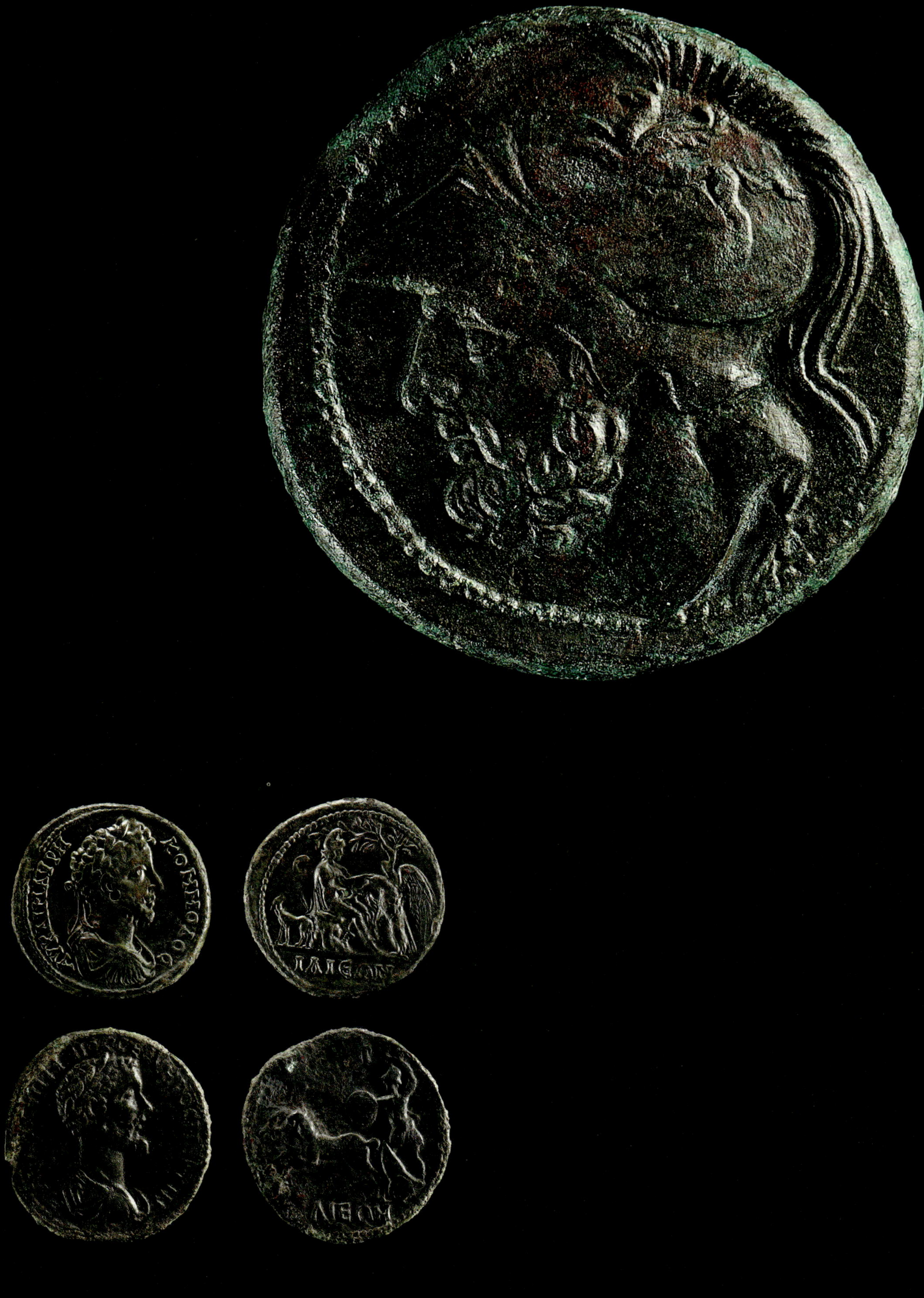

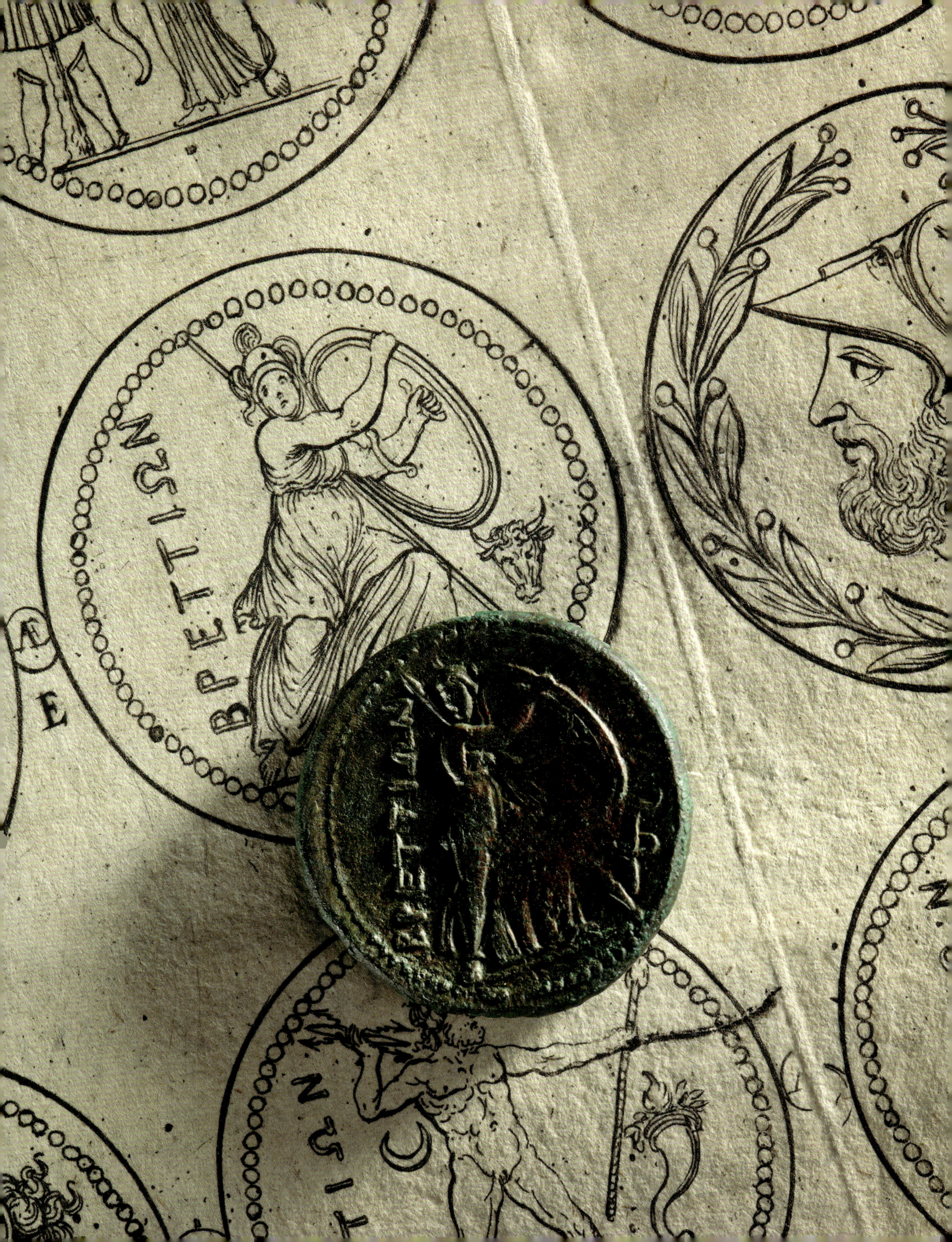
ΒΡΕΤΤΙΩΝ
Æ
E

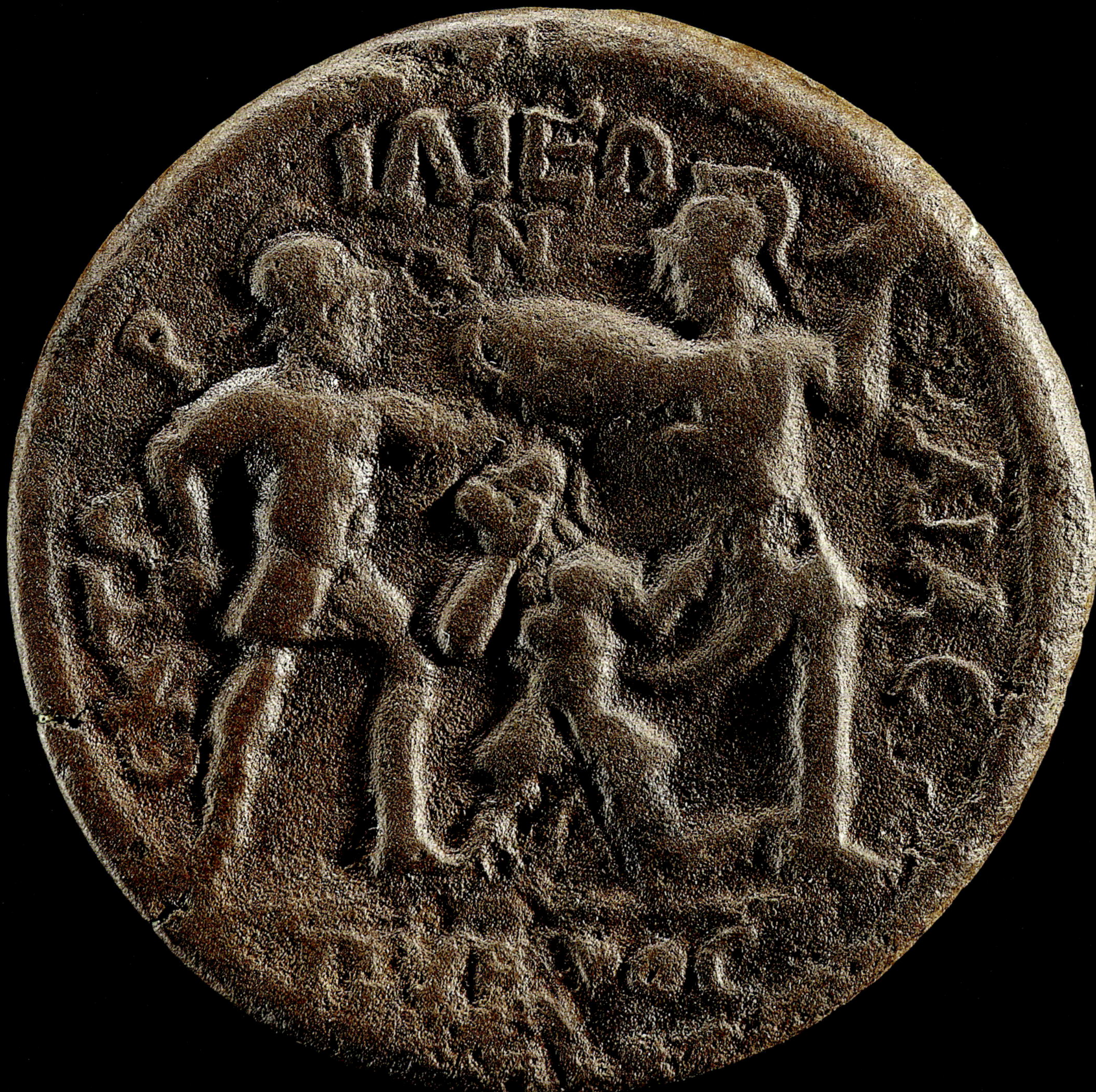

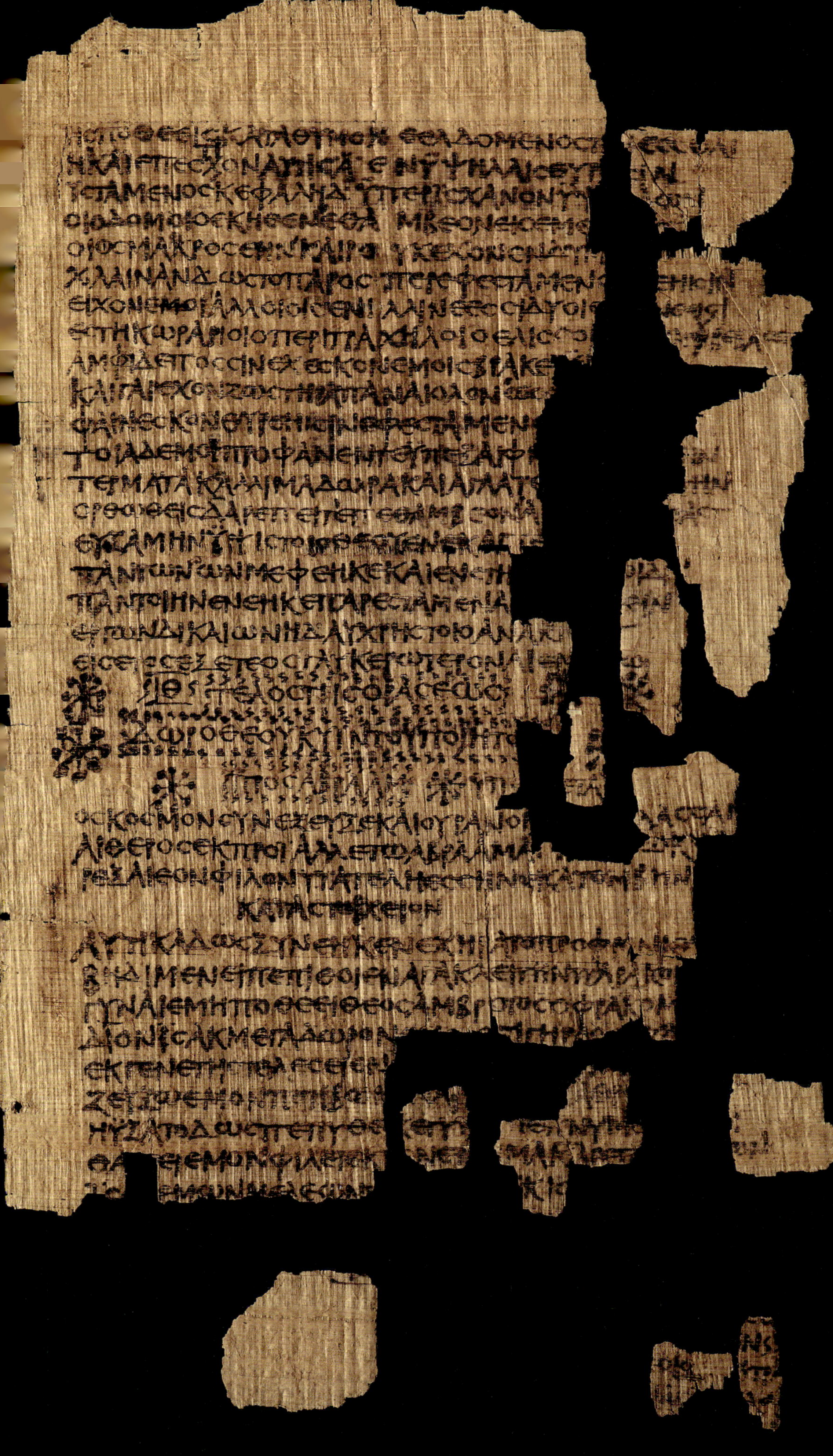
ΤΕΛΟΣ ΤΗΣ ΟΡΑΣΕΩΣ
ΔΩΡΟΘΕΟΥ ΚΥΙΝΤΟΥ ΠΟΙΗΤΟ

desired; that a small rivulet ...
such immense alluvial deposits in a few hundre[d]
of the question; in my opinion several thousan[d]
for it. The Bounarbashi-Sou inundates in ma[ny]
~~tificially heightened~~ right bank and forms in seve[ral]
the largest is at the ~~place~~ where the channel
~~From this point an uninterrupted~~ this large ~~...~~
~~four distance of ... three miles and~~
this large swamp, ~~which~~ receives all the ...
waters which do not flow off by the ...
extends for a distance of more than ~~three~~ three miles ...
abt a mile ~~north of Bounar~~bashi to the north
has a large tank ~~...~~ more than 30 ft deep
most carefully explored this swamp I ca[n]
reader that, ~~contrary~~ all the topographers
have committed an error in stating th[at]
communicates with the Scamander or ...
at all of the Bounarbashi Sou runs ...
That is most decidedly not the case. ...
in the swamp [at the foot of the height on which stands the tumulus of Hagios Demetrios Tepe] there is a slight current
it is merely the consequence of ~~produced by~~ the ~~...~~ ...
of the water in the northern part of the swamp. ...

*[1] Essay on the Original Genius and Writings of Homer London 1769

*[2] Voyage de la Troade

*[3] Journal of a tour in Asia Minor

Obiges ist von Dr. Heinrich Schliemann in Athen eigenhändig geschrieben.
Berlin 23/2 90. Rud Virchow.

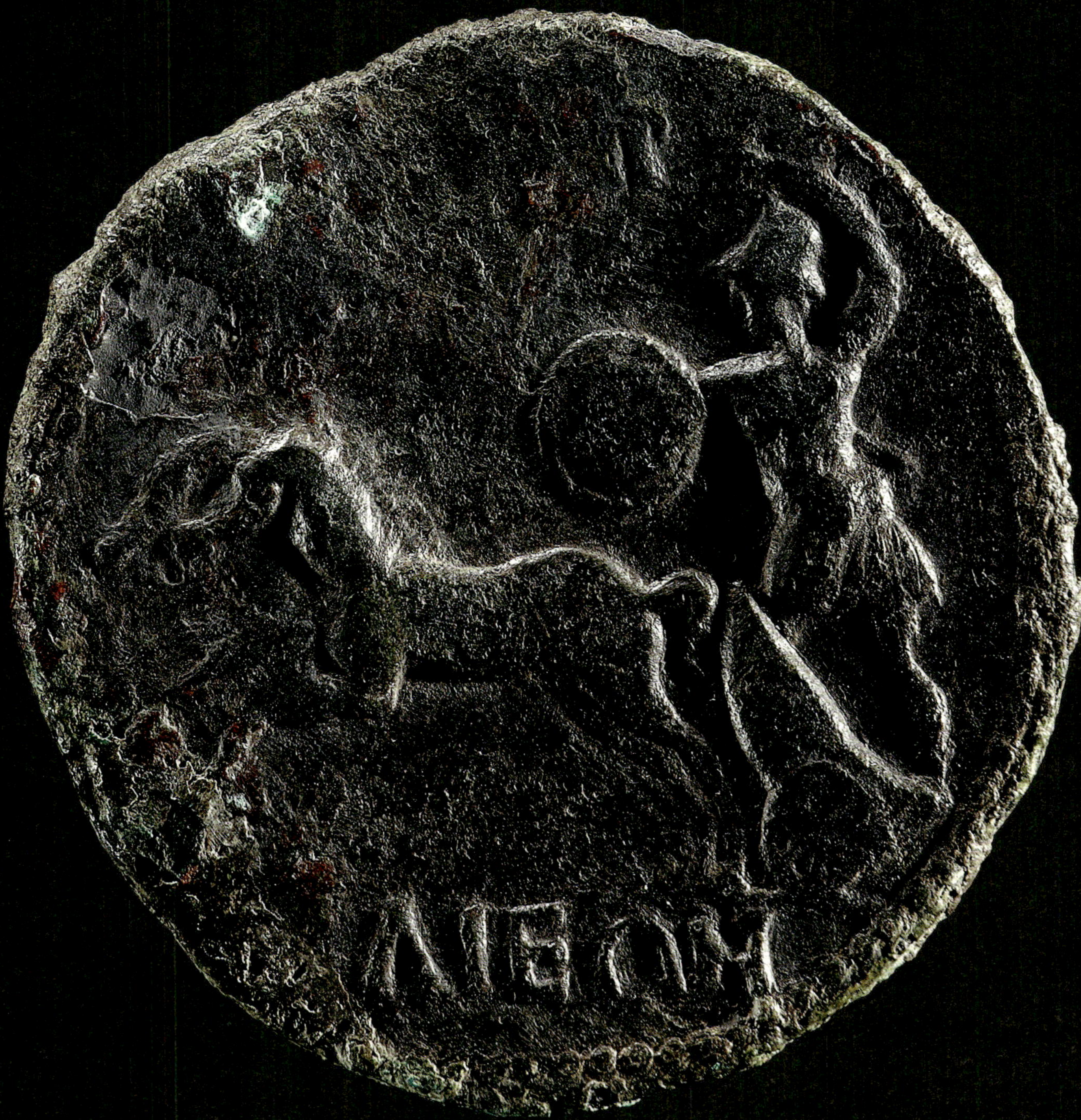

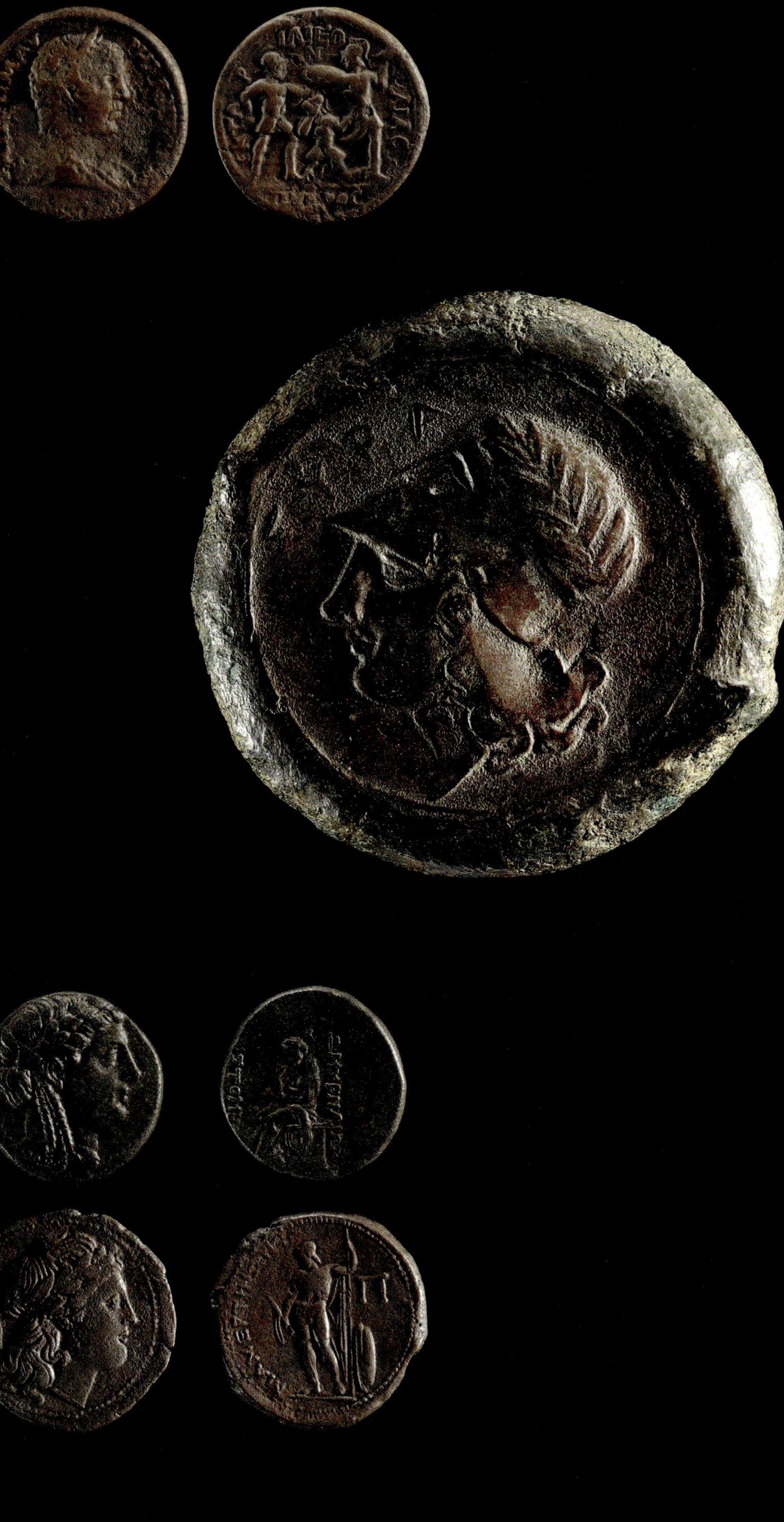

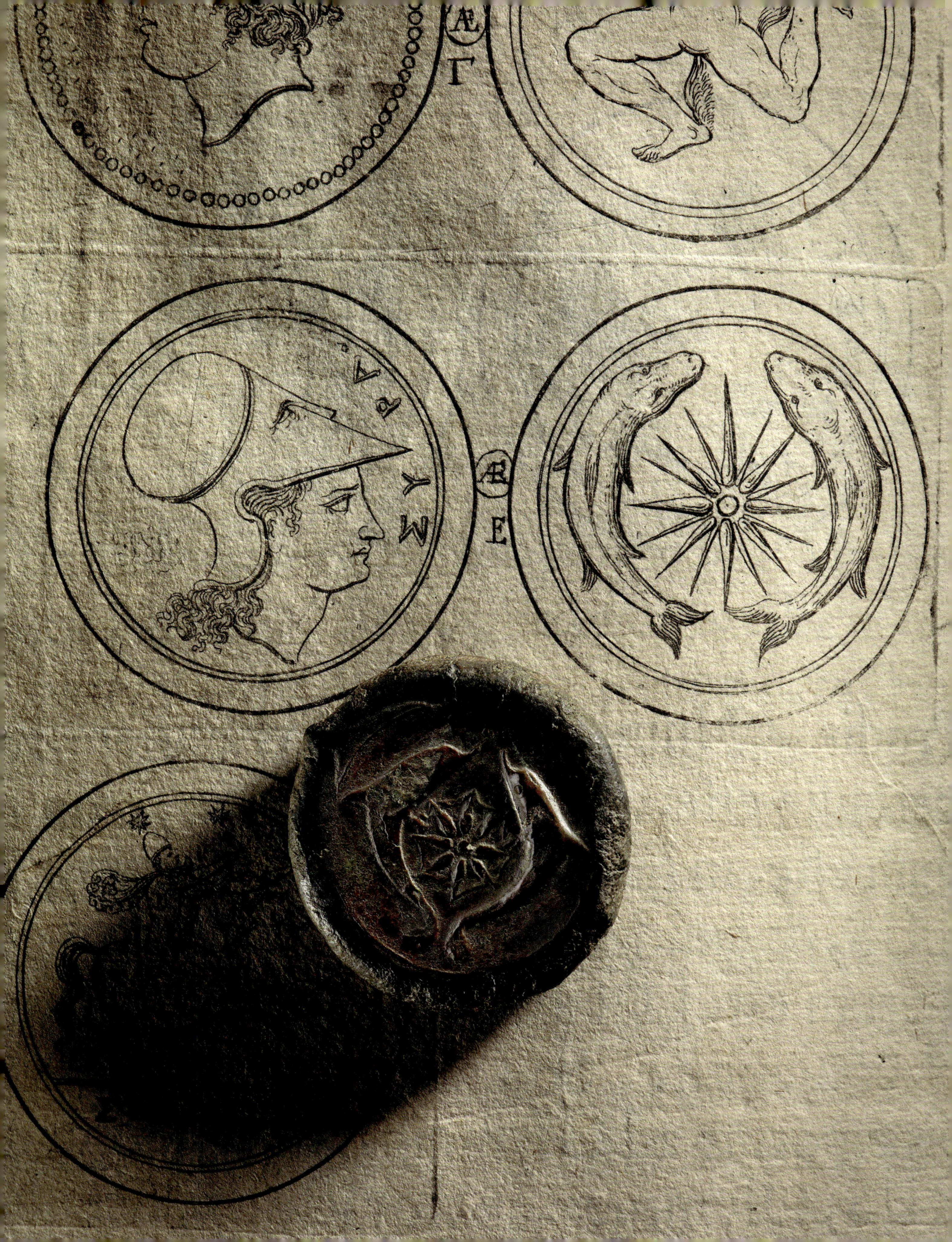
Æ
Γ
ΣΥΡΑ
Æ
E

Quant le Roy adomeon vey hector mort il
assaly achilles et la baty et naura forment
et lemporterent ses gens a sa tente sur son escu
lors furent les troyens desconfis et rentrerent en
la cite portans le corps dector a grant doleur

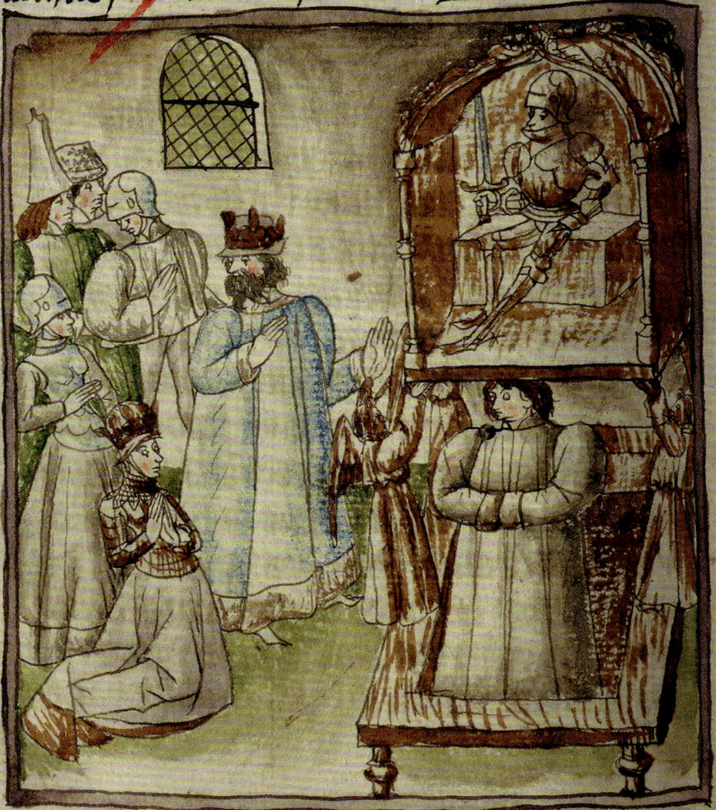

la noble et b
priant a son
Quant
en la
le deul que d
ment homm
neust mieux
et dirent tou
leur esperanc
grement dem
porterent le a
priant le be
fust mort de
demenerent
on dire du d
et puis ses s
femme certes
lamentacion
pour ce que l
durer sans c
maistres eu
le corps sans

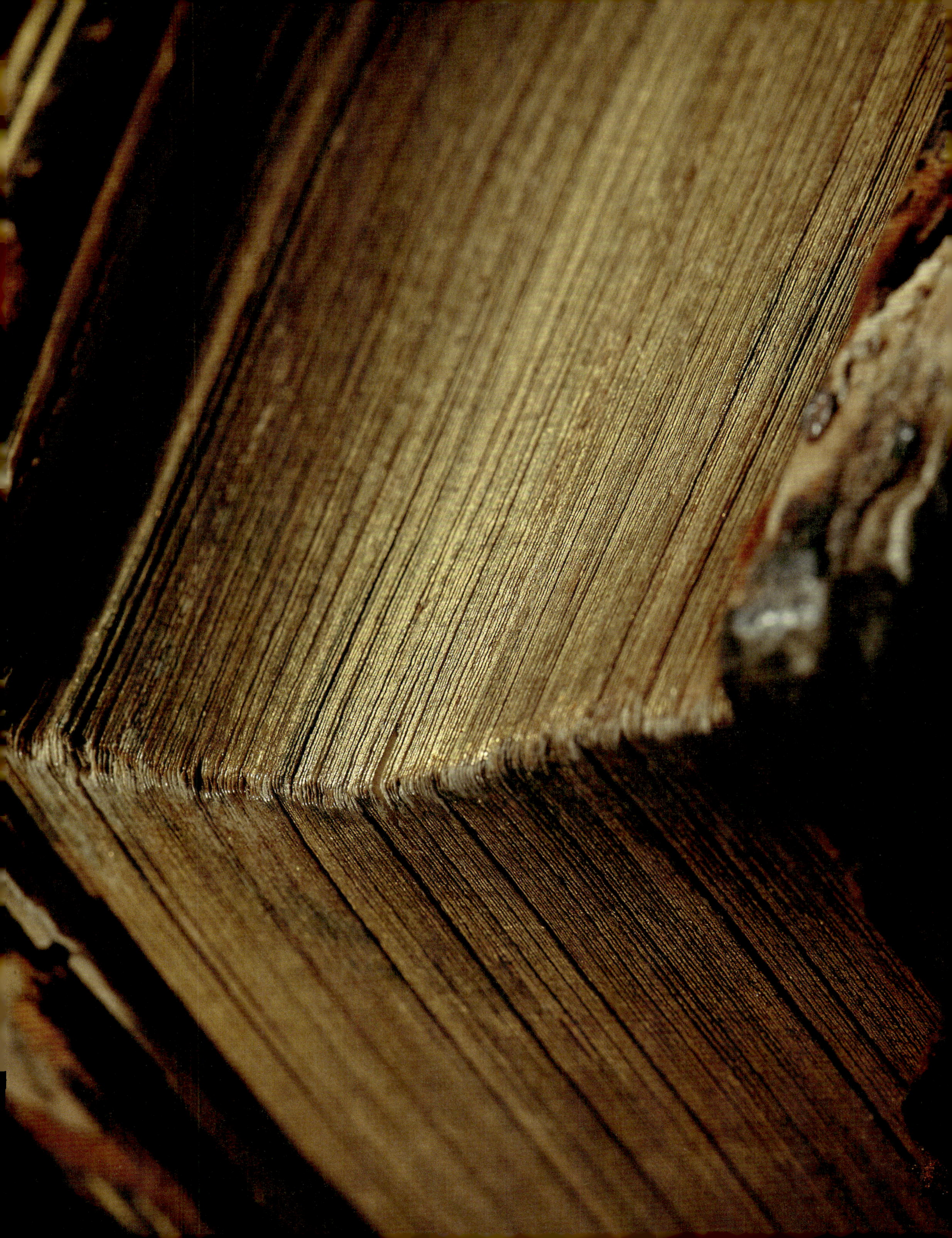

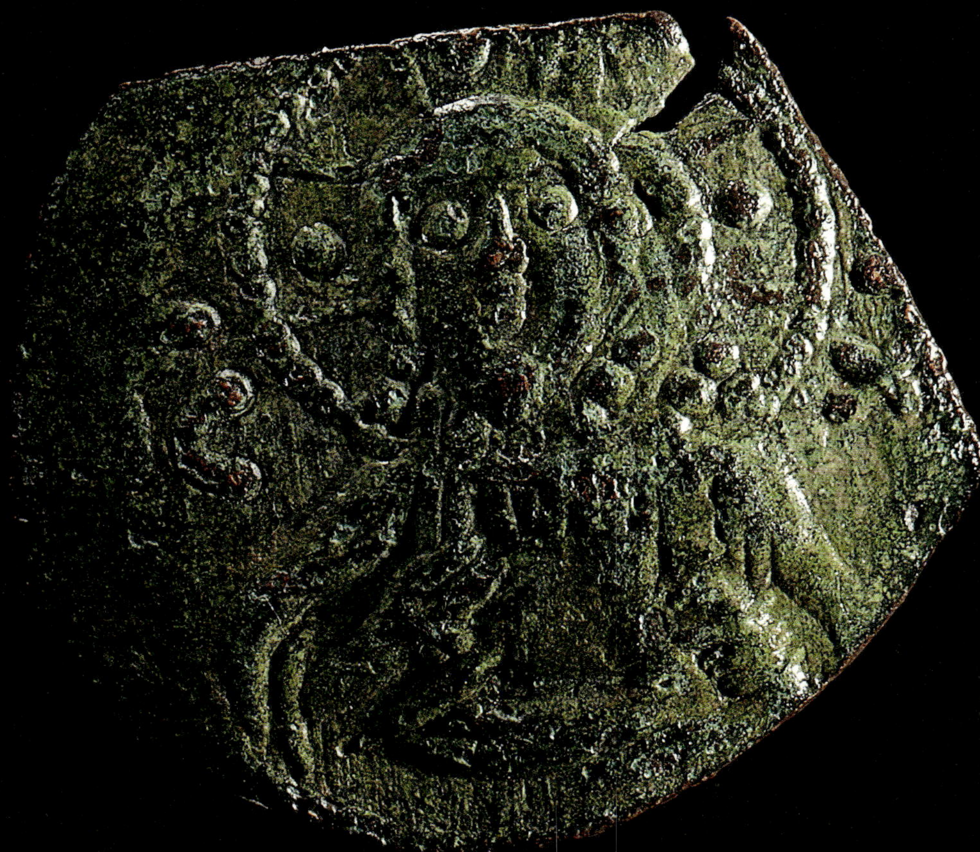

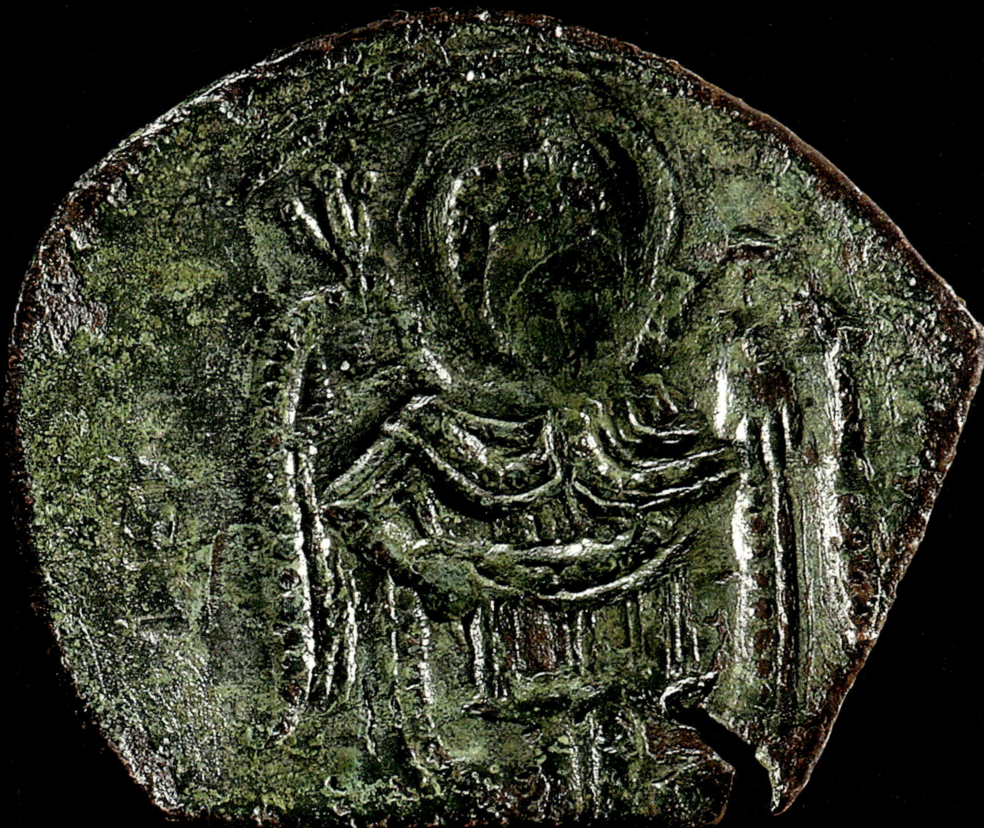

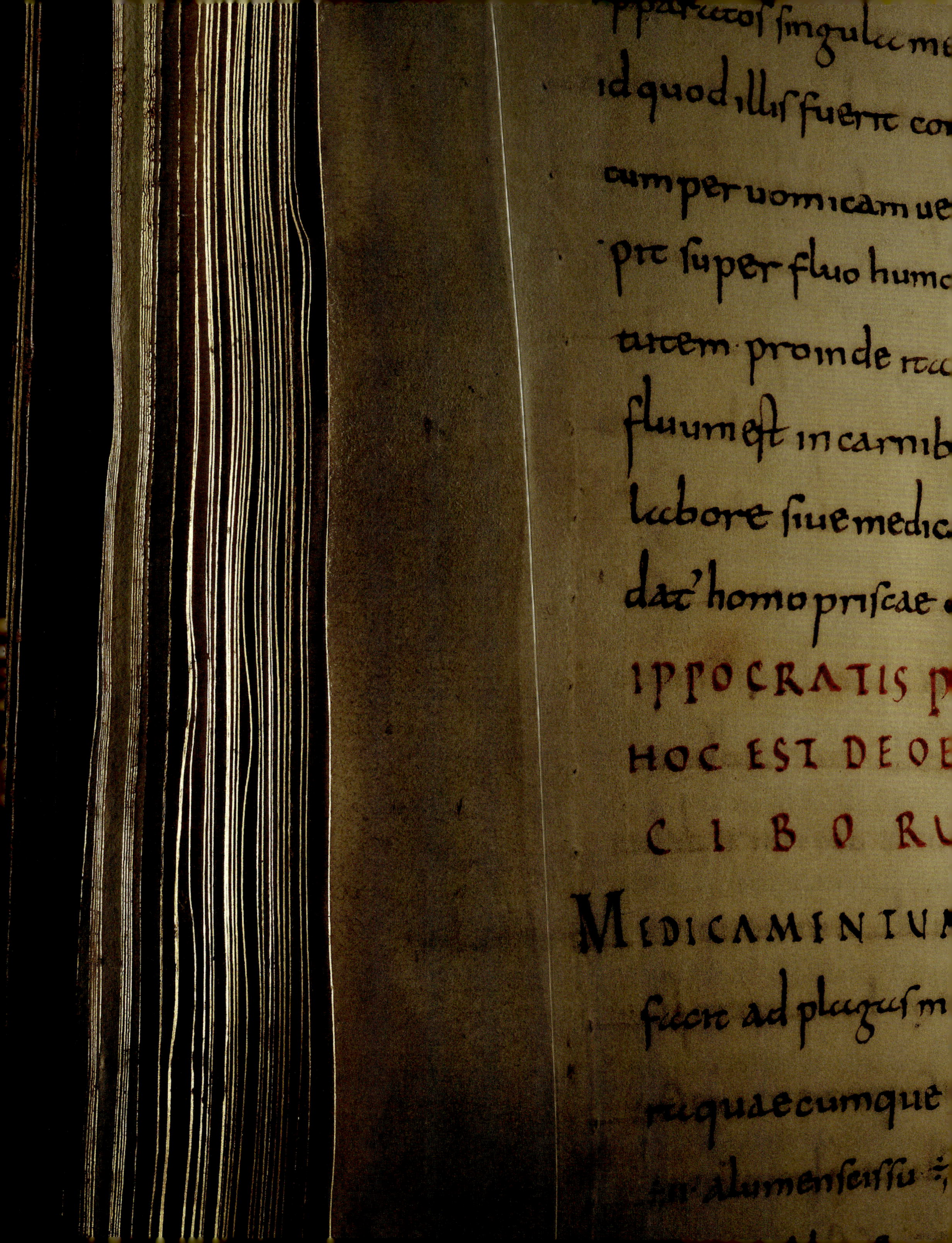
id quod illis fuerit co
cum per uomicam ue
pit super fluo hum
tatem proinde ita
fluum est in carnib
labore siue medic
dat homo priscae
IPPOCRATIS P
HOC EST DE OB
C I B O R
MEDICAMINIU
facere ad plagas m
ne quaecumque
ex alumen scissu

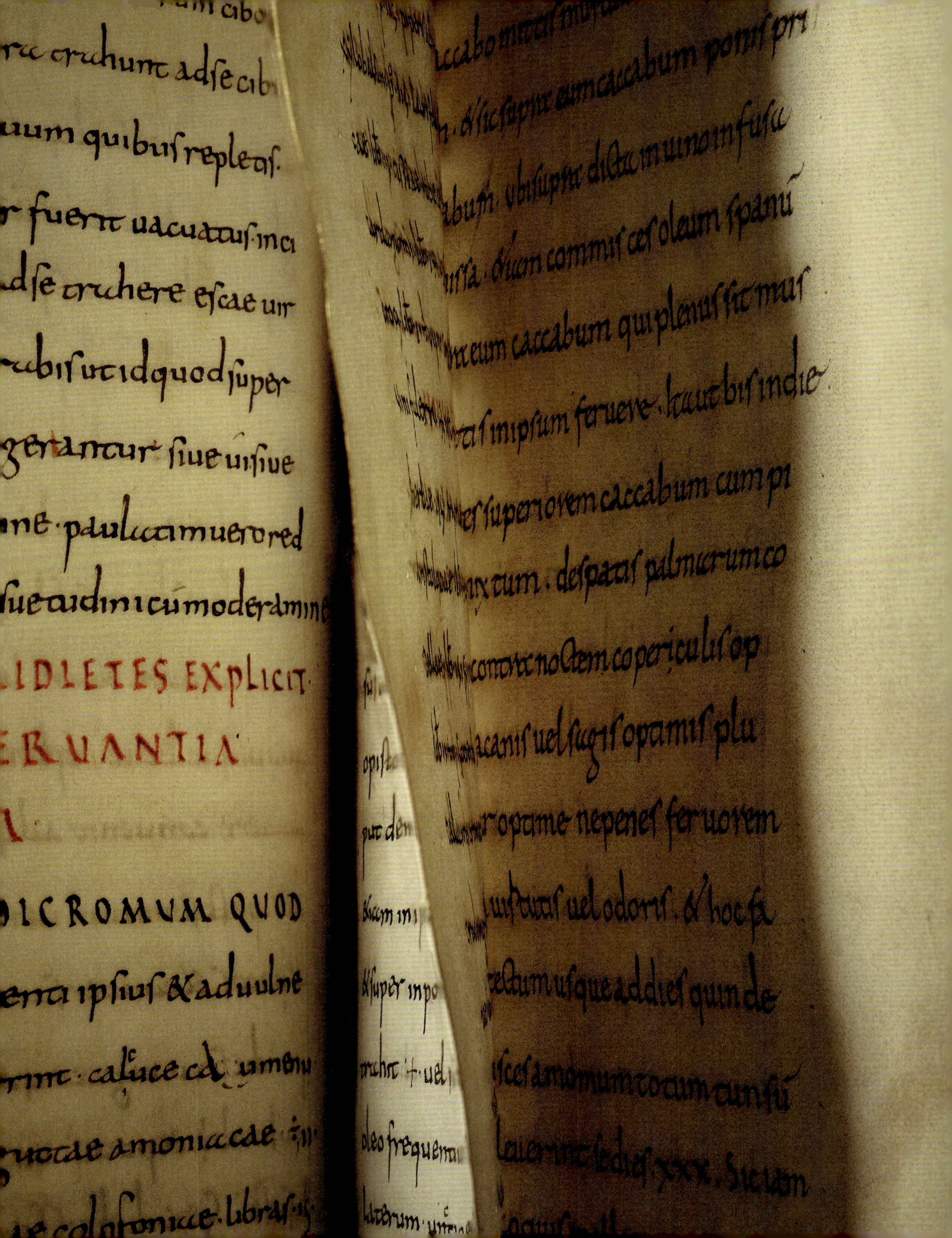
uum quibus repleas.
IDIETES EXPLICIT
ERUANTIA
ICROMUM QUOD
caccabum ponis pri
eum caccabum qui plenus sit mus
superiorem caccabum cum pi
contra noctem coperculis op
ropame ne penes feruorem
usque ad dies quinde
dies xxx. Sic tam

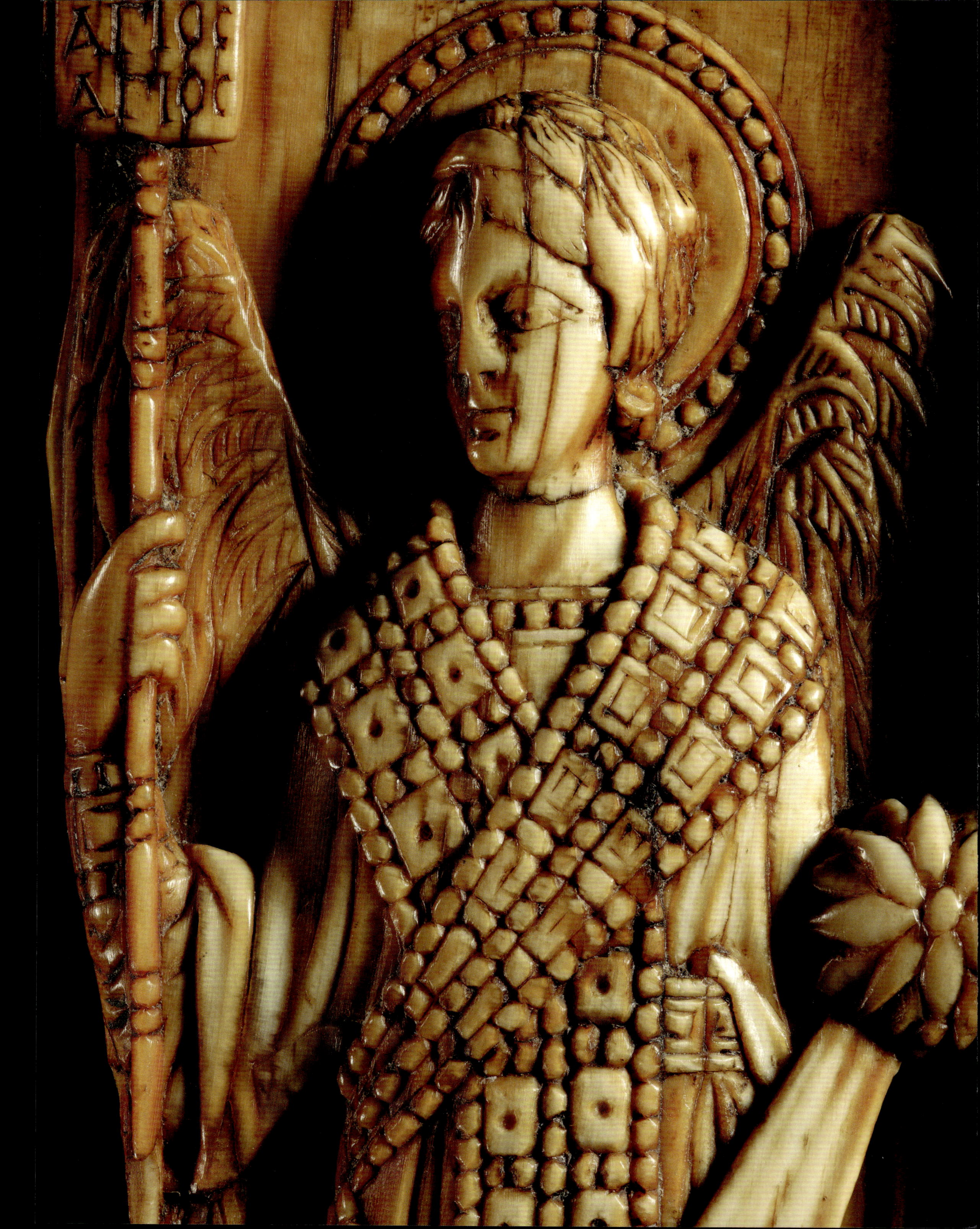
ΑΓΙΟϹ
ΑΓΙΟϹ

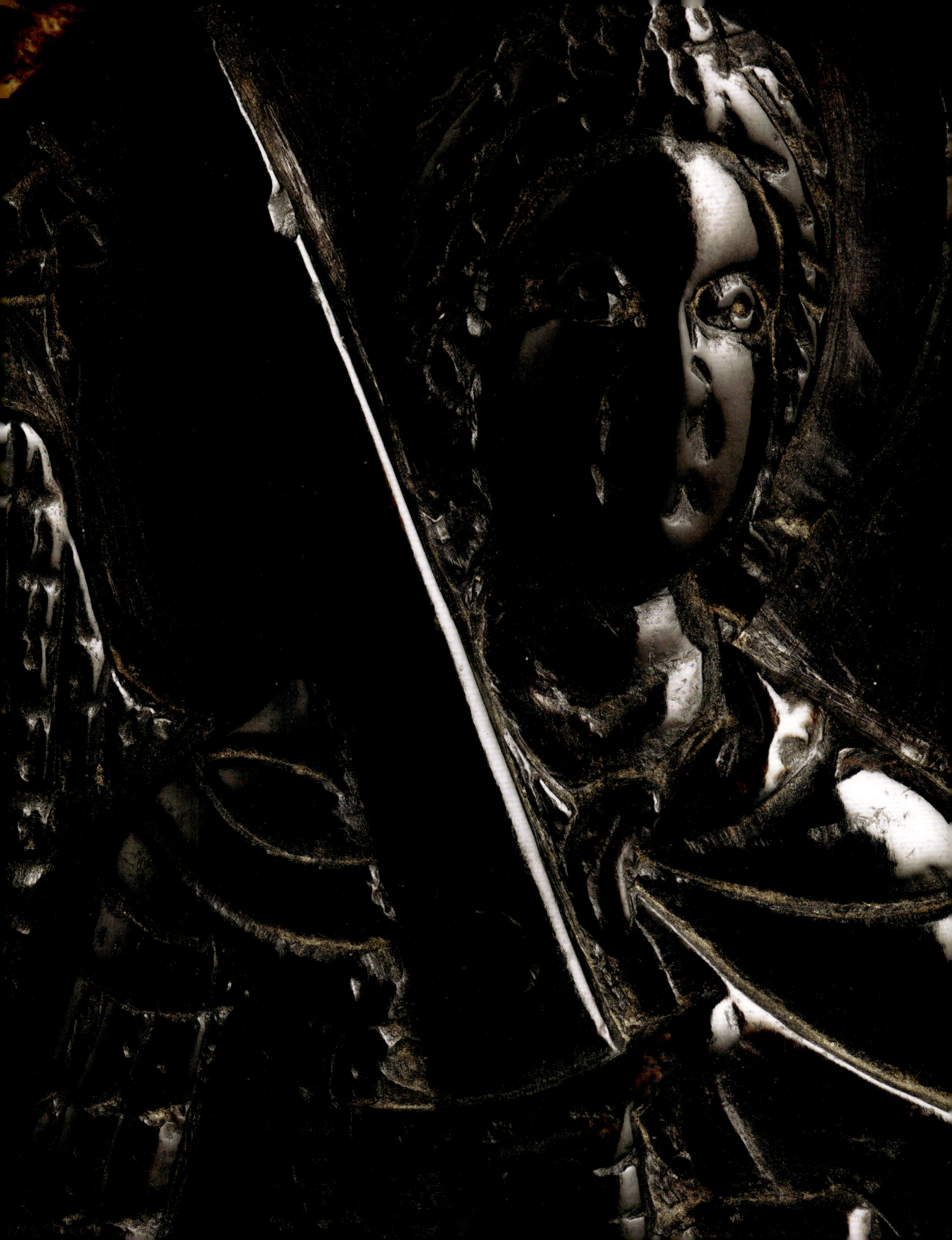

LEs hommes sages,ô Clea,
uent en leurs prieres den
der tous biés aux Dieux,
ce que plus nous desirons
tenir d'eulx, c'est la cog
sance d'eulx mesmes, au
cōme il est loisible aux h
mes d'en auoir,pource qu'il n'y a don ne plus
aux hōmes à receuoir, ne plus magnifique &
digne aux Dieux à donner,que la cognoissanc
verité : car Dieu donne aux hommes toutes a
choses dōt ils ont besoing, mais celle là il la ret
pour luy mesme & s'en sert, & n'est point b
heureux pour posseder grande quantité d'or
d'argent, ny puissant pour tenir le tonnerre
foudre en sa main, mais bien pour sa prudenc
sapience : & est vne des choses qu'Homere
mieulx & le plus sagement dictes,en parlant de
piter & de Neptune,

Ils sont tous deux de mesme extraction,
Et tous deux nez en mesme region,
Mais Iupiter en est le fils aisné,
Et de sçauoir plus grand que l'autre orné.

Il afferme que la preference & precedence de
piter estoit plus venerable & plus digne en ce c
estoit plus sçauant & plus sage. Et quant à n
i'estime que la beatitude & la felicité de la vie e
nelle,dont Iupiter iouit,cōsiste en ce qu'il n'ign
rien, & que rien de tout ce qui se fait ne le fuit

pe

e que l'immortalité,qui en osteroit la cognoif-
& intelligéce de tout ce qui est & qui se fait,
roit pas vne vie, mais vn temps seulement.
tant pouuons nous dire,que le desir d'enten-
verité est vn desir de la diuinité,mesmement
ité de la nature des Dieux, dont l'estude & le
has de telle science est comme vne profession
tree de religiõ,& œuure plus saincte que n'est
t le veu & l'obligation de chasteté, ny de la
e & closture d'aucun temple: & si est d'auan-
tresagreable à la Deesse que tu sers, attendu
le est tressage & tresscauante, ainsi comme la
ation mesme de son nom nous le donne à co-
stre, que le sçauoir & la science luy appartient
qu'à nul autre, car c'est vn mot Grec que Isis:
yphon aussi l'ennemy & aduersaire de la De-
enflé & enorgueilly par son ignorance & er-
dissipant & effaceant la saincte parole,laquel-
Deesse rassemble, remet sus & baille à ceulx
aspirent à se deifier par vne continuelle obser-
ce de vie sobre & saincte, en s'abstenãt de plu-
rs viandes, & se priuant du tout des plaisirs de
hair, pour reprimer la luxure & l'intemperãce,
n s'accoustumant de longue main à supporter
ndurer dedans les temples des durs & penibles
ices faicts aux Dieux: de toutes lesquelles ab-
ences, peines & souffrãces, la fin est la cognoif-
ce du premier,principal & plus digne obiect de
tendement, que la Deesse nous inuite & con-
à chercher, estant & demourant auec elle. Ce
mesme nous promet le nom de son temple,

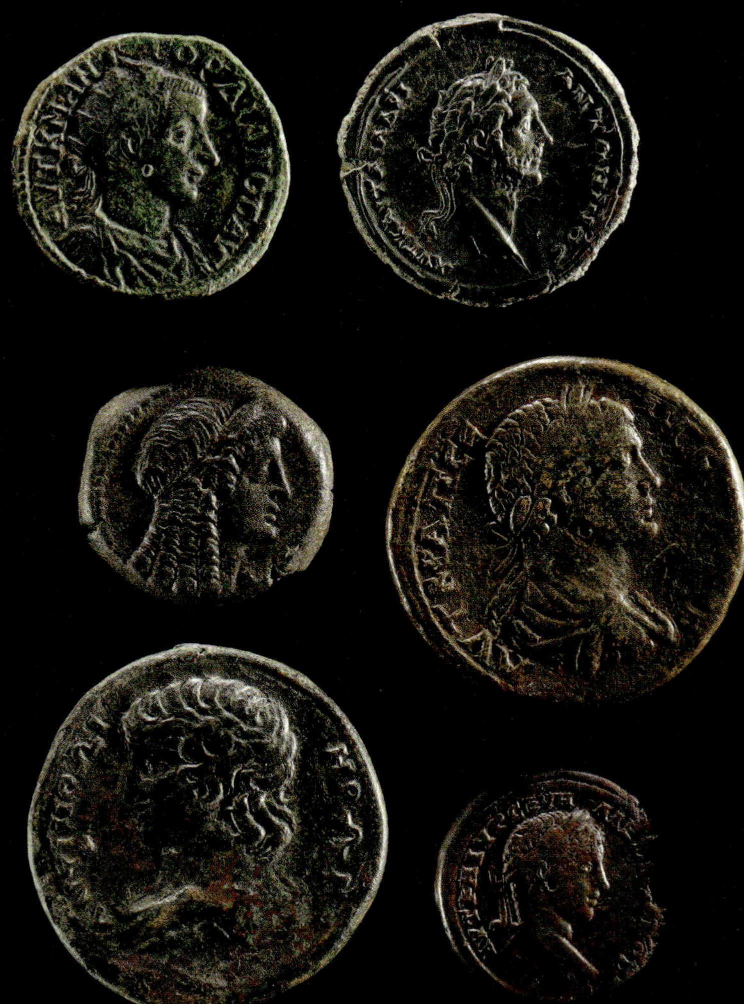

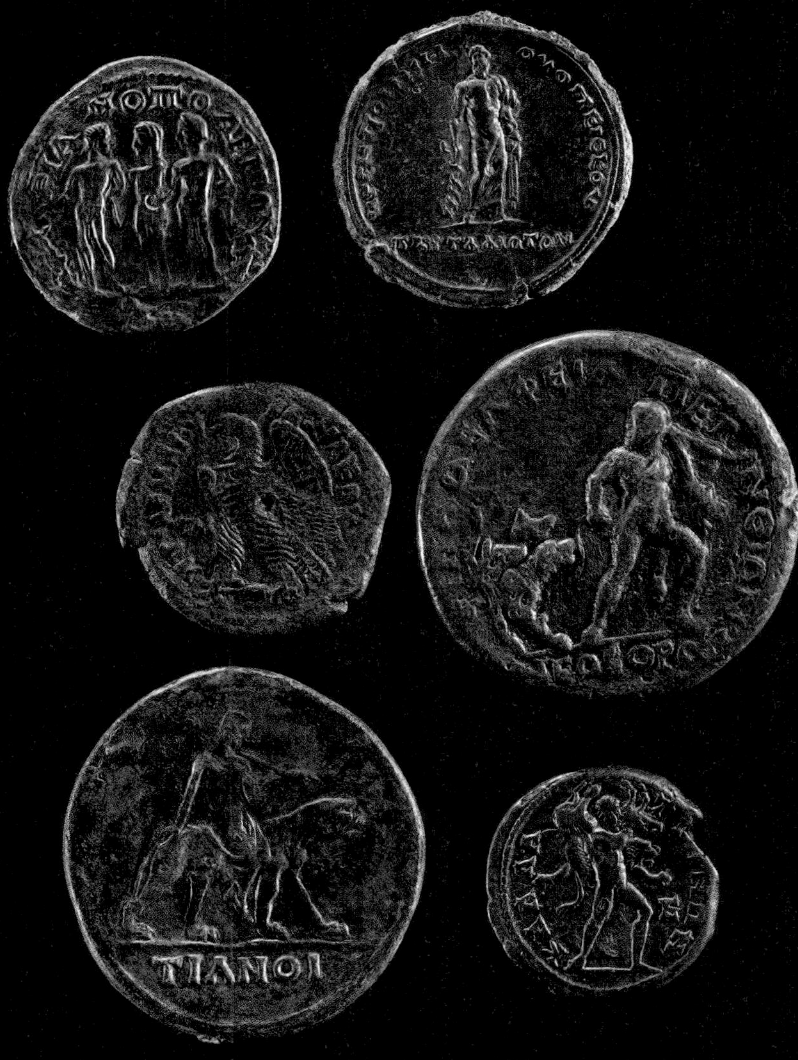
ΤΙΑΝΟΙ

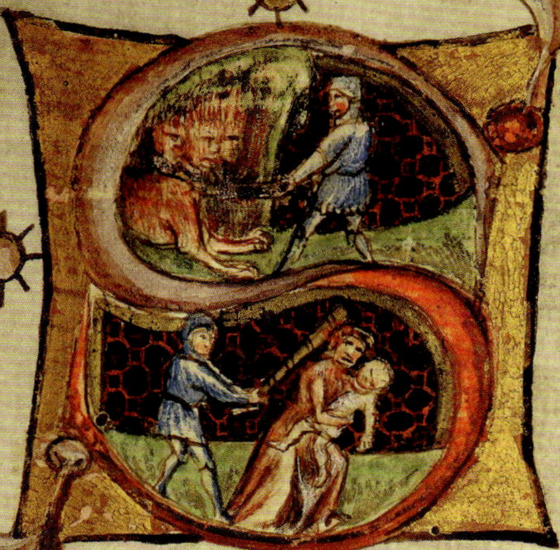

Lucii Annei Senece incipit tragedia prima Hercules furens. Iuno lo[quitur]

[S]oror tonantis hoc
enim solum michi
Nomen relictum est.
semp alienum iouem
[A]c templa summi
uidua deserui etheris.
[L]ocumque celo pulsa
pellicibus dedi.
Tellus colenda est.
pelices celum tenent.
hinc Arctos alta parte
glacialis poli
Sublime classes sidus Argolicas agit.
Hinc qua tepenti uere laxantur dies
Tirie per undas uector Europe nitet.
Illinc timendum ratibus ac ponto gregem
Passim uagantes exerunt Athlantides.
[F]erro coma hinc exterret Orion deos.
Suasque perseus aureas stellas habet.
Hinc clara gemini signa tindaride micant.
Quibusque natis mobilis tellus stetit.
Nec ipse tantum Bacus aut Bacci parens
Adiere superos. ne qua pars probro uacet
Mondus puelle serta Gnosiace gerit.
Sed uetera sero querimur una me dira ac fera
Thebana nuribus sparsa tellus impiis
Quotiens nouercam fecit. ascendat licet
Meumque uictrix teneat Alcmena locum
Pariterque natus astra promissa occupet
In cuius ortu mondus impendit diem
Tardusque eoo phebus effulxit mari
Retinere mersum iussus occeano iubar.
Non sic abibunt odia uiuaces aget
Violentus iras animus et seuus dolor
Eterna bella pace sublata geret.
Que bella. quicquid horridum tellus creat
Inimica quicquid pontus aut aer tulit
Terribile dirum pestilens atrox ferum
Fractum et perdomitum est. superat et crescit malis
Iraque nostra fruitur in laudes suas.
Mea uertit odia. dum nimis seua impero
Patrem probauit. inde qua lucem premit
Aperitque thetis qua ferens titan diem
Qua sol reuitens quaque deponens diem
Binos propinqua tingit Ethiopas face

Qualem quę lento celant sub cortice granum
Punica ferre solent: breuis est tamen usus in illo.
Nanq; male herentem, & nimia leuitate caducum
Excutiunt iidem qui prestant omnia uenti.,

ARGVMENTVM LIBRI VNDECIMI·

ORpheus undecimo qui saxa sequentia duxit·
Cęditur a nurib; Ciconum· radice tenetur·
Ecce Mydas auro torquetur· cessit in amnem
Aurea uis: luctus aures detexit aselli·
Aedificat troiam phoebus: Thetis ędit achillem·
Dędalion fit auis· fit marmor belua uasta·
Halcyone Ceyca monet· mare fluctib; albet·
Naufragus ille perit: faciunt te somnia certam
Halcyonem· lugens mutatis corpore uiso
Mutatur Ceyx: foedus quod & ante remansit·
Esacon in pontum thetis est miserata cadentem·
Fit mergus nomenq; manet quę mergitur illi.,

·P·OVIDII NASONIS METH·LIB·XI·INC·

De orpheo interfecto a mulieribus Ciconum q̄ earum spreuerat connubia· & de membris eius abscissis, & capite: quod in flumine etiam proiectum canebat· quod dum mordere serpens uellet, a phoebo est mutatus in saxum.,

CARMINE DVM TALI SILVASQVE, ANIMOSQVE FERARVM THREICIVS VATES ET SAXA SEQVENTIA DVCIT·

ra cygnis
uirtus
uti
em
tti
ostro
tuta petente
guine dentes
uit harena
ter auras
rat alis
i albas
balto
uine corpus
capillos
palmis
nia uestri
ta manebunt
s imago
na nostri.,
ruore Adoni
REM MVTA
QVONDAM
uertere mentas
eros
tem
illo
p
r hora
ine concolor ortus

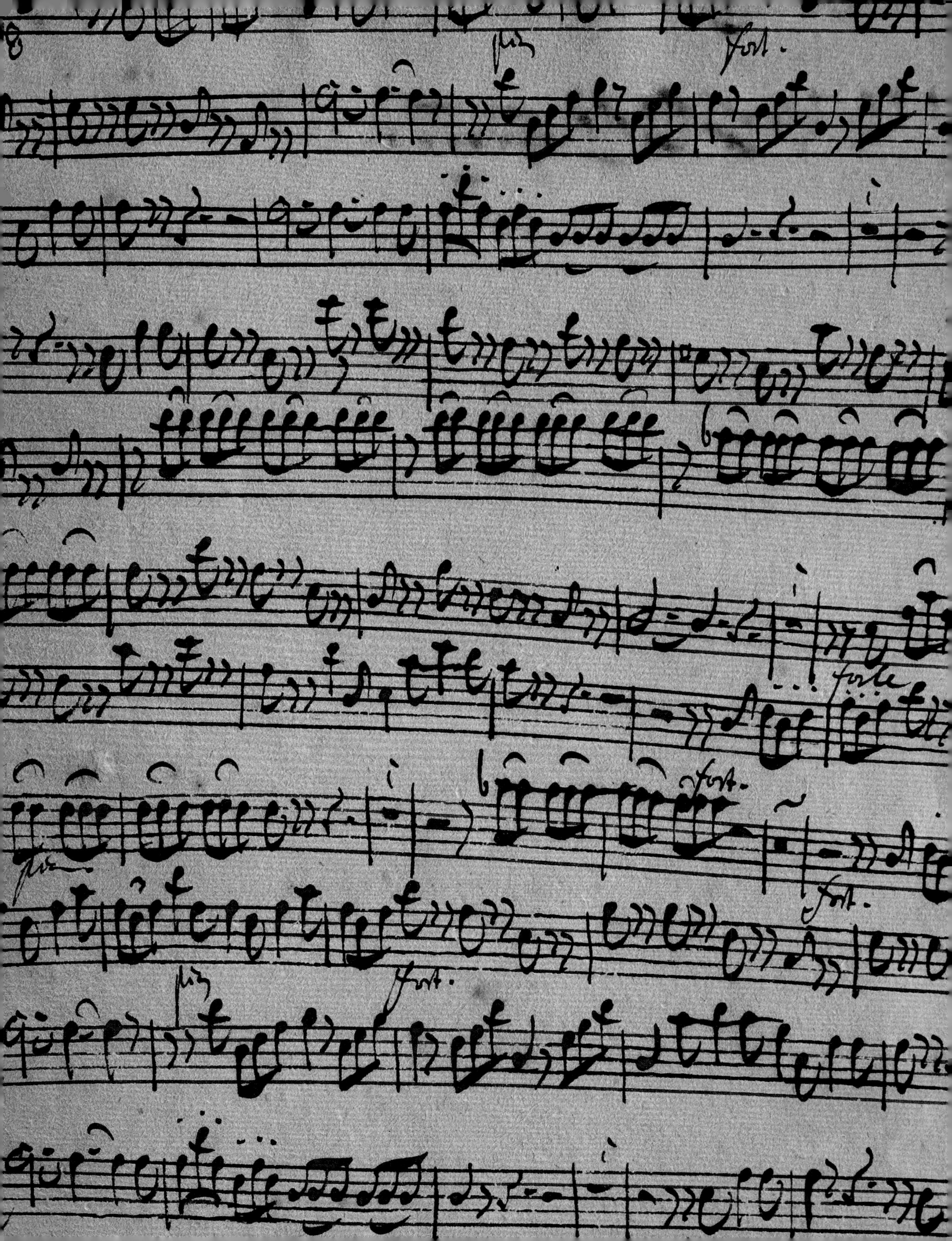
pia
fort.
forte
fort.
pia
fort.
pia
fort.

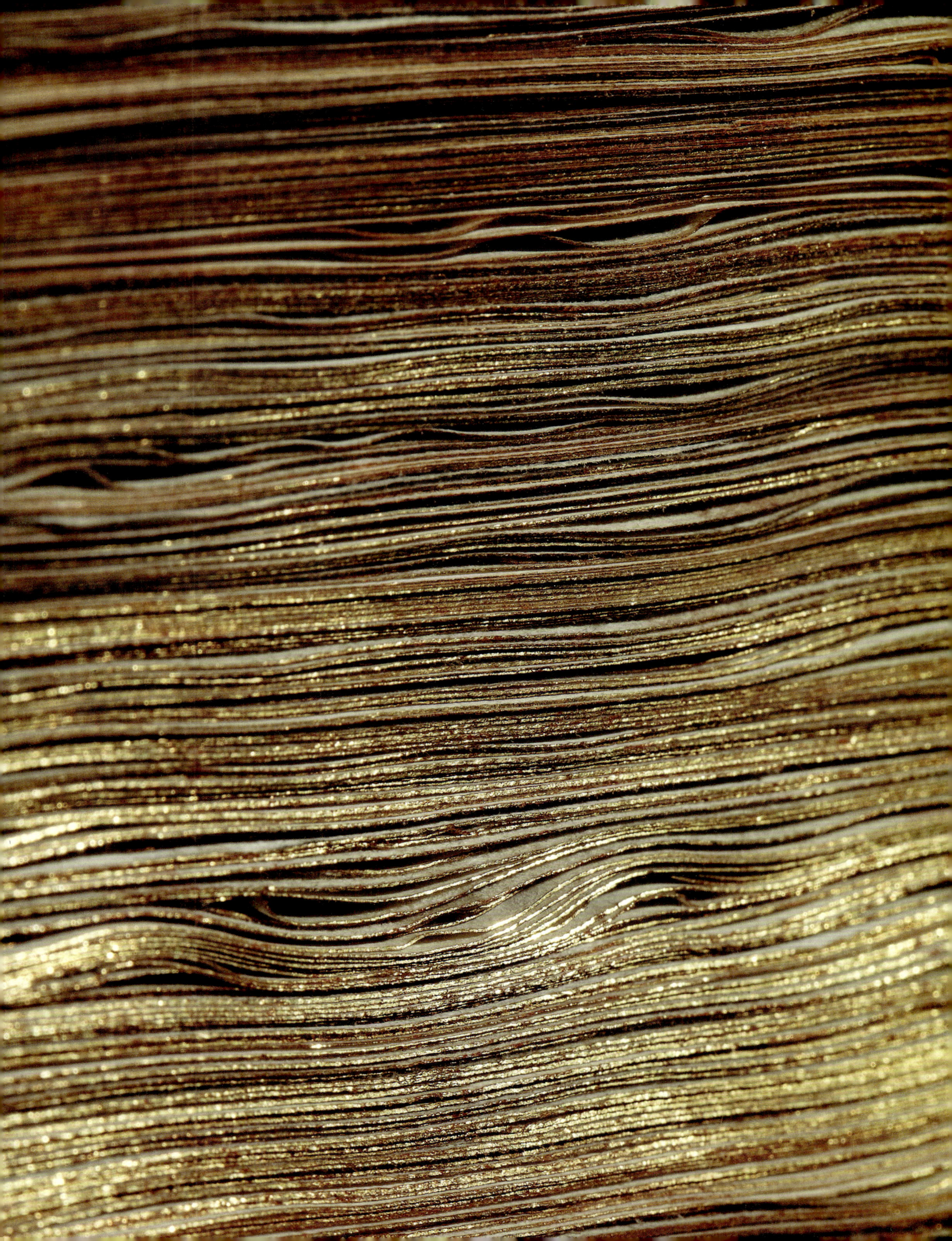

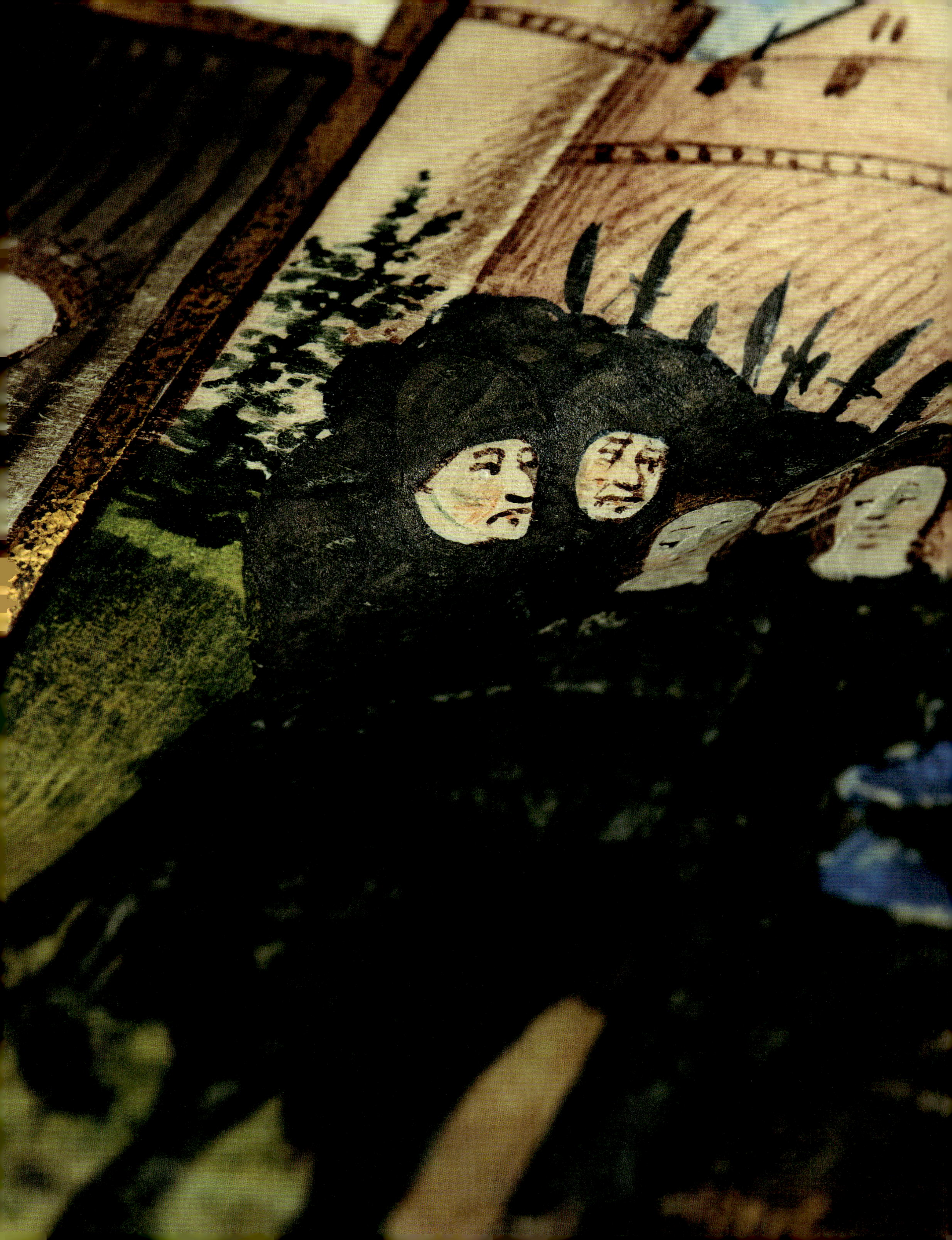

le xvi^e contient en brief les
cas dune grant compaignie
de doulereux nobles homes
et femmes

Le xvii^e contient le cas de
priam roy de troye la grant
de hecuba sa femme et de plu
sieurs autres

Le xviii^e raisonne contre les
nobles orgueilleux

Le xix^e contient les cas de
agamenon et de menelaus
freres et roys de grece

Le xx^e contient la louenge
et recommandacion de pourete

Le xxi^e contient le cas de
sanson juge et gouuerneur
du peuple disrael

Le xxii^e raisonne contre les
femmes en racomptant leurs
vices et barats

Le xxiii^e contient le cas de
plusieurs nobles grans et
plourans

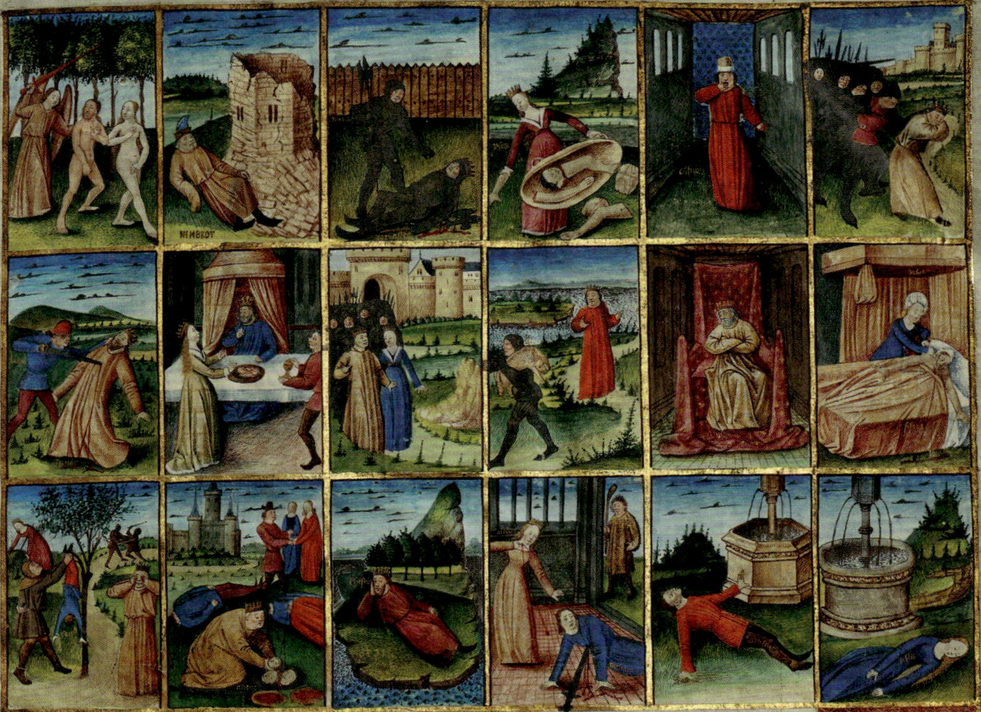

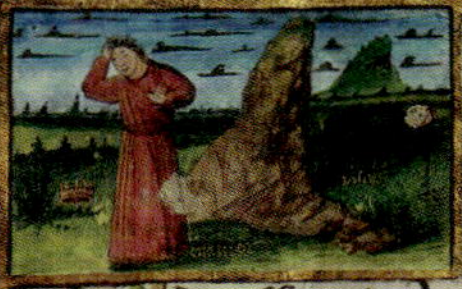

[C]omme je conside
re et pense en
diuerses manieres les plou
rables maleu
retez de noz pre
decesseurs. Acelle fin que du
grant nombre dyceulx qui par
fortune ont este tresbuches je
paruinsisse au commancement
de ce liure aucun prince tresbien
assez digne destre premier entre
les maleureux. [E]t veez cy deux
vieillars qui se arresterent de
uant moy si tres aagez et si
ancians quil sembloit quilz
ne peussent tramer leurs
membres tramblans. Lun de
ces deux vieillars cest assauoir
adam me raisonna et dist. Beau
nepueu Jehan boccasse qui cer
ches et enquiers lequel tu
mectes premier au rang des
maleureux. Je vueil que tu
saiches comme vray est que
ainsi comme nous deux qui
sommes les premiers home
et femme faiz a lymage de
dieu qui par le moyen et la
croissement de lui auons pre
miers a tenu et empli les sieges
de paradis par le merite de la
mort de Jhesucrist aussi nous
auons premiers esprouue par
lamonnestement du deable
le trebuchet de fortune. [E]t
pource aucun homme fors nous
ne donnera a ton liure plus
conuenable commancement.
Je feuz moult esbay et tom
moncay merueilleusement
regardez ces deux vieillars
qui a paine pouoient parler
qui auoient este faiz sans
ouurage de nature et qui se
disoient peres de tous les
hommes mortelz et qui ha
bitoient en paradis terrestre

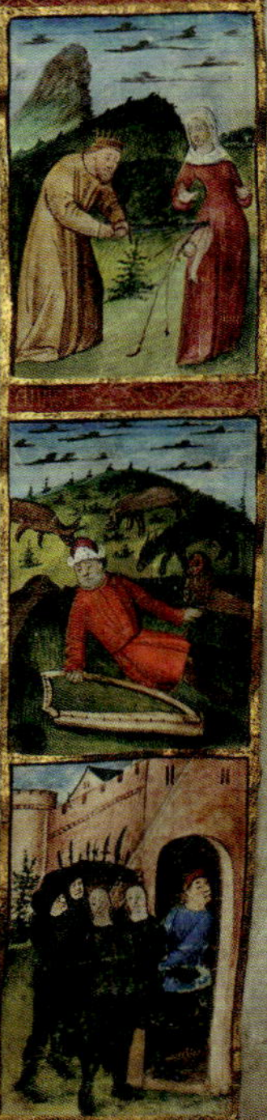

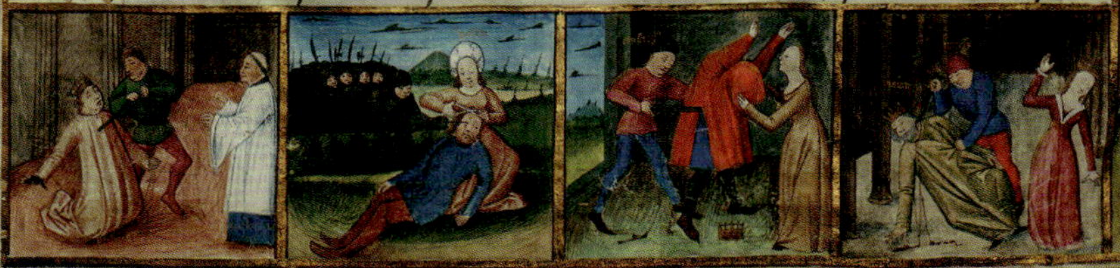

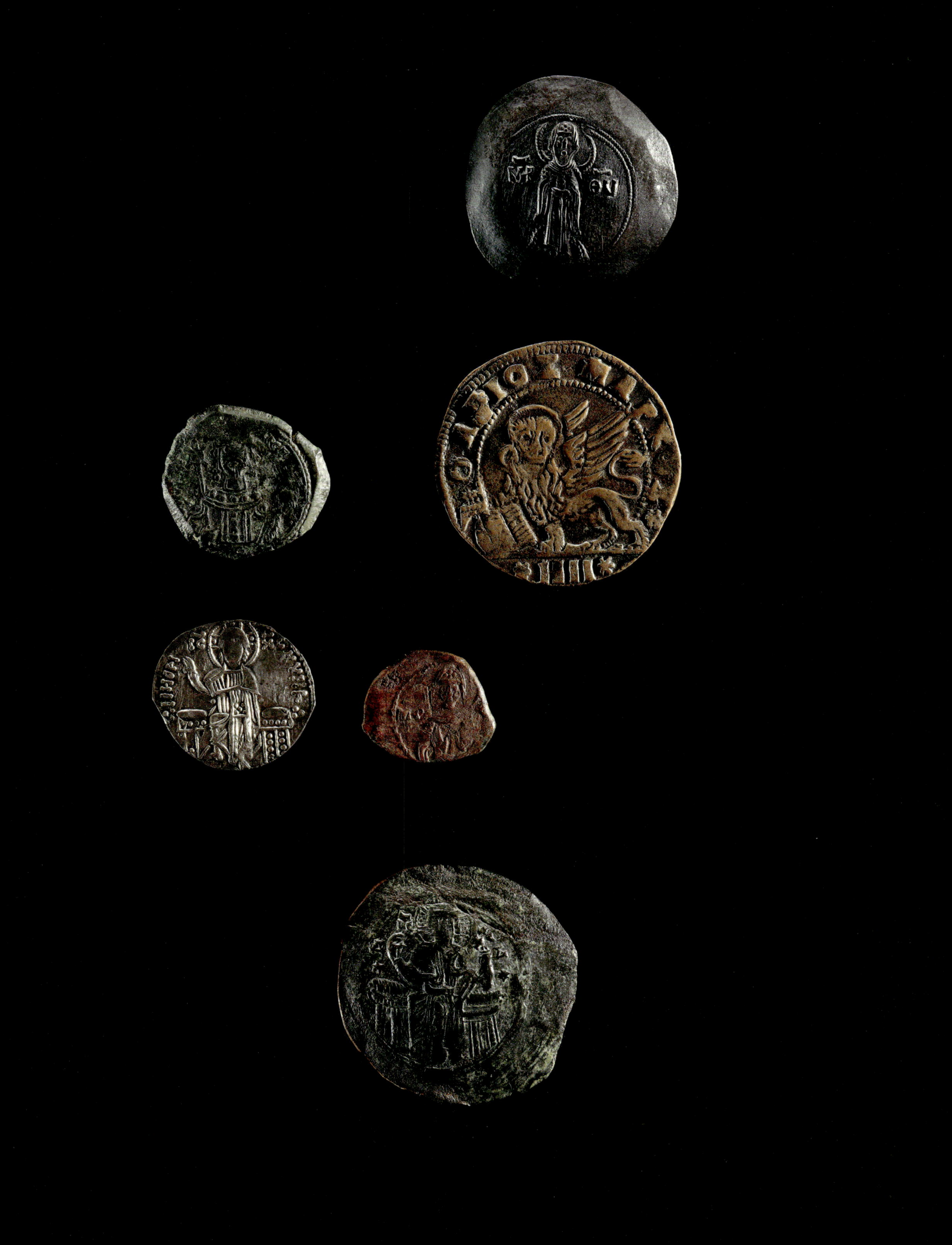

Machabei · Iohannes · Mathathias · Iudas · Eleazarus · Simon · Ionathas · Antigonus · Aristobolus · Alexander · Alexandra · Elisa · Iacob · Ioseph · Iesus natus · Antipater · Phaselus · Iosephus · Ferroras · Saloma · Cristus

Seleucus · Antiochus · Demetrius · Alexander · Tryphon · Ptolomeus · Scaurus · Gabinius · Crassus · Cassius · Iulius cesar · Augustus cesar

Quatuor uxores herodis ascalonite

Heber · Phaleg · Reu · Saruch · Nachor · Thare · Abraham · Nachor · Aran · Agar · Cetura · Ysmael · Machmas · Cedar · Adadan · Hus · Buz · Bathuel · Melcha · Loth · Sara · Rebecca · Laban · Moab · Amon · Ysaac · Esau · Iacob · Lia · Bala · Zelpha · Rachel · Ruben · Symeon · Ysachar · Leui · Zabulon · Dina · Iudas · Dan · Neptalim · Gad · Aser · Ioseph · Beniamin · Manasses · Effraym · Gerson · Caath · Merari · Her · Onam · Sela

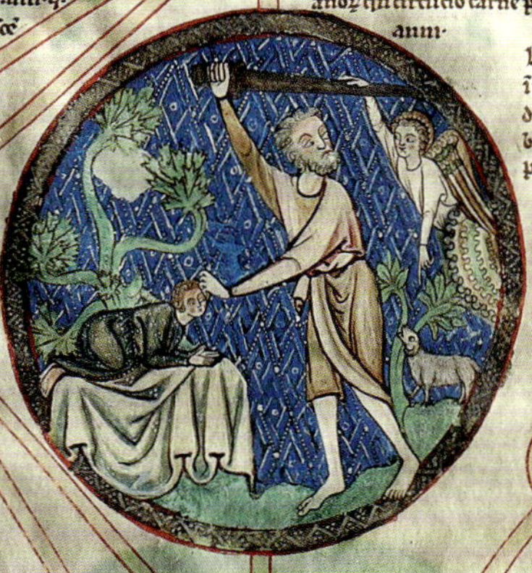

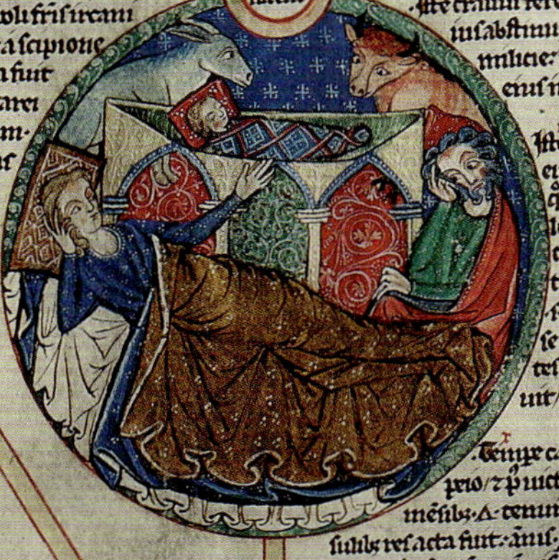

Concubina

Abraham suffocato aram adoptavit filium loth

Isti quatuor fuerunt ex Lia

.xxx. · .xxxiiii. · .cxxx. · .lxx. · .ccv.

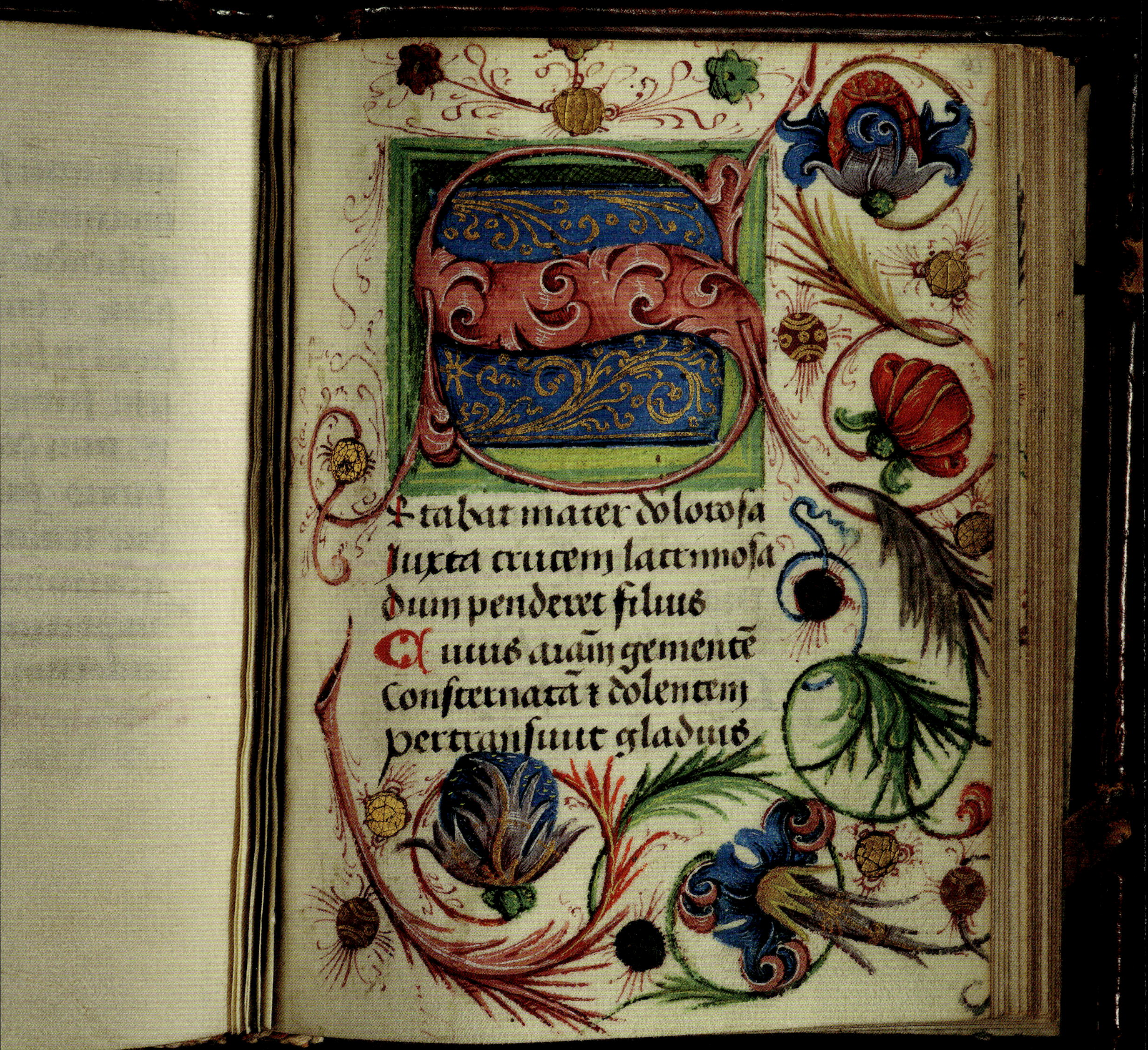
Stabat mater dolorosa
Iuxta crucem lacrimosa
dum pendebat filius
Cuius animam gementem
Contristatam et dolentem
pertransivit gladius

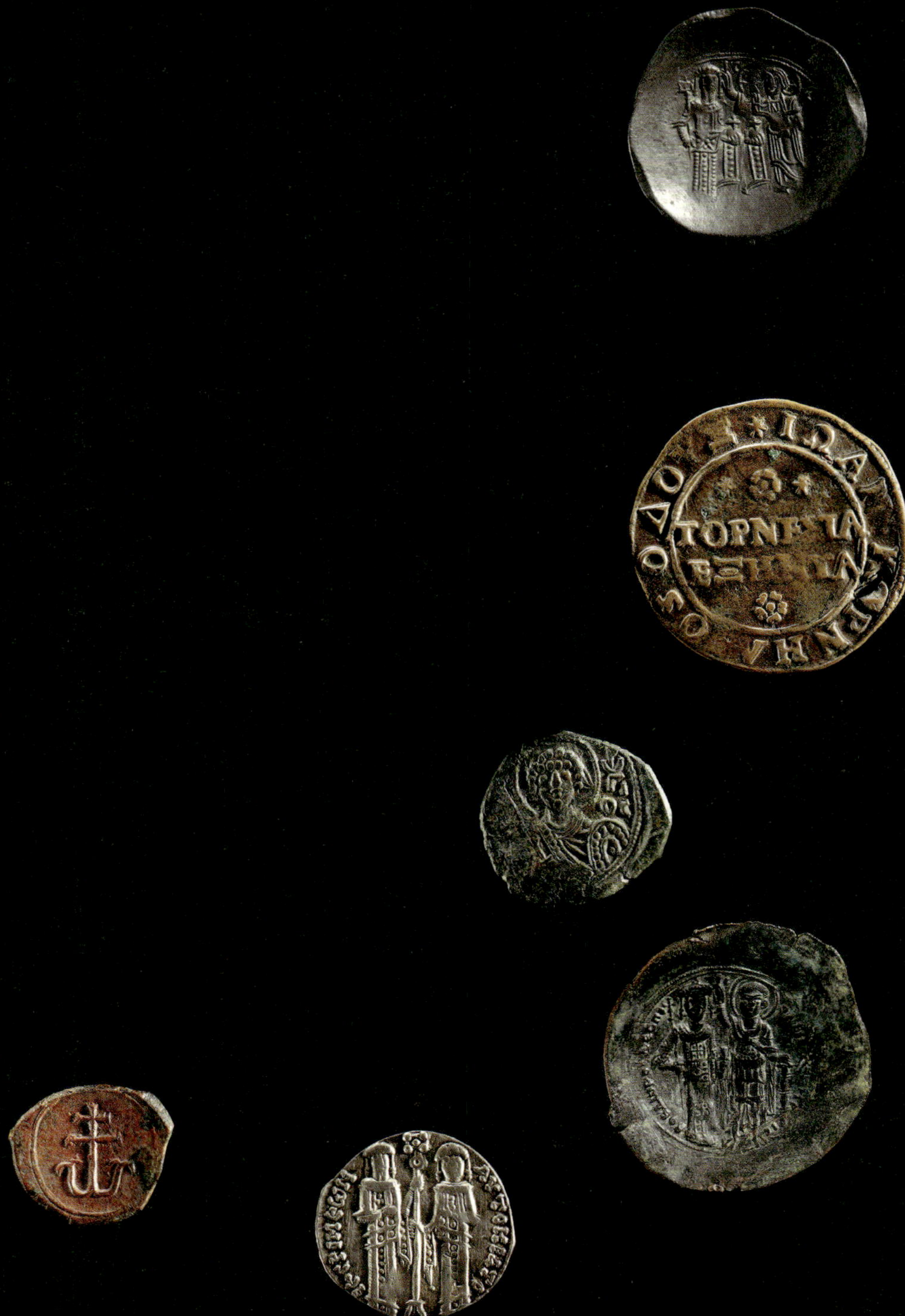

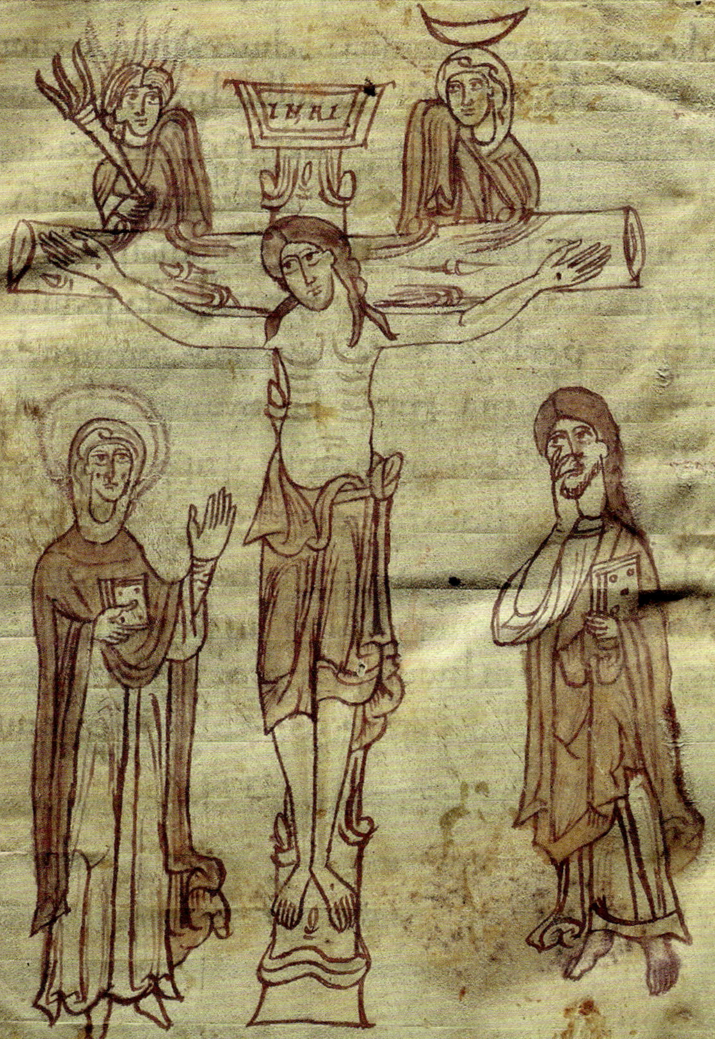

XX

152 fol.

155

Nov. 69

Deriet

D exer peg

agere

R E

Forma

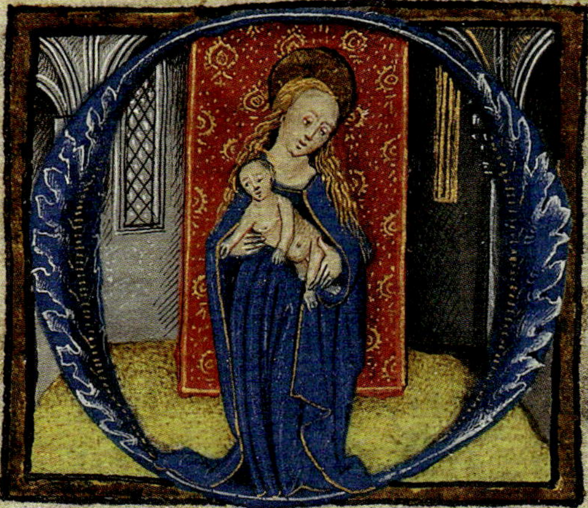

Intemerata
et in eternū
benedicta si
gularis que
īcōparabilis
uirgo dei ge
nitrix maria o gratissimū dei te
plū spiritus sancti sacrariū ia
nua regni celorū per quā post de
ū totus orbis terrarū inclina au
res tue pietatis indignis suppli
cationib; meis et esto michi pec
catori pia in omnib; auxiliatrix
Johānes xpisti beatissime famu
lus amice. qui ab eodem dño no
stro ihesu xpisto uirgo electus es
atq; inter ceteros magis dilectus

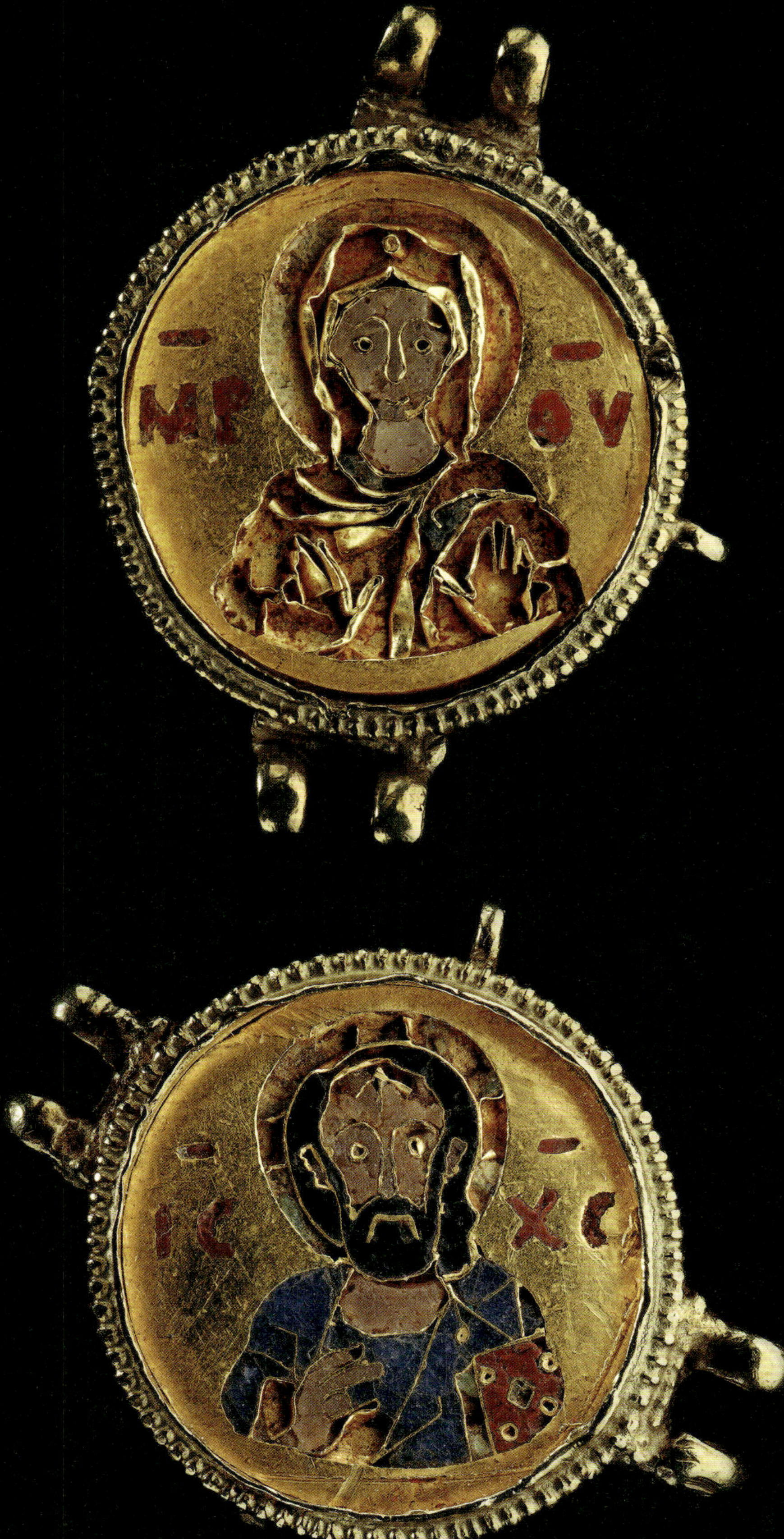
MP ΘV
IC XC

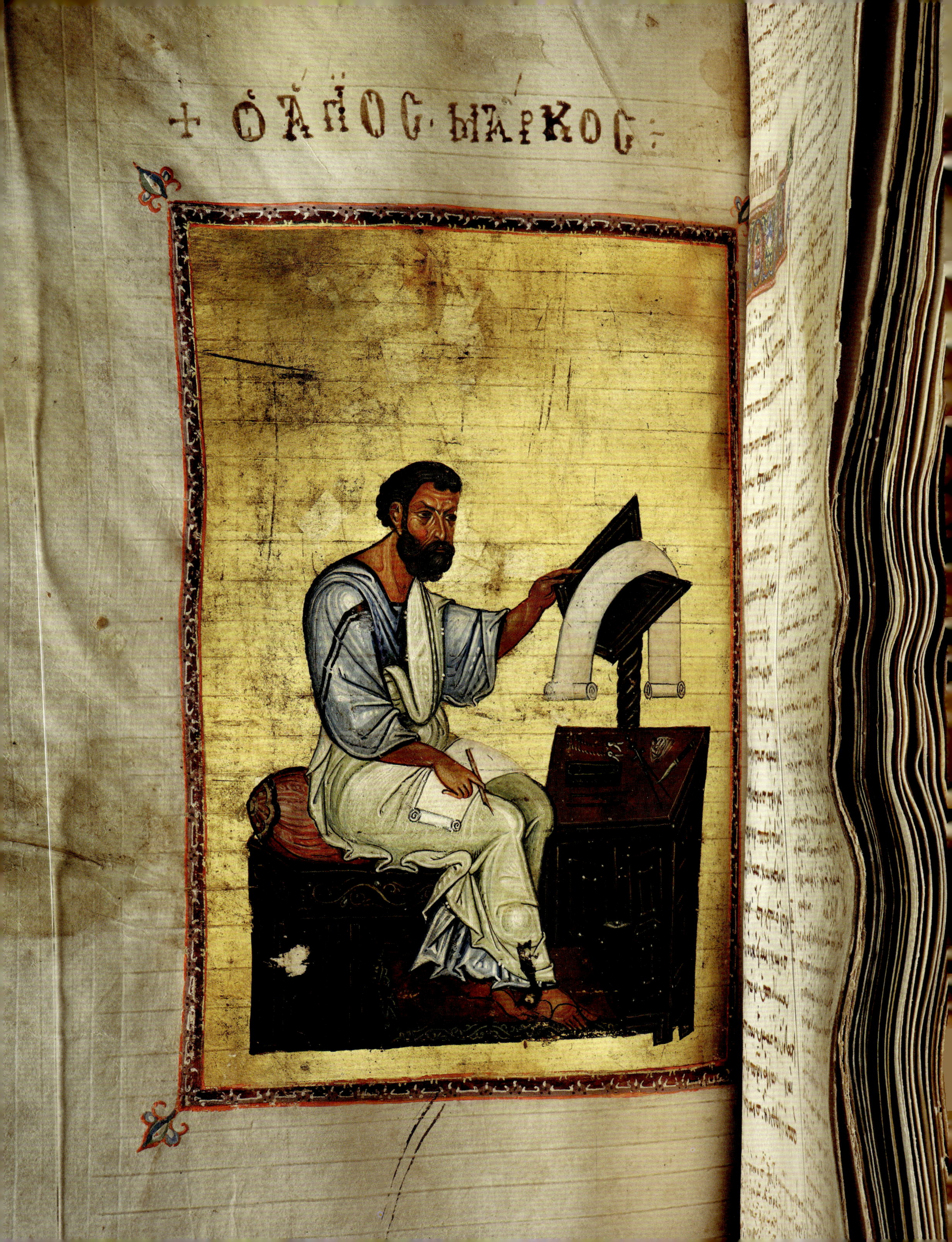
+ Ο ΑΓΙΟϹ · ΜΑΡΚΟϹ ·

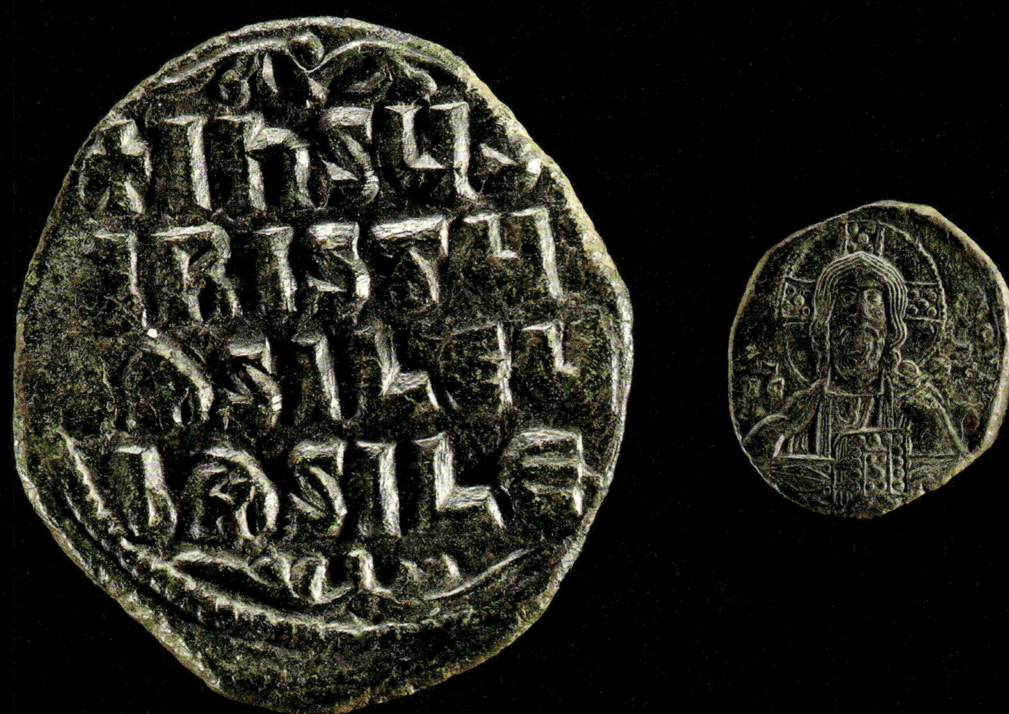

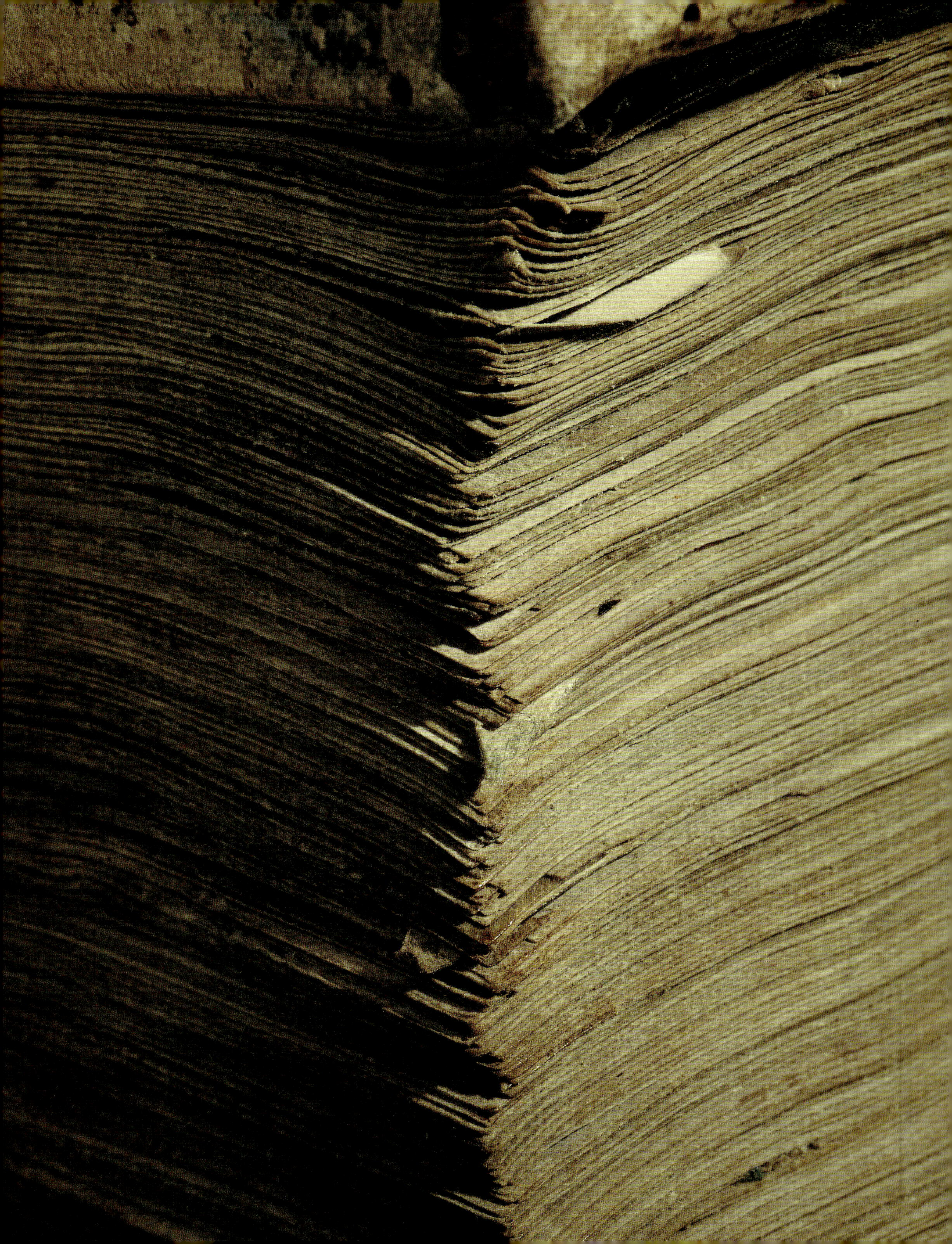

ho. q̄ uiuit & regnat cū patre &
sp̄u sc̄o in sc̄la sc̄lo⁊ am̄.

Incipit passio sc̄i Georgii martiris.

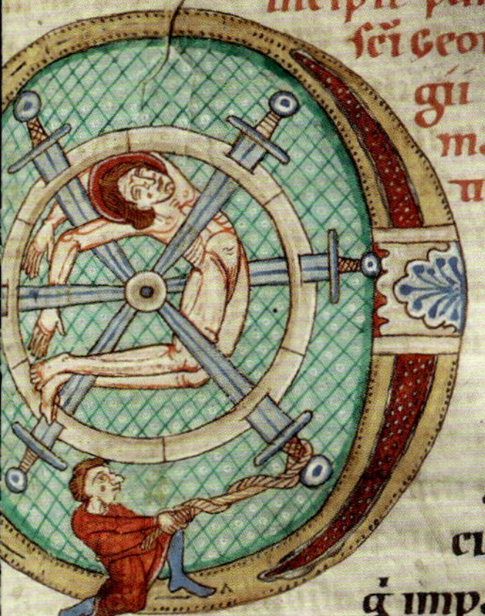

a
cian⁹
q̄ impa
r diabolica dn̄atione arrept⁹
omnē p̄uinciā sue impio di
ionis subderet. nisus ē potest
e sup reges & sup p̄sides p̄nci
ū gerere. Contigit eodē tem
re imp̄ii sui ut sacra uelocius
rgeret iussa. ut adorationē
o⁊ impiissimā uniuersus p̄p̄ls
m cū festinatione aduenisset.
sedens p̄tribunali statim im
sso p̄p̄lo q̄ ex diu̇sis ciuitatib⁹
nebant. p̄cepit ministris of
io⁊ quo⁊ fuerat cure cōmissū.
erre diuersa genera tormento⁊.
e p̄parauerat his. q̄ in dn̄o ihu
o se credere fatebant̄. Et cū al
a fuissent. dacian⁹ imp̄ ut leo
mens exclamauit dicens. Om
s q̄ n̄ curuatis genib⁹ uenera
les deos meos adorau̇it p̄strat.
his pe nis eū faciā interire.
a ut linguā ei⁹ abscida.
culos. aures. facieq; membratī
uella. Simili m̄ p̄co p̄platas cir
uit emissa forti uoce. ut un⁹

quisq; in suis diuersoriis. deos
drasq; erigerent immolando.
Talib⁹ q̄ minis cuncti p̄territi. de
relinquentes xp̄m idolis immo
labant. & magis q; diabolus in
suis argumtis insistebat. quē ad
modū innocua pectora suis laqis
irretiret. Tunc in medio apparu
it sc̄s georgi⁹ capadocie regionis
genere ort⁹. ciuitatis quoq; sue
comitatū gerens sup numerū mi
licie multe: a suis uidelicet ciui
tatū p̄imis sūmā pecunie accipi
ens quo posset a daciano impa
tore p̄mio & munere oblatū
dignitatis gradū adipisci. eo q̄d
sue patrie minis. ueridicus. do
cibilis. rectorq; habebat̄. Sc̄s ū
georgius aspiciens ex omnū p̄
uintia⁊ p̄p̄lis apd̄ imp̄iū dacianū
p̄p̄los multos adeē xp̄m dn̄m blas
phemantes & demones adoran
tes. tunc omnē pecuniā q̄m secū
attulerat egenis distribuit &
exuens se clamide ītem imp̄ii.
baltheo se induit lorice fidei.
crucis uexillo p̄tect⁹. gr̄a q; sc̄i
sp̄c mundans sic erupit sub con
spectu daciani imp̄atoris dicēs.
Om̄s dii gētiū d̄monia. dn̄s aut̄
n̄r celos fecit. Cecauit aut̄ dia
bolus oculos diffidentiū. ut n̄
cognoscant celo⁊ dn̄m ihm̄ xp̄m.
Nam dii tui imp̄ator: op̄a homi
nū s̄ aurea. & argentea. lapidea
& lignea. que uigi uigilia custo
dia⁊ seruant̄ ne nocturno si
lentio subripiant̄ a furib⁹. Hoc
audito dacian⁹ imp̄ator uehe
ment̄ exarsit. & intra semet

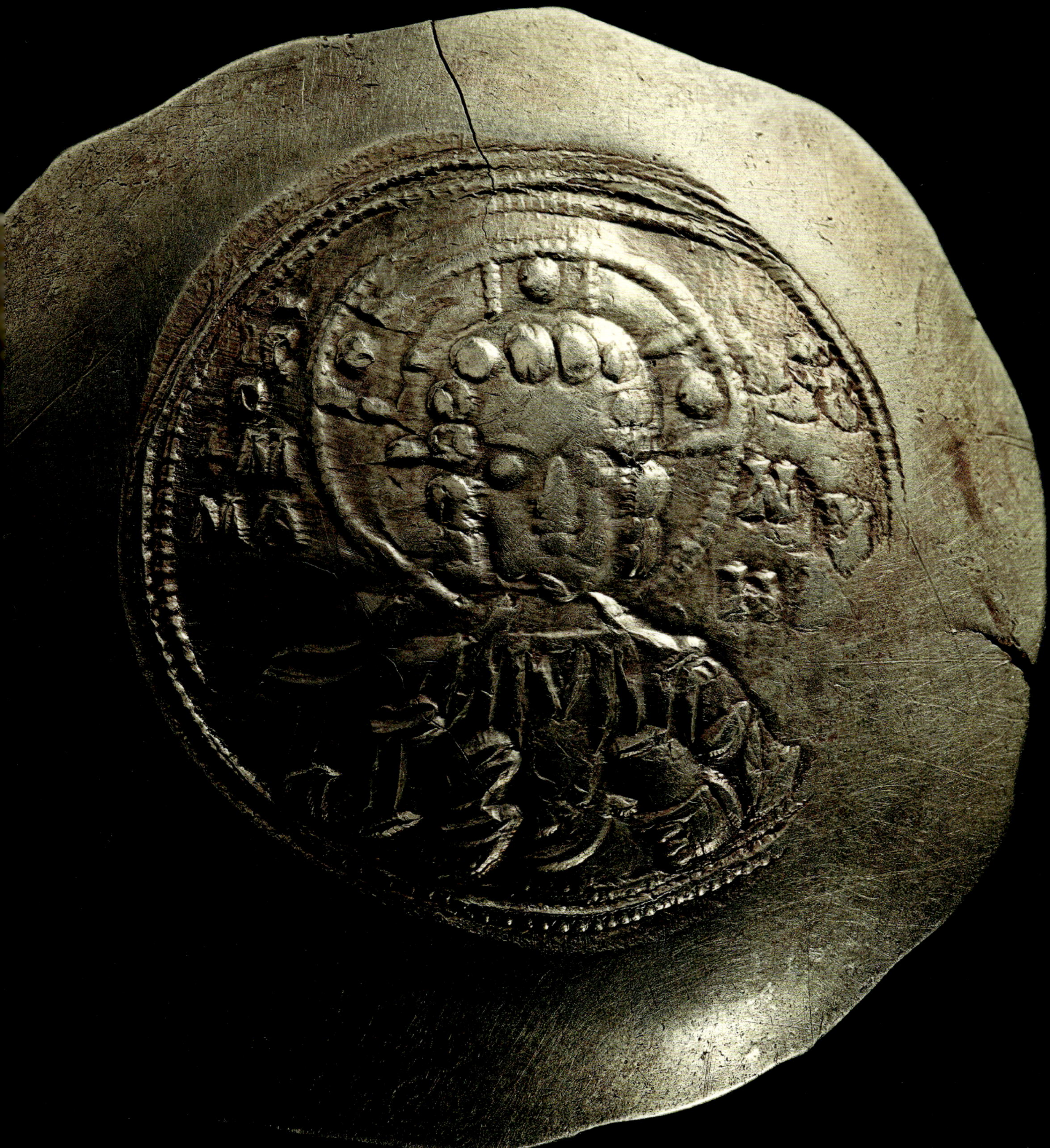

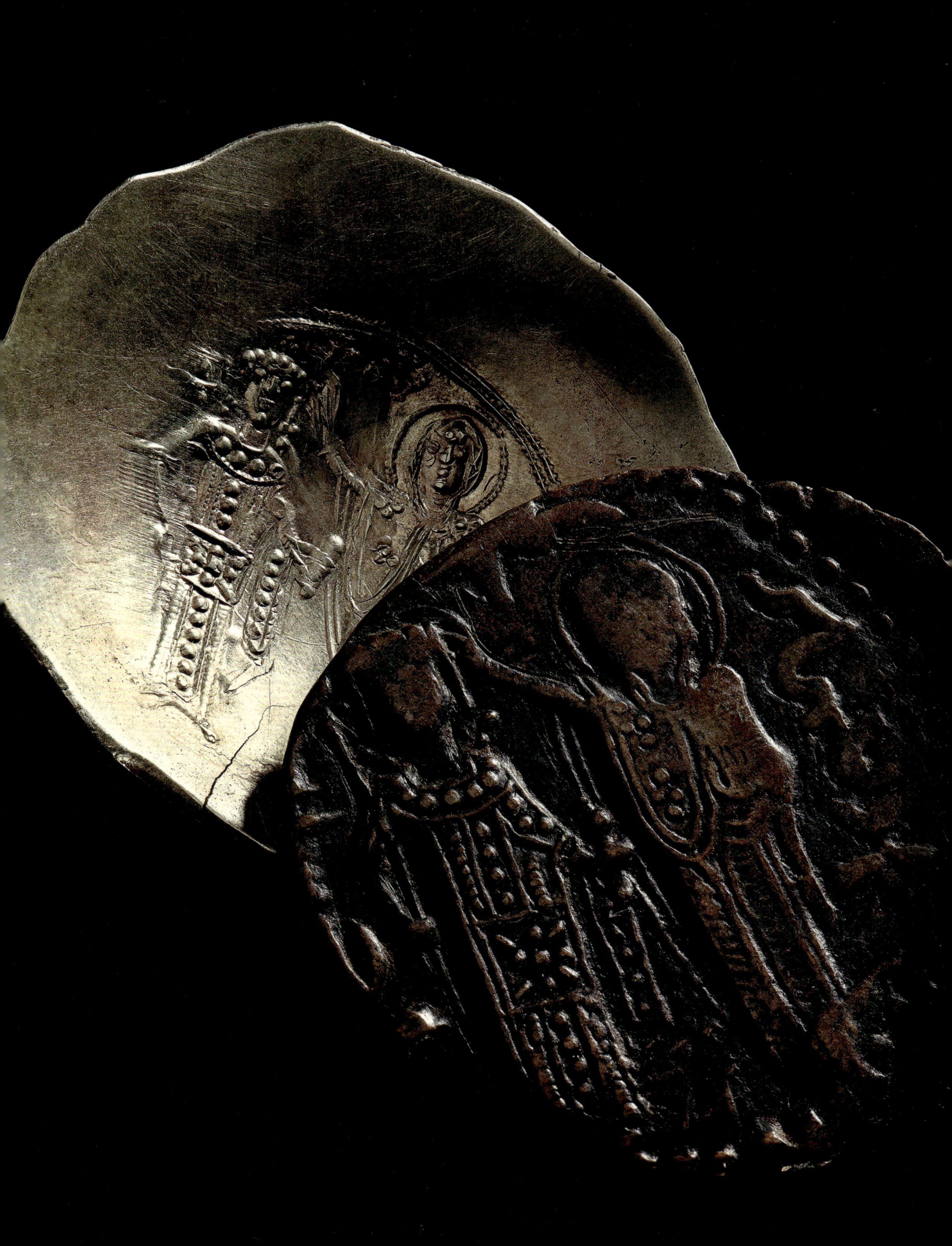

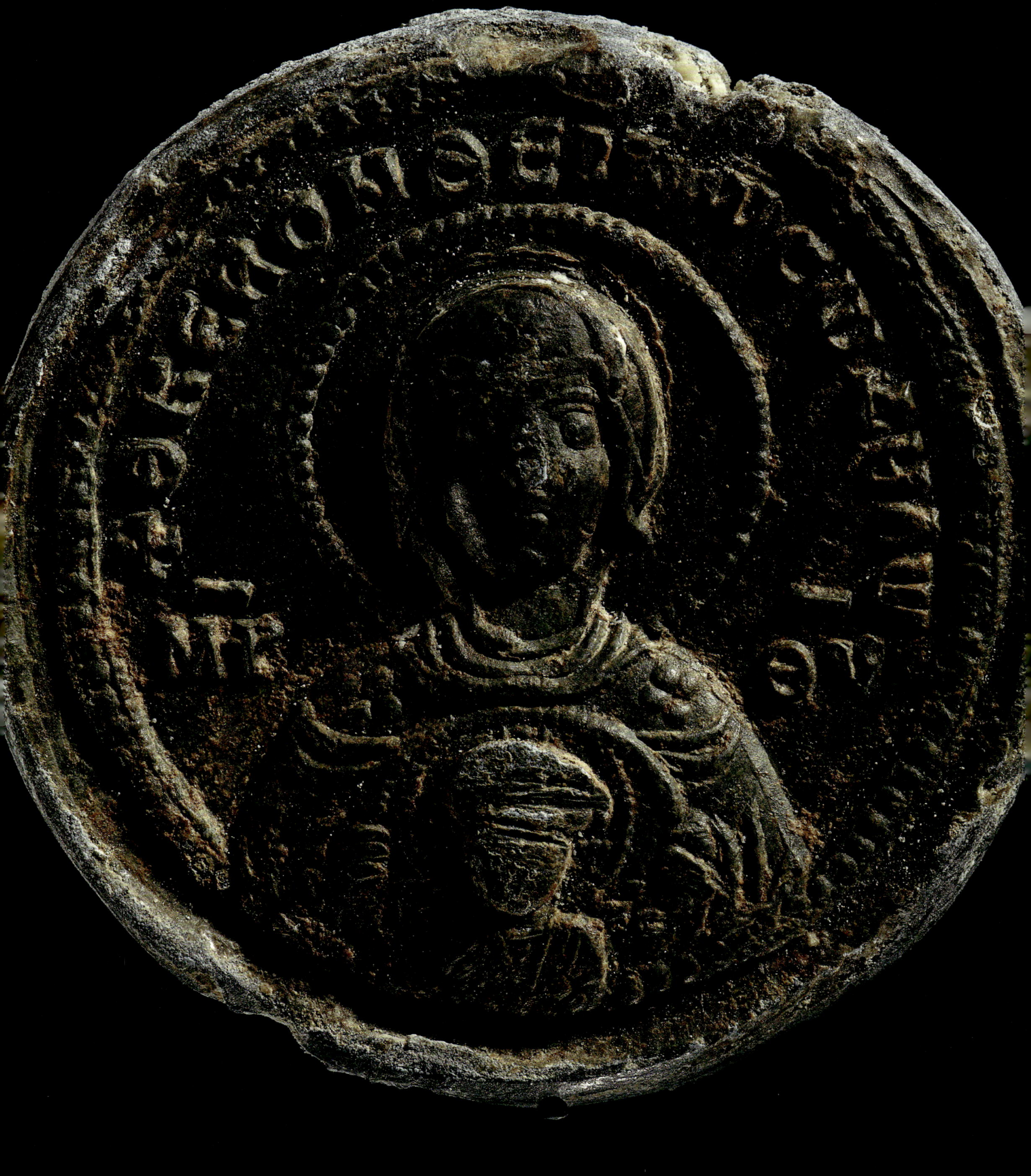
MP
ΘV

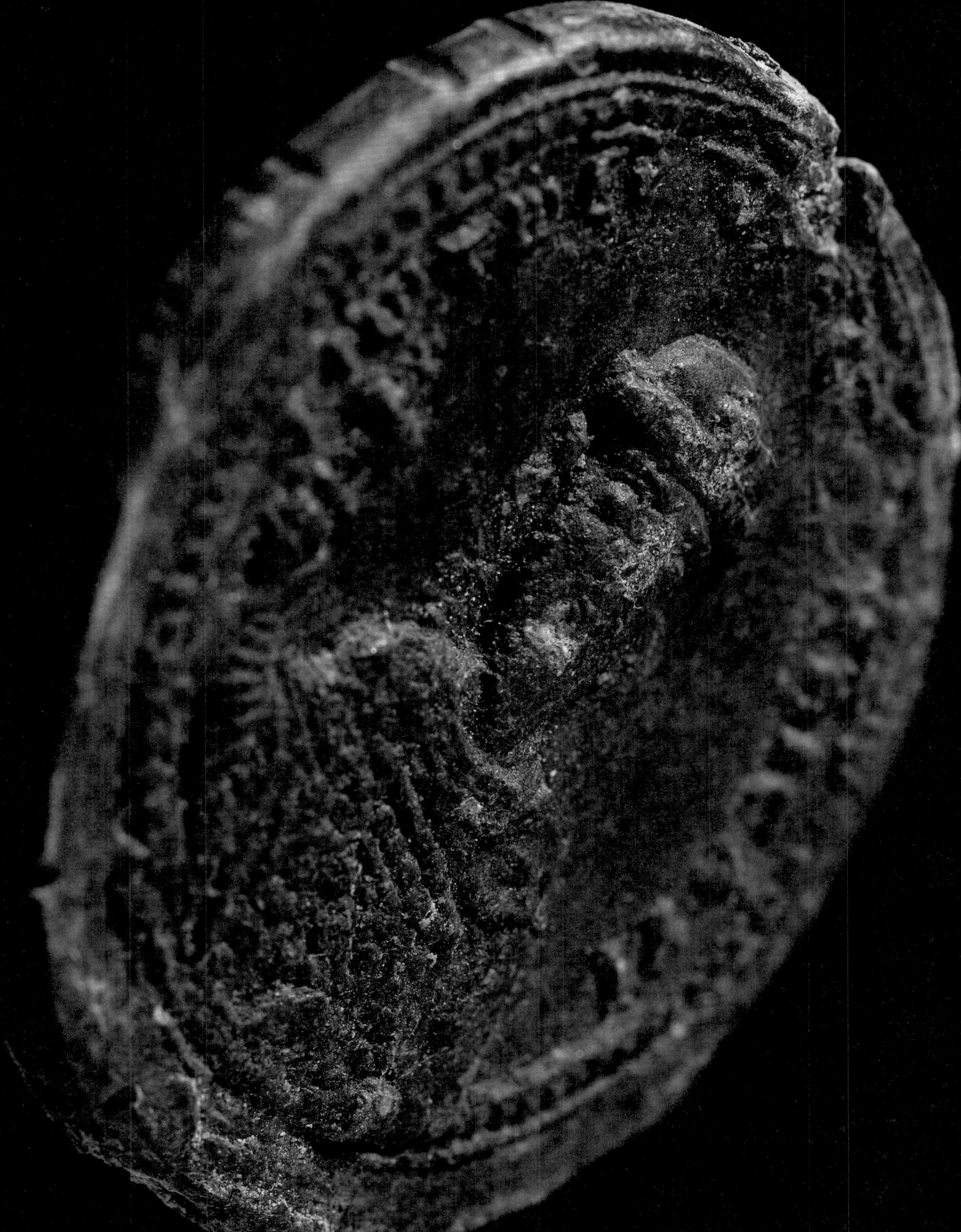

nii · cum quibus et barnabas et paulus. Quibus omnibus
pariter in gratia dei et unanimitate de gentibus · ibi pri
mum discipuli uelut ex perenni fonte superno uocabu
lo appellati sunt christiani. Qua tempestate agabus quidam
unus ex his qui aderant prophetis · famem magnam futuram
diuinis propagabat oraculis. Paulus uero et barna
bas cum ministerio a fratribus collato · quo sanctorum usibus
deseruirent · ierosolimam destinantur. · IIII ·
Interea tiberius duobus et xx · circiter annis sui principatus
exactis · uiuendi finem fecit. Post quem gaius ipsum suscepit.
et continuo iudeorum principatum tradidit agrippe simul
et philippi et lisanie tetrarchias cum quibus et pau
lo post herodem pariter contulit · ipsum uero herodem qui uel
in iohannis nece auctor extiterat uel in passione christi
interfuerat · multis excruciatum modis eterno dampnat
exilio · sic iosephus in his que supra in seruimus scribit.
Huius temporibus filo insignissimus scriptorum florebat.
qui non solum in nostra uerum et in grecorum filosophia primus
inter primos habebatur. Hic autem genere quidem apparuit
hebreus. apud alexandriam uero in omnibus clarus ac no
bilibus uiris · clarior ac nobilior erat. In diuinis
autem legibus et patriis institutis · quantus qualisque
fuerit ex his que nobis librorum suorum tradidit monu
mentis omnibus clarum est. Quis enim digne ualeat ex
plicare · quanta eius in liberalibus artibus fuerit instructio ·
quanta in philosophicis · quantusque maxime in pla
tonicis et pitagoricis fuerit disciplinis · ut que
omnes et qui secum floruerant · pene et qui precesserant
Hic igitur ipse · V · superarit.
temporibus Gaii quanta iudeis acciderint
mala · quinque uoluminibus exponit. Sed et de eius
dementis sue insania commemorat · quod in tan
tam superbiam elatus sit · ut deum se uoluerit appella
ri. Impsis autem ubi de iudeorum cladibus refert.
suam quoque legationem quam pro eorum tribulibus suis iudeis de
tulit ad urbem romam describit · et quod pro orans
apud gaium pro patriis legibus nichil amplius quam
irrisionem retulerit domum · immo et pene periculum
mortis incurrerit. Sed et iosephus meminit horum
in octauo decimo antiquitatum libro talia quedam
scribens. Et quidam cum seditio apud alexandri
am fuisset exorta · inter iudeos et grecos termi

abuerique pactio legati inuicem ad g
quibus pro parte grecorum erat quidam leg
on nomine · qui cum in ceteris quam pluri
mis lacerarer iudeos · tum maxime · quod ho
ri non deferrent ut moris esset facere om
nis facibus subiacentium · hic quod aiebat
gaio neque templa constituunt · neque
cemodi · in quibus ei diuini honores
cialibus deferuntur. Sed soli sunt qui neque
decernant · neque sacramenti nominis
uenit. Cumque hec et alia grauiora alle
on per que concitari crederet gaium · filo
ni preerat iudeorum uir in omnibus mag
alexandri alabarche frater · philosophie
potentissime purgaui obiecta · · sed abiecit eum gai
ilico e conspectu suo abscedere · dum
repletus secum ipse timeret · quod in eos con
li. Egressus autem filo cum iniuria
deos qui sibi adstabant. Bono animo nos
tet · quibus iratus est gaius · quia necesse est ad es
ubi humanum cessat auxilium. Hec q
phus. Sed et idem filo in ipso libro qu
legationem conscripsit · sigillatim de omnib
met ipso gesta sunt refert. Ex quibus
commemorabo · que legentibus euiden
os diuinam pro piaculis queque aduersi
si sunt indicent ultionem. VI
Primo quidem tempore tyberii refert.
roma fuisse ianum quendam magi
imperatorem loci · uniuersam eorum gent
ensu intime uoluisse. In iudea autem
sub quo in saluatorem facinus admissum est.
quod in ierosolimis templum adhuc manebat
profanare temptaret · maximis eos pertur
agitasse. Sed et post tyberii occasum ga
successorem eius cum ceteris quam plurimis · i
deorum genti acerbissimum extitisse quod
etiam ex ipsis scriptoris sermonibus disce
ta quidem inquit erat in gaio in geni
qua erga omnes homines tum precipue e
orum gentem ferebatur · et speciali quadam
loca eorum que in diuinis sunt suppli

…secrata in cipien…
…onē religionē moreq; gentis pfanari …
…atuis suis et signis ea atq; imaginib; replēt.
…templū quoq; scē ciuitatis qd̄ solū manebat
…pfane contagionis intactū et a maiorib;
…tituerat asilum. cōmutatr in templū ppr̄i
…ciuitauerat asilum. nobilissimi nouī
…nomis ausus ē. ut edes iouis nobilissimi noui
…gaii uocaret̄. S; et alias innumeras clades
…ut̄ omīs tragicos luctus apd̄ alexandriam
…ades irrogatas ēē sub gaio. in scd̄o opis sui
…titulatib; libro uir memorat̄ exeqt̄. Nec n̄
…ioseph; cōsona huic de pilati tēpib; scribens.
…ictis saluatoris. q̄ uniūse genti accinderit
…la. audi ut etiā ipse in scd̄o iudaici belli
…tetur libro; Ipse autē ait; Cū missus ē i iudeā
…tiberio pcurator pilat̄. noctu uelatas ierosolo
…mā inferri imagines cesaris iubet ac sta
…Quod ubi dies exortū ē. magnā ptbationē
…deoy poplis excitauit stupentib; ac pturba
…ad nouā faciē rerū. Conicieban namq;
…hoc qd̄ spnerent. & conculcarent iam legē
…& omīa instituta maioy quib; nichil ta
…habi int̄ menia urbis illi fas erat. S; hoc
…ē nimirū in quo eos in pie pfessionis su
…uelox uindicta dāpnauit. p eo qd̄ sedm
…gū relationē gens simul conclamauit
…uniuersa: non habemus regē n̄ cesarē; Tū de
…de idē scptor aliam quoq; in eos delatam
…commemorat ultionē dicens; Post hec autē etiā
…alia in eos incidit ptbatio. pro eo qd̄ sacrum
…rariū qd̄ apd̄ eos patria lingua corbanas
appellatur. cōt̄ fas in usus cōmunes puplici a
…ductus pgari uideretur. qui a trecentis sta
…is deducebat̄. Pro q̄ nimia indignatiōe po
…s cōmouebat̄; Cūq; adesset pilat̄ ierosolimis.
…dent adire eū et clamorib; fatigare. At ille p
…derat enī sedicionē futurā. milites. habitu ple
… obtectis armis multitudini miscuit. pcep
…ens dato ut ne gladiis in sediciosos. s; fustib;
…erent. Igit̄ ubi temp; fuit signo eis de tribu
…alib; dato. cedi pternīq; cepert̄. n̄ nulli uer
…antiū uulnerib;. plurimi autē dū in fugam

doloris …
in ierosolimis eis ob uenisse …
sediciosius student. idē scptor ex ponit. ostendes
qd̄ ex admissi sacrilegii tēpore nunq̄ abhein se
dicionū furor. nuq bella mortesq; cessauerint.
usq; quo ultimū & exitiabile malū tēpib; uespa
siani eos obsidionis inclusit. VII

Igit̄ iudeos p cōmisso scelere ultio diuina dāp
nat. S; et pilat̄ qui in saluatorē iniq̄ iudicis
functus officio est. isdē tēpib; gaii tantis ac ta
lib; maloy cladib; excruciat̄ ē ut ppa se ma
nu transuerberasse & nefariā uitā in abiectis
se referat̄. Nec enī poterat tanti piaculi minis
ter in punit̄ euadē. sic in historiis grecoy re
ptum ē eoy dū taxat qui olimpiadas scribunt
& annales rerū gestarū libros ad posteritatis
memoriā condiunt. VIII

Sed enī gaio q̄ttuor annis necdū tegris p̄n
cipatu ministrato. claudius imperator succe
dit. sub q̄ fames satis dira uniūsū orbē terre
obtinuit. Hoc tam̄ ita futurū longe ante nr̄i
pphe pdixerant. sic in actib; aploy refertur
agabū quendā pphā famī magnā futuram
sub imperatore claudio denuntiasse. Uerū lu
cas q̄ hec de agabo refert. cōiungit etiā hoc qd̄
p paulū & barnabā fr̄es q̄ erant antiochie p
uirib; suis unusquisq; sūptū miserint scīs
habitantib; ierosolimā. VIIII

Et p; hec addit dicens; In illo autē tēpr.
sine dubio temp; qd̄ sub claudio fuit.
cū fames erat designans. inmisit in quit he
rodes rex manus suas ut affligeret aliq̄s de ec
clesia. & interfecit iacobū fr̄em iohis gladio.
De hoc iacobo autē. clemens alexandrinus
etiā hystoriā quandā dignā memoria in sep
timo dispositionū suarū libro scrib. platam
ad se usq;. ex tradicione maioy. Qm̄ qdē inqt.
& his qui obtulerat eū iudici ad martyriū
iacobū scilicet. motus etiam ipse cōfessus
est se ēē xpianū. Ducti sunt ambo parit̄

n remanet in celo; n conti
nuatur aut apparentibz et man
ifestis et clausis et signaculis in
determinabiles s. indeterminabiles
a dico. no enim hqd sic apparen
tur dignus quibz de apparen
cos ulti h transfiguratoes sic
p sit qui videt videre ind
terminatu e e n principalis
solu qd mentu omne enim
ctu abeo qui creauit u dr. tinua
tur, que sacrificatores a sco spu
uirtutes. pdminam gra pplinire
n inmptis indigentes qui no
sit mortales, intelles u ex
sistentes. inintellectualibz locis
s. n corporali conceptu, no e co
poralis p natum signant in
tres hnt diuisiones. s qui
a intellectualis assunt corpat
ibq tristi sunt, qua n p s
pro h ul ulla est ut opari sin
qlos p talia sit differentes
amminicc non cum sol aut
qui sunt de ex nouit q o sit;
differetia aut abinuicem illu
minatorie uirtutes. su h illumi
natoes ..... uirtutes. sn
s. statione illuminationem

precepites se inuicem illumi
nates eminentia ordinis
ul natiue, manifestu de q
qui eminat inferioribz tradit
illuminatoes et cognitione; po
tes e et pon addi uolutatis ex
plere des, et ubiqz oferti inuiol
itur. itaqz dm minus uisibi
uelactate n; custodientes p
tes sue et gnatibz et locis possi
tes. sic auditore ordinans
reaq sunt s. no dispensantes
et auxiliatores nobis a q sed
diuina uolutate et ulliore si
nos entes. supracem dm existe
tes. difficile mobiles sunt ad
malu. s n imobiles; nec aut
et imobiles no natu signi.
et soli bo dei affectioe; uide
tes dm sup pos dens. et huic
abu uirtutes; sic nos existente
u incorporei erab eis corporea pa
sione enim. no tn impassibi
les; sol enim de impassibilis e; m
figurantur a adq deorz dnatoe
uisere de. et ita nobis sic appa
ret. diuina eis reuelat misteria.
In celo erit lat e unus o p
ht. primus laudare dm. cum

Intelligentia e s ... hodie ... ad par ...

stimare diuine est uoluntatis. Sicut a-
sserunt, et theologissimus ait Di-
onisius Ariopagita. omnis the-
ologia .i. diuina scriptura cele-
stes substantias nouem esse dixit. has
diuinus scilicet sacer minister interpres deno-
minat trinos ornatus; equi-
num quidem esse ait. eum qui circa de-
um est semper et proxime et immediate
unitum esse tradidit. eum quidem sex
alas habentium seraphin. et insignitos
oculis habentium cherubin. et sanctis-
simorum thronorum est. et nomen eum qui in
dominationum. et uirtutum. et potestatum
est. Tertium uero et ultimum eum qui prin-
cipatuum. et archangelorum. et angelorum
est. Quidam quidem dixit. quod ante omnes
quidem creaturas geniti sunt. ut the-
ologus dicit Gregorius. Primum quidem de-
excogitauit angelicas uirtutes.
et celestes. et excogitatio opus
fuit. Alii uero quidam post quam geni-
tum est primum celum; quidam ante hominis
plasmationem. omnes confitentur. Ego
autem theologo Gregorio consentio;
decebat enim primum intellectualem
substantiam creari. tunc sensibilem. et tunc
quod ex utroque .s. hominem. Quicumque
non autem angelos conditores cuiuscumque
esse substantie. non enim sunt patris sui dia-
boli; damnum eum existere non sunt
conditores. Eius uero autem factor et con-
ditor et protector deus est qui sol-
us incarnatus. qui in patre et filio
et sancto spiritu. pronus laudatur et
glorificatur. Sciendum autem sit. quia quod
est hominibus mors. hoc angelis est casus.
post casum enim non est eis penitentia. quemad-
modum nec hominibus post mortem. IIII

De diabolo et demone.

Ex his angelicis uirtutibus qui
preerat terrestri ordini et
cui terre custodia commissa a deo e-
rat. non natura malus factus. sed bo-
nus existens et in bono genitus. et ne-
quaquam in se ipso a conditore
malitie semita habens. non ferens
illuminationem et honorem que ipsi
conditor largitus fuerat. libri sui
arbitrii electione uersus est ex eo quod
secundum naturam in id quod preter naturam. et
eleuatus est aduersus eum qui fecerat
ipsum deum. rebellare ipsi uolens;
et primus desistens remotus
a bono in malum deuenit; nichil enim ali-
ud est malum nisi boni priuatio. sicut
et tenebre luminis sunt. uel discessio
sio uel priuatio. bonum enim lumen

Creati angeli.

Angeli nullo modo creatores.

Ex hiis angelicis [illegible] ... [illegible] spiritualis creature [illegible] in hac [illegible] ... agere de malis angelis ... demonibus ... [illegible]

Hylarius ... Quid mirum ... angelorum ... Ieronimus ... Sex milia ... Augustinus ... [illegible]

Sub dispositione uiri illustris quaestoris.

LEGES DICTANDAE · PRECES :-

Officium non habet, sed adiutores de scriniis, quos uoluerit.

Insignia uiri illustris Comitis largitionum :-

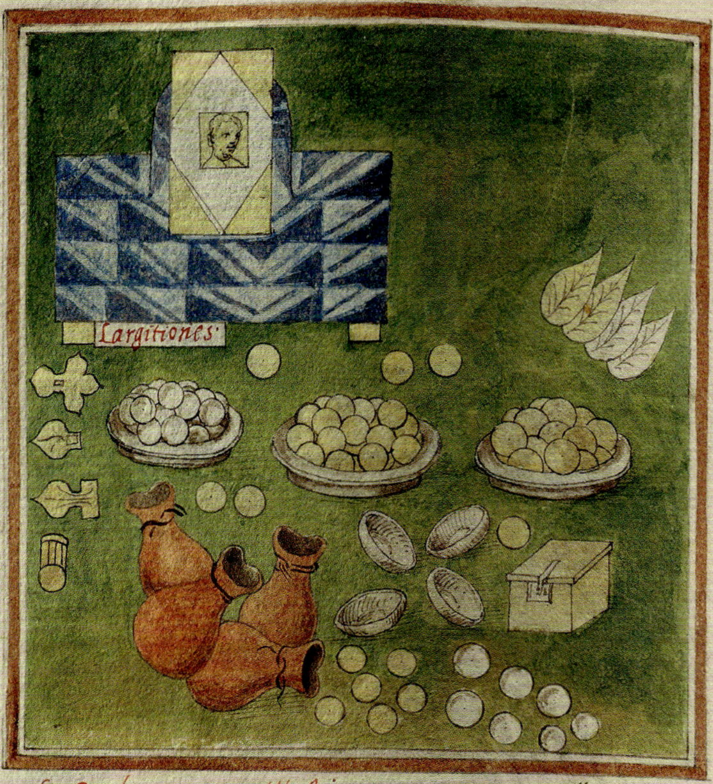

SVB dispositione · v · Illustris

Comitis sacrarum largitionum

Comites largitionu per oes dioeceses.

Comites commerciorum

Per orientem et Aegyptum.

Per Moesiam · Scythiam · et Pontu

Per Illyricum

PP · Thesaurorum.

Comes metallorum p Illyricum

Comes et Rationalis sumar Aegypti

Magri lineae uestis

Magri primarę

Procuratores Gynaeciorum

Procuratores Baphiorum

Procuratores monetarum

Praepositi bastagarum.

Procuratores linifiorum

Officium autē suprascripti V. Ill. comitis sacrar. largi-tionum habet.

Primicerium totius officij.
Primiceriū scrinij canonum.
Primicerium scrinij tabular.
Primiceriū scrinij numeror.
Primiceriū scrinij aureæ massæ.
Primiceriū scrinij aurie ad responsum. Primiceriū scrinij uestiarij sacri.
Primic. scrinij argenti.
Primic. scrinij anuliarensis.
Primiceriū scrinij a pecunijs, et cæteros scriniarios suprascriptorū scrinior. Secundocerium officij qui Primicerius est Exceptorum. Tertiocerium officij qui tractat Bastagas. Quarto loco libellos tractat, et cæteros Palatinos officij suprascripti.

Comes largitionum quotiens usus exegerit.

INSIGNIA VIRI ILLVSTRIS COMITIS PRIVATARVM.

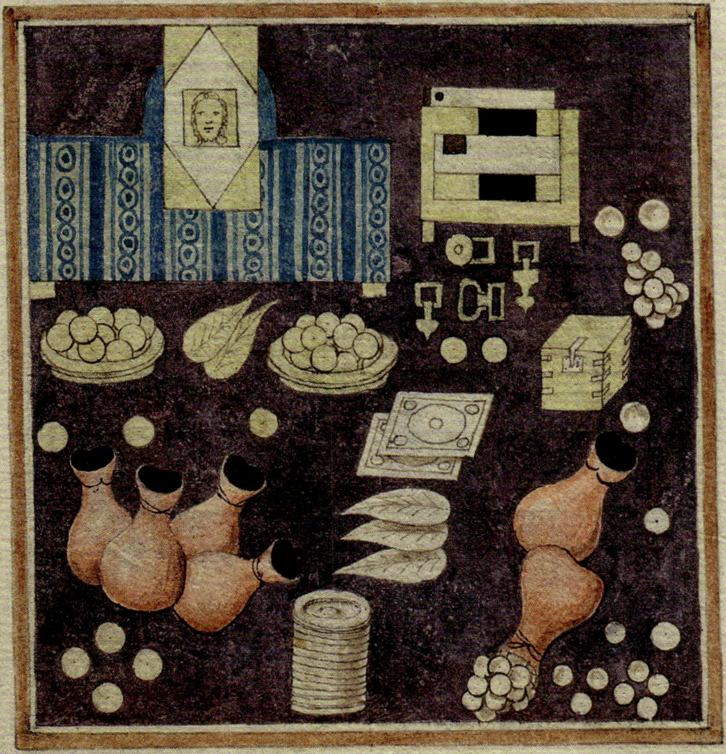

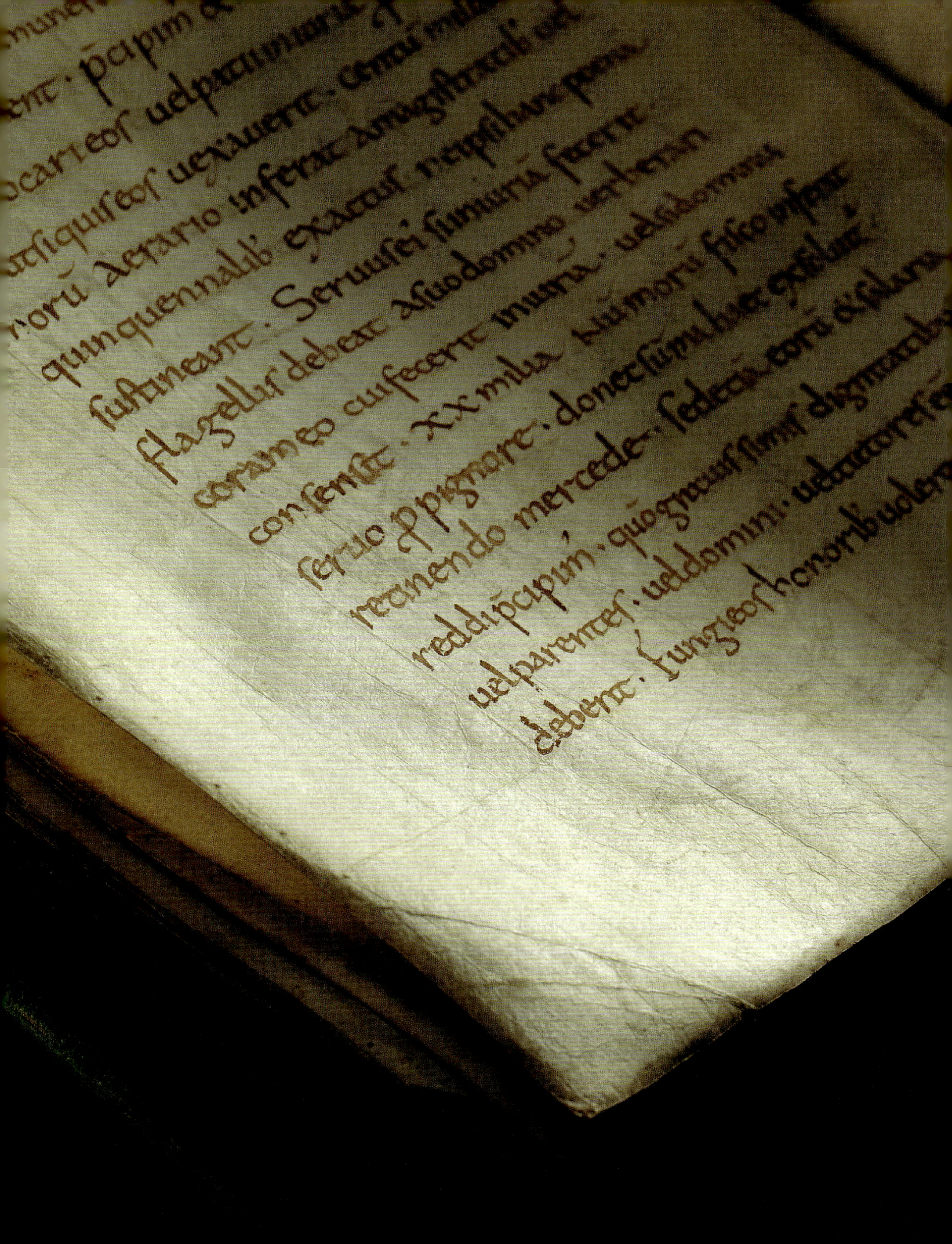

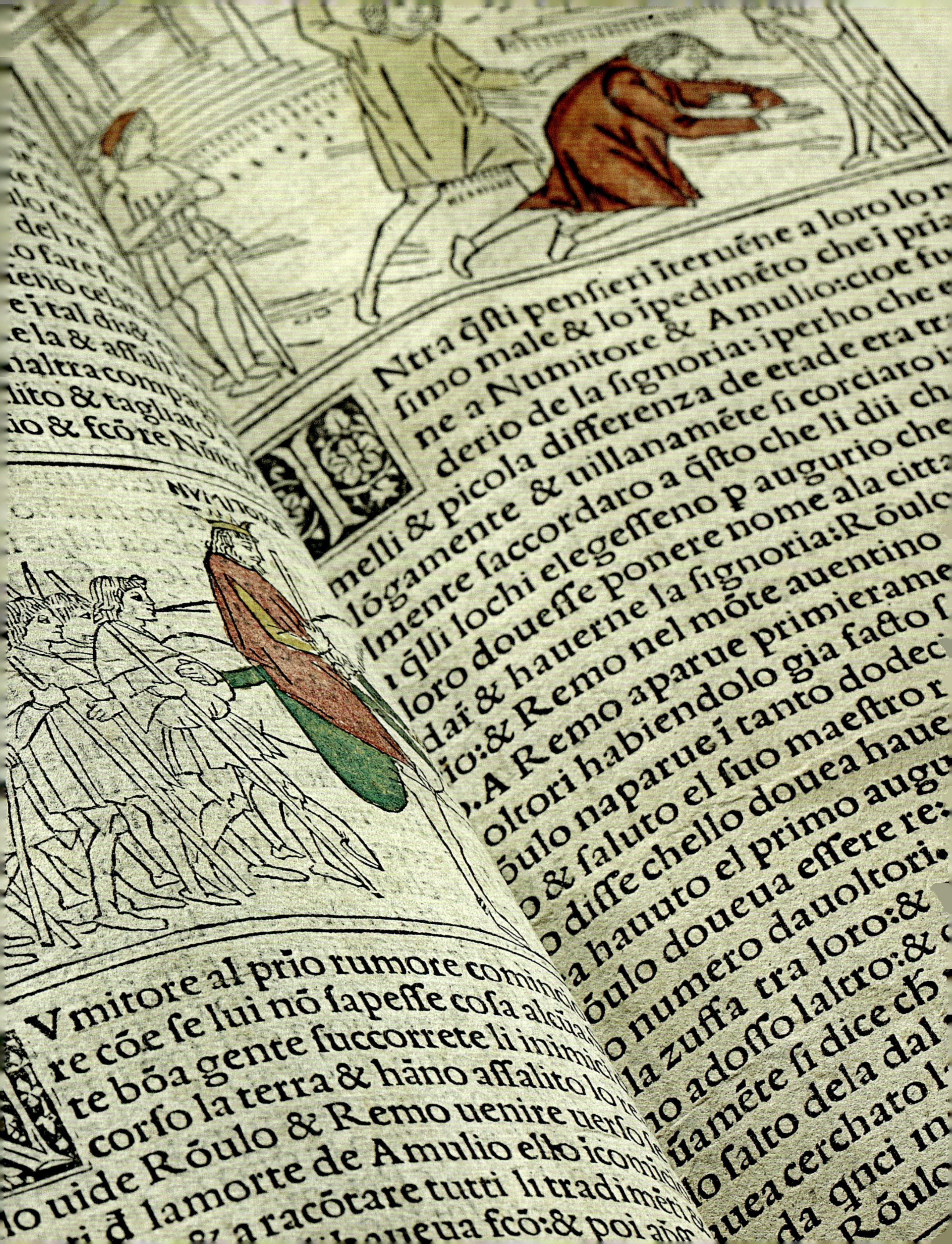
Ntra q̃sti pensieri ĩteruẽne a loro lo r
simo male & lo ipedimẽto chei pria
ne a Numitore & Amulio:cioe fu
derio de la signoria: iperho che e
melli & picola differenza de etade era tr
lõgamente & uillanamẽte si corciaro i
lmente saccordaro a q̃sto che li dii ch
ĩ q̃lli lochi elegesseno p augurio che
loro douesse ponere nome ala citta
dai & hauerne la signoria:Rõulo
io:& Remo nel mõte auentino
.A Remo aparue primierame
oltori habiendolo gia facto s
õulo naparue i tanto dodec
o & saluto el suo maestro r
o disse chello douea haue
a hauuto el primo augu
õulo doueua essere re:
o numero dauoltori.
la zuffa tra loro:&
io adosso laltro:&
ũamẽte si dice ch
lo salto dela dal
uea cerchato l
da q̃nci in
Rõulo
NVMITOR
Vmitore al prio rumore comincio
re cõe se lui nõ sapesse cosa alcuna
te bõa gente succorrete li inimici
corso la terra & hãno assalito lo re
uide Rõulo & Remo uenire uerso
lamorte de Amulio ello iconinc
a racõtare tutti li tradimẽti
haueua fcõ:& poi

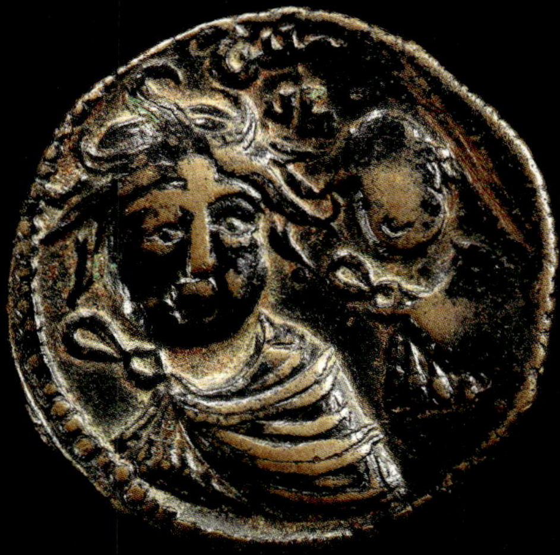

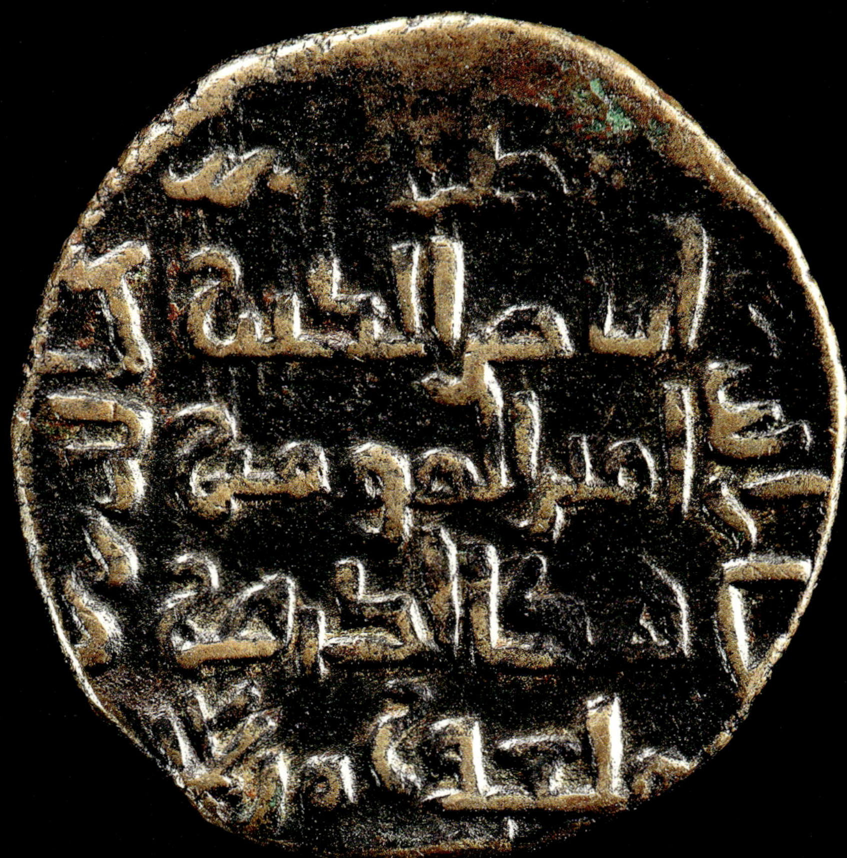

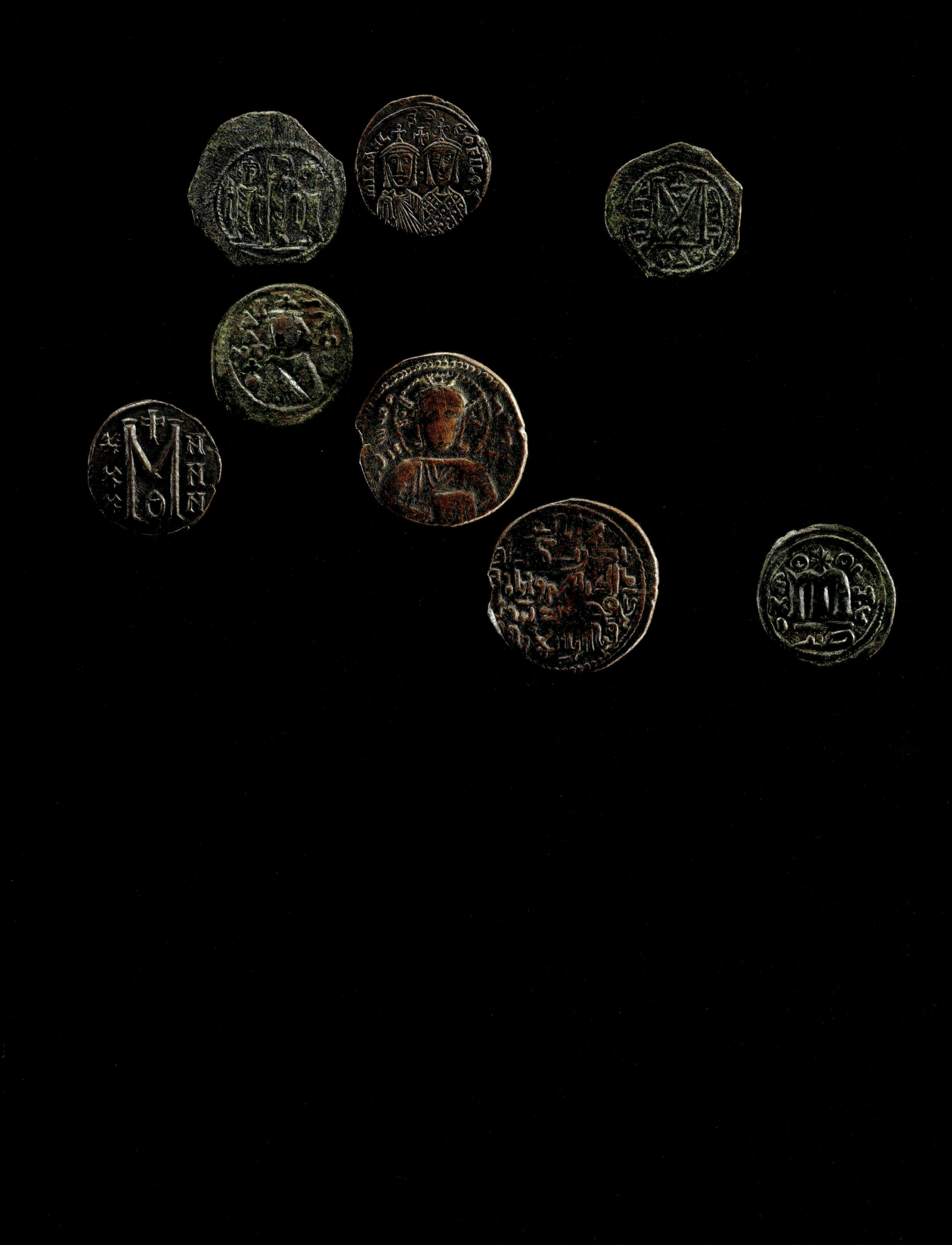

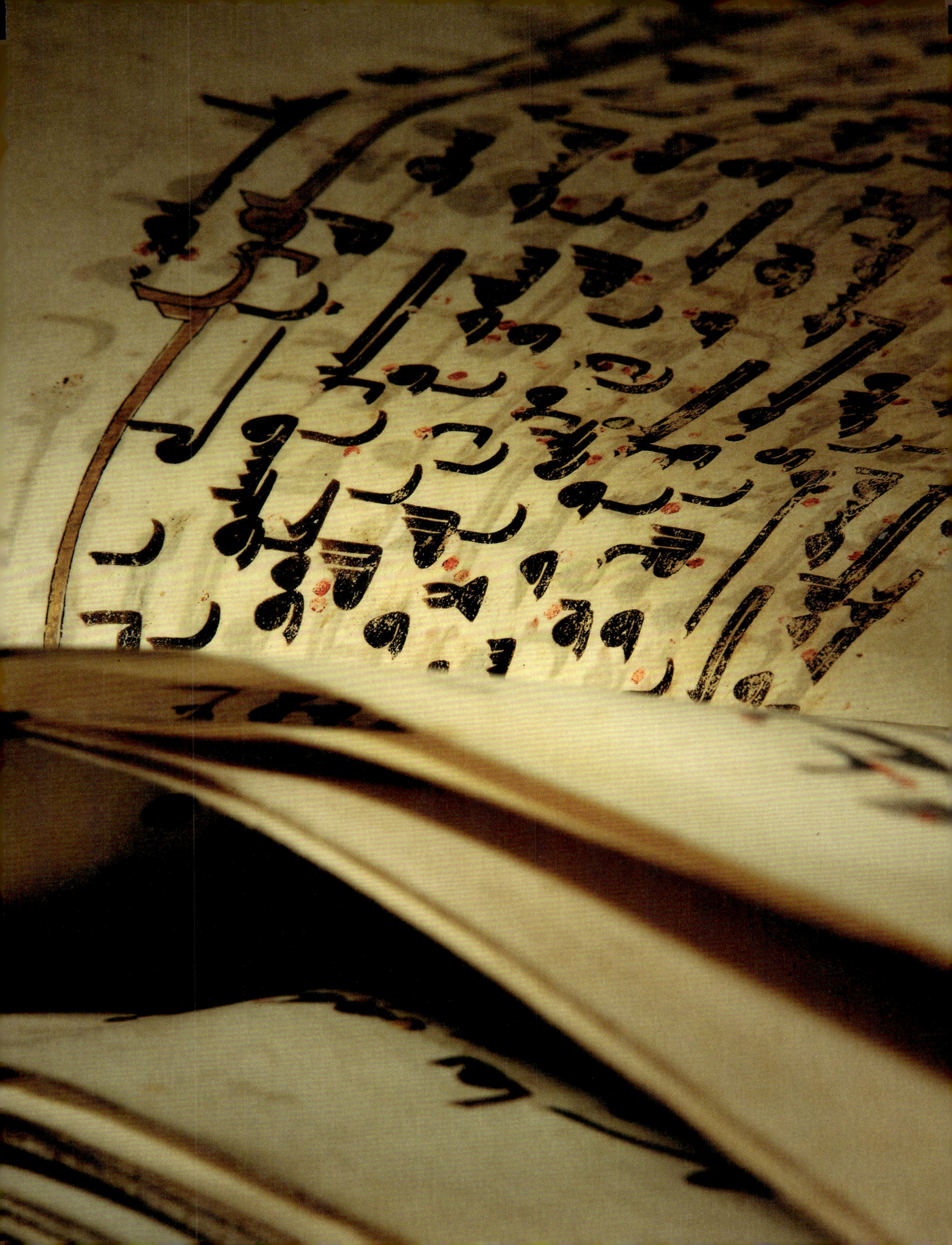

ظلموا ربنا أخرنا إلى

أولم تكونوا أقسمتم

مساكن الذين ظلموا

ضربنا لكم ا

وعند الله مكرهم وا

تحسبن الله مخلف و

تبدل الارض غير ا

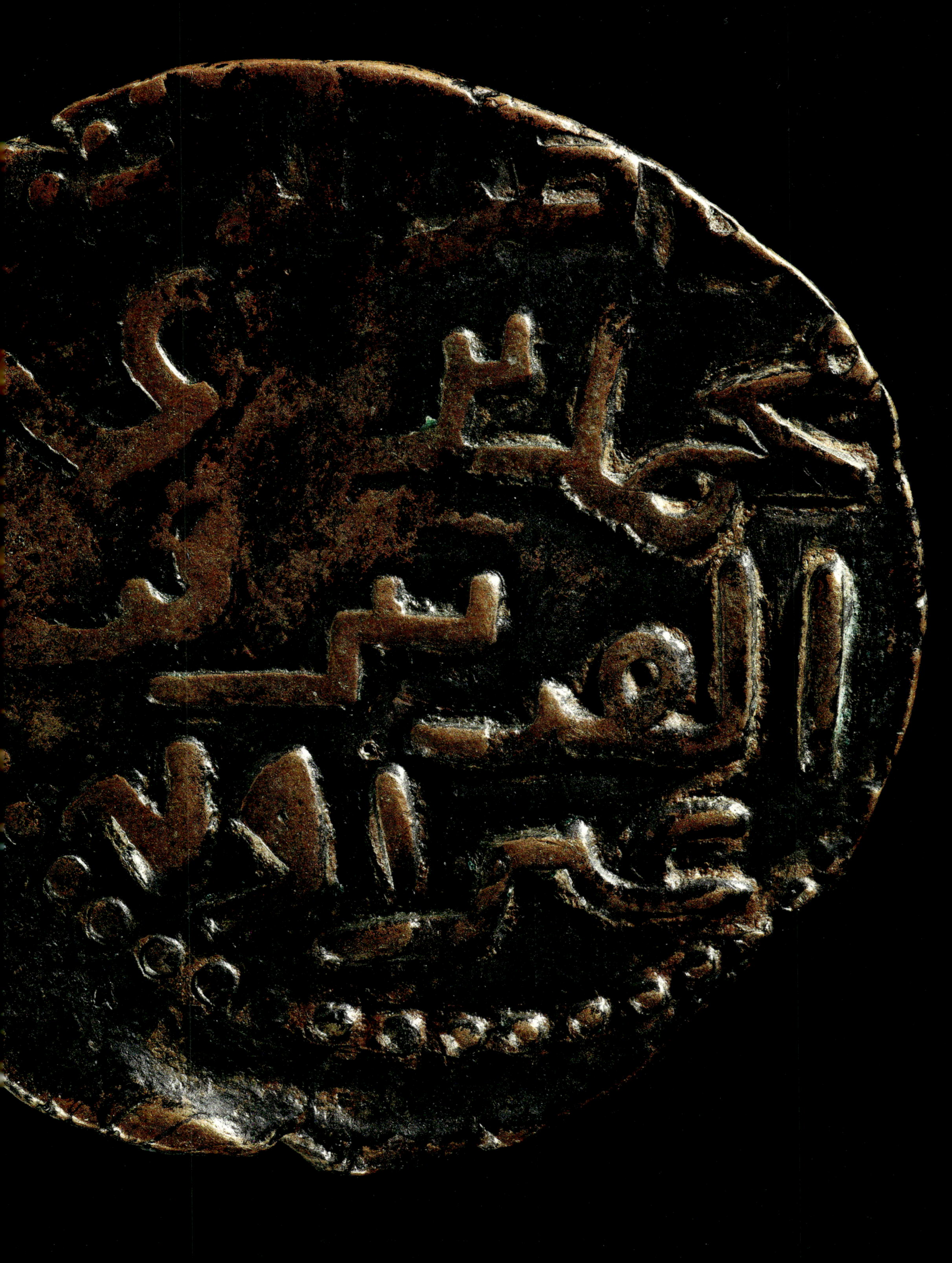

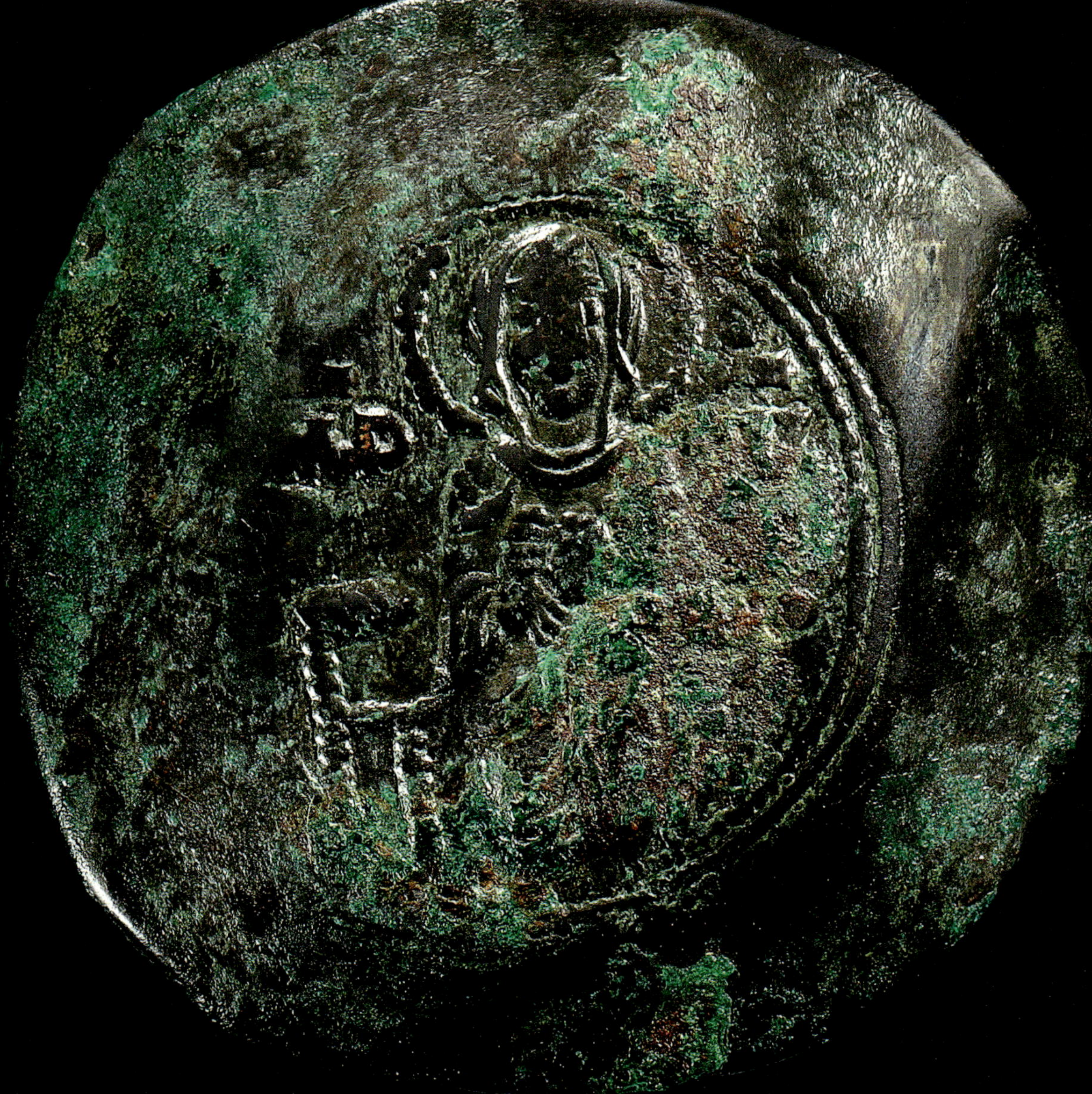

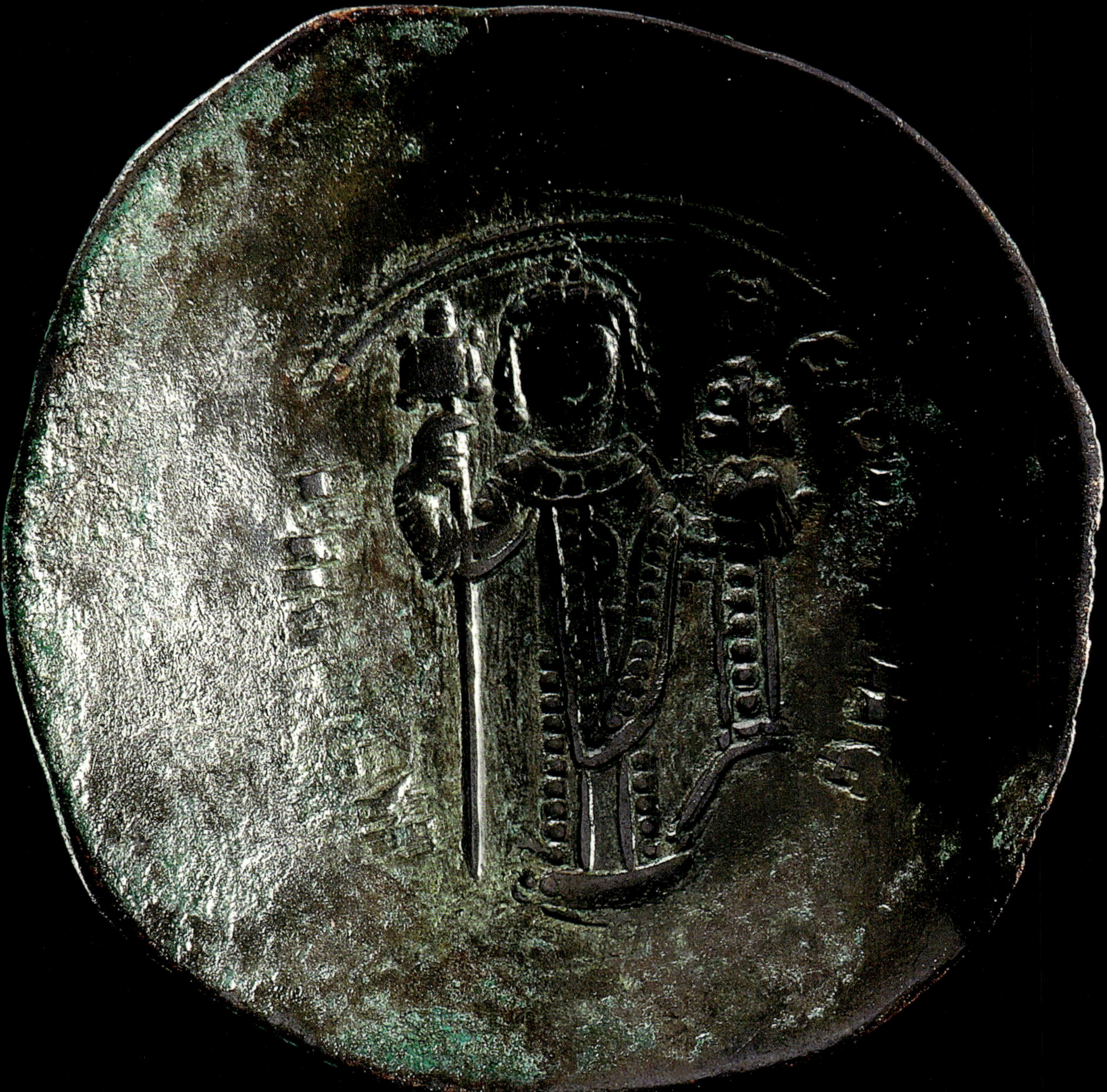

Quicumq; uel rescripti aduersus ueteres sanctio
subreptiua defensione munitur · uel deminu
culis corporib · aut certe idoneus ad p̄batur
functioni mancipatus est adiciendus.

DE MEDICIS ET PROFESSORIBUS

IMPERATOR CONSTANTIN̄

Medicos grammaticos & p̄fessores · alios
litterarū inmunes ē · cū reb' quas in ciuitatib'
suis possident · p̄cipim̄ & honorib' fungi · iniu
etiā uocari eos uel pati iniuriā p̄hibemus
ita ut si quis eos uexauerit · centū milia num
morū aerario inferat a magistratib' uel
quinquennalib' exactus ne ipsi hanc poenā
sustineant · Seruus ei si iniuriā fecerit ·
flagellis debeat a suo domino uerberari
coram eo cui fecerit iniuriā · uel si dominus
consensit · XX milia nummorū fisco infera
seruo p̄ pignore · donec sūma haec exsoluat ·
retinendo mercede · sed etiā eorū & salari
reddi p̄cipim̄ · quo g̃ neius sinit dignitatibus
uel parentes · uel domini · uel tutores ē · non
debent · fungi eos honorib' uolentes p̄mittim

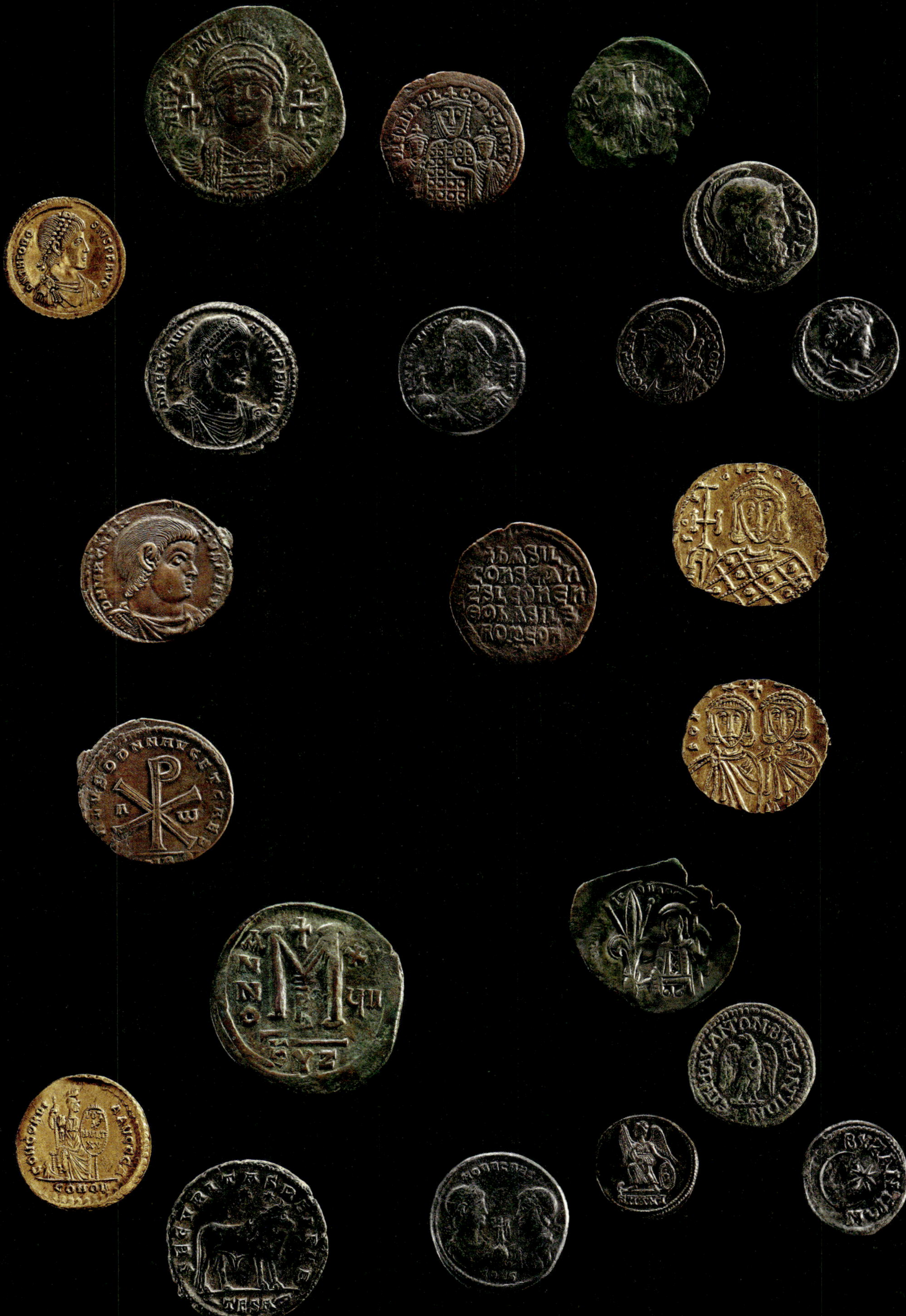

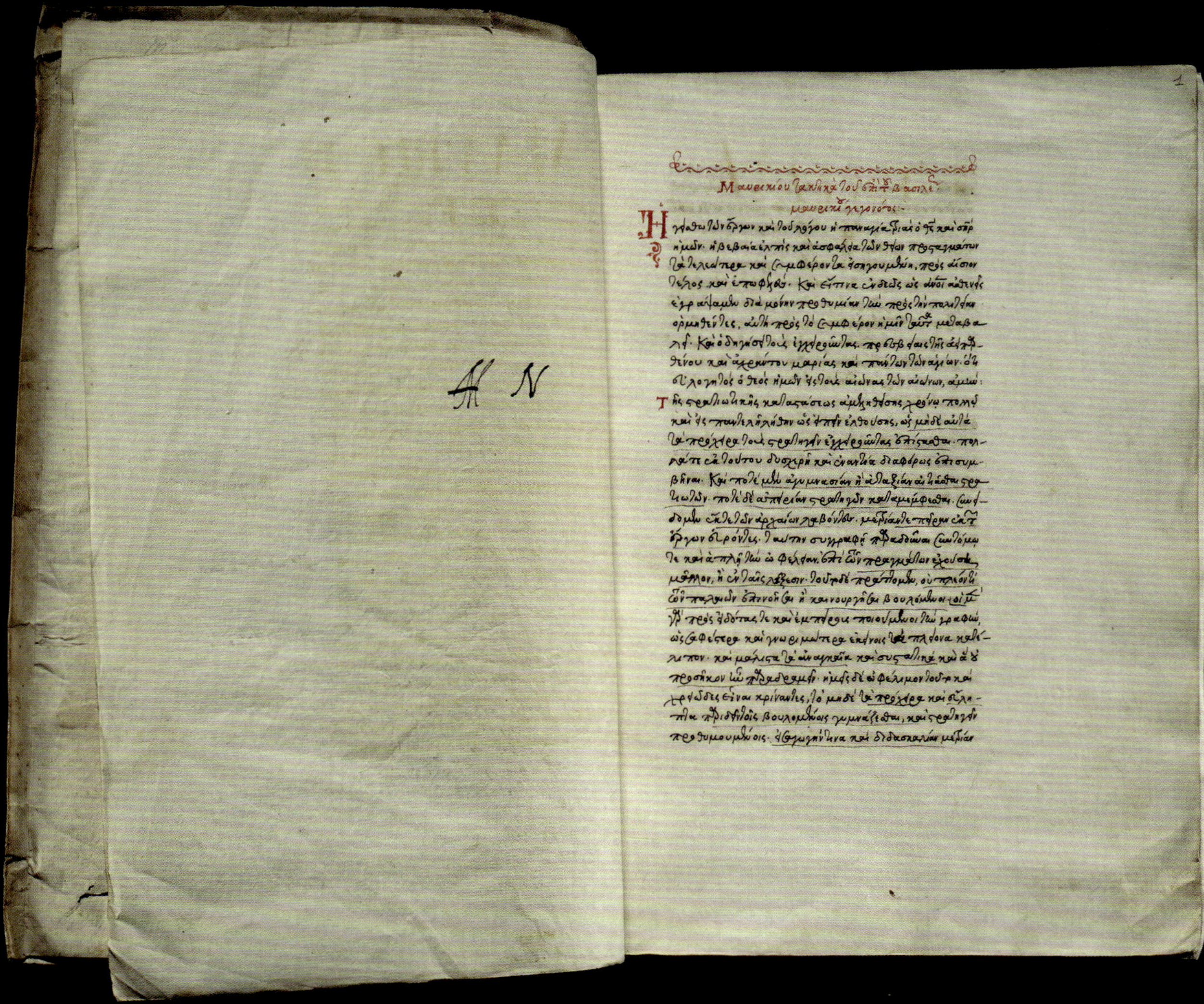
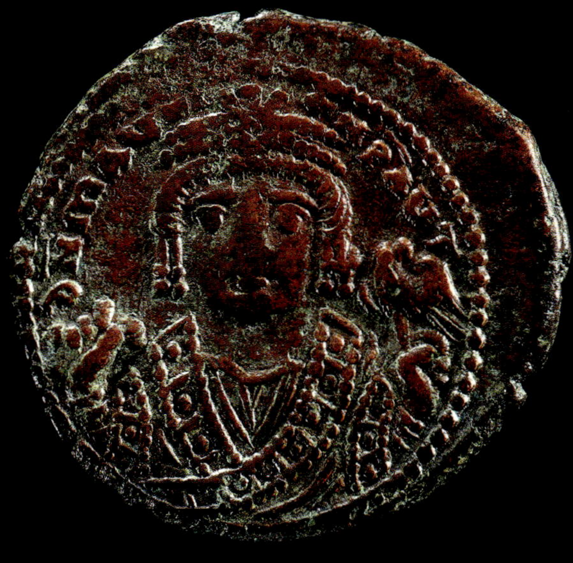
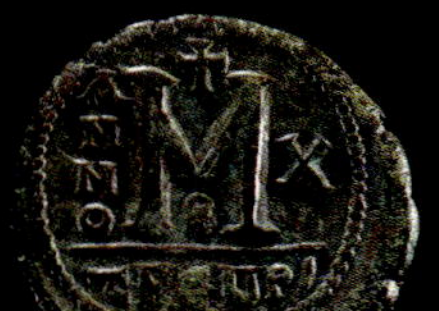

ου καὶ τῶν πατριαρχῶν τῶν τε πα-
λάτων, καὶ αὐτῶν γε τῶν μεγίστων καὶ περι-
κλυτῶν οἰκιῶν. ἃ δὴ κράτιστος κόσμος ὁ-
οῦ καὶ ὀχύρωμα τοῦ μεγίστου νεὼ τοῦ τῆς θεοῦ
φίας ὑπῆρχον· τοῖς τε πρώτοις συστᾶσαι
μιουργοῖς, καὶ τοῖς ἔπειτα προσθῆκαι γινό-
μεναι κάλλιστα, καὶ μάλα τοῖς πρώτοις ἔργοις προσήκουσαι· πάντων γὰρ ἐπ' ἴσης ς
ὲ καὶ κατάλυσις κατωρχήσατο.

sapientiæ fuerunt, tum à primis a
tectis confectæ, tum ab iis qui s
sunt pulcherrimè adiectæ, & prim
peribus admodum conuenientes:
æquè omnes corruptæ & destr
sunt.

ΤΕΛΟΣ, ΚΑΙ ΘΕΩι ΔΟΞΑ.

Apud PETRVM DE LA
ROVIERE.

1615.

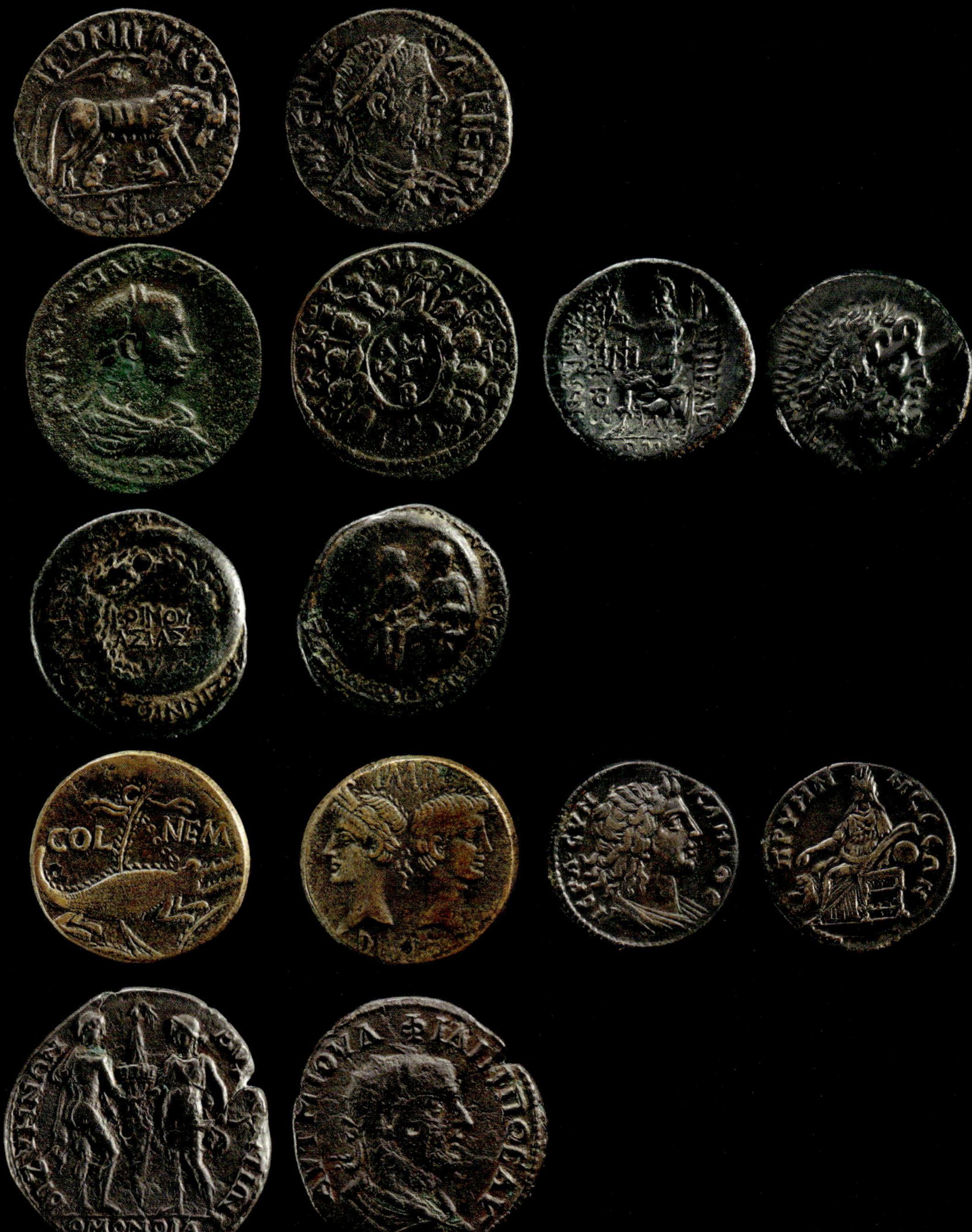
COL NEM
ΟΜΟΝΟΙΑ

CAII. IVLII. CAESARIS. COMMENTARIOꝜ. BELLI. GALLICI. LIBER. PRIMVS. INCIPIT.

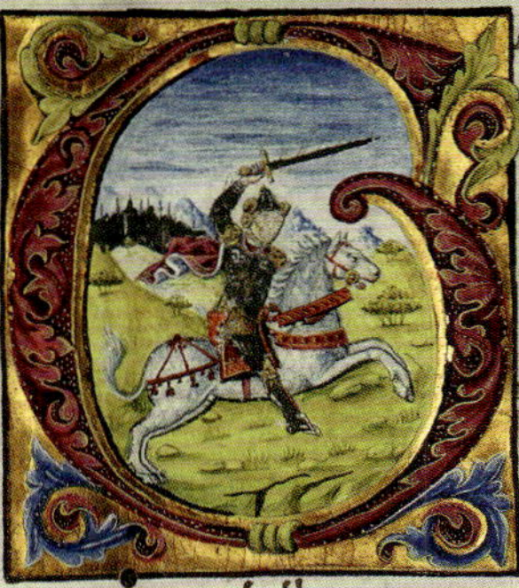

GALLIA. EST. OMNIS. DIVISA. IN PARTES. TRIS.
quarum unam incolunt belge: aliam aquitani: tertiam
qui ipsoꝝ lingua celte, nostra galli appellantur. hi om
nes lingua, institutis legibus inter se differunt. Gallos
ab aquitanis garunna flumen: a belgis matrona et seq^a
na diuidit. horum omniũ fortissimi sunt belge. ꝓpea
q̊d a cultu atq; humanitate ꝓuinciæ longissime absunt:
minimeq; ad eos mercatores sæpe cõmeant. atq; ea quæ
ad effeminandos animos ꝑtinẽt important. ꝓximiq;
sũt germanis: qui trans Rhenum incolunt: cũ quibus
continenter bellum gerunt. qua de causa heluecii quoq; reliquos gallos uirtute
præcedunt: q̃d fere quotidianis bellis præliisq; cum germanis contendũt. cũ aut
suis finib' eos ꝓhibent: aut ipi in eoꝝ finib' bellum gerũt. Eorũ una pars quã gal
los optinere dictum ẽ, initium capit a flumine rhodano, cõtineturq; garũna flu
mine occeanum fines belgaꝝ: attingit etiã ab Sequanis et heluecíis flumen rhe
num uergit ad septentrionem. belge ab extremis galliæ finib' oriuntur: ꝑtinent
ad interiorẽ ꝑtem fluminis rheni. spectant ad septentrionem et orientem solẽ. aq
tania a garunna flumine ad pyreneos montes et ad eam ꝑtem occeani quæ ẽ ad
hispaniã ꝑtinet. spectat inter occeanum solis, et septentrionẽ. Apud heluecios lon
ge nobilissim' et ditissimus fuit orgentorix. Is. M. messalla, et. P. M. pisone cõ
sulibus Regni cupiditate inductus, cõiurationem nobilitatis fecit, ac ciuitati ꝑsu
asit: ut de finibus suis, cum omnib' copiis exirent. ꝑfacile ẽẽ cum uirtute omnib'
præstarent totius galliæ imperio potiri. Id hoc facilius eis ꝑsuasit, q' undiq; loci
natura tuti heluecii cõtinerentur. una ex parte flumine rheno Latissimo atq; altis
simo: qui agrum heluecíũ a germanis diuidit. altera ex ꝑte monte iura altissimo
qui est inter Sequanos et heluecios. tertia Lacu lemãno et flumine rhodano, qui
ꝓuinciã nostram ab heluecíis diuidit. his rebus fiebat, ut min' late uagarent̃, et
minus facile finitimis bellũ inferre possent. Qua de causa homines bellandi cupi
di magno dolore afficiebantur. pro multitudine autẽ hominũ: et ꝓ gloria belli at
q; fortitudinis angustos se fines habere arbitrabant̃: qui in longitudinẽ passuũ
milia. ccxL. in latitudinẽ. cLxxx. patebant. His rebus adducti et autoritate or
gentorigis ꝑmoti cõstituerunt ea quæ ad ꝓficiscendũ ꝑtinerent compare. Iumen
toꝝ et carroꝝ q̃ maximũ numerum coemere: sementes q̃ maximas facere: ut iti
nere copia frumenti suppeteret: cum proximis ciuitatibus pacẽ, et amiciciã con
firmare: ad eas res cõficiendas bienniũ satis ẽẽ sibi duxerunt. In tertiũ annũ
ꝓfectionẽ lege confirmant. ad eas res conficiendas orgentorix deligitur. Is igr
ubi legationem ad ciuitates suscepit: in eo itinere ꝑsuadet Castico Cathamanta
Leodis filio Sequano: cuius pater Regnum in Sequanis multos annos optinuerat:

ℭ VERSVS CONTINENTES SENTENTIAM PRIMI LIBRI LVCANI.

Preponit primus liber: inuehit inuocat atq;
Causas exponit: cursus properantis ad urbem
Cesaris: & nimios huic narrat in Vrbe timores.

ℭ VERSVS SECVNDI LIBRI

Quadruplices questus libri pars prima secundi
Continet: eiusdem pars proxima uerba Catonis
Et bruti: dicit quo federe martia nupsit
Hostis in occursum dicit pars tertia magnum
Opposuisse manus: notátq; Cesaris ira
Cuncta ruant: arcesq; capit: insistẽtibus ĩstat
Domitio tribuit uitam qui nuntius hosti
Exemplumq; fuit. quo uiso magnus ad om nes
Turmas ipse suas hortandas magna minatur
Hinc pars quarta notat pompeum tũc properasse
Brundusiũ. tandemq; uidens maris hostia claudi
Experiam petiit pupes duasq; reliquit

ℭ VERSVS TERTII LIBRI.

Tertius exponit primo quid Iulia dixit
Sextus iusso patris per mundum querit amicos
Altera pars libri dicit q; Cesar in urbem
Iuit opesq; dedit rome nolente metello
Militibus. magnumq; notat que signa sequntur
Vltimaq; tendens hispanas Cesar adoras
Marsilie stetit hanc se uicit equore brutus

ℭ VERSVS Q VARTI LIBRI.

Acta quarti libri narrat ps primaq; iuit
Cesar ad hyspaneos adiussa ducesq; reue sos
Mortem Vulterii cum multis altera pars dat
Vltimaq; uarum pepulit campoq; fugauit
Curio. fraude iube cecidit & gens sua tandem

NICOLAI PEROTTI PROHEMIUM IN LIBROS POLIBII GRECI HISTORICI AD NICOLAUM QUINTUM PONTIFICEM MAXIMUM FELICITER INCIPIT.

ABSOLVI TANDEM ALIQUANDO DELEGATUM MIHI ABS TE MUNUS PONTIFEX MAXIME CONVERSIS IN LATINUM SERMONEM QUINQUE LIBRIS POLIBII QUI SOLI NOBIS SUPERSTITES EX AMPLISSIMA ILLIUS HISTORIA REMANSERE QUARE INNUMERO TALEM SUperis habeo gratiam quorum maiestate suggerente mihi favorem opus perfici. Sanctitati tue ita nisi me animus fallit gratissimum futurum. Tibi vero ingentes ago gratias agamque dum vivam quod me unum ex multis cui hoc munus delegares elegisti. Nam per immortalem deum quid mihi vel in presentiarum gratius vel ad posteritatis memoriam gloriosius iniungi potuit quam ut veterem atque reconditam sed tamen egregiam ac luculentam prestantis et sinceri auctoris hystoriam in lucem proferrem et quasi de novo scribens nostris hominibus tamquam per manus traderem. Mihi quidem ita iocundus hic labor fuit ut maiorem mihi fingere voluptatem ne voto quidem potuissem primum quod morem gerebam voluntati tue. Cuius maxima semper ac pene immortalia fuerunt erga me et meos beneficia. Deinde quod tanta varietate rerum et copia mirum in modum oblectabar. Quis enim suavior animo cibus offerri potest quam lectio hystorie huius presertim in qua cum magnitudine ac diversitate rerum gestarum splendore quoque verborum coniunctus est ut suavitas orationis quibusdam quasi luminibus sententiarum respersa ut mihi videatur uno in opere Polybius et summus hystoricus et orator maximus et optimus

ab ap
descriptiō
tuas spectare ru
alcis in obsequium m
licium nobilitatis erit.

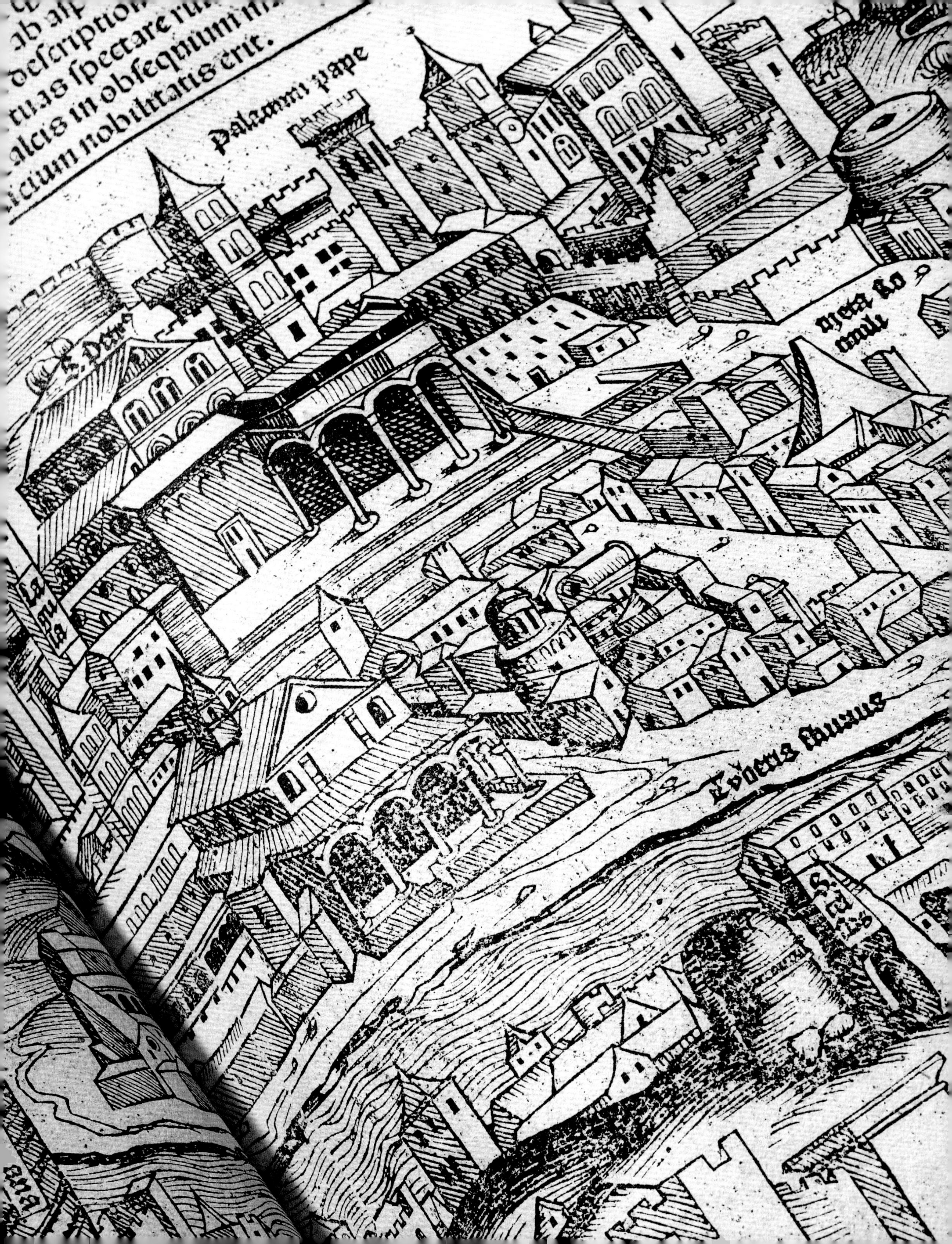

1

Diverses Corrections de mes Considerations sur les Romains

15 ~~les Boe~~ ~~beotiens les plus epaix de toutes les grecs mais~~

\+ ~~les plus sages vivoint ordinairement en paix, il~~

~~faut otter les mots mais les plus sages:~~

~~p 15 les 1 2 les beotiens les plus epaix~~

\+ il faut otter tout jusqua lalinea et mettre ainsi

les Beotiens les plus epaix de toutes les grecs,

plus vivoint ordinairement en paix et prennoint le

moins de part quils pouvoint aux affaires generales

uniquement conduits par le sentiment present du

bien et du mal ils navoint pas asses despirit pour

quil fut facile aux orateurs de les agiter:

ils estoint tombes dans une corruption qui aprochoit

de lanarchie les magistrats pour plaire a la multitude

nauroint plus les ~~[illegible]~~ le peuple de saisoit

distribuer les revenus publics ~~et de~~ voloit lui ~~[illegible]~~

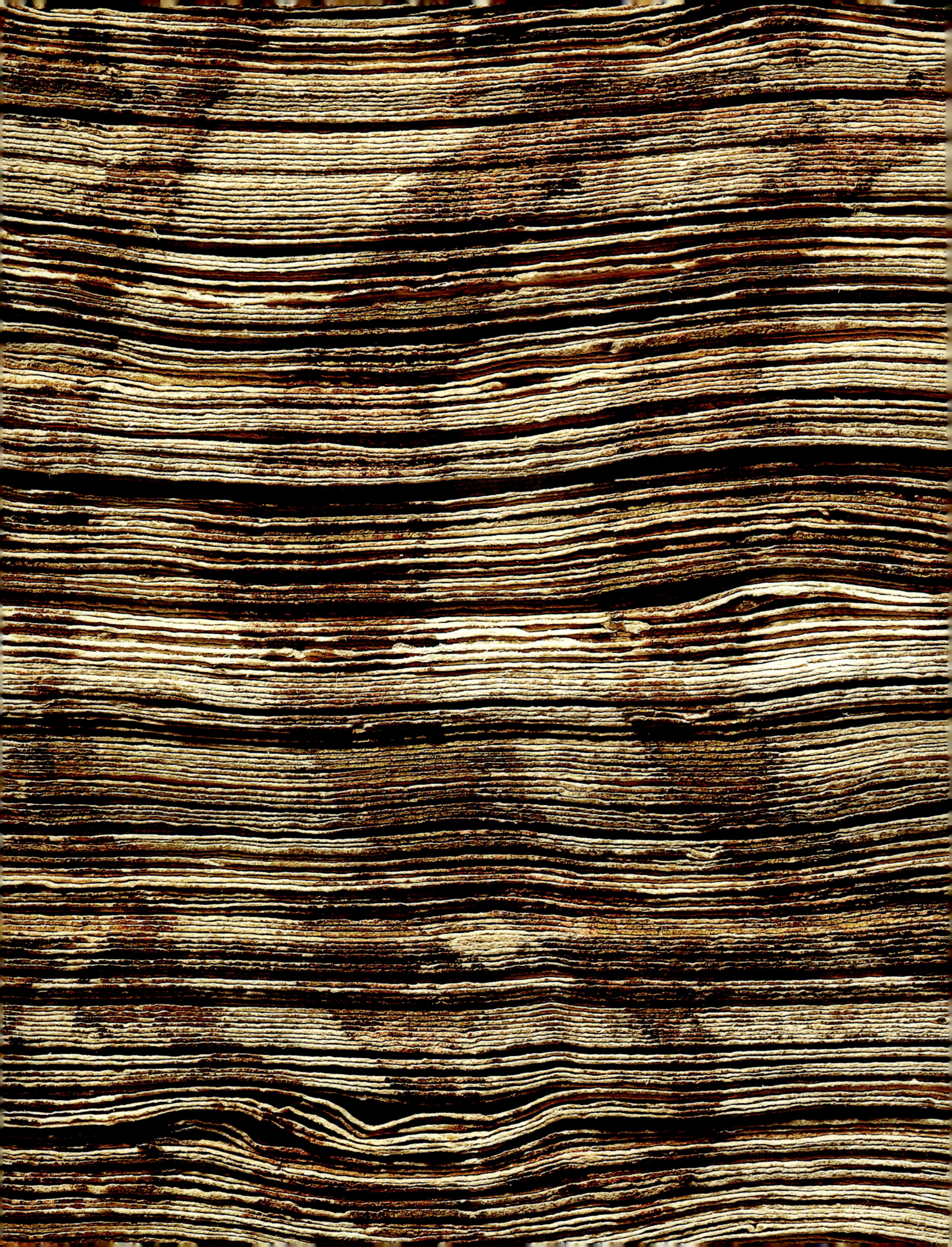

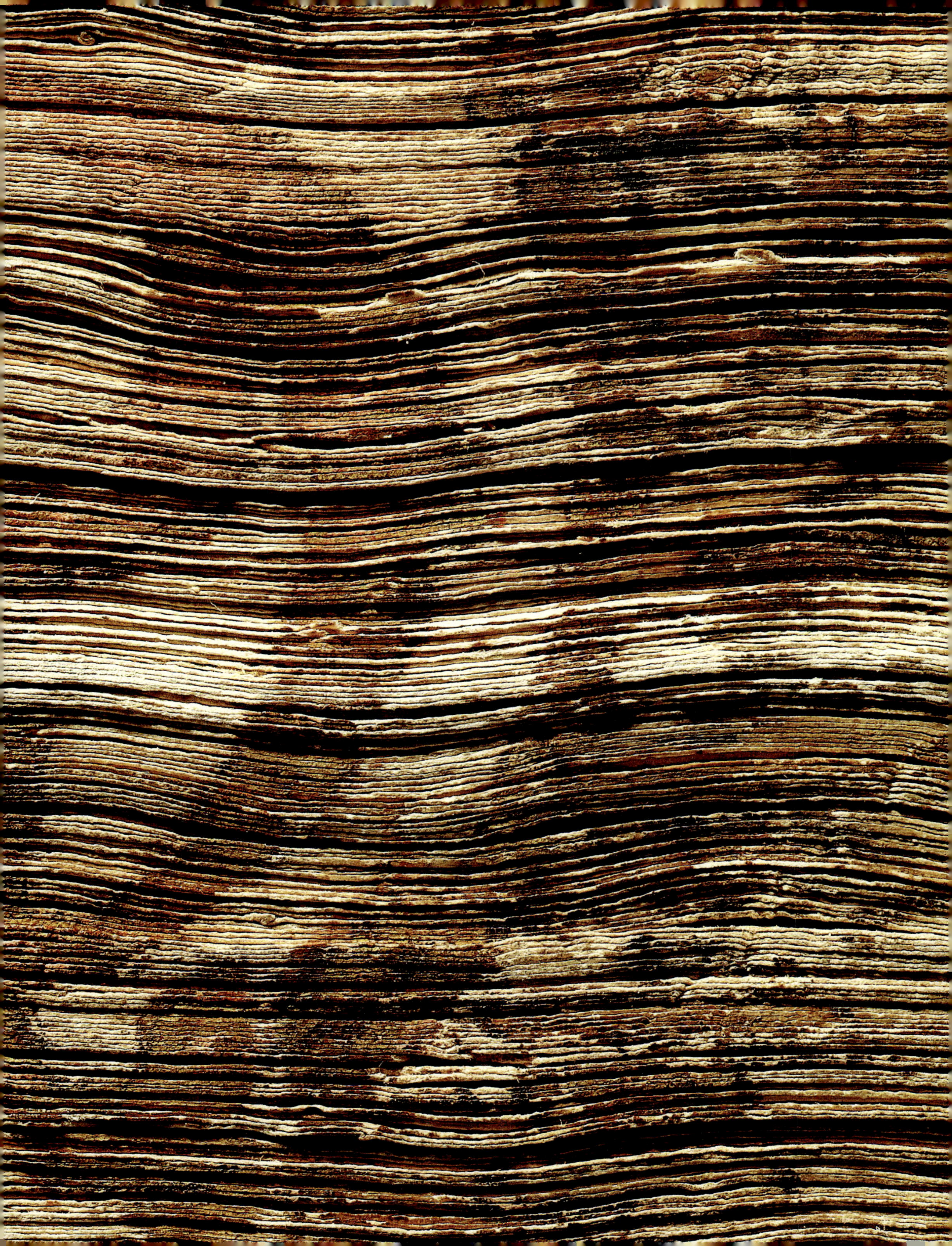

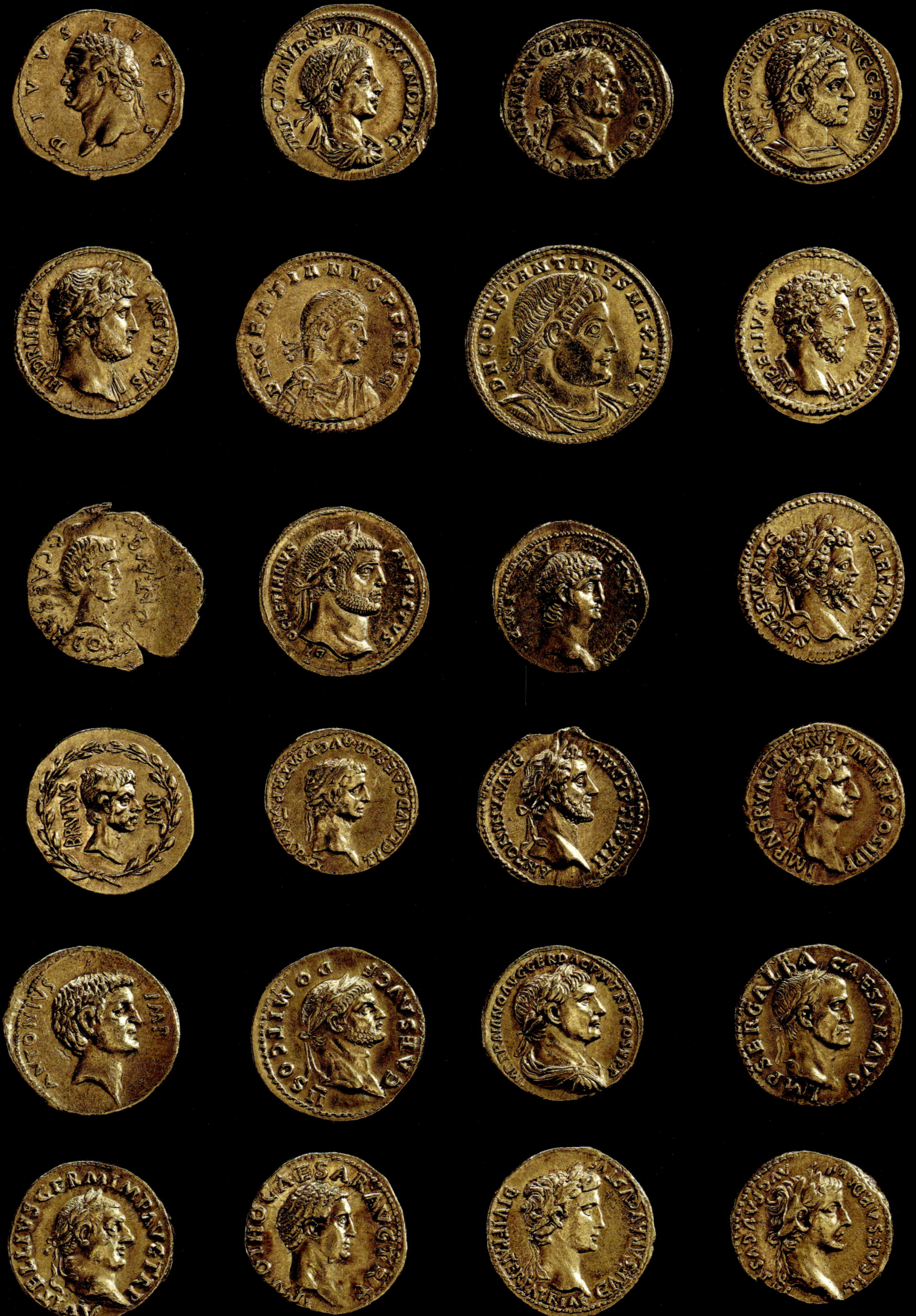

DIVVS TITVS
IMP C M AVR SEV ALEXAND AVG
ANTONINVS PIVS AVG GERM
HADRIANVS AVGVSTVS
D N CONSTANTINVS MAX AVG
AVRELIVS CAESAR AVG PII F
BRVTVS
IMP SER GALBA CAESAR AVG

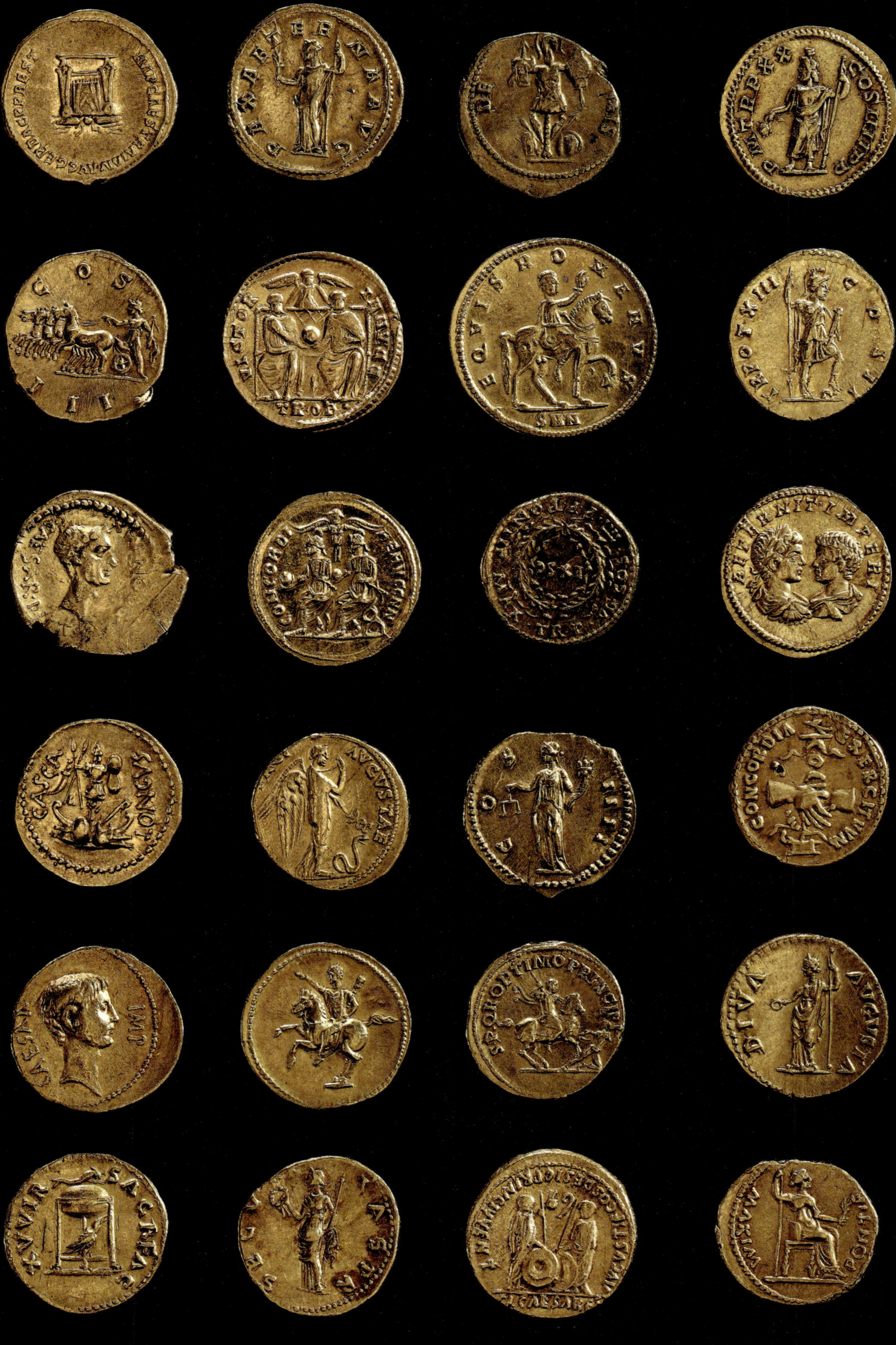

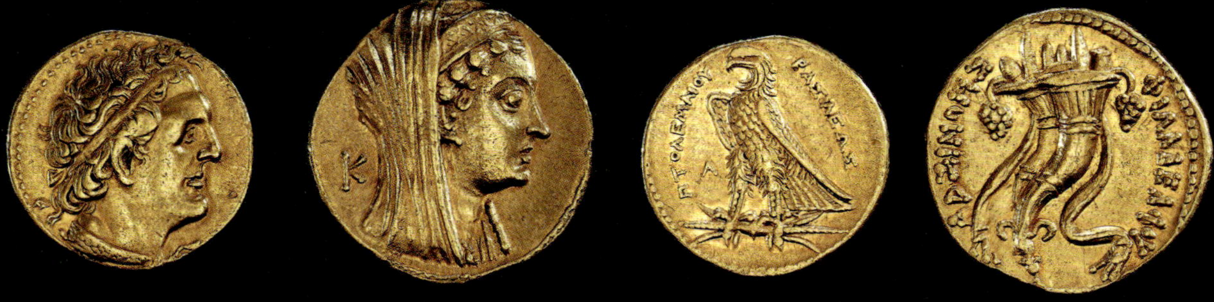

8

λομένοις πῶς τῶν περσῶν πρεσβευτὴ
ινα κατασκευάσαι· καὶ οὕτω περὶ τὰ
ἐν τάχει ἄλλετον ποιῆσαι ἐς τὴν πόλιν
ν· ὁ δὲ θεμιστοκλῆς τοὺς ἔχοντας· ἀλλὰ
πολλάκις διὰ τῶν οἰκείων ταχυτέρων ζου
νος· τραγῳδιῶν αἰσχύλος ἐνίκα φινεῖ,
καὶ προμηθεῖ: ἰστέον ὅτι τοῦ ξέρ
ξου ὁ πατὴρ ... βασιλεὺς· μητρὸς δὲ ἄτοσσα
τρίς ἡ ἀσί· κορίοτος δὲ τούτων οὖσα
ν περσῶν καὶ βασιλεύσας αὐτῶν,
τοῦ στρατηγήσαντος· μᾶλλον δὲ ἄρα
ἕλληνας· δεύτερος δὲ ὁ ἀταρξέρξης,
θας· ἔσχατος δὲ ὁ δαρεῖος ὁ ὕπαλιξαν
πρεσβείας· τινὲς δὲ καὶ δύο δαρείους·

Τὰ τοῦ δράματος πρόσωπα·
ἄτοσσα· ἄγγελος· εἴδωλον δαρείου·
ξέρξης· χορὸς γερόντων: —

Τάδε μὲν περσῶν τῶν οἰχομένων,
ἑλλάδ᾽ ἐς αἶαν πιστὰ καλεῖται·
καὶ τῶν ἀφνεῶν καὶ πολυχρύσων
ἑδράνων φύλακες, κατὰ πρεσβείαν·
οὓς αὐτὸς ἄναξ ξέρξης βασιλεὺς
δαρειογενὴς δαρείου υἱός,
εἵλετο χώρας ἐφορεύειν ἔσωθ.
ἀμφὶ δὲ νόστῳ τῷ βασιλείῳ
καὶ πολυχρύσου στρατιᾶς ἤδη
κακόμαντις ἄγαν ὀρσολοπεῖται θυμός.
πᾶσα γὰρ ἰσχὺς ἀσιατογενής,
οἴχωκε· νέον δ᾽ ἄνδρα βαΰζει·

...υδι...

...οσ π ἐφα...

...ἐμ ποιήσ φερ...

...γε καὶ σ ὑμᾶσ, κήσ αι...

...ν πολιτικῶμ ἐπιμέλειαμ φ...

...αλλωμ ὑποσ χεσ φσ διαβαλλ...

...μεμόμτωμ, ἐξ ἑξῶμ περ αὐτοσ ἐπ φαθ ημ ουτω...

...ἑ οἶμαι καὶ τοῖσ ἀλλοισ φαμερὸμ καλαστη...

λόγος πανηγυρικός

...ολλάκισ ἐθαύμασα τῶμ τὰσ πα...

...αγόμτωμ, καὶ τοὺσ γυμνικοὺσ...

...αμτωμ. ὅτι τὰσ μὲμ τῶ...

...τω μεγάλωμ δωρε...

...κοινῶμ ἰδίᾳ πο...

...ευάσασι...

...ουδ...

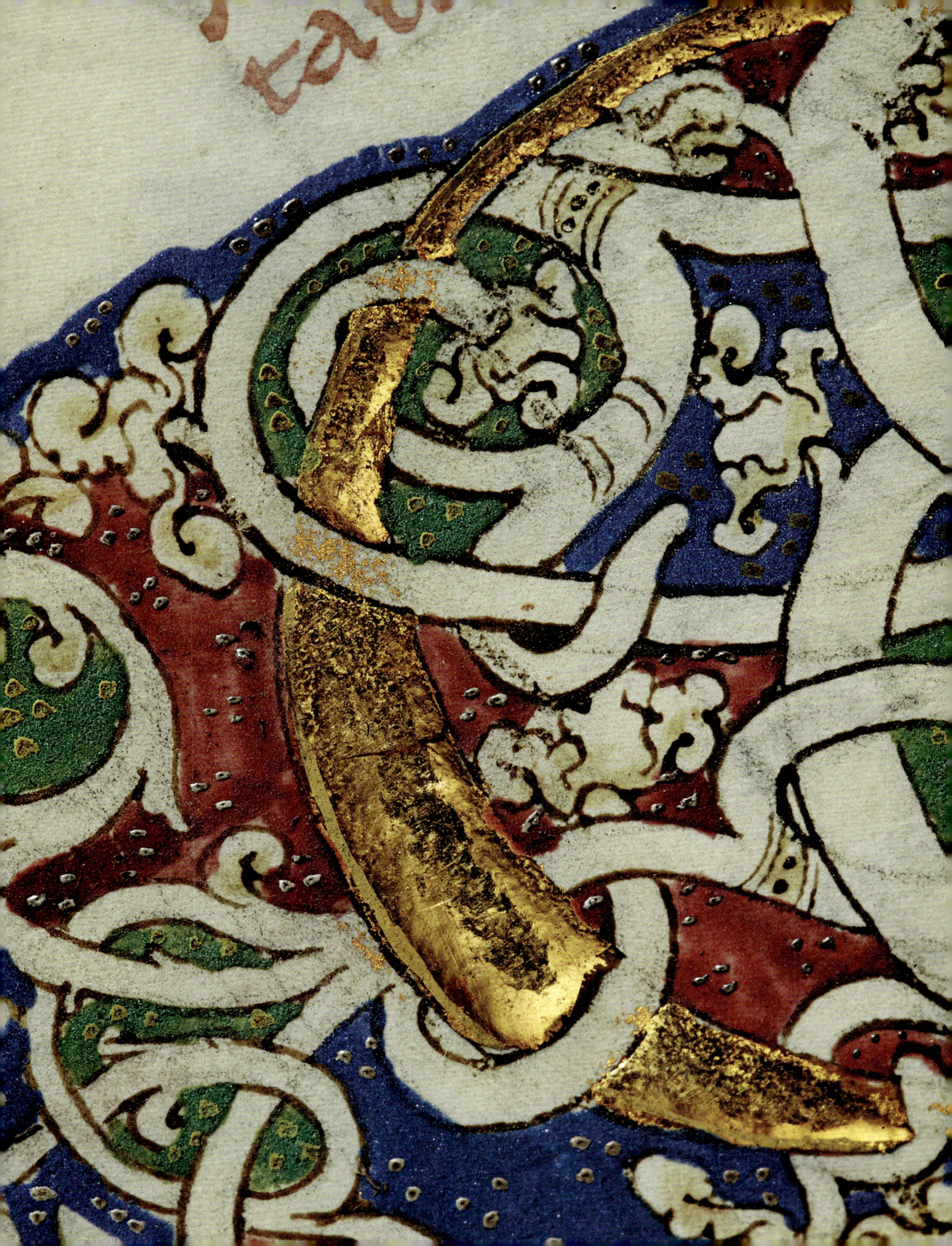

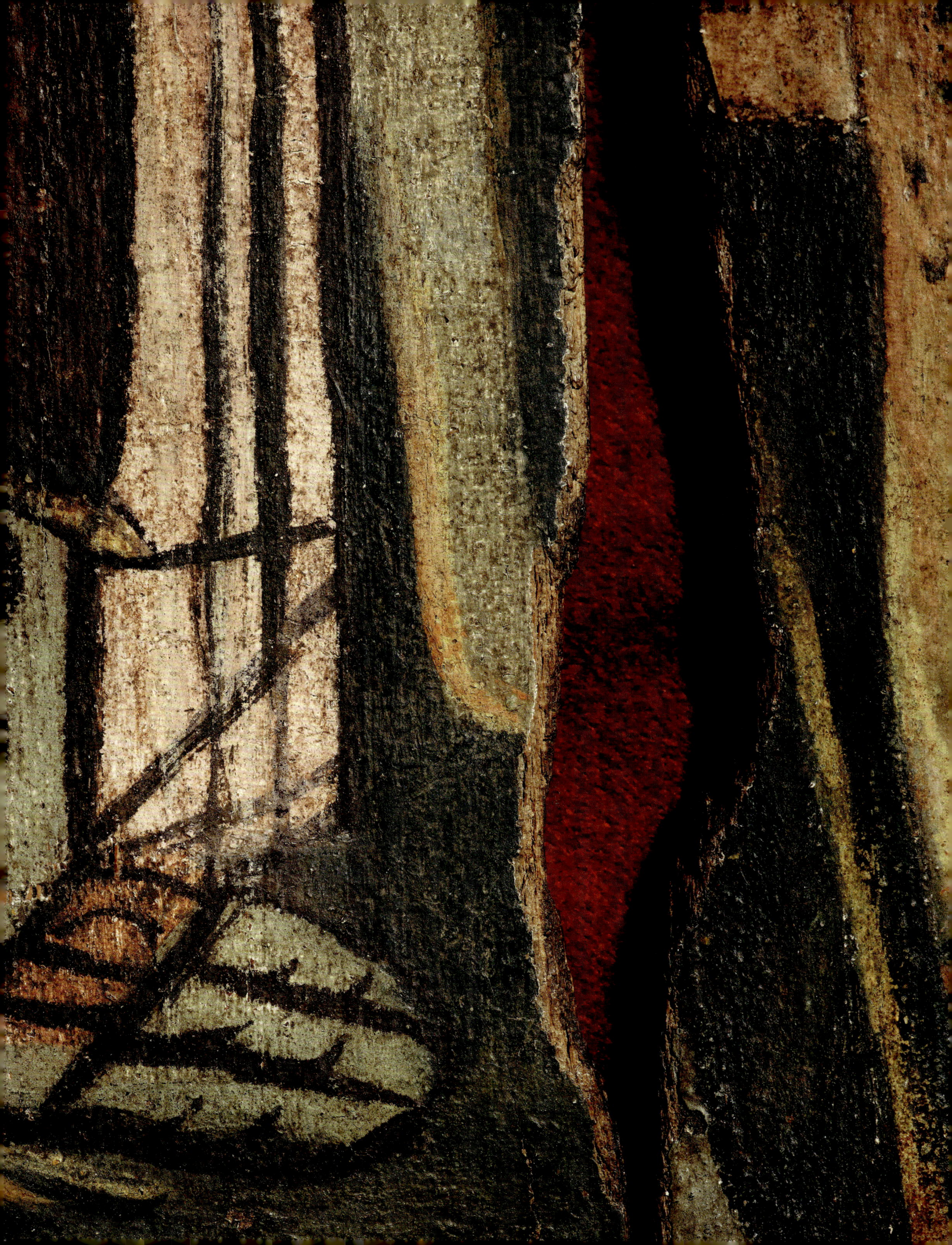

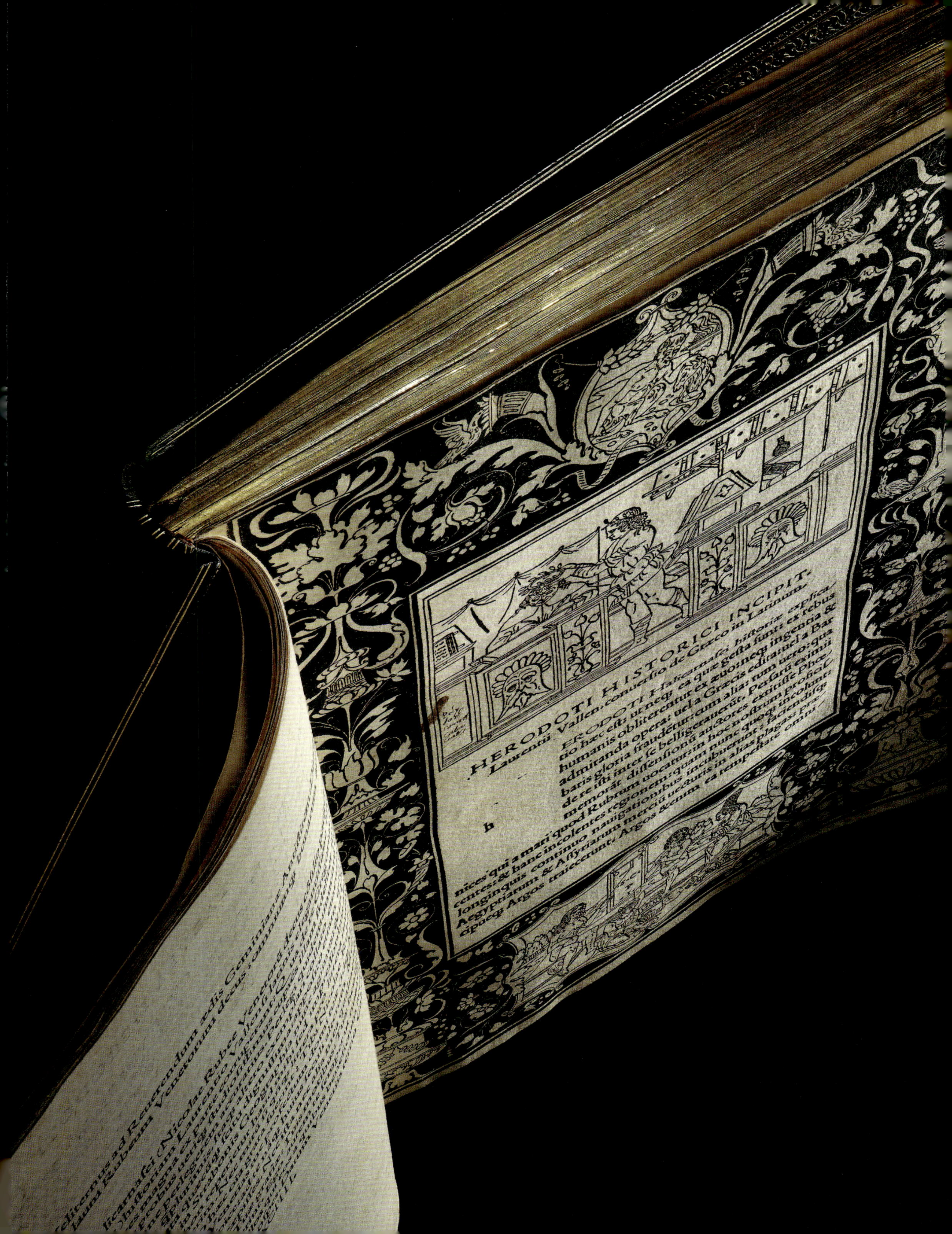
HERODOTI HISTORICI INCIPIT.

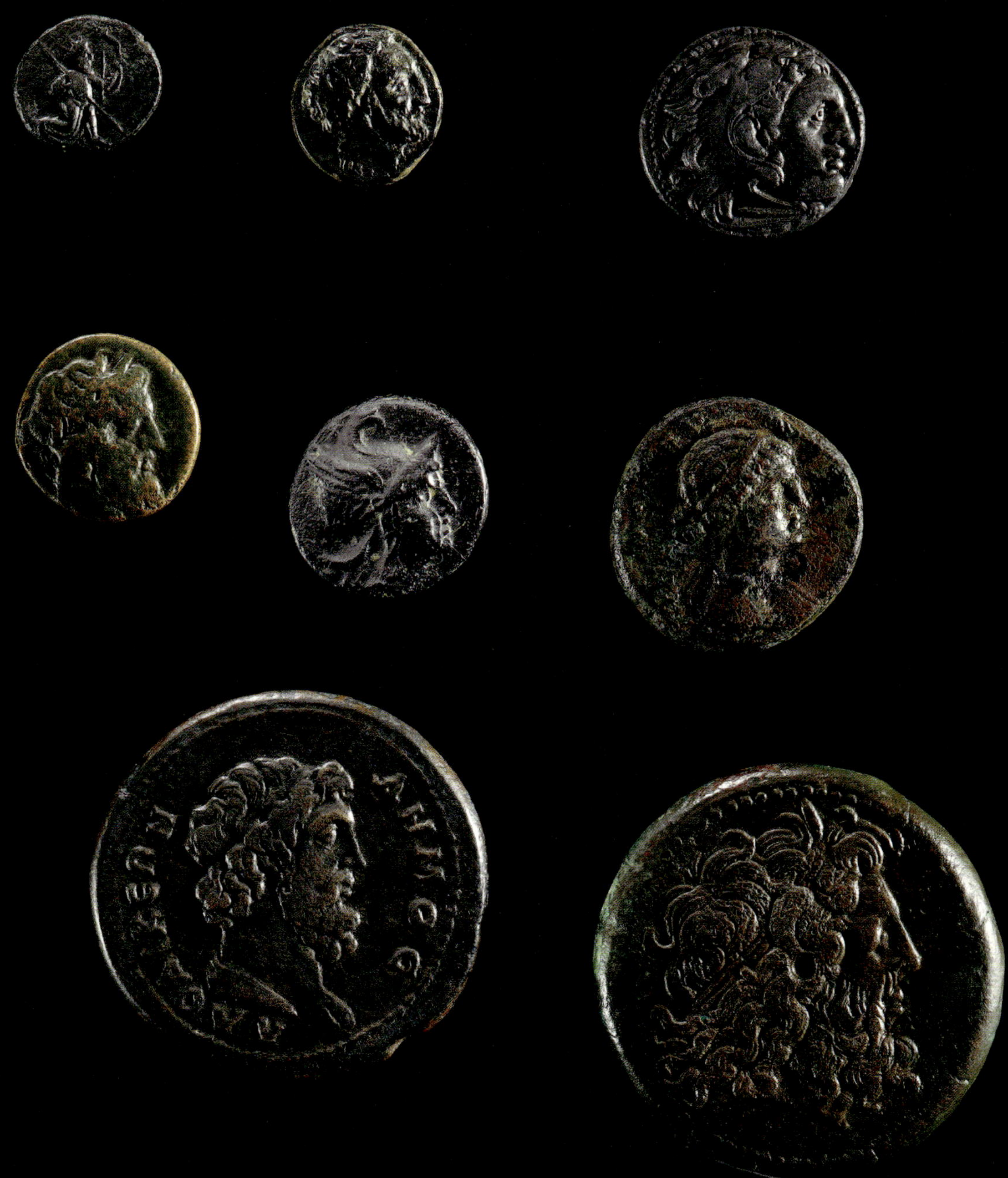

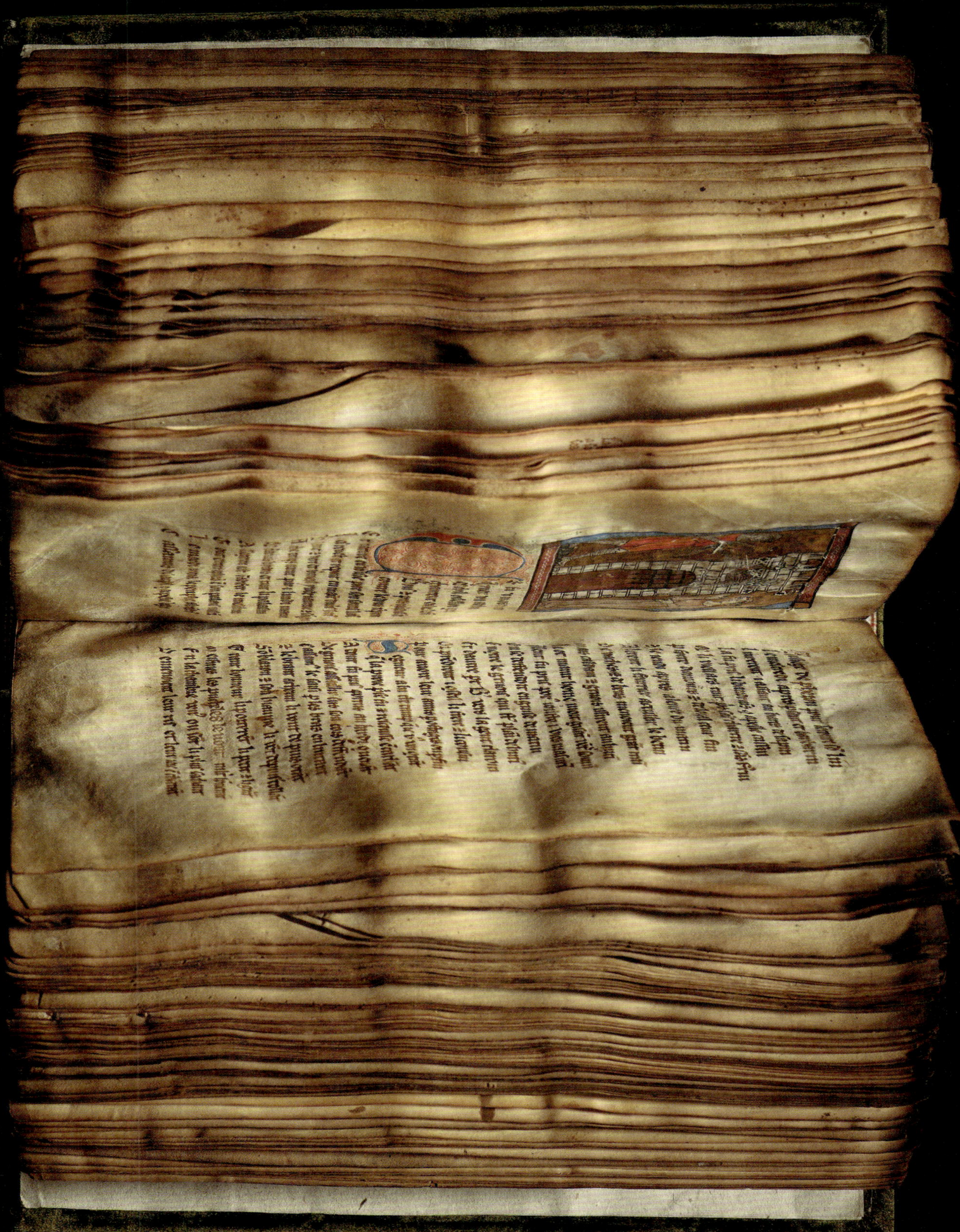

THE TRAGEDY OF
Anthony, and Cleopatra.

Actus Primus. Scæna Prima.

Enter Demetrius, and Philo.

Philo.

NAy, but this dotage of our Generall
Ore-flowes the measure: those his goodly eyes
That o're the files and Musters of the Warre,
Have glow'd like plated Mars:
Now bend, now turne
The Office and Devotion of their view
Vpon a Tawny Front. His Captaines heart,
Which in the scuffles of great fights hath burst
The Buckles on his brest, reneages all temper,
And is become the Bellowes and the Fan
To coole a Gypsies Lust.

Enter Anthony, Cleopatra, her Ladies, the Traine, with Eunuchs fanning her.

Looke where they come:
Take but good note, and you shall see in him
The triple Pillar of the world transform'd
Into a Strumpets Foole. Behold and see.

Cleo. If it be Love indeed, tell me how much.

Ant. Theres beggery in the love that can be reckon'd

Cleo. Ile set a bourne how farre to be belov'd.

Ant. Then must thou needes find out new heaven, new Earth.

Enter a Messenger.

Mes. Newes (my good Lord) from Rome.

Ant. Rate me, the summe.

Cleo. Nay heare them *Anthony.*
Fulvia perchance is angry: Or who knowes,
If the scarse-bearded *Cæsar* have not sent
His powerfull Mandate to you. Doe this, or this;
Take in that Kingdome, and infranchise that:
Perform't, or else we damne thee.

Ant. How, my Love?

Cleo. Perchance? Nay, and most like;
You must not stay heere longer, your dismission
Is come from *Cæsar*, therefore heare it *Anthony.*
Wheres *Fulvias* Processe? (*Cæsars* I would say) both?
Call in the Messengers: As I am Egypts Queene,
Thou blushest *Anthony*, and that blood of thine
Is *Cæsars* homager: else so thy cheeke payes shame,
When shrill-tongu'd *Fulvia* scolds. The Messengers.

Ant. Let Rome in Tyber melt, and the wide Arch
Of the raing'd Empire fall: Heere is my space,
Kingdomes are clay: Our dungy earth alike
Feeds Beast as Man; the Noblenesse of life
Is to doe thus: when such a mutuall paire,
And such a twaine can doo't, in which I bind,
On paine of punishment, the world to weete
We stand up Peerelesse.

Cleo. Excellent falshood:
Why did he marry *Fulvia*, and not love her?
Ile seeme the Foole I am not. *Anthony* will be h

Ant. But stirr'd by *Cleopatra.*
Now for the love of love, and her soft houres,
Lets not confound the time with Conference ha
Theres not a minute of our lives should stretch
Without some pleasure now. What sport to ni

Cleo. Heare the Ambassadors.

Ant. Fye wrangling Queene:
Whom every thing becomes, to chide, to laugh,
To weepe: whose every passion fully strives
To make it selfe (in Thee) faire, and admir'd.
No Messenger but thine, and all alone, to night
We'll wander through the streets, and note
The qualities of people. Come my Queene,
Last night you did desire it. Speake not to us.

Exeunt with th

Dem. Is *Cæsar* with *Anthonius* priz'd so sligh

Philo. Sir sometimes when he is not *Anthony*
He comes too short of that great Property
Which still should goe with *Anthony.*

Dem. I am full sorry, that he approves the Lyar, who thus speakes of him at Rome: but I of better deeds to morrow. Rest you happy.

Enter Enobarbus, Lamprius, a Southsayer, Rannius, Charmian, Iras, Mardian the Eunuch, and Alexas.

Char. L. *Alexas*, sweet *Alexas*, most any thin almost most absolute *Alexas*, wheres the Soothi you prais'd so to'th'Queene? Oh that I knew t band, which you say, must change his hornes w lands.

Alex. Soothsayer.

Sooth. Your will?

Char. Is this the Man? Is't you sir that know

Sooth. In Natures infinite booke of Secrecy, can read.

Alex. Shew him your hand.

Enob. Bring in the Banket quickly: Wine en

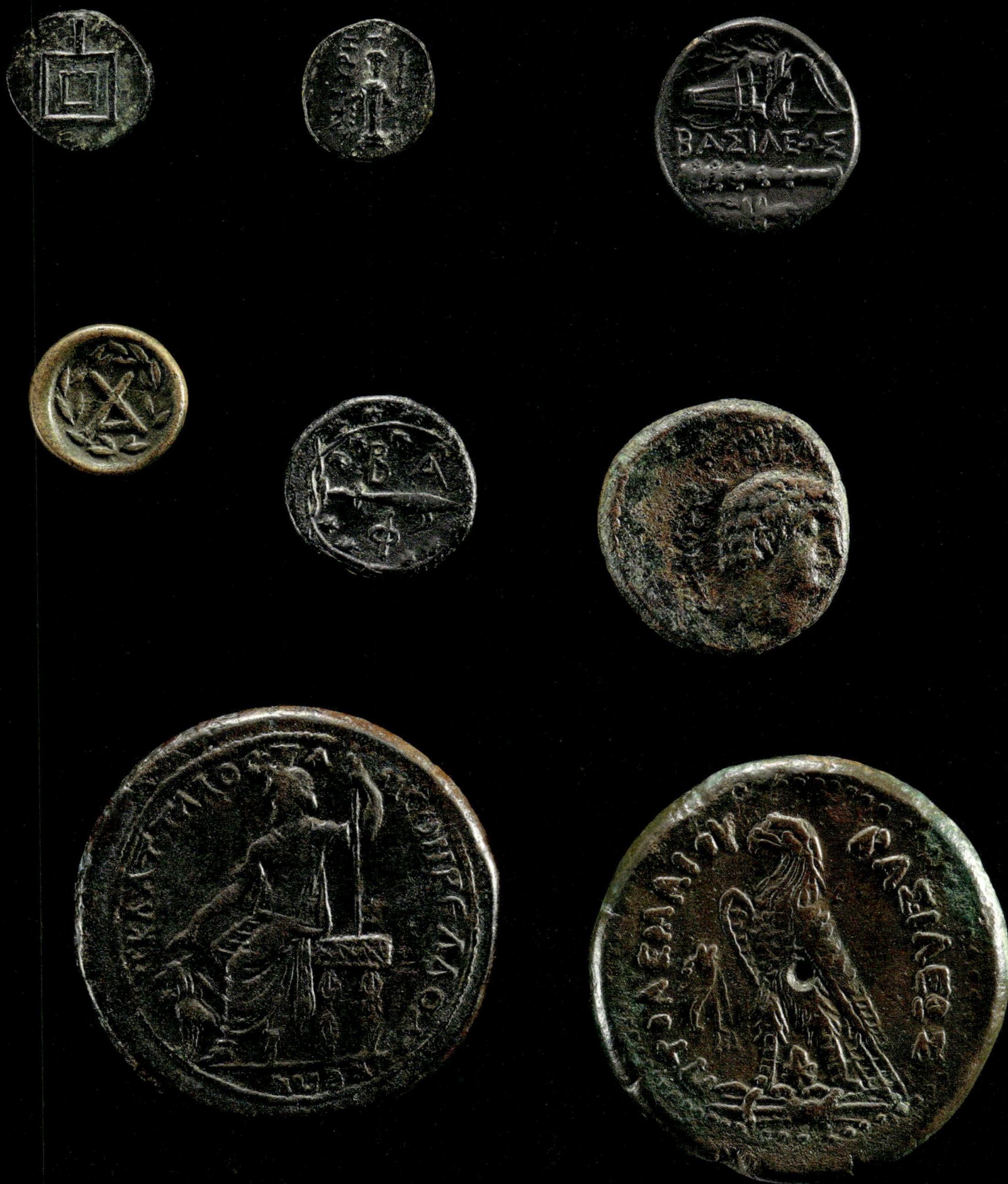
ΒΑΣΙΛΕΩΣ

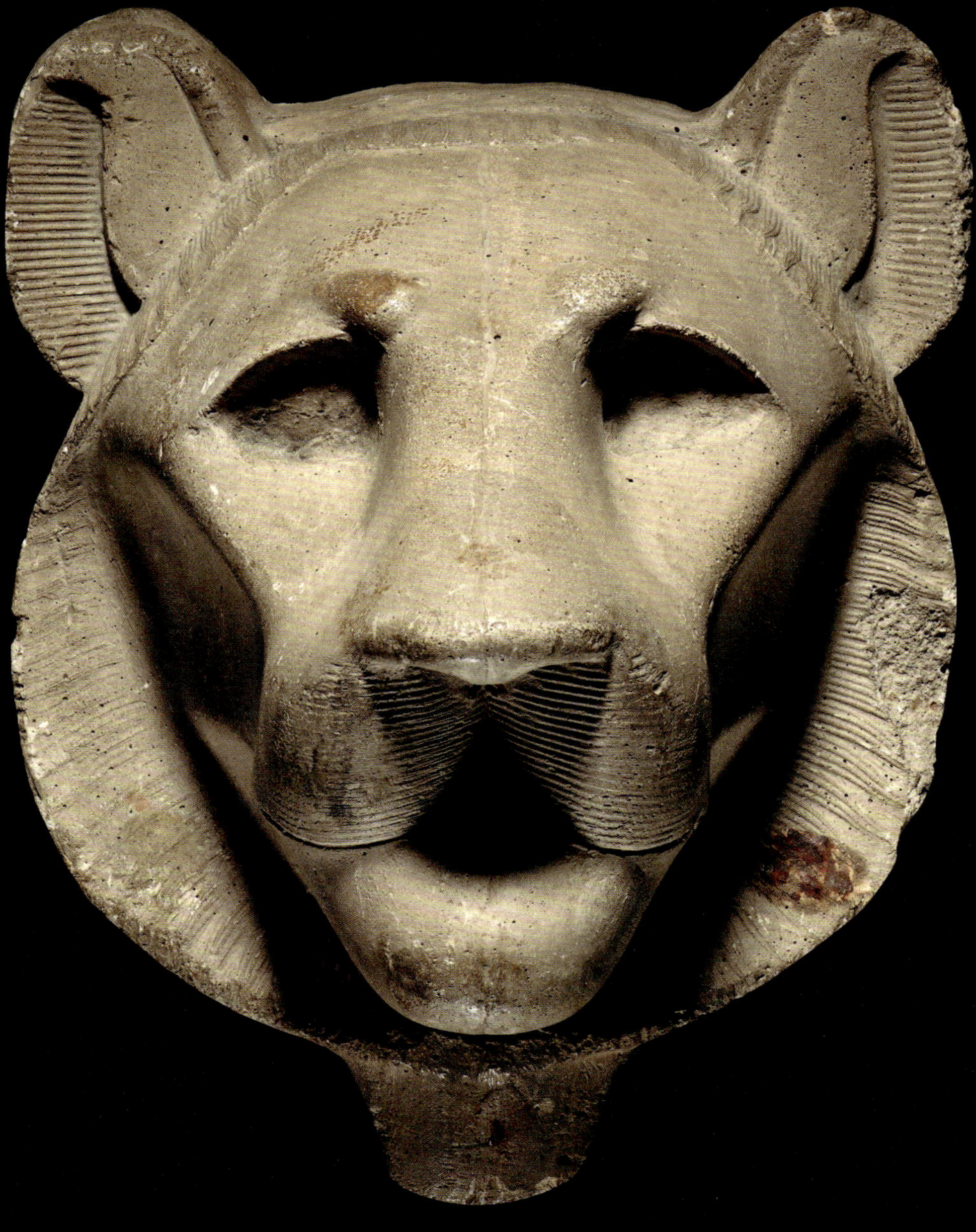

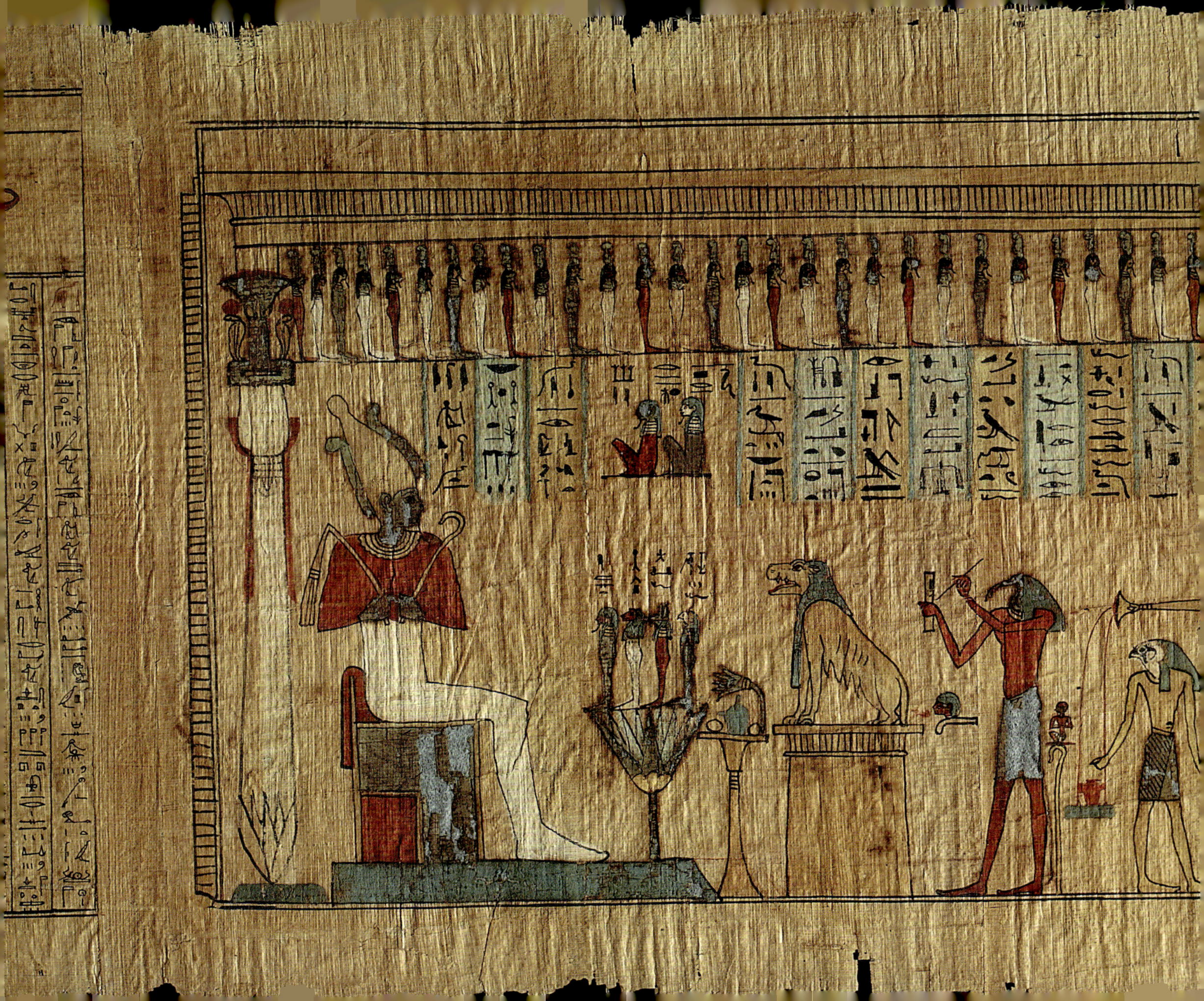

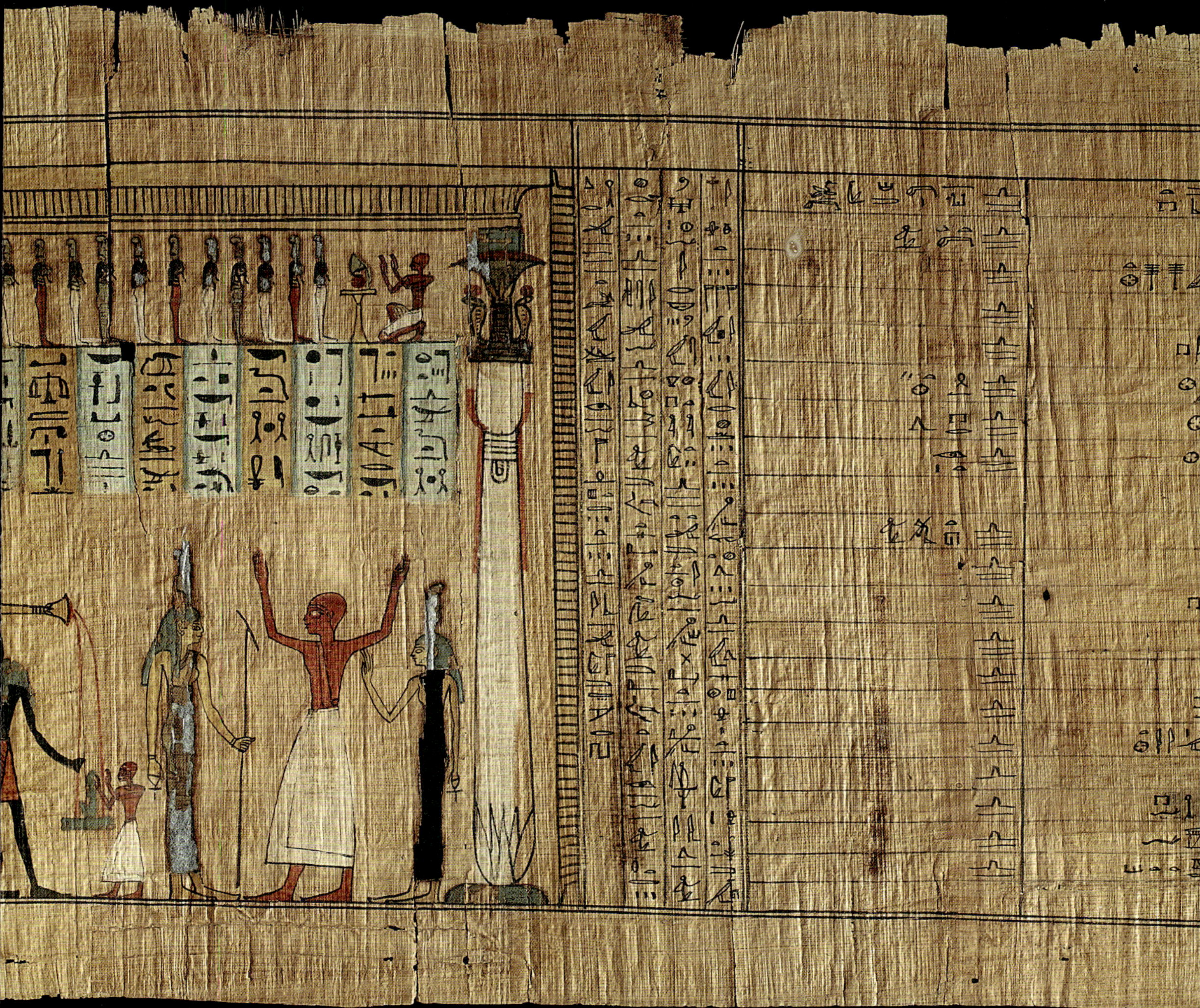

WORDS AND COINS

From Ancient Greece to Byzantium

MER

WORDS AND COINS
from Ancient Greece to Byzantium
24.11.2012 – 17.03.2013

An exhibition organized by the Fondation Martin Bodmer in collaboration with the Benaki Museum, Athens

HONORARY COMMITTEE

For Greece
Aimilia YEROULANOU, President of the Board of Trustees, Benaki Museum
Ioannis FIKIORIS, President, Welfare Foundation for Social & Cultural Affairs
Helen MOLOKOTOS, Vice-president, Public relations, Association of the Greek Ladies of Geneva
Prof. Dusan SIDJANSKI, Professor Emeritus of the University of Geneva, President of the Swiss Committee for the Return of the Parthenon Marbles

For Switzerland
Laurence GROS, President of the Fondation Martin Bodmer
Prof. André HURST, former Rector, Professor Emeritus of the University of Geneva
Prof. Pierre DUCREY, former Rector, Professor Emeritus of the University of Lausanne, Director of the Fondation Hardt
Mario BOTTA, Architect

SCIENTIFIC COMMITTEE OF THE EXHIBITION
Charles MÉLA, Professor Emeritus of the University of Geneva, President of the European Cultural Centre, Director of the Fondation Martin Bodmer
Angelos DELIVORRIAS, Professor Emeritus of the University of Athens, Director of the Benaki Museum
Vasiliki PENNA, Ass. Professor of the University of the Peloponnese, Advisor for Numismatics, KIKPE Foundation
Sylviane MESSERLI, Doctor of the University of Geneva, Fondation Martin Bodmer

CONCEPT
Vasiliki PENNA

EXHIBITION CURATOR
Vasiliki PENNA in collaboration with *Sylviane* MESSERLI

ARTISTIC CURATOR OF THE EXHIBITION
ÉLISABETH MACHERET, Artistic advisor, Scenographer of the Museum of the Fondation Martin Bodmer

EXHIBITION STAFF
Jean-Michel LANDECY, Architect, Collaborator for the scenography
Florence DARBRE, Curator and restorer, FMB
Patrizia RONCADI, Museum Management, FMB
Stasha BIBIC, Scientific collaborator, FMB
Claire DUBOIS, Administrative coordination, FMB
Stéphanie CHASSOT, Communication matters, FMB
Yannis STOYAS, Numismatist, Researcher, KIKPE Numismatic Collection
Evangelia GEORGIOU, Numismatist, Scientific collaborator, KIKPE Numismatic Collection
Electra GEORGOULA, Archaeologist, Exhibitions and Publications Department, Benaki Museum

Catalogue edited by *Vasiliki* PENNA, Editor in chief and published by MER Paper Kunsthalle, Gent

EDITORIAL TEAM
Yannis STOYAS
Evangelia GEORGIOU
Alexandra DOUMAS

ESSAYS BY
Prof. Charles MÉLA
Prof. Angelos DELIVORRIAS
Ass. Prof. Vasiliki PENNA
Sylviane MESSERLI
Prof. André HURST
Ute WARTENBERG KAGAN, Executive Director, American Numismatic Society
Yannis STOYAS, Researcher, KIKPE Numismatic Collection
Andrew MEADOWS, Deputy Director, American Numismatic Society
Prof. François DE CALLATAŸ, Head of curatorial departments of the Royal Library of Belgium, Professor at the Université libre de Bruxelles, Director of Studies at the École pratique des hautes études, Paris
Charikleia PAPAGEORGIADOU-BANIS, Research Director, National Hellenic Research Foundation, Athens
Prof. Ioli KALAVREZOU, Dumbarton Oaks Professor of the History of Byzantine Art, Harvard University
Cécile MORRISSON, Research Director Emeritus, National Centre for Scientific Research, Paris, Advisor for Byzantine Numismatics, Dumbarton Oaks

ENTRIES BY
Ass. Prof. Vasiliki PENNA
Yannis STOYAS
Nicolas DUCIMETIÈRE, Deputy Director, Head Librarian, Fondation Martin Bodmer

TRANSLATIONS BY
Alexandra DOUMAS (Greek-English)
Maria XANTHOPOULOU (French-English)
Lilliam HURST (Translation of the essay 'Writing and coining: Egality, legality?')

PHOTOGRAPHERS
Laziz HAMANI
Kostas MANOLIS, (Essay X, figs 1 and 7)
Leonidas PAPADOPOULOS (exhibit cat. no. 46)

GRAPHIC DESIGN
Studio Luc Derycke, *Luc* DERYCKE, *Jeroen* WILLE

LAYOUT ASSISTANCE
Jan RUTTEN, *Ellen* DEBUCQUOY

PRINTER
Printer Trento, Italy

ISBN: 978-94-9069-364-0
D/2012/7852/133

MER Paper Kunsthalle
Molenaarsstraat 29
B-9000 Gent
Belgium
t +32 (09) 329 31 22
f +32 (09) 329 31 23
info@merpaperkunsthalle.org
www.merpaperkunsthalle.org

FONDATION MARTIN BODMER
BIBLIOTHÈQUE ET MUSÉE

BENAKI MUSEUM

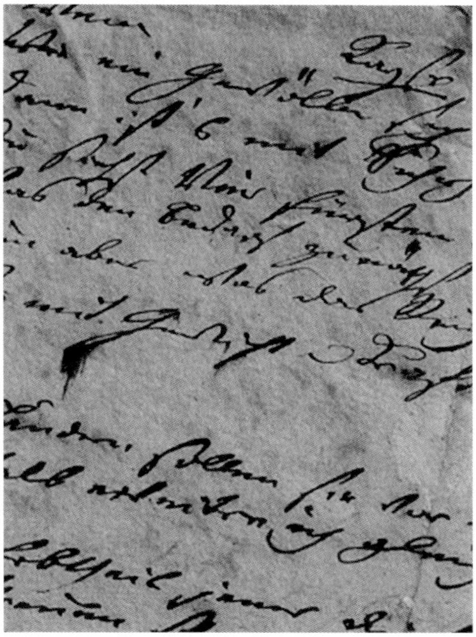

'ONE SILVER DOLLAR, CHANGING HANDS, CHANGING HEARTS, CHANGING LIVES'

How could we forget Marilyn's song at the saloon in Otto Preminger's redemption film *River of No Return* (1954)? The refrain sums up in one sentence the power, both real and imaginary, of a coin, worn from handling, ravaging random hearts as it changes hands. So many dreams cling to it as it fleets, forced to circulate without end in the economic reality that consumes our lives.

It was during the Roman Imperial period, around AD 125, when the coins of the philhellene emperor Hadrian and, later, of Faustina the Elder featured an enigmatic E suspended below the pediment of Apollo's temple at Delphi, that Plutarch, most beloved to Montaigne, wrote, shortly before his death, his famous dialogue on this religious offering, in which he saw a means to salute the existence (*Ei*, 'You are') of the god who sent us our boundaries by adding 'Know thyself' (*Gnothi s'eauton*). One of the explanations given in this dialogue by one of the interlocutors, who is none other than Plutarch himself in his youth, refers to the annual alternation between the cults of Apollo and Dionysus at Delphi; like the two faces, diurnal and bright, dark and nocturnal, of the supreme divinity, the two principles at work in the universe in the form of the One and the Many, the immutable and the changing. The one and eternal divinity, transformed into fire which assimilates everything according to Heraclitus' doctrine, diversifies itself in turn by tearing and dismembering, according to the Orphic religion, in all manner of forms in order to shape the world and give it birth.

Plutarch uses here the image he borrows from Heraclitus in order to refer to this first cause, which shapes the world through itself and later reproduces itself through the world: '... fire changes into all other substances and these in turn into fire, like a gold ingot that is turned into coins and coins that are turned again into an ingot'. Philosophy, religion, and trade thus exchange their representations in order to tell the mystery of the world, both static and ever changing, being and becoming, together and in opposition. It is coinage that gives here the concrete form to metaphysical speculation, included between the solar fire of gold, one and incorruptible, and the multiplicity of coins dispersed throughout the world.

However, it is from Greek thought that the decisive analysis on the nature of coinage came. Karl Marx was not wrong when, in formulating the theory of commodities and money in the first volume of his *Capital* (1867), he distinguishes the use value from the exchange value. According to Marx, the question of equivalence becomes easier to understand 'if we go back to the great thinker, who first analysed the value form and so many other forms, whether of thought, of society, or of nature: we have named Aristotle'. Marx refers precisely to Book 5, Chapter 5 of the *Nicomachean Ethics*.

The chain of thoughts that leads the philosopher to talk about money cannot be stressed enough. Book 5 is indeed dedicated to the study of justice, in order to determine which form of justice participates in virtue. Because the unjust is confused with the unfair and the unlawful ('The unjust man is both he who acts against the law and he who desires more than his share and even at the expense of others'), the fair is the right average. In order to construct the relevant concept, Aristotle gives four terms and defines proportionality. The problem is clarified through mathematics. The just materializes two persons and two objects in relation to which it exists. The just is a proportion – that is, the result of the relation between at least four terms. The formula is famous and can be also applied in defining the metaphor, A: B: C: D, where A is for B what C is for D. However, the question of what the fundamentals of society are depends on the possibility of rendering comparable the things that one wants to exchange, since exchange to meet one's needs is the condition for social life. There can be no exchange without equality or equality without a common measure. One must render commensurable two objects as different from one another as a bed and a house. To say that five beds equal one house – this, originally Greek, example is explicitly reused by Marx – is no different from saying that five beds equal that much money. Money provides the standard of measure. Everything is valued in money, according to the principle of proportionality. Therefore, if A is a house, B the value of ten minae, and C a bed, and if A (house) is worth five minae (half a B) and C (bed) is worth one tenth of B, then five beds equal one house. Money became by convention a means of exchange for what we need. Hence the Greek term *nomisma*, which means both coin and law (*nomos*), because a coin (money) is an institution. Money, therefore, makes the social connection.

It is on the basis of the common value expressed by Aristotle that Marx elaborated his famous theory of commodity fetishism: what is really a relation between humans (to represent a specific amount of work) is in the end perceived as a relation between things, social relations being reified and objects personified. One may say that merchandise is only concerned with its own exchange value, with its relations as something that is bought and sold. The approach established by Aristotle was indeed fecund for political economy.

Mutatis mutandis, it is not by accident that we gave our exhibition the title *Words and Coins* to echo Michel Foucault's famous book *Les mots et les choses* (*The Order of Things*, literally *Words and Things*) of 1966.

Let us conclude with a return to the time of the great emperor who accomplished the marriage between Rome and Athens, and whose world Marguerite Yourcenar reinvented in her *Memoirs of Hadrian*. Greece created the City, with Rome the City became the State, and Hadrian wished for the 'State to be even larger, to become the order of the world, the order of things'. The beautiful words of *Humanitas*, *Felicitas*, *Libertas*, or 'Kindness', 'Happiness', 'Liberty', appeared on Hadrian's coins as a sign of a rediscovered Golden Age, while, in his desire for justice and service to his people, the philosopher emperor was concerned: 'Our coinage has dangerously devalued compared to a century ago, yet it is on the number of our gold coins that Rome's eternity is calculated: it is up to us to give back their value and their weight solidly measured in things'.

Prof. Charles Méla
Director, Fondation Martin Bodmer

WORDS AND COINS: FROM ANCIENT GREECE TO BYZANTIUM

Within an international deluge of exhibitions that compete to outdo each other in scope and scale, the exhibition of the Fondation Martin Bodmer proposes a model of another order. With its conscious indifference to quantitative magnitudes and to provocative passing impressions, it attaches weight to categories of ideas of a different quality, mobilizing intellectual alacrity and promoting the ethos of forgotten values.

I speak of those mechanisms of internal reactions which only concentration can awaken, by triggering careful observation, the disposition to read and certain additional mental processes, such as comparison, interpretation and the consequent obligatory reduction from the specific to the generic. It is precisely these mechanisms that, by heightening the magnetic force of interest, almost imperceptibly direct one's logical steps to another kind of detection of the exhibition's content, both from the standpoint of its title and from the standpoint of its material.

It is, of course, known to all that words represent for the articulation of discourse what coins – money that is – represent for the constitution of the economy. However, I have no idea whether this conceptual association can be perceived only as a direct reference to the discourse of the economy during Graeco-Roman Antiquity and the Byzantine Age more specifically, or whether, possibly, it may also conceal some oblique allusions to today's reality. The first is declared, beyond a shadow of doubt, by the literal translation of the exhibition's title. The second emerges from the self-evident disposition of every deliberative visitor to seek out the covert messages of things, whether these be events or circumstances, in the depth and not on the surface of their semantic coordinates. As is the case in those exhibitions that are distinguished by an obvious awareness of their mission, so the exhibition of the Fondation Martin Bodmer leaves a clearly discernible leeway in the perception of its organizational aims, beyond the strictures of its theme.

Therefore, we should not censure those who understand the subject of the exhibition as an indirect reference to a period overloaded with words that vainly search for their specific gravity and with coins that have long lost their essential value. That is, those who wish to see it as a critical commentary on the present European status quo, and indeed from the side of Switzerland, which has succeeded in keeping unharmed both its economy and the intellectual entity of European tradition.

Nonetheless, European tradition, at least as this is comprehended by the most zealous remaining Europeanists, implicates a critical determinant: the conspicuous absence of the invocation of image from the exhibition's title. This may be due to the perspicacity of a scientific curation which may well have considered patently obvious the identification of its definition with words and with coins. However, it may well be that it declares a gut reaction to the intensifying trends of the new age to deify images as primal factors of the present in every field and every area of everyday life.

If I have not succumbed to flights of fancy, the material in the exhibition, by transcending the above dilemmas, refers directly to the best and the most precious products of human genius from Homer onwards. Indeed, as it transcends the mental limitations of its title, it spans equally the Renaissance and the subsequent period, up to the age of Enlightenment and modern times. With starting point an easily lisible annotation of money, the outburst of its periodic relations with discourse and the catalytic presence of exhibits that have been touched by human hands. That is, with the enhancement of historical phases during which the constants of another kind of appreciation of spiritual and intellectual values flourished.

Prof. Angelos Delivorrias
Director of the Benaki Museum

WORDS AND COINS

> *"Each document bears the imprint and expression of an idea that is best be communicated visually – writing in the broadest sense of the word – for it may take the form of letters, pictures, shape, musical notes and figures. It is in this kind of documents that our principal interest lies."*
> — Martin Bodmer

Europe today is yet again at a turning point in its history. The changes are multiple, deep, inscrutable; the future is, once more, uncertain. In these fascinating and troubled times, the public would be well justified in asking why such an exhibition. It seems to us that today, more than ever, we need to converse in silence with that which is within us agile and perennial, and which founds and illuminates the fascinating adventure that is human History. The humble and secretive beauty of the objects on display lends itself admirably to this task, such is our feeling that in books and coins, glimmers, as if safeguarded for eternity, the Spirit. It would be difficult to find a venue more highly dedicated and more appropriate for this experience.

Two internationally renowned cultural institutions, the Martin Bodmer Foundation and the Benaki Museum are at the genesis of this exhibition. They were both created by two great Europeans 'without frontiers', who, although relatively distant in space, were strangely close in their shared passion for Man and all that human spirit has bequeathed us that is truly moving. As if to realize the unspoken wish of their founders, these two institutions combine today their valuable expertise.

Of all the vestiges that the passion and the humanistic vision of Martin Bodmer and Antonis Benakis have extracted from oblivion, this exhibition proposes, in a resolutely historical and iconological perspective, to put into tacit conversation those objects that most rarely are thus engaged, for obvious considerations of museological practice and cultural policy. Books and coins have remained in the confines of a narrow circle of connoisseurs for so long, that the general public rarely shows interest in them. The great fragility of an ancient book or manuscript and the diminutive size of a coin have prevented museums from allowing the public's natural curiosity to apply itself to them. The book and the manuscript call for darkness; the coin demands light. Both are equally undecipherable to the modern eye, often uninformed, more often inattentive. So many challenges to the ingenuity and creativity of an exhibition's curator or designer.

Our Foundation feels honoured and fortunate that such a beautiful compendium of its numismatic collection found its way, through a series of serendipities, into the confluence of all that has allowed this exhibition to see the light of day. Let us hope that this experience will be beneficial in teaching us to listen better to the 'voice' of these magical and marvellous 'things' that are books and coins. This alone, in our view, is our greatest contribution. Perhaps it will also give us courage for the journey.

Manos Dimitrakopoulos
Vice-president of the Board of the Welfare Foundation for Social & Cultural Affairs

Procemium

COINS AND WORDS PERCEPTION AND METAPHOR

Language is for the human species the decisive specifying difference that *par excellence* distinguishes it from every other living creature on the planet Earth and gives man the identity of the rational being. Language, critical element of identity and absolute point of reference, is perhaps the first principle underpinning the history of mankind and giving rise to culture. Gradually, with the invention of writing, language became not just a medium of oral communication but the means of following human activity and, consequently, the vehicle for perpetuating historical memory, by recording, processing, storing and transmitting information.

The introduction of coinage is, in its turn, a product of human ingenuity intended to meet everyday needs, under a convention aimed at preserving equity in a society of reciprocity, in which the value of all goods of a certain weight or a certain affinity could be estimated comparatively, fairly and logically, using one medium. Coins of electrum, coins of gold, silver, bronze, nickel, coins of billon, and later paper-money, banknotes or even today's plastic money-credit cards; all are a human invention to meet the need for guaranteeing and balancing transactions. An invention that was obliged, in the course of time, to submit and adapt to norms determined by the economic and political ambitions of each era.

The course of the coin from its place of production, the mint, is lost in mazes charted by the orbit and magnitude of human activity. It is disseminated in trade, exchanged for comestibles, chattels and adornments; it becomes remuneration for the soldier, the civil servant, the mason, the artist, for every employee; it accompanies the traveller and the pilgrim in his peregrinations, follows man in his expansionist aspirations, underpins education and the arts, becomes a means of redemption of the human soul through acts of philanthropy and offerings in temples and churches.

Thus, the coin is transformed from a medium of transaction to a medium of manifold information. Coins are eyewitnesses and, as Ernest Babelon perceptively states, 'Coins are irrefutable visual witnesses, relentlessly called upon to contribute information of every sort about humanity's past for the understanding of history'. Coins are history.

A priori, it could be said that the relationship between written discourse and therefore between words and coins is intrinsic. It is a relationship that emerges from their very nature as basic driving forces of the course of mankind and as master-craftsmen of the art of 'participating'. Products of inventiveness, they sprung up through a mental alertness and became innovative creations that were incorporated in the everyday practice of people, determining their daily intercourse at a level of intellectual and practical mutual understanding: equitable assessment of meanings, equitable evaluation of material goods, respectively. 'Words and coins are to be exchanged. They both have value… both bear a stamp of meaning which can be defaced by usage, so that what they meant originally is no longer apparent - save to the expert'.[1]

Particularly interesting is the fact that this intrinsic relationship between words and coins seems to have consciously influenced the structure of human thought, resulting in the vocabulary of money creeping into a series of figures of speech, which are used to determine human thoughts, attitudes and actions. Typical example the metaphorical expressions framing or characterizing time, such as 'Time is money', 'Save time', 'He has invested a lot of time', 'It'll cost you a few minutes'. As Buchan remarks, 'Man's great inventions… are words and money, and words about money are therefore of double interest to us'.[2]

Coins and words in a continuous communication, in a two-way conscious acceptance of the dynamic role of each.

Words on coins, that is the inscriptions, had a particular significance and endorsed, in parallel with the iconography on the two sides of the coin, the identity of the issuing authority:[3] cities, leagues, *ethne*, kings, generals, dynasts and satraps. Shortly after their appearance in the late seventh century BC, coins carried engraved inscriptions, initially on one side and later on both sides. Apart from the name of the city – at first with the least possible letters –, usually on the reverse, or the name of the ruler, various complementary inscriptions and monograms were engraved in the field on both sides, references to the mint officials and symbols of control of the issue of specific series. Coin inscriptions, besides being elements of validation and authentication of the issuing authority, functioned also as a means of transmitting information by publicizing the name of the issuing authority to a wide geographical region, analogous of course with the ambit of circulation of the coins, and preserving it for posterity.

On the other hand, apart from the traditional definition of money as a standard of value, as a medium of exchange and as a store of wealth, money, within the particular milieu in which it functioned each time, acquired a peculiar power, which had a special effect on the written word. This power was expressed by inspired texts that are landmarks in world literature.[4]

Coins and words, creations of human need for communication, forever in continuous dialogue, record history, become tools for transmitting knowledge of the past, proposing a performance that leads from the material to the spiritual world, and *vice versa*. Coins are History. Coins are People. This was the view cultivated initially in the Italian Renaissance from the fourteenth century, when the poet and scholar Petrarch (1304–1374) began being interested in Roman coins. Petrarch, as well as other of his contemporaries and colleagues, realized that the portraits of the Roman emperors, as these appear emblematically on the coins, are realistic representations of the illustrious men and began to use drawings of them to illustrate their writings, for decorative or evocative purposes. Indeed, through the ages, the narrative and pictorial language of old coins became an eyewitness of humanity's past, a visual didactic discourse and an instrument of cultural transmission (*translatio*); they help people to approach actual events and beliefs of the past, to understand the stories described and depicted in papyri, manuscripts and books over time, as well as to become participants in those values or concepts that formed and inspired the intellectual vigilance and literary wealth of various periods.

So, it is obvious that the exhibition *Words and Coins* attempts to create an artistic dialogue between written discourse and coins, so that the stories and the messages diffused through these are correlated and enhanced. The roles of each medium – coin, text – are examined in an interactive and interconnected framework. The fourteen units articulating the central idea of the exhibition, with thematic and chronological affinity, set the stage for minor histories of narration as well as histories of familiar human inquiries: the coding of these stories presupposes the activation of careful observation and active participation in the dialogue between discourse and image.

Within the time machine, coins, manuscripts and books become precious tools for enhancing historical phases of the ancient Greek world, as well as of the Roman and, in continuation, the

Byzantine Empire. Indeed, the exhibition, as it transcends the significative limitations of its title, through the diachronic correlations of the coin with the manuscripts and books, covers equally the Renaissance and the subsequent period of the Enlightenment and the Modern Age.

Hesiod's Works and Days, the Homeric epics, Ovid's *Metamorphoses*, Boccaccio's *Genealogiæ Deorum gentilium*, texts by Goethe, verses by the Alexandrian poet Constantine P. cat. nos 114, 121 Cavafy (1863–1933), to confine ourselves to some of the exhibits of the written word, in dialogue with Orpheus and Eurydice, with the gods of Olympus who ordained the fortunes and works of men, with the protagonists of the Trojan War, with mystery deities of the East, with mythical animals such as the Chimaera, and mythical persons such as the Tegean Telephos, cat. no. 91 son of Heracles and Auge, who was left exposed on Mount Parthenion in Arcadia by his grandfather Aleus, son of Arcas, and was nurtured by a doe.

In dialogue too, Heracles slaying the Lernaian Hydra on a coin of Nicopolis ad Istrum, with a miniature in the manuscript of Christine de Pisan, *Epître d'Othéa* (15th c.), which depicts the chivalrous hero in the midst of wild beasts and wielding a club with an equally forceful cat. nos 25, 30 gesture . Further, the hero, vanquisher of Hades, fulfilling his last Labour, is represented carrying Cerberus to the Upper World on a coin of Perinthus, while a similar depiction illu- cat. nos 118, 125 minates the upper part of an initial letter from the narrative of *Hercules Furens* in a fifteenth-century manuscript of Seneca's *Tragœdiae*. Tragic figure in the lower part, struck down by the curse of Hera, he is shown killing his wife and children.

And it is Bucephalus, the famous horse of Alexander the Great, which appears in half-body galloping towards the exit gateway, in a miniature with the birth of Alexander the Great in a fifteenth-century manuscript of Quintus Curtius' *Faits et gestes du grand Alexandre*, and cat. nos 38, 39 which seems to have leapt out of the circular flan of a bronze coin of Seleucus I Nicator (312–281 BC).

Portraits of kings and rulers of Hellenistic Antiquity, as well as Roman emperors, imprinted on gold, silver and bronze coins, animate the content of Plutarch's *Vitae illustrium virorum* or even function as identity photographs next to timeless tales telling of their deeds or to texts that are documents of their period.

A gold aureus with the head of Julius Caesar accompanies the epic poem *Pharsalia*, refer- cat. nos 166, 171 ring to the Battle of Pharsalus fought in 48 BC near Pharsalus in Thessaly between Julius Caesar and the forces of the Roman Senate led by Pompey the Great.

Coin portraits of emperor Hadrian frame the Renaissance surround of a miniature from a cat. nos 23, 29 fifteenth-century manuscript with the work *Romuleon*, by Benvenuto da Imola, (14th century), which depicts a dying king handing the crown of authority to a child. The coins delimit the actual historical environment of the narrative, which recalls the legend of Trajan's succession. Trajan who had no heir, wished to die without a descendant, following the example of Alexander the Great. However, his wife, Pompeia Plotina, is said to have introduced an impersonator into the bed of the deceased emperor, who adopted Hadrian as the legal heir of the imperial throne.

And it is the book by M. Yourcenar, *Mémoires d'Hadrien* which describes in a modern manner the life and death of the Roman emperor Hadrian. The book is in the form of a letter to Hadrian's eventual successor, Marcus Aurelius. The emperor meditates on his military tri- cat. nos 116, 123 umphs, his love of poetry and music, philosophy, and his passion for the young Antinous, who after his untimely death is portrayed on a series of coins as a heroized youth.

cat. no. 180 The bronze medallion of Constantine the Great refers to the new capital of the Roman Empire, on the European shore of the Propontis, on the site where the Megarian Byzas had founded a trading colony (*emporium*) in the seventh century BC. The *solidus* of Theodosios I accompanies the manuscript of the two military treatises, De *rebus bellicis [and] Notitia dignitatum*, written in the fourth or early fifth century, the first describing the different war machines then in use and the second drawing a picture of the empire's military and administrative organization, as well as the *Codex Theodosianus* which, decreed by his grandson Theodosios II in 438, became one of the pillars of Roman Law. Next to Procopius' history *De Rebus Gothorum, Persarum ac Vandalorum* projects the vigorous bust of Justinian, while the theological texts of John of Damascus complement coins of the iconoclast Byzantine emperors Constantine V and Michael II. Last, next to the *Tetraevangelium* (Four Gospels) are the coin of the period of Venetian rule with the lion, symbol of the Evangelist Mark who is depicted in the miniature, and the bronze coin of Basil I, who in 867 founded a long-lived dynasty which remained in power for 189 years, until the death of his great-great-great-granddaughter Theodora in 1056. The Macedonian dynasty is accredited with the most splendid period in the history of the Byzantine Empire. Under the leadership of able generals-emperors the Empire defeated the Arabs, subjugated the Bulgars, cleared the Mediterranean of corsairs, strengthened its position in southern Italy and spread Greek Orthodox Christianity to the Rus (989), while enjoying a heyday in learning, literature and the arts.

cat. no. 177

cat. nos 195, 204, 205

cat. nos 182, 188

cat. nos 193, 194, 203

cat. no. 183

Coins and books are history, coins and books are people. History and people of a geographical unity, separated into states, each with different boundaries in the course of time, today united in its greater part at a monetary level. A mosaic of interconnected historical events, receiver and transmitter of ideas and spiritual inquiries between its constituent peoples, and not only, field of diverse oppositions then and now…

And it is the myths that are never silent, that have the power to remain unchanged by current events and by historical hermeneutic approaches… And it is the myths which, the world over, in all ages and under whatever circumstances, were the living inspiration for all man's mental activities, mainly for those expressed through art, either the art of discourse or the art of image.

The head of the nymph Arethusa, with its chaste severity, surrounded by four dolphins, upon the tetradrachm of Syracuse, an image of highly delicate sensitivity, is perhaps an abstract yet at once an eloquent visual rendering of the primeval history linking the peoples of the Mediterranean, and not only. Arethusa, with curls escaping from the ribbon keeping her hair in place, under the pressure of the water, narrates superbly her adventure when the river-god Alpheus fell in love with her, before she was transformed into a spring on the island of Ortygia at Syracuse in Sicily. At the same time, she appears to leap out of Ovid's *Metamorphoses*: 'then Arethusa, once of Elis, whom Alpheus loved, lifted her head from her pool, and brushed the wet hair from her forehead, saying…'.[5]

cat. no. 63

Vasiliki Penna

* A complicated and arduous project such as the realization of the exhibition *Words and Coins: from Ancient Greece to Byzantium* consists the culmination of the efforts of many people, as it can be reflected in the credits of this book. Additionally, acknowledgements should include certain members of the staff of the Benaki Museum: special thanks are due for their contribution to Irine Papageorgiou, Angeliki Ziva and Panayiotis Papastavrou, as well as to Anastasia Drandaki and Mara Verikokou. The (KIKPE) coins and the other (Benaki) artefacts were conserved by Despina Kotzamani, Maria Zacharia, Georgia Karydi and Anthia Phoca in the Conservation Department of the Benaki Museum.

Notes

1. Ch. Bode, 'A Mercia of the Mind: Geoffrey Hill's Mercian Hymns and the Poetical Transcendence of Time and Place', in: L. Fietz *et al.* (eds), *Regionalität, Nationalität und Internationalität in der zeitgenössischen Lyrik*, Tübingen 1992, pp. 313-42 and esp. p. 332.
2. J. Buchan, *Frozen Desire – an Inquiry into the Meaning of Money*, London 1997, p. 127; J. Gribb, 'Money as Metaphor', *Numismatic Chronicle* 165 (2005), pp. 417–8.
3. For the inscriptions on ancient Greek and Roman coins see indicatively F. Rebuffat, *La monnaie dans l'antiquité*, Paris 1996, pp. 189–201; see also in the present volume the contribution by A. Meadows, 'Coinage and the Writing of Ancient Greek History'; see also T. R. Volk, 'From Phanes to Pisanello: 2000 years of numismatic Greek' in: P. Easterling and C. Handley (eds), *Greek Scripts, An illustrated introduction*, London 2001, pp. 31–40. For the inscriptions on Byzantine coins see indicatively in the present volume the contribution by C. Morrisson, '*Kharaktēr*: the history of Byzantium and beyond in words and images'. For the numismatic iconography see indicatively in the present volume the contributions by: V. Penna, 'Glimpses of the past: coin issues of illustrious men'; U. Wartenberg Kagan, 'The Perception of Ancient Myths: Narratives and Representations'.
4. See in the present volume the contributions by: S. Messerli, 'Words and Money'.
5. Ovid, *Metamorphoses*, 5.487. Following the narration of Ovid, the myth of Arethusa's transformation begins when she was bathing in a clear stream without knowing that it was the river-god Alpheus. He fell in love during their encounter, but she fled after discovering his presence and intentions, as she wished to remain a chaste attendant of Artemis. After a long chase, she prayed to her goddess for protection. Artemis hid her in a cloud, but Alpheus was persistent. Soon Arethusa was transformed into a stream. Artemis then broke the ground, allowing Arethusa another attempt to flee. Her stream travelled under the earth to the island of Ortygia, but Alpheus flowed through the sea to reach her and mingle with her waters; see Ovid, *Metamorphoses*, 5.572–641.

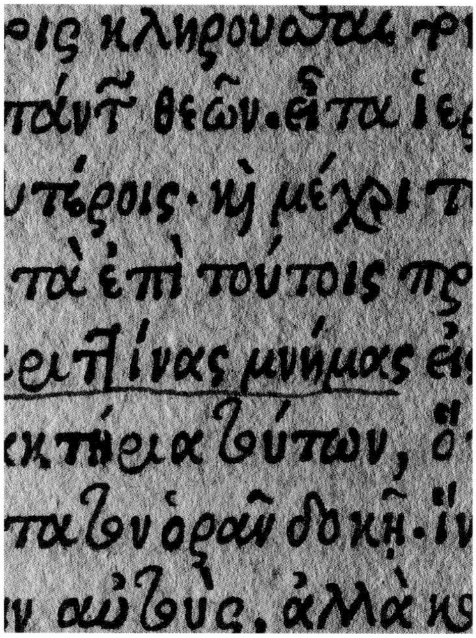
οις κληρουσθαι
πάντων θεῶν. εἶτα ἱε
υτέροις. καὶ μέχρι τ
τὰ ἐπὶ τούτοις πρ
ειτ ἵνας μνήμας ἐ
τεια τούτων, ὅ
τα τὸν ὁρᾶν δοκῇ. ἵν
αὐτούς. ἀλλὰ κ

I
WORDS AND MONEY

Sylviane Messerli

Ex Ioue et Moneta, Musae

Some say that the word 'money' comes from the goddess Juno's epithet '*moneta*', meaning 'she who warns, she who counsels'. Cicero tells of a time after an earthquake when a voice ordering the Romans to sacrifice a pregnant sow was heard to come from her temple: 'From this fact the goddess was called Juno the Adviser [Moneta]'.[1] Her temple in the Capitol housed a mint for Roman coins. For others, the epithet came from an Italian deity honoured in the Capitol's original sanctuary, the geese of which had warned the Romans against an attack by the Gauls. The *Souda* reports yet another legend: during Pyrrhus' war against the Tarantines, the Romans, who were short of money, prayed to Juno for help. The goddess replied that as long as they fought with the weapons of justice, they would not be without means; '...having confirmed the truth of these words, the Romans named her *Juno Moneta*'.[2] More prosaically, Isidore of Seville affirms: 'She was named *Moneta* because she warned (*monet*) against using fraudulent metals and weights'.[3]

These etymological games, however, are weak; early on, scholars demonstrated their limits. In reality, Juno's epithet derived most probably from the Greek *moneres* (μονήρης), which means 'single' or 'unique'. Moreover, *moneta* in the sense of money (coinage) is probably of Phoenician or Etruscan origin. Nevertheless, popular etymology associates the word 'money' with warnings. More particularly, the justification of this etymology led to the development of a series of legends, which profoundly united words and money.

The first written reference to the goddess Moneta supports this hypothesis. It is found in Livius Andronicus' adaptation of Homer's *Odyssey* in Saturnian verse.[4] Livius Andronicus translates Odysseus's words honouring the poets 'because they are inspired by the Muse' as: *nam divina Monetas filia docuit*.[5] He thus makes of Moneta the mother of the Muse of poetry. Continuing in this vein, the fabulist Hyginus explains the association: 'From Jove and Moneta, the Muses [were born]'.[6] Interestingly, in Hesiod and Apollodorus, for example, Moneta is replaced by Mnemosyne.[7] Indeed, Mnemosyne (Μνημοσύνη, or Memory) is traditionally considered the mother of the Muses. In fact, one of the functions attributed to money (coins) is that of transmitting the present memories to future generations. Thus, Cassiodorus establishes a new etymology (*commonere*: to remind):

> *Verum hanc liberalitatem nostram alio decoras obsequio, ut figura uultus nostri metallis usualibus inprimatur, monetamque facis des nostris temporibus futura saecula commonere.*[8]

the coins that forever glitter in history and in fable

When you think about it, should one be surprised at this naïve association between words and money?

The study of vocabulary offers one first caution to this approach: the Latin word *moneta* can also designate more specifically the imprint of a coin. In fact the rare occurrences when this term is used in a figurative manner refer specifically to the style of an author.[9] Juvenal, for example, speaks thus of a poet 'who has a vein of genius all his own, one who spins no hackneyed lays, and whose pieces are struck from no common mint' (*nec qui / communi feriat carmen triuiale moneta*).[10]

It is, in fact, to the poets that we must turn in order to better understand what is at stake. We know that the motif of the coin perfuses the work of Jorge Luis Borges.[11]

cat. no. 27

In *The Zahir*, a short story published in *The Aleph*, the Argentinian author chooses a 20 *centavos* coin as a *zahir*, an unforgettable object that the narrator cannot erase from his memory. The lines describing his first encounter with the coin give a good example:

> *I ordered a glass of orange gin. In my change I was given the zahir. I stared at it for a moment, and then I went out into the street, perhaps already feverish. It occurred to me that every coin in the world is a symbol for all the coins that forever glitter in history and in fable. I recalled the obol of Charon; and the obol which Belisarius sought; Judas' thirty pieces; the drachmas of Laïs, the courtesal; the ancient coin proffered by one of the Seven Sleepers of Ephesus; the shining coins of the wizard of* The Thousand and One Nights*, which turned into paper circles; Isaac Laquedem's inexhaustible penny; the 60,000 pieces of silver – one for each line of an epic poem – which Firdusi returned to a king because they were not gold; the gold piece which Ahab had nailed to the mast; Leopold Bloom's irreversible florin; the louis d'or whose effigy informed against the fugitive Louis*

> *XVI close by Varennes. As in a dream the thought that every coin allows such illustrious connotations struck me as of vast, if inexplicable, importance.*[12]

Borges's recounting is literally fabulous. Reading it is enough to make whole universes appear contained as seeds in the simple evocation of facts and names, and to give birth to the desire to relate their stories. The list is an incitement to return to the sources for more details. It is also an invitation to crown it with one's own recollections: Jupiter's transformation into golden rain in order to impregnate Danae; the charity refused by Isolde to Tristan disguised as a leper beggar; the coin stolen by Jean Valjean from the young chimneysweep from Savoy... Indeed, one coin alone reflects all the coins 'in history and in fable', so long as one takes the time to consider it.

On the other hand, Orhan Pamuk, the recent Nobel laureate for literature, gives money a voice of its own: 'Behold! I am a[n] ... Ottoman ... gold coin'.[13] Seven years of the coin's travels while changing hands 560 times allow the writer to recount the life of Istanbul in full. What adventures, hopes, sorrows, banalities has the coin that I hold in my hand witnessed?

The evocative power of the coin itself is the key to open a world of narrative doubles when we consider the design on its faces. Very early, men represented their gods and masters, the planets, cities, heroes and legends on their coins. An emblematic scene, a face accompanied by initials, a stereotype profile, a star, an animal, a lyre or a quiver, a cross... The effigies are, of course, the affirmation of a political and religious identity. They potentially contain a thousand narratives. How many stories does the combat between Ajax and Hector evoke, or the struggle of Heracles against the Lernaian cat. no. 104
Hydra or the Nemean Lion, Athena standing before the olive tree she gave to the first cat. no. 25
Athenians, or Leander's dead body washed up at the tower where Hero awaited him? cat. nos 92, 98
The bust of Antinous on the coins issued by Hadrian, the face of Cleopatra on those cat. nos 93, 99, 116
issued by Anthony, the portraits of Caesar and Brutus, Saint George holding a lance cat. nos 148, 165, 166
and shield, the Virgin and Child, Constantine the Great, Alexander... they all carry cat. nos 134, 201, 180
the weight of history and legend.

to take from or place in the hand of someone else a coin in silence

In a revelatory manner, this almost intrinsic bond between coins and words is activated by the writers themselves when they define their relationship to language. Numerous examples awaken reflections on language and literature so that it would be worth bringing them together in an anthology. We will mention a few, chosen randomly, and will present them without commentary so as to allow the questions that they raise to germinate.

Stéphane Mallarmé makes the point:

> *Narrate, teach, even describe, that's fine and even if it were enough for each of us perhaps, in order to exchange human thought, to take from or place in the hand of someone else a coin in silence, the elementary use of discourse serves the needs of universal reportage, of which, with the exception of literature, all the genres of contemporary writings contain elements.*[14]

In *Render unto Caesar*,[15] Marguerite Yourcenar connects two episodes 'voluntarily unconnected, or rather placed sideways one against the other' taking place in fascist Italy in 1933 'through the story of a coin changing hands'. She also spins the metaphor, reactivating Mallarmé's idea: 'In *Render unto Caesar*, the quasi-automatic verbal exchange of everyday life is the equivalent of a coin changing hands'.

In a more anticipated – though just as open to interpretation – affirmation, Goethe uses the image of the coin, the effigy and legend of which are erased by time, to assert that the original meaning of words is progressively worn.[16]

Often the connection between the coin and the literary creation only emerges in the interpretation. One must probably be a seasoned medievalist to taste Rutebeuf's masterly art in the *La Grièche d'été* (referring to a dice game). This text, one of his most characteristic works, places the figure of an amateur poet in a tavern. Play on words after play on words, the author defines himself using precisely the motif of money. *Li argens art gent* (Money [*argent*] burns people [*les gens*], l. 74) is a characteristic pun; as is his use of the second reading of the *bourgeois*, the coins featuring the Bourges cross:

> *Quar dui tornois*
> *Trois paresis, cinq vienois*
> *Ne pueent pas fere un borgois*
> *D'un nu despris*[17]
> *'For two tournois [coins of Tours], three parisis [coins of Paris], five viennois [coins of Vienne] cannot render bourgeois a man who is naked and despised' [or someone naked in spirit, i.e. 'a man devoid of intelligence']*

Even if he loses his clothes at dice, the poet nevertheless weaves his text – and his identity.

Dante also takes hold of the monetary metaphor to say what is impossible to say. Thus, upon arriving in Paradise, he understands without difficulty the sense of profound things, hidden from the eyes of those on earth. His definition of faith, which, though complex, is clear enough to the eyes of Saint Peter, who interrogates him, ends with the familiar image of a coin:

> *This speech was breathed from that enkindled love.*
> *He added: "Now this coin is well-examined,*
> *and now we know its alloy and its weight.*
> *But tell me: do you have it in your purse?"*
> *And I: "Indeed I do—so bright and round*
> *that nothing in its stamp leads me to doubt".*[18]

Finally, these associations will not surprise those literary critics and linguists, whose studies were founded on the works of Ferdinand de Saussure, who defines the linguistic signifier by comparing it to a coin.[19]

truths are (…) used coins with faded engravings

We know that to define one's relation to literature or language is to define one's relation to the world. Is there a better example than Friedrich Nietzsche, who in turn seizes the monetary image in his *On Truth and Lies in a Nonmoral Sense*? In this text, the philosopher defines the principal elements of the manner in which he considers language the foundation of the world's structure:

> *What then is truth? A movable host of metaphors, metonymies, and anthropomorphisms: in short, a sum of human relations which have been poetically and rhetorically intensified, transferred, and embellished, and which, after long usage, seem to a people to be fixed, canonical, and binding. Truths are illusions which we have forgotten are illusions, they are metaphors that have become worn out and have been drained of sensuous force, coins which have lost their embossing and are now considered as metal and no longer as coins.*[20]

As for Arthur Schnitzler, he talks of our inability to express the truth of a thought, which is always received by another independently of our intention and depending on what he wants to hear. In this relation 'truth as such has no value, as little as a coin in a country where it is not current'.[21]

Here is the iron coin

The reverse and the obverse. Every coin has two faces. So too does their metaphorical use. Coins give hope that the memory of ancient times will last with them, but their wear signals the loss of memory. They contain a thousand stories, but when their effigies become unknown to us they sometimes impose a cruel silence. They do lead, however, to questions that inspire reflection…

At the end of a course conceived as an invitation to read, let us keep poetry as our only point of reference. Let us ask one last question, with Borges, while holding a coin in our clenched fists:

> *Here is the iron coin. Let us interrogate*
> *The two opposing faces what will be the answer*
> *To the demanding question nobody has put:*
> *Why does a man require that a woman should love him?*
> *(…)*
> *In the other's shadow we are seeking our own shadow,*
> *And the other's glass, our complementary glass.*[22]

Notes

1. Cicero, *De divinatione*, 1.45.101: *Atque etiam scriptum a multis est, cum terrae motus factus esset, ut sue plena procuratio fieret, uocem ab aede Iunonis ex arce exstitisse; quocirca Iunonem illam appellatam Monetam* (… [it] has been reported by many writers … that a voice coming from Juno's temple in the Capitol after an earthquake advised that they sacrifice a pregnant sow and from this fact the goddess was called Juno the Adviser). However, in the second book, Cicero used the example of Juno Moneta to denounce the futility of divine signs: *Quod idem dici de Moneta potest; a qua praeterquam de sue plena quid umquam moniti sumus?* (Your Juno Moneta may likewise be dismissed with a question: What did she ever admonish us about except the pregnant sow?); Cicero, *De divinatione*, 2.32.69. Cicero, *De Senectute, De Amicitia, De Divinatione*, transl. W. A. Falconer, Cambridge, MA / London 1923.
2. *Suidae Lexicon*, ed. A. Adler, III, Leipzig 1933 (Stuttgart 1967), p. 408, 1220: *Μονήτα: Ἡ Ἥρα παρὰ Ῥωμαίοις ἐξ αἰτίας τοιᾶσδε. Ῥωμαῖοι δεηθέντες χρημάτων ἐν τῷ πρὸς Πύρρον καὶ Ταραντίνους πολέμῳ ηὔξαντο τῇ Ἥρᾳ· τὴν δὲ χρῆσαι αὐτοῖς, εἰ τῶν ὅπλων ἀνθέξονται μετὰ δικαιοσύνης, χρήματα αὐτοῖς μὴ ἐπιλείψειν. Τύχοντες οὖν οἱ Ῥωμαῖοι τῆς αἰτήσεως ἐτίμησαν Ἥραν Μονήταν, τουτέστι σύμβουλον, τὸ νόμισμα ἐν τῷ ἱερῷ αὐτῆς ὁρίσαντες χαράττεσθαι.*
3. Isidore of Seville, *Etymologiae*, 16.18.8: *Moneta appellata est quia monet ne qua fraus in metallo uel in pondere fiat.*
4. Born at Tarentum *ca* 280 BC, Livius Andronicus is the earliest Roman poet whose name is known. Bridging Greek culture with the new Latin literature, he was also the first dramatist to be staged at Rome. His work is known to us only from fragments cited by other authors. Read and assimilated by his successors, his work thus escaped oblivion; it is a vivid example of the work of Memory.
5. Homer, *Odyssey*, VIII 480. On Livius Andronicus: G. Pontiggia and M. C. Grandi, *Letteratura latina. Storia e testi*, Milan 1996.
6. *Ex Ioue et Moneta, Musae, Fabulae* Preface in *The Myths of Hyginus*, M. Grant (transl. and ed.), Lawrence, KS 1960.
7. Hesiod, *Theogony*, 75ff. and 915ff; Apollodorus, *Bibliotheca*, 1.3.1. Hyginus had already associated Moneta and Mnemosyne, in the introduction of his genealogy, where he counts Moneta, instead of Mnemosyne, among the children of Aether and Earth; see *Fabulae* Preface in *The Myths of Hyginus*, M. Grant (transl. and ed.), Lawrence, KS 1960.
8. Cassiodorus, *Variae*, 6.7.3: 'It is your business to see that our face is imprinted on our coins, a reminder to our subjects of our ceaseless care on their behalf, and a memorial of our reign to future ages' (Formula of the office of *Comes Sacrarum Largitionum*), transl. T. Hodgkin, *The Letters of Cassiodorus…*, London 1886, pp. 303–4. Cassiodorus lists the charges of the House of Theodoric.
9. *Cf.* L. Nadjo, *L'argent et les affaires à Rome des origines au IIe siècle avant J.-C. Etude d'un vocabulaire technique*, Louvain / Paris 1989, p. 177, who, besides Juvenal, mentions Apuleius (*Apologia sive de Magia*), Symmachus (*Epistolae*), and Ennodius (*Epistolae*).
10. *Satire* 7, 54–55; *Juvenal and Persius*, transl. G. G. Ramsay, London / New York 1918.
11. From *Thirteen Coins*, published in *The Gold of the Tigers*, to the collection entitled *The Iron Coin*, Borges demonstrates his interest for coins. In *The Other* (*The Book of Sand*), the date on a banknote exchanged for a coin allows the young Borges living in Geneva in the early twentieth century to understand that he is meeting Borges living north of Boston in 1969. María Kodama, the writer's companion during the latter years of his life, reports that it was while playing with his father, who paraded before him coins from a pile, that Borges understood that it was impossible to recover the past: *En otro de los juegos,* [Borges's father] *utilizando una moneda como base de una pila de ellas, le enseñó que el recuperar el pasado es imposible. Le explicó que el recuerdo de la moneda que había visto, de la imagen de la moneda que había visto, no era ya exactamente el mismo, porque el recuerdo primero, la imagen primera, se va distorsionando a medida que vuelve a nosotros aquello que guardamos en nuestra memoria. La última moneda no es la primera de la pila; imposible recuperar la nitidez de la impresión original*; M. Kodama, *La memoria de Borges / Η μνήμη του Μπόρχες*, Athens 2002, pp. 16–7. I wish to thank Yannis Stoyas for indicating this text.

12. J. L. Borges, *The Zahir*, in *A Personal Anthology*, New York, Grove Press, 1967, pp. 128ff, 130–1 (transl. A. Kerrigan); Original text: *Pedí una caña de naranja; en el vuelto me dieron el Zahir; lo miré un instante; salí a la calle tal vez con un principio de fiebre. Pensé que no hay moneda que no sea símbolo de las monedas que sin fin resplandecen en la historia y la fábula. Pensé en el óbolo de Caronte; en el óbolo que pidió Belisario; en los treinta dineros de Judas; en las dracmas de la cortesana Laís; en la anrigua moneda que ofreció uno de los durmientes de Éfeso; en las claras monedas del hechicero de las* 1001 *Noches, que después eran círculos de papel; en el denario inagotable de Isaac Laquedem; en las sesenta mil piezas de plata, una por cada verso de una epopeya, que Firdusi devolvió a un rey porque no eran de oro; en la onza de oro que hizo clavar Ahab en el mástil; en el florín irreversible de Leopold Bloom; en el luis cuya efigie delató, cerca de Varennes, al fugitivo Luis XVI. Como en un sueño, el pensamiento de que toda moneda permite esas iluestres connotaciones me pareció de vasta, aunque inexplicable, importancia*, in J. L. Borges, *Obras completas*, vol. 7, Buenos Aires, 1966.
13. O. Pamuk, *My Name is Red*, transl. E. M. Göknar, New York 2002, p. 113.
14. S. Mallarmé, *Crisis in Poetry*. The passage is taken from his *Avant-Dire* in R. Ghil's *Treatise on the Verb*, published in Paris 1866.
15. M. Yourcenar, *Histoire et examen d'une pièce*, in *Théâtre I. Rendre à César, La petite sirène, La dialogue dans le marécage*, Paris 1971, pp. 9 and 21. For a translation of *Render unto Caesar* into English, see M. Yourcenar, *Plays*, transl. D. Katz, New York 1984. The play *Render unto Caesar* resumes the discourse of the novel *A Coin in Nine Hands*, which Yourcenar published 1934 and in which she used the same process.
16. *Cf.* G. J. Romanes, *Mental Evolution in Man: Origin of Human Faculty*, Cambridge 2011, p. 284.
17. Rutebeuf, *La Grièche d'été*, ll. 66–69, in *Œuvres complètes*, published by E. Faral and J. Bastin, Paris 1977, Vol. I, p. 528ff.
18. Dante, *Paradiso*, XXIV, 82–87: *Cosí spirò di quello amore acceso; / indi soggiunse: "Assai bene è trascorsa / d'esta moneta già la lega e 'l peso; / ma dimmi se tu l'hai ne la tua borsa". / Ond' io: "Sí ho, sí lucida e sí tonda, / che nel suo conio nulla mi s'inforsa".*
19. F. de Saussure, *Course in General Linguistics*, transl. W. Baskin, New York 1959, pp. 118–9: 'In addition, it is impossible for sound alone, a material element, to belong to language. It is only a secondary thing, substance to be put to use. All our conventional values have the characteristic of not being confused with the tangible element which supports them. For instance, it is not the metal in a piece of money that fixes its value. A coin nominally worth five francs may contain less than half its worth of silver.
Its value will vary according to the ammount stamped upon it and according to its use inside or outside a political boundary. This is even more true of the linguistic signifier, which is not phonic but incorporeal-constituted not by its material substance but by the differences that separate its sound image from all others'.
20. F. Nietzsche, *On Truth and Lie in a Nonmoral Sense*, transl. W. Kaufmann, *The Portable Nietzsche*, New York 1976, pp. 46–7. Original text: *Was ist also Wahrheit? Ein bewegliches Heer von Metaphern, Metonymien, Anthropomorphismen kurz eine Summe von menschlichen Relationen, die, poetisch und rhetorisch gesteigert, übertragen, geschmückt wurden, und die nach langem Gebrauche einem Volke fest, canonisch und verbindlich dünken: die Wahrheiten sind Illusionen, von denen man vergessen hat, dass sie welche sind, Metaphern, die abgenutzt und sinnlich kraftlos geworden sind, Münzen, die ihr Bild verloren haben und nun als Metall, nicht mehr als Münzen in Betracht kommen* in *Sämtliche Werke, Kritische Studienausgabe in 15 Bände*, herausgegeben von G. Colli und M. Montinari, Bd I (Nachgelassene Schriften 1870–1873, *Über Wahrheit und Lüge im außermoralischen Sinn*), Munich / New York 1980, pp. 880–1.
21. A. Schnitzler, *Aphorismen und Betrachtung*, herausgegeben von R. O. Weiss, Frankfurt 1967, p. 250: *Schmerzlicher, als dass wir niemals die Wahrheit zu hören bekommen, ist, dass wir sie auch beim besten Willen niemals aussprechen können. Denn was wir auch sagen, der andere hört die Wahrheit nicht, die wir ihm vermitteln wollten. Was von unseren Lippen kam und was in des anderen Seele dringt, ist niemals das gleiche. Es ist schon im nächsten Augenblick nicht dasselbe mehr: es kommt auf so viel an, was mit deiner Wahrheit und mit deiner Wahrheitsabsicht nichts mehr zu tun hatte: es kommt darauf an, was der andere*

hören wollte, wie er zu dir steht und so weiter. Und die Wahrheit um ihrer selbst willen ist kein Wert, so wenig wie ein Geldstück in einem Land, wo es keinen Kurs hat. (More painful than to never get to hear the truth is that we can never express, despite our best intentions. Because whatever we say, the other does not hear the truth that we want to communicate. What comes out of our mouths and what goes into the mind of another is never the same (...) it depends on so many things that have nothing to do with your truth or your truth intention, but it depends on what the other wants to hear, on how he is with you, etc. And truth as such has no value, as little as a coin in a country where it is not current).

22. J. L. Borges, *The Iron Coin*, in *The American Poetry Review*, March/April 1996, vol. 25, n. 22. Original text: *La moneda de hierro / Aquí está la moneda de hierro. Interroguemos / las dos contrarias caras que serán la respuesta / de la terca demanda que nadie no se ha hecho: / ¿Por qué precisa un hombre que una mujer lo quiera? / (...) / En la sombra del otro buscamos nuestra sombra; / en el cristal del otro, nuestro cristal recíproco*, in J. L. Borges, *La moneda de hierro*, Buenos Aires 1976. Borges wrote 'The Iron Coin', last poem of the homonymous collection, between 1975 and 1976, the year following his mother's death, while Argentina sank into the dark years.

II
WRITING AND COINING: EQUALITY, LEGALITY?

André Hurst

When we say the word money, we have no doubt as to its meaning. But where does the word come from? In general, we do not know. So, let us remember that when we say 'money' we are unwittingly perpetuating the name of *Juno Moneta*, the Roman Juno who, according to Cicero, 'warned' the Romans about an earthquake (*moneta = she who warns*).[1] It is in her temple, transformed into a public treasury, that the pieces of metal which for this reason took her name, that is to say pieces of *Moneta* – money, that is coins, were made. Therefore, when we say 'money' we are keeping alive the memory of a Roman institution, most often unknowingly – but not without knowing what we mean.

This is not the case for the Greeks: the word they use to designate coinage, *nomisma* (νόμισμα), is perfectly intelligible in their language system. The meaning of the word carries the sense of 'estimation', since the word is formed on the verb which means 'to estimate', and any speaker could easily understand what meaning this term *nomisma* gave to the pieces of metal it referred to. Here is a particularly clear testimony by Aristotle: cat. no. 15

> *For an association for interchanges of services is not formed between two physicians, but between a physician and a farmer, and generally between persons who are different, and who may be unequal,*

> *though in that case they have to be equalized. Hence all commodities exchanged must be able to be compared in some way. It is to meet this requirement that men have introduced money; money constitutes in a manner a middle term, for it is a measure of all things, and so of their superior or inferior value, that is to say, how many shoes are equivalent to a house or to a given quantity of food. As therefore a builder is to a shoemaker, so must such and such a number of shoes be to a house [or to a given quantity of food]; for without this reciprocal proportion, there can be no exchange and no association; and it cannot be secured unless the commodities in question be equal in a sense. It is therefore necessary that all commodities shall be measured by some one standard, as was said before. And this standard is in reality demand, which is what holds everything together, since if men cease to have wants or if their wants alter, exchange will go on no longer, or will be on different lines. But demand has come to be conventionally represented by money; this is why money is called 'nomisma' (='estimation'), because it does not exist by nature but by culture ('nomos'), and can be altered and rendered useless at will.*[2]

It is the 'conventional' facet of money which is emphasized in its function. It is used as a means of 'estimating' the value of diverse labours and to ensure the necessary passage of the value of one job to that of another. To pay is to make a value judgement, so to speak, but a judgement which is always set out with the same vocabulary, to wit the series of numbers and the units of 'estimation': money.

Hence the question of the appearance of coinage. In the brief history of humanity, we can observe that even the Neolithic Revolution, though relatively recent, did not lead to the immediate invention of money in the form of coins, as we know them. Nevertheless, as soon as human groups distribute tasks, it necessarily follows that goods circulate, even if only from the farmer to the maker of his tools, since the latter must be able to feed himself even if he does not produce anything edible. However, 'merchandise is incapable of transporting itself to market and exchanging itself', as Karl Marx wrote.[3] Human intervention is essential, quite obviously, for exchanges between people, between individuals who have the same needs (to go back to Aristotle's account), and one is led to postulate the existence of a form of 'money' before the invention of stamped coins.

It is necessarily a form of estimation, whether it be of the quality of the goods or the quality of the interlocutors within the exchange. Aristotle says it implicitly: exchange existed before the invention of what we commonly call 'money'. It is clear that for him money was not always present, since it is not a gift of nature. Moreover, the Greek names of the different coins which are collectively designated as *nomisma* bear the trace of an earlier state of evaluation by means of pieces of metal: *obolos* is none other than a 'spit', a shaft of metal, while *drachme* is a 'handful' of spits.

In truth, money as we know it now, in the form of metal coins bearing a mark that indicates their value and their place of issue, came into being around the mid-seventh century BC in the kingdom of Lydia in Asia Minor. It is Herodotus who informs us on this matter.[4] Lydia is the country of King 'Croesus', the country crossed by the

fig. 1: see cat. no. 1
cat. no. 14

River 'Pactolus', in short, a place associated with fabulous names and which are still mythical references for designating the most thriving wealth.

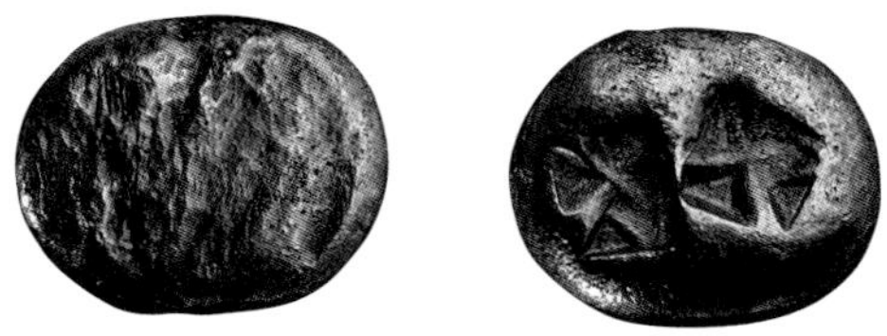

fig. 1

Electrum *hekte*, uncertain Ionian mint, *ca.* 630–600 BC.
KIKPE Collection, Athens

With such an origin, we might think that this form of money was, first and foremost, the affair of wealthy monarchies. But the kingdom of Lydia is small, and the invention did not come from the great affluent kingdoms of the Middle East. Moreover, money seems to have taken on the role of equalizer, through circumstantial serendipity. It is the privileged tool of commerce, and hence of social relationships. Its usage spread in Greece at the same time as we observe the sudden rise of two other remarkable features: the aspiration to equality and the spread of writing (this will not be the case in Persia, where the Lydians' invention will be borrowed after the defeat of the Lydians by the Persians at Sardis in 546 BC).

In the field, archeologically speaking, the aspiration to equality can be seen in the transformation of urbanism. In intellectual life, as we can grasp it, we are in the presence of the 'writing down' of texts such as laws (with their accompanying publication) and the Homeric poems (in view of their public recitations).

Urbanism first. From the eighth century BC onwards, at Megara Hyblaia in Sicily, we can observe the emergence of the 'grid' city plan, which will subsequently be so successful. This city was founded by the Megarians around 729 BC.[5] The very idea of going somewhere else to found a new city could also (or not) be accompanied by the desire to found a better society, aside from the fact that it was also a solution to the problem of over-population in the original city and an initiative linked to the expansion of trade. Nevertheless, and indisputably, the grid plan expressed the will to allocate equal parts of habitable land to the inhabitants of a given city.

Scholars have not failed to underscore the coincidence of this reality of urbanism with currents of thought which, even if they remain difficult to comprehend, seem nevertheless to reveal at the same time, or in the time immediately following, an aspiration to establish a justice equal for all.

We can observe this in Hesiod's poetry, which dates from the mid-seventh century BC. In his poem *Works and Days*, we can clearly perceive the echo of a demand for equality when the poet shows 'Justice' (*Dikē*) chased from among humans and brought to heel by the manoeuvrings of corrupt judges.[6] 'Equality is the first component of justice', Montaigne will write much later.[7]

We observe equality amongst the 'pre-Socratic' thinkers too. Alongside visions of the world considering one or other of the natural elements as the foundation for everything, along comes Anaximander (early 6th century BC) with a vision in which the 'beings' are equivalent, even having the same origin and the same end in the 'in(de)-finite', alternating along a time line like a form of equality.[8] Jean-Pierre Vernant will write about Anaximander, opposing him to Anaximenes:

> *For Anaximander, on the contrary, no singular element, no portion of the world could be considered to dominate other elements. It is the equality and the symmetry of the various powers that make up the 'cosmos' which characterize the new order of nature. The supremacy belongs exclusively to a law of equilibrium and constant reciprocity. A regime of 'isonomia' has taken the place of 'monarchia' in nature as in the city.*[9]

Isonomia, 'equality (of all) before the law', is here a key element. It could well be that the idea it expresses is closer to that of 'democracy' than the translation 'equality before the law', but the concept remains clear. Actually, the word *isonomia* itself is only attested later, from the fifth century BC onwards, yet at the beginning of the sixth century BC. Solon expresses himself unequivocally on the question, and he explicates clearly the existence of equality, which was still only an underlying element in Hesiod. In reality, we know, facts will resist *isonomia*, which detracts nothing from the observation of the striving towards it by the human groups who will organize the cities. After all, we can observe the same phenomenon in other domains: the Greeks have a word to designate peace, they make it a positive idea, attested most notably by a comedy by Aristophanes, even if, in fact, periods of peace were not the norm for them. And yet, the aspiration to equality will find an ally in the circulation of money and we are tempted to say that money is worth the use that was made of it.

An emblematic figure of his time, Solon is known for the determining role he played in Athenian politics at the beginning of the sixth century BC, and he expresses very clearly the demands of equality. We are here right in the period when the use of money was spreading and Solon is even supposed to have intervened in the monetary reform.[10] However, the demand for equality brings on with Solon, almost necessarily, the writing down and the publication of laws. The question that can now be asked is as follows: is there a link between the use of money and the publication of laws? Is it not possible to focus on such a relationship in the citizens' aspiration to equality? On second thought, it becomes apparent that the potential equality of the citizens before the political structure is guaranteed by the possibility offered to each and every one to consult the laws. In the same way or very nearly so, the potential equality of these same citizens before the economic realities is guaranteed by the existence of a reference value accepted by all, namely money; an 'estimation' of material value which comes to replace a form of access to goods which could be linked to birth or to martial worth, as was the case in the Archaic world unfurled in the epic poems. It is no longer one's potential kingly position that will permit one to acquire something, but the possession of a piece of money – a coin – which someone else can also own without being one's social equal. Let us note in passing that during the twentieth century, in the political systems that extolled the virtues of equality without practising it, the manipulation of money became one of the means used by those in power to foil the pretended equality. Shops were created which were accessible only to a small portion of the population, depending on their status: consequently, owning a coin did not give one access to the goods if one did not belong to the privileged caste. Here we have the negative of the phenomenon: if owning the same coin gives one the same rights of access to the same goods, it will become necessary in one way or another to strike out at money to challenge this equality.

It is in the wake of the demand for social equality, explicit in certain measures taken by Solon,[11] implicit in the recourse to money, that we observe the writing down and the publication of laws: put in charge of re-establishing civil concord in Athens, Solon was caught between the contradictory expectations of the powerful in the city, and those of the less fortunate. He describes the situation in one of his poems, a manifesto of sorts in which he clearly evokes the writing down of laws destined to insure the equality of the citizens:

I wrote down (ἔγραψα) *laws equal for the poor and the rich, I linked everyone to rectitude and justice.*[12]

From this declaration which predates the earliest coins of Athens,[13] we should retain two essential aspects: equality and writing down, or the side of 'money' and the side of 'literature'.

On the side of money, we have an insight into the role played by this new form of 'estimation' in a political struggle. We have, in the opposing camps, the powerful on the one hand and the 'poor' on the other, amongst whom some risked enslavement for debts. And yet, Solon had precisely annulled debts.[14] The annulment of a debt, aside from the fact that it tends to 'equalize' the partners, can be held for one of the most extreme concrete manifestations of the operation of 'estimation', that is to say the estimation that one of the commodities within the framework of an exchange possesses a value equal to zero. But this reasoning alone remains fragile, and the annulment of debts only takes on all its significance, even if we cannot understand it entirely, if we remember at the same time the reform of the monetary system desired by Solon.

'*I wrote down*' constitutes the other side.[15] Not only will the laws be the same for all, but also they will be written down. Each and every one must have access to the text, which will be made public by being posted publicly. We can thus observe the appearance of a triangle, the angles of which are equality, money and writing. The 'writing down' will not be limited to the domain of legislation, it will also spread over into what we call 'literature': Solon's successor, Peisistratos, presided over the writing down of the Homeric poems. This measure follows almost logically on the heels of the writing down of the laws, insomuch as the epic texts can be considered as 'oral encyclopaedias' of society,[16] offering their recipients a code of conduct of which the laws are a sort of subgroup.

Were it necessary, on the question of money, to have a contrast to the Athenian situation, we would certainly find it in Sparta. Solon, legislator in Athens, has often been compared with Lycurgus, legislator in Sparta. Lycurgus, if one is to believe Plutarch, is, even more than Solon, the champion of the idea of equality. On the other hand, he will transform money into an instrument of closing down as much as an instrument of equality amongst the citizens.

Plutarch reports that Lycurgus did not hesitate to redistribute the land,[17] where Solon only dared the annulment of debts. But for coinage, he offers us an extreme case: to avoid the inequalities brought on by riches, Lycurgus introduced an iron coin[18] (treated with vinegar so that the metal could not be salvaged for another use).[19] This coinage was not very desirable, due both to its weight and to the fact that it was shorn of value outside of Spartan society. It was therefore supposed to favour the equality of citizens, but equality in austerity.[20] Solon, as we have seen, seemed to favour rather the equality of chances. We can imagine that a coinage that aims at the closure of a society upon itself can lead to an impasse: indeed, to strike coinage which offers the guarantee of being of 'controlled origin' implies that the coinage can circulate beyond the territory in which it was issued. This is a new common ground between coinage and literature, because the texts travel, as Pindar proudly sings when he opposes his poems and the sculptures of the famous Aegina statuary (483 BC):

> *No sculptor am I, that I should carve statues doomed to linger only on the pedestal where they stand: No! I would bid my sweet song speed from Aegina, in every argosy, and in every skiff...*[21]

The contrast between Athens and Sparta perhaps rests more on the schematizations than on the realities, and this contrast will know developments that we need not recall at length here. Let us nevertheless retain the fact that this opposition will be one of the motors driving the reflection of Plato in his dialogue *The Laws*. Plato confronts a Cretan (Clinias), a Spartan (Megillos) along with their 'Athenian host' (the identity of whom has given rise to a great deal of speculation). Together they undertake to create laws which are to permit a real city, the city of 'Magnetes' as it is called at this juncture, to live in the best possible manner. The choice of the interlocutors is eloquent: they represent the opposed traditions of Athenian and Spartan culture, as Thucycides magnificently outlines them in his funerary oration delivered by Pericles,[22] while the home of good laws, the Crete of Minos and Rhadamanthys, is present in the person of Clinias. As concerns the usage of money, the Athenian hosts makes a comment which includes it in the general problem of commercial exchanges: any form of falsification will be severely punished, whether it be of goods offered for sale or of the money destined to acquire them: 'He that exchanges for money either money or anything else, living or not living, shall give and receive every such article unadulterated, conforming to the law'.[23]

'Adulterated' (*kibdēlon*) obviously opens the trail of counterfeit money. We are not surprised: no money without counterfeit money. Nevertheless, this trail might just lead us farther than we think with Plato. An Athenian, Plato used an Attic coinage guaranteed by the civic community. Indeed, when we read on an Athenian coin the three letters ΑΘΕ, these letters are the abbreviation of *Athenaiōn*, that is to say '*(coinage) of the Athenians*'. It sometimes happens that the indication of origin is written in full, as is the case on the coinage of Syracuse (to mention another coinage that Plato must have used). To counterfeit coins bearing such an inscription is to undermine the trust in the honesty of the society which is supposed to guarantee their value. The link between the coinage and the citizenry did not escape treatment on the comic scene. This is how Aristophanes, in his comedy *The Frogs* (405 BC), criticizes his fellow-citizens' choice by explicitly assimilating Athenians and coins (it is the chorus leader who speaks in the part of the play in which one traditionally expects the poet to give advice to the spectators): cat. no. 16

Often has it crossed my fancy, that the city loves to deal
With the very best and noblest members of her commonweal,
just as with our ancient coinage, and the newly-minted gold.
Yea for these, our sterling pieces, all of pure Athenian mould,
All of perfect die and metal, all the fairest of the fair,
All of workmanship unequalled, proved and valued everywhere
Both amongst our own Hellenes and Barbarians far away,
These we use not: but the worthless pinchbeck coins of yesterday,
Vilest die and basest metal, now we always use instead.
Even so, our sterling townsmen, nobly born and nobly bred,
Men of worth and rank and mettle, men of honourable fame,
Trained in every liberal science, choral dance and manly game,
These we treat with scorn and insult, but the strangers newliest come,
Worthless sons of worthless fathers, pinchbeck townsmen, yellowy scum,
Whom in earlier days the city hardly would have stooped to use
Even for her scapegoat victims, these for every task we choose.
O unwise and foolish people, yet to mend your ways begin.[24]

fig. 2: see cat. no. 5

These bad coins were not 'authentic' due to the fact that they were struck in bronze: at that time, the finances of Athens are being undermined by war. Later, these coins would be declared valueless.[25]

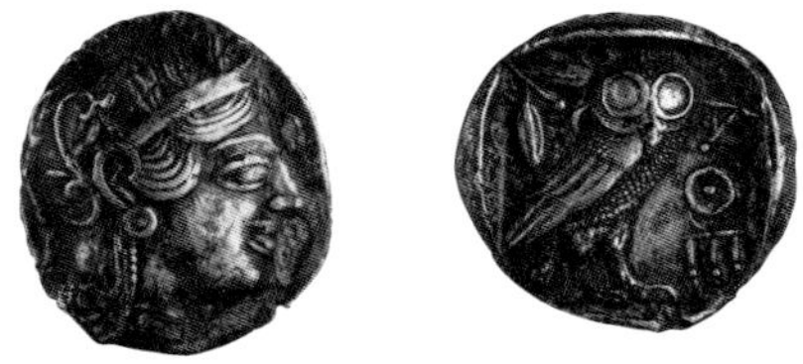

fig. 2

Subaerate tetradrachm, Athens, 406/5 BC.
KIKPE Collection, Athens

We shall conclude with two cases of a relationship between money and literature.

The first is a very unusual case that we hesitate to call a purchase. A tradition recorded by Galen in his commentary on the *Epidemics* of Hippocrates, reports that the 'official' copy of the tragics, established in Athens in the fourth century BC in the time of the politician and orator Lycurgus, was borrowed by Ptolemy III (student of Apollonius of Rhodes) against the deposit of the exorbitant guarantee of fifteen talents.[26] Once the precious text – more than three hundred scrolls – arrived in the Museum of Alexandria, a copy was made. It is this copy that was sent back to Athens and the Athenians were informed that they could keep the fifteen talents, while the Alexandrians kept the original. It is believed that this text played an important role in the transmission of the texts of the great tragic poets.[27]

This case of a relationship between literature and money is interesting in many respects. First of all, we cannot properly speak of a sale. At best, it is a case of unexpected sale, forced even: the owners were not dreaming of giving up their copy of the text and the guarantee demanded was therefore not considered to be the equivalent of the value of the scrolls. The deposit, as is the case of all deposits, was only meant as a guarantee and as a potential means of retaliatory measure. Secondly, we will observe that we find ourselves before the perfect illustration of *nomisma*: there is 'estimation' on both sides, as in Aristotle's analysis explaining the notion of money, but without there being any 'payment'. A payment would imply agreement between the two parties concerned. Here the Athenians' 'estimation' corresponded to the resolute will to see the manuscript return, it is at most the estimation of non-sale (the partner of the operation is supposed to be incapable of giving up such a sum of money), while the estimation of Ptolemy III implies that in his eyes possession of the text was worth not only the sum in question, but was even worth undermining the future trust that could be granted to him. In short, we find here two points of our triangle, and we could say that as concerns literature, the divergent views of the confronting parties annul the relations of money and the estimation. This, incidentally, grants tenability to Aristotle when he says that it is in our power to make money useless. For Ptolemy III, the point that prevailed was that of 'need'.

The second case can surprise us and amuse us: in ancient Greece, a text and a coin could both come out of one's mouth. Indeed, we know, notably thanks to the comedies of Aristophanes, that in daily life coins were carried in one's mouth.[28] As concerns texts, if they are not physically carried in one's mouth, they come out of a mouth when one first hears them, as a text is generally read out loud. We will not enter into the argument as to whether silent reading, with the mouth closed, was known or not before the fourth century AD, date of Augustine's famous account about being astounded when he saw Ambrose read without opening his mouth.[29] This reaction, and several others,[30] would not be comprehensible if reading with one's mouth closed was not exceptional, if not entirely unknown in Antiquity.

Hence, money and texts knew the same passage: that which, to repeat the Homeric expression, consisted of 'passing through the enclosure of the teeth'.

This could prove to be the most immediately physical reason justifying a connection between texts and coinage. But still it is only anecdotal. We will retain more specially what appears essential, to wit, the emergence, at the origins of the usage of money in Greece, of a significant constellation in which an aspiration towards equality took with it the will to accede to a written form of texts even as it fixed the notion of 'estimation' upon the quintessential instrument which would become that of commercial exchanges: money.

Notes

1. It could be a 'popular etymology'. *Moneta* is, in fact, the name of a Roman divinity identified with the mother of the Muses; her name is an attribute of Juno. From the same Latin verb *monere*, we still have the English word *monitor*.
2. Aristotle, *Nichomachean Ethics*, 1133a; transl. H. Rackham, London / Cambridge, MA 1962, with changes in the last sentence. Original translation: *But demand has come to be conventionally represented by money; this is why money is called* nomisma *(customary currency), because it does not exist by nature but by custom* (nomos)*, and can be altered and rendered useless at will.*
3. Marx 2007, vol. 1, p. 95: 'Die Waren können nicht selbst zu Markte gehn und sich nicht selbst austauschen'.
4. Herodotus, 1.94.
5. Thucydides, 6.4.
6. Hesiod, *Works and Days*, ll. 220–4.
7. Montaigne, Essais, 1.20: 'Que philosopher, c'est apprendre à mourir'.
8. *FdV*, 12 B 1.

9. Vernant 1983, p. 122.
10. Aristotle, *Constitution of Athens*, 9.2.
11. The clearest measure of this was the admittance of all the categories of citizen, whatever their censual rank granted by the constitution, to sit in the tribunals (Plutarch, *Life of Solon*, 87F-88C; Aristotle, *Constitution of Athens*, 9, with the magnificent formula: 'the citizen, being the master of the suffrage, becomes the master of the State'; *κύριος γὰρ ὢν ὁ δῆμος τῆς ψήφου κύριος γίνεται τῆς πολιτείας*).
12. Solon, *fr.* 36, ll. 18-20; M.L. West (ed.), *Iambi et elegi Graeci*…, Oxford 1989.
13. Franke and Hirmer 1964, pp. 88–90, pl. 114.
14. Plutarch, *Life of Solon* 86D-E.
15. On the coincidence between the writing down of the laws, the introduction of coins and the development of commerce in the case of the 'Gortyn Law Code', *cf.* Willetts 1967, p. 9.
16. See notably Havelock 1963.
17. Plutarch, *Life of Lycurgus*, 44A-D.
18. *Op. cit.*, 44D-45A.
19. *Op. cit.*, 44F.
20. *Cf.* the legend according to which Lycurgus paid for his combat for equality with the loss of an eye. (Plutarch, *Live of Lycurgus*, 45D-E, *Life of Solon*, 87B-C).
21. Pindar, *Nemean Odes* 5, 1–2; transl. J. Sandys, *The Odes of Pindar*, Cambridge, MA 1915.
22. Thucydides, 2.35–46.
23. Plato, *Laws*, 11.916d.
24. Aristophanes, *The Frogs*, ll. 717–35.
25. *Cf.* Aristophanes, *The Assembly of Women*, ll. 815–22.
26. It is difficult to evaluate the purchasing power that this sum represented. Let us simply point out that at the trial of Socrates (399 BC), the fine proposed as an alternative to the death penalty was 30 minas, the sum that Socrates' friends would have been able to raise together in order to save him. It is half a talent, that is to say thirty times less than the guarantee deposited for the manuscript of the tragics (1 talent is 60 minas). The inscriptions in Delos show that at the time of our episode, an architect received a salary varying from 1.5 to 3 drachmas per day (Franke and Hirmer 1964, p. 33). Fifteen talents would theoretically have been sufficient to pay an architect at these tariffs for one or two centuries.
27. Irigoin 2003, pp.190–1. The antique source is Galen, in his commentary on the *Epidemics III of Hippocrates* II.4, (17.1. p. 607, ed. Kühn = *CMG* V.10.2, 79–80, ed. E.Wenkebach, 1936).
28. Aristophanes, *Wasps*, l. 609; *The Birds*, l. 503; *The Assembly of Women*, l. 818.
29. Augustine, *Confessions*, 6.3.3: 'Sed cum legebat, oculi ducebantur per paginas et cor intellectum rimabatur, vox autem et lingua quiescebant'.
30. E.g. Lucian, 31.19 (*The Ignorant Book-Collector*): the cynic Demetrius observes an 'ignoramus' reading Euripides' *Bacchae*. He snatches the book away from him, exclaiming: 'Better, that Pentheus should suffer one rending at my hands than many at yours'. The anecdote implies that Demetrius *had heard* the ignoramus reading the text, and that he was reading aloud.

Bibliography & Abbreviations

CMG:	*Corpus Medicorum Graecorum*, Berlin 1907.
FdV:	Diels, H. and Kranz, W. (eds), *Die Fragmente der Vorsokratiker*, Berlin 1952.
Franke and Hirmer 1964:	Franke, P. R. and Hirmer, M., *Die griechische Münzen*, Munich.
Havelock 1963:	Havelock, E. A., *Preface to Plato*, Harvard.
Irigoin 2003:	Irigoin, J., *La tradition des textes grecs. Pour une critique historique*, Paris.
Marx 2007:	Marx, K., *Das Kapital*, Leipzig (new edition).
Vernant 1983:	Vernant, J.-P., *Les origines de la pensée grecque*, Paris.
Willetts 1967:	Willetts, R. F., *The Law Code of Gortyn*, Berlin.

III
GLIMPSES OF THE PAST: COIN ISSUES OF ILLUSTRIOUS MEN

Vasiliki Penna

The development of the art of photography, from the early decades of the nineteenth century, was, without doubt, a turning point in human history. Photography, by immortalizing significant moments and diverse activities in man's life, from infancy to old age, recycles memories both happy and sad, deciphers ephemeral expressions and reactions, and in general pictorially unwinds the bobbin of the human course and augments our understanding of the everyday life of people in the past. Moreover, photography imprints facial features and decodes unseen aspects of the personality and disposition of the figure depicted.

Today, it is difficult to imagine a time when the concept of an individualized likeness did not exist. The truth is that the concept was born in Greece, in the first half or second quarter of the fifth century BC.[1] However, Greek Antiquity proved rather sparing in the realistic rendering of the human figure. Although the human representation reached the zenith of its beauty, it moved, regardless of the identity of the subject, within a virtual world in which overemphasis of the spirit subjugates reality, in which the special aesthetic vision differs greatly from the common everyday vision. Pliny, referring to the statue of Pericles on the Acropolis, remarks that 'it is a marvellous thing that in this art noble men were made to appear still nobler'.[2] Goethe, in the same vein, declares that Greek art elevates man, giving him dizzying spiritual and intellectual dimensions, yet at the same time it is underpinned by the awareness of the limits of human power.[3]

Unfortunately, original images from Greek Antiquity, those that could bring us closer to personalities of this period, are few and of these several present difficulties regarding their identification. Most works are known only from Roman copies, found mainly in Italy, since it was in their homeland that the Romans liked to surround themselves with images of the distinguished Greeks they so ardently admired.

Strikingly, it was not customary for Greeks of pre-Hellenistic times to put portraits on their coins, although from the mid-seventh century BC, when coinage first appeared in the ancient Greek world, each city began to engrave on its coins representations that were transformed into symbols of authority and functioned as an ideal medium for projecting political and economic prestige.[4] On the small circular flan of the coins, the city-states represent gods and patron deities, sacred symbols, holy animals and birds, mythical heroes and monsters, as well as products that were a source of their wealth and prosperity. cat. no. 19

The reluctance of Greeks in the Archaic and Classical periods to represent on their coins historic figures of the past, as well as their own present – statesmen, generals, philosophers and poets – was possibly due to a conscious mental approach to the divine, which protects man, both man as an individual and man as a collectivity within a specific political system and regime. The 'emblem' of each city, as this is imprinted on the two sides of its coin issues, is an interpretation, a secret window through which man can glimpse at the inexhaustible forces of the universe and the powers controlling the world, as well as at the relation of human beings and of the places where they live and are animated to these powers. The use and the circulation of coinage functions as a transmitter relaying messages to a wide audience inside and outside the geographical boundaries of each issuing city, and becomes a visual didactic discourse in which the ephemeral is overshadowed by divine intervention, in which diverse public activity in the political, intellectual or artistic life of a place is included in the dynamic of the whole and is governed by the concept that the deity is a cosmic mind that creates nature, history, justice and morality.

The narrative and pictorial language of the ancient coin in the Archaic and Classical periods is synoptic and leaves the portrayal of illustrious men of the time to the domain of the visual arts, which too, as we have said, were sparing in the realistic representation of figures. Throughout this long period of development, the Greek portraitist, even in his most realistic achievements, was always mindful that he must penetrate the psychology of the model and sum up his personality; he must capture something more intangible and more important than just a faithful reproduction of the outward appearance.

Signs of change in the criteria for selecting coin iconography are evident already from the time the King of Macedon, Philip II (360/59–336 BC), who dynamically entered the political forestage of Greece. On his earliest silver coins, a splendid and dignified representation of Olympian Zeus adorns the obverse. On the reverse is Philip himself, riding a war-horse advancing to the left. He is bearded, wears a military mantle and the traditional Macedonian brimmed hat, the *kausia*, and he raises his right hand in salute. The monarch imprints on his coins his status as political leader and isolates a single moment in his public communication with his army or his people. fig. 1

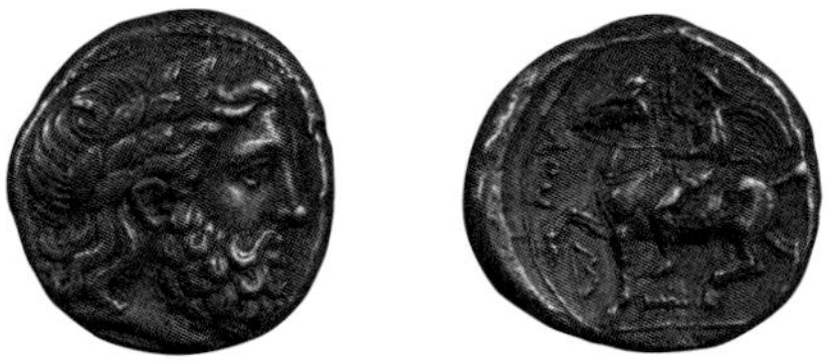

fig. 1

Silver tetradrachm of Philip II of Macedon (360–336 BC),
Amphipolis, *ca.* 355–349/8 BC.
Benaki Museum, Athens

Similarly, the laureate head of Apollo on the obverse of Philip's gold staters, with the bounding chariot in commemoration of his great victory in the Olympian chariot races in 357 BC on the reverse, and the replacement of the mounted king on the reverse of his later silver coinage with the slim figure of a little jockey, holding the palm-branch of victory and riding a racehorse, also in commemoration of a horse race won by Philip, reflect the spirit of the new political age. In this case the monarch imprints on his coins events that project agonistic competitiveness, a combination of physical and mental virtues, events that publicize faith in traditions and institutions, and sketch a new political thinking or a new political ambition, that of the king's powerful leadership under the protection of Zeus, the supreme god for all the Greeks. cat. no. 31

The coinage of Alexander the Great (336–323 BC) continues in the same direction as that of his father.[5] The head of Athena Promachos, goddess of wisdom and war, on the obverse of his gold staters, and the beautiful figure of Nike (Victory) bearing the *stylis* and a laurel wreath, on the reverse, are symbolic references to the naval successes of the Greeks in the Persian Wars, and this on the wake of Alexander's Eastern campaign. cat. no. 32

The panhellenic spirit is reflected also in the iconography of the young monarch's silver tetradrachms. On the obverse is the head of Heracles, the legendary genarch of the Macedonian dynasty, but also the greatest of the mythical Greek heroes, and on the reverse is the enthroned Olympian Zeus holding in his left hand a sceptre and in his right an eagle, the sacred symbol of the god.[6] Heracles appears also on the obverse of certain bronze issue of Alexander III, while the club and the bow in a case, on the reverse, refer to the hero's Labours; with his Twelve Labours Heracles became the symbol of power as well as the perfect embodiment of the virtuous struggle and suffering which led him to immortality. cat. no. 145

Although the representation of Heracles, as well as of his weapons, on the coins of Alexander the Great belongs in the realm of symbolism, there are many who still erroneously believe, particularly the general public, that the hero's head is a portrait of the Macedonian king. The truth is that Alexander the Great does not seem to have been depicted on any coin issue during his lifetime and that any difference in the depiction of Heracles on Alexander's coins, primarily on the various tetradrachms, is due to the different technique of each engraver.

The depiction of Alexander on coins was adopted, however, by his successors, pioneers being Ptolemy I Soter (323–283 BC) and Lysimachus (306–281 BC).[7] The head of Alexander the Great on some relatively rare tetradrachms of Ptolemy I Soter of Egypt, which were most probably commemorative issues of Alexander's funeral in Alexandria in 322 BC, appears to be quite realistic. The king is represented with an elephant skin on his head, funerary reference to the conquest of distant India. This iconographic type also appears occasionally on some bronze issues of Ptolemy I's successors, as well as on a few bronze issues and gold double and single darics from Ecbatana, Susa and Babylon of Seleucus I Nicator (*ca.* 300–298 BC). Lysimachus' gold and silver coins of around 297 BC bear on their obverse the splendid, still idealized head of the hero Alexander, adorned with the ram's horns of Ammon. A similar image of Alexander as an idealized sovereign-hero features also on some bronze issues of Ptolemy I of Egypt: on the obverse the Macedonian king is shown with long hair and wearing a diadem.

cat. no. 34
cat. no. 36
cat. no. 33
fig. 2: see cat. no. 35

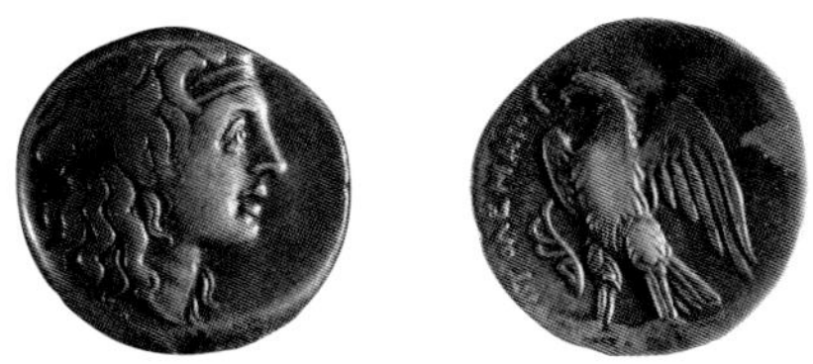

fig. 2

Bronze coin of Ptolemy I of Egypt, Cyrene, *ca.* 300–285 BC.
KIKPE Collection, Athens

At this point it is worth mentioning some rare posthumous staters of Philip II, most probably issues of the mints of Magnesia and Colophon. These beautiful gold coins probably date to the time when the late Alexander's half-brother, Philip III Arrhidaeus (323–317 BC), was the nominal head of state together with the conqueror's infant son by Roxane, Alexander IV.[8] The supposed head of Apollo on the obverse, with its distinctive features, has been identified as a true portrait of Alexander III.

fig. 3

Without doubt, the conquests of Alexander the Great brought seminal changes in the character of the ancient world. The Hellenistic kingdoms created after his death led to the break up of the traditional body politic of the city-state. We are now on the threshold of a new era, the Hellenistic Age of the successors, during which art starts to move in other directions. The artist now had to deal with the powerful Hellenistic ruler who desired to immortalize his victory, to proclaim his presence, to be portrayed. In reality, the posthumous portraits of Alexander the Great on coins of his successors are a landmark in the development of the portrayal of mortals in ancient Greek coinage. The role of the coin now becomes more political and the coin iconography is influenced by personal aspirations of the various rulers. The divine figure is displaced to the reverse, while the portrait of the ruler is established as basic numismatic type with a tendency for political imposition and equation with the divine. Furthermore, this is the period of the transition from the depiction of a divine or heroic figure with human features to the engraving of the head of one specific mortal. On the coins of Alexander the Great's successors we can admire the high artistic quality of portraits on coins and the engravers' ability to render the particular physiognomic features of the various sovereigns.[9]

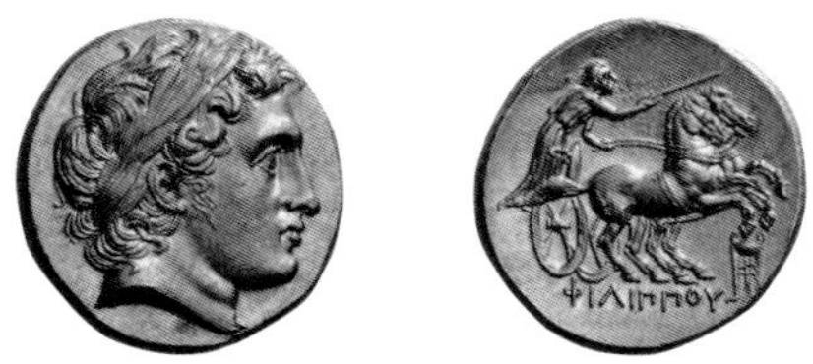

fig. 3

Gold stater of Philip III of Macedon, Colophon, *ca.* 323–317 BC.
Nomos AG, Auction 6 (8.05.2012), lot 48

The coins of the satraps of the East, who had begun engraving their portraits on their coin series already from the last quarter of the fifth century BC, could, of course, be considered the forerunner of the Hellenistic coin portraits.

cat. no. 144

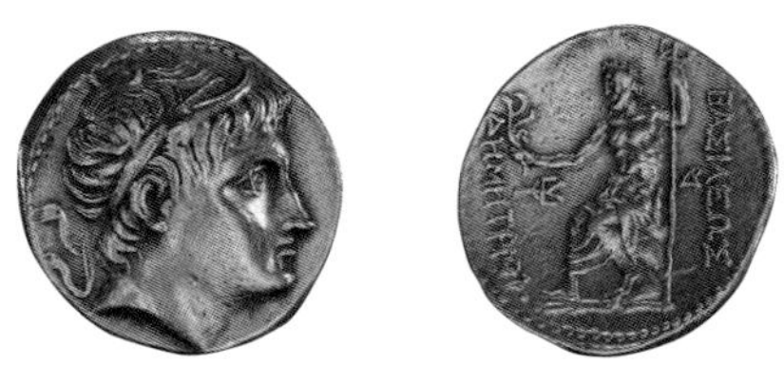

fig. 4

Silver tetradrachm of Demetrius I Poliorcetes of Macedon (306–283 BC),
Amphipolis, *ca.* 291–290 BC.
Fondation Martin Bodmer, Cologny

The King of Macedonia Demetrius Poliorcetes (306–283 BC) was the first of Alexander the Great's successors to dare to engrave his figure on his silver tetradrachms and later his gold staters. After him, the superb portraits of the other kings of Macedonia,[10] of the Seleucids and the Antiochids of Syria, of the Ptolemies of Egypt, of the kings of

fig. 4: see cat. no. 211
cat. nos 212, 149

fig. 5: see cat. no. 213

Bithynia, of Pontus and of Pergamum, as well as those of Cappadocia,[11] Parthia,[12] Bactria, and also of the rulers of Sicily, are impressive for their realism and iconize the new world of the Hellenistic period.

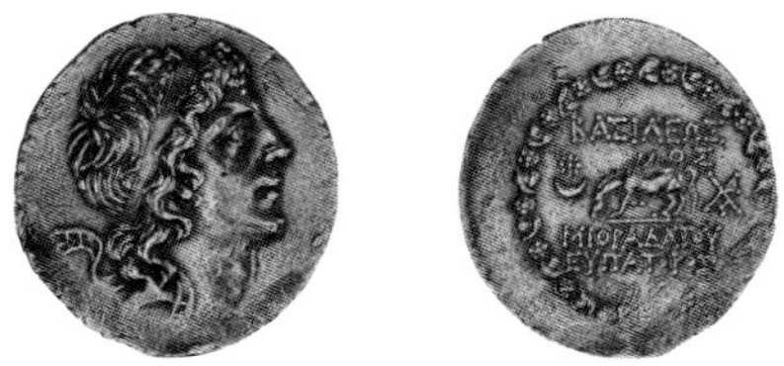

fig. 5

Silver tetradrachm of Mithridates VI of Pontus (120–63 BC), 89–88 BC.
Fondation Martin Bodmer, Cologny

The numismatic iconography during the Roman period moved within the same sphere, equipped with its own peculiarities, products of a different cultural conception and worldview, as well as of the coexistence of East and West. Truly, the Roman world, which too was to make innovations in the historical evolution of coinage, imprinted the human figure on the flans with remarkable skill and showed originality in rendering individual personal features of the subjects portrayed.[13]

Common too during Roman times was the Greek cities' tactic of choosing famous persons of the past, personalities associated with them historically or professionally, for representation on their coins.[14] Busts or heads or full figures, seated or in motion, of poets, philosophers, physicians and political personalities, on coins of the period of Roman rule give us an image of these particular men, at least as this had been preserved in the eyes of contemporary artists, by tradition or even by some earlier visual documents possibly available to artists of the day in their workshops.[15] These numismatic depictions of distinguished citizens of the past were modelled on now-lost statues that were set up in conspicuous positions in the cities, as a gesture of respect and remembrance of the works and days of these men. They are anachronistic commemorations of an illustrious past in a milieu of cultural pluralism and a social tissue in which the 'by convention' *civis Romanus*, in the geographical area in which he lives, desires and is permitted to project his own ethnicity. The specific coins with the anachronistic representations of eminent persons are transformed into an instrument of cultural transmission (*translatio*) by providing an overview of intellectual heritage and by establishing a new cultural stronghold and a new cultural elite in the eastern provinces of the Roman Empire, always, however, under the strict tutelage of Rome.[16]

It is understandable that the glory and the reputation of a city or a region was enhanced even more when this was able to boast a long or glorious past, engraving on its coins, for example, a founder-god or a founder-hero or even an eponymous historical or mythical figure whose fame surpassed the narrow geographical bounds of the issuing city.[17]

For example, on bronze coins of Byzantium of the third century AD, the obverse carries the helmeted head of the hero Byzas, the mythical founder of this ancient Megarian colony at the entrance to the Black Sea, following the pronouncement of the Delphic oracle. cat. no. 177

On coins of cities that claimed to have been the place of Homer's birth or death, such as Chios, Colophon, Amastris, Nicaea and Tios, the blind poet of the *Iliad* and the *Odyssey* is represented sometimes in bust and sometimes seated, along with his writing implements. It is worth noting here, as an aside, that the representation of Homer on didrachms and bronze coins of the Aegean island of Ios, in the second half of the fourth and the early third century BC,[18] is an interesting novelty in ancient Greek numismatic iconography. The poet appears also on coins of Smyrna, of the second century BC, as well as on coins of the city of Colophon of the first century BC. cat. no. 100 cat. no. 101

Bronze coins of Athens of the second and third centuries AD show for the first time the Athenian general Miltiades with a Persian captive and a trophy,[19] as well as Themistocles, in panoply on a galley, holding trophy and wreath.[20] It is notable that, whereas Athens was dilatory in minting coins in the name of Themistocles, the victor of Salamis, Magnesia, to which he came after being ostracized by the citizens of his homeland, and where he was guest of the Persian king Artaxerxes, seems to have struck coins in his honour as early as fifth century BC.[21]

Among the renowned persons of the past who were represented widely on Graeco-Roman coins, Alexander the Great merits special attention.[22] We mention indicatively some bronze pseudo-autonomous issues of the *koinon* of Macedonia (3rd century AD),[23] featuring on the obverse the young king's diademed head with flowing hair, while on the reverse he is depicted riding Bucephalus. This late coin portrait of Alexander the Great keeps something of the heroized expression of the Macedonian monarch, as this was promoted after his death by his immediate successors. On other contemporary issues of the Macedonian *Koinon*, the head of Alexander is represented with *leontē*, in the type of Heracles,[24] or even with helmet. The reverse types of these particular issues either show critical moments in the king's life – Alexander taming Bucephalus, Alexander on horseback galloping proudly – or allude to symbols of the past Macedonian kingdom, symbols linked simultaneously with the Labours of the mythical hero Heracles – lion and club or quiver, bow, and club. These issues, just as the beautiful gold medallions the third century AD from the two famous gold hoards,[25] with the diverse depictions of the figure of Alexander on the obverse, in more or less the same repertoire as the bronze issues of the *Koinon*, and the intricate representations on the reverse, among them Alexander on horseback hunting a lion or Alexander hunting a boar, bring the young general's reputation back into the Roman Imperial world, visually bridging the 'reality' of the man and his 'journey' to immortality; they focus on Alexander's colourful legend and his divine origins. cat. no. 37

Even under Roman domination, the Greeks continued to be sparing in their representation of living persons, apart from the 'obligatory' portrayals of emperors or the 'bespoke' depictions of some local rulers. Antinous, emperor Hadrian's favourite who was drowned in suspicious circumstances while sailing on the Nile, in AD 130, could perhaps be considered an exception. The Hellenic world's participation in the emperor's deep mourning was expressed in many ways, while the youth's figure was engraved on several contemporary coinages of Asia Minor and Greece, as well as in Alexandria.[26] We mention indicatively the large commemorative coins issued in his honour at Tios (Tium) in Bithynia, Antinous' birthplace, with the figure of a deified youth and the dedicatory inscription ΑΝΤΙΝΩΙ ΗΡΩΙ, on the obverse. On the reverse, Antinous is depicted as Dionysus, riding panther right, with thyrsus over the shoulder. The association of Antinous with Dionysus is attested also on other coins issued in his honour, as well as by a series of free-standing statues and relief panels, and, of course, texts.[27] Without doubt, the correlation of Antinous with Dionysus belongs in the framework of a symbolism connected with the many versions of the god's myth, and indeed as this developed in Hellenistic and Roman times, with the incorporation of new oriental elements.[28] Dionysus, a suffering yet indomitable deity, son of the supreme god Zeus and a mortal woman, puts his enemies to flight, brings salvation to the dispossessed and the wretched of the earth, and in the end is put to death, to rise again triumphantly; he is the master of all immortals, the soul of the natural and the moral world, and guarantor of its perpetuation.[29] The correlation of Antinous with Dionysus, with whatever additional or different implications could be proposed, seems to be linked with the notion of *apotheosis*. The representation of the heroized youth mounted on a panther and holding the sacred attribute of the thyrsus is an artistic, nonetheless abstract, rendering of the process of ascension into the sphere of the invisible and the divine, a representation of the transcendence of mortality.

fig. 6: see cat. no. 116

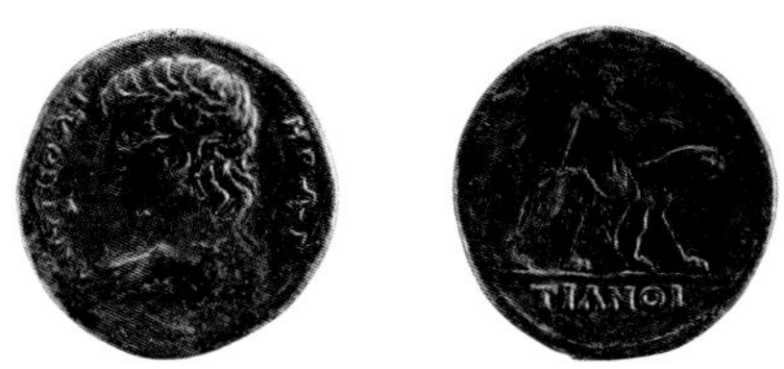

fig. 6

Bronze 'medallion' in honour of Antinous under Hadrian,
Tium, after 130 AD.
KIKPE Collection, Athens

The anxiety over death, the inability to comprehend the ephemeral state of life, the discomfiture before the gateway to the Underworld and the hope of a life after death are enduring concepts that are identified with all the watersheds in the history of mankind, regardless of religious or cultural environment. The symbolisms of these mental, yet conscious, emotions upon artworks of Greek Antiquity are an alloy in which variations of myths, legends and traditions with a historical kernel, popular beliefs and genuine poetic imagination are fused. To confine ourselves to the world of coins, their sparing narrative iconography with regard to the depiction of ideas or sentiments during Classical and Hellenistic times should be emphasized once more. The symbolisms are limited to the domain of divine protection and divine intervention, in an austere and summary manner, in a head-on dialogue between the representations on the two sides of the coins, where solitary figures predominate. For example, the Labours of Heracles are not depicted but are hinted at by the figure of the demigod and the interpolation of his attributes and weapons. Nevertheless, the Labours of Heracles are widely diffused in the iconography of the Greek provincial coins. For example, on the Roman provincial coins Heracles is depicted carrying in celebration the Erymanthian Boar on his shoulders or even carrying Cerberus, guard-dog of Hades, to the upper world, using only the strength of his bare hands. The representations of Heracles' Labours allude by association to the notion of the continual human trials in order to attain *apotheosis*; as reward for finishing the Twelve Labours, Heracles was given after his death the gift of immortality by his father Zeus. Irrespective of the degree to which the specific symbolism is conceptually close to the historical substrate of each issuing authority, in this period it was sufficient to project in narrative manner the values and the feats of the past, as has been said already, as well as to function didactically through art or even to insinuate the ideal values of an illustrious man and distinguished citizen, and of a mighty ruler, that is the Roman emperor.[30]

cat. no. 119

fig. 7: see cat. no. 118

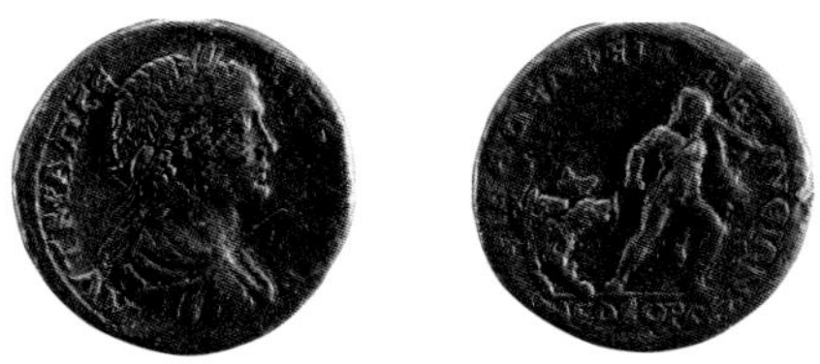

fig. 7

Bronze 'medallion' in the name of Geta, Perinthus, *ca.* 209–212 AD.
KIKPE Collection, Athens.

There was in this period a conspicuous presence of deities of mainly oriental provenance, such as the Egyptian goddess Isis, given that they held out the promise of bringing their devotees, through the process of initiation, close to the divine and securing their salvation. It was within this same clime that the cult of the healing god Asclepius spread, and although his representation on Greek coins goes back to the closing decades of the fifth century BC, in Roman times, as expression of seeking

cat. no. 115

fig. 8: see cat. no. 117

the emperor's protection, it appears with greater frequency and wide geographical diffusion.[31] The time had come when the old gods were struggling to hold on to their gains, while the new religion of Christianity endeavours to oust them.

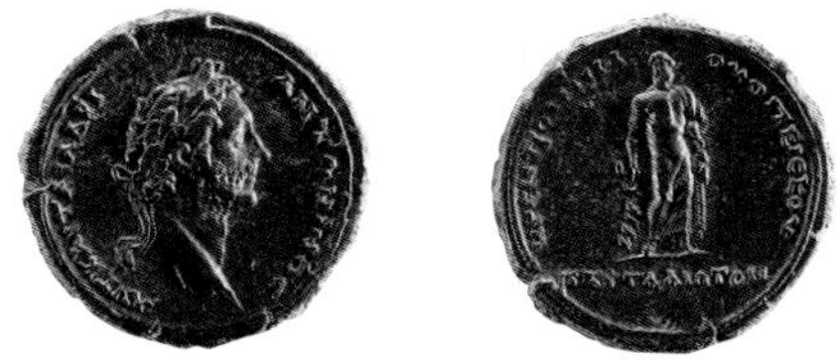

fig. 8

Bronze 'medallion' under Antoninus Pius, Pautalia, 138–161 AD.
KIKPE Collection, Athens

During the reign of emperor Gallienus (253–268 AD), the Greek coin, as this had been redefined under the shadow of the Roman Empire, ceased to be minted, due to economic difficulties, while a little later, at the end of the third century, the administrative and economic reforms of Diocletian (285–305 AD) led to a uniform monetary system throughout the Empire. The Greek coin was no longer a rich visual narration of concepts, sentiments and diverse cults, and was no longer inspired by the works of illustrious men and mythical heroes of the past.

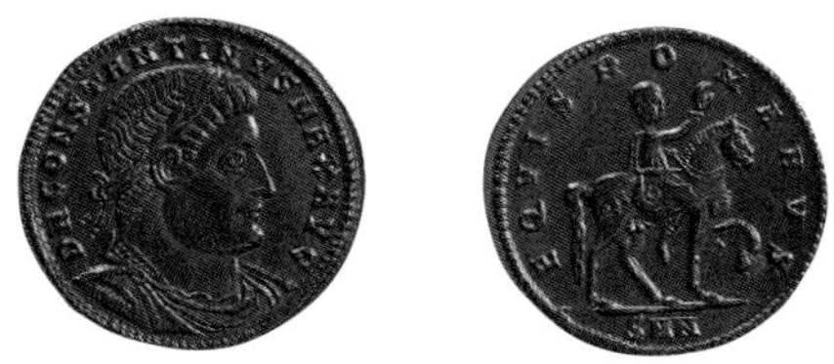

fig. 9

Gold 'medallion', Constantine I (306–337 AD), Nicomedia, 324–325 AD.
Fondation Martin Bodmer, Cologny

The transfer of the capital of the Roman State to the East, the founding of Constantinople and the adoption of Christianity as official religion of the Empire brought essential changes in the way of life, and consequently the modes and manners of artistic expression. The Church, the imperial court, secular circles, monastic circles, the society of the entire Empire, guided by the above factors and enriched with different experiences and expediencies, have left us a wide array of monuments and works of art.

However, in the Byzantine world, as in Classical Antiquity, the realistic representation of figures and, primarily, the representation of secular and transient personalities, is scarce. Moreover, few representations of the Byzantine emperors have survived. Byzantine coins are thus fated to fill out our knowledge of the figure of the Byzantine emperor, as well as of specific events in his public and private life, such as the ascent to the throne, the coronation of the co-emperor, the celebration of some anniversary or imperial marriage, secret machinations of co-rulers against legitimate emperors born in the purple (*porphyrogennētoi*), personal preferences of specific members of the imperial family, religious convictions, etc.[32] Symbol and mirror, cornerstone and weapon of a mighty Empire, Byzantine coinage became an ideal means of projecting the imperial ideal and promoting imperial policy.

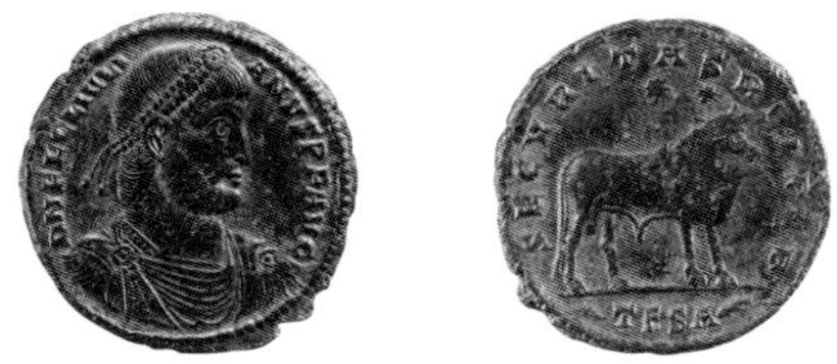

fig. 10

Bronze coin, Julian, Thessalonike, 361–363 AD.
KIKPE Collection, Athens

The thematic repertoire revolves around imperial values, those values that determine the religious mission of the supreme archon, his role on earth, the fount of his power and authority. It is expressed with diverse stylistic solutions, fascinates with its pictorial innuendoes, is specified by the symbols of the imperial costume and the insignia of power, and, last, transcends the symbolism by juxtaposing the imperial figure on the one side to the divine or saintly figure on the other. On Byzantine coins the secular and the sacred coexist in harmony, and outline in the best possible way the development of Byzantine thought in the course of its long history.

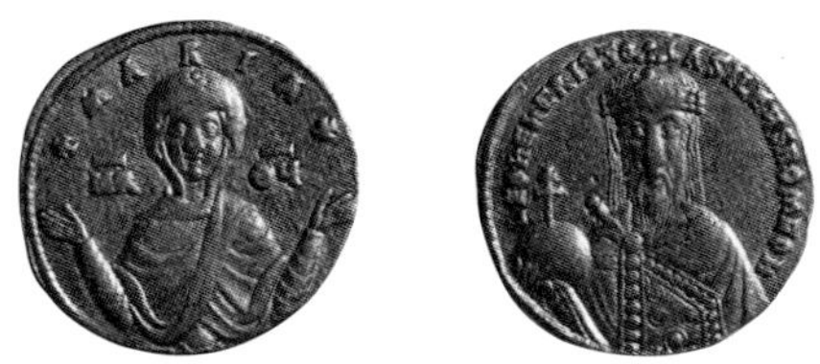

fig. 11

Gold *nomisma* of Leo VI (886–912 AD), Constantinople, *ca.* 905–908 AD.
Benaki Museum, Athens

The characteristic portraiture of the ruler, which was normal during the first three centuries of the Roman Empire, had already started to lose ground under the Tetrarchy. However, the Constantinian portrait was basically realistic, although with a certain idealization in later years. In any case, during the fourth century emperors were still broadly represented as young, old, heavily or lightly built, bearded or beardless. From the fifth century onwards the obverses of coins tell us virtually nothing about the physiognomic features of the emperor or of the beauty of his empress. From now on

fig. 9: see cat. no. 191
fig. 10: see cat. no. 181

fig. 11 coin portraiture is characterized, with very few exceptions, by linearity and abstraction, and the portrait constitutes, in essence, a conceptual rendering of the emperor, transfiguring him finally into a cult image.

Notes

1. For a general overview of ancient Greek portraiture see Richter and Smith 1984. For a comprehensive study on the interaction of visual representation and classical culture from the fifth century BC to the fourth century AD, see Zanker 1995.
2. Plinius, *Naturalis historia*, 34.19.74.
3. Trevelyan 1981, pp. 70–83.
4. For the iconography of ancient Greek coins see indicatively: Kraay and Hirmer 1966; Kraay 1976. For a general overview on the iconography of ancient Greek, Hellenistic and Roman coins, see indicatively: Howgego 1995, pp. 62–184; Rebuffat 1996, pp. 165–88; Carradice and Price 2004, pp. 56–60, 122–4.
5. For the coinages of Philip II and Alexander III, see in the present volume the contribution by F. de Callataÿ, 'Les fabuleuses richesses des rois hellénistiques : monnayages et *Weltmachtpolitik*'.
6. See (*supra* n. 5) de Callataÿ, fig. 3.
7. For a comprehensive overview of Alexander's depiction on coins, see Dahmen 2007; especially for the period after his death until Roman times, see pp. 6–18, 48–50, 58–60, 108–22. In general for Alexander's portraiture, see Steward 1993.
8. Nomos, Auction 6 (8.05.2012), lot 48; see also *SNG Aplha Bank* 260. For the chronology of this rare issue, see Thompson 1982, pp. 57–63, Pl. VI, 4, 5, 12; Price 1991, p. 248.
9. For the development of portraiture on Hellenistic coins, see indicatively Smith 1988; see also Mørkholm 1991.
10. See (*supra* n. 5) de Callataÿ, fig. 8.
11. See (*supra* n. 5) de Callataÿ, fig. 7.
12. See (*supra* n. 5) de Callataÿ, fig. 9.
13. For the Roman coinage, see in the present volume the contribution by Ch. Papageorgiadou, 'Writing and imprinting the history of the Roman world'; see also indicatively Burnett 2004, pp. 66–79; see also *supra* n. 4.
14. Rome, almost from the outset of its hegemony in Greece and Asia Minor, in many cases conceded to the Greek cities there the right to issue their own coins, mainly bronze ones. For a classification of this coinage, also known as 'Greek Imperials' or referred to recently as Roman provincial coinage, see Heuchert 2005, pp. 29–31. For a review of the iconography of Greek provincial issues under Roman rule, see indicatively: Burnett 2004, pp. 80–5; Howgego *et al.* 2005; with epicentre Asia Minor, see Franke 1968; see also *supra* n. 4.
15. Franke 1968, pp. 18–9; Heuchert 2005, p. 52
16. Williamson 2005.
17. Howgego 2005, p. 6.
18. Hoover 2010, p. 192.
19. For the type, see SNG *Cop*. 320. See also Kroll 1993, p. 132 , no. 190 (*ca.* 120s–140s or later AD); for the chronology, see Kroll 1993, p. 116, 128.
20. For the type, see SNG *Cop*. 318, 319, 344–345. See also Kroll 1993, p. 130, nos 182, 183 (*ca.* 120s–140s AD or later), p. 144, nos 278, 279 (*ca.* 140s or 150s–*ca.* 175 AD), p. 158, no. 374 (264–267 AD); for the chronology, see Kroll 1993, pp. 116, 118, 128, 140, 146.
21. On Themistocles' Magnesian coins, see Nollé and Wenninger 1998/9.
22. For the depiction of Alexander the Great on Roman provincial issues both in Greece and in Asia Minor, see Dahmen 2007, pp. 20–38, 43–6, 51–5, 60–4, 123–55.
23. For the numerous 'Alexander' types of the *Koinon* under Elagabalus, see Kremydi-Sicilianou 2005, p. 102.

24. See (*supra* n. 5) de Callataÿ, fig. 4.
25. For the famous Tarsus and Aboukir gold medallions, see Dahmen 2007, pp. 144–52; Dahmen 2008; Touratsoglou 2008.
26. Price 1984, p. 68.
27. Heath 2006, p. 67.
28. It is charcteristic that in the fifth century AD Nonnus of Panopolis, an author who was also well acquainted with Christianity, since he translated the Gospel of St John (see Whitby 2007), presents Dionysus travelling across Phrygia, Cilicia, Phoenicia and reaching as far as India, in order to converse as an equal with the gods of those regions.
29. For the myth of Dionysus and the ramifications of his cult, see indicatively Kerényi 1996.
30. Price 1984, p. 184.
31. Penn 1994.
32. For an overview on the representation of Byzantine emperors on coins, see indicatively Grierson 1999, pp. 24–31; Grierson 1982, pp. 29–34; Penna 2002, pp. 125–38.

Bibliography & Abbreviations

AJN: *American Journal of Numismatics*

Burnett 2004: Burnett, A., *Coinage in the Roman World*, London.

Carradice and Price 2004: Carradice, I. and Price, M. J., *Coinage in the Greek World*, London.

Dahmen 2007: Dahmen, K., *The Legend of Alexander the Great on Greek and Roman Coins*, London / New York.

Dahmen 2008: Dahmen, K., 'Alexander in Gold and Silver. Reassessing Third-century AD Medallions from Aboukir, Tarsos, and Related Objects' *AJN* 20 (2008), pp. 493–546.

Franke 1968: Franke, P. R., *Kleinasien zur Römerzeit. Griechisches Leben im Spegel der Münzen*, Munich.

Grierson 1999: Grierson, Ph., *Byzantine Coins*, Berkeley / Los Angeles.

Grierson 1999: Grierson, Ph., *Byzantine Coinage*, Washington, D.C.

Heath 2006: Heath, S., 'A Box Mirror Made from Two Antinous Medallions of Smyrna', *AJN* 18 (2006), pp. 61–72.

Heuchert 2005: Heuchert, V., 'The Chronological Development of Roman Provincial Coin Iconography'in: C. Howgego, V. Heuchert and A. Burnett (eds), *Coinage and Identity in the Roman Provinces*, Oxford / New York, pp. 29–56.

Howgego 1995: Howgego, C., *Ancient History from Coins*, London / New York.

Howgego 2005: Howgego, C., 'Coinage and Identity in the Roman Provinces, in: C. Howgego, V. Heuchert and A. Burnett (eds), *Coinage and Identity in the Roman Provinces*, Oxford / New York, pp. 1–17.

Howgego *et al.* 2005: Howgego, C., Heuchert, V. and Burnett, A. (eds), *Coinage and Identity in the Roman Provinces*, Oxford / New York.

JNG: *Jahrbuch für Numismatik und Geldgeschichte*

Kerényi 1996: Kerényi, C., *Dionysos: Archetypal Image of Indestructible Life*, Princeton.

Kraay and Hirmer 1966: Kraay, C. M. and Hirmer, M., *Greek Coins*, London.

Kraay 1976: Kraay, C. M., *Archaic and Classical Greek Coins*, London.

Kremydi-Sicilianou 2005: Kremydi-Sicilianou, S., '«Belonging» to Rome, «Remaining» Greek: Coinage and Identity in Roman Macedonia', in: C. Howgego, V. Heuchert and A. Burnett (eds), *Coinage and Identity in the Roman Provinces*, Oxford / New York, pp. 95–106.

Kroll 1993: Kroll, J., *The Athenian Agora. Volume XXVI. Greek Coins*, Princeton.

Mørkholm 1991: Mørkholm, O., *Early Hellenistic Coinage from the accession of Alexander to the Peace of Apamea (336–188 B.C.)*, Cambridge.

Nollé and Wenninger 1998/9: Nollé, J. and Wenninger, A., 'Themistokles and Archepolis', *JNG* 48/49 (1998/9), pp. 29–70.

Penn 1994: Penn, R. G., *Medicine on Ancient Greek and Roman Coins*, London.

Penna 2002: Penna, V., *Byzantine Coinage. Medium of transaction and manifestation of imperial propaganda*, Nicosia.

Price 1991: Price, M. J., *The Coinage in the name of Alexander the Great and Philip Arrhidaeus*, Zurich / London.

Price 1984: Price, S. F. R., *Rituals and Power. The Roman Imperial Cult in Asia Minor*, Cambridge / London / New York / New Rochelle / Melbourne / Sydney.

Rebuffat 1996: Rebuffat, F., *La Monnaie dans l'antiquité*, Paris.

Richter and Smith 1984: Richter, G. M. A. and Smith, R. R. R., *The Portraits of the Greeks*, Oxford.

Steward 1993: Steward, A., *Faces of Power: Alexander's Image and Hellenistic Politics*, Berkeley / Los Angeles.

Smith 1988: Smith, R. R. R., *Hellenistic Royal Portraits*, Oxford.

***SNG Cop.*:** *Sylloge Nummorum Graecorum. The Royal Collection of Coins and Medals, Danish National Museum*, Copenhagen 1942–1979.

Spanoudakis 2007: Spanoudakis, K., 'Icarius Jesus Christ? Dionysiac Passion and Biblical Narrative in Nonnus' Icarius Episode (*Dion.* 47, 1–264)', *Wiener Studien* 120 (2007), pp. 35–92.

Thompson 1982: Thompson, M., 'Posthumous Philip II staters of Asia Minor', in *Studia Paulo Naster Oblata*, I, *Numismatica Antiqua*, Leuven.

Trevelyan 1981: Trevelyan, H., *Goethe and the Greeks*, Cambridge.

Touratsoglou 2008: Touratsoglou, I., 'Tarsos, Aboukir, etc.; before and after. Once again', *AJN* 20 (2008), pp. 479–92.

Zanker 1995: Zanker, P., The Mask of Socrates: *The Image of the Intellectual in Antiquity*, Berkeley / Los Angeles / Oxford.

Williamson 2005: Williamson, G., 'Aspects of Identity', in: C. Howgego, V. Heuchert and A. Burnett (eds), *Coinage and Identity in the Roman Provinces*, Oxford / New York, pp. 19–27.

Whitby 2007: Whitby, M., 'The Bible Hellenized: Nonnus' Paraphrase of St. John's Gospel and Eudocia's Homeric Centos', in: J. H. D. Scourfield (ed.), *Texts and Culture in Late Antiquity: Inheritance, Authority, and Change*, Swansea, pp. 195–232.

IV
THE PERCEPTION OF ANCIENT MYTHS: NARRATIVES AND REPRESENTATIONS

Ute Wartenberg Kagan

Greek and Roman coins are among our sources on ancient religion, which continues to be known to this day, through its celebrated myths and gods. It was revived for the modern era in particular during its *Nachleben*, or Afterlife, in the scholarship, art and literature from the Renaissance onwards and particularly in the eighteenth and nineteenth centuries. A well-educated person of that period might well have read the *Iliad*, known the Muses, or at any rate been familiar with the principal myths from Antiquity. Today, even a broad, popular audience consumes Hollywood films such as *Troy* or *Clash of the Titans*, which adapt myths and legends for the big screen. The attraction of the ancient myths lies in their stories, which reflect timeless sensibilities and experiences of war, exile, love, family life.

The narrative of ancient mythology is known from the classical authors, foremost from Homer's *Iliad* and *Odyssey*, Hesiod's *Theogony*, the Attic playwrights, and the Roman poets Virgil and Ovid. Often, however, their polytheistic world of gods and heroes is so multifarious that even ancient authors cannot agree on what the primary story was. In the fifth century BC, Pindar wrote victory odes redacting obscure myths of Greek cities, while the historian Herodotus reconstructed the origins of a bewildering array of cities and peoples.

cat. nos 112, 28, 121

In the Hellenistic period, the tradition of aetiology – the explanation of how particular names or customs came to exist – became a defining feature of literature. In his *Aitia* ('Causes') the poet Callimachus compared the differences between multiple-versions myths, while Apollonius of Rhodes recounted the foundation myths of various cities in his *Ktiseis* ('Foundations'), of which only fragments survive.[1]

Where the surviving literature ends, the stories of ancient myth are taken up today by the archeological record, prominently including coinage. While the Olympian gods are familiar from epic poetry, the numismatic evidence in particular extends to another level of local, less prominent deities and myths. These were often barely known beyond the boundaries of their *polis*, and today few accounts survive that could attest to their names, rites or temples. These local traditions, however, are very much extant on the many thousand coin issues from ancient Greek and Roman times.

Although the custom of using deities as coin designs became widespread in the ancient world, it was highly unusual when the first coins were minted, after the early seventh century BC, by the Lydian kings and some Greek cities in Asia Minor.[2] The new medium permitted the choice of practically any image as a sign of origin or value. Like engraved gems or painted shields, coins of the Archaic period often show animals. The main Lydian emblem for coinage is a lion, sometimes facing a second one, although
cat. nos 2–3 a boar is also used. The Greek coinage of Aegina depicts a turtle, while Athens has a variety of animals and even human body parts, such as a leg.

A few mythical creatures sometimes appear, although rarely in any narrative context.[3] The city of Corinth, a major trading power, produced a long-standing series of staters showing Pegasus, the famous winged horse. Athens showed Athena Parthenos on the
cat. no. 4 obverse and her bird, the owl, on the reverse. Although there is little evidence for the reasons behind the choice of most coin devices, ancient authors do mention them in a few instances. The Greek poet Simonides, for example, refers to a statue of Artemis whose price was 'two hundred Parian drachmas, which bear the emblem of a goat'.[4] In one common practice, the emblem could be a pun on the name of a city, like that of Selinous, which uses the leaf of the wild celery plant (*selinon*).

In Classical and Hellenistic times, however, a clear preference emerged for deities, as opposed to animals or objects such as buildings. The ancient Greeks' polytheistic religion typically offered a city many choices for its official coinage, since numerous divinities were usually worshipped in any single place and a variety of myths might be associated with it. When the emblems for *poleis* begin to appear in the late sixth century BC, deities and their various attributes are clearly popular. At this early stage, before 400 BC, they noticeably favoured minor and local cults over the major ancient Pantheon.[5]

Remarkably, the first coinage depicting any of the Olympian gods appeared far from the centre of the Classical world, at Cyrene, a Greek colony in northern Africa.

The subject was none other than Zeus, the father of the gods, identified here as Zeus Ammon, whose principal sanctuary was the Egyptian oasis of Siwa. Cities on the Greek mainland shied away from displaying an anthropomorphic representation of Zeus until later in the fifth century BC, even though he was well established in sculpture or vase-painting. Instead, designs alluded to the ruler of Mount Olympus only by incorporating his well-known attributes. Even on the coinage of Elis, for example, home to the sanctuary where the Olympic Games were held, only the thunderbolt of Zeus appears during the fifth century BC, or an eagle in flight with snakes in its
talons.[6] Only in the late fifth century BC did this mint begin to portray the heads of fig. 1
Zeus and Hera. The earliest depiction of any god's head can be identified on the
coinage of Sicilian Naxos.[7] Sicily also provides the earliest depiction of a full figure fig. 2
of a god, with Poseidon on the coinage of the city of Poseidonia.[8] fig. 3

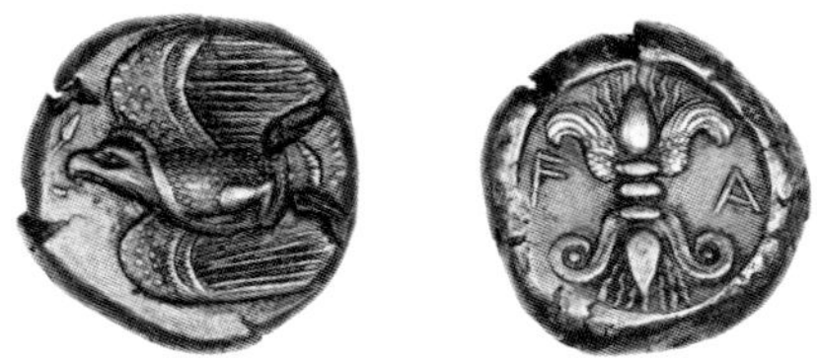

fig. 1

Silver stater, Olympia, 5th century BC.
American Numismatic Collection, New York

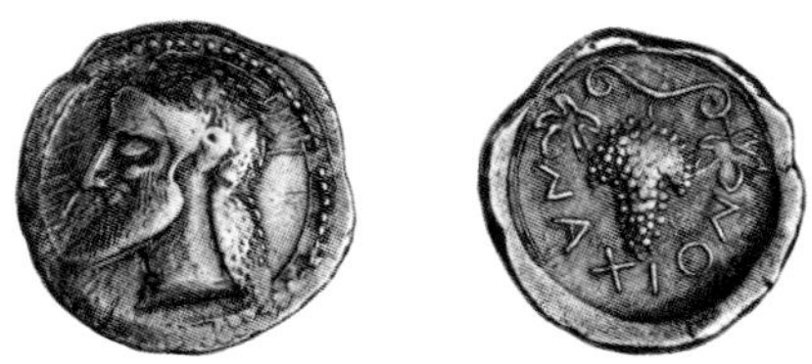

fig. 2

Silver drachm, Naxos, Sicily, 6th century BC.
American Numismatic Collection, New York

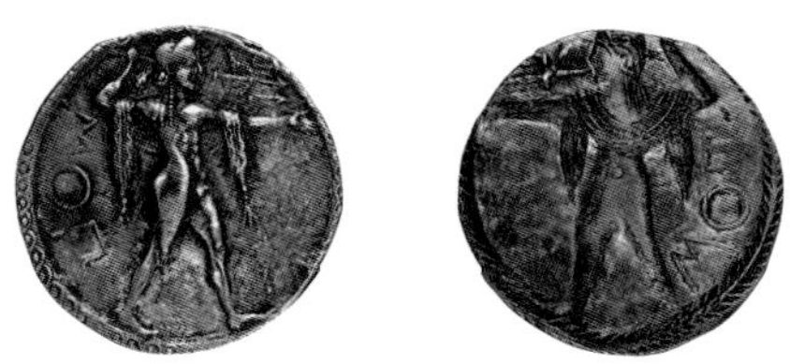

fig. 3

Silver stater, Poseidonia, *ca.* 530–510 BC.
American Numismatic Collection, New York

By far the most popular deity on coins of the Archaic and early Classical age is Apollo.[9] On tetradrachms of Selinous in Sicily he is depicted as a standing figure,

fig. 4 with his bow drawn, riding in a chariot together with Artemis.[10] This elaborate scene is unusual on coins, which mostly show only heads or animals. That this has more to do with the artistic ambitions of the Sicilian die-cutters than with the city itself is clear when we look at the reverse of this coin, which shows the river-god Selinous pouring a libation over a flaming altar engraved with a cock, next to a smaller altar showing a bull. Since the cock is typically an attribute of Asclepius, it suggests that the altar is dedicated to the healing god, in memory of the city's deliverance from the miasmic pollution of its two rivers.[11] The ability to depict action and indeed interactions on coins is clearly in place, however rare it was in practice. On the coins of Selinous it clearly expressed a complex set of ideas, involving on the one hand the archer Apollo, presumably in his capacity as an alternate healer-god, together with Artemis, and on the other hand the river deity sacrificing to Asclepius.

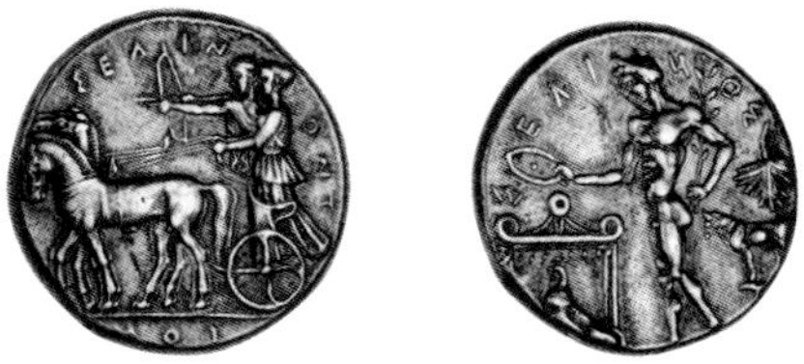

fig. 4

Silver tetradrachm, Selinous, *ca*. 440-435 BC.
American Numismatic Collection, New York

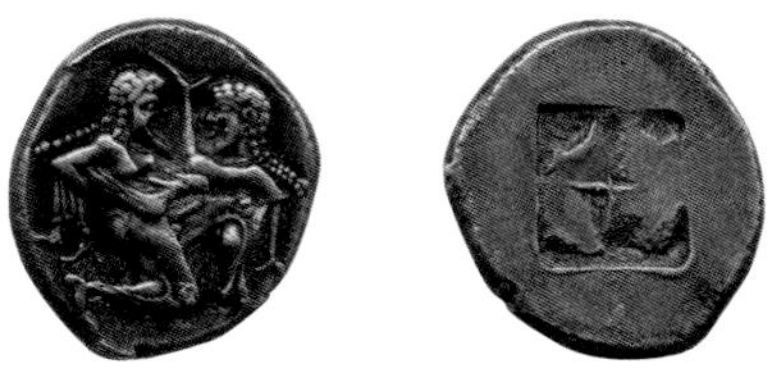

fig. 5

Silver stater, Thasos, *ca*. 520 BC.
American Numismatic Collection, New York

Such sophisticated iconography is rare on ancient Greek coins, except in one intriguing and prolific group of Dionysiac scenes from Thrace and Macedonia, where it was quite common. The coinage of Thasos, which begins striking around 520 BC, appears to be the earliest showing action, indeed of a dramatic character. It depicts a satyr carfig. 5 rying off a nymph, clearly in great excitement with erect phallus.[12] The silver staters of the Orreskioi, minted in the late sixth century BC, show a different version of the same scene, this time with a centaur abducting the nymph. Other coinages of the region display more peaceful manifestations of the Dionysiac rite, such as that of Maroneia, with a bunch of grapes, or of Mende, showing the god Dionysus himself lying on a donkey while holding a kantharos full of wine. The Sicilian city of Naxos minted one of the most beautiful ancient depictions of Dionysus, on which his head is shown on the obverse, while the reverse shows him seated, with his legs crossed and clearly drunk.[13] Although Dionysiac scenes of ecstatic women or satyrs appear on sixth-century BC vases, most cities presumably regarded them as inappropriate for their official coinage. fig. 6

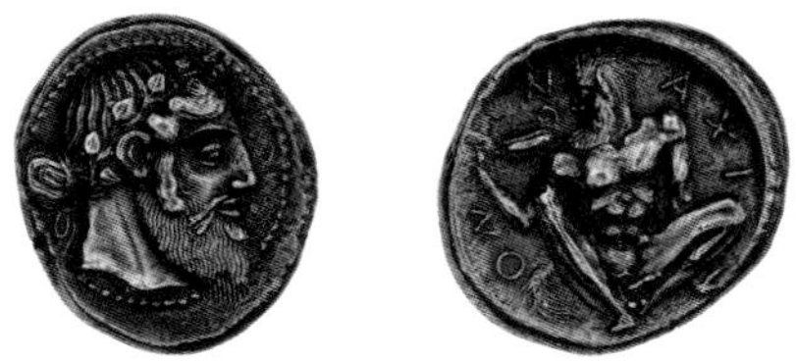

fig. 6

Silver drachm, Naxos, Sicily, *ca.* 461–440 BC.
American Numismatic Collection, New York

The abundance of mythological and religious subjects shows how deeply coinage was rooted in Greek culture. The function of coins themselves, which enabled payments to citizens, facilitated transaction in the market place, or financed wars, was integral to the Greek city-state. Although coins were minted and used in other parts of the Mediterranean, some of which were not Greek, the overall influence on designs comes from the shared body of imagery in Greek myth and religion. It is no coincidence that this was the same period in which Greek cities concentrated their efforts on erecting monumental temples for their principal deities, intended to define the *polis* both to the inhabitants and to foreign visitors.

By the fourth century BC, coinage in silver, gold and bronze had spread to many parts of the Mediterranean world. Hundreds of new cities and mints emerged in areas that had not issued coinage before. Much of this proliferation came from smaller, less wealthy Greek city-states, which increasingly became dependent on currency, but typically could only afford to introduce it in the form of lower-value bronze coins for local use. As such, these coins display a more regional character, in many cases illustrating obscure cults associated with a city. Often such coins are today the only evidence for the existence of a particular cult in a city.

The region of Thessaly, in particular, was the most prolific in coinages depicting lesser-known myths or deities. Especially remarkable is the prevalence of designs incorporating symbols that alluded to a specific episode in a myth involving a local god or hero. The coinage of Larissa, for example, provides an otherwise unknown depiction of a myth: on its earliest coins, minted around 479–460 BC, various types show a female head, probably of the nymph Larissa, on one side, and a sandal on the other.[14] The sandal clearly refers to the famous myth of the Argonauts' quest for the Golden Fleece. The hero Jason loses one of his sandals in an icy Thessalian river fig. 7

while carrying an old woman – actually the goddess Hera in disguise – across it on his back. He consequently arrives in Iolkos with one of his feet bare, to the horror of King Pelias, who had been told by an oracle that he would lose his kingdom to a man with one sandal. It is in the hope of averting this fate that Pelias sends Jason off to recover the Golden Fleece from remote Colchis, on the coast of the Euxine Pontus (pres. Black Sea). Why the city of Larissa chose a single sandal as one of its earliest coin designs is not clear, although we can assume that the sandal's significance for Thessalian mythology would have been clear to users of these small coins.

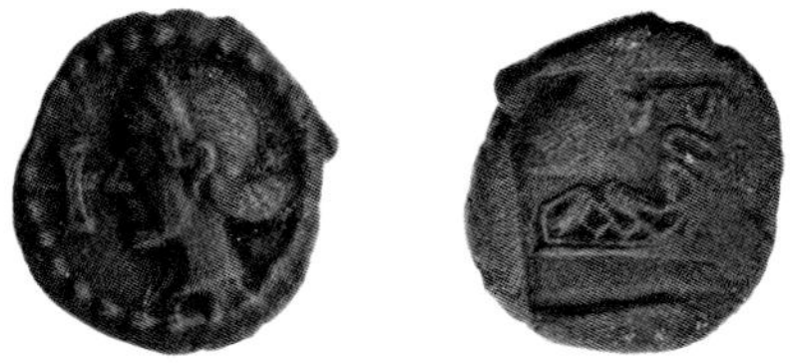

fig. 7

Silver obol, Larissa, 5th century BC.
American Numismatic Collection, New York

As for other, less mainstream myths or semi-historical legends, Thessalian mints offer many examples of these, often with the additional aim of promoting their particular story beyond a purely local group, most likely for political propaganda. Silver coins of Larissa, dating to the second half of the fourth century BC, show a facing head of a man wearing a helmet. Next to the face is a small double-axe and clearly visible is
fig. 8 the inscription ΑΛΕΥΑ.[15] There are various interpretations for this coinage, but it is clear that the head is that of King Aleuas, the ancestor of the aristocratic family of the Aleuadai, presumably to assert his descendants' claim to the title of *tagos*, the office whose symbol is the double-axe.[16]

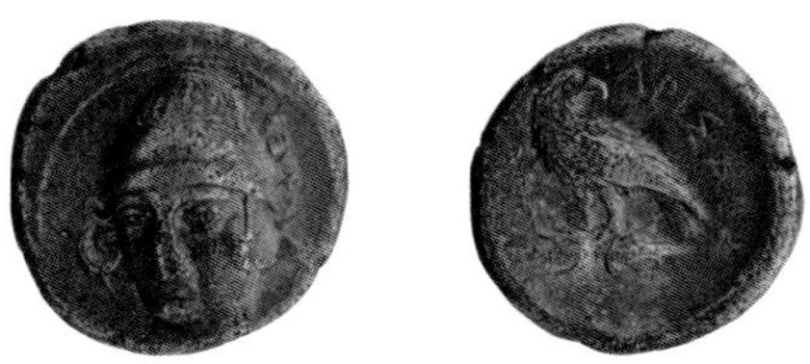

fig. 8

Silver drachm, Larissa, 5th century BC.
American Numismatic Collection, New York

The city of Pherae produced a spectacular set of coins under the tyrant Alexander of Pherae (369–358 BC), showing the Thessalian goddess Ennodia. These silver pieces show a wreathed female head with a small torch in front of the neck; on some speci-
fig. 9 mens the inscription ΕΝΝΟΔΙΑΣ is visible along the lower edge.[17] Alexander clearly

intended these ambitious coins for a wider circulation, in particular to finance his wars with other Thessalian cities and with Thebes. The identification of the goddess as Ennodia could be expected to tell the viewer that the coin had originated in the city of Pherae, where one of her primary sanctuaries was situated. Presumably to the same end, these coins are also the first in Thessaly to bear the name of the ruler himself, as opposed to that of the *polis*. Recent scholarship on archaic Thessaly has focused on the connections between the cities and the *ethne*, or tribal confederacies, among which the region was divided. In this context, the deployment of various ancestors, such as Aleuas or Skopas, would have been assertions of claims by particular cities, or factions within them, to wider domination in an *ethnos*. These changing coin designs in Thessaly, frequently incorporating distinct political messages, stand in stark contrast to those of major cities such as Athens, which remain completely static for centuries.

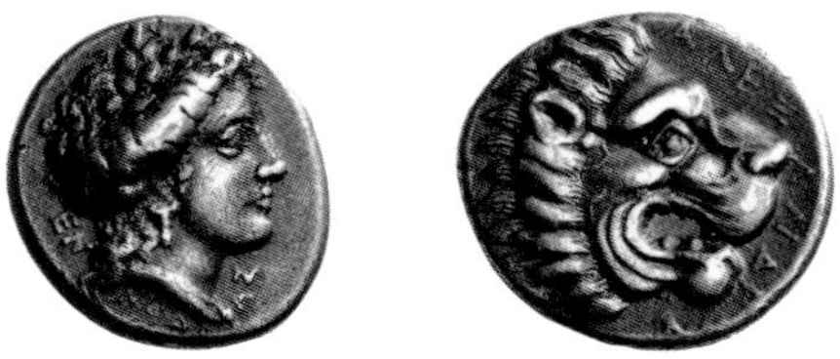

fig. 9

Silver drachm, Alexander tyrant of Pherae, 369–358 BC.
Nomos, Auction 4 (10.05.2011), Coins of Thessaly, the BCD Collection, lot 1310

When Rome became the dominant power in the Mediterranean world by the second century BC, the narrative of its coin images took up the practice of celebrating some episode in the moneyer's ancestry. In some cases, it actually reinvents an established myth, adjusted to fit contemporary mores and political expediency. The Trojan War and the web of narratives extending from it remained perennially popular throughout the Greek and later Roman world, including on coinage. The Romans, for their part, took up with unique fascination the myth of the Trojan hero Aeneas, to whom they ascribed the founding of their city. The episode frequently depicted is Aeneas' flight from the sack of Troy with his family.

The earliest numismatic representation of this scene is Greek, on silver tetradrachms of Aeneia in Macedonia (*ca.* 490–480 BC), which established the classic composition. They show Aeneas carrying on his back his aged father, Anchises, from the burning city, while his wife Creusa leads their young son Ascanius.[18] The subject was a natural fig. 10
choice for Aeneia, which claimed to have been founded by the hero himself. While its tetradrachms could depict the famous scene of the fleeing family, the smaller denominations were confined to a head of the helmeted hero. In this Greek version of the story, Aeneas's wife is still prominent, whereas later versions on Roman coinage show only the

cat. no. 28 male members of the three different generations.[19] In his epic, the *Aeneid*, Virgil largely invented a new foundation myth of Rome, which tied the new world power in the first century BC to the mythical past of the Greeks as represented in the Trojan Wars. The role of Aeneas's wife Creusa in Virgil is transitory, and significantly different from the early Classical renderings. In his telling, Creusa falls behind the others and is lost amid the smoke and chaos. When Aeneas returns to look for her, he finds himself speaking only to her shadow. On the early tetradrachms of Aeneia, by contrast, as well as in Greek vase-paintings Creusa, actually leads the way, carrying the boy Ascanius on her own back.

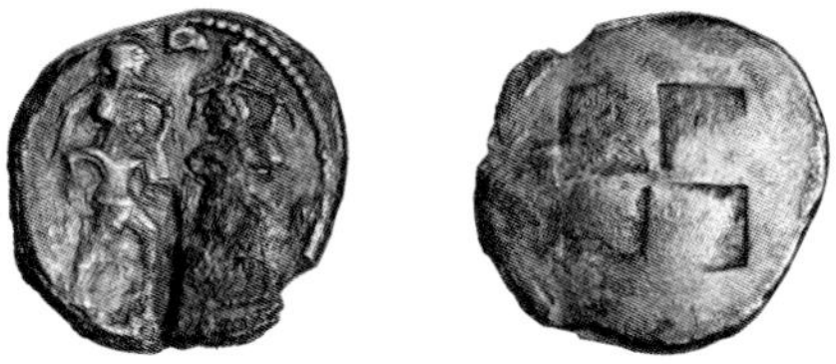

fig. 10

Silver tetradrachm, Aeneia, *ca.* 525–480 BC.
American Numismatic Collection, New York

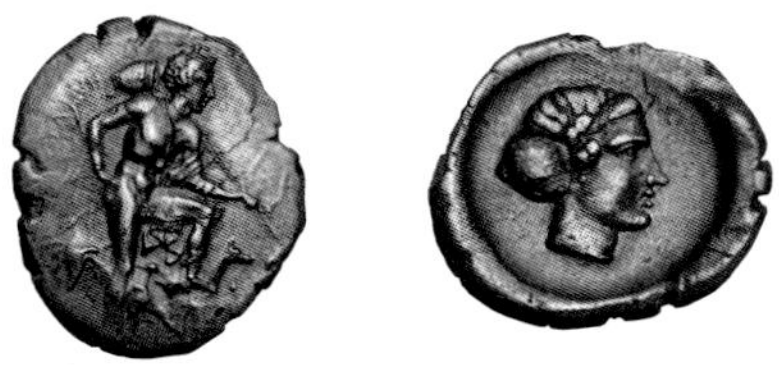

fig. 11

Silver tetradrachm, Segesta, *ca.* 470–405 BC.
American Numismatic Collection, New York

In the first century BC, the motif of Aeneas carrying Anchises suddenly gains new popularity on coins. Again it does so in the form of a foundation myth, this time in the case of the city of Segesta in Sicily. Here, Virgil's retelling replaces an older tradition, which too claims a Trojan origin: in the version known from the fifth century BC, the historian Thucydides[20] writes in his history that the Elymians displaced Trojans, founded Egesta; Aigestes, son of a Trojan woman, is credited with the actual foundation. Silver tetradrachms of the fifth century BC probably allude to this particular fig. 11 founder-hero.[21] In the description in the *Aeneid* of Aeneas'visit to Sicily, a different, somewhat more elaborate foundation myth for Segesta can be found. Here, Aeneas leaves behind Akestes with some other Trojans, who do not want to continue their long journey, preferring to settle and found the city Akesta/Segesta:

Meanwhile Aeneas is ploughing out the city limits,
assigning homes by the lot. One sector, as he decrees,
called Troy, another Ilium. Trojan-born Acestes

relishes his new kingdom, holding court,
giving laws to the elders called in session.[22]

As commentators have pointed out, this foundation passage is Roman in character and language, anticipating the foundation of Rome.[23] Virgil's version of the founding of Segesta is reflected on some bronze coins of this city, which are now generally dated to the early years of Augustus' reign.[24] Aeneas' role as a Roman ancestor seems well established in the earlier Roman tradition of the third century BC, but its renewal in the first century BC is hardly surprising if one considers the political arena, in which one of the most prominent Roman families, the *gens Iulia*, grew to importance. This family claimed direct descent from Iulus, an alternate name for Ascanius, who was the son of the goddess Venus and Aeneas. On a popular series of *denarii* of Julius Caesar, minted in 48/47 BC, both ancestors, Venus and Aeneas, are shown.[25] Aeneas carries fig. 12 his father and the famous Palladium, a wooden statue of Athena, which was stolen by Diomedes and Odysseus from the citadel of Troy. This sculpture was said to have stood in the temple of Vesta in the Roman Forum. Later Imperial coins, in particular under the emperor Elagabalus, who transferred the famous wooden statue to his own temple, make use of the Aeneas myth and other Trojan myths again.

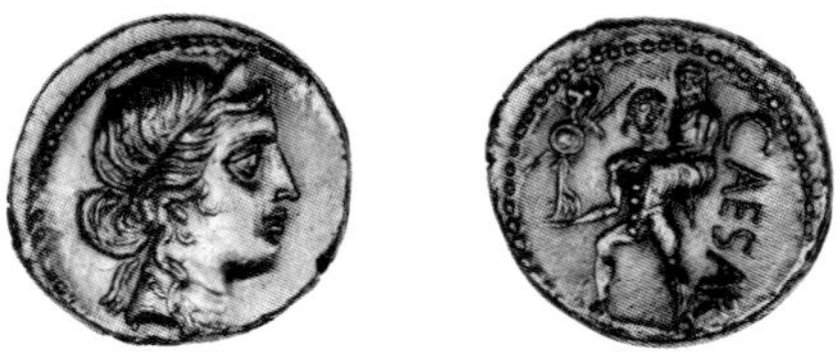

fig. 12

Silver *denarius*, Julius Caesar, Africa, 47–46 BC.
American Numismatic Collection, New York

The power of religious imagery on coins plays an even more important part on Byzantine and Medieval coinage than on ancient coins, where the roots for this development lay. The strong religious connection between State and Church led towards a set of almost fixed numismatic imagery, which was sponsored and designed by the State.

Notes

1. For an overview of the various Hellenistic authors see Clauss and Cuypers 2010.
2. On coin types see the book of McDonald 1905, which is still useful as a collection of coin types. For an introduction to various ancient Greek and Roman coinages see: Metcalf 2012; Price and Carradice 1988; Kraay 1976.
3. Such emblems on Archaic gems and coins have been discussed by Spier 1990.
4. Simonides quoted by Diogenes Laërtius, 4.45.

5. The secondary literature on ancient Greek religion is enormous. Standard works such Burkert 1985 offer an overview of the gods discussed below.
6. ANS 1960.176.22, gift of B.Y. Berry. For the coinage of Olympia see Seltman 1921.
7. ANS 1944.100.10047. For the coinage of Naxos see Cahn 1944.
8. ANS 1957.172.313, H. Miller Bequest.
9. See for examples the cities of Caulonia, Colophon, Siphnos, Leontini.
10. ANS 1997.9.129, J. Leggett Bequest.
11. Diogenes Laërtius 8.70; *HN*[2], pp. 167–8; Robertson 2010, pp. 152–3.
12. ANS 1941.153.341, W. Gedney Beatty Bequest.
13. ANS 1997.9.132, J. Leggett Bequest.
14. ANS 1944.100.16904, E.T. Newell Bequest. For an overview of this coinage see Kagan 2004, pp. 79–86. Also Moustaka 1983, p. 70, nos 171–2.
15. ANS 1944.100.16949, E.T. Newell Bequest.
16. Moustaka 1983, pp. 58–60, pl. 5, 6. For the somewhat mysterious office of the *tagos* see: Sordi 1958; Helly 1995; reviewed by Trevett 1999.
17. On this coin the full inscription is visible, Nomos, Auction 4 (10.05.2011), Coins of Thessaly, The BCD Collection, lot 1310; *ex* Leu, Auktion 30 (28.04.1982), lot 105; *ex* Ars Classica, Auction 16 (3.07.1933), lot 1128; *ex* Ars Classica, Auction 14 (2.07.1929), lot 238; *ex* J. Hirsch, Auktion 13 (15.05.1905), lot 1446 (A. Rhousopoulos collection).
18. ANS 1950.53.5. Four specimens of this tetradrachm are known: *SNG ANS Macedonia* 67 (*Jameson* 932: 'found in Fayoum'); Berlin (*Traité*, pl. XLIX, 15); *Asyut* 194; private collection. For an overview of the iconographic evidence for Aeneas and this scene see *LIMC* I. 1–2, pp. 386 ff.
19. For the foundation the city by Aeneas, see Hellanicus, *FGrHist* 4. Fr.31; for an overview of history see *IACP*, no 557; iconographical analysis in Fuchs 1973, pp. 615–32 and more recently *LIMC*, *s.v.* Aeneias.
20. Thucydides, 6.2.3.
21. ANS 1997.9.125, J. Leggett Bequest. For this coinage see Hurter Mani 2008.
22. Virgil, *Aeneid*, V, ll. 838–842.
23. For book V see Galinsky 1968, pp. 157–85; for an overview of Aeneas and his Sicilian and Roman connections see Galinsky 1969.
24. *RPC* I, p. 173; the date is based on Grant 1946, p. 335.
25. ANS 1944.100.3301, E. T. Newell Bequest. *RRC* I, 458/1; Sydenham 1952, 1013.

Bibliography & Abbreviations

***Asyut*:** Price, M. and Waggoner, N., *Archaic Greek Coinage. The Asyut Hoard*, London 1975.

Burkert 1985: Burkert, W., *Greek Religion*, transl. J. Raffan, Cambridge, MA.

Cahn 1944: Cahn, H. A., *Die Münzen der sizilischen Stadt Naxos. Ein Beitrag zur Kunstgeschichte des griechischen Westens*, Basel.

Clauss and Cuypers 2010: Clauss, J. J. and Cuypers, M. (eds), *A Companion to Hellenistic Literature*, Oxford.

Galinsky 1968: Galinsky, G. K., 'Aeneid V and the Aeneid', *American Journal of Philology* 89.2 (1968), pp. 157–85.

Galinsky 1969: Galinsky, G. K., *Aeneas, Sicily and Rome*, Princeton.

Helly 1995: Helly, B., *L'état thessalien. Aleuas le Roux, les tetrads et les tagoi*, Lyon.

***HN*[2]:** Head, B. V., *Historia Numorum*, London 1911[2].

Hurter Mani 2008: Hurter Mani, S., *Die Didrachmenprägung von Segesta: mit einem Anhang der Hybriden, Teilstücke und Tetradrachmen sowie mit einem Überblick über die Bronzeprägung*, Bern.

IACP: Hansen, H. H. and Nielsen, Th. N. (eds), *Inventory of Archaic and Classical Poleis*, Oxford 2004.

Jameson: Jameson, R., *Collection R. Jameson des monnaies grecques et romaines impériales* I–IV, Paris 1913–1932.

Kagan 2004: Kagan, J., 'The so-called Persian Weight Coins of Larissa', in: *Obolos 7, Coins in the Thessalian Region, Proceedings of the third Scientific Meeting, Volos 24–27 May 2001*, Athens 2004, pp. 79–86.

Kraay 1976: Kraay, C. M., *Archaic and Classical Greek Coins*, Berkeley / Los Angeles.

MacDonald 1905: MacDonald, G., *Coins Types. Their Origins and Development*, Glasgow.

Metcalf 2012: Metcalf, W. E. (ed.), *The Oxford Handbook of Greek and Roman Coinage*, Oxford.

Morgan 2003: Morgan, C., *Early Greek States beyond the Polis*, London / New York.

Moustaka 1983: Moustaka, A., *Kulte und Mythen auf Thessalischen Münzen*, Würzburg.

Price and Carradice 1988: Price, M. J. and Carradice, I., *Coinage in the Greek World*, London.

Robertson 2010: Robertson, N., *Religion and Reconciliation in Greek Cities: The sacred laws of Selinus and Cyrene*, Oxford.

RPC: Burnett, A., Amandry, M. and Ripollès, P. P. (eds), *Roman Provincial Coinage, Vol. I: From the death of Caesar to the death of Vitellius (44 BC–AD 69)*, London 1992.

RRC: Crawford, M. H., *Roman Republican Coinage*, Cambridge 1974.

Seltman 1921: Seltman, C. T., *The Temple Coins of Olympia*, Cambridge.

Sordi 1958: Sordi, M., *La lega Tessala: fino ad Alesandro Magno*, Rome.

Spier 1990: Spier, J., 'Emblems in Archaic Greece', *Bulletin of the Institute of Classical Studies* 37.1 (1990), pp. 107–30.

SNG ANS *Macedonia*: *Sylloge Nummorum Graecorum. The Collection of the American Numismatic Society, Part 7, Macedonia 1: Cities, Thraco-Macedonian Tribes, Paeonian Kings*, New York 1987.

Sydenham 1952: Sydenham, E., *The Coinage of The Roman Republic*, London.

Traité: Babelon, E., *Traité des monnaies grecques et romaines, Description historique*, 1–4, Paris 1907–1932.

Trevett 1999: Trevett, J., Review of: Helly, B., 'L'état thessalien. Aleuas le Roux, les tetrads et les *tagoi*', *Journal of Hellenic Studies* 119 (1999), p. 213.

V
REFLECTIONS OF THE EARTH AND THE COSMOS ON ANCIENT AND MEDIEVAL COINS

Yannis Stoyas

The impulse to describe the world originates largely from man's primordial need to get his bearings and somehow to arrange his position in relation to other things, finding a notion of comfort in surrounding space. From early on, conventions were established in the form of maps, attempting more or less accurately to 'convey the complexity and chaos that is reality'.[1] At the same time, the necessity to orientate within a local environment, alongside man's innate curiosity and desire to comprehend the universe, led to abstract or more graphic depictions, as well as to symbolic representations of parts of territories, whole areas or even spatial conceptions. Initial endeavours to attain some perception of the world were rather instinctually articulated through religious and mythological perspectives.[2]

'Out of old mythologies'

A turning point in perceiving the world can be noted at the end of the seventh century BC, as from that time onwards the philosophical inquiries of a number of Greek thinkers[3] ventured towards rational interpretations of the Cosmos and a critical scrutiny of the old perceptions.[4] Anaximander of Miletos has been famously credited with having

drawn on a tablet the entire inhabited world (*oikoumenē*) then known to Greeks and of being a pioneer in publishing such a map. Pythagoras of Samos was the first to call the sum of the whole *kosmos* (ornament), because of the order it displayed;[5] he also expressed his theoretical belief that the world has a perfect form, that of a sphere. Later, Aristotle provided observational arguments supporting the idea that the world was round.[6] Already in the fifth century BC, Parmenides of Elea had imagined the earth as a globe; he envisaged it hanging in heaven, which was engulfed by the *aithēr*, the quintessential element surrounding the universe.[7] About the same time, Empedokles of Akragas proposed the theory of the four essential elements (fire, air, water and earth)[8] from which all the structures of the Cosmos were thought to be made. During the Hellenistic age, there were major advances in both cosmography and geography. Beyond doubt, of great significance was the contribution of scientists such as Eratosthenes of Cyrene, who attempted, *inter alia*, to calculate the circumference and the size of the earth – with astonishing precision for that era; his cartographic work, introducing the use of parallels and meridians in map drawing, was important too. By the early imperial period descriptive *opera magna* appeared, such as the *Γεωγραφικὰ* (*Geography*) of Strabo (end of first century BC – beginning of first century AD), becom-
cat. no. 57 ing a reference point for the then-known world.[9] Under the title *Naturalis historia*, a comprehensive encyclopaedia was produced (*ca*. AD 77–79) by Pliny the Elder; part
cat. no. 61 of this monumental *opus* deals with cosmo-geographical matters. Pausanias, a traveller of the second century AD, focused on the topographical description and cultural
cat. no. 60 geography of certain areas of mainland Greece. Claudius Ptolemaeus distinguished himself primarily as a geographer and an astronomer; his treatise *Cosmographia or Γεωγραφικὴ ὑφήγησις* was to have a lasting impact from his day well into the
cat. no. 56 Middle Ages. Probably in the sixth century AD, Stephanus of Byzantium compiled a geographical lexicon (*Ἐθνικά*), of which only a part was preserved. At that time, writers such as Constantine of Antioch and Kosmas Indikopleustes[10] believed in the notion of a flat earth, but such views were not very influential; others, like Jacob (or James) of Edessa, continued to support the idea of a spherical world. In any case, the Ptolemaic *Cosmographia* remained until the Late Byzantine period a celebrated work from which important copies with maps were produced, while some additions were also made.[11] Moreover, medieval knowledge benefited greatly from the contribution of Islamic cartography and cosmography.[12]

'Money alone sets all the world in motion'[13]

Coin-shaped money probably emerged in the last third of the seventh century BC in Lydia and thence was diffused from Ionia to Greece. Besides greatly facilitating local and more distant exchanges, the new medium combined within it practicality and ideology; as was the case with other crafts, social conventions and aspects of everyday life, the old ways of tradition made their presence felt pictorially on coinage, but gradually new trends blended in, starting to show a sense of pragmatism.[14] Taking into account the reach of the vehicle in question, an attempt to isolate glimpses of the world and the universe on ancient and medieval coinage seems quite intriguing. However, within the limits of this essay, such an overview of coin types is inevitably selective.

The lie of the land

It can be said *a priori* that charting territories on coins was rather uncommon in Antiquity. However, it has been proposed that the incuse reverse of certain coins,[15] struck probably somewhere in western Asia Minor, resembles the relief of the hinterland of Ephesus. In the case that a physical map should be viewed, landmasses may be discerned on the granulated irregular shapes, which might correspond to the Tmolus and Mes(s)ogis mountains, as well as to the Kaystros and Maiandros valleys.[16] A connection to Memnon the Rhodian, a general in the employ of the Persian king (*ca.* 336–334 BC), had been hypothesized,[17] but chronological objections have been raised since then.[18] Recently, a higher dating in the early fourth century BC was suggested;[19] at the same time, the map theory remains attractive but unproven, since the reverse design could be just a roughly formulated pattern.[20]

fig. 1: see cat. no. 46

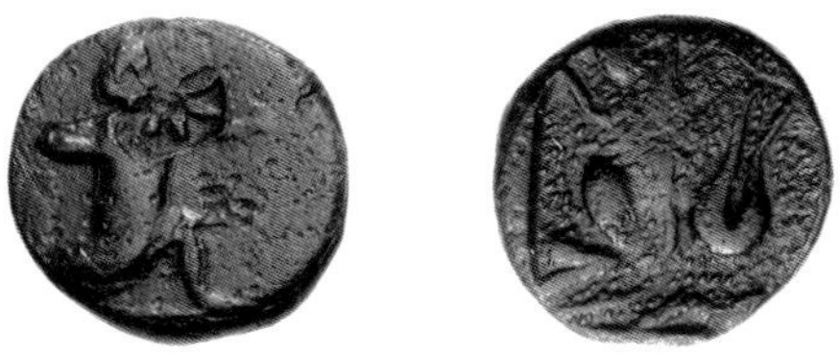

fig. 1

Bronze coin, satrapal issue (?), mint in Ionia (?), early 4th century BC (?).
KIKPE Collection, Athens

On the other hand, a numismatic representation of Mother Earth, drawn from the sphere of myth, is known from the second half of the fifth century BC: on an electrum *stater* issue of Cyzicus, Gaia is emerging from the ground holding her infant son Erichthonius, ready to hand him over to Athena. Much later, a similar deity under the Latin name Tellus[21] appears on Roman imperial coins: on issues of Hadrian (AD 134–138) Tellus is standing or reclining, accompanied by the legend TELLVS STABIL[*ita*].[22] The reverse of an exceptional 'medallion' of Commodus is inscribed with same legend, but here the composition is more elaborate: Tellus is reclining, her left arm resting on a basket with fruits and holding a vine-branch, while her right hand is placed on a star-studded globe, around which pass four figures representing fig. 2 the seasons; the scene heralds a new idyllic age, probably beginning on 1 January AD 187, at a time of relative stability for the *imperium*.

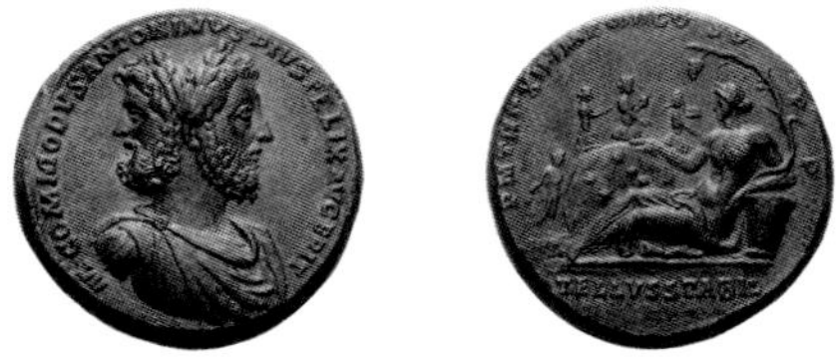

fig. 2

Bronze 'medallion' of Commodus, Rome, AD 186–7.
Numismatica Ars Classica, Auction 40 (16.05.2007), lot 748

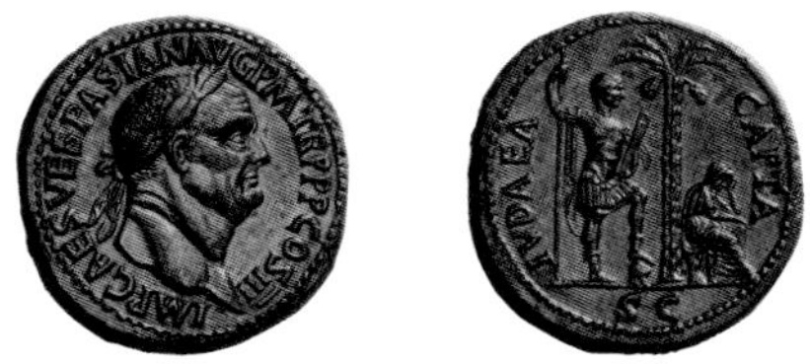

fig. 3

Bronze *sestertius* of Vespasian, Rome, AD 71.
Numismatica Ars Classica, Auction 41 (20.11.2007), lot 60

Symbolic representations of regions feature more frequently on ancient coins.
cat. no. 69 The olive- or myrtle-wreathed female head on the coins of Herbessos is thought to be the personification of Sikelia (Sicily); a similar wreathed head appears also on
cat. no. 43 bronze coins of another Sicilian city, Morgantina.[23] The female head wearing an
cat. no. 44 elephant-scalp on the coins of Juba I of Numidia signifies that country or alternatively Africa. Sometimes a distinctive animal, such as an elephant, is used to symbolize a
cat. no. 45 region. In an analogous manner, conquered Egypt is denoted on Octavian's coins by a crocodile or a hippopotamus, accompanied by the legend AEGVPTO CAPTA.[24] During imperial times the representation of Roman provinces and of vanquished or annexed territories is a recurring theme. A well-known case in point is that of captive Judaea on coins struck by Vespasian and Titus in association with the dramatic events
cat. no. 50 of the First Jewish War (AD 66–73/4) and the fall of Jerusalem. The personification
fig. 3 of mourning Judaea is a fine example of the transmission of a coin type into a written medium, that of literature — a form of *translatio studii* after a fashion. This becomes manifest through an old treatise of Joseph Addison,[25] commenting on such a piece, with a sketch also included in the illustrations;[26] the essay is prefaced, moreover, by a poem by Alexander Pope,[27] speaking of the grandeur that was Rome and making reference to this coin and others:

Convinc'd, she now contracts her vast design;
And all her triumphs shrink into a Coin.

A narrow orb each crowded conquest keeps;
Beneath her Palm here sad Judaea weeps …

Mountains are represented on coins very rarely, *par excellence* when they are numinous places. During the imperial period, silver and bronze issues of Caesarea in Cappadocia often feature the nearby Mount Argaios (pres. Erciyes), usually with a statue of Helios or with a star on its summit.[28] Another sacred site was Mount Gerizim, where the most important sanctuary of the Samaritans was located. Hadrian tried to suppress the local cult by erecting a large shrine in honour of Jupiter Optimus Maximus; the mountain is frequently depicted on the coins of Neapolis in Samaria, with a colonnade at the foot and a stairway leading to the temple on the top, while to the right a side path goes up to an altar.[29] On the Severan coinage of Kleonai, a rare subject appears, the peak of Mount Apesas, with an eagle standing on an altar.[30] Legend had it that the altar on this high-point overlooking Nemea had been dedicated by the hero Perseus to Zeus Apesantios.

Furthermore, a rare and interesting representation of a part of land is that on certain imperial issues of Corinth showing the personified Isthmos, sometimes sitting on a rock.[31]

City faces and cityscapes

Cities made their presence felt on their coinages in various ways; in some cases their names were implied through canting puns (λαλοῦντα σύμβολα) effective as civic badges, while in others their products were employed somehow like trademarks. Foundation legends were also important, as the practice of portraying the founding hero (*oikistēs* or *ktistēs*) on the flan of a coin was a manifestation of the city itself.[32] At some point later, it seems that city as a concept started to be associated with its fortune, an idea that came to be visualized in the form of a turreted head: the word for the walls (τείχη) of a city, on which its protection usually depended, is homophone in Greek with Τύχη (Fortune, Chance, Fate).[33] Tracing the iconographic type in the fourth century BC can be rather dicey;[34] in any event, the appearance of the well-known sculpture of the Tyche of Antioch by Eutychides, after the foundation of the city on the Orontes (300 BC),[35] was seemingly crucial for the image's dissemination.[36] Turreted heads abound on Hellenistic civic coinages, notably in Cilicia, Syria, Phoenice, Phrygia, Ionia (particularly Smyrna) and elsewhere; certain Roman Republican issues cat. no. 22
followed suit,[37] such as a remarkable example with the turreted head of Alexandria.[38]
This trend was continued in imperial times[39] and even survived during the Late Ro- cat. nos 47, iv
man period, mainly in the form of the turreted personification of Constantinople.[40] cat. no. 233

On the coins of the Roman Republic a helmeted head, possibly representing Roma, occurs from the second quarter of the third century BC; largely standardized after 211 BC, this representation probably signified more the authority of the Roman cat. no. 163 State and less the city itself.[41] The iconographic type of helmeted Rome persisted for cat. no. 233 a long time; however, a portrayal hinting more at a geographical connotation can be traced centuries later. In the twelfth century AD the Roman Senate started to mint coins outside papal authority; after AD 1254 and for about a century, *grossi* were issued bearing the image of seated Rome, wearing crown, holding globe and palm-branch, and with the legend *Roma caput mundi*.[42] This is a theme known also from other media,[43] which gained importance during that period due to political implications.[44]

Although more 'naturalistic' illustrations of cities were not common on coins, they still had their share, and so a couple of characteristic examples should be mentioned. On a bronze emission of Marcianopolis under Gordian III (AD 238–244) the city is cat. no. 48 shown from aerial perspective; the city wall[45] is punctuated by thirteen towers, while an arched colonnade runs along its rear side and there is a temple precinct in the interior.[46] A counterpart to this example can be seen on *hyperpyra* of Michael VIII Palaiologos (dated 1261–1282), where the half-figure of Virgin *orans* stands within the city walls of Constantinople; six triple towers are included in the curtain wall, in a however schematic representation of the city.[47]

Water element(al)s

A vital element on our planet's surface, water had several incarnations on the fields of coins; one was the numismatic representations of fountain nymphs. A nymph of this kind was Arethusa,[48] who gave her name to the fountain on Ortygia island at Syracuse cat. no. 63 and became famous through coin masterpieces. Another case from Kierion in Thessaly (fourth century BC) is that of the nymph Arnē.[49] Last but not least, Peirene at Corinth appears as a personification and more rarely is denoted as a location.[50]

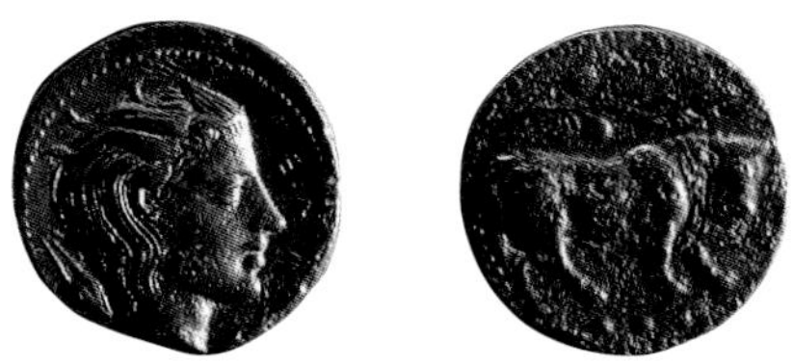

fig. 4

Bronze coin of Gela, *ca*. 420–405 BC.
KIKPE Collection, Athens

A major manifestation of the aquatic element is shown through the coin iconography of rivers, in a multitude of examples, some better known than others. The embodiment of a river-god as a man-headed bull is quite common: Gelas and Achelous,[51] but cat. no. 53 also Sepeithos,[52] etc. More anthropomorphic personifications abound too: Akragas, fig. 4: see cat. no. 54; cat. nos 24, 65, 66 Gelas, Arachthos,[53] Hebros, Strymon, Tiber, etc. Among some interesting cases is the swimming figure of Pyramos (Hierapolis-Kastabala) and, of course, the majestic personification of the Nile. Sometimes rivers appear in couple, such as Savus and Colapis, flanking Siscia, or Tigris and Euphrates, flanking Armenia. fig. 5

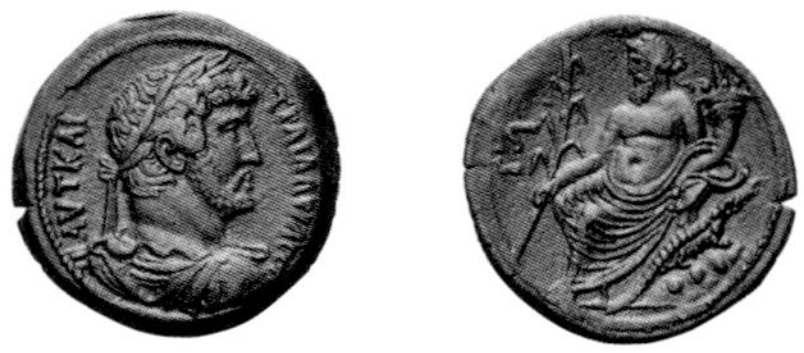

fig. 5

Bronze 'drachm' of Alexandria under Hadrian, AD 131/2.
UBS Gold & Numismatics, Auction 78 (09.09.2008), lot 1636

Harbours are seldom represented on coins, making such pieces particularly interesting. An impressive example is the curved breakwater appearing on coins of Zancle-Messana (*ca.* 525–500 BC); quay buildings can be discerned on early specimens,[54] while gradually the pier becomes linear and C-shaped.[55] Besides its importance, the sickle-shaped harbour mole served also as a canting pun on the city's name (*zanklon* = sickle in Sicilian). Ostia was of great importance to Rome; a major construction project was launched by Claudius and completed by Nero, the latter choosing an outstanding image of the port on his *sestertii*.[56] Due to siltation problems, Trajan later created a second inner port, hexagonal in shape.[57] A more charming representation comes up from the imperial coin series of Corinth: the two ports of the city, Lechaion and Kenchreai, take the form of two nymphs standing side by side.[58]

The representation of the sea flows back and forth on coins, resembling its perpetual motion. Sometimes a portion provides the marine scenery for a myth, as in the case of the Hellespont on coins of Abydos illustrating the legend of Hero and Leander.[59] cat. nos 93, 99
In other cases, a personification (Pontus) makes evident in a conventional way a city's connection with the sea. cat. no. 64

'... *ad astra mollis e terris via*'

From the views of the Atomists and the Pythagoreans to Aristotle's *Περὶ οὐρανοῦ* and Aristarchus' heliocentric system, to the commentaries on the *Phainomena* of Aratus[60] and cat. no. 77
on Cicero's *Somnium Scipionis*[61], through to later Medieval cosmological treatises, cat. nos 80, 76
envisaging and describing the universe was a rather perplexing matter.

From another angle, astronomical objects are quite often attested numismatically, rather more closely in association with legendary conceptions. The personification of the Sun (Helios) adorned the coins of several issuing authorities,[62] most notably those of Rhodos; more rarely the solar disc appears as a supplementary motif.[63] An cat. nos 74, 75 anonymous *uncia* issue of the Roman Republic bears a bust of Sol on the obverse and a crescent and two stars on the reverse.[64] In 19/18 BC a *denarius* issue of Augustus featured a six-rayed star with crescent moon; another example of the star and crescent theme appears on the reverse of a pseudo-autonomous issue of Byzantium. cat. no. 178 Constantine I famously associated his fortune with *Sol Invictus*, which is represented on a number of his coin issues.

Byzantine coinage is seemingly lacking in pictorial references to celestial bodies. However, the testimony of balance-weights and of a couple of documents (from the 1030s) refers to a numismatic term coming from that context: *ἡλιοσεληνάτον*, a peculiar word combining the sun and the moon; it has been suggested that this appellation should be linked to the last issue of gold *histamena* of Basil II (975–1025) and to the *histamena* of Constantine VIII (1025–1028). fig. 6 The attribution may be correct, but the main argument seems weak, as it attempts to explain the term on the basis of two small circles or crescents in the upper quarters of Christ's halo.[65] Without going into further details here, it seems more possible that the term is due to the triple dotted border appearing on Basil's last *histamena*, in differentiation to his smaller gold *tetartera* (as in an annular eclipse when the moon covers the sun, leaving a glowing ring).

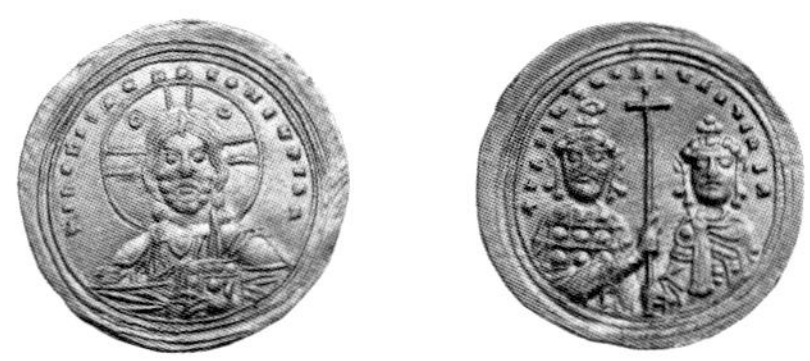

fig. 6

Gold *histamenon* of Basil II, Constantinople, *ca.* 1005–1025 AD.
Ira & Larry Goldberg Coins & Collectibles, Auction 67 (31.01.2012), lot 3319

Stars in generic renderings are another common subject on coins of various issuing authorities: the Campani mercenaries, Corcyra, Gambreion, Thymbra, Hecatomnus, Alexandros Iannaios, etc. A particularly interesting case is that of Ouranopolis, on the bronze coins of which is an eight-rayed star and a figure with a star above head, seated on a globe and holding a sceptre; usually considered as Aphrodite Ourania, this should be a representation of Helios[66] or rather Ouranos, the personification of the sky. fig. 7: see cat. no. 73 On the rare silver *staters* of this city the solar disc is used on the obverse.[67] Another brilliant example is the star placed on the rare anonymous half-*siliquae* which are associated with the dedication of Constantinople (11 May 330).[68] This obviously hints at the celebrated heavenly sign of the Vision of Constantine, and appears also cat. no. 233 on other issues of his family (bronzes of Helena and Fausta).

The appearance of celestial objects most times caused quite an impression and on occasion received a special interpretation; such was the case of the comet in July

44 BC, which was *a posteriori* associated with the deification of Julius Caesar (*sidus Iulium*);[69] on propagandistic coin issues of Augustus the comet is shown as an eight-rayed star with a flaming tail. fig. 8

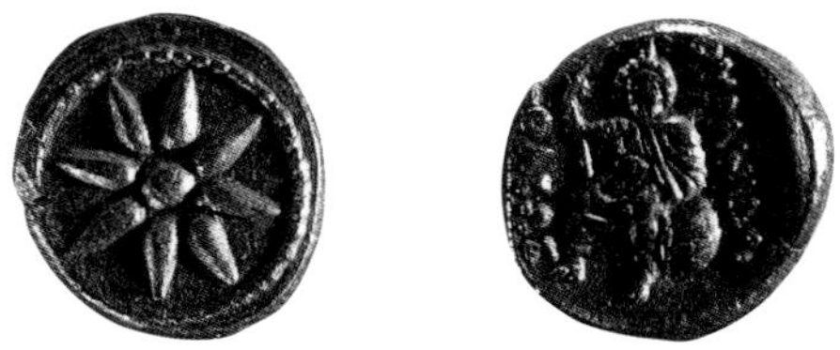

fig. 7

Bronze coin of Ouranopolis, *ca.* 300 BC.
KIKPE Collection, Athens

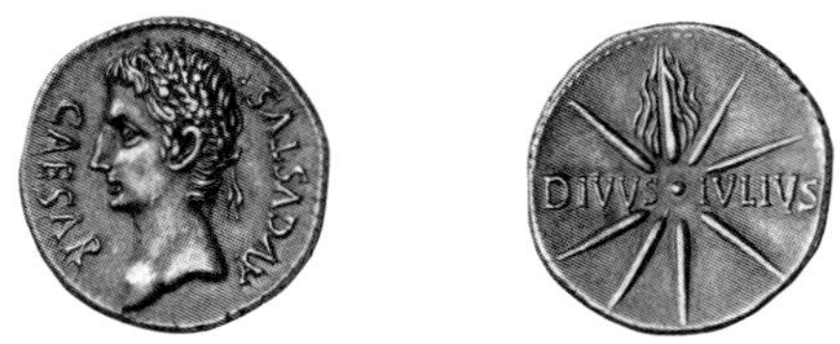

fig. 8

Silver *denarius* of Augustus, Colonia Caesaraugusta, 19/8 BC.
LHS Numismatik, Auktion 102 (29.04.2008), lot 334

Ex astris, scientia?

Constellations, either implied or denoted more directly, feature in certain numismatic representations. On the coins of Karthaia is the radiate forepart of a dog, i.e. Sirius. The heads of the Dioscuri, usually surmounted by stars, are quite commonly represented. cat. no. 70 On a *denarius* issue of Lucius Lucretius Trio (76 BC)[70] the head of Sol appears on the obverse, while a crescent and seven stars on the reverse, a clear allusion to the moneyer's name, as the sun and the moon shed their *lux* and the constellation employed was called *Septem Triones* (*Ursa Major*). Augustus used the sign of Capricorn on a significant number of emissions. fig. 9 Although Augustus had been born under the sun sign of Libra, he probably believed that he was influenced by Capricorn rising or even as his moon sign.[71] In any case, this had an impact and Capricorn appears also on coins of Juba II of Mauritania (25 BC – AD 23) and of Antiochus IV of Commagene (AD 38–72), as well as on imperial emissions (e.g. Vespasian) and provincial issues. cat. no. 72 An interesting case is presented on coins of Domitian and his wife, where their dead and deified infant is shown on a globe, surrounded by seven stars (*Ursa Major*). The depiction of a bull on Julian's bronze coins became a controversial matter; cat. no. 181 it has been suggested that, besides other syncretic connotations (Apis, Mithras, etc), the bull with the two stars above him signified the emperor's zodiac sign: Taurus.[72]

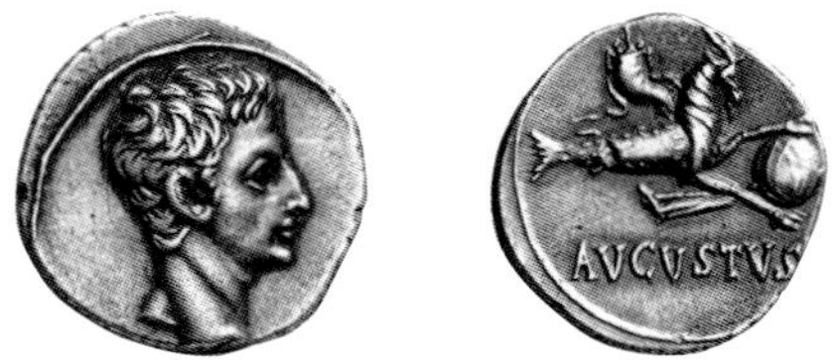

fig. 9

Silver *denarius* of Augustus, uncertain mint, 27 BC onwards.
Gorny & Mosch Giessener Munzhandlung, Auktion 151 (09.10.2006), lot 375

Zodiac signs appeared rather haphazardly on coins, but usually in connection to specific occasions. In Egypt, the completion of a Sothic cycle of 1,460 years, associated with the rise of Sirius, happened during the reign of Antoninus Pius, in the year AD 139. This important event was followed by a series of issues illustrating planets and signs (Venus and Taurus, Sun and Leo, Mars and Scorpio, etc) and an emission with two zodiacs aligned.[73] Analogous representations of zodiacs are also known from other provincial issues, such as an emission of Sardeis at the time of Gordian III (238–244)[74]
fig. 10 or the magnificent emission of Perinthus under Severus Alexander: Zeus on throne takes the centre; above him fly the chariots of Helios and Selene, while at his feet are the reclining figures of Gaia and Thalassa (the Sea), all encircled by the zodiac wheel.

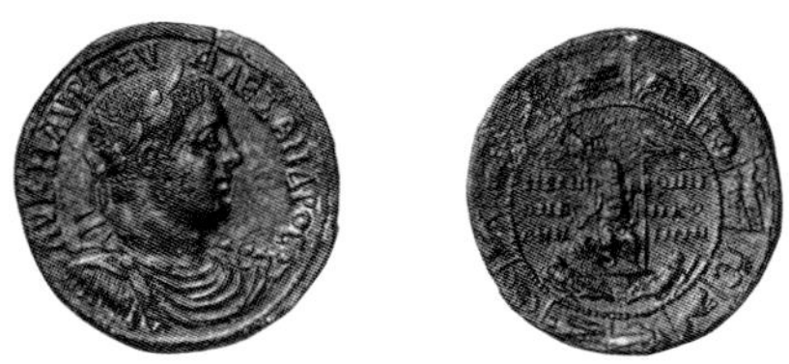

fig. 10

Bronze 'medallion' of Severus Alexander,
The New York Sale XIV (10.01.2007), lot 153

As a final addition, mention should be made of Islamic culture's fascination with astrology, expressed after a fashion on Turkoman coins of the twelfth century AD, an example being a bronze coin issue of Najm al-Din Alpi (1152–1176 AD), Artuqid ruler
fig. 11: see cat. no. 71 of Mardin, on which the facing busts on the obverse have an astrological connotation, since the issue was produced *ca.* 1154, at a time 'with Gemini in the ascendant'.[75]

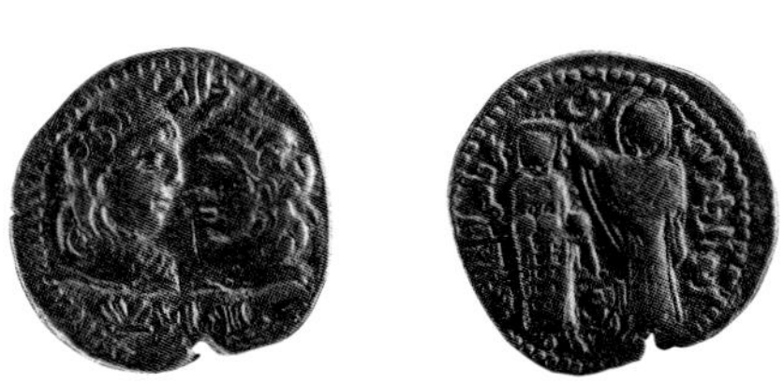

fig. 11

Bronze coin of Najm al-Din Alpi (1152–1176 AD),
Artuqid ruler of Mardin, *ca.* 1154 AD.
KIKPE Collection, Athens

The end of the Middle Ages was heralded by the discovery of a New World, alongside with a radical change in the perception of the world as a whole in human minds. This retrospective could have been more extensive, however, as has been marvellously phrased in an Afterword[76] by Borges:

> *A man sets himself the task of outlining the world. Through the years he peoples a space with images of provinces, kingdoms, mountains, bays, ships, islands, fishes, rooms, instruments, stars, horses, and persons. Shortly before his death, he discovers that this patient labyrinth of lines traces the image of his face.*

Notes

1. Carlucci and Barber 2001, p. 6.
2. It has been rather aptly suggested that '... the purpose of myth is to provide a logical model capable of overcoming a contradiction (an impossible achievement if, as it happens, the contradiction is real) ...'; Lévi-Strauss 1963, p. 229.
3. Such as Thales, Anaximander, Anaximenes, Pythagoras, Xenophanes and (later) Parmenides, Heraclitus, Anaxagoras, Empedocles, Zenon, Democritus, etc. See indicatively Dreyer 1905, pp. 11–52; Heath 1932, pp. XVIII–XXXIX, 1–39; Wright 1995, esp. pp. 19–24, 39–44, 52–4, 78–89, 166–72.
4. For, as Karl Popper stated, 'science must begin with myths, and with the criticism of myths'; Popper 1957, p. 177.
5. Aëtius the doxographer (*De placitis reliquiae*, ed. H. Diels, Berlin 1879, p. 327) attests that Pythagoras *«πρῶτος ὠνόμασε τὴν τῶν ὅλων περιοχὴν κόσμον ἐκ τῆς ἐν αὐτῷ τάξεως»*. See also Wright 1995, pp. 3–4, further noting: 'To this word [i.e. *kosmos*]...was added *logos*, meaning "a reasoned and rational account", to give the compound noun *cosmology*...'.
6. Whitfield 1994, p. 6.
7. Aëtius, *De placitis reliquiae*, ed. H. Diels, Berlin 1879, pp. 335–6.
8. These were termed ῥιζώματα (rootings, foundations) by Empedocles; the designation στοιχεῖα (elements, components) became more common after Plato (*Timaios*, 48b).
9. It is worth mentioning that numismatic catalogues still follow, with some modifications, the arrangement of B. V. Head (*Historia Numorum*, Oxford 1911^2), who largely adopted J. H. Eckhel's system (*Doctrina numorum veterum*, Vienna 1792–1798); the latter had in turn based his overview on the geographical outline of Strabon's work – starting from Spain and moving towards the East.
10. For the *Χριστιανικὴ τοπογραφία* of Kosmas see indicatively: Winstedt 1909; Harley and Woodward 1987–1998, Vol. 1, pp. 261–3; Faller 2011. The text of Kosmas was written around AD 548 and *inter alia* provides information on the distant island of Taprobane (Sri Lanka, formerly Ceylon). Kosmas, according to a 'Mosaic model' of his own, imagined the earth as a rectangular table (τράπεζα) enclosed by the Ocean; on a separate land beyond the sea, to the far east, lay Paradise; Faller 2011, pp. 209–10.
11. At the end of the thirteenth century Maximos Planoudes found a manuscript of *Cosmographia* which contained no maps and then drew a map based on information from this document; Nikephoros Gregoras (fourteenth century) is known to have added *scholia in margine* to the text and is supposedly the one to take credit for the four-page world map appearing in certain manuscripts; Bagrow and Skelton 1985, p. 36.
12. Further on the history of cartography see, indicatively, Harley and Woodward 1987–1998, Vol. 1 (1987), esp. pp. 130–257 (Greek and Roman world), 258–75 (Byzantium); Vol. 2 (1992), esp. pp. 3–188 (Islamic world).
13. Bartlett 1968, p. 126; the rendering of the maxim *Pecunia ... regimen est rerum omnium* of Publilius Syrus (*Sententiae*, P 9) is rather free. In the text there is a missing word (*lacuna*) to be surmised: *Pecunia* [*summum* or *unum* or *una*] *regimen est rerum omnium*. The meaning has been phrased in several ways: 'Money alone is the ruling principle of the world'; 'All things obey money'; or 'Money is the one controller of all things'.

14. For a refined perspective of *mythos* and *logos* see Fowler 2011.
15. Silver tetradrachms and (more rare) bronze pieces; Johnston 1967, pp. 86, 93–4.
16. Johnston 1967, esp. pp. 91–3; the engraver may have placed the West at the top of the design (p. 94).
17. Johnston 1967, p. 89.
18. Mildenberg 1993, pp. 71–2 (attributing the issue to Artaxerxes III, *ca.* 340 BC), 79, pls 12.110–111, 13.112; Meadows 2002, p. 209 (tetradrachm; *ante* 341/0 BC), pl. 30, first row, no. 1.
19. Weisser 2009, pp. 154–5, nos 8–9 (tetradrachms). The connection to a certain Pythagores, whose name appears on a few silver specimens, is still enigmatic.
20. See Brodersen 2001, p. 10.
21. Tellus was patron goddess of the cultivable land, while Ceres of fertility and agriculture (Ovid, *Fasti*, 1.671–674).
22. A claim not only for the re-establishment of agriculture, but also for making the earth firm, i.e. secure. *À propos*, the third chapter of Marguerite Yourcenar's *Memoirs of Hadrian* (see cat. no. 123) is entitled 'Tellus stabilita'.
23. Later, the figure of Sicily appears on Roman *denarii*: on emissions of Mn. Aquillius (71 BC) and L. Aquillius Florus (19/18 BC) slumped Sicilia is raised by their ancestor Manius Aquillius, who took command as consul on the island during the Second Servile War (104–100 BC).
24. A crocodile chained to a palm-branch, symbolizing the conquest of Egypt, is depicted also on bronzes of Nemausus under Augustus (see cat. no. 167).
25. Addison 1761, pp. XII, XVIII, 413ff. The treatise of J. Addison (1672–1719) was published posthumously in 1721. For an analysis of Addison's perspective see Alvarez 2005.
26. Addison 1761, pp. 498–500, 534, 525 (*recte* 537), no. 13.
27. Addison 1761, pp. 415–7: Verses occasioned by Mr. Addison's Treatise of Medals. Pope wrote the larger part of the poem by 1715, at a time when Addison intended to publish his treatise; a few verses were added probably in 1719 and finally in 1720. See Ault 1941, pp. 429, 443–8.
28. Earlier depictions of Mount Argaios appear during the time of Cappadocian ruler Archelaus (36 BC – AD 17), on coins of Eusebeia (formerly named Caesarea).
29. See e.g. Ira & Larry Goldberg Coins & Collectibles, Auction 41 (27.05.2007), lot 2691 (Antoninus Pius).
30. See e.g. LHS Numismatics, Auction 96 (08–09.05.2006), Coins of Peloponnesos. The BCD Collection, lot 1326 (Iulia Domna).
31. See e.g. BCD Korinth, lot 620 (Hadrian).
32. For city-founders on coins see Tselekas 2011b, p. 210ff, esp. pp. 214–6. Founding heroes were often eponymous for the cities and sometimes homonymous; for a few examples see cat. nos 20 (Kydonia / Kydon), 21 (Aineia / Aeneas), 42 (Taras / Taras) and 177 (Byzantium / Byzas).
33. For the role of Tyche in general, from the late fourth century BC onwards, see Matheson 1994a, esp. p. 22ff.
34. Turreted heads on coins are seemingly rare during the fourth century BC; they should not be confused with some heads wearing *polos* or *stephane*; see e.g. Broucke 1994, p. 39, fig. 20. The female head wearing a mural crown on coins of Euagoras II (361–351 BC) and Pnytagoras (351–332 BC), kings of Salamis in Cyprus — see Broucke 1994, p. 36, fig. 17, and Matheson 1994b, p. 111, no. 22, respectively — may be better identified as Aphrodite than Tyche.
35. Eutychides of Sicyon *floruit ca.* 296–293 BC (Plinius, *Naturalis historia*, 34.51). Eutychides' original is lost and known only from Roman copies; the earliest depiction of the entire statue appears on the coins of Tigranes II the 'Great' of Armenia, after 83 BC; Stansbury-O'Donnell 1994, p. 55, fig. 32 (as Tigranes 'I').
36. Pollitt 1986, p. 3; Broucke 1994, p. 39ff. Generally speaking, it may not be easy each time to discern an artist's intention to render Tyche, or a city goddess, or the assimilation of both. In any case, if '[t]he iconography of the city Tyche is in need of a new approach, which should start *not* from an attempt to recover the work by Eutychides… …but from a study of the personification within the context of the Syro-Phoenician towns and their traditions' (Ridgway 1990, pp. 233ff, 243, n. 24, esp. p. 244), this should be examined also in numismatic terms.
37. Bronze *semuncia* with turreted bust (Roma?), 217–215 BC; *RRC* 39/5.

38. The legend under the head reads ALEXANDREA or ALEXSANDREA; *denarii* of moneyer M. Aemilius Lepidus, 61 BC (*RRC* 419/2). This issue was struck probably in honour of the moneyer's homonymous ancestor, who had been reportedly sent as an ambassador and guardian to the minor Ptolemy V in 201 BC.
39. See also e.g. Tselekas 2011b, p. 217, nos 460–1 (Smyrna).
40. Some other cases can be mentioned, such as the gold multiples of Magnentius with the turreted figure of Aquileia (AD 351), or the half-*siliquae* of Julius Nepos (AD 474–5), Romulus Augustus (AD 475–6) and Zeno with the personification of Ravenna (AD 476–477, 480–491).
41. *Cf.* the *Urbs Roma* 'medallion' series struck *ca.* AD 330–354 at Rome (*RIC* VII 315–6, 349, *RIC* VIII 390–1) and by other mints too.
42. See e.g. Numismatica Ars Classica, Auction 65 (19.05.2012), lot 3442.
43. There is a striking *comparandum* in the Hamburg Staats- und Universitätsbibliothek, Ms. 151 (*Liber historiarum Romanorum* or *Storie de Troja et de Roma*, *ca.* 1282), fol. 97v: Seated Rome holds palm-branch and a T-O map globe; in such a map the world is divided into three sectors formed by a 'T' placed within an 'O'.
44. The theme was employed by Cola di Rienzo (1313–1354) for one of his banners in the takeover of Rome (May 1347): 'The first banner ... depicted Rome, sitting ... with the world in one hand and a palm in the other' (*Vita di Cola di Rienzo*, *ca.* 1358; transl. J. Wright, *The Life of Cola di Rienzo*, Toronto 1975, p. 41). Coins issued by Cola as tribune also bear the legend *Roma caput mundi*.
45. For an analogous representation of the city walls of Nicaea in the period AD 253–268 see Holt 2010.
46. See in the present volume, H. Papageorgiadou, 'Writing and imprinting the history of the Roman world', fig. 11.
47. See in the present volume, C. Morrisson, '*Kharaktēr*: the history of Byzantium and beyond in words and images', fig. 5.
48. Tsangari 2011b, p. 153; Tselekas 2011a, p. 205, no. 422.
49. Tsangari 2011b, p. 154, no. 332.
50. BCD Korinth, lots 867 (nymph), 865 (location); both under Septimius Severus.
51. Tsangari 2011a, pp. 147–8; Tselekas 2011a, p. 419.
52. Neapolis in Campania; see *HN Italy* 558 and p. 68.
53. Ravel 1928, nos 116, 123.
54. Robinson 1946, pp. 17, 19, no. 24, pl. V.24.
55. Robinson 1946, p. 19, nos 25–8, pl. V.25–6.
56. *RIC* I^2 440–1 (*ca.* 65 AD); see also in the present volume, H. Papageorgiadou, 'Writing and imprinting the history of the Roman world', fig. 8.
57. *RIC* II 631–2.
58. BCD Korinth, lot 625 (Hadrian).
59. Correlating literary evidence and coin imagery can lead to fascinating paths, however it may be true to an extent, especially during (Classical) antiquity, that '[a]rtists were illustrating stories, not texts'; for this discussion see Small 2003, esp. pp. 6–7, 36, 143–5, 114–6, 152–4.
60. Wright 1995, p. 35.
61. Wright 1995, esp. pp. 34, 41, 125.
62. See further Tsangari 2011c.
63. As e.g. on the gold staters of Cyrene; *SNG Cop.* 1209.
64. *RRC* 39/4 and p. 719.
65. *DOC* 3/1, pp. 57–8.
66. Tsigarida 2011, p. 155, n. 95.
67. The New York Sale XXVII (04.01.2012), The Prospero Collection of Ancient Greek Coins, lot 290.
68. Numismatica Ars Classica, Auction 33 (06.04.2006), lot 598.
69. For an overview see Gurval 1997.
70. *RRC* 390/1.
71. On this matter see indicatively: Barton 1995; Lewis 2008.

72. Gilliard 1964, esp. p. 141.
73. The New York Sale XVII (09.01.2008), lot 144; for this series see Maravelia 2010, p. 38ff.
74. Classical Numismatic Group, Triton V (15.01.2001), lot 1729.
75. Spengler and Sayles 1992, pp. 81–3, esp. 82.
76. J. L. Borges, *Dreamtigers* (or *The Maker*), Austin, TX 1964 (originally *El hacedor*, Buenos Aires 1960).

Bibliography & Abbreviations

Addison 1761: Addison, J., 'Dialogues upon the usefulness of ancient medals...', in: *The Works of the Late Right Honorable Joseph Addison, Esq., Volume the First*, Birmingham 1761 (London 1721), pp. 413–537.

Alvarez 2005: Alvarez, D., '«Poetical Cash»: Joseph Addison, antiquarianism, and aesthetic value', *Eighteenth-Century Studies* 38/3 (2005), pp. 509–31.

Ault 1941: Ault, N., 'Pope and Addison', *Review of English Studies* 17, no. 68 (1941), pp. 428–51.

Bagrow and Skelton 1985: Bagrow, L. and Skelton, R. A., *History of Cartography*, Chicago (2nd ed.).

Bartlett 1968: Bartlett, J., *Familiar Quotations*, Boston (14th ed.).

Barton 1995: Barton, T., 'Augustus and Capricorn: astrological polyvalency and imperial rhetoric', *Journal of Roman Studies* 85 (1995), pp. 33–51.

BCD Korinth: Numismatik Lanz München, Auktion 105 (26.11.2001), Münzen von Korinth, Sammlung BCD.

Brodersen 2001: Brodersen, K., 'The presentation of geographical knowledge for travel and transport in the Roman world: *itineraria non tantum adnotata sed etiam picta*', in: C. Adams and R. Laurence (eds), *Travel and Geography in the Roman Empire*, London / New York, pp. 7–21.

Broucke 1994: Broucke, P. B. F. J., 'Tyche and the fortune of cities in the Greek and Roman world', in: S. B. Matheson (ed.), *An Obsession with Fortune: Tyche in Greek and Roman Art*, Yale University Art Gallery Bulletin, New Haven, pp. 34–49.

Carlucci and Barber 2001: Carlucci, A. and Barber, P. (eds), *Lie of the Land: The Secret Life of Maps*, London.

***DOC* 3:** Grierson, Ph., *Catalogue of the Byzantine Coins in the Dumbarton Oaks Collection and in the Whittemore Collection. Vol. 3. Part 1: Leo III to Michael III, 717–867. Part 2: Basil I to Nicephorus III, 867–1081*, Washington, DC 1973.

Dreyer 1905: Dreyer, J. L. E., *A History of Astronomy from Thales to Kepler*, New York 1953 (originally titled *History of the Planetary Systems from Thales to Kepler*, Cambridge 1905).

Faller 2011: Faller, S. A., 'The world according to Cosmas Indicopleustes – Concepts and illustrations of an Alexandrian merchant and monk', *Transcultural Studies* 1 (2011), pp. 193–232.

Fowler 2011: Fowler, R. L., '*Mythos* and *logos*', *Journal of Hellenic Studies* 131 (2011), pp. 45–66.

Gilliard 1964: Gilliard, F. D., 'Notes on the coinage of Julian the Apostate', *Journal of Roman Studies* 54 (1964), pp. 135–41.

Gurval 1997: Gurval, R. A., 'Caesar's comet: the politics and poetics of an Augustan myth', *Memoirs of the American Academy in Rome* 42 (1997), pp. 39–71.

Harley and Woodward 1987–1998: Harley, J. B. and Woodward, D., *The History of Cartography*, 4 vols, Chicago / London.

Heath 1932: Heath, T. L., *Greek Astronomy*, New York 1991 (London 1932).

***HN Italy*:** Rutter, N. K. *et al.* (eds), *Historia Numorum: Italy*, London 2001.

Holt 2010: Holt, W. C., 'The walls of Nicaea', *Celator* 24/4 (April 2010), pp. 6–18.

Johnston 1967: Johnston, A. E. M., 'The earliest preserved Greek map: a new Ionian coin type', *Journal of Hellenic Studies* 87 (1967), pp. 86–94.

Lévi-Strauss 1963: Lévi-Strauss, C., *Structural Anthropology*, transl. C. Jacobson and B. Grundfest Schoepf, New York.

Lewis 2008: Lewis, A.-M., 'Augustus and his horoscope reconsidered', *Phoenix* 62 (2008), pp. 308–37.

Maravelia 2010: A.-A. Maravelia, 'Coins in the World and the World (=Cosmos) in Coins: A Cosmographic Approach', in: *Proceedings of The Fourth International Forum of Calligraphy, Writing and Inscriptions in the World throughout the Ages "Coins in the World" (16–18 March 2009), Abgadiyat* 5, Alexandria, pp. 33–49.

Matheson 1994a: Matheson, S. B., 'The goddess Tyche', in: S. B. Matheson (ed.), *An Obsession with Fortune: Tyche in Greek and Roman Art*, Yale University Art Gallery Bulletin, New Haven, pp. 18–33.

Matheson 1994b: Matheson, S. B., 'Catalogue of the exhibition', in: S. B. Matheson (ed.), *An Obsession with Fortune: Tyche in Greek and Roman Art*, Yale University Art Gallery Bulletin, New Haven, pp. 106–18.

Meadows 2002: Meadows, A. R., '«Satrapal» issue', in: A. Meadows and U. Wartenberg (eds), *Coin Hoards, Vol. IX: Greek Hoards*, London, p. 209 [part of: R. H. J. Ashton *et al.*, 'The Pixodarus Hoard (*CH* 9.421)', pp. 159–243].

Mildenberg 1993: Mildenberg, L., 'Über das Münzwesen im Reich der Achämeniden', *Archäologische Mitteilungen aus Iran* 26 (1993), pp. 55–79 [republished in: U. Hübner and E. A. Knauf (eds), *Vestigia Leonis: Studien zur antiken Numismatik Israels, Palästinas und der östlichen Mittelmeerwelt*, Fribourg / Göttingen 1998, pp. 3–30].

Pollitt 1986: Pollitt, J. J., *Art in the Hellenistic Age*, Cambridge.

Popper 1957: Popper, K., 'Philosophy of science: a personal report', in: C. A. Mace (ed.), *British Philosophy in the Mid-Century*, New York, pp. 153–91.

Ravel 1928: Ravel, O., *The "Colts" of Ambracia*, New York.

***RIC* I^2:** Sutherland, C. H. V., *The Roman Imperial Coinage, Vol. I: From 31 BC to AD 69*, London 19842.

***RIC* II:** Mattingly, H. and Sydenham, E., *The Roman Imperial Coinage, Vol. II: Vespasian to Hadrian*, London 1926.

***RIC* VII:** Bruun, P. M., *The Roman Imperial Coinage, Vol. VII: Constantine and Licinius, A.D. 313–337*, London 1966.

***RIC* VIII:** Kent, J. P. C., *The Roman Imperial Coinage, Vol. VIII: The Family of Constantine I, A.D. 337–364*, London 1981.

Ridgway 1990: Ridgway, S. B., *Hellenistic Sculpture I: The Styles of ca. 331–200 B.C.*, Bristol.

Robinson 1946: Robinson, E. S. G., 'Rhegion, Zankle-Messana and the Samians', *Journal of Hellenic Studies* 66 (1946), pp. 13–20.

***RRC*:** Crawford, M. H., *Roman Republican Coinage*, Cambridge 1974.

Small 2003: Small, J. P., *The Parallel Worlds of Classical Art and Text*, Cambridge.

***SNG Cop.*:** *Sylloge Nummorum Graecorum. The Royal Collection of Coins and Medals, Danish National Museum*, Copenhagen 1942–1979.

Spengler and Sayles 1992: Spengler, W. F. and Sayles, W. G., *Turkoman Figural Bronze Coins and Their Iconography. Vol. I: The Artuqids*, Lodi, WI.

Stansbury-O'Donnell 1994: Stansbury-O'Donnell, M. D., 'Reflections of the Tyche of Antioch in literary sources and on coins', in: S. B. Matheson (ed.), *An Obsession with Fortune: Tyche in Greek and Roman Art*, Yale University Art Gallery Bulletin, New Haven, pp. 50–63.

Tsangari 2011a: Tsangari, D., 'River deities', in: D. Tsangari (ed.), *Myth and Coinage. Representations, Symbolisms and Interpretations from the Greek Mythology*, Athens 2011, pp. 146–9.

Tsangari 2011b: Tsangari, D., 'Nymphs', in: D. Tsangari (ed.), *Myth and Coinage. Representations, Symbolisms and Interpretations from the Greek Mythology*, Athens 2011, pp. 150–55.

Tsangari 2011c: Tsangari, D., 'Helios', in: D. Tsangari (ed.), *Myth and Coinage. Representations, Symbolisms and Interpretations from the Greek Mythology*, Athens 2011, pp. 156–9.

Tselekas 2011a: Tselekas, P., 'Nature and myth', in: D. Tsangari (ed.), *Myth and Coinage. Representations, Symbolisms and Interpretations from the Greek Mythology*, Athens 2011, pp. 204–9.

Tselekas 2011b: Tselekas, P., 'Foundation myths of cities', in: D. Tsangari (ed.), *Myth and Coinage. Representations, Symbolisms and Interpretations from the Greek Mythology*, Athens 2011, pp. 210–7.

Tsigarida 2011: Trigarida, B., 'Chalcidice', in: R. J. Lane Fox (ed.), *Brill's Companion to Ancient Macedon: Studies in the Archaeology and History of Macedon, 650 BC – 300 AD*, Leiden / Boston, pp. 137–58.

Weisser 2009: Weisser, B., 'Funde aus Milet: XXIII. Ein Hort in Milet mit Silbermünzen aus dem frühen 4. Jh. v. Chr.', *Archäologischer Anzeiger*, 2009/1, pp. 151–8.

Whitfield 1994: Whitfield, P., *The Image of the World. 20 Centuries of World Maps*, London.

Winstedt 1909: Winstedt, E. O. (ed.), *The Christian Topography of Cosmas Indicopleustes*, Cambridge.

Wright 1995: Wright, M. R., *Cosmology in Antiquity*, London / New York.

VI
COINAGE AND THE WRITING OF ANCIENT GREEK HISTORY

Andrew Meadows

The Ancient Greeks invented many things but, interestingly, neither writing nor coinage. As Herodotus tells us,[1] it was the Lydians 'who were the first people of whom we know to strike and use coins of gold and silver', probably in the late seventh century BC. Writing, on the other hand, is attested in Mesopotamia and Egypt as early as the fourth millennium BC. In origin, perhaps around 3200 BC, it seems to have come into being as an accounting tool – a means to quantify things and keep a record thereof. Written documents from the third millennium BC onwards record the purchase and sale of land and people, the rental of buildings and animals, and marriages, births and deaths. From the outset, therefore, writing had a close liaison with the concept of money and value.[2]

cat. no. 1; fig. 1: see cat. no. 12

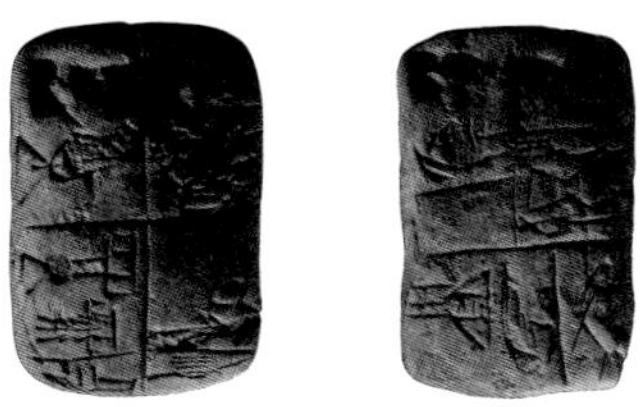

fig. 1

Texts with pictographic characters on red clay tablets, Mesopotamia, Uruk, *ca*. 3100–2850 BC.
Fondation Martin Bodmer, Cologny

This close liaison served to reinforce a restriction of use, however. Money before the advent of coinage was highly limited in form and function. Weighed amounts of precious metal might serve the function of money, as might some commodities. But the transfer of wealth by such means was limited to societal elites. For the vast majority of the populations of the empires of the Near East, there was no disposable wealth. Writing was a professional activity largely limited to the recording of the legal and economic activities of the elites. Few had the skills and leisure time to pursue the use of writing for such economically redundant activities as pleasure or curiosity.

But while they may not have invented the concept of writing or developed the new monetary form of coinage, it was the Greeks who saw the value of these and transformed them into the forms and uses that we recognize today. Coinage spread from its origins in Lydia to the city-states of Archaic and Classical Greece, where it became firmly entrenched within the economic activity of their citizens. From the gold and silver of the Lydians, coinage moved down the monetary scale in the fourth century BC to encompass also bronze. These lower-value coins facilitated transactions at a day-to-day level, as never before in human history.

fig. 2: see cat. no. 21

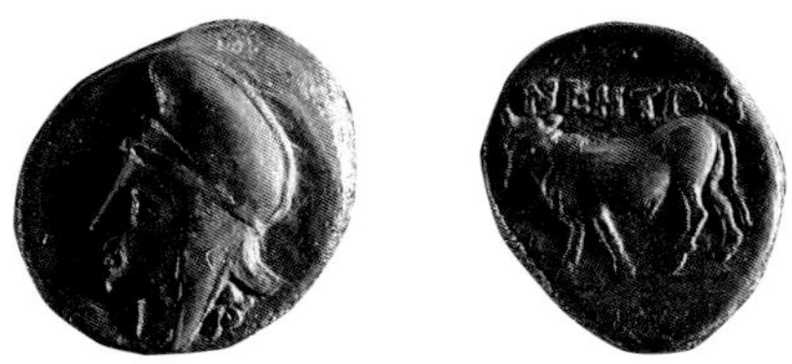

fig. 2

Bronze coin, Aineia, *ca.* 400–357/349 BC.
KIKPE Collection, Athens

Writing too was similarly taken up in the world of the city-state and moved beyond the realm of dry record-keeping to facilitate a whole host of activities. Citizens rights could be recorded, legal decisions published, political debate could be published. Plays, personal poetry, philosophical and genealogical treatises were transcribed, and amidst and out of these various creative endeavours emerged the first written histories.

Coinage and history were thus intertwined at a number of different levels. Coinage, on the one hand, stimulated the development of an environment wherein men might accumulate disposable income. As Aristotle saw it:

> *So when coinage had been now invented as an outcome of the necessary interchange of goods, there came into existence the other form of wealth-getting, trade, which at first no doubt went on in a simple form, but later became more highly organized as experience discovered the sources and methods of exchange that would cause most profit. Hence arises the idea that the art of wealth-getting deals specially with money, and that its function is to be able to discern from what source a large supply can be procured, as this art is supposed to be creative of riches and wealth;...*[3]

Success at business brought with it time for leisure, for which the Greek word was σχολὴ (*scholē*), and the appropriate use for such leisure time was inquiry. Hence the word for leisure came to be mean study and gives rise to the modern English words of school and scholarship.[4] The word for inquiry, ἱστορία (*historia*) gives rise to the modern words for History in many languages. But history did not spring fully formed into the world of literary endeavour. The earliest historians saw themselves as successors to a tradition of poets who recorded the deeds of the remote past. The most familiar of these to us today is Homer, the 'author' of the *Iliad* and the *Odyssey*, but no less important in the development of the historical genre is the poet Hesiod, whose works have their origins in part in the 'wisdom literature' of the Near East. In part practical didactic (*Works and Days*), in part catalogues owing a clear debt the bureaucratic origins of writing (*Theogony*, *Catalogue of Women*), the work of Hesiod is a crucial link between the old world of functional writing and the new world of literary endeavour. Hesiod the man, insofar as we can reconstruct his biography, is also emblematic of this change. He is the first poet to have left us his own name, and his claimed origins – the son of a poor emigrant from Asia Minor, cheated in part out of his inheritance – exemplifies the ability of the low-born individual to find his voice in the new economic environment of central Greece. In Hesiod too,[5] we find the first indications of the divisive nature of the accumulation of wealth: 'a neighbour envies his neighbour if he sees him hastening towards wealth'. fig. 3: see cat. no. 95

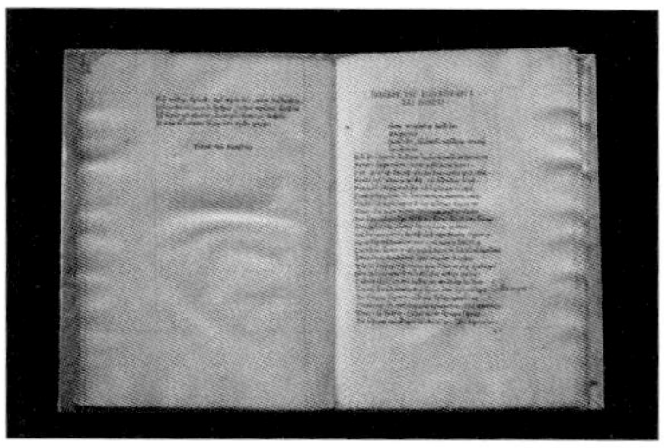

fig. 3

Hesiod, *Opera et Dies*, *ca*. 1479/80.
Fondation Martin Bodmer, Cologny

If Hesiod's catalogues were focused on what was (to us, but perhaps not to him) a mythical past, his successors sought to close the gap by cataloguing the lives of mortal men who intervened between the days of gods and heroes and the times of the authors themselves. A tradition of genealogies, again recording the administrative lists in which writing has its origins, sprang up, and was exemplified by the proto-father of History, Hecataeus of Miletus. Hecataeus, we are told, travelled 'to Thebes in Egypt, where he compiled a genealogy connecting himself in descent through sixteen generations with a god'. This information is passed down to us by the man usually described as the

Father of History, Herodotus.[6] Herodotus, whose work survives in its entirety, wrote around the middle of the fifth century BC. He is the first author to provide us with an explicit statement of the 'historical' aims of his work:

> *This is the account of the enquiry (ἱστορία, historia), of Herodotos of Halicarnassos, provided so that mortal events shall not be erased with time, and so that the great and marvellous deeds of Greeks and Barbarians shall not go without honour, in all other respects, but particularly regarding the reasons why they went to war with each other.*[7]

Herodotus emphasizes that his interest is in the actions of mortals, a preoccupation that places him in the new tradition of 'history' rather than 'mythology'. His motivation is to record these events, to make sure that they are not forgotten, again reminding us of one of the primary functions of writing. But at the last he betrays his particular interest in undertaking this activity. He wants to explain why a war broke out. In tracing the origins of history and of the spread of coinage, conflict – whether between Greek and Barbarian or neighbour and neighbour – is never far from the surface.

fig. 4: see cat. no. 14

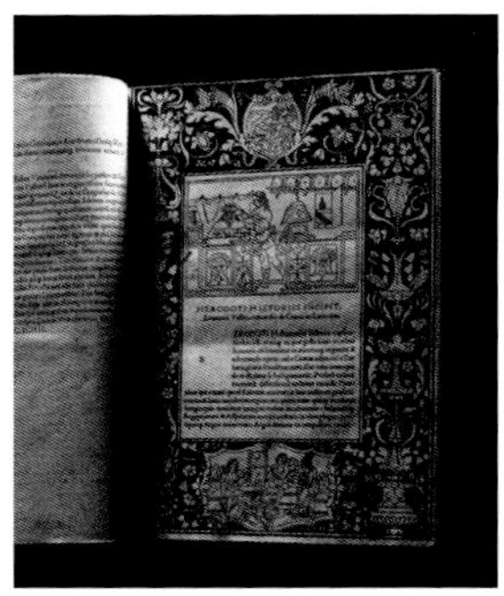

fig. 4

Herodotus, *Historiae…*, Venice, 1494.
Fondation Martin Bodmer, Cologny

But if it is Herodotus who first brings us explicit statement of the desire to explain the conflicts between men through historical discourse, it is his successor, Thucydides, who is the first fully to articulate the role of money in the power-rivalries that give rise to war. Writing in the later fifth century BC, Thucydides, an Athenian, sought to lay out the causes and course of the great conflict between his home city and its empire and the Spartans and theirs. For Thucydides it was the accumulation of money (χρήματα, *chremata*) that enabled a state to be truly prepared for war. As the Spartan king Archidamus is made to say:

> *Let no one call us cowards if we many cities decide not to attack a single city immediately. For their allies are as numerous as ours, and they pay money (chremata). And war is not so much a matter of arms as it is of expense, through which arms come to be used, particularly for a land power fighting against a naval power. Let us first, therefore, provide for this expense, rather than being carried away by the words of our allies.*[8]

From Hesiod to Thucydides the circle is complete: wealth gives rise to conflict; but wealth is also required to be successful in conflict.

There is, then, a set of strong conceptual, even causal, links between the development of writing and coinage. Coinage provided the opportunity to write more than just legal documents. Coinage and the accumulation of wealth also provided some of central themes of the early historians. On the other hand, while there no doubt exists a causal relationship between the adoption of coinage by the Greeks and the invention of history, there is a far more pragmatic link in that the coins issued by many early Greek states also serve as some of the best evidence for the nature of those cities and their preoccupations.

It is, of course, no coincidence that the import of coinage to the Greek world around the middle of the sixth century BC coincides with the first stirrings of the Greek literary efflorescence. So, some of the first coins of the Greeks and their neighbours can often serve as supplements to the historians born at the same time. To take one early example, the statement of Herodotus quoted above, that the Lydians were the first to use coins of gold and silver is spectacularly confirmed by the evidence of the first gold and silver coins. Long known as Croeseids, after the legendarily wealthy Lydian king Croesus, recent archaeological excavation at the Lydian capital city of Sardis has confirmed that these were first issued during the reign of this king. The importance of such confirmation is not to be underestimated. As we have seen above, Herodotus and his contemporaries were pioneers in the recording of 'facts' about people, within a literary discourse that had its origins in the recording of myth. For Herodotus, writing in the mid-fifth century BC, king Croesus and his Lydian predecessors were a century and more in the past, and had left no historical accounts of their activities. The circumstances he is here describing are as remote from him as the First World War is from us, but with no contemporary documents or histories to draw on. The evidence of coinage thus counts for a lot in the verification of the stories Herodotus tells.

We can in this way test individual statements of the ancient historians, but we can also examine their preconceptions. So, the comments of Thucydides on the monetary disparity between Athens and its allies and the Peloponnesians during the Peloponnesian War can be seen reflected in the coinages produced by the two sides. That of Athens is colossal, the largest to that date ever produced. That of Sparta is non-existent: the slack was taken up to a certain extent by the mints of Corinth and Sicyon, but even these produced just a fraction of the output of the Athenian mint. The sheer size of Athenian output confirms also Archidamus' assessment of the expense involved in maintaining a naval power. And if we can trace Athens' rise and the acme of her political power in her coinage, then we can also see her demise. When catastrophe arrived, towards the end of Peloponnesian War, and the Athenian coffers were emptied, we see the very tangible result of this in the production of plated silver coins with a copper

cat. no. 4

core, in place of the solid silver coinage that had gone before. Such coins seem to be behind a passage of Aristophanes' *Frogs*,[9] where the Chorus complains about the debased nature of the city and its coinage:

> *Chorus: It has often seemed to us that the city has suffered the*
> *same thing with respect to the good and the bad among the citizens*
> *as happened to old coinage and fresh gold.*
> *For we do not use these, which are free of counterfeiting*
> *but apparently the best of all coins*
> *and the only ones struck well and true*
> *among Greeks and Barbarians everywhere.*
> *But rather we use these shabby bronzes*
> *Struck yesterday and the day before with the worst possible striking.*

fig. 5: see cat. no. 5;
fig. 6: see cat. no. 16

Again, coins meet texts and confirm a picture.[10]

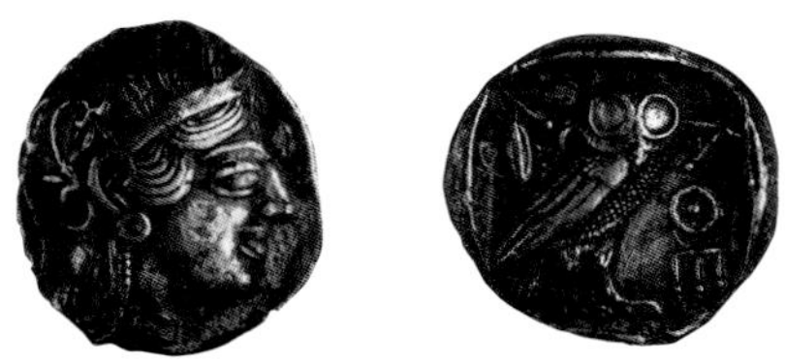

fig. 5

Subaerate tetradrachm, Athens, 406/5 BC.
KIKPE Collection, Athens

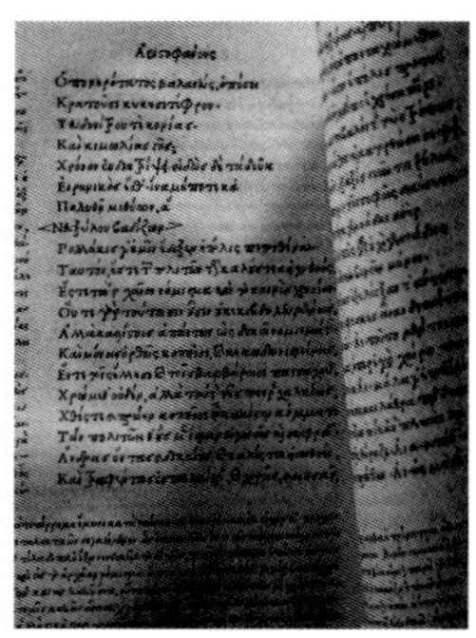

fig. 6

Aristophanes, *Comediae Novem*... Venice, 1498.
Fondation Martin Bodmer, Cologny

The fact that coins could be used to write history was not, of course, lost upon their issuers. The mass-produced nature of coinage lent itself perfectly to the transmission of messages in a world before printing presses. Potentially, tens of thousands of coins could be struck from just a single engraved die. So, when hundreds of dies were produced, as they were for some of the larger coinages, millions of coins resulted.

The medium of coinage was thus perfect for the transmission of messages to a wide audience, but also through its durable nature, coinage could guarantee the survival of those messages long beyond the lifetime of the issuer. Today, after all, we can still read the messages that the ancient Greeks left us on their coins.

The earliest coins had little to say beyond the name of the issuing people, but even this simple fact should not be forgotten. When we look at an ancient coin we often focus only on the image it bears, but the legend that accompanies this images serves an important part in telling us whose image it is. Thus, for example, the legend ΑΘΕ tells us that the head of Athena and her bird, the owl, are intended to represent the people and city of Athens. This is important information about Athens and its self-perception. Less immediately obvious is another facet of this legend. The letters used to describe the issuers (ΑΘΕ) preserve an archaic spelling of the city's name. By the end of the fifth century BC all other official documents of the city had moved to a different form (ΑΘΗ). Coinage remained archaic in appearance – archaism was a value appreciated in coinage by the Athenians, as the passage of Aristophanes quoted above confirms. So the legend on Athenian coinage is a highly-loaded messenger that tells us not just who the issuer was, but what they thought about their coins.

The power of writing and naming on coinage became powerful too for individuals who issued coins. We can observe this phenomenon right at the birth of coinage, when some of the earliest issuers are marked with personal names of the powerful men behind them. Initially this naming may have served a purely administrative function: the earliest-known Greek coin legend reads 'I am the badge of Phanes' (ΦΑΝΕΟΣ ΕΜΙ ΣΗΜΑ), a formulation that emulates some inscriptions on seals used to sign documents. It seems that the legend on the coin was designed to 'seal' or guarantee its value.[11]

But the legends subsequently applied to coins by individuals in the Classical and Hellenistic period go far beyond such mundane administrative purpose, and serve rather to monumentalize the individuals they name and, increasingly, boast of their position in the world. The major change in this context was brought by Alexander the Great. Alexander did not introduce his portrait to his coinage, but his name was omnipresent. His coins, in both gold and silver, read ΒΑΣΙΛΕΩΣ ΑΛΕΞΑΝΔΡΟΥ or just plain ΑΛΕΞΑΝΔΡΟΥ. But, by virtue of the fact that they were produced at some 30 different mints throughout his empire, they became testament to the extent of his conquests, and served long after his death as evidence of the massive change he brought to the political and economic life of the Greek East. Moreover, even after his death, 'posthumous' issues in the name of Alexander continued to be produced by kings and cities, signed as if they were coins of Alexander himself.

But other kings would introduce their portraits to their coins, and gradually began to make their inscriptions more elaborate too. In addition to the royal title it became

fig. 7: see cat. no. 152

common to add epithets, sometimes more than one, recording the virtues or divinity of the ruler. These served both to monumentalize the ruler in question and to disambiguate kings who may have shared their throne-name with a number of predecessors. Such inscriptions are thus self-conscious attempts by their issuers to preserve their place in a historical line. In some cases, such as the Greek kings in Bactria, the coin legends become some of our best evidence for the names and sequence of the rulers.

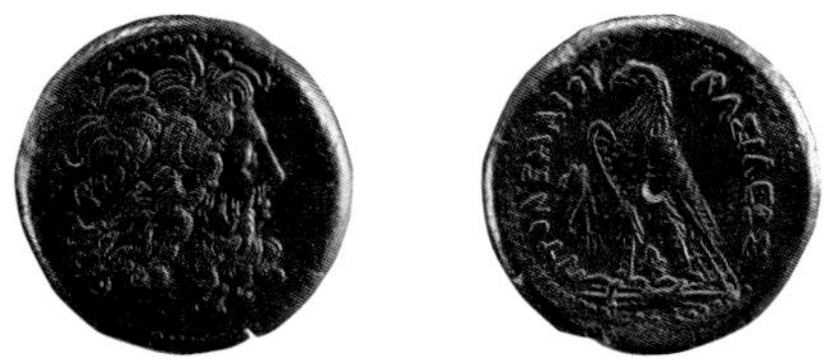

fig. 7

Bronze coin, Ptolemy III Euergetes (247/6–221 BC),
Alexandria, *ca.* 245–222 BC.
KIKPE Collection, Athens

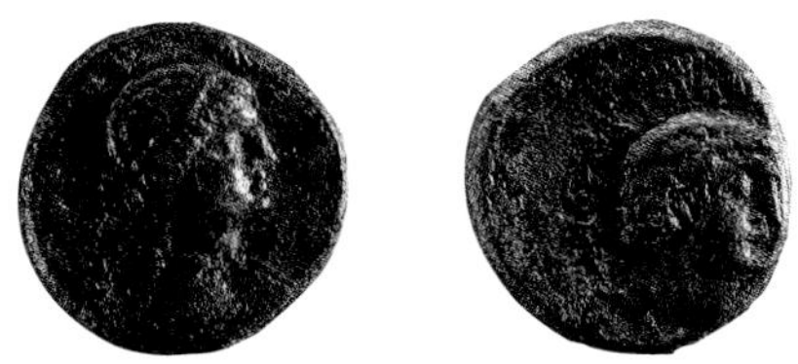

fig. 8

Bronze coin, Cleopatra VII (51–30 BC) and Mark Antony,
Chalcis sub Libano, 32/31 BC.
KIKPE Collection, Athens

In the writing that appeared on Greek coins we can trace another movement that took place in the Hellenistic period: the growing influence of Rome. On the one hand this influence can be as simple as the change in disposition of the legend. Roman coins tended to have circular legends, rather than words in straight lines, and by the first century BC, legends were common on both sides of a Roman coin, not just on the reverse. And so Greek coins of the later first century BC begin to adopt both of these features. But the influence extends to content too. Roman coin inscriptions tend to tell us much more about the issuer. This tendency to become more verbose and to contain statements, not just words, also extended to Greek coinage by the end of the Hellenistic period. A fine example is provided by the coinage struck, apparently jointly, by Cleopatra VII and Mark Antony, in Coele Syria in the 30s BC. The legends on these coins, in Greek, ΒΑΣΙΛΙΣΣΑ ΚΛΕΟΠΑΤΡΑ ΘΕΑ ΝΕΩΤΕΡΑ (*Basilissa Kleopatra Thea Neōtera*) and ΑΝΤΩΝΙΟΣ ΑΥΤΟΚΡΑΤΩΡ ΤΡΙΤΟΝ ΤΡΙΩΝ ΑΝΔΡΩΝ (*Antōnios Autokratōr Triton Triōn Andrōn*), describe Cleopatra as the second goddess of that name, but Antony as a

Triumvir of the Roman Republic. They give us a fulsome statement about the nature of the royal couple's rule – she a queen, he a Roman magistrate – and their ambitions. fig. 8: see cat. no. 148

Thus, by the end of Greek coinage, writing has moved from beyond an adjunct to the design to occupy an independent position on the coin. In a sense we have come full circle from the first Greek coin inscription of Phanes. In these cases we do not need to infer our historical reconstruction from a single word. Rather, we can read the history straight from the object. Coin has become text, and communicates with us directly.

Notes

1. Herodotus, 1.94.
2. For a useful survey of the origins and early history of writing see Bottéro *et al.* 2000.
3. Aristotle, *Politics*,1257b. On the relationship between money and development of 'self-sufficiency' see Seaford 2004, pp. 242–55.
4. On coinage as a 'technology of the mind' see Meadows 2008, pp. 769–77.
5. Hesiod, *Works and Days*, ll. 23–24.
6. Herodotus, 2.143.
7. Herodotus, 1.1.
8. Thucydides, 1.83. On the relationship between Thucydides and money see Kallet-Marx 1993.
9. Aristophanes, *Frogs*, ll. 718–726.
10. For discussion of this passage and the plated coinage attributed to this period, see Figueira 1998, chapter 19.
11. On the relationship between seals and early coin design see, for example, von Reden 1995.

Bibliography & Abbreviations

Bottéro *et al.* 2000: Bottéro, J., Herrenschmidt, C. and Vernant, J. P., *Ancestor of the West: Writing, reasoning, and religion in Mesopotamia, Elam, and Greece*, Chicago.

Figueira 1998: Figueira, T. J., *The Power of Money: Coinage and Politics in the Athenian Empire*, Philadelphia.

Kallet-Marx 1993: Kallet-Marx, L., *Money, Expense, and Naval Power in Thucydides' History 1-5.24*, Berkeley / Los Angeles.

Meadows 2008: Meadows, A. R., 'Coinage', in: J. P. Oleson (ed.), *The Oxford Handbook of Engineering and Technology in the Classical World*, Oxford, pp. 769–77.

Seaford 2004: Seaford, R., *Money and the Early Greek Mind: Homer, philosophy, tragedy*, Cambridge.

von Reden 1995: von Reden, S., *Exchange in Ancient Greece*, London.

VII
THE FABULOUS WEALTH OF THE HELLENISTIC KINGS: COINAGE AND *WELTMACHTPOLITIK*

François de Callataÿ

Plutarch states clearly in his *Life of Cleomenes* that money is the driving force of war:

> *But he who first declared that money is the sinews of affairs would seem to have spoken with special reference to the affairs of war. … And indeed, just as athletes who have taken a full course of training, in time bear down and overpower those who are merely graceful and skilful, so also did Antigonus, who engaged in the war with large resources, wear out and prostrate Cleomenes, who could only meagrely and with difficulty provide pay for his mercenaries and sustenance for his citizen-soldiers…*[1]

The history of Hellenistic royal coinage rarely deviates from this diction. The two major figures who begin and end this practice, Alexander the Great of Macedon and Mithridates VI Eupator of Pontus respectively, illustrate it best.[2]

When Alexander launched his campaign against the Persian Empire in the spring of 334 BC, the treasury of the Macedonian State was empty. Within a few years, he seized the immense wealth of the treasuries that the great Achaemenid kings had accumulated over many centuries.[3] The conquest of Darius's camp after Alexander's victory at the Battle of Issus in November 333 BC allowed the Macedonians to acquire an astonishing amount of wealth early on.[4] But the peak came with the sack of Persepolis, as described by Quintus Curtius:

He had either stormed or received in surrender many cities filled with regal opulence, but the riches of this city surpassed all that had gone before. Into it the barbarians had heaped the wealth of all Persia; gold and silver had been amassed, a vast amount of clothing, furniture designed not for use but for luxurious display ... They rent the royal robes, as each one dragged a part into his possession, they broke with mattocks vases of priceless art, nothing was left un-injured or carried off whole, each one carried the broken limbs of statues as he had torn them off ... So vast an amount of wealth is said to have been takenas almost to be beyond belief. But we shall either have to feel doubtful about other particulars also, or believe that there was in this city a treasure of 120,000 talents. For transporting this — for the king had decided to take it with him for use in war — he ordered camels and other beasts of burden to be brought together from Susa and Babylon.[5]

One hundred and twenty thousand talents did in fact represent a sum never seen before in the Greek and Mediterranean world: some 3,100 tons of silver — that is, almost the total yield of the Laurion mines yielded in more than two centuries of exploitation (estimated at approximately 3,500 tons) — or 720 million drachmas, enough to pay 100,000 men one drachma a day for 20 years.

fig. 1: see cat. no. 32

It was to pay the soldiers that the precious metal was originally converted into coins, just as Alexander's father, Philip, had done when he took over the Crenides mines:

After this he went to the city of Crenides, and having increased its size with a large number of inhabitants, changed its name to Philippi, giving it his own name, and then, turning to the gold mines in its territory, which were very scanty and insignificant, he increased their output so much by his improvements that they could bring him a revenue of more than a thousand talents. And because he had soon amassed a fortune from these mines, with the abundance of money he raised the Macedonian kingdom higher and higher to a greatly superior position, for with the gold coins which he struck, which came to be known from his name as Philippeioi, he organized a large force of mercenaries, and by using these coins for bribes induced many Greeks to become betrayers of their native lands.[6]

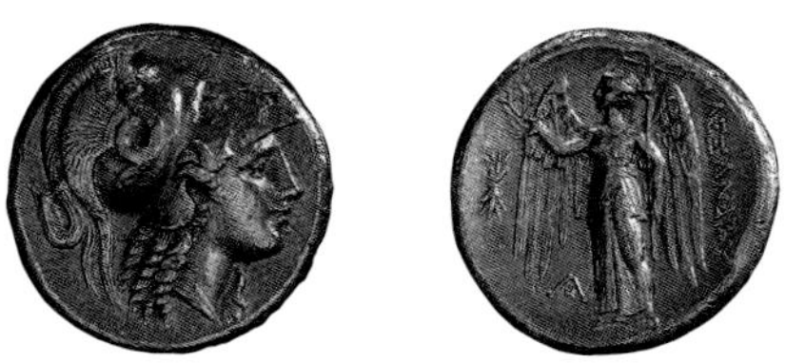

fig. 1

Gold double stater, Alexander the Great (336–323 BC), Aigeai(?), 336–323 BC.
Fondation Martin Bodmer, Cologny

Alexander, who had founded a new silver coinage in his name directly after his victory at Issus, struck enormous quantities of coins while he was still alive, even before his *Diadochoi*, or successors, prolonged and elaborated on these 'Alexander' issues, which, through the army, quickly became the international currency of the time.[7] Alexander did not share the vanity of his father, who chose to depict his own Olympic victories on his gold coins.[8] Instead, the silver 'Alexanders' depicted the head of a beardless fig. 2: see cat. no. 31 Heracles wearing the Nemean lion's hide on the obverse, as had the coins of most of the other kings who preceded him on the Macedonian throne. Although Alexander fig. 3 adopted, in late 333 BC, an ancient coin type without the intention of being identified with Heracles, his portrait was evident on it already in antiquity, as illustrated by the tetradrachms of Agathocles of Bactria in *ca.* 185–180 BC and the bronze coins of the Macedonian *koinon* in the third century AD.[9] fig. 4

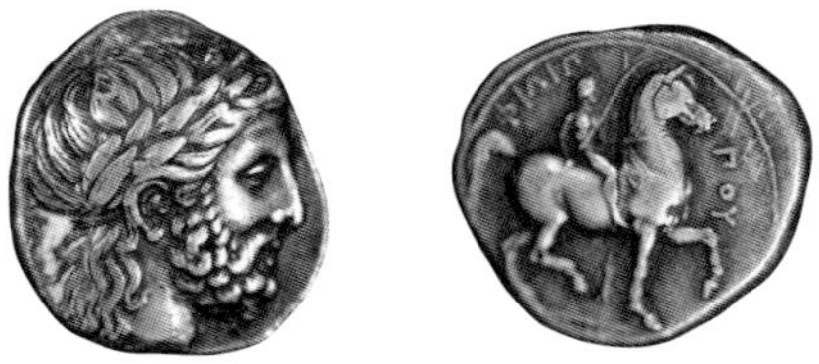

fig. 2

Silver tetradrachm, Philip II of Macedon (360/359–336 BC), Pella, 342/1–337/6 BC.
Fondation Martin Bodmer, Cologny

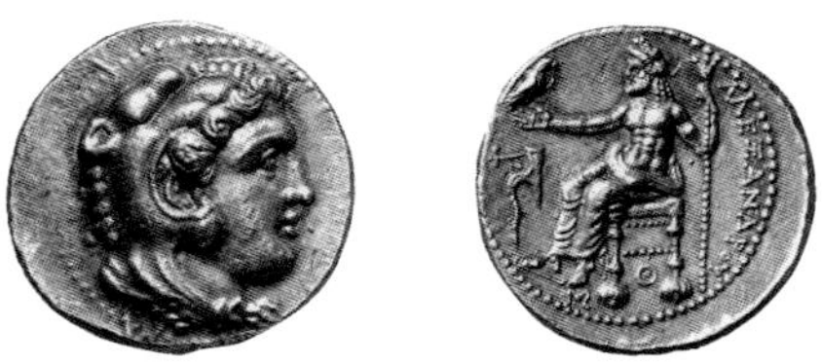

fig. 3

Tetradrachm of Alexander III the Great (336–323 BC), Tarsus, *ca.* 327–323 BC.
Triton XIV (04.01.2011), lot 71

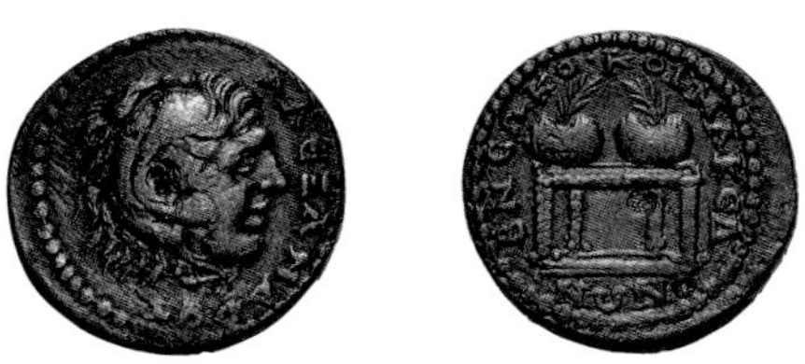

fig. 4

Bronze coin of the Macedonian *koinon* depicting Alexander as Heracles, Beroia (?), 3rd century AD.
Rauch, Auktion 88 (17.05.2011), lot 113

On the other hand, Alexander innovated on the reverse by adapting the iconographical type of the god Baal from the coinage of the Tarsus satrapy: Zeus sitting on a throne holding an eagle in his outstretched hand. Alexander granted only the best artists of his time the right to create his portrait: Lysippus in sculpture, Apelles in painting, and Pyrgoteles in miniature carving.[10] Plutarch left the following physical description of Alexander: '… the poise of the neck, which was bent slightly to the left, and the melting glance of his eyes, [Lysippus] has accurately observed'.[11]

fig. 5: see cat. no. 33

Alexander's most famous monetary portrait and probably the closest to the Lysippan model is that on the obverse of the Lysimachus coins. The diadem tying the king's hair is decorated with a ram's horn, a clear reference to the oracle he had received at the sanctuary of Zeus-Ammon at Siwa.

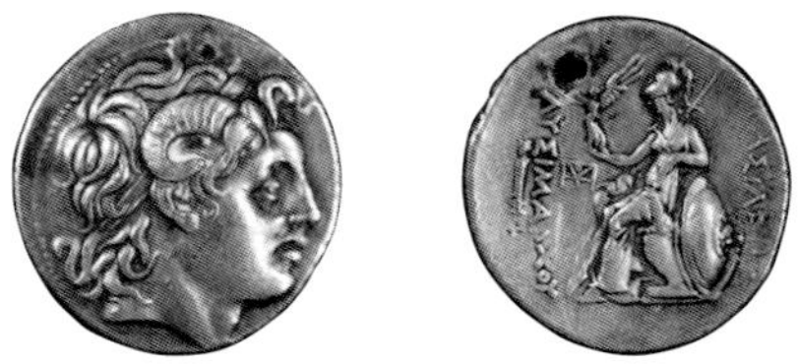

fig. 5

Silver tetradrachm, Lysimachus (306–281 BC), Lampsacus, 297/6–282/1 BC.
Fondation Martin Bodmer, Cologny

fig. 6: see cat. no. 34

Ptolemy, who was born a few years before Alexander but outlived him by a half century (367–283 BC) as ruler of Egypt, was the first to place Alexander's image on coins. On the reverse of the tetradrachms that he minted in 318 BC is Alexander's head covered by an elephant hide, as befits the conqueror of India, and a diadem with a ram's horn attached to it. According to Diodorus, Ptolemy used precious metals in order to engage mercenaries: 'In Asia, of those who had shared in the division of the satrapies, Ptolemy took over Egypt without difficulty and treated the inhabitants with kindness. Finding eight thousand talents in the treasury, he began to collect mercenaries and to form an army'.[12] Alternatively, when one had an army but not the means to pay for it, one also had to turn to war, as it is said of Pyrrhus: 'He returned to Epirus with eight thousand foot and five hundred horse, and since he had no money he sought for a war by which he could maintain his army. Some Gauls joined him, and he thereupon made an incursion into Macedonia, where Antigonus, the son of Demetrius, was reigning, designing to strip and plunder the country'.[13] And Plutarch adds: 'But the Gauls, a race insatiable of wealth, set themselves to digging up the tombs of the kings who had been buried there [at Aigeai/Vergina]; the treasure they plundered, the bones they insolently cast to the four winds'.[14] Manolis Andronikos spectacular discoveries at Vergina in November 1977 suggest that the Gauls did not take everything. In his *City of God*, Saint Augustine captured the violence of that time:

Justice being taken away, then, what are kingdoms but great robberies? … Indeed, that was an apt and true reply, which was given to Alexander the Great by a pirate who had been seized. For when that king had asked the man what he meant by keeping hostile possession of the sea, he answered with bold pride: 'What you mean by seizing the whole earth; but because I do it with a petty ship, I am called a robber, while you who does it with a great fleet are styled emperor'.[15]

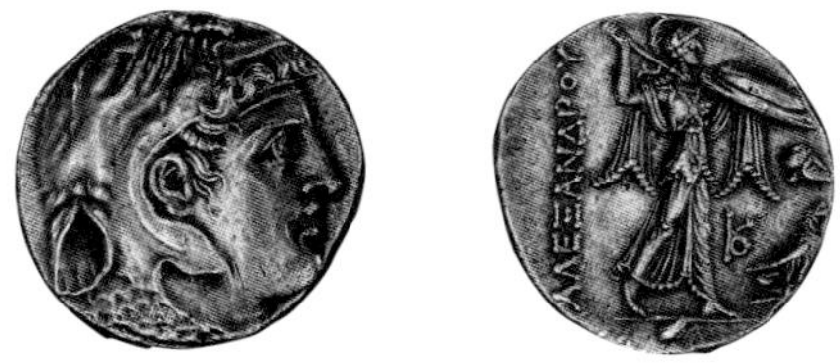

fig. 6

Silver tetradrachm, Ptolemy I Soter (311–281 BC), Alexandria, *ca.* 310–305 BC.
Fondation Martin Bodmer, Cologny

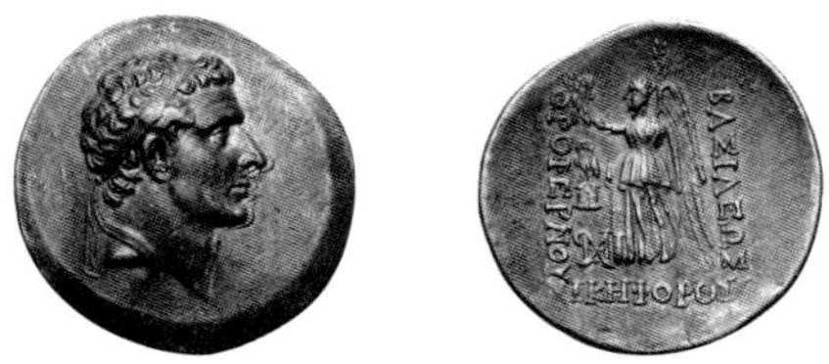

fig. 7

Silver tetradrachm of Orophernes (160–156 BC).
Gemini, Auction IV (08.01.2008), lot 211

During the first chaotic decades of the Hellenistic period, enormous stores were regularly captured allowing some to try their luck and sometimes even to found a kingdom, as in the case of Philetairus of Pergamon. The insatiability of kings or of those who sought to be kings often ended badly: 'Not a few men from lust for gain have sacrificed even their lives for money, among them Orophernes, the king of Cappadocia, who falling a victim to this passion perished him and lost his kingdom'.[16] Some sumptuous and very rare tetradrachms of Orophernes, the ephemeral king of Cappadocia, were found at Priene in Ionia where he was killed.[17] Constantine Cavafy evokes these coins in the eponymous poem he composed for this ruler: fig. 7

Orophernes[18]

The figure on this four drachma coin
who seems to have a smile on his face—
his beautiful, delicate face—
this is Orophernes, son of Ariarathes.

A child, they threw him out of Cappadocia,
out of his great ancestral palace,
and sent him to grow up in Ionia,
to be forgotten there among foreigners.

On those exquisite Ionian nights
when fearlessly, and entirely in a Greek way,
he came to know sensual pleasure totally.
In his heart, Asiatic always,
but in manners and language, a Greek;
with his turquoise jewelry, his Greek clothes,
his body perfumed with oil of jasmine,
he was the most handsome, the most perfect
of Ionia's handsome young men.

Later, when the Syrians entered Cappadocia
and made him king,
he became fully engrossed in his kingship
so as to enjoy himself in a new way each day,
greedily hoarding gold and silver,
delightedly gloating over
the piles of wealth glittering before his eyes.
As for worrying about the country and running it—
he had no idea what was going on around him.

The Cappadocians quickly got rid of him,
and he ended up in Syria, at the palace of Dimitrios,
where he spent his time amusing himself and loafing.
But one day unfamiliar thoughts
broke in on his completely idle life:
he remembered how through his mother Antiochis
and that old grandmother Stratoniki
he too was connected with the Syrian crown,
he too almost a Seleukid.
For a while he gave up lechery and drink,
and ineptly, half dazed,
tried to start an intrigue,
do something, come up with a plan;
but he failed pitifully and was reduced to nothing.

His end must have been recorded somewhere only to be lost:
or maybe history passed over it
and rightly didn't bother to notice
a thing so trivial.

The figure on this four drachma coin,
a trace of whose young charm can still be seen,
a ray of his poetic beauty—
this sensuous commemoration of an Ionian boy,
this is Orophernes, son of Ariarathes.

Fortunes changed hands in violent ways and one had to use cunning, like Eumenes of Cardia:

> *Eumenes, however, perceiving that, while they despised one another, they feared him and were on the watch for an opportunity to kill him, pretended to be in need of money, and got together many talents by borrowing from those who hated him most, in order that they might put confidence in him and refrain from killing him out of regard for the money they had lent him. The consequence was that the wealth of others was his body-guard, and that, whereas men generally preserve their lives by giving, he alone won safety by receiving.*[19]

According to the second book of the pseudo-Aristotelian *Economics*, warlords often resorted to temporary measures to appease the soldiery who were claiming their due. Large sums accompanied the armies[20] and those in charge of recruiting mercenaries.[21]

Generally, the mainland Greeks considered the Hellenistic rulers fabulously rich.[22] The pomp and great processions of Ptolemy II Philadelphus (*ca.* 279–278 BC)[23] and Antiochus IV at Daphne (166 or 165 BC)[24] have entered posterity.[25] Diodorus tells us that on that occasion Antiochus IV surpassed all of his predecessors.[26] Let us also recall how the Ptolemies and the Seleucids emulated each other when they rebuilt Rhodos after the 226 BC earthquake.[27] At approximately the same time, so Plutarch reports, king Agis of Sparta lamented that: '... he could not equal the other kings, since the servants and slaves of the satraps and overseers of Ptolemy and Seleucus had larger possessions than all the kings of Sparta put together ...'[28]. Agis, however, owned a considerable fortune of 600 silver talents in coins.[29] The plays of Plautus and Terence offer many examples of the Orient's proverbial riches, a *topos* of the New Comedy. Thus, for example, Pamphila's father 'would not earn for himself the mountains of the Persians, which are said to be of gold, to do that of which [she was] in dread',[30] whereas Demea in Terence's Adelphi refers to her brother Micio as a 'Babylonian'.[31] In Plautus's *Truculentus*, Stratophanes is the prototype of the *miles gloriosus*, the boastful, cowardly, and therefore fanfaron captain, who returned to his country enriched by conquest and was ridiculed for believing that he could conquer a heart with the gold that he had amassed.[32]

In the eyes of the Romans, even the Macedonian kings were surprisingly rich. At Paulus Aemilius's triumph in November 167 BC, after his victory at Pydna, Titus Livius marvelled at the wealth amassed by Perseus in thirty years, even though the Romans had stripped his father Philip V after their victory at Cynocephalus (Kynos Kephalai): fig. 8

> *Valerius Antias states that all the gold and silver coinage carried in the procession amounted to 120,000,000 sesterces* [i.e. 5,000 silver talents], *but from his own account of the number of wagons and the weight carried in each, the amount must undoubtedly have exceeded this. It is also asserted that a second sum equal to this had been either expended in the war or dispersed by the king during his flight to Samothrace, and this was all the more surprising, since all that money had been accumulated during the thirty years from the close of the war with Philip either as profits from the*

mines or from other sources of revenue, so that while Philip was very short of money, Perseus was able to commence his war with Rome with an overflowing exchequer.[33]

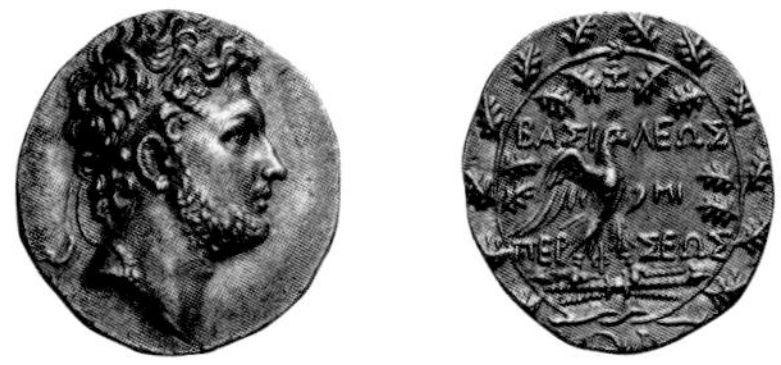

fig. 8

Silver tetradrachm of Perseus (179–168 BC).
Hess-Divo, Auktion 320 (26.10.2010), lot 121

After every military victory, the Romans fined the Hellenistic kings and states for large sums of money: 12,000 talents in twelve years was the sum specified in the Apamea Treaty (188 BC) following the defeat of Antiochus III,[34] 2,200 talents were to be paid by the Carthaginians in twenty years,[35] and 500 talents by the Aetolians in 189 BC.[36] Certainly, the money and loot exhibited in Rome during the triumphs, which Titus Livius described in detail, represent an important drain of precious metals from the Hellenistic world. It is less certain and not particularly obvious that the mass of coinage in circulation was greatly reduced as a result. Since the early second century BC, the Romans were the masters of the Mediterranean. Constantine Cavafy once again admirably describes the complexity of the cultural identities of that period in his poem *Philhellene*, which, moreover, refers to the coin engraver's art:

Philhellene[37]

Make sure the engraving is done skilfully.
The expression serious, majestic.
The diadem preferably somewhat narrow:
I don't like that broad kind the Parthians wear.
The inscription, as usual, in Greek:
nothing excessive, nothing pompous—
we don't want the proconsul to take it the wrong way:
he's always nosing things out and reporting back to Rome—
but of course giving me due honor.
Something very special on the other side:
some discus-thrower, young, good-looking.
Above all I urge you to see to it
(Sithaspis, for God's sake don't let them forget)
that after "King" and "Savior,"
they engrave "Philhellene" in elegant characters.
Now don't try to be clever

with your "where are the Greeks?" and "what things Greek
here behind Zagros, out beyond Phraata?"
Since so many others more barbarian than ourselves
choose to inscribe it, we will inscribe it too.
And besides, don't forget that sometimes
sophists do come to us from Syria,
and versifiers, and other triflers of that kind.
So we are not, I think, un-Greek.

The episode narrated is imaginary, as is the coin, but the context is plausible and the adjective 'Philhellene' was widely used by the Parthians, but also in Armenia and Characene.[38] fig. 9

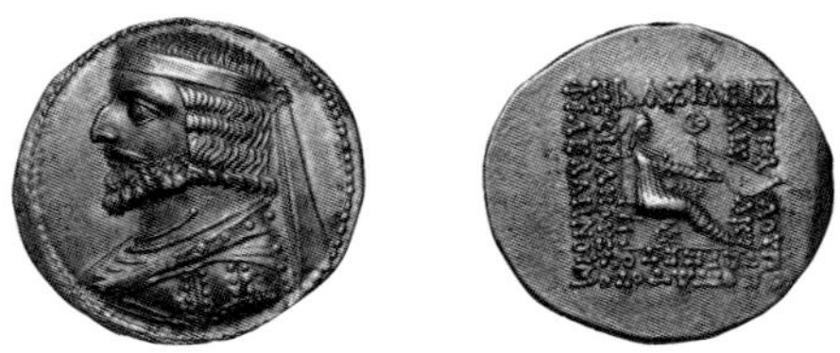

fig. 9

Silver tetradrachm of Orodes I of Parthia (90–80 BC), proclaiming himself 'Philhellene', Seleucia on the Tigris.
Roma Numismatics, Auction 3 (31.03.2012), lot 357

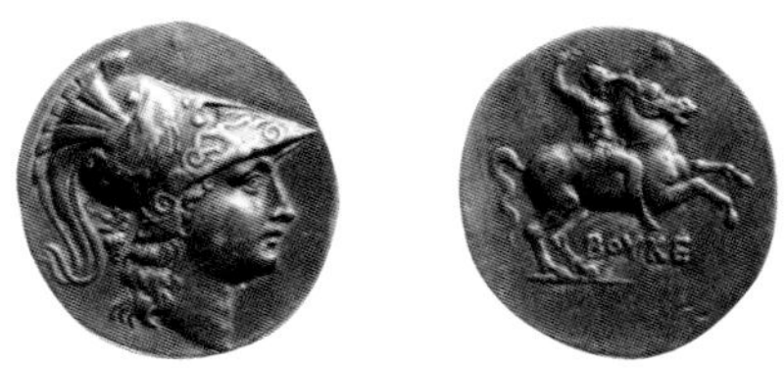

fig. 10

Renaissance medallion depicting Alexander on the obverse and Bucephalus on the reverse.
Oxford, Ashmolean Museum, Forgeries Collection, Christ Church

We usually end the Hellenistic world with Octavian's victory over Antony and Cleopatra at Actium in 31 BC. Alexander's figure, however, heroic and deified, enjoyed a huge critical success in the Middle Ages and the Renaissance, largely because of the many versions of the *Alexander Romance*. It is during the Renaissance that the iconographic subject of Alexander and Bucephalus emerged after the Athena and Pegasus figures on the unsigned coins of Corinth were mistaken for the Macedonian king and his horse.[39]

This confusion, which can only be explained by the success of the *Alexander Romance*, generated in the sixteenth century a series of metal fantasies, like the one illustrated here. Ardently enamoured with Antiquity, the curious and the antiquaries fig. 10

of the Renaissance did not only tried to write history based on medallions, the superiority of which over posthumous and biased texts Hubert Goltzius was the first to proclaim, but they also occasionally produced medallions on the basis of these texts.

Notes

1. Plutarch, *Cleomenes*, 27.1 and 27.4. On money as the driving force of war also see Cicero, *Philippics*, 5.3; Tacitus, *Histories*, 2.84.1; Quintus Curtius, *Histories of Alexander the Great*, 4.6; Diogenes Laërtius, *Lives and Opinions of Eminent Philosophers*, 4.7.48.
2. On the relation between Greek coinage and war, see among others Kraay 1984 and Callataÿ 2000.
3. Callataÿ 1989.
4. Arrian, *Anabasis*, 2.11.4 and Quintus Curtius, *Histories*, 3.11.20.
5. Quintus Curtius, *Histories*, 5.2–3.5 and 9. Ten thousand pairs of mules and five thousand camels, according to Plutarch (*Alexander*, 37.2).
6. Diodorus, *Library of History*, 16.8.6–7. On the coinage of Philip, see Le Rider 1977.
7. Price 1991; Le Rider 2003.
8. Plutarch, *Alexander*, 4.
9. Dahmen 2007. Also see Constantine Porphyrogenitus, *De Thematibus*, 2.2 [22].
10. Pliny, *Natural Histories*, 7.38 and 37.4; Cicero, *Ad familiares*, 5.12.
11. Plutarch, *Alexander*, 4.
12. Diodorus, *Library of History*, 18.14.1.
13. Plutarch, *Pyrrhus*, 26.2.
14. *Op. cit.*, 26.6.
15. Saint Augustine, *City of God*, 4.4.
16. Polybius, *Histories*, 32.11.1.
17. On this subject see Polybius, *Histories*, 33.6.1–9.
18. C. P. Cavafy, *Collected Poems*, transl. E. Keeley and Ph. Sherrard, ed. G. P. Savidis (revised edition), Princeton 1992.
19. Plutarch, *Eumenes*, 13.6.
20. See Diodorus, *Library of History*, 20.108.3.
21. *Op. cit.*, 19.57.5 and 61.5.
22. Callataÿ 2004; Le Rider and Callataÿ 2006, pp. 169–208.
23. Athenaeus, *Deipnosophistai*, 5.196–203.
24. Polybius, *Histories*, 30.25–26; Athenaeus, *Deipnosophistai*, 5.194c–195f.
25. Callataÿ 2006.
26. Diodorus, *Library of History*, 31.16.2.
27. Polybius, *Histories*, 5.89. On the Seleucid coinage, see Houghton and Lorber 2002; Houghton *et al.* 2008.
28. Plutarch, *Agis*, 7.2.
29. *Op. cit.*, 9.5.
30. Plautus, *Stichus*, 1.1.24–5.
31. Terence, *Adelphi*, 5.7.915.
32. On the coined gold brought to Macedon, see Touratsoglou 1998 and 2010.
33. Titus Livius, 45.40.1–3.
34. Polybius, *Histories*, 21.42.19; Titus Livius, 38.38.13.
35. Polybius, *Histories*, 1.62–63.
36. *Op. cit.*, 21.32.8–9; Titus Livius, 38.9.9 and 11.8.
37. C.P. Cavafy, *Collected Poems*, transl. E. Keeley and Ph. Sherrard, ed. G. P. Savidis (revised edition), Princeton 1992.
38. Callataÿ and Lorber 2011, p. 451.
39. Callataÿ 1999, p. 18, no. 6/1.

Bibliography & Abbreviations

Callataÿ 1989: Callataÿ, F. de, 'Les trésors achéménides et les monnayages d'Alexandre: espèces immobilisées et espèces circulantes?', *Revue des Études Anciennes*, 91/1–2 (1989), pp. 259–76.

Callataÿ 1999: Callataÿ, F. de, 'Athéna pour Alexandre, Pégase pour Bucéphale : les aventures métalliques d'Alexandre le Grand à la Renaissance', *Antike Kunst* 42/2 (1999), pp. 99–112, pl. 17–9.

Callataÿ 2000: Callataÿ, F. de, 'Guerre et monnayage à l'époque hellénistique. Essai de mise en perspective suivi d'une annexe sur le monnayage de Mithridate VI Eupator', in: J. Andreau, P. Briant, and R. Descat (eds), *Économie antique. La guerre dans les économies antiques*, Entretiens d'Archéologie et d'Histoire 5, Saint-Bertrand-de-Comminges, pp. 337–64.

Callataÿ 2004: Callataÿ, F. de, 'La richesse des rois séleucides et le problème de la taxation en nature', *Topoi* Suppl. 6 (2004), pp. 23–47.

Callataÿ 2006: Callataÿ, F. de, 'Réflexions quantitatives sur l'or et l'argent non monnayés à l'époque hellénistique (pompes, triomphes, réquisitions, fortunes des temples, orfèvrerie et masses métalliques disponibles)', in: R. Descat *et al.* (eds), *Approches de l'économie hellénistique*, Entretiens d'Archéologie et d'Histoire 7, Saint-Bertrand-de-Comminges, pp. 37–84.

Callataÿ and Lorber 2011: Callataÿ, F. de, and Lorber, C., 'The pattern of royal epithets on Hellenistic coinages', in: P. Iossif, A. S. Chankowski and C. C. Lorber (eds), *More than men, less than gods. Studies on royal cult and imperial worship. Proceedings of the international colloquium organized by the Belgian School at Athens (November 1–2, 2007)*, Leuven, pp. 417–55.

Dahmen 2007: Dahmen, K., *The legend of Alexander the Great on Greek and Roman coins*, London / New York.

Houghton and Lorber 2002: Houhgton, A. and Lorber, C. C., *Seleucid coins. A comprehensive catalogue. Part 1. Seleucus I through Antiochus III. Vol. II. Appendices, indices, and plates*, New York / Lancaster, PA / London.

Houghton *et al.* 2008: Houghton, A., Lorber, C. C., Hoover, O., *Seleucid coins. A comprehensive catalogue. Part II. Seleucus IV through Antiochus XIII, vol. II. Appendices, Indices, and plates*, New York / Lancaster, PA / London.

Kraay 1984: Kraay, C. M., 'Greek coinage and war', in: W. Heckel, R. Sullivan and C. M. Kraay (eds), *Ancient coins of the Graeco-Roman World: The Nickle Numismatic papers Waterloo*, Ontario, pp. 3–18.

Le Rider 1977: Le Rider, G., *Le monnayage d'argent et d'or de Philip II frappé en Macédoine de 359 à 294*, Paris.

Le Rider 2003: Le Rider, G, *Alexander le Grand. Monnaies, finances et politique*, Paris.

Le Rider and Callataÿ 2006: Le Rider, G. and Callataÿ, F. de, *Les Séleucides et les Ptolémées. L'héritage monétaire et financier of Alexander le Grand*, Paris.

Price 1991: Price, M. J., *The Coinage in the Name of Alexander the Great and Philip Arrhidaeus. A British Museum Catalogue*, Zurich / London.

Touratsoglou 1998: Toutatsoglou, I., 'Back to the future. Alexander the Great's silver and gold in the Balkans. The hoard evidence', in: A. Burnett, U. Wartenberg and R. Witschonke (eds), *Coins of Macedonia and Rome. Essays in honour of Charles Hersh*, London, pp. 71–101.

Touratsoglou 2010: Touratsoglou, I., *A contribution to the economic history of the kingdom of ancient Macedonia (6th–3rd century BC)*, KERMA II, Athens.

VIII
WRITING AND IMPRINTING THE HISTORY OF THE ROMAN WORLD

Charikleia Papageorgiadou

In an age when communication was extremely difficult, not only due to the limitations of technology, but also to the more general ignorance and illiteracy of the populations, the power of the images on coins was used by all centres of authority to disseminate political messages. The Romans, having immediately grasped the possibilities offered by coins – possibilities that the Greek cities had taken advantage to the full – represented an immense variety of subjects on their flan, in this way transmitting important messages to a wide public. The coinage of Rome, notwithstanding its differentiations, is a constant to be traced through a long period, with iconography and symbolisms as its vehicle.

Mythical tradition, the early years and the Roman Republic

Rome, the city whose name was to be linked with a vast empire, traced its founding back to the Trojan hero Aeneas, according to the poet Virgil and the tradition widespread among the upper classes, particularly in the first century BC and the early years of the Empire. In this way the Roman elite promoted the idea that the origin of the Romans was equal in nobility to that of the Greeks, on whose territories Rome's expansionist policy at that time set its sights, and that the Romans were the worthy continuers of an heroic past. However, according to another tradition, the twin brothers Romulus and Remus, direct descendants of Aeneas, were the 'historical' founders of Rome, possibly on 21 April 753 BC. This tradition is corroborated by archaeological evidence and echoes more the city's tribal past and the conflicts between the local populations.[1] The relevant myths, which allowed Titus Livius to proclaim proudly in his work *Ab urbe condita* that 'if any people ought to be allowed to consecrate their origins and refer them to a divine source…'[2] this people is the Romans, recur frequently in Roman art and are a favourite subject also in the coinage of the later periods of the Empire.

fig. 1

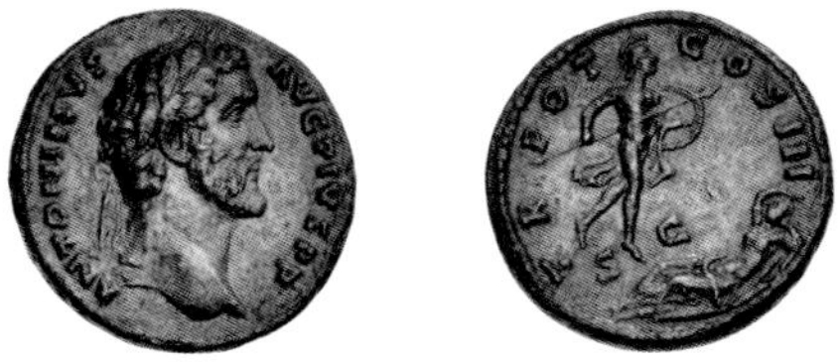

fig. 1

Bronze *as*, Antoninus Pius (138–161 AD), Rome, *ca.* 140 AD, with representation of Mars with Rhea Silvia, from whose union Romulus and Remus were born.
Traditions relating to the foundation of Rome recur frequently on imperial coins.
Classical Numismatic Group, Mail Bid Sale 84 (05.05.2010), lot 1029

Around the end of the sixth century BC, the aristocratic families ousted the last kings and took power, establishing the Senate (*Senatus*) as supreme authority, which together with the people, *Senatus populusque Romanus*, constituted henceforth the 'personification' of the Roman Republic.[3] In this period, in 211 BC, the *denarius*, the silver coin that was to be associated as no other with the history of Rome,[4] was introduced. Its iconography, with clear influences from the Greek cities of Italy and Sicily, revolves around deities associated with the Romans' heroic past and present.

In this period, moreover, the sense of Rome's omnipotence is consolidated, as described *inter alia* by Titus Livius.[5] This omnipotence is now represented on the coins too, not as a goddess but as the personification of the Roman State, the *res publica* or the fatherland (*patria*).[6] Much later, in imperial times, Roma, with the characteristics of a martial goddess, such as Athena, is identified in many cases with *Minerva*,[7] while she is encountered also on coins of Greek cities, where she was worshipped in the same temple as the emperors.

fig. 2: see cat. no. 163

As coinage increased and Rome was opening up to its new possessions and was moving away from the austere archaic tradition, the officials responsible for producing coins, the *monetales* (moneyers), felt free to seek also other sources of iconography and indeed from their family past, considering that coins were a medium of personal enhancement in the desired *cursus honorum*.[8] The specific types, although passing essentially unnoticed by the general public, which had no idea about the events depicted, nonetheless projected the appropriate messages to the circles of power.

fig. 3

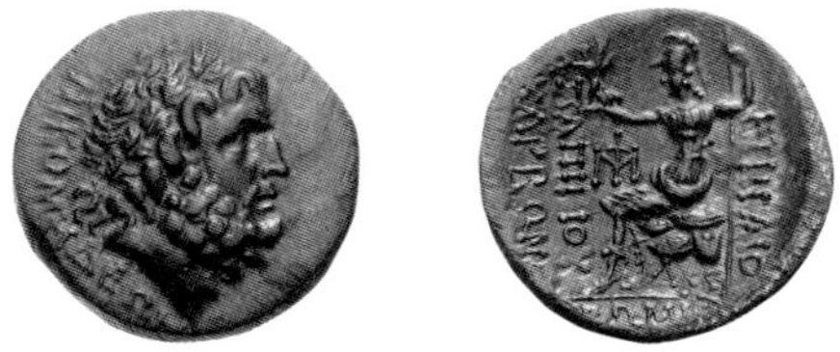

fig. 2

Bronze coin, Nicomedia, C. Papirius Carbo, 59/8 BC.
The assimilation of Roma with the Greek goddess Athena is observed already in the years of the Republic.
KIKPE Collection, Athens

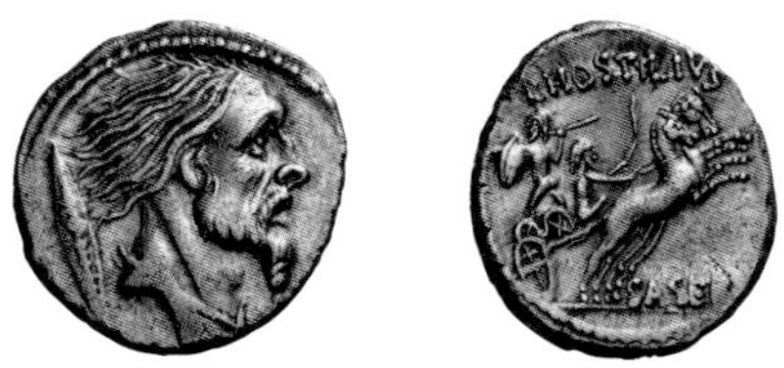

fig. 3

Silver *denarius*, L. Hostilius Saserna, 48 BC.
The numismatic representations refer to Julius Caesar's victories in Gaul. Indeed, the figure on the obverse is identified as the legendary Gallic chieftain, Vercingetorix.
Nomos, Auction 3 (10.05.2011), lot 167

The Empire

The assassination of Julius Caesar on 15 March 44 BC ushered in a ten-year period of civil wars, from which his direct descendant and successor, Octavian,[9] emerged as the monarch of the Roman world and, in actual fact, the founder of the Empire.

Augustus, the first to link inextricably the emperor's actions with the fate of the Empire, exploited to the utmost the potential of coins[10] — and indeed of every art form or other medium — to project the guidelines of his policy, by utilizing iconography.[11] The emperor is portrayed on coins as imperishable and ageless, with idealized features, just as the Empire should be too. The development and the maturing of Augustus' policy are distinguished only by the corresponding inscriptions, according to which he is transformed from *Imperator Caesar Divi Filius*, Caesar's son and worthy continuer, to *Pater Patriae*, Patriarch of the Nation.

The use of coins as agents of promoting the imperial house that began from Augustus — in a way, the *monetales* of the Republic had preceded — is one of the characteristics of Roman numismatics and has generated much debate as to whether it should be considered as a means of propaganda, publicizing or projection of imperial achievement.[12] However, regardless of theoretical stance, the fact remains that coin iconography offers important information on the reconstitution of imperial policy, since the coin offers the field for the development of the messages to be publicized.

On the obverse, the portrait of the emperor, framed by a series of titles[13] following and dating his career, was the sole permitted image, which confirms the dominant figure of the period. The way in which this figure is portrayed signified not only the personality of the emperor, with specific facial features and personal traits, but also the basic axes of his governance. For the immediate imperial milieu and the higher echelons of society this kind of information could be circulated through works of art, as well as imperial literature, whether *res gestae* and autobiographies, or correspondence with distinguished persons.[14] For the rest, the rendering of the imperial portrait was open to multiple readings, given that beyond the obvious, the citizens of Rome at least were able to discover other, more covert aspects of their emperor, as in the case of Domitian, who although described by Tacitus as bold, is represented with luxuriant curly hair both on coins and in official portraits.

fig. 4: see cat. nos 215, 23, 229, 232

The coin portrait depicted the emperor as he ought or would want to appear to his citizens, depending also on the policy he applied. Those who linked their authority with major military operations and the expansion of the Empire are depicted with features revealing vigorous personalities, beginning with the Flavians or Trajan, while Caracalla instituted the profile of the emperor-general, which was adopted by subsequent rulers who had risen from the ranks of the army.

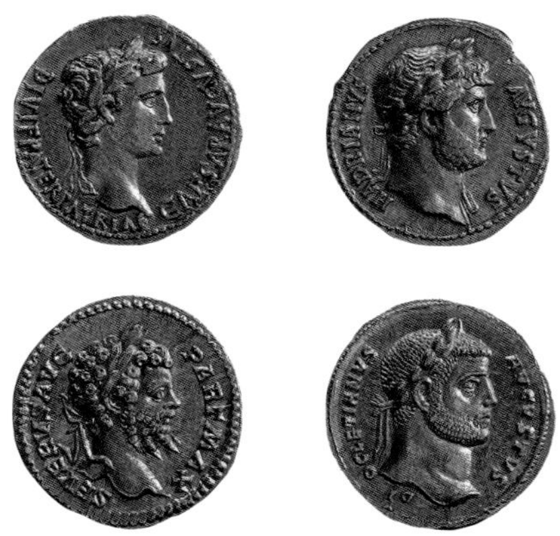

fig. 4

From Augustus to Diocletian the portraits on coins provide significant information on the emperors, as well as on the way in which they wielded their power.

Obverses of gold *aurei*: Augustus (27 BC – 14 AD), Lugdunum, 7–6 BC; Hadrian (117–138 AD), Rome, *ca.* 125–128 AD; Septimius Severus (193–211 AD), Rome, 200–201 AD; Diocletian (284–305 AD), Cyzicus, 293 AD.
Fondation Martin Bodmer, Cologny

On the contrary, the emperors-philosophers, particularly Hadrian, but also Antoninus Pius and Marcus Aurelius – emperors renowned for the serious introspective inquiries, who wanted to be presented swathed in classical beauty – adopt portraits impressive for their serene majesty. A special case is Septimius Severus, who established different types of the imperial portrait, stressing certain characteristics associated with his personal career from soldier to continuer of a lineage of emperors and divine sovereign, and last to philosopher.

The imperial issues of the third century, when the empire is collapsing and seeking salvation in divine intervention, which may also take on the form of the emperor, are placed on a more general ideological foundation. Gallienus is portrayed identical to various deities, while a few years later Aurelian, all too aware of Rome's fate, appears on his coins as RESTITUTOR ORBIS, and even more, as DEO ET DOMINO NATO AURELIANO AUGUSTO. Born god and prince, Aurelian was the first of a series of emperors who believed themselves to be born of gods and creators of gods, to which alone they give account, in order to be assimilated with them in the end. This was the case with the emperor Theodosios I, who on a relief from Ephesus is represented together with his family, in the midst of the Olympian gods.[15]

Sometimes the rendering of the imperial portraits follows contemporary aesthetic currents. A case in point is Nero, who is portrayed in meticulous detail and with obvious differences in age as the years passed. This is an exceptional example of imperial portrait in a period in which Roman art is disengaging itself from Hellenistic models and turning towards realistic representations of figures – distinctive quality of the pure Roman tradition.

Almost two hundred years were to pass before a significant change occurred in the rendering of the portrait, this time of Gallienus, whose figure is presented as a mask. This is a new artistic trend, distinguished by schematization and cubic outlines, which was to convey in the best possible way the ideological basis of the Tetrarchy, established by Diocletian in 293 AD and supported by the rulers' concord and *similitudo*, which is expressed aesthetically by the uniformity of volumes and the playing down of the different features.

If the imperial portrait is in many ways a constant, the remarkable variety of representations on the reverse of coins echoes imperial reality in its full scope. Regardless of the final recipients of the messages and the gamut of their acceptance and comprehension, regardless of the beautification of the acts and of the nature of power promoted by the imperial milieu, the numismatic types truly iconize an era for which there are only literary testimonies. Moreover, the Roman historians were not always objective and their work is informed by their personal principles and ambitions, or even by their likes and dislikes.

Indicative examples are the two main historians of the first century of the Empire, Gaius Suetonius Tranquillus (*ca*. 69 – after 122 AD) and Publius (or Gaius) Cornelius Tacitus (56–117 AD). The first, in his work *De Vita Caesarum*, focused on the adverse side of the personal life of the emperors, giving the more general picture of a corrupt, debauched, blood-loving and scandalous principle characteristic of Roman power, whereas the second, although himself a senator, in the *Annals* and the *Histories* has no qualms about describing in the darkest terms and a belittling manner the Romans in general, and specifically the members of his class.

Even the third-century historian Dio Cassius (*ca.* 150–235 AD), although referring to events of previous centuries, is critical both of his fellow Roman citizens and of their enemies, but for obvious reasons does not adopt the same stance towards his contemporaries the Severans.

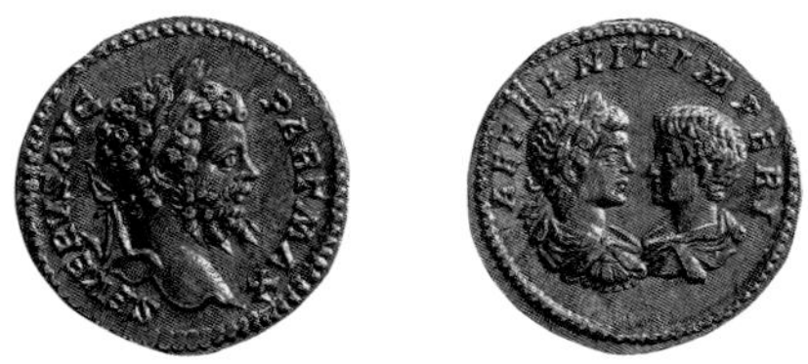

fig. 5

Gold *aureus*, Septimius Severus (193–211 AD), Rome, 200–201 AD.
Represented are his natural heirs, Caracalla and Geta. Dynastic continuity was among the emperors' principal concerns, even though the choices or the hereditary succession were not always to the benefit of Rome.
Fondation Martin Bodmer, Cologny

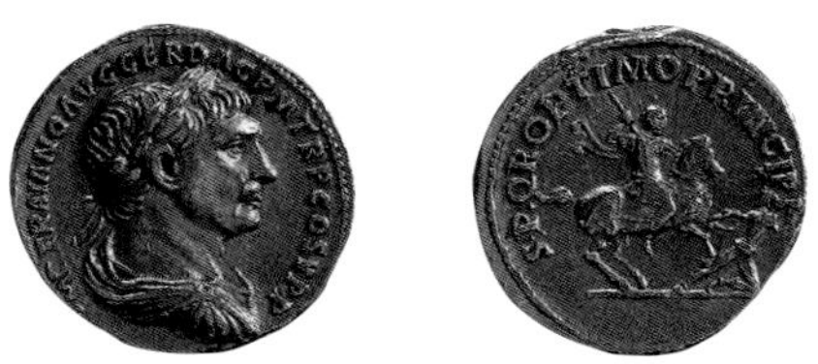

fig. 6

Gold *aureus*, Trajan (98–117 AD), Rome, 103–111 AD.
Represented is the emperor on horseback defeating his enemy.
Fondation Martin Bodmer, Cologny

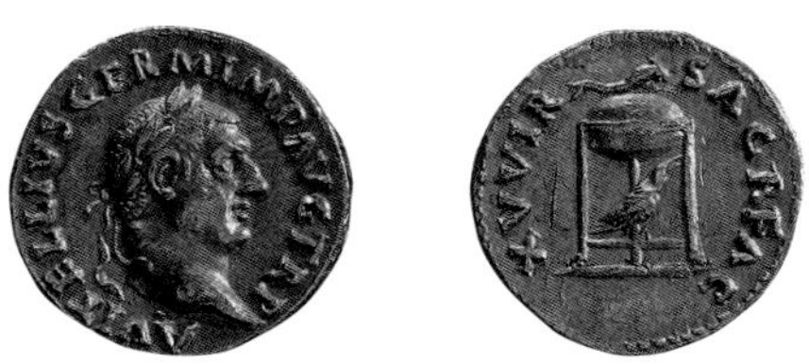

fig. 7

Gold *aureus*, Vitellius, Rome, 69 AD.
Vitellius stayed in power for eight months, before being usurped and executed by Vespasian. The reverse representation is associated with the *Quindecimviri Sacris Faciundis*, who were able to interpret the Sibylline Books in time of crisis.
Fondation Martin Bodmer, Cologny

However, there is a common axis linking the historians' texts with the coin iconography. Building projects, familial relations and dynastic continuity, military operations and spiritual inquiries are indicative and characteristic of the nature of authority and imperial power.

fig. 5: see cat. no. 230
fig. 6: see cat. no. 226
fig. 7: see cat. no. 221

Once again, a case in point is the coinage of Nero, on which the different facets of his contradictory personality are unfolded, with the detailed recording also of the emperor's acts. For although known to history as an exemplar of bestiality and insanity, he could nonetheless boast considerable achievements, as is apparent also from his coin iconography in which public works projects, such as the harbour of Ostia, and gifts to the people coexist with the conspicuous display of the artistic talent of the emperor who identified himself with Apollo.

fig. 8

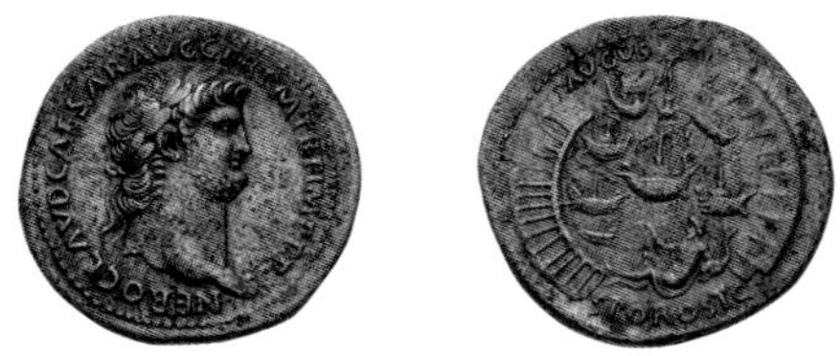

fig. 8

Sestertius, Nero (54–68 AD), Rome, 64 AD.
The harbour of Ostia, which was completed in 64 AD, is represented in meticulous detail, after the model of analogous mural paintings.
Classical Numismatic Group, Mail Bid Sale 90 (23.05.2012), lot 1471

One further field in which the emperors had to boost their image was that of domestic policy, especially in the first and second centuries when wars were no longer of vital importance for the Empire and what mattered was the well being of those living within its narrow boundaries. Characteristic is the case of Trajan, who, as is apparent also from his correspondence with Pliny, had taken serious measures to relieve the plight of the social underdogs throughout Italy. These measures are referred to on his coins, on which are engraved representations of the ITALIA RESTITUTA and ALIMENTA ITALIAE. However, the management at close hand of the problems of the far-flung provinces interested emperors such as Hadrian, who, as *Restitutor Orbis Terrarum*, imprinted on a notable series of coins the provinces he visited.

The principles on which the emperor governed, which were the hallmark of the central authority, are personified and appear on coins as allegorical figures, particularly in the time of Hadrian and his successors. Virtues such as *Liberalitas* (Liberality), *Indulgentia* (Indulgence), *Patientia* (Patience), *Pudicitia* (Modesty), *Tranquilitas* (Tranquility), *Hilaritas* (Joy) typify Hadrian's authority, whereas *Clementia* (Clemency), *Honos* (Honour) and *Justitia* (Justice), were the principles according to which Marcus Aurelius desired to reign.[16] Very often these ideological references affected

fig. 9: see cat. no. 227

also the depiction of the gods, who acquire specific characteristics, such as *Roma Felix*, or have the qualities of *Pax* (Peace) and *Salus* (Salvation), *Jupiter Conservator* or *Liberator*, *Venus Victrix*, *Minerva Pacifera*.

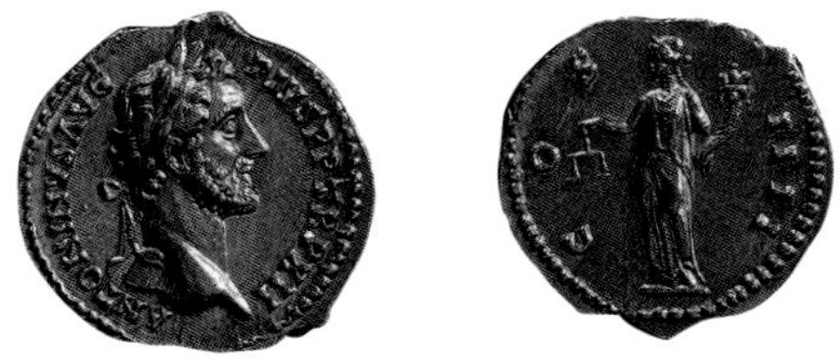

fig. 9

Gold *aureus*, Antoninus Pius (138–161 AD), Rome, 148–149 AD.
Representation of Nemesis, goddess of Justice, holding a pair of scales and a cornucopia.
Fondation Martin Bodmer, Cologny

Despite the emperors' efforts to broadcast a policy of principles, the unequivocally bellicose nature of the empire is marked from the early years of its existence by the image of Roma as a martial deity seated on breastplates, holding a spear and accompanied by related attributes. From the simpler form on the coins of Titus to the more sophisticated one that accompanies the end of the Empire and holds Victoria proffering her a wreath, while a figure of a suppliant kneels at her feet, Roma is the *par excellence* representation of the magnificence of the empire. A magnificence that was seriously threatened by barbarian incursions, as a result of which the coins now carry the image of the emperor on horseback vanquishing his foes, and gods such as *Mars* and *Minerva*, *Sol Invictus* and VICTORIA AETERNA, while of the emperor's virtues the martial VIRTUS AUGUSTI now prevails.

It is clear that the choice of the iconographic types imprinted on a coin was made with care and was the expression of kind of imperial 'ideology', the projection essentially of an emperor as he should or would like to be, and of a principle which had responsibility for maintaining the Empire, and which was unfolded on both sides of the coins. Independently of the range of recipients and the recognizability of these messages, the court wished to make its work known in the best possible way, and coins were the most suitable medium, given that they circulated quickly in large quantities and over long distances.

Roman provincial issues: merging tradition into a new reality

One of the questions concerning the actual power of coins as agents of propaganda to the far-flung regions of the Empire is connected with the coinage of the provinces.[17]

The institution of the provinces was the organizational backbone of the immense territory of the Empire, which had to impose a single administrative, economic and military system upon a series of diverse ethnic groups, peoples and tribes which had equally different roots. The division into provinces of the West and of the East, and the corresponding management of the economy and coinage with pre-existing structures as guideline, is characteristic of the effectiveness of Roman policy.

In the western provinces principal feature of this policy was the imposition and absolute establishment of Latin as the official language and of Roman administration in the local societies, the majority of which lacked analogous sturdy infrastructures, such as the cities of the East. Concurrently, the creation of new structures and infrastructures aimed at exploiting the local sources of wealth to the advantage of Rome and her elites.[18] Moreover, the frequent upheavals, due either to attacks by barbarian tribes or to insurrections of local warrior chieftains, left little leeway for a relatively autonomous development of the western provinces. It is possible that the cities' relatively limited numismatic activity, which for reasons still vague had neither the duration nor the variety[19] encountered in the eastern provinces,[20] is due to precisely these particularities of the western provinces, whose economy was based largely on Roman coins.

In the eastern provinces, including Hellenic lands, which were the historical continuation of the Hellenistic kingdoms, significant mechanisms of economic administration and coinage had developed *inter alia*, upon which the Romans relied. Indeed, from the outset they allowed the various local authorities to issue coins, mainly of small denominations, as petty currency to cover local needs.

These issues are among the most interesting,[21] as they were not determined by the central power but were under the control of the local authorities, who came primarily from the local elite. Given, moreover, that most populations in the East[22] were familiar with the tactics of the Hellenistic rulers, which aimed at publicizing and disseminating political messages through coins, a huge variety of images was created. These are important sources of information on the imperial presence, the response of the cities to the new world order, the manner of administration and the relations with the central authority, Roman control over annexed lands, the very history of the cities of the Roman Empire and the role of provincial coinage in the economy of the Roman Empire.[23]

Notwithstanding peculiarities of the provinces, with regard either to their local history or to the manner of their inclusion in the Roman Empire, certain common axes run through their numismatic activity and bear witness to a wider ideology of imperial times, with which coins are directly linked.

Indicative is the case of representations of purely local interest pertaining to deities and cults of the region, the imagery of which had been crystallized long ago. Even so, an attempt to render them in affinity with Roma is frequently observed. The case of the goddess Athena, who shares characteristics in common with the martial nature of Roma, is among the best-known examples, while very often the emperor is identified with a god,

fig. 10: see cat. no. 87

as in the case of Nero depicted as *Jupiter Liberator*, on the occasion of the 'liberation' of Achaea; the empresses too often acquire the features and attributes of female divinities.

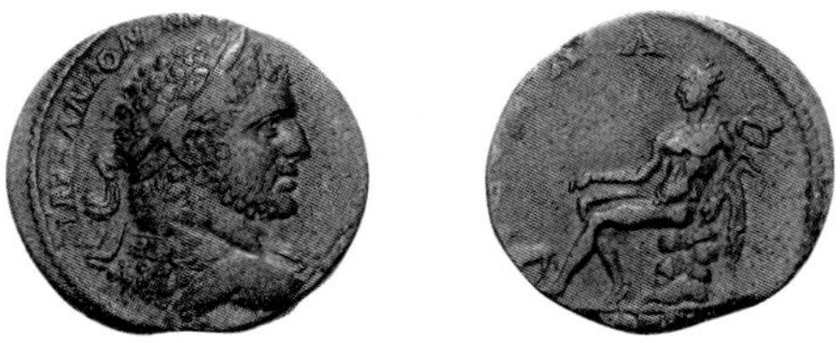

fig. 10

Bronze coin, Patrae under Caracalla (198–217 AD), 213–217 AD.
Represented is Hermes with his characteristic attribute the caduceus.
KIKPE Collection, Athens

Representations of landmark monuments and constructions of the region are one more typical choice and are associated usually with imperial building programmes, the renovation of earlier buildings on the occasion of a visit by members of the imperial family or the rebuilding on imperial initiative after natural or other destructions.[24]

fig. 11: see cat. no. 48

The local societies, either wishing to flatter the supreme authority or simply following the trends of the time, also copied representations from the Rome mint, which in reality were of no symbolic or semeiotic interest to them.

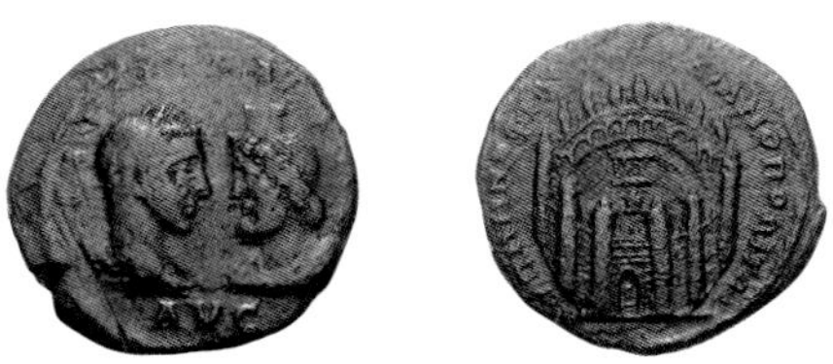

fig. 11

Bronze coin, Marcianopolis under Gordian III (238–244 AD).
Represented on the obverse is the emperor with the god Sarapis, whose cult spread from Egypt to the territories of the Empire under the Severans. On the reverse is a view of the city, showing a temple and an altar, which was surrounded by walls with thirteen towers.
KIKPE Collection, Athens

Of special character is the coinage of the Roman colonies,[25] on which types associated with their founding – colonist or priest who defines the boundaries of the colony, or the standards of the legions if it is a military colony – are among the most recognizable, as well as the coinage of the *koina*, mainly of religious character, primary concern of which was imperial cult, the centre of which – usually a sanctuary – was the commonest iconographic type.

However, for all the vast variety of representations, the iconography of the provincial mints rarely refers to major events affecting the whole of the Empire, such as great military victories. The coins of the provinces convey the sense that they were addressed solely to the local societies, with pronounced reference to the emperor, to whom they owed their well-being, and followed a flow of issues, independent of the coinage of Rome, on which events were immortalized immediately. Most probably in the distant provinces there was such a delay in keeping up with events that they preferred to continue an unbroken coinage on which were imprinted the local past and present, as this was formulated within the unified Empire and on the basis of the new ideological components.

The 'Renaissance' of the Roman coinage

Ancient coins combined art with precious metal, a fact that has always attracted the interest of affluent connoisseurs, while their size, which facilitated transport and storage, made them a favourite collector's item already in Antiquity. Moreover, the representations, which may have been familiar or have carried recognizable symbolisms, also made them ideal objects for presenting as gifts, as Suetonius records for the emperor Augustus.

The Italian Renaissance of the *Quattrocento* brought to the forestage Classical Antiquity and especially Roman art, finds of which were being brought to light in large number throughout the West. Coins in particular, not least because of the frequency of their discovery, were an economical as well as an impressive choice as collectibles. At the same time, as in Antiquity, collectible coins were appropriate as gifts, often accompanied by epistles or poems, or as keepsakes.[26]

Petrarch is accredited with being the first collector of coins in the Renaissance. As an authentic Renaissance man, he wanted to enhance and to instill in his contemporaries the virtues promoted by the Roman rulers, an endeavour that he realized through writing a collection of biographies, *De viris illustribus*, on the model of Plutarch's *Parallel Lives*.[27] Petrarch, like the highly inquisitive Leon Battista Alberti, considered coins a means of approaching the humanistic ideals of Antitiquity, which is why he offered coins as a gift to the Holy Roman emperor Charles IV in 1355 (possibly in his effort to persuade the sovereign to abandon the newly-built luxurious palace in Prague and move permanently to Rome, as expression of awakening Roman tradition and the Roman Empire). Eminent personalities of the age had created significant collections, some of which later constituted the core of modern museums, such as Elector Joachim II of Brandenburg, who founded the Coin Cabinet of Berlin.[28]

Whereas intellectuals were keen to extol and transfuse to their contemporaries the moral values and virtues of ancient times, rulers were more interested in being identified with the persons of the heroic past, just as the Roman emperors had once been identified with deities. Medallions were considered the most suitable means to this end, and these, taking as models Roman coins, began to be designed and produced in most of the Italian courts from around 1300, for the purpose of lauding the princes.

The catalogues in which coin images were copied assiduously were also models for the artists, while the profile rendering of figures was extended to painting too, where the first portraits of eponymous or anonymous persons appear.

The love of ancient coins and the interest in collecting them seem to have been a kind of measure connected with the profound knowledge of the humanistic ideals of the past, which typified the *homo universalis* of the Renaissance.

Notes

1. Gaudemet 1982², pp. 260–4, with relevant references to the excavations; Grandazzi 1997.
2. Titus Livius, *Ab urbe condita* 1.7.
3. Titus Livius, 4.2.4; Valerius Maximus 1.8.1; 9.5.1; Velleius Paterculus 2.89; *cf.* Gaudemet 19822, pp. 281, 349–53; Hoelkeskamp 2004.
4. *RRC*, pp. 616–8.
5. 'But the fates were resolved, as I suppose, upon the founding of ths great City, and the beginning of the mightiest of the Empires, next after that of Heaven'; Titus Livius, 1.4.2.
6. Mellor 1981, pp. 950–1030. The figure with helmet of Phrygian type, which is identified with Roma, is in opposition to the analogous one with Corinthian helmet, which is identified with the martial goddess Minerva. Also, Hoelkeskamp 2004, p.119.
7. Mellor 1981, pp. 973–5. Also, Fayer 1976; Fears 1978, pp. 274–86.
8. Hamilton 1969, pp. 181–99; *RRC*, pp. 725–34; *cf.* also, Harlan 1995. Concurrently, the moneyers, consistent with Roman tradition, honoured their ancestors; *cf.* Cheung 1998, pp. 53–61. Meadows and Williams 2001, pp. 27–49.
9. Edmondson 2009, with exhaustive bibliography.
10. Sydenham 1920; Sutherland 1965 and 1978. See also,Wallace-Hadrill 1986, pp. 66–87.
11. Zanker 1990. Indicative of the manipulation, by all means, is the fact that shortly before his death Augustus composed his political autobiography, the *Res Gestae*, *cf.* Scheid 2007.
12. Hannestad 1986, with earlier relevant bibliography. See also, Sutherland 1951; Jones 1974, pp. 61–8; Crawford 1983, 47–64; Levick 1982, p. 104.
13. Fears 1981, pp. 827–948.
14. Dilke 1957, pp. 78–97.
15. Given the fact that Theodosios was mainly interested in the imposition of Christianity, it is more probable that this was a local initiative, on the occasion of the reconstruction of Hadrian's temple, in order to honour the imperial family.
16. Birley 1987².
17. Howgego 1985; Butcher 1988; Ando 2000²; Heuchert 2003, pp. 313–43; Howgego *et al.* 2005.
18. Leveau 2007, pp. 651–70.
19. Norena 2011; Haeussler and King 2007.
20. *RPC* I, pp. 18–20.
21. Harl 1987.
22. Alcock 2007, pp. 671-97.
23. Franke 1968.
24. Price and Trell 1977.
25. Papageorgiadou-Banis 2004.
26. Cunnally 1994, pp. 129–43.
27. Kohl 1974, pp. 132–44.
28. Cunnally 1984; Cunnally 1999.

Bibliography & Abbreviations

Alcock 2007: Alcock, S., 'The eastern Mediterranean', in: W. Scheidel, I. Morris and R. Saller (eds), *The Cambridge Economic History of the Greco-Roman World*, Cambridge, pp. 671–97.

Ando 2000²: Ando, Cl., *Imperial Ideology and Provincial Loyalty in the Roman Empire*, Berkeley.

ANRW: *Aufstieg und Niedergang der Römischen Welt*

Birley 1987²: Birley, A. R., *Marcus Aurelius: A Biography*, London.

Butcher 1988: Butcher, K., *Roman Provincial Coins. An Introduction to the 'Greek Imperials'*, London.

Cheung 1998: Cheung, A., 'The Political Significance of Roman Imperial Coin Types', *Scwhweizer Münzblätter* 48 (1998), pp. 53–61.

Crawford 1983: Crawford, M. H., 'Roman imperial coin types and the formation of public opinion', in: C. Brooke, B. Steward, J. Pollard and T. Volk (eds), *Studies in Numismatic Method Presented to Philip Grierson*, Cambridge, pp. 47–64.

Cunnally 1984: Cunnally, J., The Role of Greek and Roman Coins in the Art of the Italian Renaissance, PhD dissertation, University of Pensylvania, Philadelphia.

Cunnally 1994: Cunnally, J., 'Ancient Coins as Gifts and Tokens of Friendship during the Renaissance', *Journal of the History of Collections* 6/2 (1994), pp. 129–43.

Cunnally 1999: Cunnally, J., *Images of the Illustrious: The Numismatic Presence in the Renaissance*, Princeton.

Dilke 1957: Dilke, O. A. W., 'The Literary Output of the Roman Emperors', *Greece & Rome*, Second Series, Vol. 4/1 (March 1957), pp. 78–97.

Edmondson 2009: Edmondson, J., *Augustus*, Edinburgh.

Franke 1968: Franke, P. R., *Kleinasien zur Römerzeit. Griechisches Leben im Spiegel der Münzen*, Munich.

Fayer 1976: Fayer, C., *Il culto della dea Roma. Origine e diffusione nell'Impero*, Collana di Saggi e Ricerche 9, Pescara.

Fears 1978: Fears, J. R., 'A Note on the Origins of Dea Roma', *Mnemosyne* 31 (1978), pp. 274–86.

Fears 1981: Fears, J. R., 'The Cult of Virtues and Roman Imperial Ideology', ANRW II, 17.2, Berlin / New York 1981, pp. 827–948.

Gaudemet 1982²: Gaudemet, J., *Institutions de l'Antiquité*, Paris.

Grandazzi 1997: Grandazzi, A., *The Foundation of Rome: Myth and History*, transl. J. M. Todd, Ithaca, NY / London.

Haeussler and King 2007: Haeussler, R. and King, A. C. (eds), *Continuity and Innovation in Religion in the Roman West*, Portsmouth, RI, JRA Supplementary Series, 2 vols.

Hamilton 1969: Hamilton, C. H., 'The Tresviri Monetales and the Republican Cursus Honorum', *Transactions of the American Philological Association* 100 (1969), pp. 181–99.

Hannestad 1986: Hannestad, N., *Roman Art and Imperial Policy*, Aarhus.

Harlan 1995: Harlan, M., *Roman Republican Moneyers and their Coins*, 63 *B.C.*–49 *B.C.*, London.

Harl 1987: Harl, K., *Civic Coins and Civic Politics in the Roman East A.D.* 180–275, Berkeley.

Hoelkeskamp 2004: Hoelkeskamp, K.-J., *Senatus populusque romanus. Die politische Kultur der Republik: Dimensionen und Deutungen*, Wiesbaden.

Heuchert 2003: Heuchert, V., 'Roman Provincial Coinage', in: C. Alfaro and A. Burnett (eds), *A Survey of Numismatic Research* 1996–2001, Madrid, pp. 313–43

Howgego 1985: Howgego, C., *Greek Imperial Countermarks: Studies in the Provincial Coinage of the Roman Empire*, London.

Howgego *et al.* 2005: Howgego, C., Heuchert, V. and Burnett, A. (eds), *Coinage and Identity in the Roman Provinces*, Oxford.

Jones 1974: Jones, A. H. M., 'Numismatics and History', in: P. Brunt (ed.), *The Roman Economy*, pp. 61–8.

***JRS*:** *Journal of Roman Studies*

Kohl 1974: Kohl, B., 'Petrarch's Prefaces to *De Viris Illustribus*', *History and Theory* 13/2 (1974), pp. 132–44.

Leveau 2007: Leveau, Ph., 'The western provinces', in: W. Scheidel, I. Morris and R. Saller (eds), *The Cambridge Economic History of the Greco-Roman World*, pp. 651–70.

Levick 1982: Levick, B., 'Propaganda and imperial coinage', *Antichthon* 16 (1982), pp. 104–16.

Meadows and Williams 2001: Meadows, A. and Williams, J., 'Moneta and the Monuments: Coinage and Politics in Republican Rome', *JRS* 91 (2001), pp. 27–49.

Mellor 1981: Mellor, R., 'The Goddess Roma', in: W. Haase and H. Temporini (eds), *ANRW*, II, 17.2, Berlin / New York 1981, pp. 950–1030.

Norena 2011: Norena, C. F., *Imperial Ideals in the Roman West. Representation, Circulation, Power*, Cambridge.

Papageorgiadou-Banis 2004: Papageorgiadou-Banis, Ch., *The Numismatic Iconography of the Roman Colonies in the East. Local Spirit and the Expression of Imperial Policy*, ΜΕΛΕΤΗΜΑΤΑ 39, Athens.

Price and Trell 1977: Price, M. J. and Trell, B. L., *Coins and Their Cities. Architecture on the Ancient Coins of Greece, Rome, and Palestine*, London.

***RPC* I:** Burnett, A. and Amandry, M. (eds), *Roman Provincial Coinage*, Vol. I, London / Paris 1992.

***RRC*:** Crawford, M. H., *Roman Republican Coinage*, Cambridge.

Scheid 2007: Scheid, J., *Res gestae divi Augusti. Hauts faits du divin Auguste*, Paris.

Sydenham 1920: Sydenham, E. A., 'The coinages of Augustus', *Numismatic Chronicle* 29 (1920), pp. 17–56.

Sutherland 1951: Sutherland, C. H. V., *Coinage in the Roman Imperial Policy, 31 B.C. – A.D. 68*, London.

Sutherland 1965: Sutherland, C. H. V., 'The symbolism of the early Aes coinages under Augustus', *Revue Numismatique* 7^6 (1965), pp. 94–109.

Sutherland 1978: Sutherland, C. H. V., 'Some observations on the coinage of Augustus', *Quaderni Ticinesi, Numismatica e antichità classiche* 7 (1978), pp. 163–78.

Wallace-Hadrill 1986: Wallace-Hadrill, A., 'Image and Authority in the Coinage of Augustus', *JRS* 76 (1986), pp. 66–87.

Zanker 1990: Zanker, P., *The Power of Images in the Age of Augustus*, Ann Arbor, MI.

IX
IMAGES OF THE SACRED OR HOLY IN BYZANTIUM

Ioli Kalavrezou

When we speak of the holy or sacred in Byzantine society what immediately comes to mind are symbols, figures, images and buildings that are associated with Christianity and the practices connected with it. The sacred was experienced in words and in images, and when in liturgies it was accompanied by chant. The visual component, however, was well integrated in the everyday life of the Byzantines and was present in all aspects of it, especially in expressions of private piety. Whenever we think of the Byzantine world, what first comes to mind are its extraordinary images. Over the centuries the Byzantines had developed an easy and very precise visual language for their religious art, a language that remained standard for centuries. In other words, this art – religious as well as imperial and public – had a strong iconographic continuity which seems to vary little to those not versed in its rules. One of its rules, however, is that the art gives the viewer hints at or guides how a picture is to be read. Thus, this continuity of iconographic themes can become a flexible vehicle with the slightest of variation. This can be seen in particular in small images in minimal space, as on coins, where a small variation can give the representation of the figure of Christ, for example, a different meaning.[1]

Because of its firm iconographic continuity this representational vocabulary was available, so to speak, and could be used by the whole population without any distinctions of class, education or other criterion. Everyone could own or address the same images and symbols, and turn to them for their personal devotional needs. Thus Christ, the Virgin Mary or any other saintly figure and their images were there for all, and all could look at them and find the personal connection with the sacred that they were hoping for. The non-flexible iconographic types that were developed facilitated this process and created a universal world of images and symbols that have become the Byzantine visual expression of the holy.

Where does it find its manifestation and how is it articulated? The Byzantines throughout the Middle Ages were famous for the interior decoration of their churches, especially when these were surfaced with mosaics. This was done in such a way as to express the presence of the divine within these structures. The exterior of the building was kept quite simple in terms of materials, usually brick with some marble, which defined the architectural unit. But once inside the interior space one would find oneself in a different world. In particular, mosaic decorations with gold tesserae covering the surfaces between the images of Christ, the Virgin Mary and the other holy figures created the feeling of standing within an otherworldly place. Surrounded by the holy figures, Christ above all in the centre of the church, the Virgin in the apse where Holy Communion was celebrated, and the saints around the walls, the pious found himself in heaven on earth. Light played a most important role in this experience. Reflecting off the glass and gold *tesserae*, it created rays that appeared, wherever one stood, to descend from heaven, illuminating different areas and figures within the space. It was perceived as divine light, which penetrated those sacred places. This was the kind of encounter with the holy that the layman experienced when in church listening to the word of God and the hymns that filled the air. Even today, when visiting those few surviving monuments with mosaic surfaces, one can sense the extraordinary uplifting feeling that those architecturally intricate spaces with the holy figures on their walls could arouse.

But the Byzantine in his daily existence had other resources with which to pay his respect and express devotion to the holy. These were objects and images much closer to the real daily life with all its ups and downs that often bring the need to turn to the holy for help and gratitude. From the early centuries of Christianity the pious felt the need to have something tangible to hold or to look at while establishing contact with some power, which might be of assistance. For example, we find a number of small, carved semiprecious stones, mainly cameos, depicting the scene of the Annunciation.
fig. 1a These were used as personal amulets, or *enkolpia* worn by women.[2] They seem to have served as phylacteries, or charms for protection and good luck, and the Annunciation is an obvious theme to be associated with the desire to have children and more generally with fertility. Thus it seems that the Virgin of the Annunciation became a very popular image on personal objects of devotion used by women. Trends of this type,

which express the desire to connect to Mary in a more personal way, were becoming popular. They related to the desire to find protection and help, as was hoped for with certain other saints, as for example with the healing saints Cosmas and Damian, or with the military saints Demetrios or Theodore.

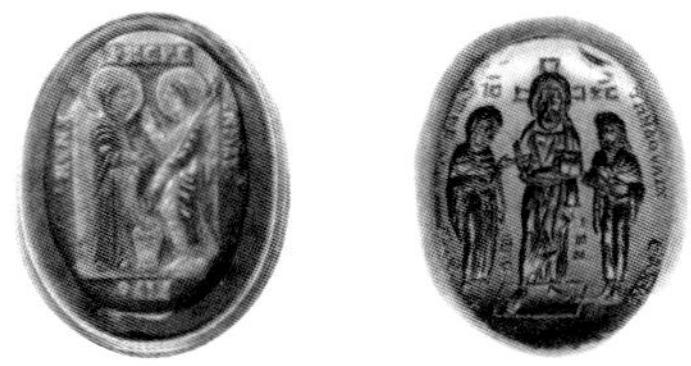

fig. 1 a, b

Two-sided cameo with the scenes of the Annunciation (6th century AD)
and the *Deēsis* (10th century AD?).
Bibl. nationale, Cabinet des Médailles, Paris

However, especially after the period of Iconoclasm, during a time when any kind of figural representation of holy figures was repressed and the pious had only the symbol of the cross to venerate,[3] we find an approach to the holy that will dominate the entire practice and relationship between the individual and the divine: this is the notion of intercession. Intercession as a concept was expressed in visual terms already by the sixth century when, for example, in the icon of the enthroned Virgin and Child from Sinai we have two martyr saints flanking her.[4] These seem to function as intercessors between mankind and Christ and the Virgin, since they look directly outward, establishing eye contact with the viewer, in contrast to the holy figures with their distant gaze. Possibly these kind of images were popular during this period but since only a few examples survive we cannot speculate further. fig. 2

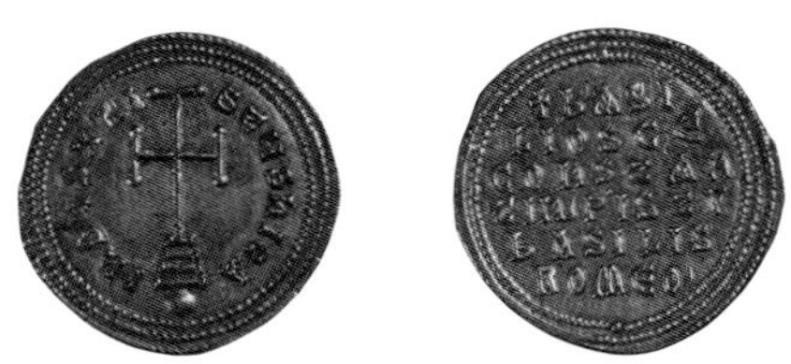

fig. 2

Silver *miliaresion*, Basil I, Constantinople, *ca*. 868–879.
Benaki Museum, Athens

However, the discussions and debates during the period of Iconoclasm as to the nature of the divine and the question whether mankind, mere human beings, can or should represent the Holy, brought to the fore what was defined at the Council of Ephesus of 431. There it was decided that through the humanity of the Virgin – the Theotokos – Christ became man, and it was argued in favour of depicting Christ because it is only his human nature that is represented and not the divine. Now Mary's human qualities, rather than her utility as a source of doctrine, were brought out directly. The promotion of the motherhood of Mary became explicit in texts and was followed by a new visual language. As the mother of Christ she is seen as the most appropriate figure to address Christ. She has become the ultimate intercessor for everyone.[5]

fig. 3: see cat. no. x

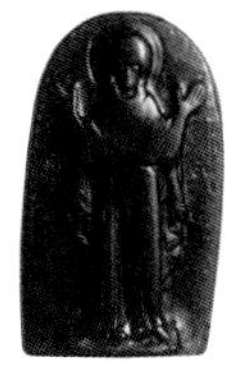

fig. 3

Virgin orant, haematite (?), 10th–11th centuries AD.
Benaki Museum, Athens

A new image was developed, in which this intercessional role the Virgin now had was made very clear. She stands together with John the Baptist, the other human figure close to Christ, also in his capacity as the last of the prophets, to intercede with Him. So, in the ninth century, with the end of Iconoclasm, a new composition, that of the *Deēsis*, was created to express the role that appropriately was given to the Virgin and to John. It is one of the simplest but most expressive images of the concept of prayer or supplication between man and the holy that have been conceived. In its simple symmetry Christ, either standing or enthroned, is placed at the centre of the composition and is flanked by John on the one side and the Virgin Mary on the other, who, turned slightly towards him, pray and communicate with him on behalf of mankind. One of the most splendid examples in mosaic of the *Deēsis* is found in the south gallery of Hagia Sophia, probably of the very late twelfth century. Although here we see it in a monumental mosaic representing the highest quality of that art in the cathedral of Constantinople, this image was very much used privately on small icons kept in homes or in private chapels, as for example in the apse of the Pammakaristos funerary chapel.[6] It is the subject also that has been incorporated in the compositions of the Last Judgement, where truly there Mary and John address Christ the judge to save humanity.[7]

fig. 4

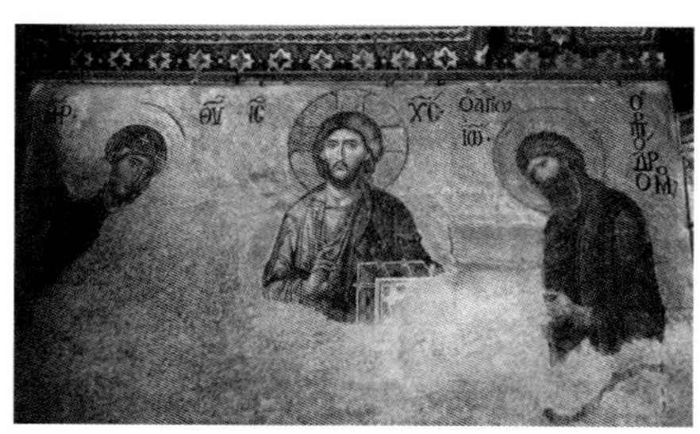

fig. 4

Deēsis, wall mosaic, south gallery, Hagia Sophia, Constantinople.
Photo by the author

In terms of private icons of the *Deēsis*, we even have three imperial examples of different periods. One was made for Constantine VII and probably was the first to include all categories of holy figures and not just the triad of Christ, Mary and John. It is an example of what has been seen as the extended *Deēsis*, where intercession includes apostles, Church fathers, martyrs and military saints participating in this process. In this case specifically, God's heavenly court is participating and assisting Constantine VII to be well and victorious in his military and other struggles.[8] The popularity of the *Deēsis* as a private icon is even found on one of the Annunciation amulets mentioned above, of the sixth-seventh centuries. On the cameo in Paris at some later date, probably in the tenth century, the scene of the *Deēsis* has been carved on its reverse side and the inscription added: Θ(εοτό)κε βοήθι τὴν δούλιν σ(ου) Ἄνα; 'Theotokos, help thy servant Anna'.[9] It is interesting to observe that by adding the *Deēsis*, the prayer in image and word, several centuries later, the purpose of the Annunciation scene becomes much more forceful for the new wearer, and in addition it clearly points out to us, as we are studying these objects, the intention of the amulet and the lasting and continuous practice of turning to the Virgin to ask for assistance and protection. fig. 1b

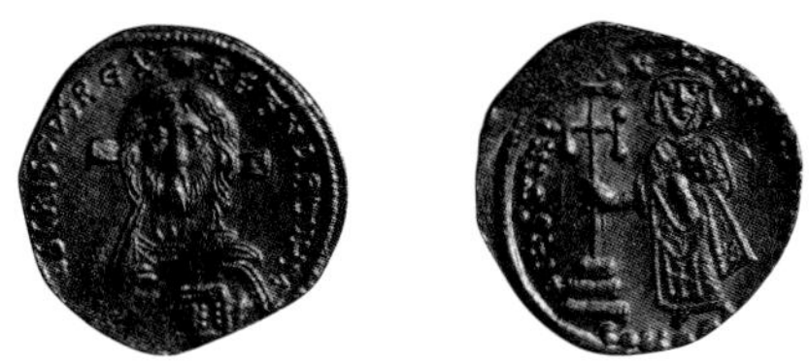

fig. 5

Gold *solidus*, Justinian II, Constantinople, 692–695.
Benaki Museum, Athens

The recognition of Mary's motherhood, her being ΜΗΤΗΡ ΘΕΟΥ, changed much in the way the holy entered into the life of the Byzantines. A gold issue of Leo VI (886–912), of the early tenth century, is very good example of the introduction of the Virgin in the coinage. Christ was first placed on the obverse of the gold coins of Justinian II in 692–695, a most daring move to depict the most holy figure on the surface of money pieces. However, we have to recognize in these portraits of Christ Pantokrator not the holy as we have been discussing above, but the authority through which the emperor was validating his rulership, an image of the imperial ideology at the time. As the inscriptions make clear, Christ is the king of those who rule and the emperor is his servant.[10] Leo VI, when introducing the Virgin on his gold coin, had a different intention. Probably in great need of an heir to establish a dynasty, Leo turned not to the scene of the Annunciation but to Mary herself to intercede for him. The gold issue was struck with the Virgin represented in the orant, that is the praying and intercessory pose, with the title +MARIA+ above her head and in addition the newly established fig. 5 fig. 6

abbreviated legend ΜΡ ΘV (ΜΗΤΗΡ ΘΕΟΥ – Mother of God) flanking her image.[11] It is the first time that the figure of the Virgin Mary is placed on the gold coinage in Byzantium. We can almost sense the desperation that drove Leo to this decision. It is also probably one of the first times that her title 'Mother of God' is used officially. This adjective/title, from that period until today, did become the standard inscription next to her head. In this coin she is not only the intercessor, but also her role as the Mother has been especially emphasized, most appropriately for Leo's request for his needs. Her representation as the one who assists and helps the emperors and approves their rule will become something of a commonplace in the later centuries.[12]

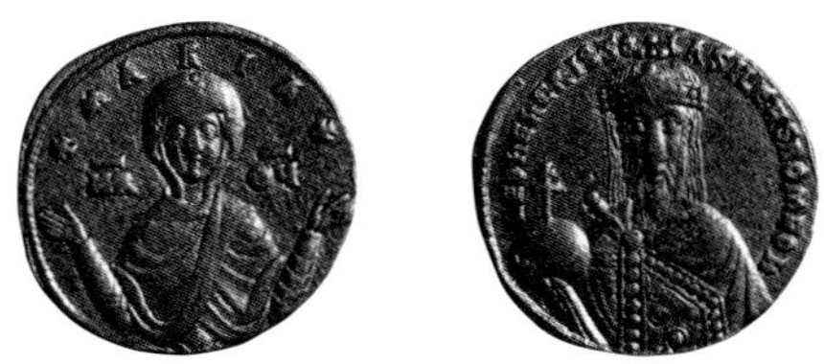

fig. 6

Gold *solidus*, Leo VI, Constantinople, *ca.* 905–908.
Benaki Museum, Athens

Although these are images that are imperial in their subject, they represent well the relation, devotion and regard that all Byzantines had for this holy figure. What is expressed in these small objects can be found represented on icons in the churches or on those kept privately at home. Owning an icon with the image, for example, of the saint one has been named after created a special relation with that holy figure who was one's direct protector. These kinds of connections and associations can be seen also in the choice of figures of saints that appear on coins. The archangel Michael is found on the coins of Isaak II Angelos because of his last name (Angel), or on the coins of Michael VIII Palaeologos because of his first name, shown clearly as his protector in the issues post-1261 after his re-conquest of Constantinople.[13] These saints, like most of the holy figures, in a sense participate or, better said, are through their images present in the life of the Byzantines.

An emperor turns not only to the Virgin to help him fight the enemy – another aspect of the Virgin since she was seen on the walls of the city of Constantinople defending it during the Arab siege in the seventh century –, he has the series of military saints stand by his side during military campaigns and battles. In the great Psalter manuscript produced for the emperor Basil II in the early years of the eleventh century he is depicted frontally in military attire, holding his sword and with a long spear at his side, with the enemy de-
fig. 7 feated at his feet. But the most important element in this composition is Basil's relation to the holy, which has been introduced into the image. First, Christ above recognizes his victory and crowns him by sending a crown through angels to be placed on his head. This

is the privileged and special relationship that emperors had with the divine, since they were chosen by God to rule. Most interesting in this image, however, are the six portraits of military saints who have been represented as icons on the page. They are the protectors who stood on his side, as they would have been for any other soldier in the battlefield. The emperor and the common man alike would have turned to these intercessors for assistance. This image shows in a sophisticated composition the way the Byzantines related to the holy. It is a rather direct and unveiled manner of simultaneous respect, devotion and familiarity, which are expressed in their love for those sacred and holy heavenly figures to which they can feel close. Through their icons, crosses or other *enkolpia* the Byzantines brought the holy closer to their world and their needs. It provided them with a sense of security and trust. Military saints accompany emperors on their coins beginning with the Komnenoi, a dynasty coming from the military aristocracy.[14]

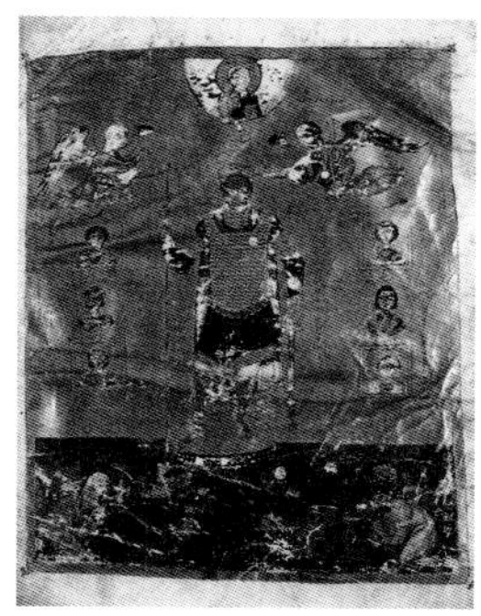

fig. 7

Basil II crowned by Christ with military saints to his aid,
full page illustration, *ca.* 1000.
Bibl. Marciana, Ms gr. Z 17, fol. IIIr, Venice

In another type of icon, not those of individual saints, Christ or the Virgin Mary, a similar but broader way of approaching the holy can be observed. These are a few selected moments from the life of Christ and of the Virgin, which, like the Annunciation amulets, had their place in the Byzantines' everyday life. When surveying the subject matter of private icons for personal devotions, and limiting it for example to those icons made of ivory, one can observe that one-third of the total number of ivory icons represents the Crucifixion. The second most popular of the narrative themes is the Dormition (*Koimesis*) of the Virgin.[15] The Crucifixion of Christ represents salvation, through his death, and the Virgin's *Koimesis*, in a very literal visual way, shows how there is hope for the resurrection after death. This narrow selection of themes suggests that these have been chosen because their subject has to do with a general relevance to living one's life. They are broadly seen as themes of salvation, providing the believer with the assurance of an eventual triumph over death. They offer consolation in life's difficult moments in one's world. Both are representations of the most holy figures of Christianity, who themselves suffered for mankind. Christ with his own death on the cross, the Virgin Mary with the motherly suffering of the loss of her son. So, even in these images we see the holy brought in direct relevance to the experience of the everyday human being. Thus, we can say that the visual component of piety and devotion towards the holy had found a place in the daily surroundings and activities of the Byzantines, participating in their successes as much as their sorrows.

This visual language that had developed over the centuries was carefully protected. Images were much discussed, especially during the debates of the Iconoclastic period but also afterwards, so that their place and role in Church and society was well defined, and all were very much aware of their authority and power. This wide-ranging phenomenon, however, did not reach over to the coinage, where Christ, the Virgin and selected saints were also depicted. Coinage had another use and the images of the holy on the coins served a different function. As mentioned above, it was already daring in the late seventh century to place the face of Christ on money designated for material transactions. There, however, these sacred figures served the imperial ideology, which in Byzantium was tied to a theocratic worldview. On the one hand the holy figures were placed on the coins to define the relation of the emperor to Christ, or on the other to display or solicit assistance with the presence for example of military saints. Narrative scenes were never placed on coins. The holy figures were closely related to the emperor, his position and his actions. As Bellinger stated some time ago, these were different worlds relating to the holy, which should not be confused.[16]

Notes

1. Christ can be blessing in a general way with his right hand in front of his body or blessing with his right arm extended towards the right, directing the viewer to the other side of the coin where the imperial family is depicted. i.e. see gold issues of Leo VI with his son Constantine (*DOC* 3/2, p. 513, Class II, Pl. XXXIV, no. 2.3).
2. We know this because of inscriptions on them mentioning the female name of the wearer; see Pitarakis 2005, p. 158.
3. During Iconoclasm the silver *miliaresion* is introduced by Leo III (*ca.* 720), adopting the image of the cross accompanied by the legend 'Jesus Christ conquers'. This non-figurative trend was continued until Alexander (912–3).
4. Weitzmann 1976, vol. I, pp. 18–21, no. B3.
5. Kalavrezou 1990.
6. Belting *et al.* 1978.
7. There are two icons of the Last Judgement on Mt. Sinai, and in monumental art a well represented *Deēsis* can be seen in the eleventh century wall mosaic in Torcello, in the church of Santa Maria Assunta, see *Glory of Byzantium*, 1997, p. 437.
8. Oikonomides 1995, pp. 73, 76
9. Avisseau 1992, pp. 277–8, no. 184. The *Deēsis* as a visual representation becomes established by the ninth century and is quite popular by the tenth century. It is very possible that this newer subject with a new owner was added to the cameo, expressing most clearly the intention of this amulet.

10. For the iconography of Justinian II's coinage see Breckenridge 1959; see also *DOC* 2/2, pp. 568–70 and 644–5.
11. *DOC* 3/2, pp. 508, 512 (Class I), pl. XXXIV, nos 1a, 1b.2; Kalavrezou 1990, pp. 170–1. This being a coin, as tradition had it, the letter P (rho) is written with the Latin R in both inscriptions and not the Greek.
12. The Virgin appears together with an emperor holding the cross sceptre for the first time on the coins of Nikephoros Phokas (963–9). For a study of the Virgin on coins see Penna 2000, pp. 209–17.
13. See in the present volume, C. Morrisson, '*Kharaktēr*: the history of Byzantium and beyond in words and images', fig. 5.
14. As discussed also for lead seals by Cheynet and Morrisson 1995, pp. 28–30.
15. There are several also of the Nativity, which I would consider placing in this category of icons that directly address birth and death as one would experience them in one's family, and the hope for salvation.
16 Bellinger 1956, p. 70; Penna 2002, p. 13.

Bibliography & Abbreviations

Avisseau 1992: Avisseau, M., (catalogue entry) in: J. Durand (ed.), *Byzance. L'art byzantin dans les collections publiques françaises* (exhibtion catalogue, Louvre, 3 November 1992–February 1993), Paris, pp. 277–8, no. 184.

Bellinger 1956: Bellinger, A.R., 'The coins and Byzantine imperial policy', *Speculum* 31 (1956), 70–81.

Belting *et al.* 1978: Belting, H., Mango, C. and Mouriki, D., *The Mosaics and Frescoes of St. Mary Pammakaristos (Fetiye Camii) at Istanbul* [Dumbarton Oaks Studies 15], Washington, DC.

Breckenridge 1959: Breckenridge, J. D., *The Numismatic Iconography of Justinian II*, American Numismatic Society, Numismatic Notes and Monographs 144, New York.

Cheynet and Morrisson 1995: Cheynet, J.-C. and Morrisson, C., 'Texte et image sur les sceaux byzantines: les raisons d'un choix iconographique', in: N. Oikonomides (ed.), *Studies in Byzantine Sigillography* 4 (1995), pp. 9–32.

DOC 2: Ph. Grierson, *Catalogue of the Byzantine Coins in the Dumbarton Oaks Collection and in the Whittemore Collection. Vol. 2. Part 1: Phocas to Heraclius, 602–641. Part 2: Heraclius Constantine to Tiberius III, 641–717*, Washington, DC 1968.

DOC 3: Grierson, Ph., *Catalogue of the Byzantine Coins in the Dumbarton Oaks Collection and in the Whittemore Collection. Vol. 3. Part 1: Leo III to Michael III, 717–867. Part 2: Basil I to Nicephorus III, 867–1081*, Washington, DC 1973.

Glory of Byzantium, 1997: Evans, H.C and Wixom, W.D. (eds), *The Glory of Byzantium: Art and Culture of the Middle Byzantine Era, A.D. 843-1261*, New York.

Kalavrezou 1990: Kalavrezou, I., 'Images of the Mother: When the Virgin Mary Became *Meter Theou*', *DOP* 44 (1990), pp. 165–72.

Oikonomides 1995: Oikonomides, N., 'The Concept of "Holy War" and Two Tenth-Century Byzantine Ivories', in: T. Miller and J. Nesbitt (eds), *Peace and War in Byzantium: Essays in Honor of George T. Dennis, S.J.*, Washington, DC, pp. 62–86.

Penna 2000: Penna, V., 'The Mother of God on Coins and Lead Seals' in: M. Vassilaki (ed.), *Mother of God. Representations of the Virgin in Byzantine Art* (Benaki Museum, 20 October 2000 – 20 January 2001), Milan, pp. 208–17.

Penna 2002: Penna, V., *Byzantine Coinage, Medium of transaction and manifestation of imperial propaganda*, Nicosia.

Pitarakis 2005: Pitarakis, B., 'Female piety in context: understanding developments in private devotional practices' in: M. Vassilaki (ed.), *Images of the Mother of God*, Aldershot, pp. 153–66.

Weitzmann 1976: Weitzmann, K., *The Monastery of Saint Catherine at Mount Sinai: The Icons. Vol. I: From the Sixth to the Tenth Century*, Princeton.

X
KHARAKTĒR: THE HISTORY OF BYZANTIUM AND BEYOND IN WORDS AND IMAGES

Cécile Morrisson

Kharaktēr is an appropriate motto for the display of books and images envisaged in the present exhibition, particularly as regards Byzantine coins.

Technically this term designated the engraved mark on the die, which was essential for giving the coin its currency value, together with its weight and fineness. *Parakharattein* – counterfeiting – was a lese majesty crime whose perpetrator would have had his hand cut off in the ninth century, while earlier, if he forged the highest value gold coin, he would have been subjected to the most severe punishments (e.g. scalded in boiling water).[1] The Anonymous fourth century treatise *De rebus bellicis* counted counterfeiting 'among the injuries to the State that are not to be borne, [since] it disturbs the population in several ways and diminishes the portrait of imperial majesty when they [the solidi] are refused through the fault of the mint'.[2] cat. no. 204

When print was invented, the 'engraved mark' (*caractère*) became in French the word for the printed signs or fonts; and the word kept this meaning before being extended to defining qualities, negative or positive alike, such as in the famous *Caractères* of La Bruyère (1688).[3] It is precisely those fonts, designed in the Renaissance on the basis of the Greek humanists' calligraphy, that were used to disseminate the works of Byzantine historians from the early sixteenth century onwards, when in the

West the memory of Constantinople and the Empire was not of a phantom but of a recent and still vital past.[4]

cat. no. 186

Byzantine coins rarely feature prominently in texts except for a few occasions when a new type, such as the anonymous eleventh century *folles* on which the emperor's image or name was replaced by that of Christ or the Virgin, or a misunderstood one, such as that of Isaak I Komnenos, portrayed with his drawn sword, stir the chroniclers' attention.[5] But Byzantine coins were struck in the millions, had a vast diffusion in a relatively literate society, at least by the standards of the time, and aimed at conveying the emperor's words together with his image. According to an often-cited text by Cassiodorus, the coin imprinted with the ruler's face was intended to 'inform future ages'.[6] How much the ordinary people understood of these words is difficult to tell, although they could certainly recognize the portraits and some of them could read the accompanying inscriptions: the emperor Julian scolded the people of Antioch in the *Misopogon*: 'you insult your own Sovereign, yes even the very hairs on his chin and the devices engraved on his coins',[7] an allusion to the philosopher's beard which he bore on all his coins. In the sixth century, still in Antioch, a street juggler earned money with a trained dog who could bring coins back when told the emperor's name.[8]

cat. no. 128

cat. no. 181

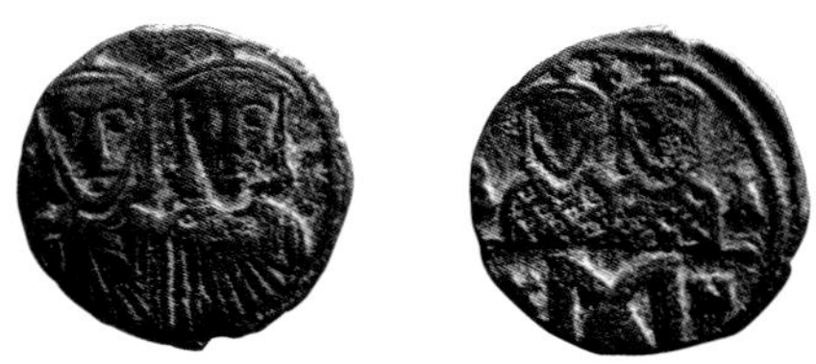

fig. 1

Bronze *follis*, Leo IV (775–780).
KIKPE Collection, Athens

Since already at that time the portraits had become quite stereotyped, the imperial names featuring on the coins were probably decisive for the identification. They would be even more indispensable in the Iconoclast period, when the elongated diademed faces of the rulers were as impersonal as they ever could be. Compare for instance the busts on the *folles* of Michael II and Theophilos with those of Leo IV and his son Constantine VI. The latter had no inscription and were only identified by referring to the contemporaneous gold coins bearing a full legend which took great pains to explain the whole family relationship of the four generations accommodated on the two sides of the coin: LEON VS S EGGON CONSTANTINOS O NEOS on the obverse and LEON PAP CONSTANTINOS PATHP on the reverse (*Leon uios kai eggonos Constantinos o neos / Leon pappos Constantinos patēr*: Leon son and grandson, Constantine the new / Leon grandfather, Constantine father).[9]

cat. no. 194

fig. 1

fig. 2

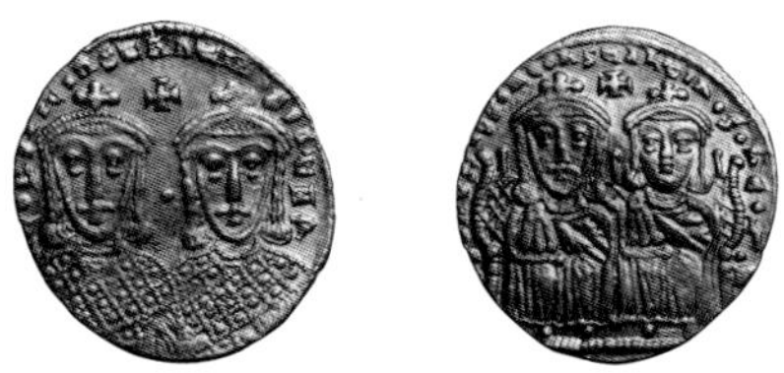

fig. 2

Gold *nomisma*, Leo IV (775–780), Constantinople.
Collection of Dumbarton Oaks, Washington, DC

The close association of the emperor's name(s) and his image is a feature that Byzantine coins inherited from Rome and maintained, with very few exceptions, throughout, as can be seen here from coin no. 180 (Constantine and sons), through nos 181 (Julian), 182 (Justinian), 183 (Basil I) to no. 185 (Michael VIII). The first shows a bust of Constantine with the pearl diadem, holding the globe with Victory, the same one as is shared by his two sons, Constantine II and Constantius, on the reverse. The legend gives Constantine the title of MAGNVS, later associated with him on the basis of his reputation as the first Christian emperor but here stressing the fact that he is now the only and therefore great Augustus, while his sons, not named on the reverse, bear only the title of NOBB(ilissimi) CAESS(ares). The last coin features Michael VIII with a large fleur-de-lis and the legend (ΜΙΧΑΗΛ ΔΕϹΠΟΤΙϹ Ο ΠΑΛΕ), an example of the tradition of adding the family name of the emperor to the titulature, which became systematic practice from Constantine X Doukas (1059–67) onwards and was retained by the Komnenoi, the Angeloi, the Laskarids and the Palaiologoi, down to the Fall of Constantinople. When this last dynasty was well established, as was the case under Andronikos II (1282–1328), the emperor had himself and his son Michael IX Palaiologos portrayed, initially, with an inscription stating both their first names and sometimes their imperial title, all abbreviated in varying fashion, but in the second half of his reign (*ca.* 1305–1320) issued an abundant series of gold, silver and copper coins with the legend ΑΥΤΟΚΡΑΤΟΡΕϹ ΡΟΜΑΙΩΝ ('emperors of the Romans'). 'Why the personal names of the emperors should have been dropped we can only conjecture', writes Philip Grierson, 'possibly it was to emphasize the fact that both rulers, and not the senior one only, enjoyed the title and rank of *autocrator*'.[10] However, the full imperial titulature on chrysobulls read: '... ἐν Χριστῷ τῷ Θεῷ πιστὸς βασιλεὺς καὶ αὐτοκράτωρ Ῥομαίων (... in Christ God faithful Emperor and autokrator of the Romans' and is found on the earlier *hyperpyra* of Andronikos II.[11] fig. 3

The large silver coins that replaced the debased gold *hyperpyron* in the last century of the Byzantine Empire, from *ca.* 1367 onwards, had a new design with two circular borders, which allowed for a long, less abbreviated inscription. As far as can be reconstructed from several specimens, it now read in full: '... *despotis ho Palaiologos theou chariti basileus tōn Romeōn*', the '*theou chariti*' being borrowed from the Western *Dei*

fig. 4 *gratia* formula.[12] Nonetheless, the careless production and the frequent clipping of the coins often resulted in part of the outer legend, where the emperor's name was located, being illegible.

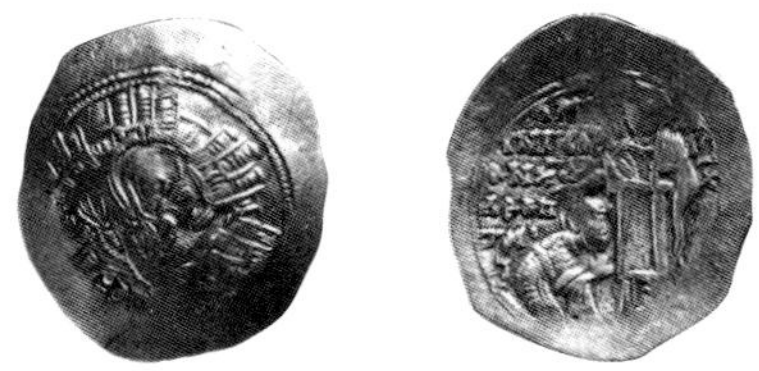

fig. 3

Gold *hyperpyron*, Andronikos II Palaiologos (1282–1328), Constantinople.
Collection of Dumbarton Oaks, Washington, DC

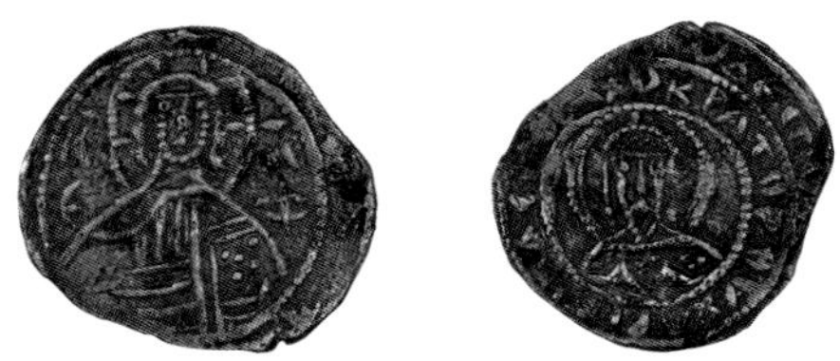

fig. 4

Silver *stavraton*, John V Palaiologos, Constantinople.
Collection of Dumbarton Oaks, Washington, DC

Apart from the imperial titulature on one side, intended to identify coins to the users, words on coins had another purpose; generally occupying the reverse and in association with a certain type, they might disseminate a message to the public. 'Propaganda' is sometimes used to characterize this function, but it is an anachronistic term and should be qualified. There is no direct proof that the emperors or even their entourage paid particular attention to their coin types and decided upon their design, although this cannot be ruled out completely. In a few cases changes in coin types can be related to specific political events, such as the *hyperpyron* of Michael VIII, showing him and the Virgin within the walls of the City, which is associated with the recapture
fig. 5 of Constantinople from the Latins in 1261.[13] The imagery of this coin encapsulates elements known from other media, such as the column on which the emperor was represented offering a model of the capital city to Archangel Michael, or celebrated by himself in deeds – when he entered the city on foot, preceded by the icon of the
cat. no. 190 Virgin Hodegetria, as related by Georgios Akropolites – or in his own words, preserved in the Typikon for the Monastery of St Demetrios of the Palaiologoi-Kellibara in Constantinople, where he boasts that 'Constantinople, the citadel of the inhabited world, the imperial capital of the Romans, had, with the permission of God, come under the control of the Latins. By God's gift it was returned to the Romans through us … this deed had not been accomplished by the hand of men but was a triumph of

God's great power'.[14] The image of the kneeling emperor on the coin, as well as on the column, was clearly conveying the idea of offering and consecrating the imperial city to divine protection, as stated by George Pachymeres.[15]

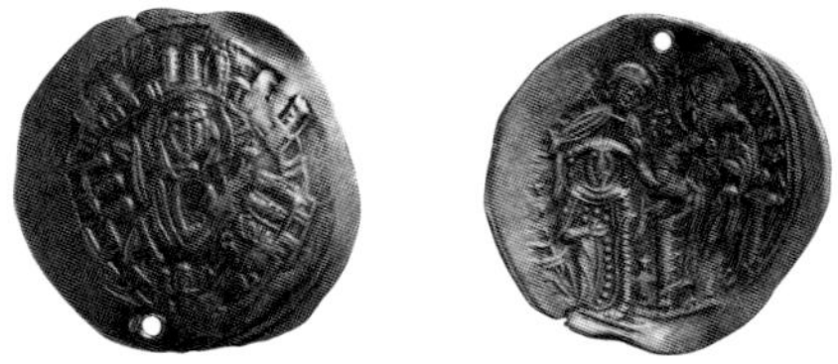

fig. 5

Gold *hyperpyron*, Michael VIII Palaiologos (1259–1282), Constantinople.
Collection of Dumbarton Oaks, Washington, DC

In the long run, the evolution of Byzantine coin types mirrors that of the general belief and culture of the people, or at least of the elite, and the growing ascendancy of Christianity. Nevertheless, the two coins of Constantine presented here serve as a reminder of how slow and piecemeal the emperor's conversion translated into coin subjects. The personification of Constantinopolis played a far more important role in the coin issues than the Christian motifs, especially at the time of the dedication of the new capital whose Tyche (*Fortuna*) was symbolized by the prow at her feet. The sign of the cross, which according to Eusebius had given to Constantine the victory over Maxentius, made very few and limited appearances on Constantine's coins, except for the *nummus* celebrating the ultimate victory over Licinius in 326, which shows the labarum treading upon a serpent symbolizing the arch enemy, with the legend SPES PVBLICA.[16] The Christogram was first made highly conspicuous on the reverse of the *centenionales* of the usurper Magnentius (350–353), struck in Amiens, Trier, Lyon and Arles in 353. The *alpha* and *omega* added on both sides of the cross stressed the eternity of Christ and were intended to mark Magnentius' support of the Orthodox Christians in Gaul who opposed Constantius II's Arianism.[17] The legend around the motif, SALVS DD NN AVG ET CAES brought divine support to Magnentius and his caesar Decentius, whose names alternately featured on the obverse, but it was not an outright religious one, as would be the case later. Only the contemporary coin of Vetranio, struck in Siscia and Sirmium in the name of Constantius (350), showed the labarum with Christogram in the hands of the emperor, together with HOC SIGNO VICTOR ERIS 'in this sign be victorious',[18] the words that Eusebius recalls in his description of Constantine's vision.[19]

cat. nos 179 and 180

cat. no. 202

cat. no. 192

It was not until the troubled times of the seventh century and the early stages of the conflict with Islam that the same words appear in Greek on the *folles* of Constans II (642–668): ЄN TȢTO NIKA.[20] These coins, like Heraclius' silver ones asking the Lord to help the Romans [against the Persians] – ƊЄЧS AƊIЧTA ROMANIS *Deus adiuta*

fig. 6

Romanis, transmitted the increasing role of Christian prayers and invocations in the preparation for battle, as prescribed in the military treatise (*Strategikon*) of emperor
cat. no. 206 Maurice (582–602).[21]

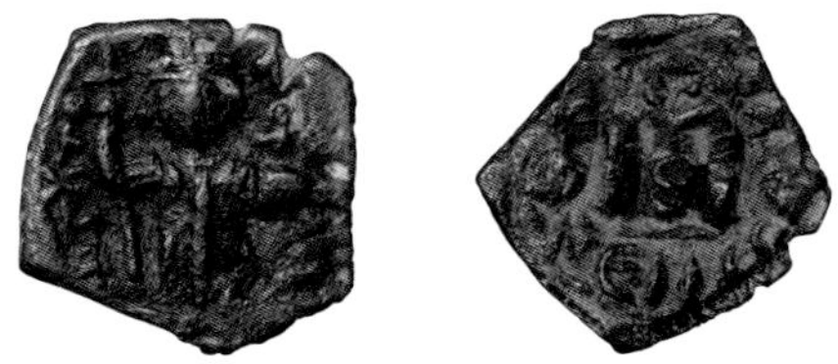

fig. 6

Bronze *follis*, Constans II (641–668), Constantinople (642/643).
Collection of Dumbarton Oaks, Washington, DC

The influence of the military, to whom the coin 'propaganda' had been mainly directed from the third and above all the fourth century onwards, together with that of court ceremonial, so closely interwoven with proper religious liturgy, was decisive in shaping the contents and expression of the whole monetary typology. Retracing the process of its Christianization, its dramatic progress in the fifth century under Theodosios II and its later vicissitudes in the Iconoclast period, before the Triumph of Orthodoxy and the Restoration of the Icons in 843, is beyond the scope of the present essay. Suffice it to consider here the two examples of this culmination in the Komnenian era. The emperor now appears as an intermediary between heaven and his earthly subjects, always supported and blessed by a religious figure. Either Christ or the Virgin is depicted on the obverse,[22] while the emperor stands on the reverse,
cat. no. 129 either alone, as on this *stamenon* of Manuel I Komnenos, or blessed by Christ, as on
cat. no. 132 the *stamenon* of Andronikos I Komnenos.

The image of the *basileus* standing and blessed by Christ is a classical motif of coin imagery on all denominations in gold, electrum or silver and copper since the eleventh century – and was to remain so till the mid-thirteenth century –, as well as a recurring theme in the *encomia* or panegyrics that praised the emperor but always attributed the origin of his power and his actual or exaggerated victories to divine support.[23] It was so familiar in the increasingly abundant circulating medium of the period that it is one of the sources of inspiration for the syncretic coinage of the Turkomans in Anatolia in the 12th and 13th centuries.

This is not the first instance of cultural borrowing between Byzantium and Islam; military and political conflict was not the sole interface in their multi-secular relations, as even the Digenis epic, relating the feats and adventures of a Byzantine frontier warrior in the tenth century, reflects. In the first seven decades after the conquest, local and central authorities in Syria and Egypt issued a coinage that presented a large

variety of figural images of Byzantine inspiration, combined with Greek and Arabic inscriptions. The transition started with more or less faithful imitations of Byzantine bronze issues of the seventh century and continued with more remote bilingual ones before the Standing Caliph issues of 694–697 (AH 74–77) and the complete Islamization of the Umayyad coinage in 696/697 (AH 77). The two types shown here belong to the bilingual series dated in the reign of Muawiya (660–680): the first one cat. no. 198
comes from a plentiful issue struck in Homs (ancient Emesa) with the name of the city in Greek (EMICHC) and the epithet ΚΑΛΟΝ / *tayib* (good) around the figure of the contemporaneous Byzantine emperor Constans II, while the second, struck in cat. no. 197
Tiberias/*Tabariya*, goes back to show the deceased emperor Heraclius with his two sons.[24] The coinage reflects both the prestige of the imperial authority even among its opponents and how the issuing authorities adapted to the dominant symbolism accepted by the population, which was still Christian in its majority. That the public's acceptance or rejection of a currency had to be taken into account is attested by a passage from a Syriac chronicle: 'In the year 971 [of the Seleucid era, counting from 312 BC], Constans's 18th year [AD 660], many Arabs gathered at Jerusalem and made Muawiya king… He also minted gold and silver, but it was not accepted, because it had no cross on it'.[25]

The Turkoman coins follow a different pattern. There is no linear evolution as was the case with the Arab-Byzantine earlier series. The Islamic identity is clearly asserted from the start on the obverses of the Danishmendid and Artuqid coins: they bear the *laqab*, the name of the ruler with the title *malik* and that of his father, grand-father and great grand-father, together with the name of the caliph: on no. 200, for instance, one reads 'Malik al-umara Qara Arslan bin Da'ud bin Sukman bin Artuq'. The reverses feature a wide array of figural themes, borrowed from ancient (Greek and Roman) or contemporaneous Byzantine issues, or inspired by other Islamic (Arabic or Persian) media.[26] Most of the Byzantine models are easily identified: the Danishmendid ruler of Malatya, Nasir al-Din Muhammad (1162–70 / AH 557–65 and 1175–78 / AH 570/73) copies rather closely the electrum *aspron trachy* of Manuel I Komnenos' first coinage, on the earliest of Turkoman issues, the Artuqid of Hisn Kayfa and Amid Fakhr al-Din Qara Arslan (1144 / AH 539, 1174 / AH 570) reproduces a bust of Christ Pantokrator cat. no. 200
taken from the countless anonymous *folles* first class of the eleventh century. The case of is less obvious: the American experts Spengler and Sayles consider the frontal bust with long hair as a representation of an auspicious planet (Jupiter) taken from twelfth century Islamic art. The depiction of the face with its prominent cheekbones and pellet-like chin reminds me of Christ Emmanuel on the *hyperpyra* of Manuel I Komnenos. Whatever the case, this figural coinage emphasizes the adoption by the nomad newcomers and rulers of elements that they could integrate in their own cul-

ture, while aiming at getting recognition from their then mainly Christian (Greek or Armenian) subjects and claiming sovereignty on the 'land of Rum'. This coinage offers a paradigm of the increasingly diverse society of Anatolia in the thirteenth century, where the numerous mixed marriages had led to the adoption of Christian elements, including the cross, in popular belief and practices.[27]

Among the subjects they chose, not illustrated here, that of the warrior saint, George, on horseback, served perfectly the ideal of the nomad conquerors and was venerated as Khidir Elias. It is not fortuitous that he too was adopted in the same region by other cavalrymen and conquerors from the West, the Normans, when they became princes of Antioch on the occasion of the First Crusade. The coin of Roger (1112–1119) is another example of the adoption by the new rulers of identity elements from their subjects: the obverse has the name of the ruler inscribed in Greek (ΡΟΤΕΡ / ΠΡΙΓΚΠ/ ΟC ΑΝΤΙ/ΟΧ, Roger prince of Antioch) in four lines – the city had been a Byzantine possession since it was won back from the Arabs in 969) – and the reverse St George on horseback with a spear.

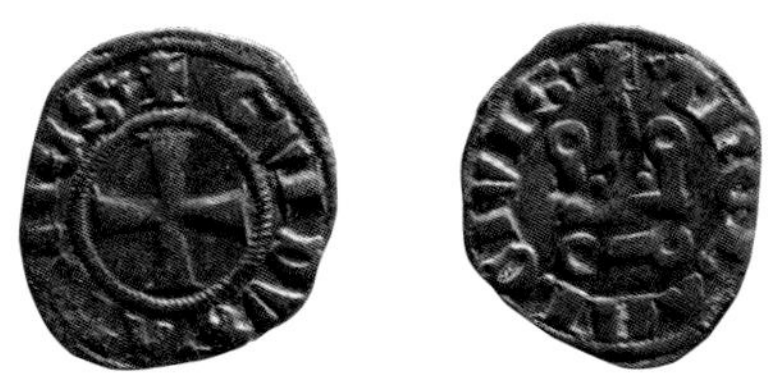

fig. 7

Denier tournois, Duke of Athens Guy de la Roche (1287–1308),Thebes.
KIKPE Collection, Athens

fig. 7 On the contrary, the last coin in this timeline offers a reversed example: the *denier tournois* of the Duke of Athens Guy de la Roche (1287–1308; GVI DVX.ATENES), minted in Thebes (ThEBANI.CIVIS), is one of the many silver coins struck by the Frankish rulers established in Greece after the Empire's partition in 1204, following the Fourth Crusade. It copies the model of the French coins from Tours, which had first dominated Greece's currency together with English pennies (the so-called *esterlins*, sterling). In the thirteenth century economic domination was supporting political conquest and the Horatian saying *Graecia capta ferum uictorem cepit* no longer applied entirely.

Note: The special fonts used here for coins (or seals) inscriptions, created by the late Professor Nicolas Oikonomides in 1986, were subsequently enriched by Glenn Ruby and the Publications Department of Dumbarton Oaks (Washington, DC). The author is very grateful to DO's program in Byzantine Studies for graciously releasing these fonts for use in scholarly publications.

Notes

1. On the details of a complex and changing legislation that punished less severely the counterfeiting of bronze coinage, see Hendy 1985, pp. 320–8.
2. *De rebus bellicis*, III, seems to imply that counterfeiting was often occurring within the mint itself and advised that the moneyers should be confined to an island!
3. La Bruyère happens to have mocked wittily the numismatists of his time (*Caractères*, Ch. XIII).
4. Among a vast bibliography, see Spieser 2000, and Dagron 2007, and the various papers assembled in Auzépy ed. 2003, Spieser ed. 2007.
5. Morrisson (in press).
6. *Variae* 6.7, *MGH AA*, XII, 180–181: The Count of Sacred Largesses is commissioned 'ut figura vultus nostri metallis usualibus inprimatur, monetamque facis de nostris temporibus futura saecula commonere …ut et imago principum subiectos videretur pascere per commercium, quorum consilia invigilare non desinunt pro salute cunctorum'.
7. Julian, *Misopogon*, VII, 27, p. 256.
8. Malalas, *Chronographia*, ed. L. Dindorf [CSHB], Bonn 1831, p. 453. ll. 22–23: *διαφόρων βασιλέων νόμισματα μυρία ἐπεδίδου κατ' ὄνομα*.
9. Dumbarton Oaks Collection: *DOC* 3/1, no. 2.2; BZC.1957.4.70.S1999.
10. Grierson 1999, p. 143.
11. Dumbarton Oaks Collection: *DOC* 5/2, no. 220; BZC 1948.17.3602.
12. Dumbarton Oaks Collection: *DOC* 5/2, no. 1294; BZC 1960.88.5359.
13. Dumbarton Oaks Collection: *DOC* 5/2, no. 12; BZC 1948.17.3592.
14. Grégoire 1959/60, § 8, p. 457.
15. *Cf.* Pachymère, ed. Failler 1984, pp. 259–61.
16. *RIC* VII, Constantinople, nos 19, 26.
17. Bastien 1983, p. 69.
18. *RIC* VIII, nos 270–84 (Siscia).
19. Eusebius, *Vita Constantini* I, 27–32.
20. Dumbarton Oaks Collection: *DOC* 2/2, no. 61e.2; BZC 1960.125.1131.
21. Maurice, *Strategikon*; McCormick 1986, pp. 245–7.
22. In the Dumbarton Oaks catalogue and other reference books the convex side of the so-called '*scyphates*' (cup-shaped) coins is described as the obverse. This usage is observed here although technically this side is the reverse, being struck by the upper, mobile, die and described as such (*opisthen*) by Pachymeres in his description of Michael VIII's *hyperpyron* (above, fig. 5).
23. Angelov 2007, particularly pp. 78–115.
24. Foss 2008 for an introduction to the historical context and the dates of issues; pp. 50–2 for the two KIKPE coin types.
25. Palmer 1993, pp. 31f.
26. Popular accessible presentation in Spengler and Sayles 1992. Historical study in Shukurov 2004.
27. Zachariadou 2011, pp. 373–4.

Bibliography & Abbreviations

Angelov 2007: Angelov, D., *Imperial Ideology and Political Thought in Byzantium, 1204–1330*, Cambridge.

Auzépy 2003: Auzépy, M.-F. (ed.), *Byzance en Europe*, Saint-Denis.

Bastien 1983: Bastien, P., *Le monnayage de Magnence (350–353)*, 2nd edn, Wetteren.

Dagron 2007: Dagron, G., 'Oublier Byzance, Eclipses et retours de Byzance dans la conscience européenne', *Praktika tès Akadèmias Athènôn*, 82/2 (2007), pp. 141–58.

DOC 2: Ph. Grierson, *Catalogue of the Byzantine Coins in the Dumbarton Oaks Collection and in the Whittemore Collection. Vol. 2. Part 1: Phocas to Heraclius, 602–641. Part 2: Heraclius Constantine to Tiberius III, 641–717*, Washington, DC 1968.

DOC 3: Grierson, Ph., *Catalogue of the Byzantine Coins in the Dumbarton Oaks Collection and in the Whittemore Collection. Vol. 3. Part 1: Leo III to Michael III, 717–867. Part 2: Basil I to Nicephorus III, 867–1081*, Washington, DC 1973.

DOC 5: Ph. Grierson, *Catalogue of the Byzantine Coins in the Dumbarton Oaks Collection and in the Whittemore Collection. Vol. 5: Michael VIII to Constantine XI, 1258–1453. Parts 1–2*, Washington, DC 1999.

Foss 2008: Foss, C., *Arab-Byzantine Coins: An Introduction, With a Catalogue of the Dumbarton Oaks Collection*, Washington DC.

Grégoire 1959/60: Grégoire H., 'Imperatoris Michaelis Palaeologi de vita sua', *Byzantion* 29–30 (1959–1960), pp. 447–74, transl. G. Dennis, in *Byzantine Monastic Foundation Documents*, Washington, DC 2000, 1245.

Hendy 1985: Hendy, M. F., *Studies in the Byzantine Monetary Economy, c. 300–1450*, Cambridge.

Julian, *Misopogon*: Julian (emperor), *Misopogon*, transl. W. C. Wright, Cambridge, MA 1913.

Maurice, *Strategikon*: *Das Strategikon des Maurikios* [Corpus fontium historiae byzantinae], G. T. Dennis (ed.) and transl. E. Gamillscheg, Vienna 1981; *Maurice's Strategikon: Handbook of Byzantine Military Strategy*, G. T. Dennis (ed. and transl.), Philadelphia, PA 1984.

McCormick 1980: McCormick, M., *Eternal Victory. Triumphal Rulership in Late Antiquity, Byzantium, and the Early Medieval West*, Cambridge, Paris.

Morrisson (in press): Morrisson, C., 'Displaying the emperor's authority and kharakter in the marketplace', in: Ch. Roueché, P. Armstrong *et al.* (eds), *Authority in Byzantium*, Farnham (in press).

Pachymère: Pachymère Georges, *Relations Historiques*, 5 vol., ed. A. Failler, transl. V. Laurent [CFHB, 24], Paris 1984.

Palmer 1993: Palmer, A., *The Seventh Century in the West-Syrian Chronicles*, Liverpool.

Shukurov 2004: Shukurov, R., 'Christian elements in the identity of the Anatolian Turkmens (12th–13th centuries)', *Cristianità d'Occidente e Cristianità d'Oriente (sec. VI–XI)*, (Settim. LI), Spoleto, pp. 707–64.

Spengler and Sayles 1992: Spengler, W. F. and Sayles, W. G., *Turkoman Figural Bronze Coins and their Iconography*, vol. 1, *The Artuqids*, Lodi, MI.

Spieser 2000: Spieser, J.-M., 'Du Cange and Byzantium', in: R. Cormack and E. Jeffreys (eds), *Through the Looking Glass: Byzantium Through British Eyes*, Aldershot, pp. 199–210.

Zachariadou 2011: Zachariadou, E., 'L'Asie Mineure turque', in: C. Morrisson (ed.), *Le monde byzantin* III. L'Empire grec et ses voisins (XIIIe–XVe siècle), Paris.

CATALOGUE OF EXHIBITS

i — l

PLATES